W9-DEW-413

Global History
and
Geography
The Growth of Civilizations

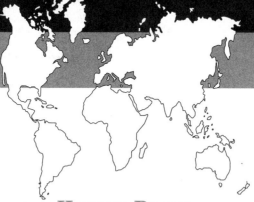

HENRY BRUN
Principal (Ret.), John Jay High School
New York City

LILLIAN FORMAN
Social Studies Writer and Researcher

HERBERT BRODSKY
District Coordinator for Social Studies
Freeport School District, N.Y.

AMSCO

AMSCO SCHOOL PUBLICATIONS, INC.
315 Hudson Street, New York, N.Y. 10013

Reviewers and Consultants

Vincent Asaro
Teacher, Social Studies
Franklin Delano Roosevelt High School
New York City

Edward W. Berg
Assistant Principal, Social Studies
Murry Bergtraum High School
New York City

Cornelius Cahill
Social Studies Department Chairperson
Highland High School
Highland, N.Y.

Sheila Kavovit
Assistant Principal, Social Studies
John F. Kennedy High School
New York City

Ann-Jean Paci
Assistant Principal, Social Studies
Bushwick High School
New York City

Mary Ann Pluchino
Global Studies Teacher
Kings Park High School
Kings Park, N.Y.

Mark D. Rothman
Social Studies Department Chairperson
Paul D. Schreiber High School
Port Washington, N.Y.

Stephen A. Shultz
Assistant Principal, Social Studies
Boys and Girls High School
New York City

Cover and Text Design: Merrill Haber

Maps, Charts, Graphs: Tech-Graphics

Photo Research: Linda Sykes

Compositor: UG

Cover Illustrations:

Front (top to bottom): Greece: Parthenon, Athens; Leo de Wys Inc./W. Hille

China: Great Wall at Beijing, Bada Range; © Yat Nin Chan

Zimbabwe: Great Zimbabwe, ruins of the great enclosure; CORBIS/Robert Holmes

Back: Lascaux, France: cave painting; The Bridgeman Art Library International, Ltd.

When ordering this book, please specify:
R 674 H *or*
GLOBAL HISTORY *Hardbound*
or
R 674 P *or*
GLOBAL HISTORY *Softbound*

Please visit our Web site at:
www.amscopub.com

ISBN 1-56765-606-4 / *NYC Item 56765-606-3* Hardbound
ISBN 1-56765-607-2 / *NYC Item 56765-607-1* Softbound

Copyright © 2001, 2000 by Amsco School Publications, Inc.

No part of this book may be reproduced in any form
without written permission from the publisher.

Printed in the United States of America

6 7 8 9 10   04 03 02 01

PREFACE

The New York State Scope and Sequence for Global History and Geography for grades nine and ten social studies classes presents teachers and students with a major challenge. The two-year course of study features a topical and chronological approach to the broad sweep of human history, beginning with the origins of societies and civilizations and continuing to the present. The course, organized by time periods, is followed by a rigorous New York State Regents Examination. The Regents exam—required of all students—tests content knowledge and students' ability to apply that content through responses to objective multiple-choice questions, thematic essays, and document-based questions.

Global History and Geography: The Growth of Civilizations has been written and designed to assist students and teachers to successfully respond to this course of study and to the Regents examination. *Global History and Geography*'s organization into eight units is identical to the content that appears in the Scope and Sequence. The text is divided into thirty-five chapters.

An overview of methods of the social sciences is presented in the first five chapters of the text. Students are introduced to the tools and methods of the historian, geographer, economist, and political scientist as each examines and describes human experience from the perspective of the particular discipline. An extended definition and discussion of *culture* and *civilization* is also included. The thematic strands established in these five chapters are integrated into the following thirty chapters.

Students in grades nine and ten often find global history or world history courses to be somewhat abstract; they deal with events and topics that students perceive as being unrelated to their daily lives and personal concerns. Yet students are told that they must learn this subject matter in order to pass the Regents examination and earn a high school diploma. Thus, it falls largely on the teacher to infuse color and life into each time period and help students see ways their lives relate to the sweep of human experience. To help make this course more interesting and lively, *Global History and Geography* contains many special features:

- Careful attention is given to appropriate ninth and tenth grade reading levels.

- Human interest vignettes that open each chapter introduce realistic characters that help illustrate larger historical issues, events, and movements.

- Many time lines throughout the text help students link historical events and developments to specific points in time.

- "Boxed" features in each chapter highlight social history, cultural and economic trends, and political figures and issues.

- Frequent "surveys of the physical environment" place historical developments in their geographic contexts.

- A full range of illustrations, photos, historic prints, cartoons, maps, charts, and graphs enliven and clarify the text and lend themselves to a variety of instructional approaches and classroom activities.

- Info Check questions are strategically placed within each chapter to provide opportunities in class to periodically elicit oral or written responses. These questions are designed to help students to think critically and engage in expository writing and/or discussion.

- Regents examination review and preparation will be aided by Regents-type questions at the end of each chapter and unit.

Global History and Geography is intended to be an in-class instructional tool. Its organization and design includes a variety of teaching/learning styles, such as discussion-based lessons, materials-based activities, and co-operative learning. *Global History and Geography* opens the door to achieving the most desired characteristics of a successful lesson—maximum student participation in reaching conclusions responsive to an aim and a clear, concise set of notes for future reference. Further, the text is accompanied by a Teacher's Manual that contains unit and chapter objectives, lesson plans and suggestions to aid in implementing instruction, and activities for extending lessons.

In summary, *Global History and Geography* provides all the content, skills development, activities, and assessments required for a two-year course of study. To all who use this text and its ancillaries, we wish you success.

HENRY BRUN
LILLIAN FORMAN
HERBERT BRODSKY

CONTENTS

Methods of the
Social Sciences

The World Today

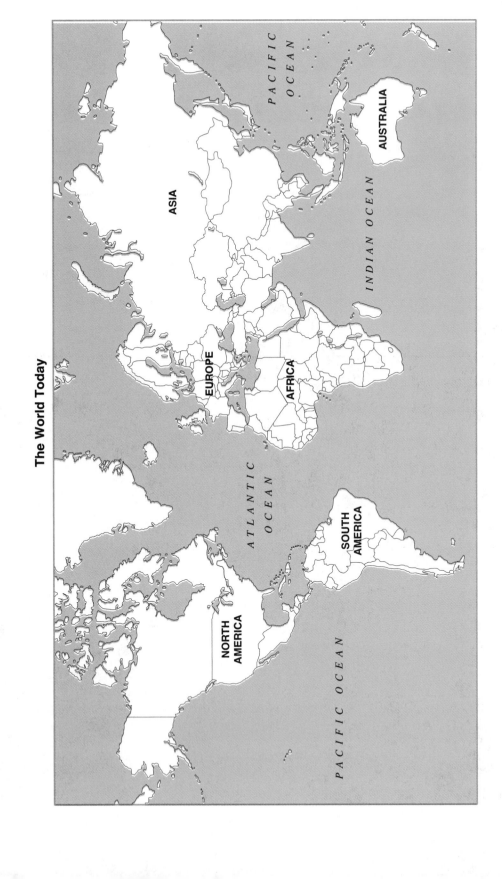

C H A P T E R
1

History: Looking Into the Past

We live in a shrinking world. In the past, it was easier to consider ourselves separately from other cultures and other countries. Now, because of instant communications, we must be more aware of the relationships between all people of the planet. Technology makes it difficult to ignore any of our world neighbors. The study of the social sciences helps us to understand the rapid pace of technological change and how we are all connected in a larger global community. By studying the social sciences, we can also better understand how societies are interdependent, relying on one another socially, politically, economically, and culturally.

The social sciences are the tools we use to understand the forces that link all people together in one global community. These areas of study are history, geography, economics, political science, and culture and civilization. Each provides us with a different way of learning about the past, interpreting events, and planning for the future. They are all essential to an understanding of global history and the growth of civilizations.

HISTORY: THE HUMAN STORY

History tells the chronological story of the human race and its many civilizations. In order to understand the world today, it is necessary to study the significant events of the past. We need to know the many ways in which people have grown, developed, resolved problems, and responded to their environment. Historians examine the ideas, actions, and words of our ancestors as well as the great political, geographic, economic, military, and cultural forces that have shaped their lives. Studying these patterns helps us to understand their impact on the contemporary world and our lives.

Kinds of Historical Evidence

Like any scientist, the historian must be a detective. The historian combines logical thinking with a careful search for the evidence that reveals the past. This historical evidence comes in many forms. The most common forms are:

1. *Documentary evidence*: the written records of a people—their books, reports, letters, and government documents.
2. *Epigraphical evidence*: the inscriptions on monuments and buildings.
3. *Artifactal evidence*: the artifacts, or physical remains of a people—their tools, weapons, clothes, money, household goods, and food, and the people themselves.
4. *Literary evidence*: the poetry, stories, myths, and legends of a civilization or culture reveal how its people thought, what they believed, how they worshiped, and what they valued.
5. *Graphic evidence*: the art, architecture, sculpture, jewelry, and interior decoration that people used.

Neolithic tools uncovered in eastern Europe

Evidence in its many forms must be researched, analyzed, and interpreted by historians whose thinking is objective and unbiased. In other words, a historian must be willing to accept the conclusions to which the examination of evidence leads. The objective scholar does not seek to hold onto theories that cannot be supported by evidence. Consider the examples below:

The Oldest Human Communities

Most historians agree that modern Homo Sapiens—people who looked like us modern folks—first appeared in Africa. Bone fragments that appear modern and date from about 120,000 years ago have been found in both Ethiopia and southern Africa. However, there are questions to which answers must be found. Where in Africa did modern humans first appear? How did they live? When did they begin thinking in the way humans do today?

In 1997, scientists working on the southwest coast of South Africa found evidence that brought them closer to answering these questions. On the shore of a lagoon 60 miles north of Cape Town, two fossil human footprints were discovered. They were pressed into an ancient sand dune that became rock. The rock was dated to 117,000 years ago. These footprints, therefore, are among the oldest known fossilized traces of modern humans.

The location of the footprints supports the belief that South Africa's coast and central region was the place of origin of modern humans. More evidence has been found at the Klasies River mouth,

Fossilized human footprints 117,000 years old, in South Africa

about 375 miles from the footprint site. People sheltered in caves there between 60,000 and 120,000 years ago. A spearpoint lodged in a giant buffalo's remains proves that Klasies hunters were advanced enough to defeat a large, dangerous animal. Other artifacts found at the site suggest that these hunters may have designed tools to trade with neighboring groups. Red ocher "crayons" found on the site have been interpreted as a symbolic use of color. This could indicate religious or magical beliefs. Continuing investigation of these sites will add to our knowledge of these early humans and will reveal more about their origin.

Records of an Empire

For more than 300 years, England was the northernmost province of the mighty Roman Empire. Dr. Robin Birley, an archaeologist and a historian, has spent decades excavating a Roman fortification in northern England. The Romans arrived in Vindolanda in the 1st century A.D. and occupied it until about the year 400. In 1973, Birley began finding the remains of writing tablets. On these wooden panels, Roman soldiers had written personal letters, reports about the strength and condition of their garrison, and accounts of food and supplies. Birley and his assistants were able to read the Latin script by photographing the tablets with infrared film. They then had to

Excavation of a Roman commanding officer's house at Vindolanda, England

interpret this cursive script, which is a forerunner of our modern handwriting.

By 1993, approximately 1,900 writing tablets had been unearthed. For Birley and other historians, this combination of artifactal and documentary evidence creates a picture of life on the northern frontier of the Roman Empire nearly 2,000 years ago. It also helps them to arrive at conclusions about how these ancient Romans lived and worked. Additional artifactal evidence—in the form of the remains of buildings, textiles, leather goods, and wooden objects—provides even more information about Roman military life.

The First Historians

Every society has had individuals who were knowledgeable about the past. Some early historians relied upon memory rather than on written records. Consider the following:

In A.D. 986, Earl Hakon, ruler of most of Norway, won a great sea victory over an invading fleet of Danes. Sailing with Earl Hakon were five skalds from Iceland. *Skalds* were poet-historians. It was their task to observe the great naval battle in which the Norse dragon ships sank or captured the Danish vessels. The skalds would note the courage and skills of the warriors as they fought with sword, spear, and

Fierce animal carved in wood decorates the prow of a Norse ship

axe. And what the skalds observed would be woven into long historical poems called sagas. These *sagas* were recited at feasts in the halls
of kings, nobles, and chieftains. While the smoke rose from great slabs
of meat roasting on spits and wine, ale, and mead were passed in
curved drinking horns, the warriors would shout their approval of
heroic deeds.

Oral History. The Norse sagas were great entertainment, but
they were also history. They contained the genealogies of royal families, important events, and stories of how gods and goddesses helped
and hindered mortals. The skalds who created and recited the sagas
were trained to perform great feats of memorization. The sagas were
not written. They were passed down through the generations by word
of mouth as *oral histories.*

The use of oral history has been common to many societies. In
ancient India, two great epic poems about princes, heroes, and gods—
the *Mahabharata* and the *Ramayana*—were recited long before they
were written down. In some places, the practice has lasted into modern times. Local historians and storytellers called *seanachies* are
found in contemporary Ireland. In the villages of western Africa, the
people who perform the same function are known as *griots.*

Written History. As time went on, written history became much
more common than oral history. Most of us are familiar with infor-
mational sources that are printed as books, magazines, or reports, or
in electronic form on the Internet. However, the skalds and griots
acted as preservers and transmitters of history long before the societies in which they lived developed written languages. After these
societies began to use written language, many of the sagas and epics
were written down. Whether it is written or oral, history reveals both
the memorable events of a society and the development of its
language.

TIME FRAMES AND PERIODIZATION

In the year A.D. 1324, King Mansa Musa made a pilgrimage to
the holy city of Mecca. A dedicated Muslim, Mansa Musa ruled the
great West African empire of Mali. For generations, the king's long
journey was well remembered. He was accompanied by 60,000 people.
His caravan carried 24,000 pounds of gold loaded on 80 camels. In
addition, 500 servants carried about six pounds of gold each. Few
kings of the Middle Ages (A.D. 500–1500) could display such wealth.

Time Frames. During the Middle Ages, three great empires—
Ghana, Mali, and Songhai—flourished in western Africa. Great
things were also happening in other parts of the world in this *time
frame* or *period.* Germanic kingdoms replaced the Roman Empire.
The Byzantine Empire dominated Asia Minor (Turkey), the Balkan
region of southern Europe, North Africa, and much of the Middle

East. The power of Europe's Christian rulers was threatened by the armies of Islam. They swept out of Arabia to create a Muslim Empire in the lands taken from the Byzantines and others. The Mayas, builders of great cities in Central America, were conquered by the Toltecs. During the same period, the Aztecs of central Mexico put together a great empire. Significant change also came to East Asia. Muslims conquered India, and Mongols took control of China.

It is important to understand that the exciting Middle Ages, or medieval period, is only one of the many time frames into which human history is divided by historians. During the Classical Age (500 B.C.–A.D. 500), for example, many civilizations contributed to the development of humankind. Two of these—the Roman Empire in Europe and the Han Empire in China—developed political, economic, and cultural systems that greatly influenced other parts of the world.

Periodization. This is a tool used by historians to help us understand how the cultures and civilizations that existed during the same time frame interacted. It is also a means of expanding our knowledge of any period by examining important developments in different regions.

It is exciting to learn the details of Mansa Musa's fabulous pilgrimage to Mecca in 1324. We can appreciate this event better if we discover more about the period in which the journey was made. What was happening elsewhere in Africa and in the world? How and why do historians distinguish one historical period from another? Usually, there are great themes or patterns of political, cultural, and economic development and change occurring in a particular period. This theme or pattern makes the period different from others. For example, the Stone Age (2.5 million to 5,000 years ago) is divided into the Paleolithic (2.5 million to 10,000 years ago), the Mesolithic (10,000 to 8,000 years ago), and the Neolithic (8,000 to 5,000 years ago) periods.

During each of these periods, people responded to their environments in particular ways. The greatest change came during the Neolithic period, or New Stone Age. It was then that people learned to grow their food, instead of hunting or gathering it. The beginning of agriculture made possible the first towns and villages. Some of them became the first cities. Every period of time has patterns of development. Often, perhaps usually, they are only seen when historians look back at the events of the period.

CRITICAL-THINKING SKILLS

In order to reach conclusions based on evidence, historians must be able to analyze, infer, judge, hypothesize, generalize, predict, and make decisions. Collectively, these processes are called *critical-thinking skills*. They are not unique to the study of history, but are used in all disciplines or areas of study. Critical-thinking skills enable us to obtain and process information or data and to use it to arrive at conclusions.

The following definitions will help you to better understand the skills needed to think critically:

1. We *analyze* when we separate the basic facts and ideas of an issue or problem in order to better understand it.

2. We *infer* when we arrive at a conclusion after noting individual facts or ideas.

3. We *judge* by forming an opinion about something through careful weighing of evidence.

4. We *hypothesize* when we develop ideas or theories that must be tested to be proven and accepted as fact.

5. We *generalize* when we make statements of opinion that are not particular or specific.

6. We *predict* by declaring an event or a result in advance, before it actually occurs, on the basis of observation, experience, or reasoning.

It is the investigation of evidence, combined with the critical-thinking process, that makes the historian a scientist.

CHAPTER REVIEW

Multiple Choice

1. Which of the following is *not* one of the social sciences?

   1. history
   2. geography
   3. biology
   4. economics.

2. Historical evidence includes

   1. documents
   2. inscriptions
   3. artifacts
   4. all of the above.

3. Historians search for

   1. mineral deposits
   2. bacteria
   3. sunspots
   4. cause-and-effect relationships.

4. *Sagas* and *epics* are examples of

   1. oral history
   2. folktales
   3. myths
   4. written history.

5. To enable us to understand the development of different cultures during the same time frame, historians use

   1. mathematical computations
   2. chemical formulas
   3. periodization
   4. literary anthologies.

6. When we analyze, infer, and judge, we are using

   1. computational skills
   2. literacy skills
   3. computer skills
   4. critical-thinking skills.

Thematic Essays

1. Write an essay about *one* of the following themes.

    -   History: A Tool for Examining the Past
    -   The Historian as Detective
    -   Skills of Historical Analysis

2. Explain why you AGREE or DISAGREE with the following statement made by an American industrialist in 1916.

    "History is more or less bunk. We want to live in the present, and the only history that is worthwhile is the history we make today."

    Henry Ford

C H A P T E R

2

Geography: A Physical View of the World

Like history, geography is necessary for a thorough view of the world and its civilizations. Geographers are the scientists who study the Earth and its place in the universe. They study, among other things, the distribution of people, animals, plants, resources, and industry around the world. The Earth is home to the human race. It is populated by over 5 billion people who are as unique as they are similar. What we learn from the study of the Earth's surface and how it is populated helps us to survive in an ever-changing world.

THE WORLD IN SPATIAL TERMS

Geographers must study the Earth in measurable terms. They must examine the Earth as if it were beneath a magnifying glass in order to see the shapes, sizes, and locations of all its regions, land masses, and bodies of water. Globes and maps help us to understand the world in *spatial* terms. They show us how the Earth is put together physically and where the people and places are in relation to each other. Since globes are round, they are the most accurate models of the Earth. Globes enable us to see most easily what part of the Earth is occupied by each continent and ocean and how these features are shaped. Location also provides us with information about climate, time zones, and distance.

Maps also provide this information and are easier to transport and store. However, maps are not as accurate as globes. Since the surface of the earth is curved rather than flat, maps distort the shapes of portions of the Earth.

When astronauts look at the Earth from space, they see arrangements of mountains, plateaus, canyons, plains, valleys, lakes, rivers, and oceans. These *landforms* and bodies of water give the world its appearance and influence the ways in which people live and work. The study of this interaction is an important geographer's task.

The interaction of people with landforms and bodies of water has always been determined by geography. Consider the following:

The Mayas of Central America

Nearly 2,000 years ago, the Mayas of Central America built cities in the tropical rain forests of Mexico, Guatemala, and Belize. Skilled architects and mathematicians, they were also farmers. They cleared small plots of land out of the rain forests. In the hot, humid climate, Mayan farmers grew corn, beans, peppers, and tomatoes. They also raised sweet potatoes, tobacco, cotton, fruits, and cacao (the main ingredient of chocolate). These products, together with beautifully designed pottery and objects of jade, were carried by Mayan traders over rain forest trails. Cacao was so highly valued that cacao beans were used as money.

The closeness of the Caribbean Sea brought frequent heavy rainfall that helped the Mayan farmers. In order to farm, they had to clear the dense forest. To do this, they used a method called *slash and burn.* Some of their descendants continue to use this method to create new fields to plant. The land has not changed.

Stone Age Russia

Zaraysk is a small city near Moscow in Russia. The soil is poor. The winds are harsh, and the winters are brutally cold. It was even colder 22,000 years ago when the first inhabitants of the area arrived. They were Stone Age hunters who migrated from Central Europe. They did not go to more inviting lands farther south because they

Steps in food production depicted on the frieze of a Maya temple

were in pursuit of *mammoths*, the lumbering ancestors of elephants. The flat plain was perfect for slow-moving, grass-eating mammals. There were no forests nearby. Predators that might threaten the mammoths were easy to spot. The flatness of the plain and the high grass kept the mammoths in the area for a long time. A broad river provided water. The early human hunters also stayed, even though the climate was extremely cold for them. In the course of 6,000 years, at least three waves of settlers made permanent homes in the area. Without trees for lumber, the hunters were forced to dig living quarters out of the hard ground. These dugout homes were roofed with mammoth tusks.

The mammoths were not bothered by the cold. However, they needed dry weather. As the Ice Age ended, the climate became warmer and wetter. High humidity and dampness killed the mammoths. When their thick, furry hair got wet and then froze, they became sick and died. The humans who had hunted them had to find other ways of obtaining food and clothing.

The Ural Mountains discouraged the mammoths and the early humans from moving farther east. This is important to geographers, who believe that Europe ends at the Urals. Beyond them, Asia begins.

Places and Regions

The lives of people are rooted in particular places. Geographers look at the physical and human characteristics of places. To assist this study, geographers have divided the world into regions. They examine the physical features, resources, lifestyles, and cultural, economic, political, and historical patterns of each region.

INTERPRETATION OF THE PAST

Historical developments often have geographic causes. The importance of river valleys to the rise of the world's first great civilizations is an example. The fertile lands, water supplies, and opportunities for transportation and communication provided by great rivers such as the Nile, Tigris, Euphrates, Indus, and Huang He made possible agriculture, trade, cities, and government. As a result, the Egyptian, Mesopotamian, Indus, and Chinese civilizations arose in the vicinities of these rivers. (See the map on page 15.)

Greece is a land of high mountain ranges enclosing fertile valleys. In ancient times, these valleys were isolated because traveling over the mountains was dangerous. Such geographic barriers kept the Greeks divided. As a result, they organized independent city-states instead of a unified nation under a central government. The mountains helped cause political disunity. Therefore, the first loyalty of the people was to their own city-state, rather than to Greece as a nation.

Sites of the Earliest Agricultural Communities

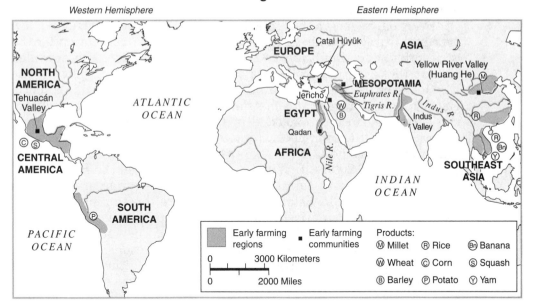

Geography affected the development of Greek civilization in other ways. Greece is a peninsula jutting into the Aegean and Mediterranean seas. Its rugged coastline is irregular, and provides many harbors. Because Greece lacks good farmland, many Greeks turned to the sea. They became merchants and traders who sailed the surrounding seas. Between 750 and 500 B.C., they established colonies on the shores of the Mediterranean and Black seas. In this way, Greek civilization spread to Italy, Sicily, France, and Turkey.

Geography has also played a role in the decline of civilizations. Consider the following:

Around 2300 B.C., a number of the major civilizations of the world collapsed. The Akkadian Empire in Mesopotamia, the Old Kingdom in Egypt, the early Bronze Age societies in Israel, Turkey, and Greece, as well as the Indus Valley civilization in India and the Hongshan culture in China were the first urban civilizations. They built the first cities. However, they all fell into ruin at about the same time. A thousand years later, around 1200 B.C., many of the civilizations of the same regions again collapsed.

The reasons for these widespread disasters have long been a fascinating mystery. Historians have considered warfare and famine. However, there is no physical or written evidence of such causes. Eventually, historians turned to geographers and other natural scientists, such as astronomers, for answers to the mystery. These researchers found evidence of natural causes, such as climate change, volcanic activity, and earthquakes, for the fall of so many civilizations at the same time. However, there has been disagreement about which natural cause was most responsible.

Eventually, geographers and astronomers began to consider a new type of natural disaster as the most likely single explanation for the widespread and simultaneous collapse of civilizations. The new idea is that these cultural collapses were caused by the impact on the Earth of comets, asteroids, or other kinds of debris from outer space. Geographers believe that comets and asteroids have, at times, struck the earth's surface or exploded in the air after entering the atmosphere. At least ten impact craters are known around the world. They date from after the last Ice Age. At least seven of these date from around 3000 to 2000 B.C. Whether impacting upon the Earth's surface or exploding in the air, the results have been the creation of great amounts of dust. Clouds of dust that obscure the sun for months or years can cause dramatic drops in global temperature, which disrupt or curtail agriculture for long periods of time. The sudden interruption in food supplies can cause the fall of civilizations. The idea that comet impact causes civilization to collapse and cultures to change is a *hypothesis*. Geographers will have to provide more evidence before historians accept it as fact. History involves the study of cause-and-effect relationships. Geography is an essential part of that process.

INTERPRETING THE PRESENT AND PLANNING FOR THE FUTURE

In recent years, theatergoers have been entertained by a musical based on a famous biblical story about a wise young man named Joseph. The pharaoh, or ruler, of ancient Egypt was troubled by a dream in which seven fat cows were eaten by seven lean cows. He asked Joseph to interpret the dream. Joseph told the pharaoh that Egypt would experience seven years of prosperity during which crops would grow well and food supplies would be plentiful. The seven fat years would be followed, however, by seven lean years of crop failures and food shortages. Joseph advised the pharaoh to prepare for the lean years by storing up food supplies that could be distributed to the people during the bad times. The pharaoh was so impressed by Joseph's analysis that he appointed the young man to the post of chief minister and placed him in charge of the project.

Modern-day geographers do not interpret dreams. It is their task, and that of other social scientists, to assist governments in understanding present-day problems and planning for the future.

To do this, they must focus the attention of public officials on questions that must be answered. For example:

If lumbering and farming activities are allowed to continue destroying the Amazon rain forests in South America, what outcomes can be predicted for the humans, plant species, and wildlife inhabiting that *ecosystem*? What consequences will there be for ecosystems

Ancient Egyptian model in stucco and painted wood showing granary workers

around the world? What steps must be taken to limit these predicted outcomes and compensate for them?

If the world's industrial nations continue to pollute the atmosphere with carbon dioxide and other *greenhouse gases,* how will the *global environment* be changed? What will be the impact of warmer temperatures, rising ocean levels, and other climate changes on industries, agriculture, and lifestyles?

How might the extinction of whales, tigers, and other *endangered species* affect the global environment?

The pursuit of answers to such questions involves the study of maps, charts, and graphs of land and climate. Statistical studies, field research, and computer technology compile and analyze the data needed for effective interpretation and planning.

Among the many ways in which geographers use these skills and procedures is to analyze natural disasters, such as volcanic eruptions and hurricanes. They assess the impact of these events on people and places and determine the effectiveness of government reactions. For example, the response of U.S. authorities to Hurricane Andrew in 1992 might be compared to the response of the authorities in Bangladesh to the floods caused by monsoon rains in that country in the same year. The objective would be to improve the ways in which local and national governments respond to such disasters wherever they occur.

One of the important tasks of the geographer, therefore, to help people and governments better understand and respond to a wide range of problems in the present and future.

CHAPTER REVIEW

Multiple Choice

1. To study the world in spatial terms, geographers find globes more accurate than maps because
   1. the surface of the earth is curved
   2. globes are three dimensional
   3. maps distort the shapes of portions of the earth
   4. all of the above.

2. Geography studies the interaction of people with
   1. other life forms
   2. landforms and bodies of water
   3. governments
   4. economic institutions.

3. To assist their study of the physical characteristics of places, geographers have divided the world into
   1. regions
   2. departments
   3. countries
   4. communities.

4. Historical developments often have geographic causes. An example of this is the primary importance to the first great civilizations of
   1. mountain ranges
   2. rain forests
   3. lakes and streams
   4. river valleys.

5. Some geographers connect the collapse of major civilizations around the year 2300 B.C. to
   1. glaciers
   2. sunspots
   3. comets and asteroids
   4. heatwaves.

6. To interpret the present and plan for the future, geographers analyze the reaction of people and governments to
   1. natural disasters
   2. political movements
   3. military operations
   4. economic crises.

Thematic Essays

1. Write two or three sentences to further explain each of the following statements. Give specific examples from the chapter to support your information.
   - Globes and maps help us to understand the world in spatial terms.
   - Geography has affected the development of civilizations.
   - Geographers often focus the attention of governments on important questions.

2. Reread page 14 and study the map on page 15. Then decide which of the following statements are true and which are false. Write a brief explanation of your answers.
   1. Each region of the world has physical and human characteristics.
   2. Africa and the Indus Valley lie in the Eastern Hemisphere.
   3. Southeast Asia and North America are both in the Western Hemisphere.
   4. Central America is *not* one of the *regions* into which geographers have divided the world.
   5. Geographers study a variety of regional patterns.

C H A P T E R

3

Economics: The Search for Security and Prosperity

Economics is the study of the production and consumption of goods and services. Economics is also concerned with a variety of other matters, including taxation, business organization and operation, banking, money, and insurance. Since we are all producers and consumers of goods and services, we are all affected by economics. Economic forces determine our ability to obtain the goods and services we require and the degree of comfort with which we live. Some of the most basic and important aspects of our lives, such as where and how we live and work, are economic decisions. How well we make those decisions depends upon our understanding of this particular social science.

MAJOR ECONOMIC CONCEPTS

People have always tried to satisfy their needs and wants by producing or obtaining things. From the earliest times, humans have developed economic means of obtaining what they do not have. Before money was invented, people used barter. They traded their goods and services in return for things that they needed or wanted. For example, one group of Stone Age hunters might have been able to kill enough animals to have a *surplus* of food, but the group might have lacked the materials needed to make new tools and weapons. They might have traded some of their extra food to another group of early humans skilled at making axes and spears. Later, people assigned value to ordinary goods such as salt, cacao beans, shells, or furs. They became a type of *currency*, or money. People would then exchange these forms of money for whatever they needed or wanted. Whether the object desired was necessary for survival or a luxury purely for enjoyment, the process was the same. Decisions were made about what was essential and what was not and about how to obtain the goods one needed. Economics is the study of how such decisions are made in a society of buyers and sellers.

Economic Vocabulary. The study of economics has its own vocabulary. It is important to understand that all people are *consumers*. Consumers buy *goods* and *services*. Goods are items of value that we can see or touch—a computer, an automobile, or a book. Services, such as health care, education, and legal advice, also have value. Consumers have unlimited needs and wants. Societies, however, have limited *resources*, or natural sources of wealth. This causes *scarcity*. Resources with a high degree of scarcity, such as gold or diamonds, have a high value. Soil and weeds, because there is so much of them available, have little value.

The laws of *supply* and *demand* determine how resources are allocated or distributed. Supply refers to the quantity of goods and services available to consumers at whatever prices are placed on them. Demand is the quantity of goods and services consumers want to purchase at fair prices. *Price* is the deciding factor. If prices are too low, sellers will not make a profit, even though they may sell a great quantity of goods. If prices are too high, consumers will not buy. The price of a good or service, therefore, is determined by supply and demand. If consumers want a particular item, more of the item will be produced. If consumers reject certain goods, fewer of them will be produced.

ECONOMIC SYSTEMS

Economists investigate how societies meet their unlimited demands. To do this, they must be concerned about the role of governments in economic activity. This leads to a study of the three types of economic systems existing in the world today. They are the *traditional, command,* and *market* systems. In the traditional economy, families and the community produce the basic necessities of daily life. Usually, a traditional economy depends on farming, herding, fishing, or a combination of such activities. By contrast, the command economy operates in response to government orders. The government controls industry and agriculture and decides what goods will be produced, in what quantity, by whom, with what resources, and what prices shall be paid by consumers. Very different from the command economy is the market economy. Also called the *capitalist system,* it permits individuals and businesses to decide what will be produced, offered for sale, and purchased. It is the market economy that is most strongly responsive to the laws of supply and demand. Business organizations produce what they think consumers want and sell at prices consumers are willing to pay. All three economic systems have played important roles in global history. Consider the following:

Traditional Economy

Life was hard in the countryside villages of England in the 7th century. Most farmers hunted and fished in addition to raising crops and livestock. A quiet determination drove the poorer people. For the children, work began as soon as they were physically able, and it never stopped. For people of all ages, the work went on from dawn to dusk and often beyond. There was always more to do—more wool to comb; more fuel to find and cut and gather; more pastures to move the animals to; more corn to grind; more walls and roofs to repair; more vegetable gardens and small strips of field to tend; more deer and birds to be stalked and, with luck, killed; more nuts and berries to be gathered; more clothes to be made. A visitor might be welcomed, but the work went on, and the visitor was expected to help.

These English farmers of the early Middle Ages lived in a traditional economy. They made their own decisions about what to grow and what to do with their products. They exchanged (bartered) goods and services with one another whenever they needed things that they

Person-to-person trading (barter) on the Russian-Chinese border in the 1990s

could not produce themselves. Their survival depended on their economic decisions, and on their labor.

Command Economy

Communism in the Soviet Union (1918–1991) was an economic and political system in which the government had total control over the production of goods and services. It was the ultimate command economy, with both strengths and weaknesses. Through centralized economic planning, Communist leaders transformed the Soviet Union from an agricultural into a leading manufacturing nation. They largely succeeded in avoiding such capitalistic problems as unemployment, inflation, and depression. A pool of skilled technicians and engineers produced complex space vehicles and modern military equipment. The Soviet Union became the world's second largest industrial power. (The first was the United States.)

There were many negative aspects to this command economy. Centralized economic control often resulted in poor management, waste, and costly errors in industry. Costs of production were high. Goods were often of poor quality. Consumer products were scarce, and there was a housing shortage. Soviet agriculture also did not operate efficiently. Food production barely kept pace with the increase in population.

By 1990, Soviet production of goods and services had dropped sharply. Shortages of consumer goods became worse than ever. The ruble (Soviet currency) became nearly worthless. Lines of people at government-run food stores became longer. As fear of even worse shortages grew, consumers began resorting to barter.

By the end of 1991, the Soviet Union had broken up into independent republics. Russia and some of the other republics began to de-

A Volgograd steel works, operated non-stop under the Soviet command economy

velop market economies. The new leaders believed that privately owned businesses, run for profit, would do a better job of strengthening their economies and meeting consumer needs.

Market Economy

Nations that are developing market economies usually also seek to make their governments more democratic. Democracy and market economies seem to go hand in hand. This is the case in the United States, the world's strongest and most successful market economy. In China, however, things have been different. In the 1990s, China remained the world's largest Communist power. As industrialization expanded at a rapid rate, the Asian giant became an economic powerhouse.

The leadership of the Communist Party continued the dictatorship established in 1949 by Mao Zedong. Following Mao's death in 1976, a more practical Communist leadership began reforms in education, culture, and industry in an attempt to stimulate China's backward economy. By the mid-1980s, movement away from the command economy had begun. Economic reforms led to the abandonment of rigid government control of industry and agriculture. Instead, private enterprise was encouraged. As private ownership of businesses expanded, China enjoyed more consumer goods and a rising standard of living.

To make its state-owned businesses profitable, the Chinese government *privatized* many of them. This means that it sold the businesses to private investors. The buyers invested new *capital* (money).

Street signs proclaim the lively market economy of Hong Kong

Many of these investors were foreigners. Businesspeople from Hong Kong, Taiwan, and elsewhere improved China's economy by bringing to it new capital and advanced production and management skills. Corporate giants from the West invested billions of dollars in China's telecommunications, automobile, and electronics industries.

Another departure from traditional Communist policies was the encouragement of private enterprise among ordinary Chinese. Throughout the country, individuals were encouraged to engage in business activity for profit. This sparked an economic and social revolution. As China's market economy grew, economists predicted that China would be one of the world's top five economic powers by the beginning of the 21st century. Despite these great economic changes, however, the Communist party remained firmly in power.

GLOBAL ECONOMIC INTERDEPENDENCE

The year 1997 was a terrible one for the economies of many Asian nations. In Japan, Taiwan, Thailand, South Korea, Hong Kong, and Indonesia, banks failed and stock prices dropped sharply. Years of poor banking and investment practices had resulted in too much money being spent too fast. Also, the banks had loaned too much to people who were unable to repay the debt. This Asian economic crisis caused declines in the value of shares sold on stock markets of the United States, Britain, France, and Germany. The United States government responded quickly. It asked the International Monetary Fund (IMF) to assist the faltering Asian nations with loans of money and "bailout" plans designed to stabilize their economies. The U.S. secretary of the Treasury and other American economic officials met with the Asian leaders to persuade them to make the difficult economic improvements required by the IMF. At first, the American stock markets rallied, and prices began to rise on the European markets. Economists, however, warned that the Asian crisis would have long-range effects in Europe and the United States. Asians would have less money to spend on American and European products. And, as the prices of Asian products fell, Western customers would buy more of them. But if the U.S. economy slowed down, American consumers would cut back on spending. A worldwide recession might occur.

The events of late 1997 and 1998 demonstrated the *interdependence* of the Asian, American, and European economies. The Asian nations had experienced rapid economic growth in the 1980s and 1990s. They had become important trading partners of the United States and Western Europe. And Americans and Europeans had invested heavily in Asian businesses. This, too, is a form of interdependence.

Regional Associations

The rise of regional economic associations in the late 20th century also strengthened interdependence. The 15 nations that are members of the European Union (EU) agreed to remove *tariffs* (taxes on imported goods) and other barriers to the free movement of goods and services across their borders. These efforts also included the establishment of a European central bank and the use of a single European currency called the *Euro* by the year 2002. Across the Atlantic, the North American Free Trade Agreement (NAFTA) provided for free trade between Canada, the United States, and Mexico. Similar agreements were made by groups of Latin American nations. And in Asia, the Chinese Economic Area (CEA) linked the economies of China, Hong Kong, and Taiwan. This particular interdependence was further strengthened in 1997 when Hong Kong ceased to be a British crown colony and was returned to the rule of China.

In the late 20th century, another aspect of global economic interdependence became evident. Political and economic leaders showed a preference for greater cooperation, rather than unlimited competition, as the path to prosperity.

CHAPTER REVIEW

Multiple Choice

1. Among the matters of concern to economists are

   1. production of goods and services
   2. banking
   3. money
   4. all of the above.

2. The price of any good or service is determined mainly by

   1. consumers
   2. producers
   3. supply and demand
   4. currency changes.

3. Government control of the production of goods is found in which type of economic system?

   1. traditional
   2. command
   3. market
   4. barter.

4. The world's most successful market economy was

   1. the United States in the 1990s
   2. the Soviet Union in the 1980s
   3. China in the 1960s
   4. England in the 600s.

5. An example of global economic interdependence is

   1. forming regional associations such as the European Union
   2. using high tariffs to keep out foreign products
   3. refusing to cooperate with the International Monetary Fund
   4. profiting from bank failures in other nations.

6. The Asian economic crisis of 1997–1998 demonstrated the interdependence of Asian economies with those of

   1. Latin America
   2. Africa
   3. the former Soviet republics
   4. the United States and Europe.

Thematic Essays

1. Reread Economic Systems on page 20. Then develop a chart to show the following:

   - the difference between traditional, command, and market economies
   - the strengths and weaknesses of each economic system

2. Explain why you AGREE or DISAGREE with this statement: Economics is just a boring subject taught in schools. It has nothing to do with my life and has no influence in the *real* world.

C H A P T E R

4

Political Science: The Governing of Nations and Peoples

Every nation of the world has developed its own system of keeping the peace and making decisions—its government. The roots of government are to be found in the customs and laws that people developed to help them live with one another and with other groups. Political scientists are people who study different forms of government and the ideas or beliefs that gave rise to them. (*Politics* is the art or science of government.) How these different forms of government operate and how their citizens relate to them are also the concerns of political scientists. They also study the making and enforcement of laws, the choosing of leaders, and the means by which group decisions are made.

Most people in the modern world live under a particular form of government. Therefore, even those who have little or no interest in government and law are affected by them. It is wise, therefore, to learn about them. As a modern political leader said, "People get the government they deserve!"

THE PURPOSES OF GOVERNMENT

The preamble to the Constitution of the United States, written in 1787, identifies the goals of the new American government:

> We, the people of the United States, in order to form a more perfect union, establish justice, insure domestic tranquillity, provide for a common defense, promote the general welfare, and secure the blessings of liberty to ourselves and our posterity, do ordain and establish this Constitution for the United States of America.

The authors of the Constitution believed that governments should exist to protect people's rights and property, to defend the nation against external threats and internal disorder, and to ensure that economic activity could take place. To achieve these goals, they established a form of government that was both a *republic* and a *democracy*. This means that our government is led by elected officials. These officials are responsible to the citizens who elected them.

Regulation and Controls. Governments have existed since the beginning of human history. More than 5,000 years ago, the Sumerians of ancient Mesopotamia (present(day Iraq) created the world's first system of government. Ruled by kings who were also priests, the Sumerian government regulated and controlled the land, resources, and people. To strengthen their control, the priest-kings required their people to pay taxes to the government. This income was used by the government to pay the soldiers who enforced royal authority, the workers who built palaces for the kings and their families, and for the luxury goods and slaves purchased for the rulers' comfort.

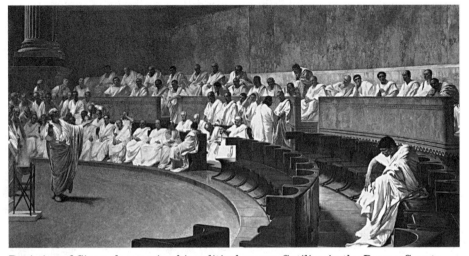

Depiction of Cicero denouncing his political enemy Catiline in the Roman Senate

Members of the U.S. House of Representatives assembled in the Capitol

The dual goals of regulation and control were seen in the governments of many ancient societies. The pharaohs who ruled Egypt, for example, were regarded by their people as gods. As such, the pharaohs owned everything and everyone in Egypt. All land and other property was loaned by pharaoh to his nobles and people and could be taken away by pharaoh. Pharaoh's word was law.

Natural Rights. In time, ideas about the purposes of government became more sophisticated. It became accepted that governments were responsible for the well-being of their people. It was not until the 17th and 18th centuries, however, that British and French political scientists developed the theory of *natural rights*. This theory stated that people were born with rights—to liberty and to possess property in particular—and that governments were formed to protect these rights. Some people came to believe that if governments did not fulfill this basic purpose, citizens had the right to overthrow them by revolution.

Rule of Law. The citizens of the United States and many other nations in the late 20th century benefit from the *rule of law* and all the rights and freedoms guaranteed to individuals in democratic societies. To maintain these benefits, citizens must act in a responsible manner. Most people understand this to mean obeying the laws and paying their taxes. Some people believe that the responsibilities of citizenship also include full participation in the political life of the community and the nation. To do this, one must vote in elections and be sufficiently informed about candidates and issues to make wise decisions. History has proven that when citizens neglect their responsibilities, governments abuse their authority.

POWER, AUTHORITY, GOVERNANCE, AND LAW

Democracy Versus Totalitarianism

Since its invention over 2,000 years ago by the ancient Greeks, democracy has been a popular political philosophy. Certain societies, however, have at times rejected democracy. Their governments have demanded loyalty to a particular political party and its leaders. Some examples are fascism, which controlled Italy from 1922 to 1943; nazism, which flourished in Germany from 1933 to 1945; and the Communist systems that ruled the former Soviet Union (1918–1991) and continue in present-day China and North Korea. All have demanded loyalty to a particular political party and its leaders. Such dictatorships are called *totalitarian* because their leaders maintain power by attempting to impose total control over their nations and citizens.

Citizens of totalitarian nations have few rights. They are required to place the needs of their governments before their own. Under a totalitarian government, citizens give unquestioning loyalty and obedience to their government and its leaders. Following orders and performing services for the state are what is expected of them.

In contrast, the citizens of democracies expect their governments to guarantee basic freedoms such as speech, press, religion, and assembly, and to act in the best interests of their people. Democratic governments are elected by citizens voting to promote and protect their well-being. In addition to rights, the citizens of democracies also have responsibilities. Chief among them is the responsibility to be

First democratic election in Morocco open to all adults, 1997

educated about political, economic, and legal matters so that they can make informed decisions about the issues and the candidates for public office.

Totalitarian governments enact laws designed to maintain the power and authority of a political party and its leaders. The lawmakers are chosen by the party in power. Disagreement with and criticism of government policies are usually not tolerated.

Democracies, on the other hand, enact laws that reflect the concerns, problems, and needs of their citizens. The lawmakers are elected by eligible voters. Systems of checks and balances are established to ensure that power is shared by those who make the laws and those who carry them out.

The police and military forces of totalitarian nations exist to control their populations and prevent opposition to the government and ruling party. Law enforcement officers and security forces are feared and hated because the people are powerless to resist them.

In democracies, police and security services exist to defend the population against military threats and to maintain public law and order. They are responsible to elected local and national officials who ensure that they function as servants of the people.

In all political systems, the manner in which governments use power is important. The degree to which power is shared between government and citizens determines the amount of freedom enjoyed by all in the society. Consider the following:

Indonesia—a Modern Dictatorship

Indonesia is an Asian nation of 210 million people. Although not a totalitarian state, it was ruled by a dictator for much of the 20th century. President Suharto was sole ruler of the country from 1967 to 1998. Under his regime, political opponents and critics of the government were jailed. There were no direct elections for president. Instead, candidates were proposed by an assembly. The candidates, including those of the opposition parties, had to be approved by the government. In the seven elections held after Suharto took office, he was the sole presidential candidate of all three parties. In addition to unlimited political power, Suharto also controlled the Indonesian economy. His children and close associates were placed in charge of major industries, banks, and other economic institutions.

In May 1998, Suharto was driven from office by a national uprising. An economic crisis increased popular resentment of the corruption and inefficiency of his dictatorship. Thousands of Indonesians rioted, demanding Suharto's resignation. A new leader promised to establish democracy in Indonesia by passing new laws and holding free elections. Political scientists, however, were doubtful that true reform could be accomplished. Although Suharto had stepped down, his government remained in power. And the powerful armed forces had the ability to block any reforms. As a result, Indonesia's political future remained in doubt.

CITIZENSHIP ACROSS TIME AND SPACE

Ancient Greece. Throughout history, societies have had their own particular ideas about citizenship. From 461 B.C. to 429 B.C., for example, the Greek city-state of Athens was led by a great statesman named Pericles. One of Pericles' goals was to develop Athenian democracy to its fullest extent. He expressed his ideas about the role of citizens by saying, "We alone regard a man who takes no interest in public affairs, not as harmless, but as a useless character." Although Athenian women were denied voting and other rights, Athenian men had many responsibilities as citizens. These included voting in the assembly, holding administrative offices, and serving on juries. Religious duties required the citizen to participate in the 60 days of religious festivals held each year. The first and most important responsibility of an Athenian citizen, however, was military service.

The Athenian Greeks' ideas about the rights and responsibilities of citizens influence most Western societies to this day. The Greeks also passed on the belief that written laws should protect individuals from one another and from the state. However, the Greek city-states did not extend citizenship to foreigners. It was the Romans who made citizenship a prize sought by millions. Rome was a multiracial empire that expanded over three continents from 100 B.C. to A.D. 500.

Ancient Rome. Until the 5th century A.D., citizens of the Roman Empire enjoyed rights and privileges not given to noncitizens. A great benefit of Roman citizenship was the protection of its laws. Citizens accused of crimes had the right to trial by jury and to appeal a court's decisions to the emperor. Rome also showed genius in making citizenship a privilege obtainable even by former enemies. In return for services to the empire, citizenship was granted to individuals, communities, and military units.

In addition to rights and privileges, Roman citizens also had responsibilities. Military service was compulsory in times of emergency. Citizens were expected to pay their taxes and honor the state religion—the government-approved list of gods, goddesses, and emperors worshiped as gods. In addition, Roman men of the higher social classes were expected to serve the empire by moving up a career ladder of military and administrative posts.

Ancient China. The rule of law and the rights of citizenship are so central to Western civilization that most people today take them for granted. This has not always been so in Eastern civilizations. Under the rule of ancient China's imperial dynasties, life was different. The great Chinese teacher named Confucius (Kong Fuzi, who lived from 551–479 B.C.) and his disciples distrusted written laws. They chose to rely on the goodness of the people as the best guarantee of a well-ordered society. Confucius defined the rights and responsibilities of citizens by developing a code of ethical conduct. He urged citizens to observe ancient traditions; respect learning and honesty; care for parents, family, and friends; and avoid doing to others what they did not want done to themselves. Confucius further taught that citizens should participate actively in the life of their community and that government should act vigorously to solve problems. He believed that an emperor who practiced Confucian virtues would govern almost as a parent. In the Confucian system, therefore, the primary responsibility of the citizen was to preserve the harmony of society through proper conduct. It was the responsibility of government to do the same while seeing to the well-being of its citizens.

CHAPTER REVIEW

Multiple Choice

1. Political scientists study

   1. global banking practices
   2. the rise and fall of ancient civilizations
   3. the operation of different forms of government
   4. environmental crises.

2. The basic purposes of the governments of ancient societies were

   1. protection of natural rights and civil liberties
   2. regulation and control of land, people, and wealth
   3. limitation of nuclear weapons
   4. organization of school districts.

3. The theory of *natural rights* was developed in the 17th and 18th centuries by

   1. Sumerian priest-kings
   2. Egyptian pharaohs
   3. Greek statesmen
   4. British and French political scientists.

4. Which of the following statements about totalitarian nations is correct?

   1. Citizens have few political rights.
   2. Following orders and serving the state is expected of citizens.
   3. Laws are enacted to maintain the power and authority of a political party and its leaders.
   4. All of these.

5. Which of the following statements about democratic nations is correct?

   1. Citizens expect their governments to guarantee basic freedoms.
   2. Systems of checks and balances are prohibited.
   3. Police and military forces exist to control the population and prevent opposition to the government.
   4. All of these.

6. Confucius defined the rights and responsibilities of the citizens of imperial China by

   1. formulating a law code
   2. writing rules for elections

3. developing a code of ethical conduct

4. drawing up lists of candidates for public office.

Thematic Essays

1. Select ONE of the following themes and write an essay of three or four paragraphs by doing the following: Define the topic or theme, and provide examples that clarify it.

themes
- The Purposes of Government
- Power, Governance, Authority, and Law
- Citizenship Across Time and Space

2. Reread the preamble to the Constitution of the United States on page 28. Explain how it relates to the study of political science.

C H A P T E R
5

Culture and Civilization

The story of how people built their many cultures and civilizations through the centuries is really what global history is all about. How cultures grew into civilizations and how they have interacted is an important part of our human experience. We are all products of one culture or another, just as we all belong to one or another of the world's civilizations. Therefore, our cultural background and the civilization in which we live determine our view the world and our reaction to the many experiences with which we are presented.

THE MEANING OF CULTURE

The wide range of ideas, feelings, beliefs, and habits that an individual shares with other members of his or her society is a major part of culture. It is our culture that tells us what to think and believe and how to act. To understand any culture, we must examine its many elements, especially its language, dress, religion, art, architecture, family structure, education, economic organization, government, and technology. Consider the following:

Islamic Culture

Islam is one of the world's great religions. Worldwide, Muslims number approximately 1 billion people. They are the majority popu-

African Muslim children
studying the Quran

lation in many countries, particularly in the Middle East and South
Asia. Despite the great diversity among Muslims, common beliefs and
customs make Islam a culture as well as a religion. Much of Islamic
culture arises from the Quran, or holy book.

Muslims believe that the teachings of God (Allah) were revealed
to Muhammad the Prophet. Muhammad was a 7th-century Arab who
lived in Mecca, a city in present-day Saudi Arabia. Among the Arabs,
he was the first to believe in one Supreme Being, rather than in many
gods. He converted others to his beliefs, which spread throughout
Arabia, the Middle East, and beyond. By the 8th century, a Muslim
Empire extended into Europe. It was ruled by *caliphs*, who were descendants of Muhammad the Prophet.

Muhammad's teachings were written by his followers in the
Quran. This holy book has influenced Muslim culture through rules
about language, art, diet, clothing, family organization, and, of
course, religious practice. For example, Arabic is the sacred language
of the Quran. Muslims believe that passages of the Quran should be
memorized in Arabic, even by those whose native language is not
Arabic. And Muslims do not use human and animal images in their
art. Instead, they prefer abstract symbols and geometric patterns to
decorate buildings, homes, and books. Calligraphy, in the form of
highly stylized Arabic script, is another art form popular in Islamic
culture.

THE SIGNIFICANCE OF CIVILIZATION

Throughout history, cultures have grouped together to form civilizations. (A *civilization* is a large group of cultures with a high degree
of social and technological development.) As the Muslim Empire ex-

panded, the cultures of many lands were affected by Islam and by the Arabic culture in which Islam had its roots. This process caused great changes in the civilizations of the Middle East and North Africa.

Social scientists often use the term *Western civilization* to indicate the grouping of the many cultures of the Americas and Europe. All of Asia's cultures, whether of China and Japan, the Indian subcontinent, or the island chains of the vast Pacific region, form *Eastern civilization*. Smaller geographic regions have also given rise to civilizations. Consider the following:

Ancient Civilizations

Indus Valley. For more than 4,000 years, agricultural and pastoral communities in what is now Pakistan and western India traded with one another and shared religious practices and customs. In time, a vast civilization emerged with large, well-planned cities, a common writing system, and religious beliefs and symbols. The *Indus civilization,* named for the river that watered its farming and grazing lands, flourished between 2600 and 1900 B.C. Its two greatest centers were the cities of Harappa and Mohenjo-Daro.

Classical Age. Rich and colorful civilizations arose during the *Classical Age* (500 B.C.–A.D. 500). In the city-states of ancient Greece, much was created that is important to us today. Democratic

Excavation of the Indus Valley city of Mohenjo-Daro in present-day Pakistan

Rhinoceros and bull seals of the Indus Valley civilization

government, the use of philosophy to search for truth, dramatic performances to entertain and enlighten the people, and a distinctive style of architecture seen in many modern cities, are only a few. These accomplishments of Greek, or *Hellenic, civilization* continue to excite the interest of historians and others. It so impressed King Philip of Macedon that he employed Greek teachers to educate his son, Alexander. From 336–323 B.C., Alexander led Macedonian and Greek troops eastward against the Persian Empire. They conquered most of the Middle East, Central Asia, and the Indus River region in India. Alexander's soldiers carried Hellenic civilization with them, especially to the cities they built along their line of march. In these cities, a rich cultural blending took place. The enrichment of Hellenic civilization by contact with the cultures of Egypt, Mesopotamia, Persia, and India created *Hellenistic civilization.*

By their conquest of the remains of Alexander's empire, the Roman people became masters of the Mediterranean world by 30 B.C. The art, architecture, and philosophy of the Hellenistic cities dazzled the Romans and changed their culture. Recognizing the superiority of the advanced Hellenistic civilization, the Romans purchased books, statues, vases, and other objects in the East for shipment to Rome and other Roman cities in the West. Educated Greeks were purchased as slaves or hired to serve as teachers, actors, writers, and scientists. Wealthy Romans learned to speak Greek as easily as Latin, and they imitated the ways of Greek civilization. The result of this new blending was the development of *Greco-Roman civilization.* Until the collapse of the Roman Empire in Western Europe, around A.D. 500, this rich and powerful civilization dominated the Western world. Historians regard Greco-Roman civilization as the foundation of Western civilization.

THE IMPORTANCE OF CITIES, LITERACY, AND TECHNOLOGY

Some historians have defined civilization as the *culture of cities*. They believe that the first characteristic of a civilized society is the existence of cities as political, social, and cultural centers. The great civilizations of the ancient world were centered on cities such as Babylon, Nineveh, Jerusalem, Athens, Rome, Constantinople, and Mecca. The forms of art, architecture, religion, commerce, and government that distinguished each civilization were developed in these and other cities. By road and sea, these cultural features moved out of the cities to influence the rest of the world. Consider the following:

Timbuktu: A Center of African Civilization

By the beginning of the 14th century, the West African empire of Mali was famous for its wealth. Its capital city of Timbuktu impressed travelers with its many commercial activities and its law and order. Goods, such as salt, from North Africa were exchanged in Timbuktu for gold and products from the rain forests and grasslands of West

Artist's rendering of the fabled West African city of Timbuktu

Africa. Camel caravans carried the products from North Africa. Arab traders, traveling overland or along the Niger River, also brought slaves.

Along with the traders who flowed into and out of Timbuktu came Muslim scholars. Many of them had studied in Arabia and Egypt. They attracted students from other lands to their courses in Arabic grammar, theology, law, and science. Timbuktu became known as a center of Islamic learning in Africa. Those who studied in the city brought the knowledge they gained to their own lands, thus extending the growth of Islamic civilization in Africa.

Written Languages and Civilization

Literacy is a key element of any civilization. Writing systems were developed by civilized societies to keep their records and to pass on to future generations their literature, history, science, and everything else reflecting their way of life. The Sumerians of ancient Mesopotamia invented the first system of writing around 4000 B.C. Called *cuneiform,* it consisted of wedge-shaped marks. The marks were pressed into wet clay tablets with a stylus, or pointed stick. The Sumerians' written language contained more than 700 cuneiform symbols. Each one stood for the name of something, an idea, or a sound. The cuneiform system of writing was later used by other peoples of Mesopotamia.

From 1200 to 800 B.C., the Phoenicians built a kingdom on the Eastern Mediterranean coast. The Phoenicians were seafaring merchants. They traded throughout the Mediterranean and even sailed to the Atlantic coasts of Europe and Africa. As merchants, the Phoenicians needed a simple alphabet to ease the burden of keeping records. They replaced the cumbersome cuneiform system with a phonetic alphabet, based on distinct sounds, consisting of only 22 letters. After further alterations and additions by the Greeks and Romans,

4000-year-old Sumerian clay tablet showing a medical text in cuneiform writing

this alphabet became the one we use today. The writing system based upon the Latin alphabet, as it came to be called, is used by most of the cultures of Western civilization.

Technological Development

The development of *technology* is another important characteristic of civilization. Civilized societies understand the uses of metals and power sources to produce tools, weapons, and other products, including those developed for luxury and amusement. Historians have established the following time frames or periods for the acquisition of this knowledge by people.

During the *Copper and Bronze Age* (4000–1000 B.C.), people learned how to use metals to make daggers, swords, spear and arrowheads, axes, and hammers. At first, they worked with copper. Later, they added tin to the copper to create a harder metal called bronze. During this period, the first civilizations developed in the Middle East, Asia, Africa, and Europe.

The *Iron Age* started 3,000 years ago around 1000 B.C. and continues into modern times. People forged iron into tools and weapons that were stronger than those made of bronze. Today's complex industrial civilizations depend on iron and on steel, made by mixing carbon with iron. Therefore, social scientists consider our own time to be part of the Iron Age.

Cultural Diffusion

The borrowing by one culture of attractive elements from another culture is known as *cultural diffusion*. In the 20th century, American baseball became popular in Latin America and Asia, especially Japan. And soccer, the European and Latin American form of football, was adopted in the United States. Also, Americanisms have crept into the languages of many nations. Thanks to films, television, and commerce, people in many diverse cultures understand the meaning of phrases such as "OK" and "Big Mac."

One of the most significant instances of cultural diffusion occurred during the Crusades (A.D. 1095–1291). For 200 years, European armies attempted to take control of portions of the Middle East from the Muslim Empire. The main objective of the Crusaders was to drive the Turks out of the Holy Land, or present-day Israel. Despite fierce fighting, in which many lives were lost, the Europeans failed. All they permanently won in the Middle East was the right of Christians to visit the city of Jerusalem.

Although the Crusaders did not change much in the Middle East, they were changed by their experiences. They came into contact with Islamic culture, which was more advanced than the culture of Europe.

This contact brought about a flow of new products and ideas into Europe. The exchange contributed to the development of the Renaissance, a great flowering of art, learning, and commerce that enriched Western Europe and led its people into modern times.

CHAPTER REVIEW

Multiple Choice

1. Which of the following is NOT an element of culture?
   1. language
   2. religion
   3. transportation
   4. family structure.

2. Which of the following reflects the influence of the Quran on Islamic culture?
   1. Human and animal images are not used in Islamic art.
   2. Lightweight clothing is preferred in warmer Islamic countries.
   3. Low-fat foods are a dietary staple for many Muslims.
   4. Oil revenues help to finance social services in some Islamic countries.

3. The term *civilization* refers to
   1. the grouping of cultures
   2. the culture of cities
   3. the development by cultures of literacy and technology
   4. all of these.

4. Which of the following statements is correct?
   1. The terms *culture* and *civilization* mean the same thing.
   2. A civilization can embrace many cultures.
   3. A culture can consist of many civilizations.
   4. A culture cannot exist in the same time and place as a civilization.

5. The sharing of cultural elements by people in different geographic locations is referred to by social scientists as
   1. cultural communication
   2. cultural transportation
   3. cultural diffusion
   4. cultural dilution.

6. The popularity of American-style baseball in Japan is an example of
   1. cultural communication
   2. cultural transportation
   3. cultural diffusion
   4. cultural dilution.

Thematic Essays

1. List the cultural elements that are most evident in your life. Select ONE of these elements and explain how it operates as a cultural element and how it enriches your life.

2. Reread The Significance of Civilization on pages 36–38 and do the following:
   - Trace the development of *Greco-Roman civilization* and relate it to Western civilization.
   - Identify THREE contemporary cultures or geographic areas that belong to Eastern civilization.

3. Reread Cultural Diffusion on page 41. Write two or three paragraphs on this theme by doing the following:

   - Explain why you regard cultural diffusion as a beneficial or nonbeneficial process.

   - Describe examples of cultural diffusion other than those discussed in this chapter.

   - Use your imagination to create a cultural-diffusion model, including geographic locations and time frames.

Facing page: Wall painting of Egyptian grain agriculture and harvesting
decorating a tomb in the Valley of the Kings, Thebes

UNIT I

The Ancient World: Civilizations and Religion (4000 B.C.–A.D. 500)

The Ancient World:
Civilizations and Religion (4000 B.C.–A.D. 500)

Year	Dates and Events
B.C. **4000**	**4000 B.C.:** Rise of Sumer civilization in the Fertile Crescent (Mesopotamia)
	3000 B.C.: Unification of kingdoms of Upper and Lower Egypt
	Peak of Yellow River (Huang He) civilization in China
	2500–1500 B.C.: Rise and decline of Indus Valley civilization
	1750–1122 B.C.: Shang Dynasty in China
3001	**1650 B.C.:** Rise of Minoan civilization (Crete) and Mycenaean civilization
	(Greece)
3000	**1122–221 B.C.:** Zhou Dynasty in China
	587–538 B.C.: Babylonian Captivity of the Jews
	550 B.C.: Spread of Persian rule from India to Aegean Sea
	509–508 B.C.: Romans overthrow Etruscans, set up first democratic republic
2001	**480–479 B.C.:** Persians defeat Spartans at Thermopylae; Athenians defeat
	Persians at Salamis
2000	**431–404 B.C.:** Three Peloponnesian wars between Athens and Sparta
	343 B.C.: End of 30th (last) Dynasty in Egypt
	Rome begins conquest of Italy, makes Latin the official language
1001	**334 B.C.:** Alexander the Great begins 11-year territorial conquest from Greece
	to Indus River Valley
1000	**321–185 B.C.:** Maurya Dynasty in India; rise and spread of Buddhism
	200s B.C.: Rise of the Silk Road trade between China and India, Middle East,
	and Mediterranean
	264–146 B.C.: Punic Wars; Carthage destroyed, Rome controls Mediterranean
1	**206 B.C.–A.D. 220:** Han Dynasty in China
	27 B.C.–A.D. 180: Golden Age of Roman civilization (Pax Romana)
A.D.	**A.D. 33:** Crucifixion of Jesus; rise of Christianity
1	**A.D. 232:** Beginning of spread of Buddhism to Southeast Asia, China, Korea,
	Japan
	A.D. 320–567: Gupta Empire, India's golden age
	A.D. 324: Emperor Constantine reunites Roman Empire, moves capital to
	Constantinople
1000	**A.D. 622:** Muhammad's Hegira to Medina; rise of Islam

C H A P T E R
6

Societies and Civilizations Begin

A girl crouched on the riverbank gathering the tender young sprouts that grew there. She had done a good morning's work—her basket was nearly full. There would be enough for the whole family.

Stopping for a moment, she held one of the green sprigs in the palm of her hand and examined it. It was growing out of another part of the plant. In another season, this part made a different kind of food. What if she put sprouts like this in the ground where scarcely anything grew? But, no, that wouldn't work. These plants only grew near the river. Plants need water to grow. It didn't rain much here. So why not make little rivers flow out from the big one? The water could run through the dry, dusty places and bring water to the plants. All she needed to do was dig long channels from the sides of the river to the dry spots.

The girl smiled to herself and shook her head. How her family would laugh if she told them her idea. "Why," they would ask, "should we break our backs digging and planting? All we have to do now is make a few days' journey to fresh supplies of food. It's much pleasanter walking from place to place than grubbing in the dirt." They always complained that she brought back more daydreams than food to the camp.

EARLY PEOPLES

For a long period of time, prehistoric people did not plant crops. They kept alive by gathering wild plants and hunting animals. No one knows just how they learned to farm. Probably, like the girl in the story, many had fleeting ideas about planting seeds to grow crops and ensure a reliable source of food. But their traditional way of getting food kept them supplied with all they needed. Over time, changes in the climate made it necessary for them to put their new ideas to work. When people began to farm, great changes took places in human societies.

Hunters and Gatherers—Nomadic Groups

Human beings originated in central and southern Africa. There they inhabited vast grasslands known as savannas. They traveled together in small groups. They stopped in one place only as long as the plants and animals there could supply them with food and clothing. Sometimes they left because they had picked all the edible plants and killed all the animals that lived in one place. Sometimes they left because, with a change in season, the weather had become too cold or too dry for vegetation to grow.

Pattern of Life. The hunters and gatherers did not wander around aimlessly. They followed a predetermined path within a large territory. Whether they had picked a place clean or bad weather had killed all the plants, they knew that the area would become filled with good things again if they left it alone for a while. Therefore, they made a circuit of the same campsites, returning to each at fixed intervals of time. Anthropologists point out that in order to survive successfully for thousands of years, these people must have been able to construct mental maps and hold them in their memories.

In the cold or rainy seasons, hunter-gatherers stayed in caves. In warm, dry seasons, they made huts of branches or camped near rocks that served as wind shields. They may have stretched animal hides over the huts to make them waterproof.

Although hunter-gatherers generally followed set routes, they had to be flexible at times. Often drastic and long-term climate changes forced them to look for new areas that were rich in the resources they needed. These explorations were not hit-or-miss, however. Hunter-gatherers knew what kind of environments would support human beings and could make educated guesses about where to find them.

Often they changed their travel patterns because the number of people in the band (group) had increased. It was difficult to find an environment that could support a large number of people indefinitely. Therefore, from time to time, a few couples would split off and form the nucleus (core) of a new group. The new group then staked out its own territory.

Spreading Outward. As hunter-gatherer bands multiplied, they spread northward in Africa. They may have migrated northward because of changes in climate or rainfall. Food plants and animals may have become scarce. Or they may have been curious to see other places. Most of this movement occurred between 300,000 and 100,000 years ago. Not only did the northern climate become warmer then, the weather, in general, became wetter. Much of the desert between Central Africa and North Africa, now known as the Sahara, changed to grasslands. This meant that early people, once confined to Central Africa, could now move more easily into North Africa. From there they branched out into the Middle East and Europe.

The Neanderthals

Those *hominids* (early humans) who migrated to Europe and the Middle East had to adapt to different climates and terrain (land features). As a result, they developed different traits from the people who stayed behind. The most famous of these early humans were the Neanderthals. Although they were fully human, some of their characteristics were different from those of modern humans. Also, their cultures were not as advanced. The Neanderthals are known as *Homo sapiens* (wise human being). Modern humans are called *Homo sapiens sapiens* (wise, wise human being).

Adapting to Conditions. Neanderthals flourished between 100,000 and 30,000 years ago. Their superior intelligence helped them to survive during the last Ice Age. In caves containing Neanderthal bones, complex tools and weapons that date back 70,000 years have been found. At that time, glaciers covered much of Europe and Asia. These discoveries suggest that, as living conditions grew more difficult, the Neanderthals became more inventive. Because fewer resources were available during the frigid Ice Age winters, the Neanderthals must have had to use every part of the plants and animals they found. They needed a variety of tools to process these different parts.

Archaeologists believe that when the climate got colder and plants got harder to find, the Neanderthals had to concentrate mainly on hunting. As they faced larger, more dangerous animals, they learned to cooperate with one another to kill the animals. From examining the caves in which Neanderthals lived, archaeologists have learned that they built hearths to protect their fires and make the fuel burn more efficiently. Such advanced behavior suggests that Neanderthals also knew how to use animal skins for clothing and for windscreens at cave entrances.

Art and Beliefs. Besides improved survival techniques, the Neanderthals also demonstrated advances in culture. They may have been the first hominids to bury their dead. Archaeologists have found many Neanderthal skeletons in what seem to be graves. Some scholars claim that the Neanderthals believed in an afterlife. To support this theory, they point to Neanderthal grave sites in which they have found pollen from ancient flowers, red ochre dye, and objects made of goat horns. They feel that these things may have been put there deliberately for the dead to use in an afterlife. Other scholars argue that the presence of the items in the graves may have been merely accidental.

As they excavate more and more Neanderthal campsites, archaeologists find *artifacts* (objects) that suggest the beginnings of artistic activity. For example, they have found small tubular bones with holes in them. Because the holes are in a line and all on one side, archaeologists assume that they had been deliberately punched into the bone. These artifacts are very similar to flutes found at sites once occupied by more advanced people. Pieces of stone with holes pierced in their tops that the Neanderthals may have used as jewelry have also been found.

Disappearance. Eventually, a more advanced group of humans displaced the Neanderthals. During the time that Neanderthals existed, a new wave of hominids began migrating out of Africa. These were *Homo sapiens sapiens*, the direct ancestors of people living today. For a while, this new group coexisted with the Neanderthals. Then all traces of the Neanderthals disappeared.

Although it is possible that the modern humans killed off the Ne-

Sites of Prehistoric Peoples and the Spread of Modern Humans

The Spread of Modern Humans
(*Homo Sapiens Sapiens*)

- Australopithecus
- Homo habilis
- Homo erectus
- Homo sapiens

anderthals, no evidence supports this theory. In fact, interactions between the two groups seemed to have been peaceful and productive. Some groups of Neanderthals imitated the modern humans' superior methods of making tools.

Most anthropologists feel that members of the *Homo sapiens sapiens* group replaced Neanderthals because they were more adaptable. This means that they could quickly create new kinds of shelters, tools, and hunting techniques. The culture of the modern humans may have helped them survive environmental changes that eventually destroyed the Neanderthals.

The Cro-Magnon People

Scientists once believed that the Cro-Magnon people were the link between Neanderthals and modern humans. But they have since learned that the Cro-Magnons lived at the same time as their supposed ancestors did and, therefore, could not have evolved from them. Today, most scientists accept the theory that the early humans whose remains were found in Asia and Europe did not evolve into *Homo sapiens sapiens* but developed only as far as *Homo sapiens*. They believe that the Cro-Magnon people were the modern humans who had come from Africa.

Culture. The way of life, skills, and belief systems—culture—of the Cro-Magnons was more complex than that of the Neanderthals. The Cro-Magnons used a greater variety of tools and weapons than the Neanderthals did. They were better craftspeople and often decorated their products with patterns or carved them into the shape of animals. They learned to use materials—such as bone, antler, and ivory—in ways that the Neanderthals did not. From these materials, they made such delicate weapons as harpoons. They even used the new materials to make needles. This meant that they could sew animal hides into more comfortable, better-fitting clothes.

The Cro-Magnon people buried their dead in a way that showed a belief in an afterlife. The Cro-Magnon skeletons found in grave pits often wear remains of fine clothes and personal ornaments such as necklaces and bracelets. Tools and carved figurines lay at their sides. Anthropologists believe that these articles were meant to accompany the dead into another world.

Art. The Cro-Magnons painted pictures and made carvings considered by anthropologists as evidence that they believed in magic. For example, the Cro-Magnons may have thought that painting images of animals on the walls of their caves would increase the number of animals for their hunts. The figures of pregnant women that Cro-Magnons carved probably represented the life-giving aspect of nature. Early humans may have felt that owning such an image gave them some control over this power.

Prehistoric painting of a leaping cow and small horses, Lascaux caves, France

INFO CHECK

1. Explain how environmental change affected the ability of hunters and gatherers to expand outward.

2. Define the following terms: hominids, homo sapiens, homo sapiens sapiens, Neanderthals, Cro-Magnons.

3. State two ways in which Neaderthals and Cro-Magnons differed.

THE NEOLITHIC REVOLUTION

All the cultural changes that hominids experienced while evolving from prehumans into *Homo sapiens sapiens* occurred during the Stone Age. It is called the Stone Age because tools and weapons were made from stone, wood, and bone rather than from metal. This age is further divided into Old Stone Age (500,000 to 10,000 years ago), Middle Stone Age (10,000 to 8,000 years ago), and New Stone Age (8,000 to 5,000 years ago). In each of these periods, technology and other aspects of culture improved. The Old Stone Age began when the first hominid chipped rocks into shapes suitable for cutting, chopping, or scraping. It was during this period that early people moved into Europe, Asia, Australia, and North and South America.

The Middle Stone Age

Human technology advanced rapidly during the Middle Stone Age. This was partly due to modern humans' creativity and partly due to drastic changes in the environment. At this time, the last Ice Age was drawing to an end. The glaciers that covered the northern parts of the earth began to thaw. The water that melted from them ran off into the ocean, which overflowed its shores. Grassy plains became marshes. Fields of ice became grassy plains.

As the world warmed, the huge animals that had thrived in the extreme cold died off. When they became extinct, people lost an important source of meat and hides. The animals that took their place were smaller. Hunters had to hunt more frequently and kill more animals to get enough food for their communities. In order to kill more animals faster, people invented new weapons. One important invention was the *microlith*—a small, triangular-shaped stone blade used for knives and spears. Its sharp edge could pierce an animal's hide better than earlier weapons. Another invention, the bow and arrow, allowed hunters to bring down animals more quickly and from a safer distance than spears did.

People who lived near bodies of water invented tools to help them catch fish. These included the fishhook, the fish net, and boats made from hollowed logs.

The New Stone Age

During the New Stone Age, technology advanced so rapidly that scientists call it the *Neolithic Revolution*. ("Neolithic" is the scientific term for New Stone Age. "Revolution" refers to a sudden or complete change in the state of things.)

The Development of Agriculture. The greatest change of the Neolithic period was in how people obtained food. *Agriculture*, or farming, became more important than hunting and gathering. The replacement of large animals with smaller animals contributed to this change. Large animals breed very slowly. Sometimes hunters had to wait as long as ten years before an area became repopulated with prey. Meanwhile, people had to find areas that had not been overhunted. This was one reason for their constant traveling. Smaller animals breed very quickly. When small animals replaced large animals, hunters no longer had to move so frequently.

The plants that grew in the warmer climate also reproduced very quickly. No longer did years have to pass for an overpicked area to yield food again. Gradually, the members of hunter-gatherer bands began to settle down in one place and to build permanent shelters. To ensure that the areas where they lived would continue to produce, they learned to plant the grains they gathered. They also learned to keep herds of animals for a constant source of meat and hides.

No one knows how agriculture started. Possibly someone got the idea while gathering food, just as the young girl in the opening story did. Grain growing began around 8000 B.C. in the Middle East—possibly in southern Turkey. The change from the hunter-gatherer way of life to farming took place all over the world in roughly the same time period. (See map, page 15.)

Impact of Farming. Agriculture allowed people to store surplus food for future use. This meant that some people did not have to farm. They could exchange their skills for the extra food grown by others. These people became full-time priests, craftsworkers, and traders.

Farmers need tools that hunter-gatherers had no use for. A hoe was devised to prepare the ground for planting seeds. To harvest the grain, farmers used a curved-bladed tool called a sickle. The blade had to be sharp to cut the grain stalks. Farm households needed storage containers. They learned to make pots out of clay. Gradually, farmers realized that they could tame, or *domesticate*, sheep, cattle, pigs, and goats. Keeping domesticated animals close by gave the people a steady supply of meat and milk. About the same time, they learned to make thread out of animal hair and plant fibers. They wove the thread into cloth for clothes and other coverings.

Social Class and Conflict. With a reliable source of food, people could compete with one another without using up all the resources in one area. Consequently, some had a great many possessions while others lacked the necessities of life. Poor people began to borrow other people's goods. If they were unable to return them, they had to work for the lenders to pay their debts. Thus began a class system, with the wealthy on top and the poor on the bottom. Some of the wealthy people became powerful enough to rule large numbers of people.

Competition also led to war. Some groups claimed areas with plentiful resources for their sole use. When neighboring groups no longer shared their food, the poorer ones often tried to take the goods of richer groups by force. Weapons designed for fighting other people and paintings of battle scenes are first found in this era. Successful warriors may have become rulers by promising protection to some people and threatening others.

Farming and Herding Societies

As time went on, farming communities flourished and grew into towns. The most famous ruin of one of these communities is Catal Hüyük in present-day central Turkey. It dates from about 9,000 years ago. The people of Catal Hüyük lived in houses built very close together. The walls of these houses were often decorated with paintings and sculptures. The villagers had a variety of occupations and were divided into different classes.

Not all farmers lived in settled communities. Some were members of *pastoral* societies that moved from place to place herding animals. Few remains of the first pastoral people have been found. Like hunter-gatherers, they did not often make permanent shelters and accumulated few possessions. Several grave sites have been found, however. From studying these sites and observing herders of more recent times, scientists have some ideas about what the earlier groups were like. Like the hunter-gatherers, their members had close family ties. They shared their resources with one another and other groups more readily than did settled farming communities. All the members of the group were important to its well-being and were, therefore, on an equal footing. Perhaps more often than in hunter-gatherer bands, pastoral women shared men's tasks.

During the late New Stone Age, people learned that tools and weapons made of metal were better than those made of stone. At first, early metal workers hammered copper into the shapes of spearheads, arrow points, knives, or any other tool they needed. After a while, they discovered that mixing melted copper and tin produced an even harder metal called *bronze*. Finally, people learned how to use *iron*. *The Age of Metals* began about 5,000 years ago in the Middle East. The ability to produce metal tools and weapons developed later in other regions.

INFO CHECK

1. Complete each sentence:

   • During the Middle Stone Age, human technology advanced because _____.

   • Among the great changes brought by the Neolithic Revolution were _____.

2. Explain how the Neolithic Revolution brought more competition and conflict to human society.

3. State the significance to anthropologists and historians of Catal Hüyuk.

EARLY RIVER CIVILIZATIONS

Civilization resulted from the development of agriculture, the increase in population that agriculture brought about, and the need to solve problems presented by the environment. The solutions civilization offered were not perfect. Nonetheless, they made it possible for large numbers of people to live and work together in relative security. The first civilizations known to scholars—the Sumerian, the Egyptian, the Indus Valley, and the Yellow River (Huang He) civilizations—all developed out of cooperative ventures. In order to grow enough crops to feed a large population, the people of these regions organized under strong governments. They needed the direction of capable and powerful leaders to construct and maintain canals that brought river water to their fields.

The Role of Environment in the Growth of Civilizations

It is no accident that all of the early civilizations arose near rivers. In the Middle East, the Sumerians settled the land between the Tigris and Euphrates rivers. In Africa, the Egyptians established cities beside the Nile. In South Asia, an early Indian people built a civilization near the Indus River. In East Asia, Chinese farmers flourished beside the Huang He. Because all these regions had hot, dry climates, the farmers in each built canals to bring river water to their fields. They also took fish from the rivers for food. Rivers gave them a way to carry surplus goods to be traded elsewhere. Although alike in many ways, the environments of these civilizations had important differences. Consequently, the people in each region grew different crops and developed different kinds of cultures.

The City-States of Mesopotamia

The Sumerian civilization was the first of several that arose in lower Mesopotamia. (It began about 4000 B.C.) Mesopotamia was located in part of an area known as the *Fertile Crescent*. The Fertile Crescent is a large arc of land that starts at the eastern end of the Mediterranean Sea and curves northward and then south, ending at

The Earliest Civilizations

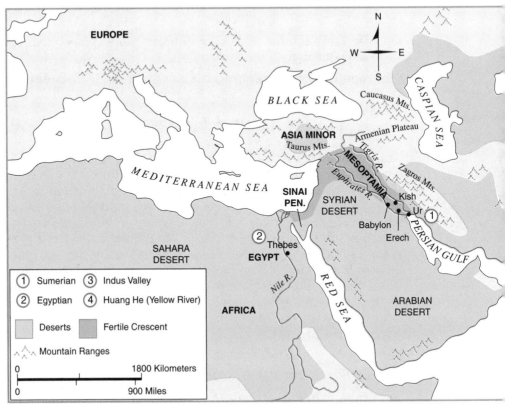

the Persian Gulf. The Tigris and Euphrates rivers made it possible to farm there.

In order to water fields located at a distance from the river, the farmers built an irrigation system. At first they simply dug ditches that brought water from the rivers to the fields. As more people came to the area, more complex irrigation systems were necessary. The ditches became a network of canals. Structures called *dikes* were built to keep the flood waters from destroying towns and crops. Methods of draining waterlogged land were devised. A strong central government with authority developed to keep the system in working order and to make sure that water was distributed to all the farms.

Not all of the areas around the Tigris and Euphrates could be protected from floods. Much of the area was marshy and unsuitable for farming. Consequently, swamps separated settled areas from each other. Each of these isolated settlements developed into a *city-state*, which included a city and the farms and villages around it.

Throughout most of their history, the Sumerian city-states fought against one another. About 2360 B.C., a strong leader named Sargon forced them to unite under his rule. Sargon's rule lasted for about 55

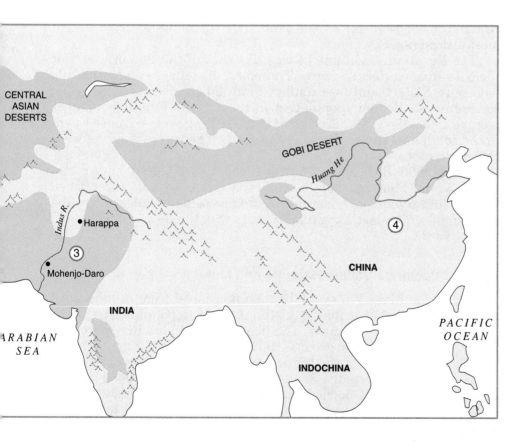

years. After his death, new wars among the city-states caused the downfall of Sumerian civilization.

The city-states finally fell to foreign invaders from a region that is now Syria. The leader of the conquerors then ruled both his own land and Mesopotamia. When a realm consists of different lands and different groups of people, it is considered to be an *empire*. A king named Hammurabi (ruled 1792–1750 B.C.) became the greatest ruler of this new empire. He made the city of Babylon his capital and called the empire Babylonia.

The rulers who followed Hammurabi could not hold the empire together. In time, mountain tribes from the north and east conquered the Babylonians.

The many different groups that formed states in the Fertile Crescent adopted the Sumerian culture. Consequently, all the civilizations that formed in the area can be referred to as Mesopotamian.

Egypt: Gift of the Nile

As civilizations were developing in the Fertile Crescent, a powerful people called the Egyptians began to build their own civilization in North Africa. Water from the Nile River and a warm climate made the area suitable for agriculture. Each fall, the flood waters of the Nile deposited rich soil on the land. The surrounding deserts kept most attackers away.

The Egyptian environment was like that of the Sumerians. But the Nile area was less swampy. Therefore, the villages along the Nile had more contact and less conflict than did the isolated Sumerian communities. As their population increased, the Egyptian villages merged into cities. The cities grew into two kingdoms—Upper Egypt in the south and Lower Egypt in the north. The rulers of Egypt were called *pharaohs*.

About 3000 B.C., a pharaoh named Menes united Upper and Lower Egypt. Menes set up his capital at Memphis and established Egypt's first *dynasty*. Dynasties are a succession of rulers from the same family. The last Egyptian dynasty was the 30th, which ended about 343 B.C.

Cities of the Indus Valley: Harappa and Mohenjo-Daro

The Indus River Valley civilization flourished from around 2500 to 1500 B.C. in what is now Pakistan. Like Mesopotamia, the Indus Valley has a hot, dry climate. The floods of the Indus River brought water and rich soil to the area, as did the Nile floods to Egypt. Unlike the Nile floods, however, the Indus floods did not occur regularly every fall but came unexpectedly. Sometimes the river did not flood for long periods. Sometimes it flooded with such force that it destroyed crops and fields. Therefore, the people of the Indus Valley had to dig irrigation ditches and build flood barriers. As in Mesopotamia and Egypt, the population of the area increased. Soon great cities, among them Harappa and Mohenjo-Daro, grew from villages and towns.

Scholars disagree about why the Indus civilization ended around 1500 B.C. Possibly the Indus River changed its course and the surrounding farmland dried up. Possibly some disease killed most of the people—the name Mohenjo-Daro means "place of the dead." Some scholars believe that the cities declined for economic reasons. Their populations may have moved away or become farmers in more fertile regions.

The Huang He Civilization

The earliest Chinese civilization arose beside the Huang He (Yellow River) between 3000 B.C. and 2500 B.C. (During that era, Egypt united under Menes.) The river gets its name from the fertile yellow soil called *loess* that it carries to the surrounding fields. Like Mesopotamia, Egypt, and India, northern China is very hot and dry. Although the soil there is fertile, farmers could not grow crops in it without water from the Huang He.

The history of early Chinese civilizations followed the same pattern as the histories of civilizations in Mesopotamia, Egypt, and India. To protect their fields from destructive flooding, Chinese farmers built dikes to keep the river within its banks. The farmers also dug irrigation canals to carry river water to their fields. With the success of agriculture, more people came to live in the valley. As in the other regions, a strong central government was needed to govern the people and to maintain the dike and canal systems that grew bigger and more complex as the population increased.

INFO CHECK

1. Describe the role played by the environment in the development of the first civilizations.

2. Explain how geography favored the Egyptians more than it did the Sumerians.

3. Complete each sentence.

   • A problem faced by the people of the Indus Valley civilization was _____.

   • Like the people of the Indus region, the early Chinese found it necessary to _____.

A COMPARISON OF THE EARLY CIVILIZATIONS

Traditional Economies

The economies of the early civilizations were all primarily based on agriculture. If crops failed for an extended period of time, the civilizations collapsed. The surpluses of food made possible by farming allowed some people to *specialize*, or do only one kind of work. Some people devoted all their time to making such goods as cloth, pottery, and jewelry. Others became merchants and traded surplus food and manufactured goods for items not available in their area. Eventually, craftwork and trade became as important as agriculture.

Government and Law

In all early civilizations, the governments controlled public works, such as irrigation systems, roads, and city walls. The population depended on these systems for survival. The governments made sure that repair and maintenance work was done. They taxed all those who used these services. Rulers also made laws to keep the citizens in order and raised armies for their defense. Often priests shared these powers and responsibilities with kings.

Mesopotamia. In Mesopotamia, the king represented the god that watched over his city-state. He oversaw the maintenance of the temples and irrigation system and commanded the army. Because he managed the affairs of the city's protective god, the king in some ways had to answer to the priests. The priests interpreted religious matters and also owned the wealthy estates that surrounded and supported the temples. King Sargon, who united the Sumerian city-states, took

Stone shaft showing Hammurabi and, inscribed below, a portion of his law code for governing Babylonia

away some of the priests' power by lessening their control over these estates.

Hammurabi, the ruler of the Babylonian empire, developed one of the first written law codes in the world. All the people in the empire who could read now knew what the laws were. Punishments would be similar throughout the empire.

The 300 laws of Hammurabi's Code strengthened the power of the central government. For example, the code gave the government a bigger role in punishing criminals. Formerly, the victims and their families had avenged the crimes committed against them. The code also increased the government's control over daily affairs. It set punishments for dishonest business practices and nonpayment of debts. It increased the legal rights of women and slaves. Punishments were harsher for people of lower rank than for the nobility.

Egypt. In Egypt, the pharaoh was not the agent of a god but the god figure himself. Egyptians believed that the gods were concerned about their well-being. Consequently, the pharaoh's main duty was to care for his people. His subjects expected his commands to be wise and just.

Pink granite figure of Queen
Hatshepsut, female pharaoh
of Egypt's 18th Dynasty

The pharaohs kept powerful armies to protect Egypt from enemies. Some pharaohs, such as Thutmose III (reigned 1490–1436 B.C.) and Ramses II (reigned 1290–1224 B.C.), used their armies to conquer more land. During the Empire Period of Egyptian history (1580–1150 B.C.), Egypt conquered many surrounding countries. The rulers of the defeated areas gave gold, silver, jewels, and food as tribute (taxes) to the pharaohs. Many of the conquered peoples became slaves in Egypt.

Egypt was too vast to be ruled by the pharaoh alone. A large group of priests, nobles, and governors shared his authority. They helped him interpret religious questions, make decisions about the ownership of land, collect taxes, and determine how the tax money should be spent. A large group of people who do government work is known as a *bureaucracy*. Only people who knew how to read and write could belong to the Egyptian bureaucracy.

The priests of Egypt were responsible for seeing that the gods were worshiped in the proper way. If the forms of worship were not correct, the gods might become angry and punish the people with failed crops or sickness.

Indus Valley. Because they are unable to translate early Indian writings, scholars do not know exactly how the Indus Valley cities were governed. No palaces where monarchs or ruling priests might have lived have been found in the ruins of Indian cities. Nonetheless, scholars believe that like the Sumerian and Egyptian governments, this civilization developed under some strong organizing influence such as councils of businessmen, craftsmen, and farmers. Only under such an influence could the people have built their beautifully planned cities and efficient irrigation systems.

Ancient China. Writings exist that refer to a very early Chinese dynasty called the Xia. Archaeologists, however, have not yet found any trace of this civilization. The next earliest was the Shang Dynasty. Its remains were not discovered until the beginning of the 20th century. This civilization probably began about 1750 B.C.

Each Shang king was believed to be the descendant of a god called Shang-di. His kinship with the god enabled him to ask the god to protect and favor his people. The king performed some of the duties of a priest. He communicated with the god to learn about future

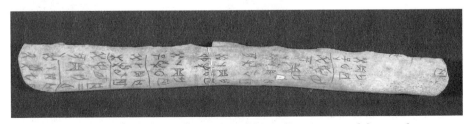

Chinese-script-engraved animal bone of the Shang Dynasty, used for prophecy

events that might affect his kingdom. This was done by writing a question about some problem in his kingdom on a large flat bone. A heated rod was placed against the bone until it cracked. The shape and length of the cracks were supposed to indicate the god's answer. The king made important decisions about agriculture and military matters based on what the cracks in the oracle bones revealed to him.

The core Shang territory included about 1,000 towns. A large number of allied towns outside of this territory sent tribute to the king. An adviser, or minister, and a number of other officials and priests made up a bureaucracy. These people helped the king govern.

Social Structure

Class structure was a feature of all early civilizations. It began when people founded the New Stone Age farming towns. When they massed together in cities and accepted the rule of kings and priests, class structure became more fixed.

In most civilizations, women did not enjoy the equality they had known in early farming communities. This was partly because the cities got much of their wealth from the products of skilled workers who received little or no pay. Most of these workers were women taken from other countries as prizes of war. Many scholars believe that the low status of these women affected men's attitudes toward women in general. Certainly, war itself influenced the roles of women. Many leaders got their power from their success as warriors. Such success was not generally possible for women.

Religious beliefs also played a part in women's loss of power. The fertility goddess was replaced by a male god who ruled all the other gods. Male priests now told people what to value and how to behave.

Mesopotamia. Mesopotamian kings and priests represented the highest class. They were followed by members of the nobility, who held large tracts of land. Commoners could also own land. Although these small landowners had a voice in the government and enjoyed the law's protection, they had less power than the nobles. Tenant farmers worked the nobles' land. In exchange, they were allowed to grow their own crops on part of it. The lowest class included criminals, debtors, and prisoners of war who had been enslaved. Mesopotamian slaves were not completely powerless. They could borrow money and engage in trade. These privileges enabled many to buy their freedom.

Mesopotamia was strongly *patriarchal*. In a patriarchal society, the father is the head of the household. The family is known by his last name and marks its descent from male ancestors. In ancient societies, fathers ruled their households and could even sell their wives and children into slavery. It was rare for Mesopotamian women to own businesses or enjoy political power.

Egypt. Egyptian society was structured much like that of Mesopotamia. The highest class consisted of the pharaoh, his family, the

Painting of an Egyptian man and wife of the 19th Dynasty harvesting wheat

priests, and the nobles. These people lived in luxurious houses sur-rounded by gardens. Wealthy farmers, merchants, scribes, and skilled workers enjoyed comfortable middle-class lives. (Scribes were people who kept records and wrote documents.) Occupying the next to lowest place in society were the hard-working peasants. Theirs was the larg-est class. These people had to pay heavy taxes, sometimes as much as 20 percent of their harvest. Tax collectors often punished them severely if they could not afford this amount.

As in Mesopotamia, slaves were the lowest class. They were forced to work for the government, digging stones for the state monuments or tending temple farms. Later in Egyptian history, they were allowed to join the army. As soldiers, they gained their freedom. They also gained the opportunity to move higher up in the class structure.

The women of Egypt enjoyed more rights and privileges than the women of Mesopotamia and China. They could legally own property, run businesses, and take part in public life. But they could not get a formal education. Because members of the government bureaucracy had to be able to read and write, most women were excluded from making political decisions. Women of the royal family were an excep-tion, however. They could become pharaohs, as Hatshepsut did.

The Indus Valley. Because scholars cannot yet understand the writing of the Indus Valley people, no one knows what their class structure was like. The ruins of Indus Valley houses give little indi-cation of social class. There are few grave sites in which privileged people were buried with costly treasures. According to a recent theory, the elite of this society were powerful merchants. Seals used to stamp signatures on possessions have been found. These may give the status as well as the name of their owners. If scholars are ever able to read the writing and interpret the images on these seals, they might learn how Indus Valley society was organized.

No one knows what life was like for women of the Indus Valley. Inability to read early Indian writing prevents scholars from knowing what roles men and women took. It is possible that the women of this civilization were more valued than those of Mesopotamia and China. If the early Indians worshiped a goddess, then their society may have been matriarchal.

Ancient China. The people of the Shang Dynasty could not move easily from one class to another. As in the other civilizations, slaves were the lowest class. The peasants were not much better off than the slaves. They worked on land owned by the nobles, whom they had to obey. Using tools with stone blades, they produced much of the country's wealth. (The metal bronze was considered too precious to waste on tools. It was used only for weapons and ceremonial objects.) Little wealth came back to the peasants.

The king and his nobles lived in palaces filled with ornaments made of bronze and gold. Because the king was dependent on the nobles to command his army and help run his government, he gave them many privileges.

Skilled workers, such as craftspeople, were above the peasants but considerably below the nobles. Craftspeople were dependent on the nobles to buy their goods. Their skills made them valuable, however, and they enjoyed some advantages.

Like Mesopotamia, China was strongly patriarchal. Women had few legal rights and privileges. At times, women of the royal court were able to lead fuller lives than ordinary women. For example, the exploits of Fu Hao, a wife of the Shang king Wu Ding (ruled in the 1300s B.C.), were described on oracle bones. Fu Hao apparently held a great deal of power because she owned land and led armies in battle. Because her grave was filled with treasures, scholars assume that she was highly honored.

INFO CHECK

1. Identify the similarities between the economies of the early civilizations.

2. For each of the societies listed, state an important fact about its government: Mesopotamia, Egypt, Indus Valley, China.

3. Determine which statements are correct.

- The women of most early civilizations did not have equality with men.
- Priests had little power in Mesopotamian society.
- Egyptian peasants paid no taxes.

- There is no evidence that the Indus Valley civilization was ruled by kings.
- Under the Shang Dynasty of China, skilled craftspeople were better off than peasants and slaves.

CONTRIBUTIONS OF EARLY CIVILIZATIONS

Religions

The religions of early civilizations were strongly influenced by their environments. The Mesopotamians, the Egyptians, the people of the Indus Valley, and the Chinese all believed that their gods controlled the forces of nature. Because the environment of each civilization was different from the others, however, the nature spirits in each were seen as having different personalities.

Mesopotamia. The people of the Fertile Crescent endured many violent floods. Consequently, they considered their gods to be rather harsh and unpredictable. In general, the gods looked and acted like human beings. Each god had his or her responsibilities and privileges. Mesopotamians believed that if they performed the proper ceremonies, they could persuade the gods not to send disasters.

According to their myths and legends, Mesopotamians believed that only the gods enjoyed true immortality (everlasting life). When humans died, they entered a realm of shadows.

Egypt. Egypt's environment had a very different effect on the religion of its people. Every summer, Egypt's farmland seemed to die as the soil dried out and the plants wilted. Every fall, the farmland came back to life when the overflowing Nile brought water and fertile mud. Egyptians, therefore, created a myth about death and rebirth. Every year the nature god Osiris died and was brought back to life by his wife, Isis. Osiris could give eternal life to the souls of humans. After a person's death, Osiris judged whether he or she had been just enough for his or her soul to be admitted to his kingdom.

Egyptians also believed that each person had *ka*, a special life force that could not be destroyed. At death, *ka* deserted the body. It could, however, return. Therefore, Egyptian priests preserved corpses. They *mummified* them by treating them with special herbs and oils and wrapping them in linen cloths. They then placed the mummies in tombs filled with the dead person's belongings. Egyptians hoped that, when the *ka* returned, it would stay in its well-furnished tomb and not haunt the living. So great was the skill of the priests that many mummies remained whole through thousands of years.

Indus Valley. Archaeologists believe that the people of the Indus Valley may have worshiped a nature goddess. They have found female statues similar to the ones made by the Cro-Magnons. Scholars are fairly sure that the early Indians performed bathing ceremonies. They have found the remains of a great public bathing pool in a large building on top of a high mound in Mohenjo-Daro. The Hindu practice of ritual, or ceremonial, bathing in the sacred Ganges River in northwest India may have originated from this practice.

Ancient China. Like the people of other early civilizations, the Chinese worshiped nature gods. The people of the Shang dynasty, however, also felt that their dead ancestors could persuade the gods to give them good crops and other advantages. Therefore, they built shrines to their ancestors and made offerings of food and drink to them in hopes of winning their good will. Eventually, this practice developed into what is known as ancestor worship.

Writing Systems

The work of scribes was extremely important to the functioning of the first civilizations. Without writing, business records could not have been kept, law codes could not have been handed down from generation to generation, and ownership of property could not have been proved. Scholars do not know for sure when writing was invented. Some point out that until civilizations arose, writing had been unnecessary.

Mesopotamia. Archaeologists found the earliest specimens of writing in the city of Uruk on the Euphrates River in present-day Iraq. These specimens date back to about 3300 B.C. The writing consists of wedge-shaped marks, called *cuneiform*. The writers used a pointed stick, called a stylus, to press the shapes into a wet clay tablet. Each symbol stood for a name of something, an idea, or a sound. The specimens show a system of 700 symbols. (See illustration, page 40.)

The Mesopotamians developed writing into an efficient means of communication. Mesopotamian merchants needed to keep records of their goods and business deals. Mesopotamians found other uses for writing besides keeping business records. Writing became a way for them to express their ideas and beliefs. Much of their literature is concerned with the creative and destructive forces of water. A poem called *Gilgamesh* describes a great flood that an angry god sent to destroy the world. Scholars believe that the Old Testament story of Noah and his ark was based on this poem.

Egypt. Specimens of Egyptian writing have been found that date from about 3000 B.C. This system of writing, called *hieroglyphics*, was similar to the cuneiform system. It used pictures to represent sounds, words, and ideas. There were about 600 symbols. At first, the Egyptians carved their hieroglyphics onto stone. Later they invented a method of making paper from papyrus plants and wrote on the paper. For pens they used sharpened reeds, which they dipped into an ink made from soot and vegetable gum. (Soot is a black substance left behind after something is burned.)

Scholars learned to read Egyptian writing from a slab of rock that had writing engraved on it. Found in A.D. 1799, it was a monument to honor a pharaoh. Luckily, it included a Greek version of the text. With the help of this Greek version, a French scholar named Jean-François Champollion solved the problem of reading the hieroglyphics. Because it was found near an Egyptian town called Rosetta, the rock is called the Rosetta Stone.

Egyptian writers created poetry, songs, myths, and fiction. The Egyptian Book of the Dead is a collection of myths, hymns, and prayers. It was placed in tombs to help the dead adjust to their new world.

Indus Valley. No one has yet translated the writing of the Indus Valley people. Scholars have found 400 different symbols. Like Egyptian hieroglyphics and Mesopotamian cuneiform, some of the symbols stand for entire words and others for sounds. Perhaps one day you will read about a scholar who has managed to solve the mystery of this language.

Ancient China. Unlike writing in Mesopotamia and Egypt, writing in ancient China was not developed by merchants. Because the king wrote questions to the gods on the oracle bones, writing was an essential part of religious ritual. It did have practical uses, of course. The king and his nobles used it to keep records of taxes and to communicate royal policy to the governors of distant villages.

Early Chinese writing was a complex system, containing at least 2,000 characters, or picture symbols. Each character stands for an object and a sound. Characters are combined to express ideas. The system took a great deal of time to learn. Chinese peasants, who worked long hours, had no leisure in which to study. Because education was available only to the ruling classes, it was considered a source of power and privilege. Consequently, Chinese people developed a deep respect for learning.

Cities and Architecture

The cities of the Mesopotamians, the Egyptians, the people of the Indus Valley, and the Chinese were alike in many ways. All the cities were important as religious centers, seats of government, and marketplaces. The cities of each civilization, however, had unique characteristics.

The architecture in each civilization also had important differences. Building materials, for example, varied with the natural resources found in each area. Different levels of technological advancement also influenced the way the people in each civilization built their homes and temples.

Mesopotamia. Mesopotamian cities were surrounded by massive walls and dominated by religious buildings called *ziggurats*, which towered over the temple and the king's palace. The houses of wealthy people had several stories and were built around a central patio.

Mesopotamia had few stone quarries and forests. Therefore, the ziggurats, palaces, and temples were built mainly of bricks. Building techniques were very advanced, however. The Mesopotamians invented the arch, a curved structure built to support weight over an opening in a building.

Egypt. Egyptian capital cities resembled the Mesopotamian city-states to some extent. These, too, devoted a large amount of space to royal buildings and temples. They were, however, more magnificent. The pharaoh had two palaces. He and his family lived in the more luxurious one on the outskirts of the city. The one in the center of the city was used for business and was less imposing. A road broad enough for the pharaoh's chariot led from his residence to his city offices. Ordinary people lived outside the central city. Although the houses of wealthy people were larger than those of the poor, the designs were similar. The city's water was supplied by the Nile and, in some cases, by wells. There were no drainage pipes for sewage.

Most homes and other ordinary buildings were made of bricks. Unlike Mesopotamia, Egypt was rich in stone quarries. Builders shaped huge stone blocks to construct the great tombs and monuments called pyramids.

Indus Valley. In the Indus Valley, archaeologists have found the remains of cities that in many ways were superior to those of Mesopotamia and Egypt. Unlike the cities of these civilizations, the Indus Valley cities had not grown haphazardly from villages. They had been carefully designed. The wide, straight streets were paved and arranged in a grid pattern.

Massive structures were made from bricks. The buildings had many functions. They included places to store grain, offices where state business was done, and centers for religious ceremonies. A large pool area in one building had been made with bricks, carefully fitted together. The bricks were sealed with a glaze to make them watertight.

Ancient China. Like the cities of Mesopotamia, Shang cities were surrounded by walls. Chinese walls were more massive than those of Mesopotamia, however. The earth wall around Zhengzhou, a Shang capital, was 33 feet high and 5 miles long. Archaeologists believe that if 10,000 builders had worked on the wall 330 days a year, its completion would have taken 18 years. Unlike the cities of Mesopotamia, which sheltered people of all classes, Chinese cities protected only the king and his nobles. Craftspeople and less skilled workers lived in settlements outside the fortifications.

Even before they had begun to live in cities, Chinese builders were highly advanced. Many buildings in early villages were constructed from pieces of timber that had been joined together by the tenon-and-mortise method. This means that the ends of two boards had been cut in such a way that they could be interlocked.

Science and Technology

As civilizations developed, people could exchange ideas more easily through trade and written documents. Consequently, new inventions and intellectual achievements increased and spread faster.

Mesopotamia. The Sumerians were responsible for many improvements in technology. They originated the manufacture of bronze (a metal made from copper and tin). They were the first people to use wheels for transportation. Scholars believe that wheels used in making clay pots inspired the invention of wheeled vehicles.

The Babylonians, who took over the Sumerian civilization, also made many contributions to science and culture. Their *astronomers*, people who study the stars and planets, developed a lunar calendar. (*Lunar* means that it was based on the phases of the moon.) The calendar provided for a 12-month year, a 7-day week, and a 24-hour day. Babylonian scholars created a system of arithmetic based on the number 60. They gave us the 60-minute hour and the 360-degree circle.

Babylonians and earlier Mesopotamians apparently knew how to make maps. Archaeologists have found a map of the city of Nippur that someone had etched on a clay tablet. It dates from around the year 1500 B.C. Later analysis shows that the distances marked on the ancient map were accurate.

Egypt. To this day, no one has been able to reproduce the formula Egyptians used to preserve the dead. Egyptian mummies exist today and the bodies inside the wrappings are usually whole. Egyptian doctors performed complicated surgery and prescribed drugs to lessen their patients' pain.

Like the Babylonians, the Egyptians had a calendar. It divided the year into 12 months of 30 days each. Five feast days, or holidays, were added to the end of the year to make 365 days. Mathematicians created a number system based on ten and developed a system of geometry to help landowners measure their land. A knowledge of geometry was important to the pyramid builders.

Indus Valley. The remains of the cities of the early Indus people reveal their technological achievements. They built a very advanced drainage system in the cities. Sewers under the streets carried off waste and water. Many of the homes had indoor bathrooms. These were connected to the public sewage system by underground pipes.

Clay models of carts showed that the Indus Valley peoples used wheels for transportation. Many of their figurines demonstrate that

The Faces of Djed

In the Egyptian city of Thebes, in the 9th century B.C., a middle-class woman named *Djedmaatesankh* lived with her husband, *Paankhntof*. They were respectable, religious people, who lived comfortably. Both were employed and therefore enjoyed a double income, but they had no children. This was unusual in Egypt at that time.

Djed was a musician at the great temple of the god Amon Ra at nearby Karnak. Her husband was employed as a temple doorkeeper. However, their main income would have come from their ownership of a plot of fertile Nile farmland.

Djed's small mummy, on display at the Royal Ontario Museum, in Canada, kept the secrets of her life and death until 1995. Then, modern medical technology made it possible to examine her body electronically, without cutting it open. Thus, the sanctity of the human body, so important to the Egyptians, was preserved.

While still inside her protective mummy case, Djed underwent a full body CT (cat) scan. The images revealed that she had been a beautiful woman. They also indicated that she had died of an infected cyst in her upper left jaw. The cyst had probably burst and poisoned her. She was approximately 35 years of age.

Worn teeth and other dental problems were common among ancient peoples. Food was often very coarse. The daily bread of the Egyptians had a high sand content, which ground down teeth as it was chewed. Cavities were widespread in Egypt as honey, other sweet foods, and beer were staples of the diet, at least among the wealthy. Without modern antibiotics, Djed probably died painfully.

The CT technology revealed other things about Djed. The state of preservation of her body was excellent. By her time, mummification was available to those who could afford it, not just the pharaohs. She was wearing a gold, vulture-shaped amulet and a stone heart scarab. The inscriptions on her mummy case referred to Osiris, the god of the realm of the dead, and the sun god, Ra.

The name of her mother accompanied her own name on the mummy case. This was usual. However, her husband's name was also present. This was unusual. It indicated that he may have paid part of the costs of mummification and burial. Such an expense may have cost him his income for a year. Djedmaatesankh's name means "the goddess Maat has said that she will live."

- What does the story of Djed tell us about the civilization of ancient Egypt?

they were able to manufacture bronze and were skillful at molding it into a variety of shapes.

Ancient China. Many craftspeople of the Shang Dynasty used advanced technology in working with metal. They knew a method of casting bronze that was superior to the one used in more western civilizations. This method enabled them to make richly ornamented weapons and ceremonial objects. Potters used kaolin, a fine white clay, for making dishes and ornaments. Cloth makers spun the fibers from silkworm cocoons into silk. Jewelers fashioned ornaments from stone, jade, and bone.

INFO CHECK

1. Contrast the religious beliefs of Egypt and Mesopotamia.

2. Describe the origins of ancestor worship in China.

3. Why do you think writing systems are important characteristics of civilizations?

4. Explain the relationship between architecture, natural resources, and technology in the cities of the early civilizations.

5. What technological achievements of the Indus Valley civilization made their cities somewhat like modern cities?

DEMOGRAPHIC PATTERNS OF EARLY CIVILIZATIONS

The characteristics of the populations—the demographics—of early communities reveal much information about their way of life. Cities had more varied populations than small farming villages. The people of small farm villages were usually related to one another or had at least known each other for several generations. The people who moved into walled cities for protection often came from different villages or even from nomadic herding groups. Many city inhabitants came from the different towns that the cities had absorbed as they expanded.

As cities developed into civilizations, their rulers took over distant peoples. When they made slaves of the conquered people, they introduced more foreign elements into the populations of their cities.

Perhaps the most important cause of population diversity was the increasing variety of social classes and kinds of work. No longer did people who lived in the same area all have the same interests and patterns of behavior. In spite of almost daily contact with one another, nobles, craftsworkers, and peasants all lived in different worlds.

Most early civilizations did not develop in isolation. Much evidence exists that their populations traded and sometimes fought with each other and with nomadic groups. Because of trade, there was considerable exchange of ideas, goods, and customs among Mesopotamia, Egypt, and the cities of the Indus Valley. Many scholars feel that the earliest Chinese civilizations developed with little or no contact from the more western cultures.

Time Line

Year	Dates and Events
B.C. **35,000**	**500,000–10,000 B.C.:** Beginning of Old Stone Age; migrations to Australia and North and South America
10,001	**100,000–30,000 B.C.:** Migrations of Neanderthals from southern and central Africa to northern Africa, Asia, southern Europe
10,000	**35,000–10,000 B.C.:** Northward migrations of African Cro-Magnons
	10,000 B.C.: Beginning of Middle Stone Age; end of last Ice Age
8,001	**8000 B.C.:** Beginning of grain agriculture in Middle East (southern Turkey) Beginning of New Stone Age; agriculture and permanent settlements
8,000	**5000 B.C.:** Early use of copper, bronze, iron in Middle East
	4000 B.C.: Rise of Sumerian civilization in Mesopotamia's Fertile Crescent
6,001	**3300 B.C.:** Cuneiform, earliest known writing, used in Uruk, Mesopotamia
	3000 B.C.: Peak of Yellow River (Huang He) civilization in China
6,000	**2500–1500 B.C.:** Rise and decline of Indus Valley civilization (Pakistan)
	2360 B.C.: Unification of Sumerians under Sargon
4,001	**1813–612 B.C.:** Rise and decline of Assyrian empire and its capital of Nineveh
	1792–1750 B.C.: Babylonian empire under Hammurabi; his code of 300 laws
4,000	**1750 B.C.:** Rise of Shang Dynasty in China
	1640–1570 B.C.: Hyksos invasions of Egypt; horse-drawn chariots, new military technology
2,001	**1580–1150 B.C.:** Egyptian territorial conquests, including Kush (Nubia)
	1122 B.C.: Beginning of 900-year rule of northern China by Zhou Dynasty
2,000	**750 B.C.:** Kush annexes southern Egypt, preserving its culture
	605–562 B.C.: New Babylonian (Chaldean) empire under Nebuchadnezzar II
1	**343 B.C.:** End of 30th (last) Dynasty in Egypt

Trade Between Mesopotamia, Egypt, and the Indus Valley

Water routes were the most popular trade routes. Boats were a cheap and easy way to transport goods. Popular trade items were metals, precious stones, and incense, such as myrrh and frankincense. Less expensive objects, such as razors and mirrors, were also traded.

Through trade, early civilizations influenced one another. Significant similarities exist between Sumerian and Egyptian writings, art, and vocabulary. A few scholars feel that Sumerian civilization set the example for Egyptian civilization. Most, however, believe that other factors were more important in the development of Egyptian culture.

No information exists about the influence that the Indus Valley civilization might have had on other civilizations. It shares many features with the Mesopotamian and Egyptian civilizations. No one can say which one originated these features. Scholars feel certain that trade took place between the early Indus people and countries to the west because Mesopotamian pottery has been found in ruins of the Indus Valley cities. Also, cuneiform records mention Indus Valley merchants who were in Mesopotamia in the time of Sargon.

Assyrian Influence on Mesopotamian Civilization

As time passed, other people besides those of the four early civilizations began to leave their mark on the world. These were either warlike groups who conquered the established states or the people of prosperous areas that the established states took over.

The Assyrians, who were examples of the first group, managed to conquer a large part of the Middle East that included Mesopotamia. They originated in an area in northern Mesopotamia that had no natural features to shield it from the raids of desert tribes. Constantly forced to ward off attacks, the Assyrians learned to be skillful warriors. They soon turned to conquering nearby kingdoms in the Middle East. They succeeded in extending their empire from Egypt to Turkey and Iran. From their capital city of Nineveh, they ruled their empire by a combination of efficient administration and terror. The Assyrians were a powerful force in the Middle East from about 1813 to 612 B.C.

The Assyrians introduced military tactics that revolutionized warfare in the known world. They invented many devices and techniques for destroying the defenses of a city. They were the first to equip their soldiers entirely with iron weapons and armor. Fear also played a part in their conquests. Assyrians had a reputation for cruelty to their captives.

In spite of their warlike tendencies, the Assyrians valued the culture of their time. The last great Assyrian king, Ashurbanipal, built a fine library in Nineveh. It contained thousands of clay tablets that preserved the literature of the Sumerians and the Babylonians. Because of this library, scholars today can study the religion, medicine, poetry, and history of Mesopotamia.

Contact Between Egypt and Nubia

Nubia is an example of a conquered people that played an important part in the history of early civilization. Nubia, an area around the Nile River south of Egypt, was rich in gold. Egypt's trade routes to southern Africa passed through a part of Nubia called Kush. Nubia and Egypt exchanged ideas and customs through trade. During this time, Egypt longed to possess the riches of Kush and to have sole control over the trade routes. Thutmose I finally conquered Kush (about 1522 B.C.) and made it an Egyptian province. The princes of Kush then had to send the pharaoh large tributes of treasure.

The people of Kush adopted Egyptian culture, learning to speak and write its language and to practice its customs. Gradually, however, Kush freed itself from Egyptian rule. Around 1100 B.C., Egypt became weak. Foreign invaders swept in and divided Egypt among them. In 751 B.C., the ruler of Kush took over the southern parts of Egypt. Although Egypt was destroyed, its culture flourished in Kush for a long time. Centuries later, when the Greek historian Herodotus

Africa: Nubia and Kush

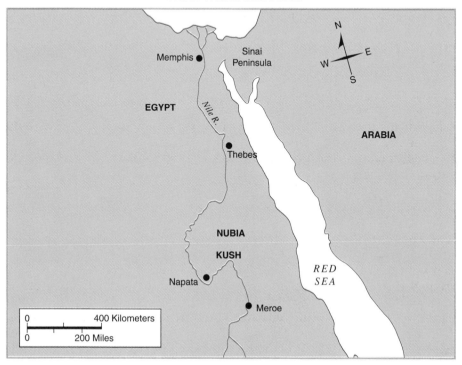

visited Kush, he incorrectly declared that Egyptian culture must have originated there.

The Isolation of Ancient China

The Himalayan and the Pamir mountains, the Gobi Desert, and the Mongolian Plateau almost entirely cut off the early Chinese from the more western civilizations. Scholars do not know how much, if any, influence from the other civilizations trickled through these barriers to the Shang Dynasty.

New influences came to the Shang kingdom from neighboring groups with whom it fought border wars. One such group, the Zhou, successfully rebelled against the Shang. They took over the empire and advanced its culture in many ways. Among these advances were the creation of the first legal documents in the region. These were written agreements between the king and the lords to whom he granted estates. The Zhou also improved roads and canals, expanded trade, introduced iron, and originated Chinese philosophy. Confucianism and Taoism are treated in Chapter 8.

Migrations of Pastoral Groups

Many early groups herded animals across vast areas. When a particularly harsh season destroyed their pastures and drove them from their territory, they traveled into more settled areas. Sometimes, they became peaceful members of the new communities. At other times, they took the communities by force. In either case, the herders brought great changes to these areas and often made significant contributions to the cultures there.

The Indo-Europeans. Indo-Europeans were several different groups of herding people from the plains of Eurasia. At various times between 2500 and 1000 B.C., waves of these people swept westward and southward into Europe, the Middle East, and South Asia. The different groups spoke closely related languages. These form the basis for most modern European languages and an early Indian language called Sanskrit.

The Indo-Europeans were skilled warriors. Using horse-drawn chariots, they easily won battles with settled farming people. In time, the Indo-Europeans merged with the people they had conquered. New cultures rose from this mixture.

Semitic Nomads. Other herding people besides the Indo-Europeans moved into civilized areas. Several different Semitic groups from the Arabian peninsula migrated into North Africa and other areas of the Middle East, looking for new pastures. They, too, gave rise to new empires and contributed to the culture of the region.

One of these groups, the Hyksos, repeatedly invaded Egypt between 1640 and 1570 B.C. They, like the Indo-Europeans, had ad-

Migrations of Indo-European Peoples

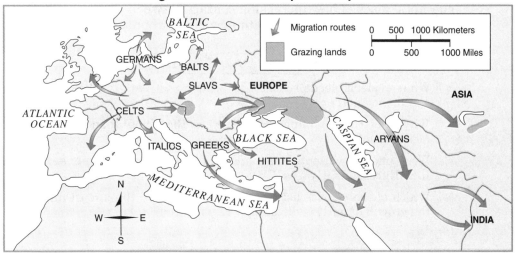

vanced military technology. The bronze weapons and armor, horse-drawn chariots, and more efficient bows that the Hyksos used were adopted by Egypt's military forces. The new technology increased Egypt's power.

The Chaldeans, also from Arabia, brought down the Assyrian Empire. The Chaldean rule is called the New Babylonian Empire. It was one of the most brilliant of its time. It reached its height under King Nebuchadnezzar II, who ruled from 605 to 562 B.C. Nebuchadnezzar is famous for beautifying the city of Babylon. He also ordered the building of the Hanging Gardens. This tall, pyramid-shaped structure was planted with exotic tropical plants. They were irrigated by pipes that brought water from the Euphrates.

The Chaldeans believed strongly in *astrology*. Astrology is an attempt to tell the future by studying the influence of the stars and planets on human events. This study may or may not have given the Chaldeans knowledge of the future. It did, however, give them accurate knowledge about the movements of heavenly bodies. Chaldean astrologers kept detailed astronomical records and were able to predict solar and lunar eclipses. Observation of the stars also made it possible for them to calculate the length of a year. The science of astronomy had its beginnings in astrology.

The Chaldeans were also mathematicians. They could add, subtract, multiply, and divide. They had some knowledge of algebra, trigonometry, and geometry. Like the Assyrians, they adapted and preserved Babylonian culture and continued the development of cuneiform writing.

As more civilizations arose, contact among different peoples increased. Much of history is the record of how great civilizations interacted with each other and the people around them. The next two chapters, discuss how increasing contact between people in different parts of the world contributed to new civilizations.

INFO CHECK

1. What evidence leads scholars to believe that early civilizations influenced one another?

2. Why was China influenced more by the Zhou than by Egypt or Mesopotamia?

3. Write one or two sentences to identify each of the following: Assyrians, Indo-Europeans, Hyksos, Chaldeans.

4. Which of the peoples listed in question 3 do you think most influenced the growth of early civilizations? Explain your answer.

CHAPTER REVIEW

Multiple Choice

1. The human beings who originated in south and central Africa moved from place to place because

   1. the weather became too hot or too cold
   2. they ate up all the plants in the area
   3. the animals they hunted had moved away
   4. all of the above.

2. People who have no permanent home and move from place to place are called

   1. farmers
   2. laborers
   3. prehistoric
   4. nomadic.

3. The two climatic changes that occurred between 100,000 to 300,000 years ago and resulted in the migration of the early humans were

   1. warmer and wetter weather
   2. colder and drier weather
   3. warmer and drier weather
   4. colder and wetter weather.

4. The Neanderthals were able to survive the last Ice Age of Europe and the Middle East because

   1. climates were warmer and food plentiful
   2. they became farmers and grew their own food supply
   3. they adapted and worked cooperatively to survive
   4. the Ice Age ended quickly, leaving much water and fish.

5. Select the group that has the correct title and lifestyle.

   1. Neanderthals—Homo sapiens, nomads—hunter-gatherers
   2. Cro-Magnon—Homo sapiens, nomads—hunter-gatherers
   3. Neanderthals—Homo sapiens sapiens, nomads—farmers
   4. Cro-Magnon—Homo sapiens sapiens, nomads—farmers.

6. In order for the hunter-gatherers to survive, tribe members

   1. worked long hours
   2. shared tasks of gathering and hunting food
   3. spent many hours tilling the soil
   4. lived near rivers and seacoasts.

7. A turning point for human society that occurred during the Stone Age Period was

   1. ending of the Ice Age and flooding of the dry lands
   2. replacing stone tools with metal and iron ones
   3. conquering the lands of Europe, Asia, Australia, and South America
   4. replacing hunting-gathering as the humans' main source of food with agriculture.

8. From the following list of societies, select the one that required men and women to fulfill the same tasks.

   1. pastoral
   2. hunter-gatherer
   3. agricultural
   4. warrior.

9. A dynasty means a

   1. succession of rulers from the same tribe
   2. succession of rulers from the same country
   3. succession of rulers from the same religion
   4. succession of rulers from the same family.

10. The growth of agriculture enabled societies

    1. to require all people to become farmers
    2. to force peoples to share their limited water supply
    3. to have people specialize in work other then farming
    4. to force cooperation among workers.

11. Using the map on pages 56–57 and your knowledge of Global History and Geography, identify three of the earliest centers of civilization.

    1. Sahara, Arabian Desert, Gobi Desert
    2. Nile River Valley, Tigris-Euphrates River Valley, Indus River Valley
    3. Black Sea, Caspian Sea, Red Sea
    4. Taurus Mountains, Caucasus Mountains, Zagros Mountains.

12. Refer to the time line on page 73 and identify the empire that existed from 1792 to 1750 B.C.

    1. Assyrian
    2. Babylonian
    3. Kushite
    4. Chaldean.

Thematic Essays

1. Select one of the civilizations presented in Chapter 6. *Task*: For the one you select, discuss how the political and economic development of that society was affected by its geographic location.

2. *Task:* Explain how and why the social, economic, or legal status of women changed in China, India, or Egypt as that civilization developed.

3. *Task:* Describe how the Neolithic Revolution affected the governmental structure of Indus Valley or Mesopotamian civilization.

Document-Based Questions

For each document or illustration, explain the message or intent of the speaker.

1. "... Furthermore, due reverence shall be shown to the gods, but to the Storm-god special reverence shall be shown. If some temple has a leaking roof, the commander of the border guards and the town commandant shall put it right, or ... if the Storm-god or any implement of any other god is in disrepair, the priests, the 'anointed' [and] the mother-of-god shall restore it."

2. "When they perform the ritual at the boundary of the enemy country they sacrifice one sheep to the Sun-goddess of Arena and the Storm-god, the Patron-god [and] all the gods ... the gods and goddesses of Turmitta ... to all the mountains [and] rivers."

3. Refer to the photograph of the oracle bone on page 62.

4. "Hail to thee, O Nile! Who manifest thyself over this land and come to give life to Egypt ... Watering the orchards created by Ra to cause all the cattle to live, thou givest the earth to drink, inexhaustible one!"

Document-Based Essay

Task: Use your answers to the previous questions to develop an essay that explains why the people of ancient civilizations believed in many gods.

C H A P T E R

7

The Brilliance of the
Classical Age

Lydia slipped away from the house. It was early evening, and she had finished her needlework. Her slave, Hermia, would make excuses for her if her mother wanted her for anything. As she had hoped, the grove between the gardens and the open fields was empty. Making her way to the rock that jutted out above a little spring, she climbed on top. Trying to make her voice ring the way the boy actor's had at yesterday's performance of *Antigone*, she began to recite:

> Living, I go down to the vaults of death.
> What is the law of heaven that I have broken?
> Why should I any longer look to the gods,
> Ill-fated as I am? Whose aid should I invoke,
> When I for piety am called impious?

Lydia was sure she had made Antigone's speech just as moving as the actor had. But was she capable of living the part as well as acting it? Was she brave enough to defy a tyrant? Would she risk death rather than let her brother 's corpse be dishonored? Lydia thought of her brother, Demetrius. If only he weren't so spoiled and conceited, it would be much easier to imagine sacrificing herself for him.

T he wealthy young Greek girl lived in Athens at the height of its glory. The citizens of her city were the freest, most politically active people in the world. Because she was a girl, however, she was not a citizen. She could not go to school, vote, or hold office. Nonetheless, she was able to enjoy one of the richest cultures of her time—which is saying a great deal. It was a time of brilliance for several civilizations.

CLASSICAL CIVILIZATIONS

Between 600 B.C. and A.D. 500, China, Greece, Rome, and India each experienced a period known as a classical age. When scholars describe a culture as *classical*, they mean that its intellectual and artistic works have enduring value. Such periods of intellectual flowering are also known as Golden Ages.

One thing most of these civilizations had in common was the concept that a government was meant to serve the people it governed. In some of these civilizations, this concept led people to claim the right to make political decisions. Once people felt that they had control over the institutions that influenced their lives, they began to ask how they could change those institutions to make their lives better. Then they began to question what exactly constituted a good life. To answer this question, many people turned to art, philosophy, and science.

China's classical age had its beginning in the 11th century B.C. when the kings of the Zhou Dynasty expanded what had been the Shang kingdom. This territory was located in the eastern part of China on the North China Plain, near the Yellow Sea.

Ancient Greece was made up of independent city-states. The two most important of these *poli* were Athens and Sparta. Athens is best known for being the birthplace of democracy in the 5th century B.C. As the leading city-state with control over the seas, Athens was at its strongest at this time. It forced the other city-states to pay money to it as tribute and became even richer by trading with them as well. Athen's statesmen, soldiers, writers, artists, architects, mathematicians, and philosophers achieved so much that the period extending from 500 to 338 B.C. is known as the Golden Age of Greece.

Rome had a long period when its culture dominated much of the known world. Historians cite the years 27 B.C. to A.D. 180 as its Golden Age. During this period, the empire prospered under a series of capable emperors.

During the Maurya Dynasty (321–184 B.C.), India was stable and prosperous. India's first great empire was established at this time. Government became centralized and efficient. The Buddhist religion became an important influence in India and began to spread to other parts of Asia.

INFO CHECK

1. Define the term "classical civilizations."

2. Which of the classical civilizations listed interests you the most? Explain your answer.

CHINA'S CLASSICAL AGE

The Zhou Dynasty: 1027–256 B.C.

The Zhou justified their rebellion against the Shang by declaring that the Shang king had not been fit to rule. They claimed that he had been incompetent and more interested in his own pleasures than in the welfare of his subjects. In denying the right of a bad ruler to keep his throne, the Zhou originated the concept of the Mandate of Heaven. A *mandate* is the authority to command or rule.

To the Chinese of the time, heaven was the source of the gods' divine force. They felt that this force willed human beings, especially kings, to be moral. If a leader was moral, heaven would make his kingdom prosperous. If he was immoral, it would send a disaster to remove him from office. Kings were considered the Sons of Heaven. Although the Mandate of Heaven gave kings a kind of divinity, it also gave the people the right to overthrow a bad king. This principle of rebellion was put into action many times during China's long history.

Adding Territory. Under Zhou rule, the kingdom expanded into the Huang He (Yellow River) plain and part of the Yangtze River Valley. To govern this large territory more easily, Wu, the first Zhou king, divided his empire into smaller states. Wu chose members of his family and the nobility to represent him in these new states.

As the Zhou added more territory to their kingdom, the new provinces needed able administrators to run their governments for the king. This gave poor but well-educated people the opportunity to earn a good living. They became members of a civil service that worked for the representatives of the king. The need for competent civil servants changed the class structure in China to some extent. Intelligence and reliability became almost as important as wealth and birth.

Trade and Money. The Zhou Dynasty was the beginning of China's classical age. During the years that it existed, important advances were made. Many cities and towns grew up. The number of skilled craftspeople and merchants increased. Metalworkers learned how to use iron. Iron plows enabled farmers to turn the soil more easily and cultivate more land. Plows made their land more productive. Money in the form of small metal coins began to be used. This enabled people to pay for goods with money instead of bartering—exchanging one item for another. Trade expanded and made the dynasty prosperous.

China: Zhou and Qin Dynasties

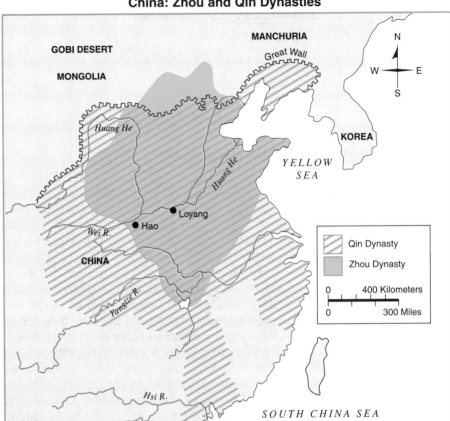

Writing. Under the Zhou, scholars refined the Shang system of writing. Modern Chinese people write their characters in almost the same way as people did during the time of the Zhou. A common writing system links all Chinese no matter where they live and gives them a common identity.

Writing had many practical uses. For example, it was used to record the land grants that the king made to his nobles. The document also listed the rights and duties of the lord who received the land.

Art and Philosophy. Art, literature, philosophy, and scholarship flourished during the Zhou Dynasty. Beautiful objects were carved from jade and other precious materials. Writers expressed their ideas and feelings on all kinds of subjects. The *Book of Songs* is a collection of poems about love, heroic deeds, and farming. The *I Ching*, or *Book of Changes*, is a book originally used to foretell the future. It is a valuable source for learning what the ancient Chinese believed about the universe. People today still consult the *I Ching* to learn what the future may hold in store.

The most important contributions to culture during the Zhou period were made by the philosophers Confucius (Kong Fuzi) and Laotzu (or Laozi). Philosophers are people who seek wisdom and truth and think about the principles that should guide a person's life. You will read more abut these philosophers in Chapter 8.

Decline. Power struggles between the Zhou kings and the nobles who ruled the provinces weakened the kings. The rulers of the smaller states often fought one another. The last 200 years of Zhou rule are called the Era of Warring States. Finally, the ruler of the Qin, the strongest of the warring states, overthrew the Zhou king in 221 B.C.

The Qin Dynasty: 221–206 B.C.

During the Qin Dynasty, the idea that a state exists for the good of the people became less important than the power of the ruler. The philosophy called Legalism influenced the Qin ruler. Legalism considered humans to be selfish and not interested in acting in the best interests of the whole community. To control the people and keep the nation or empire strong and unified, a ruler must hold all of the power. Unbending laws back up the ruler's power.

The only Qin ruler was Shi Huangdi, which means "First Emperor." He governed by the principles of Legalism. Shi Huangdi built his kingdom into an empire by extending his control southward to the South China Sea. To rule this vast empire, Shi Huangdi established a strong central government. He did this by weakening the warring nobles. He removed them from the states that they had ruled because of family ties and appointed officials to govern in their place.

To speed communications throughout his empire, Shi Huangdi ordered roads, bridges, and canals to be built. He also made sure that a uniform law code was observed throughout the provinces. The form of government established by Shi Huangdi remained basically unchanged in most of China until the 20th century A.D.

Nomadic tribes living on the plains to the north of China threatened the Qin Dynasty. In earlier times, the northern states had built walls to prevent these tribes from invading their lands. Shi Huangdi joined all these walls together in one massive fortification that extended across 1,500 miles of northern China. Posted along the Great Wall, Chinese soldiers were able to keep Mongols, Huns, and other enemies out of the empire. The Great Wall of China still stands today. (It is the only manmade object visible from orbiting satellites.)

Shi Huangdi tried to keep firm control over the thinking of his people. Scholars praised the Zhou Dynasty and criticized the Qin rule as cruel. To quiet these critics, Shi Huangdi jailed philosophers and teachers and burned their books. He tried to destroy all of the writings of Confucius.

Shi Huangdi died in 210 B.C. A power struggle among the generals of the Qin army was won by Liu Bang. He established the Han Dynasty, the next to rule China.

Great Wall of China crossing
the Bada Range near Beijing

In 1974, a farmer digging a well broke into the tomb of Shi Huangdi. What he found amazed archaeologists. Shi Huangdi had been buried with an army of life-sized terra cotta soldiers and chariots and horses. These 6,000 figures guarded the emperor's body and the many possessions buried with him.

INFO CHECK

1. How did religion influence the expansion of the Zhou kingdom?

2. Why do you think historians regard the Zhou Dynasty as the beginning of China's classical age?

3. How did Shi Huangdi create a strong central government?

GREEK CIVILIZATION

More than any other early culture, that of the early Greeks had the most influence on the Western world. The concept of democracy, for example, is a legacy from Greece. University students all over the world still study the Greek philosophers. Greek architecture and sculpture set the standards for many centuries of European art and buildings.

Crete and Mycenae

From about 1650 to 1100 B.C., advanced civilizations flourished in the Aegean Sea area. Long-distance trade nourished these civilizations—the Minoans in Crete, the Mycenaeans in Greece, the city of Troy on the east coast of Asia Minor (present-day Turkey). They traded with Mesopotamia, Egypt, and settlements in Italy and Sicily.

The Minoans had an especially advanced culture. Knossos and other cities on Crete were famous for their palaces and temples. The Mycenaeans admired and imitated the wealthier Minoans, whose navy dominated the Aegean Sea. Around 1450 B.C., the Mycenaeans invaded Crete and took over the Minoans' cities and trade routes. Between 1300 and 1000 B.C., the Mycenaean kingdom itself began to decline. Scholars believe internal warfare caused its downfall.

With the destruction of the Minoan and Mycenaean civilizations, the Aegean area entered a period of unrest and confusion. Several waves of people migrated into the area. A group called the Dorians moved into the Peloponnesus, Crete, and southwest Asia Minor (Turkey). Ionians took over Attica, Euboea, and the Aegean islands. A group of mixed people called the Aeolians settled central and northwest Asia Minor. As these peoples mingled with the Mycenaeans and one another, they began to speak a common language (Greek). They became known as the Greeks. Their settlements eventually surrounded the Aegean Sea.

The Dark Age

The period from about 1200 to 700 B.C. is known as the Dark Age of Greece. The culture and wealth of Crete and Mycenae were lost. The knowledge of writing disappeared with the Mycenaean nobility. Long-distance trade halted with the collapse of the Minoan navy. No longer able to obtain tin and copper, the Greeks could not make bronze. They could, however, make a crude kind of iron.

The Dark Age may have been a backward time, but it was also a time of change and renewal. By the beginning of the 11th century B.C., the Greeks no longer imitated Mycenaean craftwork. They had acquired new styles. Scholars believe that two epic poems, the *Iliad* and the *Odyssey*, were orally composed by poets who lived about 800 B.C. Although these poems describe events from the Mycenaean age, such as the Mycenaeans' long war against the city of Troy, they reflect the life and culture of the Dark Age. The blind poet Homer is generally given credit for popularizing these epics.

After 700 B.C., the population of Greece increased. Historians believe that the increase was caused by the expansion of farming. Farmers grew mainly wheat, olives, and grapes. Agriculture began to replace herding of sheep and cattle as the major means of making a living. With the increase in population, cities began to grow.

The Poli

In ancient Greece, rugged hills, the uneven distribution of good farmland, and an irregular coastline separated communities from one another. Like the Sumerians, the Greeks established city-states instead of great kingdoms. They called their city-states *poli*. Two of the most important of these were Sparta, which controlled the regions of Laconia and Messenia, and Athens, which ruled the peninsula of Attica.

Types of Government. Greek poli differed from Sumerian city-states in an important way. They were not ruled by god kings, but some had monarchies. Others were ruled by rich families—the *aristocracy*. In some places, groups of wealthy businesspeople and large landholders governed under a system called an *oligarchy*. Often, the leaders were elected to serve for a limited time.

Such different political systems developed for two reasons. First, the cities had small populations. Everyone was important to the economy of the city. As a result, everyone except women, slaves, and noncitizens had a say in how it was run. Second, the different city-states were frequently at war with each other. The cities did not have professional armies. Their free male citizens were obligated to serve in the military for a certain period of time. The citizen-soldiers wanted a say in how they were ruled. Male citizens elected councils and assemblies to advise their leaders.

Democracy. The modern word *democracy* (rule by the people) comes from still another kind of government system. In a democracy, all citizens, poor or rich, common or noble, have an equal say in government. In a direct democracy, which was practiced in Athens, all of the citizens voted on an issue. In a representative democracy, such as the United States, citizens elect officials to make decisions for them.

Tyrants. Still another type of government was the *tyranny*. The tyranny occurred when one man became ruler by persuading others to overthrow the existing leader and put him in that leader's place. Tyrants were sole rulers who generally favored the common people over the nobles.

Farmland was scarce in Greece. The demand for fertile land grew with the increase in population. The Greeks, like the Mycenaeans before them, had to take to the sea and trade for food and other goods. Contact with the Phoenicians gave them knowledge of shipbuilding and, perhaps, the idea of forming colonies. The Phoenicians' homeland was in modern-day Lebanon and Syria. Their colonies served as ports for their trading ships.

Tyrants tried to maintain their positions by encouraging colonization. Colonization increased the wealth of the poli by opening up trade in different parts of neighboring lands. It also enabled leaders to get rid of young, discontented men, who might cause political problems. Then, too, colonies lured away some of the population, leaving more land for those who remained in the poli. Soon the Aegean Sea was surrounded by Greek settlements. Colonists also spread to the shores of the Black Sea and the Mediterranean Sea.

Writing

The Greeks undoubtedly learned much from surviving Minoan and Mycenaean traditions. But they probably owed their greatest debt to the Phoenicians of the eastern Mediterranean. The Phoenician alphabet, which the Greeks adopted and improved, is one of the Phoenicians' most important contributions to Greek culture. The Greeks produced great works of literature and philosophy. Their writing system enabled them to share these works with the world.

Government in Athens

Athens was one of the most important cities in Greece. It developed from an ancient Mycenaean city located in Attica. As Athens grew, it took in all of Attica's fertile farmlands and became the largest of the Greek city-states. Because Athens was situated near the Aegean Sea, long-distance trade added to its wealth and influence.

Ancient Greece

Aristocracy. Early in its history, Athens was a monarchy. In 682 B.C., however, a group of aristocrats took over the government. Under the aristocracy, an assembly of landowners elected nine officials for one-year terms.

As long as the city was prosperous, Athenians accepted this form of government. Unfortunately, a period of drought occurred and many farmers could not pay their debts. People who could not pay their debts were enslaved. Many Athenians, fearing the loss of their personal freedom, became dissatisfied and rebellious.

About 632 B.C., a young aristocrat took advantage of the unrest and tried to seize power. A group of nobles who opposed his takeover murdered his followers. The young men had taken shelter in a holy place, which should have protected them from violence. Athenians were outraged by their murder and grew more rebellious. For the next ten years, various groups struggled with one another for power over Athens. Some citizens began to demand reforms in the government.

Draco. In 621 B.C., Athenians chose a judge called Draco to reform traditional laws concerning murder and revenge. His punishments for bloodshed and vengeance were extremely harsh. Today, laws considered unusually severe are called *draconian*. Although these laws discouraged violence against individuals, they did not restore political order.

Solon. Around 594 B.C., Athenians elected an aristocrat called Solon to reform the city's government. Solon outlawed the practice of enslaving people who could not pay their debts. Under the new law, debtors who had already been sold into slavery were set free. Solon also set limits to the amount of land that one man could own.

In Athens, as in other city-states, the aristocracy had always had more influence over government than any other class. Solon weakened the aristocrats' power by dividing society into four legal groups. He wanted to ensure that at least two of these groups consisted of more than one class. He therefore distributed political power to each group according to the wealth of its members rather than according to their birth. This gave many wealthy commoners, such as merchants and landowners, a larger part in government. Under this system, the poorest citizens had less power than the other groups. But they enjoyed more rights than they had under earlier systems.

Many Athenians approved of Solon's reforms and wanted him to become tyrant. He refused and left Athens. Once more, various groups struggled over control of the city. An aristocrat called Pisistratus succeeded in becoming tyrant in 546 B.C.. Today, people think of tyrants as harsh rulers with absolute power. In early Greece, they were simply men who had seized office unofficially. Although they often had a great deal of power, most of their power was based on their popularity with large portions of the population. If they took advantage of their position, they were put out of office. Although Pisistratus ruled moderately, his son, who followed him, did not. As a consequence, the son lost his office.

Democracy. In 508 B.C., Athenians chose an aristocrat called Cleisthenes as their leader. Cleisthenes created the world's first democracy. As he introduced changes to the government, he brought them before an assembly of citizens for approval and amendment.

Under this new government, all citizens were guaranteed freedom of speech and equality before the law. Citizens no longer had to own land to become members of the assembly. Cleisthenes also gave the assembly more power. While previously it could only approve laws, it could now pass them. It could also elect military leaders and act as the city's supreme court.

Athenian democracy had its limits. As under aristocratic rule, women, slaves, and foreigners had none of the benefits of citizenship. This meant that a majority of the population could not make decisions about the laws that controlled their lives. Athenian men seemed unaware that this situation contradicted the spirit of democracy. Many felt that slavery was necessary. Without slaves to do the work, they would not have had the time to take an active part in government or the military service expected of them.

The Persian Wars

The Persians lived in the region east of Mesopotamia. In 550 B.C., Cyrus the Great, a Persian general, led the Persians in a successful revolt against the Medes, their rulers.

The Empire. The victory over the Medes began a long series of conquests in the Fertile Crescent and beyond. By the time Cyrus died in 529 B.C., the Persians' rule extended from the Aegean Sea to the borders of India. They conquered Egypt in 525 B.C. and took control of southeastern Europe. This made the Persian Empire the largest and most powerful one in the Middle East.

This vast empire included many ethnic groups with different lifestyles. Persian rulers tried to prevent uprisings among all these different people by governing tolerantly and efficiently. They allowed the different groups within the empire to follow their own traditions and beliefs. The Persians did not impose heavy taxes on the conquered.

Troublesome Greeks. In general, the Persians' policy worked well. Few of their subjects rebelled. The Greeks, however, were an exception. In his sweep across Asia Minor, Cyrus had conquered Ionia, a Greek colony located along the eastern Aegean coast.

Although the Persians did not interfere with the Ionians' culture, they limited the Ionians' political freedom. The Ionians resented the taking away of their rights. In 499 B.C., during the reign of the Persian king Darius, the Athenians helped the Ionians to rebel. It took Persia five years to put down the uprising. Darius then turned his army against Athens.

In 490 B.C., the Persians landed in Attica at Marathon. The outnumbered Athenian army defeated the Persians. (A messenger ran

The Persian Empire and Sites of Battles With the Greeks

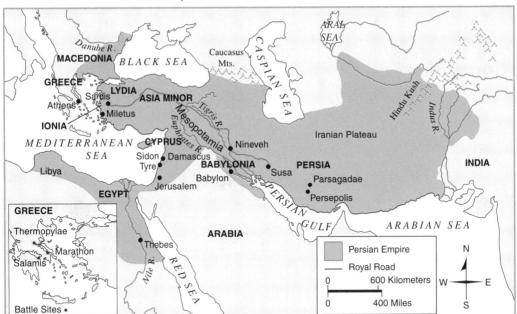

26 miles from Marathon to Athens to report the victory. Today, that run is honored whenever marathon races are held.) The Athenian victory at Marathon forced Darius to withdraw from Greece.

In 480 B.C., Xerxes, the son of Darius, tried again to conquer Greece. The Persian forces numbered in the thousands. They quickly overwhelmed the few hundred Spartans and their allies who heroically defended the mountain pass of Thermopylae. Then the Persians captured and burned Athens. The Athenians fought back at sea and defeated the Persian fleet in a great naval battle at Salamis. The next year, after repeated defeats by the Greeks, the Persians left for home.

The Greek victories saved the freedom of the city-states and the democracy of Athens. They also insured the continued development of Hellenic civilization. (The Greeks called themselves Hellenes.)

The Age of Pericles

Following the Persian Wars, Athens entered a period of glory and power. From 460 to 429 B.C., an outstanding man named Pericles led Athens. Pericles made additional democratic reforms. Through his influence, the state permitted citizens who did not own property to hold office and paid people for serving on juries. This enabled the poor to perform important civic duties.

Pericles was also responsible for the rebuilding of Athens, which had been damaged by the Persians. One of the most important of the new buildings was the Parthenon, located in a complex of shrines and temples called the Acropolis. It honored Athena, the goddess the Athenians believed protected them. Admiring visitors flocked to the city, which soon became the meeting place of the most important artists and thinkers in Greece. The Age of Pericles is regarded as the period when Greek culture reached its highest level.

Architecture and Art. The simplicity and serenity of the Parthenon show Greek architecture at its best. Like most Greek public buildings, it is a rectangle fronted by columns. The columns have been fluted to make them seem taller and thinner than they really are.

The Parthenon and the other temples around it contained beautiful statues and friezes (decorative carved bands on the walls). A favorite subject of Greek sculptors was the healthy, athletic human body. For all their admiration for the natural, however, Greek sculptors portrayed, not individual people, but ideal, or near perfect, human forms.

Artists painted scenes of everyday life on vases and pottery. Greek vases and urns often have black backgrounds with the scenes showing in red.

Drama. Greek dramas were based on myths and historical events. Plays that deal with war, death, justice, and the relationships between gods and ordinary people are called tragedies. They frequently focus on a hero who falls from a high position into ruin and death. Lighter plays that make fun of politicians, philosophers, and other dramatists are called comedies. Many ancient Greek plays are still performed today.

Some famous tragedies by Aeschylus (lived 525–456 B.C.) are *Prometheus Bound* and the *Oresteia* trilogy. *Prometheus Bound* dramatizes a myth about a heroic giant who steals fire from heaven and

The Parthenon atop the Acropolis, dedicated to Athena, patron goddess of Athens

gives it to humanity. The *Oresteia* trilogy consists of three plays about Agamemnon, the Greek king who conquered Troy, and his family.

Plays by Euripides (lived 484–406 B.C.) include *Medea* and *The Trojan Women*. Medea is a sorceress who helps a hero called Jason steal a magical treasure, the golden fleece. *The Trojan Women* depicts the suffering of the women who became captives after the fall of Troy.

Sophocles (lived 496–406 B.C.) wrote *Antigone*, the play about a young girl's defiance of a tyrant that was quoted in this chapter's introduction.

Aristophanes (lived 450–388 B.C.) wrote comedies. Two of his plays, *Lysistrata* and *The Birds*, ridicule the war policies of Athenian leaders.

Science and Mathematics. Many Greek myths, like those of other cultures, were attempts to explain natural events. Most educated Greeks, however, regarded such explanations as poetic stories. They knew that natural events had natural causes. For example, they understood that eclipses were caused, not by angry gods, but by the shadow of one heavenly body passing in front of another and cutting off the light it sheds on earth.

Greek mathematicians gave Greek scientists of a later period the tools to gain knowledge about the earth and the other planets in the solar system. The students of Pythagoras, a mathematician who lived from 580 to 500 B.C., developed the Pythagorean theory from his teachings. This theory tells us that in a right triangle the square of the hypotenuse is equal to the sum of the squares of the other two sides. By using geometry and trigonometry, Greek astronomers of a later age could calculate the circumference of the earth and the distance of the earth from the sun and the moon.

Greek scientists also studied physics and medicine. Democritus (lived 460–370 B.C.) developed the theory that all matter is composed of tiny, invisible atoms. This theory has since been proven by modern scientific instruments.

Hippocrates (lived 460–377 B.C.) became known as "the father of medicine." Unlike the doctors of earlier times, he knew that diseases had natural rather than magical or religious causes. When medical students of today graduate, they take the Hippocratic oath. It is based on the ancient physician's ideas about how medicine should be practiced.

Philosophy. Just as the Greeks believed that natural events had natural causes, so they believed that good conduct and correct thinking were governed by natural laws. The philosopher Socrates (lived 470–399 B.C.) believed that people would be good if they understood that only the pursuit of goodness brings happiness. He developed a process called the Socratic method to help people recognize true goodness. By asking them a series of questions, he showed them that by using reason anyone can make correct conclusions about values and behavior. Socrates believed in questioning everything, even the actions of Athenian leaders. In time, he angered those in authority. Socrates was tried and convicted of corrupting youth. When he refused to accept exile, he was condemned to die by drinking poison.

Plato (lived 427–347 B.C.) was Socrates' most famous pupil. He wrote about many basic ideas of life in works called *dialogues*. He established a school called the Academy in which he taught philosophy, science, and mathematics. Like Socrates, Plato asked his pupils to think about such questions as "What is good?" "What is true?" "What is beautiful?" One of Plato's main concerns was to set up an ideal form of government. Instead of democracy, Plato described an aristocracy of highly intelligent men trained to rule. He described this government in the *Republic*, his most famous written work.

Aristotle (lived 384–322 B.C.) studied under Plato. In time, Aristotle opened his own school, the Lyceum. There he wrote hundreds of essays about logic, politics, and science. Much of his scientific work was in botany and biology. Aristotle believed that people should live according to the "golden mean," which calls for practicing moderation in all things.

Sparta, the Military State

Although the Spartan government had some elements of democracy, it was primarily a military state. Most Greek city-states established colonies overseas in order to gain more farmland. The Spartans acquired territory by conquering other city-states. After 20 years of war, they conquered their neighbor Messenia in the early 700s B.C.

Helots. The Spartans not only took Messenian land, they made its people into state slaves, or *helots*. The Spartan state forced the helots to farm land that had once been their own. Outraged by harsh treatment, the Messenians revolted, and a new war broke out. It took Sparta 30 years to subdue the Messenians again.

During this second long struggle, conflicts arose between the different classes within Sparta. The common people, who did most of the fighting, began to claim equal rights with the aristocrats. After the war, the commoners and the aristocrats worked together to change their aristocracy into a combination of monarchy, oligarchy, and democracy.

Government. Under their new political system, the Spartans elected two kings every nine years. A council of elders (28 men over the age of 60) and an assembly of free Spartans over the age of 30 advised the kings. Real power, however, was in the hands of a committee of five *ephors*. These were officials elected every year by the assembly. The ephors closely watched the actions of the kings, controlled the education of children, and supervised the helots. They also tried to make sure that all citizens lived up to the standards set by the government.

Although all Spartan citizens were eligible to become ephors,

Sparta lacked the democratic spirit. Its government did not exist for the benefit of its citizens. The citizens existed for the benefit of the state. To control the helots, Sparta turned itself into a military state.

The Military. From an early age, Spartan males were trained to fight in defense of Sparta. At age seven, Spartan boys were taken from their families and placed in military training camps. At the age of twelve, they began training for combat and were taught survival skills. During this time, they learned to be courageous, resourceful, tough, and ruthless. Men stayed in the military until age 60.

Since Spartan education consisted mainly of military training, Spartans made few contributions to the culture of Greece. Although other Greeks admired Spartan discipline and patriotism, few wished to follow their example. One Greek, after tasting a Spartan soup, made of pork, blood, vinegar, and salt, said he was no longer surprised that Spartans did not fear death.

Comparing Sparta and Athens. Like the Spartans, Athenians also led lives of simplicity and physical discipline. They ate plain food—mainly grains, lentils, olives, garlic, and figs. Many were dedicated athletes. Their homes were comfortable but not luxurious.

The main difference between Sparta and Athens was the opportunity Athenians had to develop their minds and imaginations. They were not tools of the state but individuals. Instead of serving their government with unthinking obedience, Athenians tried to find ways to make their government better. When they were not engaged in political duties, many turned to art, philosophy, science, and literature.

Spartan girls were encouraged to become physically strong through athletics. Women ran the farms while the men went to war. Women could also have their own businesses.

Athenian women lacked many privileges enjoyed by Spartan women. But, like Athenian men, they could enjoy the life of the mind. Although they received no formal education, many upper-class Athenian women learned to read and write. Some became poets. Other women took part in the discussions led by the famous philosophers.

The Peloponnesian War

During the Persian wars, the Athenians joined with other Greek city-states in an alliance called the Delian League. As the leaders of the alliance, Athenians provided most of the ships and sailors and asked the other city-states to contribute money. Because of their military successes, the members of the Delian League decided to continue their alliance in order to discourage further attacks by Persia.

While under the leadership of Pericles, Athenians tried to use the league to build an empire. They demanded both land and money from the other members, sometimes taking it by force. Led by Sparta, the other city-states rebelled.

THEAGENES THE ATHLETE

The Greeks established the Olympic games to honor their gods. Every four years, athletes from all the poli, even those at war with each other, came together to compete in a variety of contests. Among the most popular events were boxing, running, and the pancration (a combination of boxing and wrestling). The victors of these contests were honored by the Greeks for their strength and skill. They were regarded as heroes.

The historian Pausanias, in his *Description of Greece*, tells us about one such Olympic victor. Theagenes of Thasos won crowns for boxing and the pancration. He was also known as a great runner. According to Pausanias, Theagenes won a total of 1,400 crowns for athletic victories.

Even as a child, Theagenes became known throughout Greece for his strength. At the age of nine, he was walking home from school when he noticed a bronze statue of a god in the marketplace of Thasos. For reasons known only to himself, the boy tore the statue from its base and took it home. The citizens of Thasos were outraged by this act of disrespect to the god. Some demanded that the boy be executed for sacrilege. Instead, they required Theagenes to return the statue to its proper place in order to save his life.

At the 75th Olympiad, in 480 B.C., Theagenes intended to win prizes for both boxing and the pancration. After defeating the champion boxer Euthymos, however, Theagenes was too tired to win a second crown for the pancration. The Olympic judges fined Theagenes for entering the boxing contest just to embarrass Euthymos. Although he went on to win the crown

for the pancration in the 76th Olympiad (476 B.C.), Theagenes did not compete in the boxing. Some of the Greeks regarded this selective competition as unsportmanlike.

After the athlete's death, the citizens of Thasos set up a bronze statue of Theagenes. A man who had never won an athletic prize came every night to beat the statue. One night the statue fell on the angry man, killing him. His sons prosecuted the statue for murder. Under Greek law, all murderers had to be punished whether they were people, animals, or objects. The statue of Theagenes was found guilty and it was dropped into the sea.

In later years, Thasos suffered from famine and plague. The people sought the advice of an oracle (a priestess through whom the gods spoke) who told them to welcome home all exiles. The Thasians did this, but the crops still did not grow. Again they consulted the oracle. The priestess reminded them that they had forgotten the great Theagenes. Fishermen retrieved the statue of the athlete from the sea. The people of Thasos then returned the statue to its original place and began to sacrifice to Theagenes. The people came to regard him as a god with the power to heal.

1. According to the Greeks, what attributes or characteristics made a person heroic?

2. Compare Theagenes with a modern-day athlete whom you admire. Would this person be heroic by the standards of the ancient Greeks? Why or why not?

From 431 to 404 B.C., Sparta and Athens fought each other over control of the Peloponnesian peninsula, the southern part of Greece where Sparta was located. The conflict between the two is called the Peloponnesian War. Eventually Sparta, with help from Persia, defeated Athens.

Sparta became the leader of Greece and ended democratic government in Athens and other city-states. But Sparta had been too weakened by war to hold power for long. In 371 B.C., the city-state of Thebes, aided by Persian money, defeated Sparta. The other city-states refused to accept Theban leadership. More wars broke out.

While the Greek city-states were destroying themselves, the kingdom of Macedonia was building its power to the north of Greece. In 338 B.C., King Philip II conquered all of the Greek city-states except Sparta. He then united the ones he had conquered. Greece and Macedonia became one kingdom.

INFO CHECK

1. Why was the period from 1200 to 700 B.C. known as the Greek Dark Age?

2. Define each of the following: poli, aristocracy, oligarchy, democracy, tyranny.

3. How was Athenian democracy more limited than modern American democracy?

4. Why was the battle of Salamis so important to the Greeks?

5. State the importance of the Age of Pericles. When did it occur?

6. List the major differences between Athens and Sparta.

7. State the cause and two results of the Peloponnesian War.

THE RISE OF HELLENISTIC CIVILIZATION

Macedonia, a mountainous country, was located north of Greece. Like Greece, Macedonia was inhabited by people whose ancestors had come from different regions. Many of them had Greek ancestors. They were farmers and herders, who lived in tribal societies. Their religion included many of the gods worshiped by the Greeks. They also spoke a version of Greek. But it was so different that most Greeks could not understand it. Most Macedonians did not share the Greek's love of learning. Their kings were absolute rulers. Feuds and tribal wars kept Macedonia in a constant state of disorder.

Philip II Conquers Greece

This disorder ended when Philip II (lived 382–336 B.C.) came to the throne. He unified his people into a nation. Then he created a powerful, well-trained, and well-disciplined army. He taught the Macedonians to fight in large, heavily armed formations called *pha-lanxes*. As a result, Macedonia became a strong military power.

Philip admired the advanced culture of the Greeks. He brought Aristotle to Macedonia to give his son, Alexander, a Greek education. When he conquered the Greek city-states, he organized them into the Hellenic League. He permitted them to govern themselves as long as they gave him military support. Sparta was not subject to Macedonia and, therefore, not part of the league.

Philip's great dream was to conquer the Persian Empire. His death prevented him from carrying out his plans. But his son, Alexander, made his dream come true.

Alexander's Empire

In 334 B.C., at age 22, Alexander started his conquest of the Persian Empire. While accomplishing this goal, he took over Egypt. Then he moved across the Middle East to the Indus River Valley. In 324, his generals made Alexander turn back toward Persia. Alexander the Great now ruled over a vast empire.

Wherever Alexander's soldiers marched, they founded cities. One of them, Alexandria in Egypt, became the most important city of the empire. It developed into a major center of learning and trade. Alexander encouraged the Greeks and Macedonians who settled in the cities of the empire to marry Persians, Egyptians, Syrians, and others of the native populations. Such marriages brought about the

Alexander the Great's Empire   323 B.C.

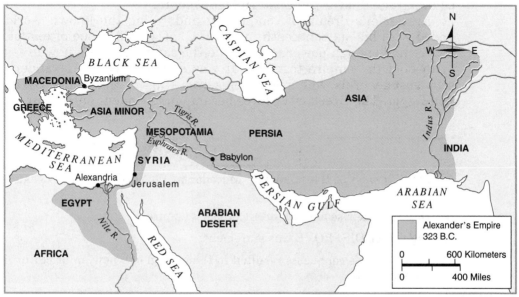

Pompeii fresco of Alexander the Great preparing to battle Darius, the Persian King

gradual blending of the Greek culture of the West with the Eastern cultures of the Middle East. The resulting mixture, called Hellenistic civilization, combined the best ideas and achievements of East and West.

As trade increased in Alexander's empire, the Hellenistic cities grew wealthy. Elaborate temples, government buildings, and theaters turned these cities into places of beauty as well as centers of learning and art. They drew scholars, artists, scientists, and merchants from all over the Eastern Hemisphere.

Alexander's dream of conquering and ruling the known world ended with his sudden death in 323 B.C. at age 33. None of his followers had enough power to continue the campaigns into new areas or to hold the empire together. It was divided among Alexander's strongest generals, who made themselves kings of Macedonia, Syria, and Egypt. The Greek city-states became independent once again.

INFO CHECK

1. Identify each of the following: Macedonia, Philip II, Hellenic League, Alexander.

2. Describe the rise and fall of Alexander's empire.

3. PROVE or DISPROVE this statement:

   • Alexander's conquests resulted in the growth of a new, multicultural civilization.

THE HELLENISTIC AGE (324 B.C.–100 B.C.)

Despite the breakup of Alexander's empire, the culture of the Hellenistic cities continued to develop. Hellenistic art and science became highly advanced. Greek was the major language of the lands around the eastern Mediterranean Sea.

Hellenistic Philosophy

Alexander and his followers purposely settled the cities they ruled with people from a variety of cultures. Adjusting to many different ideas and values made people wonder which of these were the best to live by. Consequently, interest in philosophy grew. Philosophers came up with several different answers to the question "How should I live?" "How can I make my life worthwhile?" "What do I owe the gods, the state, other people?"

Cynics. Diogenes (lived 412–323 B.C.) developed the philosophy of the Cynics. He argued that since nature provides everything humans need, they should ignore social conventions and avoid luxuries. Diogenes and his followers ate very little, wore only the most necessary clothing, and lived in humble, even poor homes. He tried to interest common people in philosophy by teaching in the streets and marketplaces. Diogenes felt that people should not regard themselves as citizens of a single country but of the whole world.

Epicureans. Epicurus (lived 340–270 B.C.) taught that people should avoid pain and seek pleasure. By this, he did not mean that people should do whatever they liked. He believed that all excess led to pain. Pleasure could be achieved through leading a life of moderation and self-discipline. He also believed that worldly ambitions disturbed the soul. Therefore, politics should be avoided. The state existed because people had agreed to cooperate for a common purpose. The form that the state's government took was unimportant.

Stoics. The Stoic philosopher Zeno (lived 335–265 B.C.) believed that nature is the expression of divine will. From this idea, he developed the concept of natural law. His followers were urged to behave in accordance with what they observed in nature. If people followed natural law, he argued, they would be virtuous. Zeno urged people to be active politically. They should not do so to fulfill ambition but to perform virtuous acts. He felt that true happiness lay in noble behavior, not in great achievements.

Hellenistic Science and Mathematics

Science made great strides during the Hellenistic period. Astronomy developed from knowledge accumulated by the astrologers of the Middle East and Greek scientific methods. An astronomer named Aristarchus (worked about 270 B.C.) concluded that the earth revolved around the sun and not vice versa. His theory was not generally believed until the 16th century A.D.

Euclid (worked about 300 B.C.) contributed to mathematics by organizing the study of geometry into a textbook called *Elements*. Today's high school geometry texts are based on Euclid's book.

A scientist called Archimedes (lived 287–212 B.C.) was a physicist and an inventor. His inventions included a catapult that hurled rocks large enough to sink ships, grappling devices to pull ships out of the water, and a pulley to move heavy objects with a minimum of effort. He also developed the principle of specific gravity.

Herophilus, a doctor, lived in the first half of the 3rd century B.C. He dissected corpses and discovered the nervous system. From his studies, he concluded that the brain was the center of intelligence.

Art and Literature

Hellenistic art and literature were more realistic than earlier Greek art and literature. Painting and sculpture emphasized people's individuality and emotions. Literature became more personal. Instead of describing the fate of heroes, plays and poetry focused on the lives and feelings of everyday people.

INFO CHECK

1. Which of the Hellenistic philosophers do you find most interesting? Explain your choice.

2. Match each scientist with an achievement: Aristarchus, Euclid, Archimedes, Herophilus.

THE ROMAN EMPIRE

In many ways, the geography of Italy was more favorable to the development of civilization than was the geography of Greece. Italy had large amounts of fertile farmland, and its mountains were not so rugged as to cut people off from one another.

Latins and Legends

In about 1200 B.C., a group of Indo-Europeans called Latins invaded Italy. They settled in the central plains called Latium. These plains were marshy but, once drained, made good farmland. The Tiber River, which flows through the area, provided a transportation route inland and access to the Mediterranean Sea. Wood for fuel and for building houses could be gathered from the forests on the nearby hills. The hills were also good lookout points. From the tops, sentries

Italy: Early Settlement and the Roman Republic

could watch for approaching enemies. In about 1000 B.C., the Latins established villages on seven of these hills. Eventually, the villages united and grew into one of the most powerful cities in the world—Rome.

Romulus and Remus. According to Roman legend, the city that produced some of the world's finest soldiers was founded by the sons of the war god, Mars. Abandoned in the wilderness as babies, Romulus and Remus were raised by a wolf. In spite of their strange childhood, the boys grew up to establish a great civilization. A sign from heaven told the brothers to build the first city of this civilization in Latium. The sign was seven vultures flying seven times around seven hills. While building their city, Romulus and Remus fought each other. Romulus killed Remus and became the first king of the city that bears his name—Rome.

Society. Scholars do not know the facts that gave rise to this legend. They know only that early in the 7th century B.C., the original villages joined to form a city-state.

The first inhabitants were farmers and herders. The basis of their society was the family. The father was the head of his household and had complete power over the other members. Some families with a common ancestor formed groups called *gentes*. The gentes held political power in early Rome. Councils, made up of men from various villages, met together to elect kings and to vote on whether or not to go to war.

The Latins lost their power to elect their own kings in the mid-600s B.C. At that time, a group called the Etruscans moved into Latium. They imposed their form of government on Rome. They also introduced the Romans to influences from Greece and other Mediterranean lands.

Rome Under Etruscan Rule

Little is known about the early history of the Etruscans. Scholars, though, have a good idea of what they were like during the time that they ruled Rome. They made excellent metal products, which they traded throughout the Mediterranean world. By exerting military and political power, they united a group of other cities into a league that extended throughout much of Italy.

The Etruscans had been strongly influenced by a group of Greeks who invaded Italy during the eighth century B.C. Etruscans adapted many Greek ways and passed them on to the Latins. Rome was transformed from a loose union of villages into a real city. Etruscans urged the Romans to trade with other Mediterranean countries. Foreign contacts increased both their wealth and their awareness of the outside world.

Soon Rome had much in common with Greek cities. Temples and public buildings replaced thatched huts. The new temples were dedicated to gods. They were more like Greek gods than the invisible spirits once worshiped by the Latins. The great Roman Forum had its beginning at this time as a paved marketplace. Wealthy people began to buy Greek art objects. Educated Romans began to use the Etruscan alphabet, which was based on the Greek alphabet.

The Roman Republic

From 616 to 509 B.C., the Etruscans ruled Rome. After a successful rebellion against the Etruscan king, Tarquin the Proud, the Romans set up a type of government called a *republic*. Elected officials instead of a king held power and made the laws.

Patricians and Plebeians. Although the new government was a type of democracy, only a small number of people had the right to decide how it was run. *Patricians*, the wealthy landowners, had organized the rebellion and created the new government. Therefore, they designed it for their own benefit. Only patricians could hold important posts in the government. The rest of the population consisted of small farmers, tradespeople, craftsworkers, and debtors. These *plebeians* made up about 90 percent of the population.

Call for Reforms. The plebeians were not without influence. Not only were they the largest part of the population, their labor and skills were necessary to the economy. Then, too, they were the soldiers. As a small city-state, Rome was constantly forced to defend its independence. The patricians needed the plebeians to fight in these border wars.

In 494 B.C., the plebeians refused to fight or do work of any kind unless the patricians granted them more rights. Faced with the loss of their state, the patricians compromised. Continuing to use such tactics, the plebeians gradually improved their status. In 287 B.C., they won full rights as citizens. As members of the Assembly of Tribes and the Assembly of Centuries, they voted on issues and passed laws.

Major Officials. During the period of the Roman Republic (509–133 B.C.), the highest officials were the *consuls*. The assemblies elected two each year. The consuls enforced the laws, ensured that the city was properly administered, and commanded the army in time of war.

Officials called *magistrates* assisted the consuls. The Assembly of Centuries elected the magistrates, who had special titles and duties. *Quaestors* handled such matters as counting the number of people in the city and determining the value of property for tax purposes. *Aediles*, officials like mayors, kept order and took care of public buildings. *Praetors*, or judges, presided over trials in the courts.

In times of emergency, when quick decisions were needed, the consuls sometimes chose one man to rule. Called a *dictator*, he could serve for no more than six months. The government followed the dictator's decisions without question.

The government body called the *Senate* had the most power. The consuls appointed members of the Senate for life terms. Originally, only patricians could be senators. Later, plebeians were allowed to hold this office. The Senate, which had about 300 members, proposed laws, handled foreign affairs, and controlled public finances.

To protect their rights, plebeians in the Assembly of Tribes elected ten men called *tribunes*. These powerful men could *veto*, or reject, decisions of the consuls and the Senate.

Citizenship. Romans felt deep loyalty to their city. They were proud to be citizens of such an honorable place. As citizens, they had obligations as well as rights. Those eligible had the duty of serving in government posts. They supported the government and the army.

The idea of being a Roman citizen was valued by outsiders. To win the loyalty of a people they conquered, the Romans might offer the reward of citizenship to the defeated.

The Beginnings of the Roman Empire

Frequent conflicts with neighboring peoples required the Romans to become skilled warriors. All male citizens between the ages of 17 and 46 could be called into the army. The discipline and training of citizen soldiers, combined with the Roman talent for military organization made the Roman legions superior to other armies. As Rome began to take over other lands, the army and its commanders became more important in public affairs.

Wars in Italy. Between 343 and 290 B.C., Romans fought several wars with their neighbors. Because Rome was one of the smaller and newer states in Italy, Romans considered nearby nations to be threats to their independence. As it conquered its neighbors, Rome grew larger and stronger. Soon other nations, in their turn, feared Roman expansion. The Greek city of Tarentum in southern Italy called on the Greek king Pyrrhus to help get rid of the powerful newcomer. After several costly defeats, the Romans finally conquered Pyrrhus in 272 B.C. With this victory, they took over all of southern Italy.

Now most of Italy came under Rome's control. Roman officials, supported by Roman legions, governed the defeated territories. Latin, the language of the Romans, became familiar to the conquered peoples. Roads were built to link the territories to Rome.

Wars of Conquest

Rome's greatest enemy was Carthage, a city-state founded by the Phoenicians in North Africa. Rome and Carthage competed with each other to control trade in the western Mediterranean area. They also competed for possession of Sicily, the major island located between Carthage and southern Italy. The Romans were afraid that if the Carthaginians took Sicily, they would invade Italy. The three destructive wars that resulted from these conflicts took place between 264 and 146 B.C. Because "Punic" means Phoenician, they were called the Punic Wars.

Punic Wars. The first Punic War lasted 23 years. At its end, Rome was in full possession of Sicily. Carthage continued its attempts to invade Italy, however, and a second war was fought. During this war, Carthaginian forces led by Hannibal invaded the Italian peninsula. Hannibal badly damaged the Roman army before it forced him to retreat. A Roman general named Scipio finally defeated Hannibal in North Africa. The third and last war ended when the Romans conquered and destroyed Carthage. They later rebuilt the city and used it as a naval base and commercial port.

The Roman Empire at Its Greatest Extent   A.D. 150

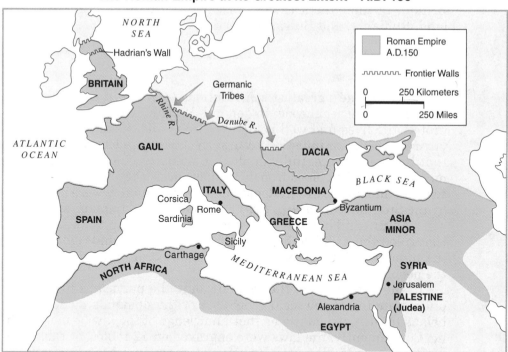

Winning the Punic Wars gave Rome control of the coast of North Africa and the areas now known as Spain, Sicily, Sardinia, and Corsica. While fighting these wars, Roman soldiers developed into some of the best fighters in the world. Their commanders became experts in planning successful battles. Contending with the Phoenicians had taught Roman leaders that, in order to be a world power, they needed a strong navy.

Pompey. By 64 B.C., Rome had conquered almost all the lands around the Mediterranean Sea, including Macedonia, Greece, Syria, and Asia Minor. These lands became Roman provinces and were ruled and taxed by Roman governors.

In these areas, the Romans came into contact with Hellenistic civilization. The philosophical, scientific, and artistic ideas of this civilization greatly affected Roman thinking and ways of living.

The person mainly responsible for the conquest and reorganization of the eastern Mediterranean lands was Pompey. He was one of the most powerful Roman generals and political leaders during the years from 78 to 48 B.C.

Julius Caesar. In the 50s B.C., the Romans began campaigns to conquer the peoples north of Italy. From 58 to 51 B.C., the armies of Julius Caesar invaded Gaul (present-day France). Caesar's victories extended the Roman empire into western Europe. Caesar also led military expeditions into Britain.

In A.D. 43, an emperor called Claudius finally conquered much of Britain. In time, the areas that became Germany, Austria, Switzerland, Rumania, and Bulgaria joined the empire.

Roman Law

One of Rome's greatest contributions to Western culture was its body of laws, or legal code. In general, Roman laws were designed to protect the lives and well-being of citizens and make amends to the victims of crime or injustice. At first the laws were based on solutions that had been successfully applied to actual problems. Because Roman laws had developed from life experiences, they tended to be practical and flexible. Later in Roman history, lawmakers were influenced by the Stoic idea of *natural law*. They felt that all humans shared the same nature and had the same needs and rights. Therefore, the laws that ruled them should be dictated by these needs and rights, not by the human will alone. Natural law benefited all humanity, not just the people in power.

In the early days of the republic, only the patricians had a clear understanding of the legal code. One of the demands made by plebeians to the patricians was that knowledge of the law be made public. Consequently, the laws were engraved on 12 tables, or tablets, of bronze. About 450 B.C., the Romans set up the tables in a public place. As part of their education, children had to memorize the laws, known as the Twelve Tables.

The Role of Roman Law in Empire Building

As Rome conquered other lands, laws had to be created to govern people who were not Roman citizens. These new laws were added to the original laws on the Twelve Tables. When making legal decisions, government officials took into consideration the laws and customs of the conquered peoples. Because of this practice, the ideas of other peoples became part of Roman law. Romans kept records of the legal decisions of judges throughout the empire. The judges in other parts of the empire then used the recorded decisions to decide new cases. In this way, the Romans were able to rule many different groups of people efficiently and humanely.

Roman ideas about law continue to influence the legal codes of countries today. Their influence is especially strong in European countries along the Mediterranean Sea and in Latin America.

In the United States, several principles of Roman law are a significant part of our idea of justice. One of the principles is that all citizens are equal under the law. Another is that an accused person is believed to be innocent until proven guilty. A third is that a person has the right to know who is accusing him or her of wrongdoing. A

Time Line

Year	Dates and Events
B.C.	**1650 B.C.:** Rise of Minoan civilization (Crete) and rival Mycenaean civilization (Greece)
1650	
	1200 B.C.: Indo-European invasion and settlement of Latium (central Italy)
1201	**1122 B.C.:** Overthrow of Shang Dynasty by Zhou Dynasty
	1000 B.C.: Decline of Mycenaean greatness; migrations into Greece and throughout Aegean Sea
1200	
	800s B.C.: Composition of epic poems *Iliad* and *Odyssey*
801	
800	**700s B.C.:** Sparta conquers Greek city-states and develops military state and culture
701	**616 B.C.:** Etruscans invade Latium and introduce Greek and Mediterranean cultures
700	**550 B.C.:** Cyrus the Great begins spread of Persian rule from India to Aegean Sea
601	**509–508 B.C.:** Romans overthrow Etruscans and set up first democratic republic
600	**490 B.C.:** Athenian victory at Marathon over invading Persians
	480–479 B.C.: Persians defeat Spartans at Thermopylae, burn Athens, but are defeated by Athenians in battle of Salamis
501	**460 B.C.:** Beginning of 30-year rule of Athens by Pericles
500	**431–404 B.C.:** Sparta and Athens fight three Peloponnesian wars, with Sparta the final victor
401	**343 B.C.:** Rome begins territorial conquest of most of Italy and imposes Latin as official language
400	**338 B.C.:** Philip II of Macedonia conquers and unites all Greek city-states except Sparta
301	**334 B.C.:** Alexander the Great begins 11 years of conquest, from Greece to Indus River Valley
300	**321 B.C.:** Beginning of 130-year rule of India by the Maurya Dynasty; rise and spread of Buddhism
201	**264 B.C.:** Beginning of 120 years of war between Rome and Carthage, ending with destruction of Carthage and Roman control of North African coast, Sicily, Sardinia, Spain
200	**221 B.C.:** Qin Dynasty overthrows Zhou Dynasty and extends rule of China southward
101	**220s B.C.:** Construction of China's Great Wall begins
100	**206 B.C.:** Beginning of 425-year Han rule of China
	58 B.C.: Julius Caesar begins conquest of Gaul (France), western Europe, and Britain
1	**27 B.C.:** Beginning of two-century golden age of Roman civilization

fourth principle is that a person should not be punished for what he or she thinks.

Trade

Trade routes that passed through southern Asia linked the Roman Empire to the empires of the East. The most famous of these routes was the Silk Road. It got its name from the great quantities of silk that the Chinese sold all over the known world. China also exported more practical goods, such as iron.

Other cultures also used the Silk Road to transport items, such as gems, gold, silver, spices, and perfumes. Parthia (now part of Iran) was famous for its fruits, rare birds, and ostrich eggs. Romans traded glassware, statuettes, and slaves who performed as jugglers and acrobats.

Sea routes also carried people, goods, and ideas to different lands. During the time of the Han Dynasty, Chinese merchants began to use the sea routes to send goods to the West. Kan Ying, the Chinese ambassador, sailed to the Roman province of Syria along one of these routes.

Architecture and Engineering

Although not as outstanding in the field of abstract science as the Greeks were, the Romans outshone the people of other cultures in the practical arts. Roman engineers improved life in the empire by building roads, dams, drainage systems, and aqueducts. Aqueducts carried water to cities through pipes stretched along bridgelike stone structures. Many of the roads and a few aqueducts that the Roman engineers built are still in use.

Roman buildings were feats of engineering as well as of architecture. Romans developed the rounded arch and the dome as features of their buildings. The domed roof could cover large spaces without the need for columns to hold it up.

Roman aqueduct still spanning the Gard River near Nîmes, France

Public baths required a knowledge of plumbing and ventilation. These huge buildings contained steam rooms, gymnasiums, hot and cold pools, and libraries.

Other buildings had to be very strong and massive to accommodate the crowds for which they had been built. Large numbers of people attended events in the Coliseum in Rome, an arena in which gladiators fought. Another structure built to withstand heavy usage was the Circus Maximus, where chariot races were held. To make sure that such structures would stand up under the weight and movement of crowds, horses, and vehicles, the Romans developed concrete as a building material.

The Spread of Roman Culture

Wherever Roman armies went, they built new cities and towns and roads to connect places to Rome. As a result, Roman architectural styles spread throughout Europe, northern Africa, and the Middle East. In England, there are ruins of Roman baths, military camps, and a great wall built by the Emperor Hadrian in northern England. Roman ruins are also found throughout France, Spain, North Africa, and Turkey. More important traces of Roman culture exist in the Latin-based languages of Italy, France, and Spain. When invaders from France conquered England in 1066, they introduced many Latin-based words into the English language. In addition, the legal codes of most Mediterranean countries are based on Roman law.

Roman ideas about life, art, and religion were also spread throughout the empire by the armies and governing officials. Because Romans were influenced by Greek and Hellenistic culture, the blend of ideas produced what is called the Greco-Roman civilization.

INFO CHECK

1. How did the early Romans benefit from Etruscan rule?

2. Describe the government of the Roman republic. Identify its democratic features.

3. What did Rome gain as a result of the Punic Wars?

4. Indicate what each of the following contributed to the growth of the Roman Empire: Pompey, Julius Caesar, Claudius.

5. Select those features of Roman law that you regard as being essential to good government.

6. Explain why you AGREE or DISAGREE with the following statement: The Romans had little knowledge of engineering or architecture.

INDIAN CIVILIZATION: THE MAURYA EMPIRE (321–185 B.C.)

Prior to their Golden Age, the Indians had gone through a period of social upheaval and had come under the influence of invaders.

Chandragupta

Alexander the Great conquered a large part of western India but died before he could organize it under Macedonian rule. Chandragupta Maurya, the ruler of a small state in the Ganges Valley, took advantage of the confusion. Little by little, he conquered the kingdoms that had been left without strong leadership. In time, he ruled all of northern India (from 321 to 298 B.C.). He used techniques

India: The Maurya Empire   250 B.C.

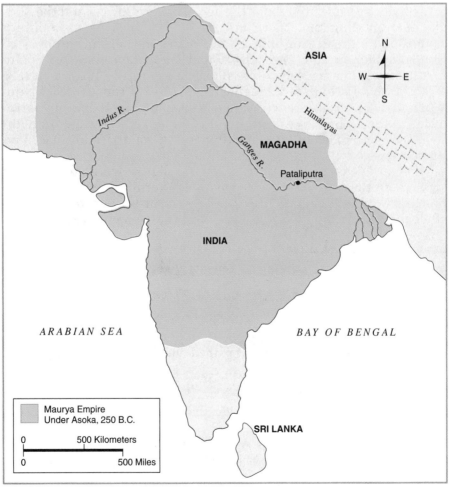

learned from the Persians about how to govern a vast territory inhabited by a large number of people. This was the beginning of the Maurya Dynasty.

Chandragupta organized his large empire by breaking it up into small provinces. He assigned a member of his family to govern each province. Agents traveled from the capital at Pataliputra to oversee the governors. The agents kept Chandragupta informed of conditions in his provinces. A large bureaucracy also helped him run his state smoothly. This body of officials was mainly responsible for the system of taxation that supported public services.

Pataliputra was a large city with great buildings and parks. A system of well-maintained roads helped government officials, traders, and armed forces to move easily about the empire.

Chandragupta was an efficient ruler who brought stability to India. He was repressive, however, and exercised tight, sometimes brutal, control over his subjects.

Asoka

Chandragupta's grandson, Asoka, expanded the Maurya Empire to include almost all of India. He was a strong ruler (272–232 B.C.) and a skilled warrior. After ruling nine years, Asoka made a change that affected the religious life not only of India but of other countries as well. His army had won a battle against a state on the east coast of India by killing an enormous number of people. After the battle, Asoka was stricken by remorse and converted to Buddhism. Buddhism stressed reverence for life. (For more details, see Chapter 8.)

From then on, Asoka ruled with unusual compassion. At his direction, holy people called monks spread Buddhist teachings to other parts of Asia, the Middle East, and North Africa.

Asoka had rules of conduct for his people carved on stone pillars. The pillars were set up throughout the empire so that everyone could see them. After Asoka's death in 232 B.C., the unity of the Maurya Empire was lost, and India was repeatedly invaded by foreigners.

In Chapter 8 you will read about the interaction between some of the civilizations described in this chapter. You will also learn that as more contact took place between different peoples, religions and philosophies began to spread throughout the world.

INFO CHECK

1. Describe the role of Chandragupta in the rise of the Maurya Empire.

2. How did Asoka change the Maurya Empire and other lands?

3. How might both Chandragupta and Asoka be compared with Greek and Roman leaders such as Alexander and Julius Caesar?

CHAPTER REVIEW

Multiple Choice

1. The concept of the Mandate of Heaven, as begun in China, was used every time

   1. a new ruler was born
   2. soldiers were sent off to fight invaders
   3. to explain why China felt itself superior to the "barbarian West"
   4. to justify rebellion and replacement of one ruler for another.

2. The creation of civil servants in China became necessary because

   1. the ruler had no family to assist in governing the provinces
   2. as the empire expanded, administrators were needed to govern the provinces
   3. the ruler never trusted the nobility to govern
   4. only the civil servants could read and write.

3. The Zhou Dynasty ended because

   1. conflict arose between the king and the nobles who ruled the provinces
   2. Viking invaders destroyed the countryside
   3. the return of the Ice Age destroyed the economy
   4. no male heir was born to the king.

4. The earliest recorded Greek civilizations were

   1. Minoan and Roman
   2. Mesopotamian and Mycenaean
   3. Assyrian and Athenian
   4. Mycenaean and Minoan.

5. The *Iliad* and the *Odyssey* were

   1. love poems written during the Golden Age of Greece
   2. tales of Homer's travels and heroic deeds
   3. epic poetry describing life during Greece's Dark Age
   4. religious folktales written by Homer.

6. In Greece many small independent city-states developed. This occurred because

   1. Greek families do not get along with their neighbors
   2. the topography of the land encouraged the development of widely scattered settlements
   3. foreign invaders divided the Greeks into smaller settlements for ease of control
   4. Greek people had many different languages and religions.

7. The only type of leadership that did not arise in Greece was

   1. tyrant
   2. aristocracy
   3. oligarchy
   4. divine king.

8. During the time of the Roman republic, the most powerful government officials were

   1. plebeians
   2. patricians
   3. consuls
   4. magistrates.

9. Philosophers who thought about the principles that a person should live

by arose in China and Greece. Select the philosopher who was put to death for seeking the truth.

1. Confucius
2. Archimedes
3. Socrates
4. Ptolomy.

10. The ruler whose conversion to Buddhism caused its spread throughout the empire was

1. Pericles
2. Alexander
3. Shi Huangdi
4. Asoka.

11. Refer to the photographs on pages 86 and 93 and select the correct statement.

1. Imperial Romans knew little about engineering.
2. The Athenians relied heavily on border fortifications.
3. A high degree of architectural skill characterized the cultures of ancient China and Greece.
4. There was little construction of monuments and buildings in Egypt.

12. Use the map on page 107 to identify two European rivers fortified by the Romans.

1. Rhine and Danube
2. Atlantic and Mediterranean
3. North and Black
4. Corsica and Sardinia.

Thematic Essays

1. "The Romans, unlike many of the other classical civilizations, concentrated on the practical sciences." *Task:* Identify any two examples of Roman civilization that support this statement and explain why you picked them.

2. "If Greece was the birthplace of democracy, then Athens was its center." *Task:* Discuss the validity of that statement as it applies to women and men who were not Athenian citizens.

Document-Based Questions

Use your knowledge of Global History and Geography and the source documents to answer the questions about governments.

1. From a description of Sparta by the Greek writer Xenophon:

"I first noted the unique position of Sparta among the states . . . the relative sparse population . . . at the same time . . . the power and prestige . . . In Sparta, the stronger a man is the more readily does he bow before constituted authority."

What, according to Xenophon, makes Sparta different from other city-states?

2. From Pericles' funeral oration:

"We are called a democracy, for the administration is in the hands of the many and not the few. If few of us are originators [creators] we are all sound judges of policy. The great impediment [block] to action is . . . not discussion but the want of knowledge . . . gained by discussion."

According to Pericles, how are decisions and policies made in a democracy?

3. Refer to the text, page 105.

List two ways that political power was divided among Roman citizens.

4. From the Roman historian Polybius:

"As for the Roman Constitution . . . it has three elements, each of them possessing sovereign power . . . and their respective share of power in the whole state has been regulated with such a . . . regard to equality and equilibrium [balance] that no one can say for certain . . . whether the constitution is an aristocracy, or democracy or despotism."

Why does Polybius admire the government established by the Roman Constitution?

Document-Based Essay

Task: Identify and discuss three Greek or Roman political practices that influenced future Western political systems.

C H A P T E R

8

Empires, Trade, and Religions in the Classical Age

Marius hurried to the town wall. Outriders had brought news of a caravan making its way to the town's gate. Quickly, he climbed to the top of the wall to get a better view. Yes, clouds of dust were visible on the horizon. In another hour or so, he'd be able to make out the camels and men that were stirring up the desert floor. Tomorrow there would be a new booth in the marketplace with new things to see and hear.

Marius wondered where the merchants were coming from. He hoped they were from India or China. Asians told such strange and wonderful stories. He remembered an Indian merchant who had once shown him the statue of a gently smiling man sitting in a cross-legged position. The merchant, who spoke a little Latin, had tried to tell him about the man. Unfortunately, Marius could barely understand what he meant. He had said something about everyone having to be born over and over again. But the cross-legged man was free of such a cycle. Marius didn't see the advantage of that freedom. For his part, he would like to have as many lives as possible. Just one didn't give you time enough to learn all there is to know about the world.

M arius lives in a remote province of the Roman Empire. Although his town is small and insignificant, it is located on one of the trade routes that link the civilizations of the East with those of the West. Because he is constantly being exposed to ideas and goods brought by merchants from distant lands, Marius is learning more about his world than boys who live in the great capital cities.

THE GROWTH OF GLOBAL TRADE ROUTES

The Phoenicians

Early traders had a strong influence on the cultures of many different regions. A seafaring people called the Phoenicians were especially active in carrying skills and ideas as well as trade items from one civilization to another. Phoenicia flourished from about 3000 B.C. until it came under Roman control in 64 B.C.

Cities and Trade. The Phoenicians lived in cities strung along the Mediterranean coast in the area that is now Lebanon. Two of their most important cities were Sidon and Tyre. Besides being ports from which merchants sailed all over the Mediterranean, these cities produced desirable trade goods. Tyre was known for a purple dye that could be obtained from certain shellfish found on its shores. Although now made synthetically, this dye is still called Tyrian purple. Other luxury items made by Phoenician craftsworkers were jewelry, blown glass, and objects from ivory and gold.

Exploration and Colonization. The Phoenicians were not just traders. They were also explorers who set up colonies on the coasts of Europe, North Africa, Sardinia, and Corsica. Carthage was one of their most famous colonies. Later in history, it became a powerful trade center in its own right. Its political downfall came when it fought Rome for control of the western Mediterranean. Under Roman rule, Carthage became an even more important center of imperial trade.

Although never a powerful military force, the Phoenicians had a significant influence on the Mediterranean area. Using their colonies as bases, the Phoenicians traded with all the nations that bordered the Mediterranean. As they did so, they adopted many ideas, skills, and customs from their trading partners. They then spread the new ideas and ways to other nations.

Literacy. Phoenicians may have taught the Greeks about shipbuilding and colonization. It is certain, however, that they introduced an advanced writing system to the Greeks. Adopting the idea of using symbols for sounds, the Phoenicians created their own alphabet. It consisted of only 22 symbols. Each symbol represented a sound. Instead of a different symbol for every different name or idea, the same symbols could be combined in various ways to form many words.

The Phoenician system was much easier to learn and use than the Sumerian, Egyptian, and Chinese systems. Early Greeks saw the advantages of the Phoenician system and adapted it to their own use.

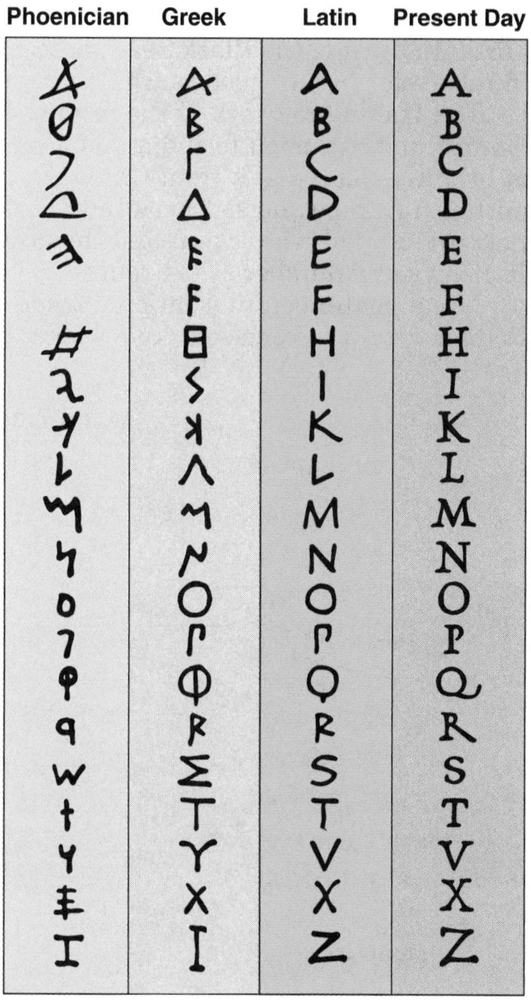

Phoenician	Greek	Latin	Present Day

Alphabets: Phoenician, Greek, Latin, and Present Day

They then passed it on to the Romans. The Latin alphabet of the Romans is the basis of the one used by most Western peoples today. See the chart above that compares Phoenician, Greek, Latin, and modern Western European alphabets.

Greek and Roman Global Trade

During the Classical Age, global trade was further developed by the Greek city-states and by the Roman Empire. Despite the hazards of long-distance travel, trade was an essential part of life in Greco-Roman civilization. Shops in Athens and Rome, for example, sold a wide range of goods imported from all over the known world.

By 500 B.C., some of the Greek poli had established trading colonies around the Aegean and Mediterranean seas and along the northern coast of the Black Sea. These colonies sent grain and timber in return for luxury goods such as pottery and jewelry.

The trading network of the Roman Empire covered the whole of Europe and extended to India and China. The Romans prized robes of brightly colored silk from China. Roman pottery was exported to northern Europe and southern India. Imperial trade flowed along the network of roads that connected the provinces of the Roman Empire. It also used a number of sea routes.

Major centers of international trade developed beyond the Greco-Roman world. Increased knowledge of monsoon winds enabled

World Trade Routes in the Classical Age

traders to sail the Indian Ocean. The ports of Taxila and Charsadda in northwest India were important trading centers by 500 B.C. Around A.D. 300, the African kingdom of Axum, in modern-day Ethiopia, gained prosperity through trade. In the Syrian desert, the city of Palmyra became famous for the wealth gained as a point of exchange for the goods of the Roman and Persian empires.

The Silk Road

The Silk Road linked Central Asian civilizations with those in the Middle East and the Mediterranean region. (See the map on these pages.) It was more than 5,000 miles long. Trade along the route

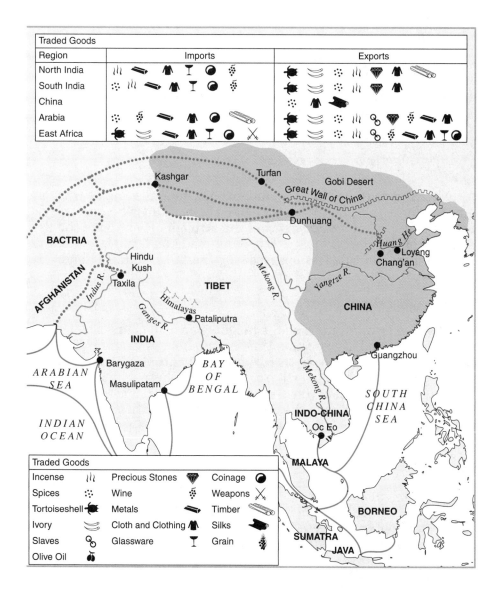

began during the Han Dynasty in China in the early 200s B.C. As market cities sprang up along this road, the inhabitants learned about Greek, Roman, and Chinese culture from the foreign merchants they did business with. The merchants, in their turn, were exposed to the arts, crafts, and ideas of the lands they visited and took these novelties home. Marius, in the chapter-opening story, shows how people in the trading towns learned about new ideas.

As the name Silk Road suggests, great amounts of silk cloth were carried to the West, along with spices and tea. In return, Westerners sent iron, copper, wool, glass, gold, and silver to the East.

INFO CHECK

1. Explain the importance of global trade to the spread of ideas and knowledge.

2. Why did the Phoenician alphabet mean so much to the development of both trade and culture in the Classical Age?

3. How did colonization spread Greek culture to other lands? Why was this beneficial to the Greeks and other peoples?

THE HAN DYNASTY: 206 B.C.–A.D. 220

After the death of the Qin emperor, his generals fought with one another for control of China. Liu Bang, a peasant who had worked his way into the bureaucracy, won the struggle. He became the first emperor of the Han Dynasty. Liu Bang made no formal political reforms, but he did rule less oppressively than Shi Huang Ti had.

Expansion of the Empire

The Han Dynasty marked the height of ancient China's power and wealth. It existed at the same time as the Roman Empire. Han emperors added new lands to their empire. Eventually, the empire included Southeast Asia, northern Korea, southern Manchuria, and Central Asia. Control of these lands made the Han one of the largest and wealthiest empires in the ancient world. Han cities were believed to be the most beautiful in the world.

Civil Service Tests

The Han ruled their empire with the help of a bureaucracy. This consisted of appointed officials, who received salaries for their services. Candidates for these jobs took tests on law, mathematics, and the writings of the philosopher. Confucius. The men who scored the

China: The Han Empire

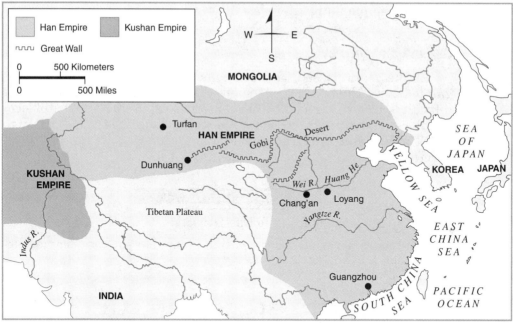

highest on these public examinations got the jobs. The best students from colleges throughout the empire had to train in an imperial school before they could take the examinations.

This examination system enabled poor but talented men to enter the Han civil service. The equality of opportunity it offered was unusual in the ancient world. The dynasties that followed the Han continued to use the examination system to fill government jobs.

Trade and Technology

As the Han extended their empire into Southeast Asia and to the borders of Persia and India, China came into more frequent contact with other cultures. Traders developed overland trade routes, such as the Silk Road, for the shipment of silk and spices.

Chinese technology advanced steadily. Craftsworkers improved methods of making lacquerware. Lacquerware objects are made of wood that has been covered with a colored, highly polished varnish. The bowls, boxes, or furniture are often red or black and decorated with gold or silver.

In A.D. 105 an inventor named Cai Lun learned to make paper from cloth, rope, and bark fibers. The world's first dictionary was written during the Han Dynasty. Metalworkers developed improved methods of making iron tools and weapons. They produced crossbows, carpenters' rules, adjustable wrenches, and machine parts, such as gear and cog wheels. Han scientists designed the first form of cartography, or mapmaking.

Decline and Unrest

As the years passed, Han rulers became weaker. Barbarians began to attack the borders of the empire. Also, the emperors found it difficult to prevent revolts by the peasants and to curb the rise of local rulers called warlords. In time, the warlords caused the dynasty to fall. The last Han emperor gave up his throne in A.D. 220. The next several hundred years were a time of great unrest.

INFO CHECK

1. Trace the rise and fall of the Han Dynasty.
2. List the two accomplishments of Han China that you consider most important. Explain your choices.

THE DECLINE OF THE ROMAN EMPIRE

The Roman Empire and the Han Dynasty had much in common. Both empires were great political and military powers in the Eastern Hemisphere. Both developed efficient forms of governments. They preserved and developed the achievements of earlier cultures. Both made contributions of their own to art, literature, science, technology, and scholarship. Unfortunately, the two empires also experienced similar problems that eventually caused their downfall. Weak economies, corrupt governments, and civil wars left them both defenseless when nomadic groups invaded from the north.

The Breakdown of Society in Imperial Rome

Development into an empire brought both benefits and problems to Rome. Contact with other peoples greatly enriched Roman culture. Romans tried to govern their provinces according to the rules and customs of their subjects. Consequently, Roman law became more flexible and universal.

The Equestrians. An increase in trade in the growing empire led to the rise of a new middle class of businesspeople called *equestrians*. As these people became more prosperous, they demanded more privileges from the government.

Plebeians. Few *plebeians* (lower-class people) had a share in the new wealth. The increased use of slave labor meant fewer jobs. Even if they found work, plebeians remained poor. In order to get the jobs that were available, they had to accept very low wages.

Plebeians who worked small farms could not compete with the

large estates worked by slaves. These estates produced larger crops more cheaply than the small plebeian farms could. The plebeians often could not earn enough from the sale of their crops to pay their taxes. As a result, many were forced to sell their lands to patricians and equestrians.

A great number of plebeians had been soldiers in the Punic Wars. While their fighting had made many of their fellow Romans wealthy, it had ruined the plebeians. When they went off to war, not enough people remained behind to do the farm work. Consequently, the farms produced few crops. Many soldiers came home to find themselves hopelessly in debt and had to sell their land to the rich estate owners.

Without work or land, large numbers of plebeians moved to the cities and became part of an unemployed mob. They lived on government handouts of grain. To keep the plebeians from rioting, the government entertained them with public games. The crowds particularly liked chariot races and armed combats. In the combats, men called gladiators fought each other, sometimes to the death.

Reform Leaders. Some leaders tried to help the poor. Two, the brothers Tiberius and Gaius Gracchus, were murdered by members of the Senate for their efforts to assist the plebians. Tiberius was killed in 133 B.C. and Gaius in 121 B.C. Tiberius angered the wealthy senators by drawing up a bill entitling the poor to small lots of public land. Gaius provoked the senators by proposing that the poor be given cheap grain. He also suggested that landless people be allowed to start colonies in southern Italy.

Gauis Marius. A third leader, a general named Marius, used the unemployed to further his career. He recruited an army from the poor and landless. Before this, most armies had consisted of *drafted* men. To be drafted means to be called by the government to serve in the army as part of one's civic duty. The volunteers Marius collected became professional soldiers, who served for long periods of time. Marius organized these professional soldiers into a standing army. Because they made their living by fighting, they took their training more seriously and fought more efficiently than the drafted soldiers had. By winning a significant victory with his army, Marius improved his political position. In order to persuade men to enlist, Marius had promised to give them land after the war. But when Marius became a political leader and drew up a bill granting land to his soldiers, the Senate refused to pass it. Despite this, a professional army of highly trained, disciplined legions became a permanent feature of Roman military and political life. These legions conquered an empire for Rome.

Civil War and Dictators. Many plebeians were left with nothing but their votes. These they sold to the politicians who would pay or promise the most. The economic problems of the plebeians and their loss of political power led to a long period of civil wars.

Many Roman citizens no longer had faith in the Republic or representative government to maintain peace and security. More and more often they turned to dictators. The dictators took advantage of the disorder and uncertainty to increase their power. Many refused to leave office after their term limit expired. During the civil wars, these political and military leaders ruled by force. Such leaders kept the peace by killing their enemies or exiling them to faraway places.

Julius Caesar

One of the most famous of the military dictators was Julius Caesar (lived 100–44 B.C.). His rise to power marked the beginning of the end of the Roman Republic.

Caesar believed that a republican government would not be able to rule the vast Roman empire effectively. He may have been the first Roman leader to have dealt with this problem. As a rising politician, Caesar won the plebeians' support by acting as a champion of their rights. In 60 B.C., he joined forces with Marcus Licinius Crassus, the richest man in Rome, and Gaius Magnus Pompey, the successful and popular general. The three men used the money of Crassus, the military power of Pompey, and the plebeian votes given to Caesar to gain control of the government. Known as the First Triumvirate, Crassus, Pompey, and Caesar had enough power to rule the Roman world and to end the civil wars. The triumvirate ruled from 60 to 53 B.C.

Caesar's military campaign in Gaul gave him command of an army. After the death of Crassus in 53 B.C., Caesar fought with Pompey for control of the Roman government. This conflict started off a new series of civil wars. In the great battles that followed, Caesar

Marble bust of Julius Caesar, general, statesman, and dictator

defeated the armies of Pompey in Greece, Spain, and North Africa. Pompey fled to Egypt, where he was killed.

In 46 B.C., Julius Caesar became sole ruler of Rome and the areas it controlled. He was a very capable dictator. He made the army and the government more efficient. The size of the Senate was increased to make it better represent the provinces. Citizenship was extended to more people in the provinces. Caesar improved the tax system and introduced a more accurate calendar. (With some changes, it is the one we use today.) By creating more jobs for the poor, he reduced by more than half the number of people receiving free grain.

Although Caesar had all the power of a king, he did not have the title. He knew that the Roman people would accept a dictator but not a king. Romans had been opposed to kings ever since Etruscan rule. While achieving his successes, Caesar had made many enemies who resented his growing power. In 44 B.C., a group led by Marcus Brutus murdered Julius Caesar. Brutus and his friends claimed that they had acted to prevent Caesar from crowning himself king.

The anger of the Roman people at Caesar's death forced the murderers to flee to the provinces. Control of Rome fell to Marc Antony, Caesar's friend and chief general. A new civil war began as the armies of Antony marched against the forces of Brutus and his supporters.

Augustus, the First Roman Emperor

A civil war followed the death of Julius Caesar. Octavian, the grandnephew and adopted son of Julius Caesar, joined forces with

Marble statue of the young Caesar Augustus, first emperor of Rome

Marc Antony. Together they defeated Brutus and his allies. Octavian and Antony ruled the Roman world until Antony's alliance with Queen Cleopatra of Egypt brought on still another civil war. In the sea battle of Actium in 31 B.C., Octavian's ships defeated the fleet of Antony and Cleopatra.

Octavian took complete control of the government and became Rome's first emperor. He ruled from 27 B.C. to A.D. 14. The Senate gave Octavian the title of Caesar Augustus. Under Augustus, the empire entered a period of peace, security, and cultural accomplishment. For the next 200 years, the Roman Empire enjoyed what is called the *Pax Romana* (Roman Peace).

Other Roman Emperors

Augustus died in A.D. 14. Tiberius, his successor (A.D. 14–37), ruled as wisely as Augustus. Unfortunately, Tiberius was followed by Caligula, who was insane. He ruled so cruelly that, in A.D. 41, a group of military officers and senators murdered him. His uncle Claudius, who succeeded him, made a wise and efficient emperor (A.D. 41–54). During his reign, Claudius added Britain to the empire.

Nero took over the empire when Claudius died. He ruled from 54 to 68. Nero, like Caligula, was insane. Among other crimes, he murdered his mother and his wife. He was suspected of causing the great fire that destroyed half of Rome in 64. Nero placed the blame for the fire on a new religious group called the Christians and ordered the execution of its members.

Most of the emperors who followed Nero were careful to choose as heirs men they believed to be good leaders. To ensure acceptance of their choices, the emperors adopted their proposed successors as their sons.

Marcus Aurelius was one of the best of the emperors. He spent most of his ruling years (161–180) defending the borders of the empire against invaders. Unfortunately, he failed to follow the example of the other emperors. Instead of adopting a good leader, he allowed his son Commodus to inherit the empire. Commodus preferred fighting in the arena as a gladiator to solving the many problems of the empire. During his reign (180–192), Rome began to decline.

When Commodus died in A.D. 192, the Pax Romana came to an end. Military leaders now took over the government. During the next 100 years or so, Rome had 26 emperors. Many of these were murdered by their own soldiers. Each time one emperor was removed, a civil war broke out over the choice of his successor. Other peoples became powerful enough to challenge the Romans. Economic and political problems increased and gradually weakened the Roman Empire.

In an attempt to strengthen the empire, an emperor named Diocletian (ruled from 284 to 305), divided it into two parts, eastern and western. Diocletian, who held most of the governing power himself,

RELIGION AND ROMANCE IN ANCIENT ROME

Valentine's Day, in February, is when people demonstrate affection and romantic interest in each other by exchanging cards and gifts. This charming custom had its origin in Roman religious practices.

The Lupercalia was a holiday celebrated by ancient Romans on Februaury 15th. Its purpose was to honor the gods Lupercus and Faunus and the twin brothers Romulus and Remus, the legendary founders of the city of Rome.

The Lupercalia ceremonies were held on the Palatine Hill, where the first Romans had built their homes. The priests of the gods Lupercus dressed in goatskins. After sacrificing goats and a dog, they smeared themselves with blood. The priests then ran around the hill carrying a goatskin thong called a *februa* (instrument of purification). Roman women placed themselves along the route around the Palatine Hill so that the priests could strike them with the *februa*. The women believed that this would assure them fertility and easy childbirth.

The ceremony also involved the pairing of the young men and women of Rome. The priests placed the names of the girls in a box. Each boy then drew a girl's name from the box and became paired with her until the next Lupercalia.

In A.D. 270, the Lupercalia was made into a Christian feast to honor St. Valentine, who was martyred (killed for his beliefs) in the 3rd century. There are many stories about him. One tale says that Valentine was an early Christian who made friends with many children. The Romans imprisoned him because he refused to sacrifice to their gods. The children missed Valentine and tossed loving notes between the bars of his cell window. According to another story, Valentine restored the sight of his jailer's blind daughter. The girl then fell in love with him.

It is believed that Valentine was executed on February 14 in A.D. 269. In 496, the pope named February 14 as St. Valentine's Day. It had become a Church practice to replace pagan festivals with Christian holidays and feasts.

1. What does the origin of Valentine's Day tell us about the influence of the past on the present?

2. What does the description of the Lupercalia tell us about Roman superstition?

ruled from his eastern capital in Asia Minor. The coemperor ruled from Milan in northern Italy, which was better located than Rome to defend the empire's northern border. The city of Rome was no longer the capital of the Roman Empire.

In 306, Constantine was named emperor. In 324, he reunited the empire and ruled alone until his death in 337. About 330, he moved the capital of the empire to Byzantium, which he renamed Constantinople. After 395, the empire was permanently divided. The western part became weaker and poorer. The eastern part grew stronger and wealthier.

Invaders From the North

Large groups of German tribes invaded the western portion of the Roman Empire in the 5th century A.D. The Romans were too weak to stop them. Twice the Germans attacked and looted the once-powerful city of Rome. As a result of the German invasions, the empire ceased to exist in Europe. Each western Roman province eventually became a German kingdom.

Other invaders followed the Germans. Among the most feared were a Central Asian people known as the Huns. Starting about A.D. 434, they conquered large parts of the Roman Empire and controlled them until about A.D. 453.

The Roman Empire and Invaders   A.D. 400

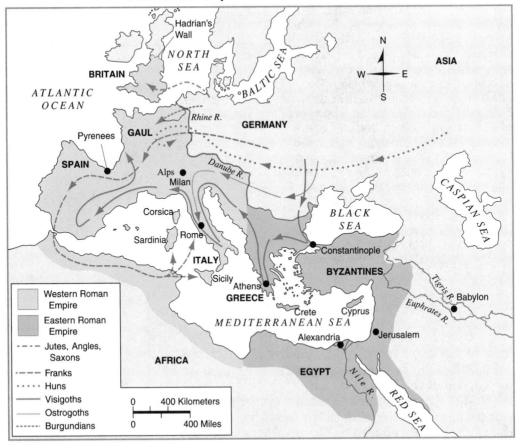

After the death of the Hun leader, Attila, in 453, the Hun Empire broke up. The German tribes then regained control of Europe and what was left of the Roman world there. The Western Roman Empire ended officially in 476, when a German general named Odoacer forced the last Roman emperor to give up his throne. Odoacer made himself king of Italy.

For most of Europe, the Classical Age was over. In the Hellenistic cities of Asia Minor and the Middle East, however, the Eastern Roman Empire continued. The Byzantine Empire, as it came to be called, lasted until 1453.

INFO CHECK

1. Explain why you AGREE or DISAGREE with this statement: The Roman Empire and the Han Dynasty had nothing in common.

2. How did each of the following change, or attempt to change, the Roman world: Tiberius and Gaius Gracchus, Gaius Marius, Julius Caesar?

3. Complete the following sentences:

   - Marcus Aurelius allowed his son _____.
   - After the death of Commodus, there were many civil wars because _____.
   - Diocletian tried to strengthen the empire by _____.
   - Around A.D. 330, Constantine _____.

4. What roles did the Germans and the Huns play in the fall of the Western Roman Empire? Why do you think the Romans were unable to prevent the loss of their empire?

THE DECLINE AND FALL OF THE HAN EMPIRE: A.D. 220

At first, the policies of the Han Dynasty made many people prosperous. In the later days of the Han Dynasty, however, only a few powerful people enjoyed China's great wealth. The peasants, who served as the empire's farmers and soldiers, were poorly paid and heavily taxed. When wars broke out on the borders of the empire, the government sent peasants to fight the invaders. Unable to serve as soldiers and to run their farms, many peasants had to sell their land to the owners of large estates. Their situation was similar to that of the plebeian farmers of Rome.

Weak Leaders

The governments of the later Han emperors were weak and corrupt. Because they did little to protect their peasants, the peasants began to revolt. The generals sent to crush the uprisings seized the peasants' land and set up their own kingdoms.

During the reign of Hsien Ti (A.D. 189–221), a peasant group called the Yellow Turbans led an uprising that brought down the Han Dynasty. While Hsien Ti's armies were away, members of his court took advantage of their absence and dethroned him.

After the Collapse

The period of the Three Kingdoms (221–280) followed the collapse of the Han Dynasty. During this time, China was divided into the kingdoms of Wei in the south, Shu in the upper Yangtze River Valley, and Wu in the lower Yangtze River Valley.

During this time, nomadic tribes from the north again began to invade the divided country. The Toba, from Mongolia, were the most successful. They took over northern China and set up their own dynasty there. Many Chinese took refuge in southern China.

After conquering much of China, the nomadic groups adopted the language, religion, agricultural techniques, and political system of their subjects. In spite of the invasion of its land and the defeat of its leaders, the culture of China remained intact.

Comparing Empires

The Roman and Han empires shared similar problems. The leaders of both empires conquered vast territories. Nomadic tribes from the north were attracted to their fertile farmlands and prosperous cities. Fighting the invaders strained the wealth and manpower of both empires. Made poor and landless by these wars, the lower classes of Rome and China became dissatisfied.

Besides defending their kingdoms against invaders, the rulers of Rome and China then had to deal with political rivalries, rebellions, and civil wars. Corruption and weakness in their governments limited their power to correct any of these problems. In an effort to pare the empires down to a manageable size, new leaders divided them into eastern and western portions. The Byzantine Empire finally replaced the Roman Empire in the 5th century, and the Three Kingdoms followed the Han Dynasty in the 3rd century.

INFO CHECK

1. PROVE or DISPROVE each of the following:

    - The Han Dynasty enjoyed continual peace and prosperity.
    - Good government kept the peasants loyal to the Han Dynasty.

2. How did the period of the Three Kingdoms affect China?

3. Identify two problems common to both the Han Dynasty and the Roman Empire.

THE BORDER PEOPLES: CELTS, GERMANS, HUNS

Not all societies developed great cities and strong central governments. Some people settled in small agricultural villages while others herded cattle from pasture to pasture. Nonetheless, the people in these societies made important contributions to culture.

Much of the technology that enriched the great cities began in small towns. Long before any cities existed, unknown villagers invented the sail, the weaving loom, and the pottery wheel. As civilizations sprang up, villagers continued to make important innovations. They learned how to use crop rotation and manure as fertilizer to make their land grow more food. They invented more efficient farm tools.

The Celts

In the ancient world, no people lived in as many lands or affected the early development of as many nations as did the Celts. They spread out through central and western Europe and the British Isles. From 700 B.C. to A.D. 100, Celtic civilizations existed in what are today Britain, Ireland, Spain, France, Germany, Switzerland, Austria, Hungary, and Czechoslovakia.

Government and Life. All of the Celts spoke similar languages and had similar ways of life. They were divided into tribes ruled by kings and, sometimes, by queens. Tribes living in the same geographic area often fought one another. The leaders of the tribes were warriors. Most Celts, however, were peaceful, hardworking farmers and herd-keepers.

Usually, Celts lived in towns and villages located on hilltops. The Celts fortified, or protected, the villages by surrounding them with deep ditches and high walls.

The knowledge of ironwork in much of Europe came from the Celts. They used iron plows to prepare the ground for planting and iron scythes to cut grain. Such tools influenced the type of farming carried on in Europe for centuries.

The Celts built roads to help them move from place to place more easily. They covered some of the roads with timber and stone to make a better surface for their horses and vehicles to move over. The Celts transported their goods in four-wheeled carts and drove two-wheeled chariots.

Literature. The Celts had no writing system. Their priests and learned men, called *Druids*, could read and write Latin, Greek, and other languages. The Celts preserved their history and stories by committing them to memory. They composed long, exciting poems about the great events in their lives and the deeds of their heroes. Specially trained men, called *bards*, memorized and recited these poems. Celtic oral literature influenced the development of European written literature. Love of adventure and heroism and an appreciation of humor were among the values handed down to writers of later times.

Roman Influence. By A.D. 100, the Romans had conquered most of western Europe. The Celts came under Roman rule. The Romans ended the Celtic tribal wars. They gave the Celts Roman law, the Latin language, and the opportunity to trade with distant lands. High-ranking Celtic officials represented their people in the Roman town and provincial governments. Celtic warriors gave up fighting or joined the Roman armies. As the Roman and Celtic cultures gradually blended, a new culture arose. The foundation of a European civilization was established.

The Germans

Many scholars believe that the Germanic peoples migrated into what is now Germany from Scandinavia and other northern parts of Europe between 1000 and 100 B.C. The Celts, who had lived in these areas, moved farther south and west into what are now Spain, France, and the British Isles.

The ancient Germans were farmers and herders who lived in log houses clustered together in villages and surrounded by fields. They owned and tilled their land communally (as a group). They were organized into many different tribes. An assembly of freemen governed each tribe. In times of war or other crises, the tribe members elected a king. While the crisis lasted, the king made all the decisions.

During periods of overpopulation, some tribes would seek new homes. The Visigoths settled in Spain, the Vandals in North Africa, and the Angles and Saxons in England.

Between 12 B.C. and A.D. 16, the Romans tried to conquer the Germanic peoples. But they only succeeded in controlling a small number of tribes. After numerous border wars, the Romans established permanent frontiers on the Rhine and Danube rivers in the 2nd century A.D. Until the early 5th century, the Roman legions guarding the frontiers kept most of the German tribes out of the empire. The Germans tended not to unify under a single state and system of laws, as other Latinized people did. Loyalty to tribal leaders and traditions prevented close cooperation.

Roman leaders recruited Germans for the Roman army. The Germans were good warriors. Many rose to positions of leadership. Contact with the Romans gave the Germans trading opportunities, which exposed them to new ideas and ways of living.

The Warrior State of the Huns

The Huns were herders who occupied the lands north of China. They were warlike nomads who did not plant crops. Little is known of their early history. Most of the information that we have about this group is based on their interactions with other peoples.

Clashes With the Chinese. When the Chinese began expanding northward in the 3rd century B.C., they took over the Huns' pastureland. In retaliation, the Huns raided Chinese towns and farms. One chieftain conquered a number of Chinese tribes and set up a small empire in the northern reaches of China. To discourage more such invasions, Shi Huang Ti of the Qin Dynasty ordered that the sections of the Great Wall be joined together.

During the Han Dynasty, the Huns once more began to harass China's northern border. In 133 B.C., Emperor Han Wu Ti began a campaign against them. Fourteen years later, he succeeded in driving them from his borders.

Westward Movement. The Huns continued to develop their fighting skills. They were known for their ability to use the bow and arrow while riding on horseback. In about A.D. 370, they swept westward, pushing the Goths out of their lands. The Goths crowded into the Roman Empire for refuge. Taking advantage of the Goths' poverty, the Romans forced them into slavery. Their treatment of the Goths was so cruel that the Goths rebelled. In A.D. 378, they defeated the Roman army at Adrianople. This victory encouraged a massive invasion of Goths and other Germanic peoples into the Roman Empire. Overwhelmed by these invaders, the Roman Empire became a collection of Germanic kingdoms.

White Huns. While Attila's Huns were fighting in eastern Europe, another group, called the White Huns, moved into the Gupta Empire in India. The Indian ruler, Skandagupta (ruled A.D. 455–467), managed to force them back. The effort was so costly, however, that it brought about the fall of the Gupta Empire. India then separated into a group of small kingdoms.

INFO CHECK

1. Explain why the Celts were so important to the development of European civilization.

2. Describe the interaction between Romans and Germans.

3. How did the Huns impact on the Chinese, Romans, and Indians?

THE EMERGENCE AND SPREAD OF BELIEF SYSTEMS

Animism

The belief systems of most early societies were based on *animism*. This is the belief that all things have *anima*, which is another word for spirit. In order to keep their environments safe and productive, early peoples acted to please the spirits in nature. They believed that success in farming, fishing, and hunting depended on the goodwill of the spirits in earth, water, seeds, forests, animals, and fish.

A class of people called priests were responsible for creating rituals that supposedly allowed them to communicate with the spirits. These priests were usually the heads of families or the chiefs of villages.

Often animism led to ancestor worship. Animists believed that the spirits of human beings lived on after their bodies died. The dead family members, animists hoped, could influence the other spirits in favor of their still-living relatives.

Indian Religions

Origins. After the fall of the Indus Valley civilization, an Indo-European group called the Aryans began migrating into the area. They conquered, then merged with the Dravidians, who are believed to be the descendants of the Indus Valley people. The Aryans were nomadic herders. They had not yet developed a system of writing. They worshiped war, fire, storms, and other powerful forces as gods. The Dravidians were a settled people who made their living by farming and trading. Scholars believe that, like their ancestors, the Dravidians worshiped nature gods and goddesses. They used the writing system of the Indus Valley people.

After conquering the Dravidians, the Aryans settled among them. Members of the two groups married one another and the two cultures blended. From the Dravidians, the Aryans learned farming techniques. They also followed the example of the Dravidians and developed a writing system. Both the Aryan writing system and their language are known as Sanskrit. The Dravidians adopted the Aryan gods and their social structure.

As the Aryans began to build cities along the Ganges River in northeastern India, they developed strong central states ruled by kings. Priests, called *Brahmins*, shared power with the kings. The priests taught that the unpredictable Aryan gods would be pleased by proper sacrifice and would grant their worshipers' wishes.

Hinduism. Some Brahmins began to break away from the idea that religion consisted of pleasing the gods by making sacrifices. These priests went alone into the forest and meditated about the meaning of death and the right way to live. Through their meditations, the Brahmins developed the concept of *reincarnation*. This means that no one truly dies. After death, people are reborn in new bodies or different forms or levels of human beings. If they have lived good lives, they will be reborn as a superior being. But if their lives have been evil, they will come back as something lower. People can, for example, be reborn as animals. The term *karma* refers to the balance of good and evil that determines the fate of a soul. The term

Hindu steplike temple at
Shrirangam, India

dharma refers to the idea that the form in which a person is reincarnated is based on the kind of life he or she had lived.

To escape the cycle of death and rebirth, a person must make amends for wrongdoing, study the Vedas, and meditate. (The Vedas are a collection of hymns, prayers, and religious teachings.) By following these practices and living a good life, a person may reach a state of inner perfection and become part of Brahma, the world soul. After death such a person will not have to be reborn but will have reached a new level of existence.

Hindus believe in thousands of gods. The principle ones are Brahma, Shiva, and Vishnu. Brahma is the creator, Shiva the destroyer, and Vishnu the preserver.

Caste System. According to traditional Hindu beliefs, each person is born into a *caste*—a social rank in society. The highest is the Brahmin, the priestly caste. Next is the Kshatriyas, or rulers and warriors. Below this rank is the Vaisyas, the merchants and professionals. The fourth rank is the Sudras. They are the workers and servants. There are hundreds of levels within each caste. Originally, there were rigid rules of behavior that caste members had to follow, particularly in their relations with other ranks.

It was believed that those of the higher castes could more easily escape the cycle of reincarnation and become part of the world soul.

Lower castes might improve their lives through reincarnation. Their goal is to end the cycles of birth and rebirth.

Outside the caste system were people called "untouchables." They worked in jobs the other castes were forbidden to do. Tanning leather was one. Collecting garbage and waste was another. Untouchables could not associate with anyone in the caste system.

In modern India, it is against the law to classify a person as untouchable. Also, the various caste distinctions have been weakened.

Buddhism. Buddhism grew out of Hinduism and the teachings of Siddhartha Gautama, who lived between 563 and 483 B.C. Gautama, an Indian prince, gave up his family and luxurious home to search for meaning in life. According to legend, Gautama saw human suffering one day when he left his palace. He then wanted to learn why there was so much suffering in the world and how to do away with it. After years of wandering and meditating, Gautama believed that he had found the answer to his question. He then became known as the "Buddha," the "Enlightened One."

Like the Hindus, Buddha believed in reincarnation. But he felt that anyone, regardless of his or her stage of reincarnation, could attain enlightenment and be free of suffering. A person need only follow the Middle Way and the Noble Eightfold Path.

The Middle Way meant avoiding uncontrolled satisfaction of desire and extreme forms of self-punishment. The Eightfold Path called for:

1. knowledge of truth

2. intention to resist evil

3. saying nothing to hurt others

4. respect for life, morality, and property

5. holding a job that does not injure others

6. working to free one's mind of evil

7. controlling one's feelings and thoughts

8. practicing proper forms of concentration (meditation)

Through this conduct, a person can avoid rebirth and enter *nirvana*, a condition in which the soul merges with the universe. Of course, people who have undergone many reincarnations are able to follow the teachings more easily.

Chinese Philosophies

Confucianism. Confucianism is a philosophy based on the teachings of Confucius, also known as Kong Fuzi. He lived in China between 551 and 479 B.C. The philosophy does not promote the worship of gods or the possibility of a life after death.

Eighteenth-century engraving of
Confucius, celebrated Chinese
philosopher

Confucius had been educated as a civil servant but worked almost all his life as a teacher. Most of his ideas have come down to us from records kept by his students. These were gathered into a book called *The Analects*.

Confucius taught that people can achieve the ideal way of life through self-control and proper conduct. Children should show respect for their parents and ancestors, pupils for their teachers, and citizens for their rulers. Rulers should also treat their subjects with respect. Kindness toward others is important. Confucius emphasized that people should live by a rule similar to the Golden Rule of Christianity: "Do not do to others what you do not want them to do to you."

Respect for tradition was an important part of Confucius's teachings. His influence on the Chinese people caused them to dislike sharp changes in their way of life. The ideas of Confucius helped to relax the rigidity of the Chinese class structure. By emphasizing proper conduct, he caused people to feel that their merit as human beings depended on their behavior, not simply on their rank of birth.

Taoism. Taoism (also spelled Daoism) was also concerned with the question of how people should live. This philosophy arose from the teachings of Lao-tzu (or Laozi), who lived at the same time as Confucius. Lao-tzu taught that by following the Tao, or the way, people could achieve inner peace. They could follow the Tao by living simply and in harmony with nature. They should not try to change what happens to them. When insulted or injured by others, they should be humble and kind.

The greatest difference between the two philosophers can be seen in their attitudes toward government. Confucius believed that good government was important. Lao-tzu thought that people were better off with as little government as possible.

Confucius and Lao-tzu lived at the same time as Siddhartha Gautama. The teachings of these three men have influenced the thinking of people in Asia and other parts of the world for more than 2,000 years.

Judaism

The Hebrews, a group of tribes in the ancient Middle East, never built a large empire. But their religious and moral ideas have had a profound effect on the world. Also called Jews, they were the first people to believe in one God. This belief is called *monotheism*. It gradually replaced *polytheism*, the belief in many gods held by other peoples of the ancient world.

The religion of the Jews is intertwined with their history. They were originally tribes of herders from Mesopotamia. Abraham, one of the leaders, brought them to Canaan, which they renamed Israel. During a time of famine, some Jews moved to Egypt, where they were made slaves. After a long period of captivity, Moses freed them and led them back to Israel. The Bible states that during the journey, God came to Moses on Mount Sinai and gave him the Ten Commandments, a code of moral behavior.

From about 1200 to 600 B.C., the Jews developed an advanced civilization. Around 1025 B.C., the tribes united under Saul, their first king. Saul led the fight against the Philistines, a neighboring people, for control of Israel. David followed Saul on the throne. This great king built the city of Jerusalem and made it his capital.

Solomon. The Jewish kingdom reached its peak of strength and wealth under David's son, Solomon. During his rule (965 to 928 B.C.), Solomon made alliances with other kings, sent ships to trade in distant lands, and beautified Jerusalem. He built a great temple there. The Temple of Solomon became the center of Jewish religious life.

After Solomon's death, his kingdom split into two parts—Israel in the north and Judah in the south. Civil wars weakened these kingdoms.

Assaults on Israel. The Assyrians made repeated assaults on Israel and eventually conquered it. The Babylonians took Judah in 587 B.C. and sent the surviving Jews to Babylon as slaves. In 538 B.C., the Persians freed about 4,000 of these exiles and allowed them to return home. In about 63 B.C., Israel became part of the Roman Empire. The Jews rebelled repeatedly. To punish them, the Romans destroyed Jerusalem in A.D. 135. They scattered the Jews to different parts of the world. Israel did not become an independent state again until 1948.

A Chosen People. Although the Jews lost their homeland and were separated from one another, their religion helped them feel united in spirit. No matter where they were, they could read their holy book, the Torah, and follow the ways of life and worship set forth in it. They believed that God had made a *covenant*, or agreement, with them. As long as they followed His commandments and worshiped no other gods, He would watch over them. As part of this covenant, they believed God had first guided them to Israel and then led them safely back from their exile in Egypt. Jews considered themselves to be God's chosen people.

During their captivity in Babylon, Hebrew prophets kept Judaism alive. They promised that God would liberate the Hebrews if they continued to believe in Him and follow His commandments. They must lead moral, upright lives and aid the poor. The prophets predicted that Israel would become a state again. A man who descended from David would be their *messiah*, or savior, and rebuild Jerusalem.

Diaspora. The period when the Babylonians exiled the Jews from Israel is called the *Diaspora*. Diaspora refers to a scattering or migration of people. The term comes from a Greek word that means "to plant seeds by scattering them." During the period when Jews moved to different places, the seeds of Judaism were sown throughout the Middle East and the Mediterranean region.

Influence. The faith of the Jews had a strong appeal. They believed in a God who was both just and merciful. Only righteousness won His favor. Other people of the time believed in gods who were impulsive, sometimes cruel, and easily moved by flattery and gifts. Many non-Jews began to see the advantage of serving a God who was concerned for the welfare and morals of His worshipers. Then, too, the oppressed people of many different societies found hope and comfort in the idea of a savior. Eventually, Judaism became the foundation of Christianity and had a strong influence on Islam, two of the major religions of the world.

The Development of Christianity

Although the Roman Empire brought stability to much of the Eastern Hemisphere, it also stirred up emotional and spiritual unrest. The Romans were tolerant of the religions and customs of the people they ruled. Nonetheless, the beliefs and ideas of the new rulers disturbed their subject's faith in the local way of doing things. Some conquered people joined the state religion of the Romans. This religion honored the gods of Mt. Olympus and the Roman emperor, who was seen as a god. The state religion was more a form of patriotism than it was a religion.

Mystery Cults. Many people looked for a faith that would give their lives value and purpose. Asian and Hellenistic mystery religions appealed to such seekers.

These cults usually centered on a god or goddess that had arisen from death and became immortal. The priests of these cults taught that the souls of humans could share the deity's immortality by uniting with him or her. To accomplish this union, worshipers underwent initiation rites intended to give them the qualities of the deity. After their initiation, the worshipers became part of a close-knit group, whose members shared their deepest experiences and beliefs. These cults brought meaning to people's lives, made them feel less isolated, and eased their fear of death.

Conflict With the Romans. Some people dealt with change and confusion by remaining faithful to their old beliefs. The Jews were such a group. But some Jews feared that the influence of other cultures would destroy the purity of their faith. If their faith weakened, God would not keep his promise to help them. Jewish fear of falling away from God increased under Roman rule.

They became increasingly rebellious and resisted the Romans. Although unsuccessful, the rebelliousness alarmed Rome. Emperor Augustus put Israel under direct Roman rule. Taxes rose. Roman officials showed less respect for Judaism. Battles broke out between Jewish patriots and Roman soldiers. In an attempt to maintain order, Roman rule became stricter and less tolerant.

Essenes. As life became harder, Jewish faith in the coming of a messiah became stronger. Some Jews cherished different hopes. One group, the Essenes (flourished 100s B.C.–A.D. 100), prophesied that a Teacher of Righteousness would appear. The teacher was not the messiah, who was supposed to deliver the Jews from foreign oppression. He was a prophet, greater than all the previous ones, who would reform and strengthen Judaism. The Essenes practiced many ceremonies similar to those later practiced by Christians. They shared ritual meals that, like Christian Communion, consisted of bread and wine. They took ritual baths that were something like Christian baptism. Essene rituals did not, however, have the same meaning as the Christian ones do.

Life of Jesus. It was during this period of violence, division, and wild hope that a religious leader called Jesus appeared. Not much is known about his early life. What we do know comes from the New Testament of the Bible. It is believed that he was born in Bethlehem in Israel during the rule of Augustus. While a youth, Jesus lived in Nazareth and was taught the Jewish faith. He worked as a carpenter. Then, when he was about 30, he began to travel about, teaching anyone who would listen to his ideas about religion. He did not seek scholars and religious leaders but preached to the poor and weak. He was not an Essene, but some of his teachings were similar to theirs. For example, his idea that the poor in spirit are blessed reflects an Essene belief.

Teachings of Jesus. Jesus told people that God loved everyone and wanted them to love others as they loved themselves. Doing this would enable them to follow God's Golden Rule, that is, to behave toward others as they wanted others to behave toward them. Jesus promised those who followed his teachings that they would enter the kingdom of heaven when they died. Jesus's teachings can be read in the New Testament of the Bible.

Jesus chose 12 men to travel with him and help him teach. These followers are called *apostles*.

Although many teachings of Jesus did not differ from Jewish law, Jewish officials felt that he was a danger to Judaism. For one thing, he claimed to be the messiah but denied all intention of trying to regain control of Israel from Rome. Some Roman leaders, on the other hand, were convinced that he planned a revolt against them.

Jesus' teachings aroused powerful feelings both for and against him. When he appeared in Jerusalem to celebrate the Jewish holiday of Passover, his presence drew huge crowds. Seeing these crowds as potential mobs, both Jewish and Roman officials felt threatened. Jesus was arrested and accused of treason against Rome. Pontius Pilate, the Roman official in charge of Israel, ordered him to be crucified. Jesus was nailed to a wooden cross, a common way to kill criminals at the time. (The year was about A.D. 33.)

Death and Resurrection. A few days after Jesus had died on the cross and been buried, his apostles claimed that they had seen and talked with him. They believed that Jesus was indeed the messiah and had risen from the dead, or been *resurrected*. Belief in the resurrection of Jesus became an important part of Christian thought. The Greek word for messiah is *Christos*. Therefore, the followers of

Christ surrounded by the Apostles, on a marble coffin from 4th-century France

Jesus are called Christians. Christians also believe that Jesus is the son of God.

Islam

Muhammad is the prophet who converted Arabians to monotheism. He belonged to the Quraysh tribe. Its members had, for generations, served as the guardian priests of a sacred black rock in a holy shrine called the *Ka'ba* in the city of Mecca. (Mecca is in Saudi Arabia.)

The Messenger. Muhammad's parents died when he was six. An uncle took him in and raised him. Muhammad was strongly religious and frequently went off into the hills around Mecca to pray and meditate. In the year A.D. 610, when he was about 40 years old, he had a vision of an angel while praying in a cave. The angel told Muhammad that God had chosen him as a messenger. He was to persuade people to give up their idols and believe in one God (or Allah, which is Arabic for God).

As a young man, Muhammad had traveled throughout the Middle East, where he had been influenced by the beliefs of the Jews and Christians he met. Muhammad's teachings about life after death and the moral obligations of Muslims are similar to some beliefs and practices of Judaism and Christianity. Muhammad regarded many Jewish and Christian religious figures, such as Moses and Jesus, as prophets and holy men. He taught his followers to respect and honor them. Muhammad did not claim to have founded a new religion. Rather, he felt that he had brought Jewish and Christian concepts into a more advanced form.

Reaction to the Message. Muhammad first told the people of Mecca about Allah's message. He preached that all who believed in Allah are equal and that the rich should give to the poor. At first, Muhammad attracted little attention. When more people began to follow him, however, the members of the Quraysh tribe became uneasy. They feared that his teachings about one God would take worshipers away from the Ka'ba, the shrine that gave the tribe its power and wealth. To stop Muhammad from influencing more people, they threatened to kill him.

In 622, Muhammad fled to Medina, another city in Arabia. His journey from Mecca to Medina is called the *Hegira* (the departure). The people of Medina accepted Muhammad's ideas more readily than the people of Mecca had.

As Muhammad gained followers, he formed an army and marched on Mecca. He forced the people there to acknowledge Allah as their only God. Muhammad made peace with the Quraysh by proclaiming Mecca a city sacred to Allah. By 632, the year of Muhammad's death, most of the people of Arabia had accepted the ideas of the Prophet.

Muhammad's teachings came to be called Islam and its followers,

The Ka'ba in Mecca, Islam's holiest shrine, which Muslims face in daily prayers

Muslims. Islam is Arabic for "surrender to the will of Allah." Muslim means "one who surrenders to God" or "believer."

Islamic Teachings. The Quran, the holy book of Islam, contains the message of Allah as delivered by Muhammad. It tells Muslims that they must follow the Five Pillars of Faith. These are: to accept Allah as the one true God and Muhammad as His Prophet, pray five times a day, fast (go without food) during the daylight hours in the holy month of Ramadan, give money to the poor, and make a pilgrimage (journey) to the holy city of Mecca at least once in a lifetime. Other duties are to avoid pork and alcoholic beverages.

The Quran also sets down ideas about good and evil, justice and injustice. It teaches that after death the soul is rewarded in heaven or punished in hell. Courage and religious devotion are important Islamic virtues. A warrior who dies fighting for Islam goes to heaven. Other Islamic teachings stress the equality of all Muslims, regardless of background; respect for parents; and the protection of the weak by the strong.

An organized priesthood did not develop among the Muslims. Men called *imams* lead the faithful in prayer. Muslim men go to mosques, the Muslim places of worship, on Fridays and holy days. Muslim women worship at home.

INFO CHECK

1. Identify or define: animism, reincarnation, the Noble Eightfold Path, Quran, Five Pillars of Faith.

2. Describe the role of the caste system in Hindu religion and society.

3. Explain why Confucianism and Taoism are philosophies rather than religions. State a central idea or teaching of each.

4. Define and explain their importance to Judaism: montheism, Torah, messiah.

5. How was the rise of Christianity affected by both mystery cults and Judaism?

THE SPREAD OF CHRISTIANITY, ISLAM, AND BUDDHISM

Christianity

In the beginning, Christianity was spread by Jesus's apostles who traveled around the eastern Mediterranean region seeking converts to the new faith. Peter, the first apostle who had joined Jesus, became the leader of the new religious group. Peter thought of himself as a traditional Jew. Under his guidance, the first Christians, even if they were converts from other religions, followed Jewish laws and customs. New practices had been added, however. Baptism initiated newcomers into the group, and a ritual meal of bread and wine commemorated the last supper that the apostles had eaten with Jesus. In the view of Peter and his followers, however, Jesus had not introduced a new religion but had fulfilled the prophecies of Judaism.

Paul. A new leader appeared who saw Christianity as different from Judaism. This was a Jew named Saul who had been converted to Christianity by a vision. After becoming a Christian, he called himself Paul, which was the Roman version of his name. He believed that while people should obey the Jewish moral code, they did not have to observe Jewish rituals. Paul also taught that Jesus had come to save everyone, not just Jews. Paul traveled throughout the eastern part of the Roman Empire to tell others about the new religion.

Paul was extremely successful at persuading people of all nations and creeds to become Christians. People who felt that their lives had become pointless were attracted to a religion based on obedience to a loving God. The poor and enslaved were drawn by the promise that their good deeds would be rewarded in heaven. Like some of the mystery religions, Christianity offered an intense emotional relationship with a divine being.

In time, Paul established the Christian church. Many church doctrines of today follow the rules he set down. Letters that he wrote to early church officials are included in the New Testament of the Bible.

Time Line

Year	Dates and Events

B.C.

3000 — **3000s B.C.:** Rise of Phoenician civilization
1200s B.C.: Beginning of 600 years of advanced Hebrew civilization under the kings
1100–750 B.C.: Phoenicia spreads control to Cyprus, Sicily, Sardinia, Corsica, Carthage
1000s B.C.: Migrations of Germans and Celts to northern Europe, France, Britain

601

600

500s B.C.: Development in China of Confucian and Taoist philosophies
401   **587 B.C.:** Beginning of 50-year Babylonian Captivity of Jews
563 B.C.: Birth of Siddartha Gautama, founder of Buddhism
400   **200s B.C.:** Rise of trade (and exchange of culture and ideas) along Silk Road
64 B.C.: Phoenicia and its territories come under Roman control
46 B.C.: Julius Caesar becomes sole ruler of Roman world
201   **31 B.C.:** Augustus becomes first Roman emperor
200   **27 B.C.:** Beginning of 200-year Pax Romana

1

A.D.   **A.D. 33:** Crucifixion of Jesus; rise of Christianity
1   **A.D. 105:** Invention of paper in China leads to first written dictionary
A.D. 220: End of Han Dynasty after peasant uprising
A.D. 221–280: Mongols invade China and adopt its culture
200   **A.D. 232:** Beginning of spread of Buddhism to Southeast Asia, China, Korea, Japan
201   **A.D. 284–305:** Rule of Emperor Diocletian; division of Roman Empire into eastern and western parts
A.D. 313: Emperor Constantine gives full official recognition to Christianity
400   **A.D. 320:** Beginning of 200-year Gupta Empire, India's golden age
401   **A.D. 324:** Emperor Constantine reunites Roman Empire and moves capital to Constantinople
A.D. 378–400s: Goths, other Germans, and Huns invade western Roman Empire
600   **A.D. 395:** Permanent division of Roman Empire into eastern and western parts
601   **A.D. 476:** Official end of western Roman Empire
A.D. 455–567: Rule of Skandagupta and fall of Gupta Empire
700   **A.D. 622:** Muhammad's Hegira to Medina; rise of Islam
A.D. 632: Death of Muhammad; spread of Islam to Middle East, North Africa, Spain

The Spread of Christianity

Roman Influence. Roman authorities became concerned about the increasing numbers of people who were deserting the Roman gods for Christianity. Many of these converts felt that it was against their new religion to join the Roman army. Roman leaders began to persecute the Christians to make them give up their beliefs. Despite the efforts of the Roman government to stamp out Christianity, the new religion continued to grow.

In A.D. 313, Emperor Constantine issued the Edict of Milan. This order made Christianity equal to all other religions in the Roman Empire. Constantine, who officially became a Christian just before he died, was the Roman Empire's first Christian emperor. By 395, under Emperor Theodosius, Christianity had become the official state religion of the Roman Empire. Christianity had expanded beyond the borders of the Roman Empire to non-Roman Europe, Africa, and Asia.

The most influential Christian church was in Rome. Known as the Catholic, or universal, Church, it was headed by a pope. He was the bishop of Rome. Peter is honored as the first pope.

Islam

According to the Quran, Allah had sent Muhammad to bring justice to the world. Because Muslims believed that only the spread of

Islam would bring justice, they felt that it was their religious duty to conquer and convert non-Muslim people.

Arab warriors were famous for their skill and bravery. Combined with these qualities, their new faith helped them win many victories. Led by Muhammad, the Muslims had first converted and then unified all the Bedouin tribes of Arabia by 632. After Muhammad's death in that year, the Muslim forces went on to conquer Syria, North Africa, and Spain. They defeated the Persians in 651. Once they had established themselves as the new rulers of Persia, they began to invade India.

The Muslims did not force conquered people to convert to Islam. Nonetheless, they won many converts. Perhaps the tolerance Muslims showed to other cultures and the special privileges they gave to those who embraced their faith persuaded people to join them.

Buddhism

After the Indian King Asoka was converted to Buddhism between 269 and 232 B.C., the religion began to spread throughout Asia. Merchants took it to Sri Lanka, parts of Southeast Asia, China, Korea, and Japan.

Buddhism became especially popular in China. Large numbers of

The Spread of Buddhism and Hinduism

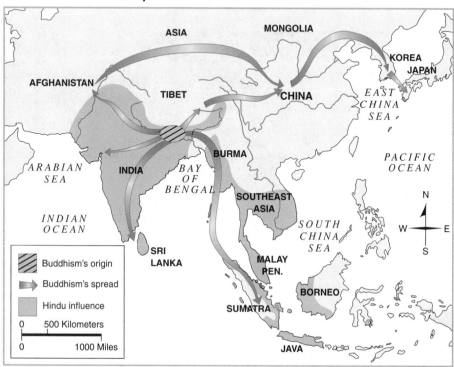

peasants, or poor farmers from the class of commoners, were attracted to this religion. As Buddhism spread, religious centers called *monasteries* were built throughout China. Within the monasteries, monks lived, meditated, and taught. Wealthy believers gave gifts of tax-free land to the monasteries. In later times, the religion of many Chinese became a blend of Buddhism and Taoism.

The chapters of Unit I discussed the beginnings of civilization and described the characteristics of the Classical Age. Chapter 8 showed how cultural features traveled to different regions. The chapters of Unit II will continue to explore the ways in which contacts among civilizations affected history. Chapter 9 discusses the further development of the Indian, Chinese, and Byzantine civilizations. Chapter 10 covers the history of the Muslim Empire. Chapter 11 describes how medieval Europe replaced the Roman Empire in the West.

INFO CHECK

1. Describe the roles of Peter and Paul in the spread of Christianity through the Roman Empire.

2. How did Christianity become the official religion of the Roman Empire?

3. What factors explain the expansion of Islam beyond Arabia?

4. Why were monasteries so important to the spread of Buddhism in Asia?

CHAPTER REVIEW

Multiple Choice

1. The advantage of the Phoenician system of writing over the Chinese, Sumerian, and Egyptian was that it
   1. used fewer sounds
   2. used fewer pictures
   3. used fewer symbols
   4. none of the above.

2. The empire that relied on a highly educated, paid, civil service bureaucracy was the
   1. Persian
   2. Chinese
   3. Roman
   4. Dravidian.

3. The Roman and the Han empires declined because
   1. they attempted to conquer too many peoples
   2. natural disasters destroyed their economies
   3. the rise of new religions divided their peoples
   4. rulers lost power because of corrupt officials and weakened economies.

4. The First Triumvirate of Rome succeeded because
   1. it was popularly elected
   2. Caesar, Crassus and Pompey joined together

3. the military supported Crassus's leadership

4. anyone could rule in a time of economic and military success.

5. Diocletian divided the empire into two parts because

   1. he had two sons and wanted each to have an empire

   2. he was giving the nobles a part of the empire

   3. his wife's family would rule the other half

   4. he believed this would strengthen the empire.

6. The plebeians of Rome and the peasants of China were similar in that

   1. both were heavily taxed and served as soldiers

   2. both voted in all elections and influenced governmental decisions

   3. both owned most of the empire's farmland and grew the majority of the crops

   4. both were mostly travelers and traders.

7. The Celts influenced the development of many European nations because they

   1. were nomadic warriors

   2. were a highly advanced people who left many written records

   3. lived in many lands and were skilled in making iron farm implements

   4. were religious people who spread their religious doctrines throughout Europe.

8. The empires formed by Alexander and Attila did not last for long periods of time. The reason was

   1. more powerful nomadic tribes appeared

   2. technology created new weapons

3. natural disasters destroyed the empires' economies

4. their deaths ended the unity of their followers.

9. The New Testament is to Christians as the

   1. Quran is to Muslims

   2. Analects is to followers of Confucius

   3. Old Testament is to Hebrews

   4. all of the above are correct.

10. The greatest difference between the Chinese philosophers Lao-tzu and Confucius was their views on

    1. how to treat and respect people

    2. the need to practice self-control

    3. the need to live modestly

    4. the individual's relationship to the government.

11. Use the map on pages 120–121 to locate the only empire in the ancient world that exported, but did not import, goods.

    1. Roman

    2. Parthian

    3. Persian

    4. Chinese.

12. With what religion is the temple in the photograph on page 137 associated?

    1. Hinduism

    2. Buddhism

    3. Christianity

    4. Islam.

Thematic Essays

1. "Hinduism and Buddhism are linked together, but Buddhism became the religion of the masses." *Task:* Explain and comment on the correctness of this statement.

2. *Task:* Compare and contrast the effects on the individual and on society of the Five Pillars of Islam and the Eightfold Path of Buddhism.

Document-Based Questions

Use your knowledge of Global History and Geography and the illustrations and maps to answer the questions.

1. From the photo on page 145, what assumptions can you make about the Muslim faith based on the numbers of people standing around the shrine?

2. According to the map on page 148, Christianity began in the Middle East and spread in what directions? What are these areas now named?

3. From the information on the map on page 149, describe the factors that aided the spread of Buddhism and Hinduism.

Document-Based Essay

Task: Discuss the social, economic, or political factors that caused so many people to accept the teachings of the major religions.

UNIT REVIEW

Thematic Essays

1. Classical civilizations affected future societies. *Task:* Compare any two of the classical civilizations you studied and discuss how they affected future societies in any two of following areas: philosophy, politics, economics, science, art, architecture, law.

2. Anthropologists and archaeologists have different ways of studying ancient civilizations. *Task:* Describe a method or practice used by each and explain how it helped us to learn about ancient peoples and their cultures.

Document-Based Questions

Use your knowledge of Global History and Geography and the documents to answer the questions.

1. From a history of ancient civilizations:

"The ancients saw man ... as part of society and society as imbedded in [part of] nature and dependent upon cosmic forces. The ancients told myths instead of presenting an analysis. ... The Babylonians ... say the gigantic bird Imdugud ... covered the sky with black storm clouds and devoured the Bull of Heaven, whose hot breath had scorched the crops. ... We would explain that certain atmospheric changes broke a drought and brought rain."

Considering the reading, what are the differences between ancient and modern humans?

2. From a history of Judaism:

"Many of the most fundamental ideas of Hebrew religion go back to the days when the Hebrews were still nomads. ... Thus God's commandments to Moses on Mount Sinai that 'Thou shall have no other gods before me,' 'Thou shall not make unto thee any graven image,' and 'Thou shall not take the name of the Lord thy god in vain' ... determined three fundamental and permanent aspects of Judaism which were new among Near Eastern religions."

Describe what makes the religion of the Hebrews unique.

3. Look at the photo on page 143. Discuss why the artists organized the scene in the way they did.

Document-Based Essay

Task: Compare and contrast the religions and religious beliefs that arose in the Middle East and India. In your discussion, include information about the number of deities and the concept and role(s) of god or gods.

UNIT II

Expanding Zones of Exchange and Encounter (A.D. 500–1200)

Expanding Zones of Exchange and Encounter
(A.D. 500–1200)

Year	Dates and Events
A.D.	**495:** Introduction of Buddhism into China
500	**527–565:** Byzantine Empire extends west to Spain, south to North Africa, east to Asia; Emperor Justinian organizes Roman law into Justinian Code
	610–641: Reign of Byzantine Emperor Heraclius, repulsion of invading Persians and Slavs
599	**618–907:** Tang Dynasty rules China
600	**622:** Muhammad's Hegira to Medina
	630: Muhammad and followers occupy Mecca; Meccans accept Islam and Muhammad as its prophet
699	**632–634:** Abu Bakr, Muhammad's successor, begins to unite Arabia
	650s–750s: Arabs, as conquerors, carry Islam to North Africa, Spain, Persia, Iraq, Iran, southern Asia, borders of China and India
700	**700s–1000s:** Vikings invade England, Scotland, Ireland, France, Italy, Sicily, Russia
	711–1212: Muslims (Moors) begin 500-year control of Spain
799	**717:** Byzantine Emperor Leo III defeats invading Arabs at Constantinople
800	**732:** Charles Martel leads French defeat of Arabs at Tours
	800: Pope Leo III crowns Charlemagne Holy Roman Emperor
	843: Division of Charlemagne's empire into three kingdoms ends political unity of western Europe
899	**878:** King Alfred of England and Viking invaders make peace
900	**900s–1000s:** Christian kingdoms Navarre, Aragon, and Castile begin to push Moors out of Spain
	900s–1171: Descendants of Muhammad's daughter, Fatima, set up dynastic rule in North Africa
999	**920–1270:** Sung Dynasty rules China
1000	**1054:** Great Schism divides Christianity into Roman Catholic and Eastern Orthodox churches
	1095: Pope Urban II calls for crusade to drive Muslims from Holy Land
1099	**1099–1187:** Christians win control of Jerusalem, then lose it to Muslim leader Saladin
1100	**1122:** Condordat of Worms defines extent of political and religious authority
1199	
1200	**1207–1213:** Pope Innocent III excommunicates King John of England; King John accepts pope's candidate for Archbishop of Canterbury
	1212: Aragon, Navarre, and Castile decisively defeat Moors at Las Navas de Tolosa (al-Iqab)

C H A P T E R

9

India, China, and Byzantium

Lin Cheng yawned and pushed aside the report he had been writing. Noticing that the room was filled with a soft glow, he looked out the window. A full moon lit up the canal below. Barges filled with rice floated by on their way to Beijing. It had been a good harvest, and the peasants were singing as they poled their barges through the water. Tonight, Lin Cheng felt like a father to these strong, hard-working people. He had been their governor for 20 years. And thanks to the policies of the emperor, he had been a just one.

Lin Cheng thought how lucky he had been. He no longer minded that his older brother had inherited the family property. He, Lin Cheng, had been the clever one. He had scored high on the civil service examination. Now, instead of acting as the manager of his brother's estate, he ruled a whole province.

What if he had been born under the previous line of emperors? Under the Sui, he would have had no opportunity for advancement. Would he have grown resentful of his brother's arrogance? Would he have escaped to this very province? Instead of bringing peace and plenty to its people, would he have urged them to rebel against their rulers?

Lin Cheng felt his pulse quicken a little. These contrasting fates would make a good poem. He turned back to his writing table and dipped his brush in the ink.

As empires grew larger and more complex, their rulers tried many methods of governing. Lin Cheng lived during the Tang Dynasty in China. For the most part, the emperors of this line ruled wisely. Lin Cheng was able to better his own life and to help the people under him prosper. However fair and just the Tang emperors might have been, they did not allow their people a voice in making government policies.

The leaders of the empires of the Gupta in India, the Tang in China, and the Byzantine in the Middle East used several methods of keeping control over vast territories. They established a close relationship between religion and the state. Their subjects, they reasoned, would be more likely to obey the laws of the state if the laws were backed by religious principles. The Gupta and Byzantine emperors made the greatest use of this method. The Tang emperors did something similar. They revived the philosophy of Confucius, which taught that people should have respect for their rulers.

THE GUPTA EMPIRE: A.D. 320–600

After the fall of the Maurya Empire in about 185 B.C., India passed through a long period of political unrest and division. When order was restored, a great civilization arose.

Three Emperors

In A.D. 320, a new ruler took over a northeastern area of India called Magadha. He had the same name as the founder of the Maurya Empire, Chandragupta. He conquered more territory and became the first in a line of Indian rulers called the Gupta Dynasty.

The second Gupta emperor, Samudragupta (ruled 330–375) tried to restore unity to India. He reconquered many of the kingdoms that had become independent after the fall of the Mauryas. Others he won back by making alliances with their rulers. At the end of his reign, Samudragupta's empire included much of the territory once ruled by the Mauryas. This new empire arose during the period in which Constantinople replaced Rome as capital of the Roman Empire.

The third Gupta emperor, Chandragupta II (ruled 375–415), defeated the Shakas, a people from the borders of China. They were trying to invade western India. With this military success, Chandragupta II won control of the trade with the Middle East and China. Foreign trade improved his empire's economy and enriched its culture with new ideas.

India: The Gupta Empire

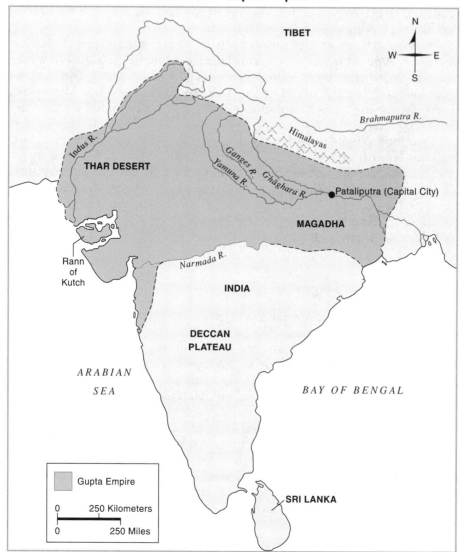

TIBET

Brahmaputra R.

Himalayas

Indus R.

THAR DESERT

Ganges R.

Yamuna R.

Ghâghara R.

Pataliputra (Capital City)

MAGADHA

Rann
of
Kutch

Narmada R.

INDIA

DECCAN
PLATEAU

ARABIAN
SEA

BAY OF BENGAL

Gupta Empire

0   250 Kilometers

0   250 Miles

SRI LANKA

Cultural Achievements

A long period of peace followed the military conquests of the early emperors. It was a time of great intellectual achievement for India. The Gupta rulers used their wealth to establish colleges and universities. The upper classes supported a rich cultural life. Consequently, Indian art, science, and scholarship flourished.

The universities and libraries protected the Sanskrit writings (literature) of the past. These institutions became famous, and people came to them from China and Southeast Asia. When the scholars returned to their own countries, they took Indian customs as well as the Sanskrit language back with them.

Indian writers and artists produced many masterpieces during this time. A great poet named Kalidasa (lived about 400 to 450) wrote plays in verse that were enjoyed by people of all classes. His themes were love, adventure, beauty of nature, and moral lessons. Music and dance forms that are still popular today were developed during the Gupta Dynasty.

Two long poems completed during this period are the *Ramayana* and the *Mahabharata*. Both were passed down through the years by oral tradition before they were written down. They are still popular. The *Ramayana* is a tale of an adventurous hero who is separated from his wife for many years. It has similarities to the *Iliad* and *Odyssey* credited to Homer in ancient Greece. The *Mahabharata* contains moral lessons and is respected as a source of religious inspiration and instruction.

Science and Mathematics

Indian scientists and mathematicians of that time developed important theories and ideas. They invented the decimal system and the concept of zero. The numbers 1 through 9 plus 0 are the ones we use today. Because they came to Europe through contacts with the Arab world, they are called Arabic numerals. The system is much easier to use for mathematical calculations than the one devised by the Romans.

A mathematician named Ayabhata calculated *pi*, a necessary concept in geometry. (Pi expresses the relationship between the circumference of a circle and its diameter.) Ayabhata also realized that the earth is a sphere. He understood that lunar eclipses are caused by the shadow of the earth falling on the moon. Other Indian scientists developed theories about gravity.

Organization of the Gupta State

Indian government under the Gupta rulers was less centralized than it had been during the Maurya Dynasty. Princes controlled areas outside the center of the empire. Their only official duty to the Gupta emperor was to send him tribute (taxes, gifts). The princes did, however, have strong ties to the emperor. It was commonly believed that the emperor was related to the gods. No one wanted to irritate the gods by disturbing the emperor. The emperor also secured the friendship and loyalty of the princes by making marriage alliances with their families.

Like the outlying kingdoms, towns and villages throughout the empire were largely self-governing. Nonetheless, the emperor exerted indirect control through religion. Hinduism was the religion favored by the Gupta dynasty, and Hindu religious leaders regulated village society. Local temples provided meetingplaces for village assemblies. The priests kept records of local history and preserved local legends. They also helped manage important public works, such as irrigation.

The Influence of Hinduism and Buddhism

Hinduism helped to make India's class structure more rigid. This class structure began when the Aryans, an invading tribe from the north, conquered large parts of India in the 1500s B.C. The Aryans introduced the caste system. It divided people into four major groups and set up strict rules for living. A person was born into a caste and could not leave it, except in rare cases. A person in one caste could not eat with anyone in another caste or marry anyone in another caste.

The Hindu concept of reincarnation reinforced this system. Since people believed that their status in society was the result of their behavior in past lives, they felt that they must accept that status. If they accepted it and lived virtuously, they would be reincarnated in a higher form in the "next life."

The Hindu religion also played a part in the spread of culture

Hindu sun god of the Gupta
Empire, 6th-century A.D.

throughout India and beyond. People on religious pilgrimages to other Indian villages learned about the inhabitants' customs and beliefs. Hindu missionaries traveled to Southeast Asia and taught the people about Hinduism. They also encouraged the use of the Sanskrit language.

Although Buddhism decreased in popularity during the Gupta Dynasty, it continued to influence the culture of the time. The magnificent temples and monasteries that Gupta architects carved into the sides of mountains were Buddhist as well as Hindu.

Though fewer in number, Buddhist schools continued to function. They taught grammar, mathematics, medicine, philosophy, and sacred writings to the young people of India.

Hinduism, however, had by far the most important influence on the people in their daily lives. Most people worshiped the idols of the Hindu gods. They followed its rules about not eating meat or drinking alcoholic beverages. They also lived by the rules of the caste system. Hinduism slowly emerged as the leading religion of India, a position it still holds today.

The Status of Women Under the Guptas

Women of the Gupta period enjoyed more freedom than they had in previous dynasties. The wealthier Indian parents taught their daughters as well as their sons how to read and write. Although no woman philosopher of Gupta India ever became famous throughout the world, they did exist. Male intellectuals sometimes mentioned their ideas in their writings. Indian women often worked as *midwives*. (Midwives are women who have been trained to deliver babies.) One Indian midwife named Rusa wrote a textbook teaching this skill. Women in Indian society were permitted to own property and engage in business.

Nonetheless, like Indian women of earlier times, those of the Gupta Dynasty were subject to their fathers and husbands. When they were small children, their fathers arranged marriages for them. The weddings took place when the girls reached their early teens. The law did not permit widows to remarry or to inherit their husbands' property.

Some widows followed a tradition called *sati* (also spelled suti and suttee). They committed suicide by throwing themselves on their husband's funeral pyre. This practice was supposed to ensure that both husband and wife would experience 35 million years of happiness in paradise. Historians speculate that many widows considered death preferable to a life of poverty and servitude. Finally in 1300, the law denying widows the right to their husbands' property was changed, and their position improved. But *sati* continued as a basic practice of Hinduism. Although outlawed, it may possibly be practiced in some remote areas of India even today.

The Decline of the Gupta Empire

During the 5th century A.D., political conflicts shook the Gupta Empire. About 450, Huns, a fierce tribe of nomadic warriors from central Asia, invaded India. (Another name for the invaders was White Huns.) The Emperor Skandagupta (ruled 455–467) was able to fight them off, but the effort strained the already weakened empire. Continued raids by the Huns drained the empire's wealth by disrupting trade with central India. Large numbers of people from north India began to migrate to other regions. In the mid-6th century, the empire fell and India once more separated into small kingdoms in constant conflict with one another.

INFO CHECK

1. How did oral history influence the literature of India during the Gupta period?

2. How did the scholars of Gupta India affect the mathematics we are familiar with today?

3. Explain how religion influenced social organization, education, and cultural life in Gupta India.

4. Indicate why you AGREE or DISAGREE with the following statement: Indian women enjoyed freedom and opportunity under Gupta rule.

THE TANG DYNASTY (618–907)

Before the Tang

From 581 to 618, a line of emperors, called the Sui, tried to bring stability to China. They reinforced the Great Wall to help keep out nomadic raiders like the Huns and introduced measures to boost China's economy. One of the most important of these works was the building of the Grand Canal that connected the Huang He to the Huai and Yangtze rivers. The new waterway improved communications between government centers in northern China and newly developed areas in the Yangtze Delta.

The Sui emperors tried to make agriculture more profitable by dividing the land more equally among the peasants. Unfortunately, their exploitation of the peasants defeated this goal. The second and last Sui emperor, Yang Ti, forced the peasants to work such long hours on public projects that they had little time or energy left to grow their own crops. He also forced them to take part in wars of expansion against Manchuria, Korea, and Tibet. These wars were unsuccessful and expensive. To finance his public projects and military campaigns, Yang Ti demanded that all his subjects pay ten years' taxes in advance.

Outraged, the Chinese people rose against him. When Yang Ti was assassinated in 618, a general named Li Yuan took over the throne and founded the Tang Dynasty.

Early Tang Rule

The Tang emperors ruled more wisely than the Sui emperors had. They improved the lot of the peasants. Extravagant projects that drained their subjects' money and strength were avoided. Under the Tang rulers, the peasants regained the prosperity they had known during the Han Dynasty.

The Tang rulers were also more successful than the Sui in expanding their empire. At the end of their dynasty, they had conquered Korea and Tibet. The map on this page shows the extent of the Tang Empire. When the Chinese occupied Korea, they were in a position to exert a strong influence on their neighbor, Japan. From observing the Chinese in Korea, the Japanese developed a system of writing and record keeping. They also adopted Chinese methods of governing.

During this period, Chinese trade revived. Merchants once more traveled along the Silk Road, exchanging goods, customs, art, and ideas.

China: The Tang Empire

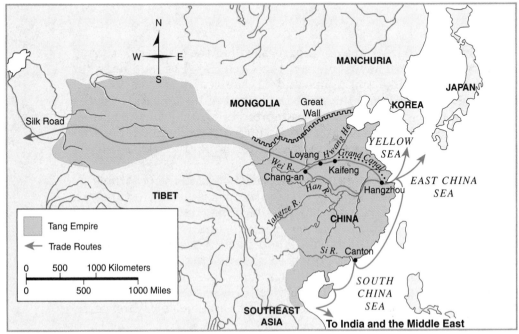

Pottery camel of the Tang Dynasty, an artifact for a noble's tomb and a token of the important Silk Road trade

Achievements of the Tang

Tang emperors are most famous for their efficient organization of the Chinese government. They assigned special departments to supervise the various aspects of government business, such as military matters, foreign affairs, justice, finance, building, transportation, and education.

A large bureaucracy was needed to staff these departments. Therefore, the Tang emperors brought back the Han system of selecting government officials through testing. The importance of appointing highly ethical people to offices of public trust revived interest in Confucian values. Confucius taught respect for authority, tradition, and scholarship. A difficult civil service examination tested the candidates' talent and memory. Those who were accepted as government officials were known as "Mandarins."

Since education became an important means of rising in the world, scholarship and artistic expression flourished. Tang painters and sculptors developed new forms and styles of expression. Scholars wrote more encyclopedias and histories than ever before. The era also produced many fine poets. One of China's greatest poets, Li Bo (or Li Po), wrote in the 700s. His principle subjects were nature, good living, and morality. The invention of printing increased the production of

MASTERS OF THE MARTIAL ARTS

Around A.D. 495, a Chinese emperor built a temple for an Indian monk who had come to China to preach Buddhism. Because the temple was located in a small forest on Shao Shi Mountain, it was called the Shao Lin Temple. The mountain is about 400 miles south of Beijing.

Through the centuries, the Shao Lin monks gained a reputation for skill in the martial arts. These skills included both unarmed combat and the use of sword, spear, and other "traditional" weapons. The monks also learned to move silently through enemy ranks and to strike with surprise. How and when the Shao Lin monks began practicing the martial arts is unknown. Most Chinese knew nothing about the Shao Lin monks until approximately A.D. 621, when the Tang Dynasty was being established. Emperor Tang Tai Zong had to fight invaders and those who opposed his rule. Thirteen Shao Lin monks joined the Tang army and contributed greatly to the defeat of the emperor's enemies. In gratitude, the emperor granted the Shao Lin warriors special status and allowed the temple to house warrior monks for protection.

Several hundred years later, during the Sung Dynasty (960–1270), the reputation of the Shao Lin rose higher. The abbot, or leader, of the temple invited 18 of the best-known martial arts masters in the country to gather at Shao Lin. Each master was a specialist in his own style of fighting. It is believed that the first Sung emperor was one of the masters at this gathering.

Knowledge of Shao Lin martial arts was spread to Japan in the 13th century by two Japanese monks who came to study at the temple.

Shao Lin's popularity and influence on the martial arts peaked during the Ming Dynasty (1368–1644). More than 10,000 monks and students entered the Shao Lin ranks during this period. In 1644, the Manchus overthrew the Ming Dynasty. The new emperor saw the Shao Lin Temple as a threat. Its army of warrior monks helped Ming loyalists. The Manchus outlawed the practice of martial arts in the Shao Lin Temple. But the monks practiced secretly and kept their skills. Discouraged by the restrictions, a number of monks left the temple. Some joined other monasteries. Others established monasteries of their own. The scattering of the monks spread knowledge of Shao Lin martial arts throughout China.

In the early 20th century, Shao Lin martial arts declined. This form of fighting did not fit in with the tactics of modern warfare. In 1928, the temple was almost completely burned down by a local warlord. Many of the temple's historical records and martial arts manuscripts were lost. However, enough of the records remained to guide the revival of the teaching of Shao Lin martial arts. By the 1990s, much of the temple had been rebuilt. Shao Lin monks again welcomed individuals who wished to study with them.

1. How does the history of the Shao Lin Temple illustrate Chinese respect for tradition?

2. Explain why you AGREE or DISAGREE with this statement: The learning of martial arts skills is useless in the modern world.

books. As a result, literature became available to greater numbers of people.

Empress Wu Zhao

One remarkable Tang ruler was a woman named Wu Zhao. She was the wife of Emperor Kao-Tsung. When he fell ill, the emperor asked his wife to help him rule the empire. Empress Wu encouraged agriculture and silk production. She lowered taxes and reduced the amount of labor that peasants were forced to contribute to the government. She commissioned scholars and artists to work for her.

After the death of her husband in 683, Wu Zhao governed China on her own. Many government officials disapproved of Wu because she was a woman. Even more officials turned against her when she established civil service examinations for women. In 705, those who opposed Wu forced her to resign and make her son the ruler. She died soon after.

The End of the Dynasty

In 907, the Tang Dynasty came to an end. The emperor had lost power to provincial governors during a long period of decline. The provinces declared themselves to be independent states. China was again weak and disunited. As the empire broke up, foreign invaders conquered and ruled China.

Painting of Tang Dynasty Empress Wu Zhao, shown with her officials

INFO CHECK

Complete the following sentences:

1. Efforts of the Sui emperor to make agriculture more profitable failed because _____.

2. The Tang rulers expanded their empire by _____.

3. Among the educational achievements of the Tang were _____.

4. Steps taken by Empress Wu Zhao to improve China included _____.

5. The Tang Dynasty ended in A.D. 907 when _____.

THE BYZANTINE EMPIRE (395–1453)

The Byzantine Empire began as the eastern part of the Roman Empire. After the fall of Rome in 476, the Byzantines kept alive many Roman ideas about law and government. Roman culture blended with the existing Greek culture of the area. Greek was the official language and Christianity the official religion. The capital of the empire, Constantinople, became a prosperous trading center. It controlled the water route between the Black Sea and the Aegean Sea.

Byzantium's location exposed it to foreign attack. A number of groups from farther east in Asia, Eastern Europe, and the Arabian

The Byzantine Empire

peninsula tried to take over Byzantium. The Byzantines were able to fight off some, but they lost territory to others over the years.

Byzantium's location also made it a buffer zone between Western Europe and the Middle East. In protecting their own empire, the Byzantines shielded Western nations from invasion by Arabs and Turks. Had it not been for Byzantium, the major religion of Europe might have been Islam instead of Christianity.

The Growth of the Empire

The Byzantine emperors were dictators. They ruled with the support of a well-trained army and navy and an efficient system of secret police and spies. The emperors controlled not only the government but also the Eastern Christian Church. Later it came to be known as the Eastern Orthodox Church. Several Byzantine emperors were women.

Conquering Territory. Early Byzantine emperors tried to increase the size of their empire. They fought the Germanic tribes who held lands that had been part of the old Roman Empire. Before Emperor Justinian, who ruled from 527 to 565, no one had succeeded in adding much territory to the empire. Justinian's armies managed to conquer many lands around the Mediterranean Sea. At the end of Justinian's rule, the empire included Italy, southern Spain, the Balkans, western Asia, and areas of North Africa. (The Balkans are the

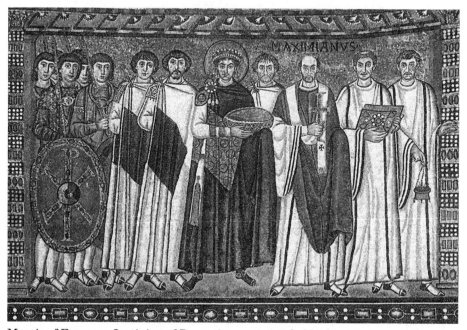

Mosaic of Emperor Justinian of Byzantium, surrounded by his court

present-day countries of Albania, Bosnia-Herzegovina, Bulgaria, Macedonia, Greece, part of Turkey, and parts of Croatia, Slovenia, Serbia, and Yugoslavia.) Justinian's conquests opened up the empire to many new enemies. To defend against these enemies, Justinian ordered forts to be put up throughout the empire.

Invasions From All Sides. The leaders who followed Justinian could not keep the empire together. His military campaigns and building programs had left little money in the treasury. The army became too weak to fight off invaders.

Movements of the same peoples who had destroyed the Western Roman Empire now threatened the Byzantine Empire. The Visigoths took over southern Spain. The Lombards swarmed into most of Italy. The Arabs gained possession of Egypt, North Africa, Syria, and Israel. The Serbs won the Balkans. The Turks conquered western Asia. At last, the empire included only Asia Minor (Turkey), southern Italy, and Greece.

Heraclius. The Emperor Heraclius (ruled 610–641) led the Byzantine army against the Persians and the Slavs. After driving off the invaders, Heraclius tried to strengthen the empire by organizing it into military districts. A general governed each district and recruited an army from the local peasants. As payment for serving in the army, the government gave the peasants land to farm. This arrangement provided economic benefits to the peasants and assured the empire of a loyal, inexpensive army. This system was especially successful in the section of the Balkans that remained part of the Byzantine Empire. The Balkan peasants fought bravely to defend their farms from invaders.

A New Weapon. The Arabs posed the most serious threat to Byzantium. They conquered Persia and took the Holy Land and Egypt from the Byzantines. Once the Arabs gained control of large areas

Illustrated history of Byzantium showing Greek fire used against an enemy boat

along the Mediterranean Sea, they built a huge navy. This enabled them to threaten Constantinople by both land and sea. Luckily, Emperor Leo III (ruled 717–741), like Heraclius, was a brilliant general. With the aid of the Byzantine invention, Greek fire, Leo defeated the Arabs in 717 at Constantinople. (Greek fire is thought to have been a mixture of oil, resin, and sulfur. The heated mixture was pumped through a tube. As the mixture came out of the tube, it was set on fire and aimed at enemy ships or other targets. It could not be put out with water.)

After this victory, the Byzantines continued to fend off Arab advances. By their successful resistance to all invaders, the Byzantines shielded Western Europe from invaders for 900 years.

Renewed Strength and Trade. About the year 1000, Byzantium became strong again. Able leaders added territory to the empire. The Byzantines created fine art and constructed great buildings. Constantinople grew in importance as a commercial center for Europe, Africa, Asia, and the Middle East. The silks, brocades, carpets, and other luxury items manufactured in Byzantium were in great demand in foreign markets. Other Mediterranean trading cities, particularly Venice, were envious.

Setbacks for the Empire

In the 1070s, the Seljuk Turks came out of Asia and stepped up their attacks on the Byzantines. The Turks were Muslims. After many years of defending the empire, the Byzantine emperor asked the pope in Rome for help against the Turks and other invaders. The pope responded by persuading various rulers in Europe to send soldiers to the Holy Land. (The Holy Land was the area now made up of Israel, Lebanon, and part of Syria.) The Turks had held the area for some 25 years. Called Crusaders, the European soldiers began arriving in the eastern Mediterranean area around 1096. The wars between Christians and Muslims went on for years.

In 1204, at the urging of Venice and against the wishes of the pope, the Crusaders captured Constantinople instead of fighting the Turks. The city-state of Venice in northern Italy wanted to control the trading routes to the Middle East.

The Byzantines won back their city in 1261, but they could not regain their former strength. Another group of Turks, called Ottomans, started raiding communities around Constantinople. Greece fell and so did most of Asia Minor. Finally, in 1453, the Ottomans captured Constantinople. The Byzantine Empire, which had existed for nearly 1,000 years, came to an end.

The Orthodox Christian Church

Early in Byzantine history, the Western and Eastern branches of the Christian Church began to grow away from each other. When

Time Line

Year	Dates and Events
A.D. 401	**A.D. 455–567:** Rule of Skandagupta, invasions by White Huns, fall of Gupta Empire
	A.D. 476: Fall of Rome makes Byzantine Empire caretaker of Greek and Roman culture
	A.D. 495: Introduction of Buddhism into China
600	**A.D. 527–565:** Emperor Justinian expands Byzantine Empire to Spain, Italy, Balkans, western Asia, and North Africa; codifies Roman law into Justinian Code, basis of many legal systems today
601	**A.D. 565–610:** Invasion of Byzantine Empire by Visigoths and Slavs (from Russia and Balkans)
	A.D. 581: Beginning of 40-year Sui Dynasty in China; construction of Grand Canal waterway
800	**A.D. 610–641:** Reign of Byzantine Emperor Heraclius; repels invading Persians and Slavs
801	**A.D. 618:** Beginning of 300-year Tang Dynasty
	A.D. 683–705: Wu Zhao, widow of Tang emperor Kao-Tsung, rules China
	A.D. 717: Defeat of Arabs invading Byzantine Empire by Emperor Leo III at Constantinople
1000	**A.D. 860s:** Byzantine missionaries to Moravia invent Cyrillic (Slavic) alphabet
	A.D. 907: End of Tang Dynasty
1001	**A.D. 920–1270:** Sung Dynasty
	A.D. 988: Russian ruler Vladimir leads his people to convert to Eastern Orthodox Christianity
	A.D. 1054: Great Schism divides Christianity into Roman Catholic and Eastern Orthodox churches
1200	**A.D. 1070s:** Increased attacks on Byzantine Empire by Seljuk (Muslim) Turks
1201	**A.D. 1096:** Byzantine emperor initiates First Crusade
	A.D. 1200s: Russia cut off from West by Mongolian invasions
	A.D. 1204: Crusaders capture Constantinople
1300	**A.D. 1261–1453:** Byzantines win back Constantinople; empire finally falls to invading Ottoman Turks

Constantine decided to rule the Roman Empire from Constantinople, he weakened royal power in the western part of the empire. The people in the West felt that their Church leaders were more powerful than the governors who represented the emperor there. As time went on, Western Church leaders claimed to have more authority than the emperor himself. During the 4th century, Ambrose, the bishop of the city of Milan in northern Italy, had a dispute with the Byzantine emperor, Theodosius, over this issue of *primacy*. Ambrose claimed that Church leaders were above kings because they were responsible for saving the souls of everyone, kings as well as commoners.

Byzantine emperors, on the other hand, assumed that they had the right to rule the Church as well as the state. They nominated the patriarch of Constantinople, who was the highest Eastern religious official. When Church leaders disagreed about religious beliefs, the emperor gathered them together in a council to resolve the problem. The emperor frequently headed the council himself.

In 1054, rivalry over territory and a dispute about religious belief finally split the Eastern and Western branches of the Christian Church. This split is called the Great Schism. The Western branch came to be called the Roman Catholic Church. The Eastern branch is known as the Eastern Orthodox Church. (The Greek Orthodox and Russian Orthodox churches came along later.)

Contributing to the East-West dispute were the differences over the use of icons in worship. Icons are painted images of Jesus, Mary, and saints. These pictures help worshipers understand religious teachings. Leaders of the Eastern Orthodox Church felt that praying to icons was a form of idolatry and banned it. The icons were to be destroyed. Emperor Leo III agreed. But the ban threatened to disrupt Byzantine society. Church leaders eventually backed down and let the icons be put in churches and homes. The leaders of the Roman Catholic Church believed that the icons gave people a deeper understanding of Christian ideals. They encouraged the use of painted images.

Byzantine Monasticism

The emperors and wealthy people of Byzantium donated money to support monasteries and nunneries, which were tax-free. Monasteries and nunneries are religious communities located in out-of-the way places. Individuals joined the communities to devote themselves to serving God. Men were called monks, women, nuns.

The monks and nuns who entered the monasteries and nunneries lived lives of moderation and engaged in acts of charity. They ran hospitals, provided refuges for victims of oppression and crime, and gave food and clothing to the poor.

Some monks and nuns became missionaries. They traveled to the Balkans and Russia to persuade the inhabitants to become Christians. Because of these missionaries, the Eastern Orthodox Church is the major Christian church in Russia and other Eastern European countries.

The Cultural Achievements of Byzantium

Because of the closeness of the Byzantine church and state, religion strongly influenced Byzantine culture. The Church set rules for marriage and family relations. During battles, holy pictures were carried like flags before the imperial troops.

Art. Religious themes dominated literature and art. Ordinary people were just as interested as Church officials in religious questions. They joined in arguments about the divine nature of Christ and whether or not it was right to worship images of holy people. Well-educated people read essays about Church doctrine. The less scholarly read stories about the lives of the saints.

Architecture. Some of the most beautiful Byzantine buildings were churches. The Hagia Sophia, which means Holy Wisdom, was one of the churches built during Justinian's reign. The architects who designed it blended Eastern and Western styles by placing a Persian dome on a rectangular Roman base. When the Muslims took over Constantinople, they admired the Hagia Sophia so much that they used it for a mosque. (Today, it is a national museum.)

Scholarship. Not all Byzantine achievements were religious in nature. This period produced many historians. The empire's fine universities and libraries protected Greco-Roman literature. Scholars wrote commentaries on the works of classical Greek and Roman writers.

Law. The Emperor Justinian helped to preserve Roman law for future cultures. He asked officials to gather together all the laws of Rome and write them down so that they could be easily understood. The resulting collection of laws is known as the Code of Justinian. This code influenced the legal systems of many present-day European and Latin American countries.

Weapons. The Byzantines made few advances in technology. Their successes in this field consisted mainly of weapons and other devices of war. They had the most advanced siege machines of the time. Using a kind of catapult called the mangon, they hurled heavy stones over the ramparts of a besieged city. They bored holes through fortress walls with large, metal-tipped drills. Their battering rams had somewhat the same effect as modern-day armored tanks. The rams were attached to wheeled towers that had small forts on top. The forts protected the soldiers as they tried to batter down the city gate. Bridges carried by ships allowed soldiers to cross moats. (A moat is a deep, water-filled ditch surrounding a castle.) Once the soldiers got across the moat, the bridges were hoisted to the top of the fortress walls so that the men could enter the city.

The most famous Byzantine invention was Greek fire. It is not surprising that the Byzantines used their inventiveness to create weapons. They were constantly defending their empire against invaders.

Byzantine Influence on Russia and Eastern Europe

In the mid-860s, the Byzantine emperor sent two missionaries to a Slavic people called the Moravians. (Moravia is a part of the present-day Czech Republic.) The missionaries, Cyril and Methodius, used their knowledge of the Slavic language to invent an alphabet for the Slavs. Although the Moravians and their neighbors eventually joined the Roman Catholic Church rather than the Eastern Orthodox Church, they adopted the alphabet. It is called Cyrillic after Cyril, who developed it. Russians, Bulgarians, and Serbs still use this alphabet today.

In 860, the Byzantines successfully turned back a Russian attack on Constantinople. For 200 years after that, the two powers remained hostile to each other. Gradually, however, the Byzantines and Russians became trading partners. As the two peoples grew to know each other, many Russians became Christians. Finally, in 988, the Russian

Kievan Russia and the Byzantine Empire

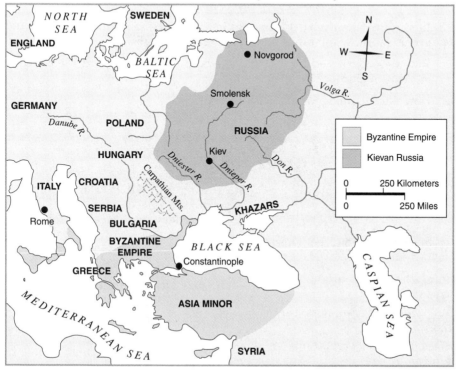

king, Vladimir, and all his people converted to Christianity as represented by the Eastern Orthodox Church.

The Russia of that time is known as Kievan Russia because its capital was Kiev. Becoming wealthy through trade with Byzantium, Kievan Russia began to make contact with Western Europe. Members of the Russian royal family married members of the royal families of Sweden and France. Russian leaders made alliances with Germanic kings. A lively trade developed between Russia and the countries of the West.

Russian contact with the West was cut off during the 13th century. During that period, the Mongols conquered Kievan Russia. No longer open to Western influence, Russians clung to the aspects of culture that they had adopted from the Byzantines. They remained Eastern Orthodox Christians. Their form of government continued to resemble that of Byzantium.

Building an empire involves more than conquering many territories. It requires skill in governing large populations. Two important methods of doing this are the establishment of a strong bond among the people through a common religion or philosophy and setting up an efficient bureaucracy. Chapter 10 describes how the Muslims of the Middle East employed these methods in ruling their vast empire.

INFO CHECK

1. Identify a Byzantine achievement in each of the following areas: art and architecture, scholarship and literature, law, military technology.

2. Who were Cyril and Methodius? How did their work affect the cultures of Eastern Europe?

3. How did the Mongols affect Kievan Russia?

CHAPTER REVIEW

Multiple Choice

1. The leaders of the Byzantine, Gupta, and Tang empires used several methods to rule their empires. These methods included

   1. dividing the empire into military districts

   2. using religion to support their authority

   3. encouraging the acceptance of Confucian beliefs

   4. all of the above.

2. During the Gupta Empire, Indian customs and culture were spread throughout Southeast Asia and China by

   1. scholars who studied at the Indian universities and took home new ideas and ways of living

   2. Indian workers who traveled to different areas to find work

   3. traders who took new ideas and ways of living to their homes in China and Southeast Asia

4. military conquest of China and Southeast Asia by the armies of the Gupta emperors.

3. The mathematical concepts of pi, zero, and the decimal system all originated under the

1. Han Dynasty

2. Gupta Dynasty

3. Byzantine Empire

4. Ottoman Empire.

4. An example of cultural diffusion would be

1. the Chinese adopting Indian customs and Sanskrit writing

2. the Buddhists adopting the Hindu caste system

3. the Tang following Sui agricultural methods

4. the Byzantine Empire adopting the Cyrillic alphabet.

5. In order to insure that government officials were honest and well educated, the Tang emperors relied on a civil service examination that was based on

1. Confucian values

2. the Twelve Tables

3. the principles of Legalism

4. the Hippocratic Oath.

6. The Empress Wu Zhao was both remarkable and unique because she

1. instituted civil service examinations for women

2. raised the peasants' taxes

3. was the only woman to hold the title empress and rule China

4. conquered other lands.

7. The Christian Church, though divided into Western and Eastern branches, remained unified until 1054. Reasons for the break included

1. Muslim conquest of Rome

2. Western Church leaders banning the use of icons and images

3. conflict over whether the pope or the emperor was the head of the Church

4. the Byzantine Church leaders introducing Latin into the prayers.

8. The Byzantines protected Western Europe from most of the attacks of the

1. Japanese

2. Arabs

3. Germanic tribes

4. Indian nomads.

9. One of the early capitals of Russia was

1. Kiev

2. Constantinople

3. Venice

4. none of the above.

10. In the 13th century, the Mongols conquered Russia. Select the answer that correctly lists one activity that ended and one that continued in Russia under the Mongols.

1. The practice of Eastern Orthodox Christianity was forbidden, but trade continued with the West.

2. Trade with the West was halted, but the practice of Eastern Orthodox Christianity continued.

3. Russian nobles no longer read Greek Epic poetry, but they continued to study Hinduism.

4. Byzantine forms of cultural and governmental practices were banned, but the Cyrillic alphabet continued to be used.

11. According to the time line on page 172, which of the following periods was important to the growth of the Byzantine Empire?

1. A.D. 527–565

2. A.D. 610–641

3. A.D. 860s

4. all of the above.

12. Compare the maps on pages 159 and 164 and select the most accurate statement about the Gupta and Tang empires.

    1. Both empires were protected by defensive walls.
    2. Major river systems aided transportation and communication in both empires.
    3. Both empires were far from the sea.
    4. The empires were separated by the Thar Desert.

Thematic Essays

1. The Gupta, Tang, and Byzantine cultures influenced future cultures. *Task:* Select two examples from Indian, Chinese, and Middle Eastern cultures and describe how they affected future cultures.

2. *Task:* Discuss the role that Byzantium played as the protector and spreader of Greek and Roman culture.

Document-Based Questions

Use the documents and your knowledge of Global History and Geography to answer the questions.

1. From the Babylonian Code of Hammurabi:

    If she [a wife] has not been a careful mistress, . . . [has] neglected her house and belittled her husband, they shall throw that woman into the water."

    According to this reading, what is expected of a woman in a household?

2. A description of the Greek family:

    " . . . Heaven so made their bodies, and set their lives, as to render man strong to endure cold and heat, journeying and warfare, so laying on him the works of the field; but to woman . . . so laying, I think, on her the works of the house . . . Those who have work indoors will be under you; and you will take charge of everything that is brought into the house . . ."

    What views are expressed in this reading about how tasks were divided between men and women and what these tasks are?

3. After viewing the picture on page 167, what can you say about the power and importance of Empress Wu Zhao?

Document-Based Essay

Task: Use information in the documents and your knowledge of Global History and Geography to compare and contrast the status of women in China to India, Rome, or Greece. Include in your answer the nature of the cultures in which the women lived.

C H A P T E R
10

The Rise of Islamic Civilization

Abdul had finished dressing. He was ready to attend the banquet his father was giving for some important people at court. Abdul was 18— he touched the silky mustache on his upper lip—a young man now. His teacher had declared that Abdul was ready to take a post at court. Abdul thought of all the books he had memorized. He remembered how proud he had been, when at seven, he had recited the entire Quran to his mother and father. Now he knew scores of books by heart and could discuss law and religion with experienced scholars. If he made a good impression on the court officials at dinner tonight, he would become an interpreter of the law. Perhaps, eventually, he would become an adviser to the caliph.

Abdul knew he should be excited, yet he felt dissatisfied. How different was his cousin Mahmoud's life in Arabia. Mahmoud did not have to work his way up from an unimportant position in the Baghdad government. At 19, he already helped make important tribal decisions. He knew how to find his way through the desert and how to survive its dangers. Mahmoud would soon be an officer in the cavalry. His father had given him a magnificent horse.

But Mahmoud's way of life belonged to the past. Abdul reminded himself of how limited his cousin had seemed on his last visit to Baghdad. He shared few interests with Abdul and his friends. Mahmoud thought only of fighting and tribal politics. He cared nothing for music, art, or poetry. He was, after all, just a herdsman. Abdul glanced in the mirror and smoothed his hair. Smiling, he hurried to join his father's guests.

A bdul, a Muslim, is part of a cultural group that established a huge empire from the eastern Mediterranean all the way to China and Southeast Asia. Muslims not only ruled a vast territory, they also introduced a religion called Islam to its inhabitants. The people of this rich culture have made significant contributions to art, literature, and science. They continue to be an important force in the modern world. About 20 percent of the world's population today is Muslim.

THE SPREAD OF ISLAM

The Muslim culture originated with a group of people living in the Arabian Peninsula, which is between Africa and Asia. While the Byzantine Empire was at its peak, the Muslim Arabs were developing into an important political and military force.

Geography and People

Although the Arabian Peninsula is mostly desert, its southwestern mountain valleys receive enough rain to support productive farms. The frankincense and myrrh produced in this region were popular trade items. They are two of the best-known substances used to

The Arabian Peninsula: Physical Map

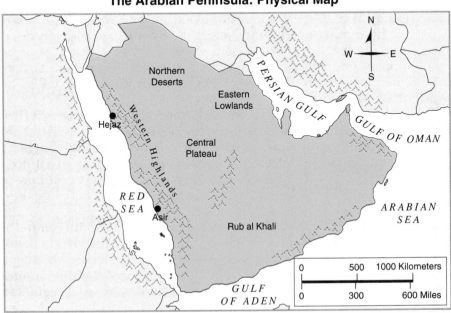

produce incense and perfumes. Religious groups burn incense in their ceremonies. The ancient Egyptians used the substances when they prepared mummies for the afterlife. The trade made the merchants of southwest Arabia very wealthy. These merchants traded their incense and other agricultural products in India, China, Africa, and the European cities along the Mediterranean Sea. Many important trade routes of the ancient world passed through Arabia.

People. A nomadic, herding people called *Bedouins* occupied the Arabian desert. This environment was extremely harsh. Nonetheless, the Bedouins were able to raise camels, sheep, and goats. They knew the location of fertile spots, called oases. There underground streams welled up to the desert's surface. Bedouins brought their herds to drink and graze at the oases.

In the larger oases, settlements formed and became important trade centers. Bedouins came to the centers to barter the leather, milk, and cheese they obtained from their herds for dates and other produce grown in the oases. They also guided parties of traders from distant regions to these settlements. The traders could stop for supplies and refreshment. Without the Bedouins, the trade between foreign merchants and those of the oasis towns and southwest Arabia would never have developed.

Tribes. The Arabic people lived in social units called tribes— groups based on common kinship through a male line. The tribal members were intensely loyal to each other and to their elected leaders, called sheiks. The different tribes were competitive with one another. Often wars broke out to control the oases that provided the

Temporary tent settlement of nomads of the Sahara

scarce water so necessary for survival. A strong warrior tradition grew out of this rivalry. The Bedouins' knowledge of the desert, their physical stamina, and their warrior tradition made them an important military power.

Law. Until the 7th century, Arabs worshiped many gods. In each city or town, a priest or holy man tended a shrine devoted to one of these gods. Since their religion forbade them to kill anyone in or near shrines, the Bedouins often used the shrines as meeting places for settling tribal disputes. The priests gained much political influence by helping them resolve the disputes. Because the position of priest was hereditary, priests' families shared their power and became an aristocracy. Scholars point out that the rules made by these priests and the roles they played as arbitrators may have been the forerunner of Islamic law, religious laws taught by Muhammad.

The Rise of the Muslim Empire

Muhammad was the messenger of Allah. He taught the Arabs about Islam. After Muhammad died in 632, the Muslims chose his close friend and father-in-law, Abu Bakr, as their leader. He took the title of *caliph*, which means "successor." Under Abu Bakr, who ruled from 632 to 634, the Arabs started military campaigns against neighboring states. In the mid-600s, they united Arabia under the rule of the caliphs.

The Muslims also attacked the Byzantine and Sassanid empires. (The Sassanids were an Iranian group that had conquered Persia.) Muslim forces easily took the present-day countries of Syria, Israel, and Egypt from the Byzantines. The Byzantines defeated the Muslims when they tried to take Constantinople. Although the Arabs seriously weakened the Byzantine Empire, they did not destroy it.

By the late 600s, Arab forces had completed the conquest of the Sassanid Empire. They had captured what are now Iraq and Iran and pushed northward into Armenia and eastward into Afghanistan and northern India.

By 711, the Arabs had taken over northern Africa. They then carried Islam into Europe, quickly conquering the Germanic Visigoths in Spain. But when the Muslim armies moved into France, they met a major defeat. At the Battle of Tours in 732, an army of Germanic Franks forced the Arabs back into Spain. (The Franks were led by Charles Martel, the grandfather of a king called Charlemagne.) The Muslims remained in Spain until 1492.

By 750, the Muslim Empire included all of southern Asia to the borders of India and China, most of Spain, and all of North Africa. In these lands, people of many different cultures lived under the rule of the caliphs. The conquered peoples followed a variety of religions, among them Judaism, Christianity, and Zoroastrianism. A great number found the teachings of Muhammad to be appealing and became Muslims.

The Arab Caliphate

In order to rule all these new territories effectively, the Muslims needed to develop a central government. The caliph and the officials directly under him were known as the *caliphate*. Each caliph considered himself to have a special tie to the Prophet Muhammad. Because of this relationship, the caliph expected to be honored as the only leader of Islam. Not every Muslim agreed, however. Conflicts between Arab and non-Arab Muslims brought about changes in government. In spite of the disputes, the caliphate form of government ruled the Muslim Empire for almost 600 years.

Reasons for Success. One of the most important reasons for the caliphate success was that the Muslims did not force a new way of life on their subjects. When Muslim leaders moved into a newly conquered area, they kept connections between the old government and the new government. They did, of course, appoint Arabs as *emirs*, or governors, to keep order, maintain an army, and collect taxes. But they assigned experienced local officials to work under the emirs. From the local officials, the emirs learned to use methods of government familiar to their new subjects.

As the needs of the empire changed, Muslim leaders established departments of government to deal with new problems. One of the new departments was the *diwan*. This agency was in charge of financing the army. One of its duties was to see that the soldiers in different parts of the empire were paid with the kind of money that was used in their local area.

As the empire grew larger, communication between the Muslim capital and its subject lands became difficult. To keep in touch with distant governors, Muslim leaders set up a relay network. The caliph and his governors used this network to send letters and important reports to each other.

Military Organization. Muslim leaders realized that military organization was important to keeping control of their far-flung empire. The empire had been won by a well organized and highly motivated army. The soldiers were Arab tribesmen who had grown up in a warrior culture. Desert life had made them physically tough and resourceful. Most were skilled horsemen (cavalrymen). They were deeply loyal to each other and to their leaders. They were also eager to spread the Islamic faith to the rest of the world. Army leaders encouraged their troops by giving them good pay, good equipment, and a fair share of the spoils of victory.

As the empire grew larger, however, the caliphs wanted their armies to be loyal to the dynasty rather than to individual tribes. They reduced some privileges previously enjoyed by the Arab troops. The caliphs also began to organize units of soldiers from different cultures. Nevertheless, the Arab forces remained a valuable military resource. The new military system never entirely replaced the old.

The Umayyad Dynasty (661–750)

At first, the center of Muslim government was in Mecca. As the empire grew, Muslim political organization became more complex. The generals and governors of newly conquered lands became more powerful than the caliphs in Mecca. In 661, the Muslim governor of Syria rebelled, made himself the caliph, and established the Umayyad Dynasty. From Damascus, the new capital, the Umayyad rulers led the Muslim world until 750.

The caliphs of Damascus sent out their armies to add more territory to the empire. Among the peoples they converted to Islam were the Berbers of North Africa. The Umayyads also conquered lands to the east of Damascus. They extended Muslim rule into areas that are known today as Afghanistan and Pakistan.

As their empire grew, the Umayyad caliphs found themselves governing people with a variety of cultures. The governors appointed by the Umayyads usually exercised tolerance. Although they encouraged their subjects to become Muslims, they allowed them to keep customs and traditions that did not conflict with Islamic law. They did not persecute unconverted Jews and Christians.

Umayyad leaders did, however, give their Arab and Muslim subjects more privileges than they did other groups. They taxed non-Muslims very heavily. The tax money paid for the luxurious lifestyle of the Umayyad leaders. These practices caused unrest within the empire.

Shi'ites. Another conflict threatened and finally ended Umayyad rule. Early in the history of this dynasty, a dissenting group called the Shiah sprang up. (Its members are Shi'ites.) When the Umayyads seized the caliphate in 661, Muhammad's cousin Ali was murdered. Many people in Mecca thought that Ali should have been caliph because he was related to the Prophet. They argued that Muhammad, who had made Ali an *imam*, or prayer leader, had meant him to be caliph. Shiah comes from *Shi'at Ali*, an Arabic phrase that means "supporters of Ali."

As time went on, the Shi'ites continued to oppose the Umayyad Dynasty. They claimed that Muhammad's blood relatives had inherited divine knowledge from him. Therefore, these relatives were better qualified than other people to be caliph. Moreover, because Muhammad's descendants had divine knowledge, they should be religious as well as political leaders.

Sunnites. The Umayyad rulers were Sunnites. Their name refers to the *Sunna*. Like the Quran, the Sunna is a collection of Muhammad's teachings written down by his followers. The Sunnis believed that the caliph did not have to be descended from Muhammad. Many Sunnis also felt that the caliph should be only a political leader. They pointed out that religious doctrine was set by the Quran and the Sunna. If these sources did not offer a clear answer to religious questions, then Islamic scholars, not the caliph, should be consulted.

The Abbassid Dynasty (750–1258)

The Abbassid family was descended from Abbas, an uncle of Muhammad. They felt that this relationship entitled them to claim the office of caliph for a member of their family. The Shi'ites became their allies. The Abbassids acted to increase the dissatisfaction of the Shi'ites with the Umayyad caliphate. They pointed out that the Umayyads used their subjects' money to pay for their comforts and pleasures. The Abbassids also stirred up unrest among non-Muslims in the conquered territories. Raising an army from these groups, the Abbassids overthrew the Umayyads in 750.

Eastern Rule. The Abbassids ordered a capital city to be built along the Tigris River in Mesopotamia (in present-day Iraq). Baghdad, the new center of government, became famous for its beauty and cultural institutions. The new location influenced the Abbassids to adopt many features of Persian culture.

In time, the Abbassid caliphs became too fond of luxury. They, like the Umayyads, lost the loyalty of their subjects by increasing taxes to pay for their pleasures. More and more people began to ignore

The Spread of Islam   634–1250

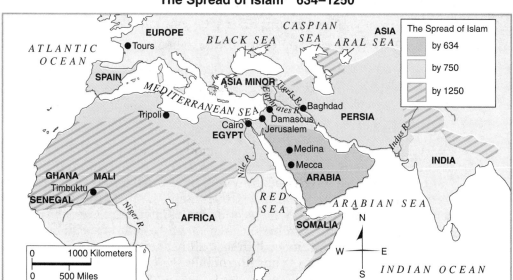

the laws. Bandits attacked trade routes, cutting off a rich source of income. Opposition to Abbassid rule spread throughout the empire.

Outside forces also threatened the Abbasids. The Seljuk Turks moved into the empire in the 1040s. Then, in 1258, Mongols from Asia conquered Baghdad. The Mongol victory ended the Abbassid Dynasty.

Western Rule. When they overthrew the Umayyads, the Abbassids took over only the eastern part of the Muslim world. Another group took over the western part. In the 750s, an Umayyad prince escaped the massacre of his family by the Abbassids and fled to Spain. There he and his descendants became rulers. Spain, therefore, remained independent of the Baghdad caliphs.

Fatimid. In the 10th century, all of North Africa broke away from the Abbassids. A new dynasty, called the Fatimid, took control of what are now Tunisia, Morocco, Libya, and Egypt. The Fatimids were descendants of the Prophet through his daughter, Fatima. The leaders also took the title of caliph and ruled the Fatimid Empire from Cairo in Egypt. This dynasty lasted until about 1171.

The Muslim world had become divided into three rival empires—the Umayyad, Abbassid, and Fatimid dynasties. Yet the people all shared the Islamic religion, the Arabic language, and a highly advanced culture.

INFO CHECK

1. Explain the importance of the Bedouins to the development of the economic and cultural life of the Arabian peninsula.

2. What role did Arab military skill play in the rise of the Muslim Empire?

3. Trace the dynastic divisions of the Muslim Empire by creating a chart giving the name of the dynasty, dates, capital city, and territories ruled.

4. How do Shi'ites and Sunnis differ in origins and beliefs?

5. Define the following: caliphate, diwan, imam, Quran, Sunna.

ISLAMIC SOCIETY

Islamic Law

Islamic law developed from religious principles set down in the Quran and the Sunna. During the Umayyad Dynasty, the caliph consulted officials called the *ulema* when he wished to use the teachings of the holy books to solve a legal problem. Eventually, the ulemas' legal interpretations became a collection of laws called the *shari'a*. As the basis for both the empire's legal code and a code of social behavior, Islamic principles influenced almost all aspects of Muslim life. Some of the most important of these principles were the duty of the rich to help the poor, the equality of all Muslims, toleration of other cultures, and respect for scholarship. Islamic law does not separate religious matters from nonreligious matters.

Status of Muslim Women

The principle that all Muslims are equal under God was a sharp contradiction to earlier beliefs about social equality. Before Islam, gender and ancestry determined a person's position in society. Women had no legal rights at all. They could be killed by their fathers, sold into marriage, and disowned by their husbands. They could not own or inherit property. (In most cultures around the world at this time, women had few rights.)

At first, the Islamic principle of equality improved the lot of women. The Quran states that a woman has the right to keep all the property she owned before marriage. Although the Quran gives her husband half of her dowry, it directs that the other half be put aside for her in case the marriage does not last. It also permits her to use her property in any way she wishes.

The Quran does not give a woman equal rights of inheritance with a man. But it does ensure that she will have something to live on if her husband or father should die.

Early in the reign of the Umayyads, women had the right to own property. They participated in politics, traveled, and attended public religious ceremonies. This freedom of action did not last, however. Military victories brought large numbers of female slaves into the empire. To a large extent, a man's wealth was measured in terms of the number of slaves he owned. This view, combined with the fact that men could have several wives at one time, brought about the renewal of the old attitude that women were men's property. Scholars began to reinterpret passages in the Quran as evidence that women were incapable of performing religious, political, or legal duties.

Social Class and Slavery in Muslim Society

Women were not the only group to be treated unequally in Muslim society. Non-Arabic converts to Islam did not have as many privileges as Arabic Muslims did. During the Umayyad Dynasty, the aristocracy was made up of descendants of Bedouin tribespeople. They had followed Muhammad and established and spread Islam.

Directly below the aristocracy were the non-Arabic converts to Islam. Many of these people believed that their cultures were superior to the Bedouin culture and resented the economic and social inferiority forced on them by the Arabs. Perhaps this need to prove their worth accounts for the fact that converts to Islam eventually made up the largest part of the empire's professional group. Non-Arabic

Muslim slave market, as illustrated in a Persian manuscript

converts served the empire as doctors, merchants, teachers, artists, and interpreters of the law.

The third class in Muslim society consisted of the so-called protected peoples. These were the Jews, Christians, and Zoroastrians who had not converted to Islam. Following the Islamic principle of tolerance, the Muslim government did not persecute Jews, Christians, and Zoroastrians. As long as these people obeyed the Muslim government, they were permitted to worship as they pleased, to own businesses, and to practice any of the professions. Although they did not enjoy the same privileges as did the members of the first and second classes, many of the protected people made valuable contributions to Muslim culture. Moses Maimonides, a Jewish doctor born in Spain in 1135, became one of the greatest philosophers of the Muslim Empire.

Slaves made up the fourth and lowest class. The Quran forbids enslavement of Muslims and protected peoples but not the institution of slavery. Muslim wars of conquest brought many captured soldiers, women, and children into the empire as slaves. Most slaves worked as soldiers and servants. The more skilled and educated slaves held responsible positions in businesses and professions. The Quran recommends that masters treat slaves humanely and encourages them to find favor with God by freeing their slaves. Many free descendants of slaves became distinguished members of society.

Trade and Commerce

Trade had always been important to Arabia. The merchants of southern Arabia and the Bedouin guides of the Sahara in Africa had amassed fortunes from trade. Muhammad praised merchants as "God's trusted servants on earth." Islamic law encouraged trade as a means of making large amounts of money, which could be used for charity and other good works.

The opportunities for profitable trade increased as the Muslim Empire gained control of almost all the known world's trade routes. Muslim traders had access to routes that crossed the Mediterranean Sea, the Black Sea, the Caspian Sea, the Volga River, the Aral Sea, the Arabian Sea, and the Indian Ocean. These routes made it possible for them to trade with European countries on the coast of the Mediterranean, Russia, China, eastern Africa, the Indian subcontinent, and eventually Indonesia and the Philippines.

Using camels, which can go for long distances without water, Arab merchants were able to travel over difficult land routes. Expert Bedouin guides led them through the Sahara into west-central Africa. They were able to go deeper into China than other traders. Some

Arab merchants beginning a long journey in search of profit

scholars believe that they got as far as Korea. They also traveled the Silk Road through Samarkand, Bukhara, and other Turkestan towns.

Most of the trade goods of the time were luxuries and rarities. From India came tigers and elephants, rubies, and fragrant woods. From China came silk, porcelain, peacocks, horses, and cinnamon. From Byzantium came silver and gold ornaments, lyres (stringed musical instruments), and slaves. From northwest Africa came leopards, felt, and falcons trained for hunting. From Egypt came donkeys, balsam oil, and topaz. From the shores of the Black Sea came slaves and fine armor. From Persia came sugar, brocades, fruit, syrups, and candy.

Muslim merchants developed many business techniques used today. For example, they originated the bill of exchange. It enables people remaining at home to order their bankers in distant locations to pay money to their business agents. Such a written order made it unnecessary for people to carry large sums of money with them on dangerous trips. It also allowed them to do business in more than one country at the same time.

Scholars believe that the Muslims originated the joint-stock company. The people at the head of a joint-stock company finance a venture, such as a trading voyage, by selling shares of the venture's future profits. The investor, or buyer, receives a portion of the profit based on the amount of money he or she has contributed. Many common English business terms, such as check and risk, come from the Arabic language.

Islamic Cultural Achievements

Navigation. Trade strongly influenced Muslim science and technology. Their travels across oceans and deserts gave Muslims knowledge of new navigational devices, which they spread all over the known world. The Muslims learned about the compass from the Chinese and brought this knowledge to Europe. Because the compass has a magnetic needle that points north, a traveler can use it to determine directions almost anywhere on the surface of earth. (It is not accurate at the North Pole.)

Although the Greeks probably invented the first astrolabe, the Muslims perfected it. (It is an instrument that helps the user to determine latitude and time of day.) Both the compass and the astrolabe played important parts in the first voyages to the Western Hemisphere that took place in the 15th century. As another result of their long trading trips, the Muslims became expert cartographers, or mapmakers.

Geography. Muslim scholars were also interested in geography. The Spanish historian Ibn-Khaldun realized that a country's climate and natural features have a strong influence on its economy. This, in

Time Line

Year	Dates and Events

A.D.
501

600

601

700

701

800

801

900

901

1000

1001

1100

1101

1200

1201

1300

570: Birth of Muhammad in Mecca

610: Muhammad begins to preach Islam to Arabs in Mecca

622: Muhammad's Hegira to Medina

630: Muhammad and followers occupy Mecca; Meccans accept Islam and Muhammad as its prophet

632: Death of Muhammad

632–634: Abu Bakr, Muhammad's father-in-law, becomes successor and chief caliph; begins military campaigns to unite Arabia

650s–750s: Arabs conquer and carry Islam to Sassanid (Persian) Empire, Iraq, Iran, southern Asia, borders of China and India, North Africa, and Spain

661: Murder of Muhammad's cousin Ali and formation of Shi'ite sect favoring succession by Muhammad's descendants

661–750: Muslim caliph of Syria rebels against Mecca, becomes first caliph of Umayyad Dynasty

718: Beginning of control of Spain and Portugal by Muslims (Moors)

732: Charles Martel leads Franks against Arabs at Tours, driving them from France back into Spain

750–1258: Abbassid Dynasty, with Shi'ite support, overthrows Umayyads, who flee west to Moorish Spain (al-Andalus) and establish Muslim stronghold; Abbassids take control of eastern part of Muslim world, move capital to Baghdad, adopt Persian culture and taste for luxury, are finally overthrown by Asian Mongols

900s–1000s: Christians establish kingdoms of Navarre, Aragon, and Castile in northern Spain; begin effort to push Moors out of Spain

900s–1171: Descendant of Muhammad's daughter, Fatima, establishes separate dynastic rule over all of North Africa, with capital at Cairo, Egypt

1212: Aragon, Navarre, Castile win decisive victory over Moors at Las Navas de Tolosa (al-Iqab)

turn, affects its people's behavior. Many scholars believe Ibn-Khaldun to be the first social scientist. He lived from 1332 to 1406.

Education. Respect for scholarship was also an important characteristic of Muslim culture. Scholarly tradition accounts for the fact that Muslim men were able to move from lower to higher positions in society. In nearly every important city of the empire, wealthy merchants helped maintain schools to educate young Muslim men. The teachers taught Muslim law and religion. They placed a great deal of emphasis on memorization. Students were expected to learn the Quran by heart by the time they were seven or eight years old. Once the student had memorized an important book, he was expected to interpret, analyze, and criticize it. Such an education prepared men to become preachers, judges, and professors.

Since women could not enter the legal, religious, and civic professions, they did not attend school. Nonetheless, Muhammad had stated that it was the duty of every Muslim to seek knowledge. Therefore, many parents educated their daughters at home. Some girls learned the same subjects as boys did.

Muslim scholars studied ideas from many other civilizations. They helped preserve works from the Greco-Roman, Semitic, Indian, and Persian cultures. These works inspired Muslim thinkers to develop new ideas. For several centuries, Muslim achievements were superior to those of Europeans.

Mathematics. Arab mathematicians used the zero and a number system developed by the Hindus. When Europeans learned about the

Illustrated segment of an Arab medical text

THE LADY AND HER FIVE SUITORS

One of the best-known collections of Islamic literature is *The Thousand and One Nights*. These many stories were written over a long period of time. It was not until the 16th century that the collection reached its final form. Some of the stories, such as *Ali Baba and the Forty Thieves* and *Aladdin and the Wonderful Lamp*, deal with magic and mystery. Most of the collection, however, is about women who use their intelligence to outwit opponents who attempt to take advantage of them. In the following story, the heroine triumphs with a clever defense against sexual harassment.

A women was married to a merchant who traveled a great deal. As a result, the woman was left alone for long periods of time. Finally, she fell in love with a handsome young man. One day, he got into a fight, was arrested, and went to jail.

The woman went to the chief of police. Claiming that the young man was her brother and that she was dependent on him for support, the woman begged for his release. The chief of police immediately fell in love with her. He offered to release the young man only if the woman would join his harem. She agreed, but only if the chief would first come to her home at an arranged time.

The woman then went to the city judge to complain about the unfairness of the chief of police. The judge also fell in love with her. He, too, offered to help her only if she joined his harem. Again, she insisted that the judge come to her house at a certain time. The time she gave him was the same she gave the chief of police.

She next appealed to the prime minister. He too, demanded that she join his harem. Once more, she arranged for him to come to her house at the same time as the others.

Finally, she went to the caliph, the highest authority, only to have the same thing happen. The woman gave him the same answer she had given the others.

The woman then hired a carpenter to build a large cabinet with four compartments, each with a door that could be locked. The carpenter also made advances to the woman. She invited him to her house as well, but instructed him to make the cabinet with five compartments. He did so and had the cabinet installed in her home.

At the agreed-upon time, her suitors began to arrive, one by one. Each was persuaded to enter the cabinet, and each was locked in. When the chief of police arrived, he gave her a letter ordering the release from prison of the young man.

The woman took the letter to the prison and obtained her lover's release. They then fled to another city where they remained in safety.

After three days, the woman's neighbors, seeing that her house was deserted, broke in to investigate. They found the cabinet and heard those locked inside groaning with hunger and thirst. The neighbors forced open the cabinet and discovered the five suitors. The men were greatly embarrassed and hurried away from the laughter of their rescuers.

1. What does this story tell us about the traditional status of women in Islamic society?

2. What makes this woman a heroine? What does she do that an Islamic man might consider to be wrong?

number system, they thought the Arabs had invented it. As a result, they called the numerals "Arabic" numerals. Al-Kwarizmi, who lived in the early 800s, improved the system of mathematics called algebra. (He may have been the first to use that term.) Another Muslim mathematician, Al-Hazan (lived 965–1039), made important discoveries in optics, the study of light rays.

Medicine. Arabs excelled in the field of medicine. Physicians, such as Rhazes (lived 865–932) and Ibn Sina, or Avecenna (lived 980–1037), wrote medical encyclopedias. For hundreds of years, European doctors used these encyclopedias as a guide for treating patients. Arab doctors developed procedures to prevent and treat such diseases as measles and smallpox. Muslim surgeons used animal gut to stitch up wounds and developed operations to remove cataracts from eyes. Arab hospitals gave far better care to the sick than did any in Europe at the time.

Literature. In literature, Persian and Indian works had a strong influence on Arabic poetry. One of the best-known poets in the Muslim Empire was Omar Khayyam. A Persian, he lived from about 1048 to 1123. He was also an astronomer and a mathematician. He wrote four-line poems on human fate, the nature of the universe, and the passage of time. These poems were put together in a collection called *The Rubaiyat*. Another famous example of Muslim literature is the *Arabian Nights*, also called *The Thousand and One Nights*. It is a collection of stories, dating from the 800s, about romance, adventure, fantasy, and humor. The stories are based on folk tales from the Middle East, North Africa, and India. Aladdin, Ali Baba, and Sinbad are characters in stories in the collection.

Philosophy. The philosopher Ibn Rusd, or Averroes, lived from 1126 to 1198. A doctor and a judge, Averroes studied and commented on the works of Aristotle and Plato, the ancient Greek philosophers. Maimonides also studied Aristotle's ideas and wrote about them. Through the writings of Averroes and Maimonides, European scholars learned about Aristotle's ideas. These ideas influenced later religious thinking in Europe.

Islamic Spain

Spain was strongly influenced by Islamic culture. Early in the 8th century, Muslim forces from Morocco defeated the Visigoths. They had taken over Spain after the fall of the Roman Empire. By 718, Muslims (or Moors) controlled almost all of the Iberian Peninsula (Portugal and Spain). This Muslim part of Spain was known as al-Andalus.

A member of the Umayyad dynasty, Abd ar-Rahman I, escaped from the Abbasids when they took over the caliphate in Syria. Supported by his tribesmen, he established a stronghold in al-Andalus in 755. Abd ar-Rahman I conquered al-Andalus and ruled it until 788.

During the reign of one of his descendants, Abd ar-Rahman III, Muslim Spain's economy and culture reached its peak. In contrast to Christian Europe, Muslim Spain had a flourishing trade and prosperous cities. This was the period when Cordoba, its capital, became a world-renowned center of learning.

In 1002, al-Andalus began to weaken, breaking up into small kingdoms. It briefly united under two new Muslim groups that invaded from North Africa. But Muslim Spain never recovered its former strength and glory.

As al-Andalus declined, the Christian kingdoms in the northern mountainous parts of Spain grew stronger. They began to push the Muslims out and enlarge their own territory. By the 10th century, the Christian kingdom of Navarre, with its strong ties to France, was firmly established in Spain.

Two other important Christian kingdoms were Aragon and Castile. They added more and more Muslim territory to their realms. Under the Castilian kings, the *Reconquistá*, or Reconquest of the Iberian Peninsula, became a religious crusade. Aiding in the fight against the Muslims was the legendary general El Cid (the lord). His real name was Rodrigo Diaz de Vivar. He conquered Valencia and ruled it until his death in 1099. El Cid's exploits made him one of Spain's national heroes.

With the support of Aragon and Navarre, Castile won a decisive victory over the Muslims in 1212. Other victories followed. By 1248, all the Muslim kingdoms except Granada had been taken over. In 1492, Granada, too, was defeated, and the Reconquest of Spain was complete.

Chapter 11 focuses on the development of medieval Europe and the consequences of a series of wars between the Muslims and the European Christians.

INFO CHECK

1. Rewrite as correct statements the following statements that are incorrect:

   - The ulemas of the Muslim Empire were similar to modern-day judges.
   - Muslim women had no rights under Islamic law.
   - Muslim society was divided into classes, with some groups enjoying more rights and privileges than others.
   - Arab traders were restricted to Arabia and dealt only in the basic necessities of life.

2. Explain why you AGREE or DISAGREE with the following statements:

   - Life in the Muslim Empire was enriched by the acquisition of knowledge, the growth of new ideas, and inventions.
   - There were few scholars, doctors, poets, or philosophers in the Islamic society of the Muslim Empire.

3. Why do you think many would have regarded Spain as a more comfortable and enjoyable place to live, during much of the Middle Ages, than other places in Europe?

CHAPTER REVIEW

Multiple Choice

1. The Arabian Peninsula was a center of agriculture, trade, and commerce because of its

   1. fertile soil
   2. production of incense and nearness to the Mediterranean Sea
   3. large crops of wheat and nearness to the Atlantic Ocean
   4. large amounts of rainfall and rapid transportation systems.

2. The Bedouins earn their living by

   1. serving as mercenaries in the emperor's armies
   2. growing large crops of palm and dates for sale
   3. using their knowledge of the desert and raising animals
   4. helping to build vast cities for their Turkish rulers.

3. Arab tribes are joined together through

   1. kinship through a male line
   2. kinship through a female line
   3. arranged marriages
   4. agreements made by kings.

4. Arab tribes never fought near any of their religious shrines. This was why

   1. travelers in the Arabian Peninsula carried icons with them
   2. the priesthood became a safe life to lead
   3. conflicts between Bedouin tribes were settled near shrines
   4. oases were always set up next to the shrines.

5. The term *caliph* was first given to

   1. Muhammad's father-in-law, as the successor and leader of the Muslim people
   2. Muhammad's, son, as the male successor and leader of the Muslim people
   3. Muhammad as the successor to the throne
   4. none of the above.

6. The battle that halted the Arab armies and stopped Islam from controlling France as well as Spain was the

   1. Battle of Constantinople in 1492
   2. Battle of Paris in 1914
   3. Battle of the Atlantic in 1940
   4. Battle of Tours in 732.

7. The Muslims peacefully ruled a vast empire. This happened because they

   1. killed and tortured any persons who did not convert to Islam
   2. had a vast army of secret police and informers to prevent native people from rebelling
   3. kept large armies in every town and city they ruled to prevent native people from rebelling
   4. allowed other religions to exist and used native officials to assist in governing.

8. The first successful rebellion that led to a Muslim dynasty and shifted the base of political power was the

   1. Wahabi Dynasty of Mecca
   2. Umayyad Dynasty of Damascus

3. Abbassid Dynasty of Baghdad

4. Fatimid Dynasty of Cairo.

9. The Sunna, like the Quran,

1. is a collection of Muhammad's teachings

2. is Islamic poetry

3. is a scientific journal

4. none of the above.

10. Select the answer that correctly arranges the four classes of Muslim society from highest to lowest.

1. Arab Muslims, protected peoples, non-Arab Muslims, and women

2. Arab Muslims, protected peoples, non-Arab Muslims, and slaves

3. Arab Muslims, non-Arab Muslims, protected peoples, and slaves

4. Arab Muslims, Arab Muslim women, non-Arab Muslims, and non-Arab Muslim women.

11. What does the illustration on page 181 indicate about Bedouin life?

1. Bedouins live in Asian cities.

2. Bedouins wander the Sahara in search of grazing land.

3. Bedouin farms are large and well irrigated.

4. Bedouins work in heavy industry.

12. According to the time line on page 191, which statement is correct?

1. Muhammad and his followers occupied Mecca in A.D. 1300.

2. The Umayyad Dynasty was established in A.D. 576.

3. Muslims took control of Spain and Portugal in A.D. 718.

4. the Abbassid Dynasty fell in A.D. 622.

Thematic Essays

1. Choose any two of the following areas: the sciences, government, arts, literature. *Task:* Describe the contributions of the Muslims in those areas and how these contributions affected future civilizations.

2. *Task:* What economic activities enabled the Abbassids to become such a culturally productive and long-lasting dynasty?

3. *Task:* How did the locations of the various Muslim dynasties affect their relations with non-Muslims?

Document-Based Questions

Use the documents presented and your knowledge of Global History and Geography to answer the questions.

1. Look at the map on page 185. Identify at least two areas where the Muslims and other empires previously studied would have come into conflict.

2. "I have been ordered to fight against people until they testify that there is no god but Allah and that Muhammad is the Messenger of Allah and . . . if they do so, they will have gained protection from me for their lives and property, unless [they do acts that are punishable] in accordance with Islam, and their reckoning will be with Allah the Almighty."

Who would use this document and for what purpose?

3. Look at the photograph on page 189. What does it show about Muslim dealings with peoples outside the Muslim Empire?

Document-Based Essay

Using specific examples, agree or disagree with the following statement: "The Muslim Empire was distinguished by its military conquests and cultural richness."

CHAPTER

11

Political, Social, and Cultural Changes in Medieval Europe (A.D. 500–1200)

The church bells had not rung for three days. The pope was angry at the king and had interdicted the whole kingdom. This meant that he had banned almost all church services. Marguerite's sister, Lady Eleanor, could not be married next Sunday. Old Jeanette at the mill could not bury her husband in the churchyard. The silence of the bells made everyone nervous. Marguerite found herself peering out the window from time to time as if she expected the arrival of someone. She had heard the kitchen maids muttering together. One swore that she had seen the devil lurking along the castle walls. "If the bells don't ring soon," she had said, "he'll find his way in."

Marguerite had overheard her father and uncles talking and had been amazed to find that they were happy about the interdiction. "Now is the time to ask the king for the land he promised us last December. He's going to need our knights very soon," Uncle Oswald had said. "Everyone knows that Count Herman has wanted to get rid of the king for years. He'll find plenty of allies now among the pope's supporters."

Marguerite sighed as she remembered the conversation. *That* was why she felt so ill at ease. There was going to be a war. All the young men would go to battle. Poor Eleanor might never be married. This very castle that seemed so strong and safe might fall to her father's enemies.

M arguerite is a young noblewoman living in medieval Europe. (This period is also called the Middle Ages. It is the name given to the years between A.D. 500 and 1500 in Europe.) She is experiencing the results of a power struggle among the king, the Church leaders of western Europe, and some members of the nobility. This chapter describes the kind of influence each group was able to exercise and how their conflicts affected the history of western Europe.

SPATIAL ORGANIZATION AND GEOGRAPHY

Europe is the western part of the great landmass that contains the continents of Asia and Europe. The Ural Mountains in central Russia mark the eastern boundary of Europe.

Europe: Physical Map and Resources

No location in western Europe is more than 300 miles from the sea. Therefore, few nations of the region are landlocked. The interplay of land and water has affected the climate and culture of the region. Travel to and from distant lands for trade and conquest has been made easy.

Along the shores of western and southern Europe are many protected harbors. Merchant ships and fishing boats have easy access to the Atlantic Ocean, the Mediterranean Sea, the North Sea, and the Baltic Sea. Rivers provide pathways into the interior: the Seine in France, the Elbe in Germany, the Danube in central Europe, and the Volga in Russia are but a few of the river systems in Europe. Where the rivers meet the seas, important port cities have grown up.

A band of mountains runs across southern Europe from Spain into Russia. The ranges include the Pyrenees, the Alps, and the Carpathians. Northern Europe, particularly Norway, is also mountainous. The ruggedness of the mountain chains has kept out invaders and made travel difficult.

The major physical feature of Europe is the vast plain that stretches from France into Russia. It contains great amounts of fertile farmland. The generally flat landscape makes travel across the central part of Europe easy.

INFO CHECK

1. Why might Europe be described as a peninsula of Asia?
2. Why is the central plain of Europe an agricultural area?

WESTERN EUROPE AFTER THE FALL OF ROME

After Rome fell in A.D. 476, the armies of Byzantium tried to hold off the invasions of Persians, Slavs, and Arabs. At the same time, Germanic tribes were transforming the western Roman Empire into a collection of small kingdoms. During the earliest part of the Middle Ages, the Germanic kings struggled with one another for more power and land. Local wars broke out. People's lives were disrupted by the fighting.

The Breakdown of Law and Order

The Roman Empire had started to decline even before the Germanic invasions. Cities had lost much of their wealth and population. Industries had begun to die. Sewage and water supply systems had fallen into disrepair.

The Germanic invasions sped up the decay. When Rome no longer ruled and protected outlying districts, roads crumbled. As the roads deteriorated, fewer people traveled long distances. Bandits lurked in areas where Roman legions had once patrolled. It became dangerous for people to travel with valuable goods or large amounts of money. Consequently, trade slowed down.

The lack of well-maintained roads cut communities off from one another. People in areas distant from one another began to speak dialects, or different forms, of Latin. These local dialects developed into the French, Italian, Romanian, Portuguese, and Spanish languages. (They are also known as the Romance languages.) People who lived in different parts of Europe could not understand one another.

A Time of Change and Growth

Many scholars, though, point out that this period of confusion and disorganization was also a time of change and growth. Although trade, learning, and the fine arts suffered, technology made some important advances. Farmers developed better plows and better methods of draining marshy land. These improvements increased crop production and made more land available for agriculture. Farmers also invented the horse collar, which was more efficient than the yoke for controlling draft animals that pulled loads. A seagoing people called the Vikings designed and built a ship that could survive the rough waters of the Atlantic Ocean.

Feudal peasants at work in March, from the Duc de Berry's *Très Riches Heures*, an illuminated manuscript of the 15th century

Changes in Political Power

Perhaps more important, the Middle Ages was a time of political change. The Germanic groups that took over large parts of the Roman Empire had a different system of government than the Romans. Throughout the empire, Roman governors had administered districts in the name of the emperor. The chief of each Germanic tribe ruled his territory independently of other authority. As a result, Western Europe no longer had a strong central government.

Many remote areas had once been important only because they contributed to the wealth of Rome. They could now use their resources to develop their own cultures and institutions. Many Germanic leaders admired Roman laws and institutions and adapted the ideas to fit local needs. In doing so, they developed new forms of government.

The Christian Church Provides New Leadership

In spite of its advantages for specific kingdoms, decentralization might have led to total disorder if the Christian Church had not served as a unifying institution. In A.D. 380, Emperor Theodosius had made Christianity the official state religion of the Roman Empire. He felt that having one official faith would bring order to an empire populated by peoples with different cultures. To show his support for the Church, Theodosius allowed its leaders to establish their own courts and their own laws. This meant that the Church, not the Roman government, could place on trial Church officials who broke Church rules. Having its own legal system made the Church a political as well as a religious institution.

Christian bishops installed their main offices, or *sees*, in the central cities of areas called *dioceses*. From their *cathedrals* (or seats of authority) in these cities, the bishops governed the religious affairs of the area. Just as the political governors had represented the Roman emperor, the bishops represented the bishop of Rome, who eventually became known as the pope. By adopting the Roman Empire's political organization, the Church had also adopted its power structure.

Conflicts in the Christian Church

The Roman Church had many disagreements with the Eastern Orthodox Church. The most important disagreement centered on the relation between church and state. Church leaders in western Europe felt that they had more power than kings and emperors. In Byzantium, the political leaders had a strong influence on Church leaders.

Because of their isolation from each other, the two branches of the Church developed other differences as well. Roman priests conducted religious services in Latin. The priests of Byzantium used Greek.

These differences contributed to the split between the Eastern

Orthodox Church and the Roman Church. Their main conflict, however, was over which of the two would control the Christian Church. This quarrel started when the political capital of the Roman Empire was moved to Byzantium. The absence of the emperors made the popes, or bishops of Rome, the only unifying force in the disorganized Europe of the Middle Ages. Consequently, the popes became the major leaders of Europe. As time went on, they began to feel that they could also set Church policy for the patriarchs, or bishops of Constantinople. The popes claimed that they had authority over all Christians and all Church affairs. The patriarchs insisted that they still presided over the churches in eastern Europe, the Middle East, and North Africa.

In 1054, the Christian Church split into two parts. The breakup is known as the Great Schism. The Roman Catholic Church had its center at Rome. The Eastern Orthodox Church had its center at Constantinople. Eastern Orthodox Christianity became the official state religion of the Byzantine Empire. The patriarchs of Constantinople recognized the authority of the Byzantine emperors over the Eastern Orthodox Church.

By the 11th century, the Eastern Orthodox Church dominated eastern Europe. Gradually, Eastern Orthodox missionaries converted Serbs, Bulgars, Russians, and other eastern Europeans to Christianity. The eastern Europeans eventually developed their own Eastern Orthodox Church by adapting Byzantine rituals, music, and architecture to their local languages and cultures.

The Roman Catholic Church became the dominant religious organization throughout western Europe. Kings and common people alike looked to Rome for spiritual guidance. The forms of worship in even the smallest local place of worship were directed by the Church officials in Rome. The pope sent missionaries to non-Christian areas of Europe to convert the rulers and the people. (The people had to follow the direction of the ruler.) By the 1200s, the Roman Catholic Church had become the strongest force in western Europe in both religious and nonreligious matters.

Monasteries and Convents: Centers of Faith and Learning

Monasteries and convents had great influence in medieval society. They provided places where men and women could withdraw from ordinary life to concentrate on devotion to God.

Women became nuns and lived in convents (also called nunneries) under the leadership of abbesses. Men became monks and friars and lived in monasteries under the leadership of abbots. Both men and women took vows of poverty, chastity, and obedience. Some of the religious orders that established monasteries were the Benedictine, the Franciscan, and the Dominican. Each order had its own set of rules.

Scholarly French monk of the 15th century scripting a manuscript copy

Monks and nuns farmed, did housekeeping tasks, and took surplus produce to the local markets and sold it. They made products, such as bread or wine, which they also sold. Monasteries and convents often became known for particular products.

In many orders, the monks and nuns spent a large part of the day studying. Many copied and illustrated manuscripts. Most orders stressed community service. The members helped the people in nearby towns and manors. They not only gave outsiders spiritual help, they also taught, gave legal advice, and took care of the sick.

INFO CHECK

1. Respond to the argument that Europe was in a "dark age" after A.D. 476, during which nothing new or important developed.

2. List some of the ways in which the Christian Church provided unity and leadership to medieval Europe.

3. Why do you think monasteries and convents attracted so many Europeans during the Middle Ages?

THE FRANKISH EMPIRE

The rise of the Merovingian Dynasty demonstrates the important role that the Church played in political developments during the early medieval period. The Merovingian family belonged to a Germanic group called the Franks, who had migrated south from an area near the mouth of the Rhine River.

Clovis and His Sons

King Clovis, a member of the Merovingian family, invaded and conquered parts of modern France, northwest Germany, and the Low Countries (now Belgium, Luxembourg, and the Netherlands). He found that he could not govern this large territory without the support of the bishops in these areas. Therefore, he converted to Christianity in about A.D. 496.

Clovis divided his kingdom among his four sons. After he died in 511, his heirs destroyed its unity by fighting with each other for more territory. They spent so much time plotting and warring against each other and so little time governing that they were called "do-nothing" kings. Little by little, much of their power fell into the hands of their chief officials. These "mayors of the palace" did most of the work of governing.

Charles Martel and Pepin

One mayor of the palace managed to make his office hereditary within his family. Charles Martel, one of the heirs to this office, was a particularly able official. He was also largely responsible for preventing the Muslims from taking over western Europe. In 732, he led a cavalry force of Frankish nobles to victory against the Muslims at Tours. Muslim forces had advanced into France from Spain.

Because of his victory over the Muslims, Martel won the loyalty of many Frankish nobles. He gained the support of the Church by helping the Benedictine monks convert northern Europeans to Christianity. Martel's son, Pepin III (the Short), strengthened this alliance with the Church. In 751, Pepin became king of the Franks with the approval of the pope.

During Pepin's reign, a group called the Lombards conquered Ravenna, a part of Italy that had remained in the eastern Roman Empire. From Ravenna, the Lombards began to take other areas that belonged to the empire. Occupied with fighting invaders from the East, the leaders of Byzantium were unable to send aid to the pope. In 753, therefore, Pope Stephen II turned to Pepin for help.

The pope traveled to France and personally anointed Pepin as king of the Franks, reinforcing his earlier approval. This blessing was to be passed along to Pepin's sons as heirs to the crown. Pepin and his army returned to Rome with the pope. They drove the Lombards out of their newly won territory. Pepin added part of the territory he took from the Lombards to his own kingdom and gave the rest to the pope.

The Roman Church called its new lands the Papal States. Having a close relationship with the Roman Church gave Pepin and his heirs more authority in Europe. Having the protection of Pepin's army lessened the dependence of the Roman Church on Byzantine officials to drive out invaders. The pope now gave more attention to leaders in western Europe.

Charlemagne and His Empire

Pepin's son, Charles, ruled from 771 to 814. He was the greatest of the Frankish kings and became known as Charlemagne, which

Depiction of the coronation of Charlemagne by Pope Leo III

means Charles the Great. His actions as ruler made people think of him as great. He was also great in size—more than six feet tall—much taller than most of his subjects.

Charlemagne conquered other Germanic kings. As he took their kingdoms, he forced their subjects to become Christians. He eventually ruled over an area that included what are now France, Germany, Austria, and Switzerland. Charlemagne also controlled northern Italy and northeastern Spain.

When a local uprising forced the pope to flee from Rome in 799, Charlemagne marched there and defeated the pope's enemies. In appreciation for returning him to his office, Pope Leo III crowned Charlemagne Holy Roman Emperor on Christmas Day in 800. This honor meant that Charlemagne was considered to be the Christian successor to the emperors of Rome.

Some scholars believe that Charlemagne would have preferred being crowned by his own people rather than by the pope. After the ceremony, Charlemagne remarked to his son that if he had known what was going to happen that day, he never would have come to the cathedral. Scholars take this remark as evidence that Charlemagne did not like what the pope had done. Perhaps he felt that if the pope had the power to make an emperor, he also might have the power to unmake one. Later, however, Charlemagne took pride in holding the title of Holy Roman Emperor.

The leaders of Byzantium were outraged at the coronation. It ignored the fact that a Byzantine emperor already ruled the Roman Empire. Then, too, they felt that the crowning of an emperor by a Church leader demonstrated that the Church was higher than the state.

The differences between the eastern and western branches of

Charlemagne's Realm and Its Division

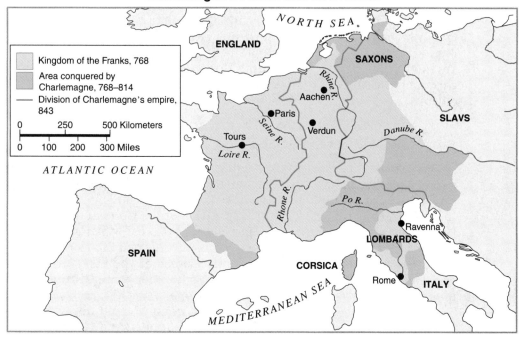

Christianity became more noticeable after Leo's action. It also led to disputes between the Church and future emperors.

The Division of Charlemagne's Empire

Charlemagne's empire did not last long after his death in 814. His son was not a good ruler. Charlemagne's grandsons went to war against one another. In the mid-800s, a formal agreement, the Treaty of Verdun, divided Charlemagne's empire into three kingdoms. The western one eventually became France. The eastern kingdom in time became Germany. European rulers fought over the middle kingdom for centuries. At last it became part of several present-day countries, such as Austria and Italy.

INFO CHECK

1. How did each of the following individuals shape the history of Europe during the Middle Ages: Clovis, Charles Martel, Pepin III, Charlemagne?

2. Explain why you AGREE or DISAGREE with this statement: During the Middle Ages, the Byzantine Empire had more influence on events in Western Europe than did the Frankish Empire.

The Culture of Medieval Europe

One of Charlemagne's great contributions to civilization in Europe was his encouragement of learning. The push he gave to education made it possible for more people to learn to read and write. It also spread knowledge of Greek and Roman philosophy and literature throughout Europe. This was important to the reshaping of European culture.

Preserving and Spreading Learning

Greek and Roman poets, scholars, and philosophers, as well as the early Church fathers, had written down their thoughts in the Greek and Latin languages. Because these works had been preserved in writing, they replaced the oral tradition of the Celts and Germans. Byzantine and Roman monks had copied classical writings and preserved them in libraries. European monks continued the work of copying these manuscripts and the Bible. Copies of the classical works and the Bible were sent to the many educational institutions and monasteries that sprang up all over Europe.

Like many people of that time, Charlemagne could not write. He could, however, read and speak Latin and understand Greek, in addition to speaking his native Frankish langauge. In spite of his own limitations, he valued learning. To further education in his kingdom, Charlemagne set up a school in Aachen, his capital city, for the children of the nobility. He appointed Alcuin, a great English clergyman and scholar, to direct the school. The presence of Alcuin attracted scholars from other lands. These scholars put special emphasis on preserving the literature of the past in their original languages of Latin and Greek. Educators throughout Europe used this school as a model when they created new schools.

As the numbers of books and schools increased, so did the knowledge of Latin and Greek. Of course, people still spoke the languages of their region, such as French and German. But now educated people could use Latin and Greek as second languages to speak and write to someone from a different region. Scholars, scientists, and professional people could exchange ideas with their peers in other language regions. Diplomats could talk to government leaders in distant kingdoms.

The Influence of the Church on Learning

Although Charlemagne set up schools and encouraged learning, he had no real influence over the intellectual community of the Middle Ages. Members of the clergy were the major teachers and scholars of the time. They had the greatest knowledge of classical learning. Both commoners and nobility went to them for advice on medicine and law as well as on religious matters. Consequently, the clergy of the Middle Ages had a great deal of control over European culture and government. For example, Alcuin wrote a book on how a Christian king should rule. He also wrote letters of advice to Charlemagne and prepared the great king's official documents. Monks dominated the medical and legal professions.

The Church and Art

The Church also ruled the world of art. Almost all works of art were created to help people worship. Most people could not read. They needed pictures to help them recall biblical stories. Music that was sung or played reminded people of God. Monks decorated the pages of the Bibles they copied. (Since there were no printing presses at that time, all copies of books had to be written by hand.) Among the most beautiful of the decorated Bibles is the *Book of Kells*, created by monks in Ireland. Artists painted scenes that represented stories from the Bible.

The most impressive buildings of the Middle Ages were the great churches in the cities and towns. Everything in these buildings was done to help the worshipers feel the presence of God and the power of the Roman Catholic Church. Two major styles of churches were built.

One style, the Romanesque, was the main type put up between 1000 and 1150. These churches had thick stone walls, very small windows, and rounded arches.

From about 1150 to 1300, a second style, the Gothic, became popular. These churches had thinner stone walls, high ceilings, large windows, pointed arches, and tall towers. Structures called flying buttresses supported the exterior walls. The windows were made of stained (colored) glass. Many pictured events from Bible stories.

INFO CHECK

1. Why were education and religion so closely connected in medieval Europe?

2. Explain the importance of Latin and Greek to trade and diplomacy.

3. How was the art of medieval Europe influenced by the Christian Church?

THE GROWTH OF PAPAL POWER

The Germanic kings who followed Charlemagne continued to value the title of Holy Roman Emperor. They traveled to Rome and received it directly from the pope. By recognizing the pope's right to crown them as emperor, they increased his political power.

The Basis of Papal Power

The popes of Rome had long considered themselves both religious and political leaders in western Europe. They based their religious supremacy on the fact that their main church was located in Rome, the ancient capital of the old empire. This is the city where Saint Peter (the first head of the organized Christian Church) had been *martyred* (killed for his beliefs). The popes claimed to be Peter's successors because they continued his work of overseeing the Christian Church. By moving to Constantinople, the Byzantine emperors had also increased the popes' political power. Their departure made the Church the most powerful institution in Europe.

When the Frankish king Pepin gave the pope part of the land he took from the Lombards, he strengthened the political position of future popes. They ruled the Papal States as kings. Popes also had some control over the land ruled by Christian kings. The rents and *tithes* (or taxes) collected from the people who lived on these lands gave Church officials great wealth and influence.

As more Europeans became Christians, the pope's legal authority increased. He could use Church courts and law to pass judgment on kings, nobles, and commoners. His two most important legal powers were *excommunication* and *interdiction*. An excommunicated person could not go to church, confess his or her sins, or take part in communion. (Through confession, a person could receive forgiveness for wrongdoing.) People believed that if they died while excommunicated, they would go to hell. If a ruler was excommunicated, his subjects might not obey him.

If a pope found a king guilty of some religious error, he could place an interdiction on the entire kingdom. This meant that the churches in that land could not perform any services except baptism and rites for the dying. No one in the land could marry, take communion, confess, or have a church service at his or her burial. People in lands where these services were banned often became very upset. Their restlessness might force their king to give in to the pope so that he would lift the interdiction. Marguerite, in the story at the beginning of the chapter, lived in a kingdom under interdiction. She feared that the people would go to war to force her king to ask forgiveness from the pope.

Like any other government, the Church needed a group of officials to manage its affairs. The cardinals ranked as the highest of the pope's officials and were often called the "princes of the Church." Next came the archbishops, then the bishops, and finally the priests. Abbots and abbesses in the monasteries and convents also represented the authority of the pope.

Conflicts Between Church and State

The Church and the kings usually relied on each other for support in governing. Monarchs in parts of Germany, for example, expected the bishops in their domain to help them govern. Therefore, they protected the lands governed by the Church. In return, the bishops paid taxes to the monarchs and sent a number of tenants who lived on Church land to serve in the army. Because this arrangement made for a stable government, the popes, at first, did not object when the German kings appointed their own bishops. The appointment of a bishop by someone who is not a member of the clergy is called *lay investiture.*

In the 11th century, reformers in the Church began to object to the practice of lay investiture. They argued that it gave kings too much power over religious matters. They also felt that the pope, as God's representative on earth, had more authority than a king.

Two main figures in the controversy over investiture were Pope Gregory VII and the German king, Henry IV. Gregory became pope in 1073. In 1075, he ruled that only members of the clergy could appoint bishops. The German bishops Henry had appointed tried to remove Gregory from office. Gregory responded by excommunicating Henry. He also claimed that Henry had no right to his throne and told Henry's subjects that they did not have to obey him.

The German nobles, who had been in conflict with Henry, sided with Pope Gregory. They told Henry that if he did not persuade the pope to reestablish him within the Church, they would remove him from the throne. Henry gave in. In January 1077, he traveled to the castle at Canossa, where the pope was visiting. Dressed in a robe made of coarse material and wearing no shoes, he stood outside the castle in the snow. Three days passed before the pope admitted him. Because Henry confessed to his sins (did penance), the pope had to pardon him. Once the pope granted the pardon, he had no reason to take away Henry's crown.

Nonetheless, Henry did not immediately regain his kingdom. During Henry's absence, the nobles chose a new ruler, Rudolf of Swabia. Henry and Rudolf fought over the German throne for three years. At the end of this period, Gregory declared that Rudolf was the rightful king. Rudolf died in battle, however, and Henry eventually regained his throne. Once Henry was back in power, the German bishops again refused to recognize Gregory as pope. Henry led his army to Rome, which he put under siege for three years. In 1084, he conquered the city and replaced Gregory with a pope of his own choosing. The new pope gave Henry the title of Holy Roman Emperor.

Resolving the Conflict

Political and religious leaders did not settle the Investiture Controversy until 1122. At a meeting held at Worms, Germany, King Henry V and Pope Calixtus II reached a compromise. Called the Concordat of Worms, this agreement made a distinction between political authority and spiritual authority. It allowed the king to invest a bishop with the worldly symbols of his office and give him land. Only members of the clergy, however, could nominate and elect a bishop. Only they could invest a bishop with his spiritual powers. The Concordat of Worms officially recognized that Church leaders and political leaders ruled entirely different realms. Today people still argue about the relationship between church and state.

The Concordat of Worms was also important because it weakened the power of kings to place an ally in an important Church position. In 1207, King John of England tried to force the church to accept the candidate he favored for the position of Archbishop of Canterbury. In 1208, Pope Innocent III excommunicated John and interdicted his kingdom. Finally, in 1213, John asked the pope's pardon and accepted the man the pope had chosen as archbishop. John even recognized the pope as lord of his own kingdom, which consisted of England, Ireland, and parts of France.

INFO CHECK

1. Define "excommunication" and "interdiction" and explain how they increased the power of the popes.

2. Describe the investiture controversy. How and when was it settled?

INVADERS AND CONQUERORS

Other factors besides the rivalry between church leaders and political leaders helped bring about changes in medieval Europe. From the 8th to the 11th centuries, a series of invasions and migrations terrified established settlements.

Invaders From the North

Starting in the late 700s, fierce raiders from northern Europe attacked settlements along the coasts of England and France. The raiders, called Northmen or Norsemen, are better known as Vikings. They came from the present-day countries of Norway, Sweden, and Denmark (together called Scandinavia).

The Vikings sailed into the Mediterranean and raided southern France. They moved up rivers to loot cities such as Paris and London. Scotland and Ireland also felt the blows of the Viking warriors. Some Vikings crossed the North Atlantic to settle in Greenland and Iceland. In A.D. 1000, a few reached the coast of North America, in the area of Newfoundland, now part of Canada. They set up at least one colony called Vinland. For a short period, the Vikings carried on trade between Newfoundland and Europe.

In 878, King Alfred kept the Vikings from overrunning all of England. The invaders agreed to stay in northeastern England. They

THE LAST VIKING

Until the 13th century, the story of the Vikings was transmitted orally in the form of *sagas,* or stories, composed by their *skalds,* or poet-historians. In these sagas, Viking leaders were praised for physical strength, courage, fighting skill, and cleverness. One such story is the *Saga of Harald Sigurdson,* King of Norway. Also, known as Harald Hardruler, his life was one of high adventure. A tall, strong man of great courage, Harald had escaped from enemies in Norway and made his way to Constantinople (now Istanbul, Turkey). There he became leader of the Varangian Guard, the English and Scandinavian soldiers who protected the Byzantine emperor and fought in his wars. As a result of many victories, Harald gained wealth and a large following.

When Harald was ready to resign from the Varangian Guard and return home, the Byzantine empress tried to prevent him from leaving Constantinople. It was rumored that she was in love with the Norse leader. The empress ordered a great chain stretched across the harbor to seal in Harald's two ships. By skillful sailing, Harald got out of the harbor.

After reaching home, Harald used his wealth and reputation to become co-ruler and then king of Norway. Years of battle followed, mainly against forces of Denmark. Harald's reputation as a powerful, able, and resourceful ruler grew. No king in the northlands was his equal in strength, skill with weapons, and wisdom.

In England in 1066, the great Viking met his end. King Edward of England had died. A noble named Harold Godwinson had been chosen to succeed him. The new king's brother, Earl Tostig, was angered by the selection. Believing that he had a greater right to the English throne, Tostig went to Norway to ask for Harald Hardruler's help. Harald agreed and sailed to England with a Norse army.

Harald won victories in England, even capturing the city of York. In September 1066, however, Harald and Tostig came up against a much larger English army. Before the battle began, the English king tried to make peace with his brother by offering Tostig a third of England. Tostig then asked what would be given to Harald Hardruler. "Seven feet of English soil, or a bit more as he is taller than other men," was the reply. Upon hearing this, Tostig refused to abandon his alliance with the Norse king.

According to the saga, the English came at the Norse from all sides. As many fell to arrow and spear, King Harald became so fighting mad that he ran out in front of the battle line, slashing with his sword. None of the English could stand against him. Finally, Harald was struck in the throat by an arrow and died.

The Norse army was defeated. But Harold Godwinson did not keep his throne for long. A short while later, England was again invaded. The forces of Duke William of Normandy defeated the English at Hastings. William the Conqueror became king of England. Historians regard Harald Hardruler's death in 1066 as the event that marked the end of the Viking Age.

1. Why do you think the skalds composed so many stories about Harald Hardruler?

2. Do you regard Harald as a hero? Why or why not?

settled down as farmers, merchants, and traders. Most also became Christians.

To stop the terrible raids in France, a Frankish king gave a Norseman a large part of the northwestern section of the country in 911. This area is still known as Normandy. In 1066, a Norman duke, William, and his army sailed to England and defeated the Anglo-Saxon king in the Battle of Hastings. William the Conqueror introduced the Norman (French) language, laws, and government into England. He drew England more closely into European affairs.

About 1000, the Vikings ended their raids. By this time, they had established settlements and kingdoms in parts of England, Scotland, Ireland, France, Italy, Sicily, and Russia. Scandinavian languages, customs, and laws influenced the culture of these areas. One of the most important Scandinavian contributions to Europe was the knowledge of shipbuilding. From the Vikings, Europeans learned how to build ships that could sail the rough Atlantic Ocean.

Invaders From the East

The Magyars had migrated westward from central Asia. They settled in Hungary, where they ruled over the Slavs and Huns. Begin-

Viking, Magyar, and Muslim Invasions of Europe

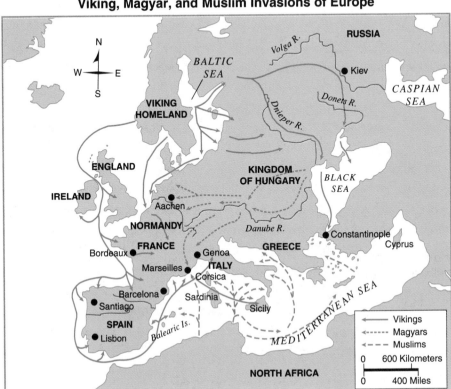

ning about 890, the Magyars began to raid France, northern Italy, and southern Germany. They looted villages and monasteries in these lands and took prisoners, whom they sold as slaves. Their attacks were so brutal that many people considered the Magyars to be monsters. Because they came from Hungary, the English called them "Hungars." Gradually, this name came to be pronounced "ogre," which today means "monster."

Muslim Invaders

Muslim Arabs invaded Spain in 711. Spain became a great center of Muslim learning and culture. In the 9th and 10th centuries, Muslims raided Italy and other places on the Mediterranean coast. They did not settle in these areas, however. Like the Magyars, they wanted treasure and slaves.

INFO CHECK

1. Complete the following sentences:

   • Medieval Europeans feared the Vikings and the Magyars because _____.

   • Among the areas explored and settled by Vikings were _____.

   • The most important Scandinavian contribution to Europe was _____.

2. Why did Spain develop differently from other European countries after A.D. 711?

DEVELOPMENT OF FEUDALISM AND MANORIALISM

The invasions of the Vikings, Magyars, and Muslim Arabs caused the landowners to develop systems to protect themselves. This effort gave rise to *feudalism*. This is the name given to a system of government or rule that involved pledges of loyalty in return for land and protection. The relationship was based on the political systems of the Germans and the Celts. The warriors in each tribe swore loyalty to their chief, who, in return, gave them food and protection in times of trouble. During the early Middle Ages, this system reappeared in a new, more complicated form.

Feudalism: A New Social, Political, and Military System

The kings who followed Charlemagne were too weak to raise armies to fight off the Vikings and other groups of raiders. They became more and more dependent on the military power of the great landowning nobles in their kingdoms. These nobles (lords) were the

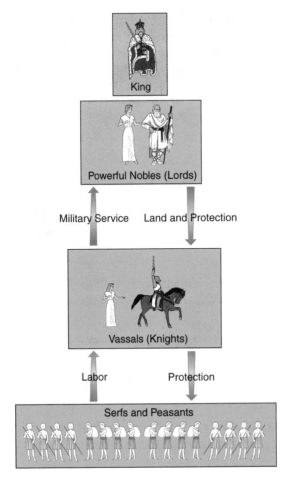

Medieval Feudal Society

descendants of political officials who had governed provinces in the Roman Empire and of Roman military commanders.

In order to raise armies to protect themselves, the kingdom, and the less wealthy people in their region, the lords gave land and protection to any noble or small landowner who would serve in their armies. Those who pledged their loyalty and service were called *vassals*.

Vassals served as knights (soldiers on horseback) in the lord's army for about five weeks a year. They paid various fees and contributed money when the lord's oldest daughter married or oldest son became a knight.

In return for the vassals' services, the lord provided money and soldiers for the common defense. He maintained roads and villages. He also acted as a judge to decide disputes among vassals. If a case was particularly complicated, he might ask the advice of vassals who were not involved with the case.

Vassals could have vassals of their own. They had the right to divide their land and give parts of it to men who promised their loyal service in return. When the vassal died, his eldest son inherited all of the property and the father's position in the feudal system. This practice is known as *primogeniture*. It preserved the large feudal landholdings rather than having them broken up equally among all male heirs.

Because the vassals were often nobles who had connections with other noble families, they held political power. Then, too, as knights in the lord's army, they represented military power.

Women could seldom own property in their own right. They were always under the protection of their father, guardian, or husband.

Training for Knighthood

To prepare for knighthood, a boy of the nobility would leave his home at the age of seven to live in the household of one of his father's friends or relatives. At first, he served as a page. A page was a kind of general servant who ran errands and waited on table during meals. When the boy reached the age of 14, he would begin formal training

Knight of the Crusades, illustrated in an Italian codex (a booklike manuscript)

Time Line

Year	Dates and Events
A.D.	

A.D.

400

476: Germanic tribes begin breakup of western Roman Empire into small kingdoms with distinctive cultures, languages, governments; Byzantium tries to hold off Russian, Slav, Arab invaders

486–751: Merovingian Dynasty rules Franks
496: King Clovis becomes Christian

500

511: Death of Clovis and decline of Merovingians

600

700

700s–1000s: Vikings from Scandinavia invade England, Scotland, Ireland, France, Italy, Sicily, Russia
711–1212: Muslims begin 500-year control of Spain
751–768: Pepin III (the Short) rules Franks as first Carolingian king
768–814: 45-year rule of Charlemagne; expansion of kingdom to Germany, Austria, Switzerland, and portions of Italy and Spain

800

800: Pope Leo III crowns Charlemagne Holy Roman Emperor
843: Treaty of Verdun divides Charlemagne's empire into three kingdoms, ending political unity of western Christian Europe
878: King Alfred of England makes peace with Viking invaders, who settle in northeastern England

900

890: Beginning of Magyar (Hungarian) invasions of France, Italy, Germany

1000

1054: Great Schism divides Christianity into Roman Catholic and Eastern Orthodox churches
1071: Turks defeat Greeks and take control of part of Asia Minor (present-day Turkey)
1075–1077: Pope Gregory VII excommunicates King Henry IV of Germany; Henry asks for and receives pope's pardon

1100

1084: King Henry becomes Holy Roman Emperor
1095: Pope Urban II calls for crusade to drive Muslims from Holy Land
1099–1187: Christians win control of Jerusalem, then lose it to Muslim leader Saladin
1122: Concordat of Worms defines extent of political and religious authority
1204–1261: Venice wins control of Constantinople from Byzantines

1200

1291: Muslims take port of Acre and drive Christians from Holy Land

as a knight. At this stage, he became a squire, the personal servant of a veteran knight. A squire took care of his knight's horse, armor, and weapons. He was taught how to fight on horseback, use heavy weapons such as pikes and lances, and develop dexterity in handling lighter ones such as swords. When the squire became older, he accompanied his master into battle.

The veteran knight provided his squire with a model of knightly behavior. The respect and admiration the squire gave his role model helped him develop the trait of loyalty.

At 21, the squire advanced into knighthood. At that time, he performed a religious ceremony to mark his new status. This ceremony involved spending the night alone at the altar of a church, watching over his weapons and armor. While he kept his vigil (as the ceremony was called), the new knight would pray and mediate on the code of chivalry. His honor as a knight depended on his following this code. It required that he be loyal to his lord, brave in battle, courteous and merciful to his enemies, and generous to the poor and helpless.

Because it emphasized loyalty, the code supported and strengthened the feudal power structure. Of course, the feudal system itself provided practical incentives for a knight to become the vassal of a great lord.

The Manorial System: Land and Power

The people of the Middle Ages measured wealth and power by the ownership of land. The more you owned, the more powerful you were. Land was important for the crops that could be grown on it. Land was also needed for raising animals and for forests, which supplied wood for fuel and building. The rents peasants and serfs paid and the work they did were another source of wealth to the landholders.

The economic relationship between the lords, the peasants, and the serfs became the *manorial system*. The lord's house, land, and all his workers were called his *manor*. The peasants and serfs lived in small houses close to the lord's great house or castle. Fields, orchards, and forests surrounded the buildings. Most of the workers were serfs. They belonged to the manor. If the ownership of the manor changed hands, the serfs stayed on the land. Some workers were free peasants. They could move from place to place.

In times of danger, peasants and serfs could take refuge in the lord's castle. A *moat*, or water-filled ditch, surrounded the thick walls of the castle. To get over the ditch, one had to cross a drawbridge that was lowered from inside the castle.

Serfs and peasants spent most of their time working in the lord's fields and taking care of his animals. They could use some of the land to raise food for themselves. But they had to pay rent for the land on which they planted their own crops. Rent was usually paid in crops or services to the lord of the manor.

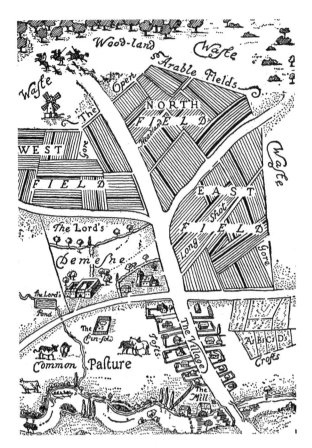

Plan of the typical medieval manor found in Europe

Serfs had few rights or freedoms. For instance, they could not marry or leave the manor without permission from the lord. Only the Church could prevent a lord from misusing his serfs. The serfs' duties were hereditary. They could not rise to a higher social position no matter how hard they worked. Most serfs spent their entire lives working on one manor. They had few chances to learn new ideas or new ways.

Manors were self-sufficient. The needs of the inhabitants were provided for without help from the outside. The peasants and serfs grew food for everyone. Each family took care of its own medical problems. Tools, weapons, clothing, furniture, and anything else required by the workers and the lord's family were also made on the manor. There were few places where goods could be bought, and factories did not exist.

Abbots and abbesses of the monasteries and convents sometimes acted as feudal lords. They had authority over the serfs who worked on the land owned by their order. The ownership of land and serfs gave the abbots and abbesses some of the political power enjoyed by the great landlords.

INFO CHECK

1. PROVE or DISPROVE:

    • The basic purpose of feudalism was to provide Europeans with security in return for service.

    • Nobles could be both lords and vassals at the same time.

2. Why do you think boys of the nobility wanted to become knights? What were the obligations of knighthood?

3. Why was the manorial system essential to feudalism?

THE CRUSADES: WARS IN THE MIDDLE EAST

In 1071, Turkish soldiers fighting for the Arabs defeated a Greek army and took over a large part of Asia Minor (now Turkey). This conquest made Byzantium more vulnerable to the Muslims than ever. The Byzantine emperor asked the leaders of Western Europe for help. It was not sent right away.

The Crusades Begin

When the Turks also conquered Jerusalem, Pope Urban II seized the opportunity to declare war against the Muslims. At the Council of Clermont in 1095, he called for a crusade to drive the Turks out of the Holy Land. (The Holy Land is at the eastern end of the Mediterranean Sea in what is now Israel and Jordan.) Thousands of peasants and knights answered his call. The First Crusade set off for the Holy Land in 1096.

After many bloody battles, the Crusaders took Jerusalem in 1099. They promptly massacred the Jewish and Muslim residents. The Roman Catholic soldiers created permanent settlements in the Holy Land. These came to be known as the Crusader States. When Muslim forces threatened over the years, calls for help went out again to the pope in Rome and kings in western Europe. Four major Crusades tried to keep the Holy Land in Christian hands. They all failed. Saladin, a Muslim ruler of Syria and Egypt, retook Jerusalem in 1187. He allowed Christians to visit their holy places.

The Crusades ended in 1291. In that year, the Muslims took Acre, the last Christian-held city in the Holy Land.

For 200 years, Crusaders had tried to drive the Turks out of the Holy Land. All they permanently won was the right of Christians to visit Jerusalem. This right cost the lives of tens of thousands of Christians, Jews, and Muslims.

Routes of the First Four Crusades

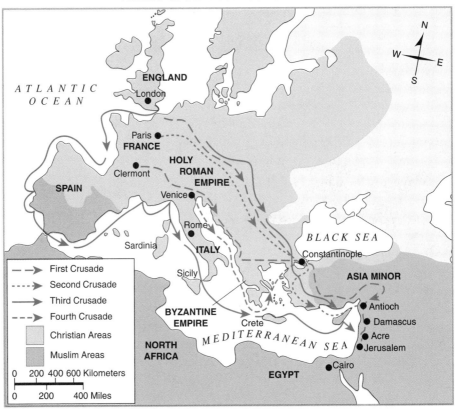

Results of the Crusades

The Crusades affected relations between Muslims and Christians in contradictory ways. The Crusaders aroused strong resentment in the Muslims. During the Christian rule of Jerusalem and other parts of the Middle East, Christian kings and religious leaders had persecuted the Muslims. Their cruelty and intolerance left a legacy of distrust that persists to the present.

The people from western Europe who went on the Crusades saw many new sights and new ways of life. They brought home new ideas and a taste for Middle Eastern products.

European merchants set up communities in the Middle East during the Crusades. They established a trade that was profitable to Muslims as well as to Europeans. When the Crusades ended and the Europeans left, the Muslim rulers continued to do business with them. Several seafaring cities in Italy—particularly Venice and Genoa—controlled this trade and profited greatly from it.

The Crusades seriously weakened Byzantium. Not only did the Byzantines have to fight the invading Turks, they also had to defend themselves against their fellow Christians. In 1204, the rulers of Venice persuaded the Crusaders to attack and capture Constantinople instead of fighting the Turks. Although the Byzantines won their city back in 1261, they could not regain their former strength. As a result, the Roman pope became stronger than the Byzantine leader.

Europe was not the only region to develop feudal and manorial systems and have knights. The next chapter describes similar systems and warriors in Japan.

INFO CHECK

1. List the major causes and results of the Crusades.

2. Explain why historians regard the Crusades as a military failure of the Christian kings that brought economic and cultural change to Western Europe.

CHAPTER REVIEW

Multiple Choice

1. During the European medieval period, there was no strong centralized government. However, advances were made in the areas of

    1. art, science, and communication
    2. agricultural technology and ship design
    3. medical knowledge
    4. all of the above.

2. Germanic rule of Europe differed from Roman rule in that

    1. rulers used fortune-tellers to guide decision making
    2. the army had a lot of influence in the selection of the ruler
    3. women played a major role in political decision making
    4. no one central political authority existed.

3. Select the pairs that correctly apply to Church leadership and responsibility.

    1. parish priest to his church as bishop is to his diocese
    2. abbot to his nuns as the priest to his convent
    3. patriarch to his church as priests to missionaries
    4. none of the above.

4. A major difference between the Roman and the Eastern Orthodox Church leadership was

    1. Eastern Orthodox priests conducted their services in Latin
    2. Roman priests allowed the use of pictures but not statues
    3. the authority of the pope was superior to that of kings
    4. in Byzantium the Church leaders made government policies.

5. The Great Schism of 1054 refers to

   1. the division of the Christian Church into two parts

   2. the major earthquake that destroyed Rome

   3. the division of the Roman Empire into two parts

   4. none of the above.

6. The rise of the Merovingian Dynasty refers to

   1. the last of the Roman emperors

   2. the first Asian hordes that conquered Europe

   3. a Germanic king who conquered portions of Europe

   4. the Muslim dynasty that ruled Spain.

7. After Clovis's death, real power in the Merovingian Dynasty was in the hands of the

   1. nobles

   2. mayors of the palace

   3. parish priests

   4. king's wife.

8. Charlemagne had many accomplishments during his reign. Select the item that correctly identifies his accomplishments.

   1. defeated the Arabs at the Battle of Tours

   2. established the Umayyad Dynasty

   3. twice prevented the overthrow of the pope and defeated the Mongols

   4. expanded the Frankish empire in Europe and established a school in Aachen to encourage learning.

9. Match the architectural style that developed in medieval Europe with its correct description.

   1. Gothic—thin walls, large windows, towers, and pointed arches

   2. Romanesque—thin walls, large windows, towers, and pointed arches

   3. Romanesque—massive marble pillars, very ornate stone carvings, and walls having no images but inlaid with multicolored stones

   4. none of the above.

10. The importance of the Concordat of Worms was

    1. the Roman Church was recognized as having power over all local rulers

    2. the local rulers continued to select and control Church bishops

    3. the ruler could provide lands and title but the Church selected and gave religious authority to the individual

    4. the Holy Roman Emperor and the pope agreed to end their quarrel.

11. What conclusion can be drawn from the manor plan on page 220?

    1. Manors were able to provide enough food for all their inhabitants.

    2. The families of lords and peasants shared the same living quarters.

    3. Manors were built near cities.

    4. Manor-grown grains were shipped to cities for grinding.

12. The map on page 214 and your knowledge or Global History and Geography tell you that

    1. the Magyar invaders of western Europe did not cross large bodies of water

    2. Muslims from North Africa invaded France and Italy

    3. the location of their homeland made the Vikings great shipbuilders and sailors

    4. all of the above are correct.

Thematic Essays

1. *Task:* Using specific examples, describe how the two separate societies of Church and lay (non-Church) people related to each other in medieval Europe.

2. Despite being a military failure, the Crusades significantly affected the social, cultural, and economic lives of Europeans. *Task:* Give examples of how European life was affected by the Crusades.

Document-Based Questions

Use the documents provided and your knowledge of Global History and Geography to answer the questions that follow.

1. Look at the picture on page 206. How could Pope Leo III use the act shown to claim political power?

2. From the letters of Pope Gregory VIII:

    The Roman church was founded by God alone.
    The Roman bishop alone is properly called universal. He alone may depose bishops and reinstate them,
    His legate, though of inferior grade, takes precedence, in a council, of all bishops and may render a decision of deposition against them. He alone may use the insignia of empire.
    The pope is the only person whose feet are kissed by all princes. His title is unique in the world. He may depose emperors.
    No council may be regarded as a general one without his consent.
    No book or chapter may he regarded as canonical without his authority.
    A decree of his may be annulled by no one; he alone may annul the decrees of all.
    He may be judged by no one, No one shall dare to condemn one who appeals to the papal see.
    The Roman Church has never erred, nor ever, by the witness of Scripture, shall err to all eternity.

    According to this document: What is the relationship of the pope to the kings? Where does the pope claim his authority comes from? When can the Church ever be corrected?

Document-Based Essay

Task: Discuss how the conflict between Church and state developed and give at least two specific examples to illustrate the conflict.

UNIT REVIEW

Thematic Essays

1. *Task:* Use examples from Islam, Buddhism, and Christianity to discuss how traders and missionaries spread the beliefs and cultures of these different societies.

2. *Task:* Select any two civilizations studied and write an essay explaining why you AGREE or DISAGREE with the following statement: Religion, philosophy, and government are essential to the development of all civilizations.

3. *Task:* Imagine you were a member of a minor noble family. Which of the societies studied would you have preferred to live in and why?

Document-Based Questions

Use the documents and your knowledge of Global History and Geography to answer the questions.

1. From the writings of a Syrian Arab.

   "I saw one of the Franks come to al-Amir . . . when he was in the Dome of the Rock and say to him, 'Dost thou want to see God as a child?' . . . The Frank walked ahead of us until he showed us the picture of Mary with Christ . . . as an infant in her lap. He then said, 'This is God as a child.' But Allah is exalted far above what the infidels say about him!"

   Describe how this passage shows different religious beliefs and attitudes.

2. Study the illustration on page 204. Why were the efforts of the monks valuable for future societies?

3. From a history of Byzantium and Rome.

   "These three elements, then, Greco-Roman classicism (including the governmental traditions of Rome), the Byzantine brand of Christianity, and what we may call the oriental component were blended by the Byzantine . . ."

   What are the cultural elements that Byzantium preserved for future generations?

4. From a history of Byzantium.

   "It is not only in the Balkans that Byzantine influence survives. . . . It was preserved in that Russia of which, in the eleventh century, Byzantium had been the tutor, and in which Byzantine tradition remained the basis of state and national life."

   How did Byzantium influence Russian society?

Document-Based Essay

Culture can be transmitted in many ways, by enemies as well as friends. *Task:* Using specific historical examples, discuss how cultural diffusion has occurred in the past and affected any two of the societies presented in Era III.

UNIT III

Global Interactions (1200–1650)

Global Interactions (1200–1650)

Year	Dates and Events
A.D. 1200	**1200s:** First invasions of China by Mongol nomads under Genghiz Khan Italian banks set up branches in Europe, North Africa, Middle East
	1237–1400s: Mongols invade and control Russia
	1260: Kublai Khan becomes first Mongol emperor of China
	1272–1292: Italian merchant Marco Polo reaches and explores China before voyaging home
	1295: Persian ruler Ghazan's conversion to Islam stimulates flow of Muslim and European culture to Asia
1299	**1300s–1500s:** Renaissance—expansion of trade, exploration, technology, interest in classic culture
1300	**1337–1453:** Hundred Years' War bankrupts Europe; Hanseatic League controls more trading markets
	1347: Bubonic plague spreads from Asia to Europe; population loss, rebellions, decline in influence of the Church
	1368–1644: Ming Dynasty in China; new cash crops increase trade with Asia, Philippines, Europe
	1394–1460: Advances in navigation by Prince Henry of Portugal spur trade by sea
1399	**1405–1433:** Zheng He opens new markets throughout Asia for Chinese goods and culture
1400	**1485–1509:** Henry II of England centralizes power, expands trade and exploration
	1492: Columbus seeks westward sea route to Asia; opens up European contact with the Americas
	1492–1500: Isabella and Ferdinand expel all unconverted Jews and Muslims from Spain
	1497–1499: Vasco da Gama's expedition sparks Portuguese domination of spice trade with India
1499	**1500s:** Portuguese control of gold trade by sea with Africa eliminates costly land routes Reformation to change Christianity as defined by Roman Catholic Church
1500	**1526:** India falls under control of Mogul (Islamic) invaders
	1534: Ignatius Loyola founds Jesuit Society of teachers and missionaries to promote Catholicism
	1542: Portuguese traders arrive in Japan
	1545–1563: Council of Trent initiates Counter-Reformation to strengthen Roman Catholic Church
	1549: Jesuit Francis Xavier begins mission to Japan
1599	**1550s:** Jesuit and Franciscan missionaries arrive in Japan and begin conversions to Christianity
1600	**1558–1603:** Elizabeth I of England spurs trade, exploration, arts
	1600s: Japan forbids teaching of Christianity, expels missionaries, executes converts
	1610–1643: Louis XIII of France and Cardinal Richelieu expand industry, foreign trade
	1618–1648: Thirty Years' War involves most of Europe, devastates German economy and population
1699	**1641:** Shoguns initiate 200-year isolation of Japan from foreign trade and culture

C H A P T E R

12

Asian Empires: Japan, China, and Mongolia

After practice, Mitsuo wiped his sword, polished its handle, and carefully placed it in its silk-lined sheath. Then he put it away in the chest under the window. There it must rest between training sessions for two more years. Mitsuo would not be entitled to wear the sword until, at age 15, he became a warrior.

Sighing, Mitsuo stripped off his sweaty clothes and took a bath. As he splashed in the cold water, he remembered the test question that the Zen teacher, Yozan, had put to a warrior. "If you were naked in the bathtub and one hundred armed men came to kill you, would you beg for your life or die fighting? Or could you, as a follower of Zen, survive without doing either?" The warrior had said that he wanted to win without pleading for his life or fighting.

Mitsuo sighed again. Well, of course. Who wouldn't? But was that possible? He had been learning swordsmanship ever since he was five. His master often praised his timing and accuracy. But he could not perform wonders. He thought of all the tales he had heard about famous warriors. One had been able to sense a threatening thought in the mind of his servant. Another had conquered an opponent simply by showing the resolve in his eyes.

Mitsuo wondered if these tales were true. He hoped they were. Perhaps the next two years would show if he were capable of such feats. During that period, he would be studying meditation under a master at the nearby monastery. He lay back in the tub and pictured himself fighting five opponents at once. He would be like a playful wind passing among them. All five would fall like leaves caught in a swirl of air.

Mitsuo felt a conceited smile curve his lips. Ah, he must be careful. Such vanity would ruin his technique. He must learn to clear his mind of daydreams about the future and to fix it firmly on the present.

Mitsuo is a young boy of noble birth living in feudal Japan. Like noble European boys living at about the same time, he is training to be a knight. In Japan, knights were called *samurai*. Zen, one form of Buddhism practiced in Japan, was very popular with the samurai. The concepts of this religion suited their active, highly disciplined way of life.

Besides Buddhism, the Japanese adopted other features of Chinese culture. All of these features eventually took on markedly Japanese qualities. What were these adaptable but highly individualistic people like? How did their civilization begin?

EARLY JAPANESE HISTORY AND FEUDALISM

People have lived in Japan for thousands of years. Because the early Japanese had no written history, much remains unknown about their beginnings. Scholars continue to search for answers to such questions as, Where did the people who settled in Japan come from? What was their society like at its very beginning?

By the time historians began to describe the Japanese, their society had already been influenced by the Chinese. Nonetheless, their way of life remained unique. Although impressed by Chinese culture, the Japanese did not let it replace their own. Instead they adapted the parts of Chinese culture that they admired to their own way of life.

The Geography of Japan

Japan is close to the eastern coast of mainland Asia. It is an archipelago, a country made up of many islands. The four largest are Kyushu, Shikoku, Honshu, and Hokkaido.

All of the islands are mountainous and have only small amounts of land flat enough for farming. Plentiful rainfall and warm summers enable the Japanese to grow rice, vegetables, and fruits. They also get an abundance of food from the sea.

Japan's rugged terrain makes land travel difficult. A body of water called the Inland Sea provides a water route between Honshu, Shikoku, and Kyushu. This water route made it possible for early Japanese groups on these islands to communicate and trade with each

Japan: Physical Map

other. For much of Japan's early history, the Korean Strait and the Sea of Japan kept out invaders from the Asian mainland. The Pacific Ocean kept away invaders from the east.

The islands have about 150 major volcanoes. About half are active. The earth's crust near Japan is unstable, causing frequent earthquakes. Underwater quakes occasionally cause tidal waves. Called *tsunamis*, they can be destructive to coastal areas.

The Development of Japanese Culture

In A.D. 297, a Chinese historian, Wei Zhi, described the Japanese as farmers and warriors. Korean histories mention warring clans in

Japan. A clan is a group of families. The leaders of the families have a common ancestor. For a long time, Japan had no central government. Separated by rugged mountains, Japanese clans remained independent of one another. As time went on, they began to compete for power. In the 300s, one of these clans, the Yamato, conquered most of the others. Yamato rulers became known as emperors.

The Yamato Years. During the early years of Yamato rule (250–710), the official state religion was Shinto, "the way of the gods." Shinto honors the spirits thought to inhabit such natural features as trees, rocks, and mountains. (Animism, a common belief system among Africans, has similar ideas about nature.)

The Yamato emperors claimed to be descendants of the sun goddess who ruled all the other nature spirits and protected Japan. This made the emperors representatives of the goddess. Consequently, they controlled both religion and the government.

From its earliest history, Japan had invaded and tried to conquer Korea to gain territory and tribute. In the 5th century, the Yamato emperors increased these efforts. Although unsuccessful, the invasions had important results. The contact between the two countries led to new developments in Japanese culture.

Korean and Chinese Influences. From the Koreans, the Japanese learned many Chinese ways. Their temple architecture, clothing styles, and methods of preparing food all began to show Chinese influence. More important, the Japanese learned the Chinese writing system and adapted it to their own language. Once the Japanese could write and keep records, they were able to imitate the Chinese bureaucratic method of governing. Writing also led to the development of Japanese literature, philosophy, and written history.

The Koreans introduced Buddhism and Confucianism to Japan. The Buddhist idea of gaining peace through discipline and methods of concentrating the mind appealed to the Japanese. A powerful group of nobles converted to Buddhism and wanted to make it the official state religion. Other members of the nobility objected. A civil war broke out and ended in the victory of the pro-Buddhist group.

A New Constitution. Once Japan's rulers accepted Buddhism, they used it as a basis for reforming their government. In 604, Prince Shotoku wrote a new constitution called the "Seventeen-Article Constitution." Using Buddhist moral principles and Confucian political theory, the constitution stated Shotoku's ideas about how to govern morally and efficiently. These ideas included the establishment of a bureaucracy similar to China's.

After a period of civil conflict, supporters of Shotoku's ideas won control of the government. (Shotoku had died in 629.) They then reformed the Japanese government to conform to Chinese political concepts.

In 710, the emperor built a new capital city, called Nara, in the same style as the Chinese imperial court. The period in Japanese

Woodblock print illustrating
the *Tale of Genji*, from a
17th-century edition

history when the rulers continued to introduce Chinese ideas from the Tang Dynasty to their society is called the Nara period.

The Move to Kyoto. About 180 years later, the emperor moved the capital to Kyoto. The ruling families in Kyoto turned away from Chinese ways and encouraged the development of a distinctive Japanese culture. The men and women of the imperial court wrote poetry and stories in their native Japanese language using the Japanese system of writing. They developed an entirely new form of literature called the novel. The *Tale of Genji*, written by a woman named Murasaki Shikibu in the early 1000s, is one of the most famous Japanese novels. It is about the romantic adventures of Prince Genji and the life of his family over a long span of time.

The Shogunate

As time passed, the emperors lost authority. Powerful clans (families) carried out the functions of the government in the name of the emperor. Sometimes, the clans fought one another to gain control of the government. In 1185, the Minamoto clan defeated its rivals. Seven years later, the emperor named the leader of the clan, Minamoto Yoritomo, the first *shogun*.

The shogun was the chief military general of the country. He also controlled the country's financial affairs, courts, and government appointments. Although the emperor still sat on the throne, the shogun actually ruled Japan. Soon, Kamakura, the city in which Yoritomo's palace was located, became more important than Kyoto. The Kamakura Shogunate lasted from 1192 to 1333.

Feudalism. Outside the capital, large landholders, or *daimyos*, controlled local affairs. In return for promises of loyalty and service,

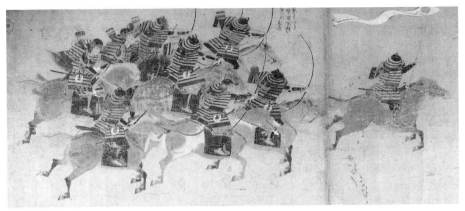

Vanguard force of samurai warriors charging into battle

warriors known as *samurai* received land from a daimyo. This warrior class kept order. The peasants who worked the land were the lowest class. They could not own land.

The daimyo-samurai relationship was like the European feudal system. Both combined features of older systems. European feudalism developed from Germanic and Roman traditions. Japanese feudalism grew out of a merging of the clan tradition with Confucianism. This philosophy encourages respect for the authority of family and state.

The two systems also had economic and social similarities. Both European and Japanese feudalism made land the most important measure of wealth. In both systems, the landowners held greater political and military power than the kings and emperors did.

Knights and samurai were also very much alike. Both swore loyalty to the lords who supported them. Both fought on horseback with carefully crafted weapons and armor. Just as knights lived by the code of chivalry, the samurai followed the Bushido, or "Way of the Warrior." The ideal samurai was obedient to authority, had a strong sense of duty, lived simply, showed kindness to others, and was honest. Samurai and knights spent many years learning the skills they would need to fight for their lords. They started young, as Mitsuo in the story at the beginning of the chapter did.

The two systems had differences, however. The manors of European lords usually included only one village and its surrounding farmland. The daimyos' holdings could include pieces of land scattered through several areas and might contain more than one village. Unlike the European peasants, the Japanese peasants never became serfs. They were free to leave the land whenever they liked. Feudalism in Europe lasted for about six centuries. In Japan, it lasted for about eight centuries.

Bushido. Although both the knights of Europe and the samurai had strict codes of honor, the samurai code was stricter. According to the Bushido, a samurai who had dishonored himself had to commit suicide. The ritual of suicide was called *seppuku* and required the samurai to slash open his belly with a knife. By having the courage to commit seppuku, a disgraced samurai could regain his honor.

The Divine Wind. During the Kamakura Shogunate, the Japanese faced two major crises. The Mongol emperor of China, Kublai Khan, decided to conquer Japan. In 1274, he sent an army through Korea to invade Kyushu. The Japanese defeated the invaders. The Mongols tried once more in 1281. Again they failed when a typhoon destroyed most of their ships and forced them to withdraw. The Japanese called the typhoon "Kamikaze," the "Divine Wind." They felt that the gods had sent the wind to help them.

A Period of Disunity

In the 1330s, the Ashikaga family took control of the government. It ruled until 1568. The Ashikagas did not have a firm hold on the shogunate. A long period of civil wars occurred. Daimyos became even more important in controlling local areas.

Finally, in 1568, one daimyo, Oda Nobunaga, captured Kyoto. He gained the loyalty of many nobles in central Japan. But he was killed in 1582 before he could take full control of Japan.

Nobunaga's chief general, Toyotomi Hideyoshi, won the support of the most important daimyos and became the ruler of a unified Japan in 1590. He then sent armies to Korea and attempted to invade China. Hideyoshi wanted to create an empire in eastern Asia. He did not get his wish. After he died in 1598, the Japanese forces returned home from Korea.

Europeans Arrive. During the time of the civil wars, Europeans first came to Japan. Before the Portuguese arrived in 1542, the Japanese had had no known contact with the West. From the Portuguese, the Japanese learned about muskets (long-barreled firearms). Such weapons changed the way the samurai fought. They now used guns as well as swords.

Along with the traders came Roman Catholic Jesuit missionaries. Led by Francis Xavier, who arrived in 1549, Jesuits converted many Japanese to Christianity. Franciscans arrived in 1593 and expanded the missionary work. Within 30 years, thousands of Japanese had converted to Christianity.

Zen Concepts. In spite of the political unrest in this period, many developments occurred that continue to influence the culture of Japan. Direct trade with China opened up. Monks introduced a different version of Buddhism called Zen. Many Buddhists believed that they could gain enlightenment through special kinds of medi-

Sixteenth-century
Portuguese traders
introduce the Japanese to
Western goods and ideas

tation. Meditation is a method of clearing and concentrating the mind. Most Buddhist groups meditated by sitting still and concentrating on breathing. Zen Buddhists also used this method. But they believed that other activities, such as painting, arranging flowers, and even training to use weapons, could also be ways of meditating. The samurai included Zen concepts in their practice of archery, swordsmanship, and hand-to-hand fighting techniques.

The Tokugawa Shogunate

In 1600, Tokugawa Ieyasu won a great battle over rival daimyos. The emperor appointed him shogun in 1603. Tokugawa made the position of shogun hereditary. His descendants governed Japan until 1868.

Bakuhan System. Tokugawa Ieyasu took measures to strengthen his position as shogun. First of all, he moved the capital to a city that could be defended more easily than Kyoto. This was Edo, now called Tokyo. He then developed the *bakuhan* form of government. This system was designed to limit the power of the daimyos. The daimyos could continue governing their own lands. But the strongest daimyos had to keep two households—one in their own territory and one in the capital. Every other year they had to live in the capital. When they returned to their own territory, they could not take their wives and children with them. If the daimyos rebelled, the shogun killed their families.

This system made the daimyos afraid of overthrowing the Tokugawa shoguns and too poor to do so. They spent most of their money

THE NINJAS OF JAPAN

During World War II (1941–1945), Japan and the United States fought over control of strategically located islands in the Pacific Ocean. A few American soldiers who fought in the battles reported seeing a different kind of Japanese soldier. Instead of wearing ordinary military uniforms, these men were dressed in black. They seemed able to move through the tropical jungles noiselessly, disappearing almost as soon as they had been seen. Since the black-clad soldiers were not involved in any major battles, little attention was given to these reports. Few, if any, Americans knew that the men so briefly glimpsed were *ninjas*.

Ninjas first appeared in feudal Japan in the 12th century. They were the descendants of warriors who were on the losing side in wars between rival warlords. As whole families went into hiding, an alternative society, or counterculture, developed. It was based on mastery of the martial arts needed for survival within a hostile larger society.

In time, dozens of regional and family *ryu*, or schools of the warrior tradition of ninjitsu, developed. Each had its own philosophy and specialized ways of fighting. Often, the ryu of a particular region would be under the control of the local daimyo, or feudal lord. During the power struggles of medieval Japan, the ninjas became extremely valuable as spies to infiltrate enemy ranks and as assassins of leaders and authority figures. With their ability to move with stealth and their reputation for mystic powers, ninjas were sometimes able to destroy the morale of armies.

In addition to the techniques of unarmed combat, the ninja was trained to fight with sword, spear, and throwing blades. Fire and explosives were also part of the ninja arsenal. Many ninjas were skilled at preparing their own explosives from natural elements. Several of the larger ninja organizations had their own chemists to produce quantities of explosives. Traditional building materials in Japan were wood, paper, and rice straw. These burn easily. Thus, the threat of fire contributed to the fear with which the ninja was regarded.

The traditional clothing of the ninja consists of special trousers that tie onto the body and a jacket with overlapping lapels. The jacket is tucked into the trousers. The ninja also wears protective arm and hand sleeves and a tied scarf used as a combination mask and hood. This costume is made of strong, dark-colored cotton cloth. It enables the ninja to move easily and to blend with the shadows.

The medieval Japanese believed that ninjas could cloud the minds of their enemies in order to make themselves invisible. In fact, ninja training did include mind control. This had more to do, however, with the ninja's mental discipline, perseverance, and endurance, than with anything magical.

1. Explain the difference between a ninja and a samurai in medieval Japan.

2. Why do you think people study ninjitsu today?

keeping their two houses furnished and staffed with servants. The daimyos also had to help pay for public projects supported by the shogun. They had no money left over to raise armies and stockpile weapons.

Rigid Social Structure. Another measure made the Japanese social structure more rigid. Society was organized into four classes. The highest class consisted of the samurai. Second in importance were the peasants, who produced food for the state. Artisans, who produced goods less necessary than food, ranked third. Because they made money from things produced by others, merchants were placed in the lowest class.

Although the Tokugawas gave special distinction to the samurai and the peasant groups, they took away some of the advantages that these groups had formerly enjoyed. The once independent samurai now had to rely on the daimyos for their salaries and weapons. The peasants lost many of their rights. The government also taxed them so heavily that their lives became almost as hard and as limited as those of European serfs. Peasants in Japan did not, however, lose their freedom of movement. Many sought better ways of life in the towns.

Isolation. The Tokugawas were strict rulers, but they brought peace to Japan. They encouraged the growth of industry and trade. However, in the early 1600s, the shoguns became suspicious of the influence of Christians and European traders. They feared that trade would give wealth and power to rivals. The Christians, who were Roman Catholics, might put their loyalty to the Church and the pope above their loyalty to the emperor and the shogun. In 1612, the shogun forbade the teaching of Christianity and began to persecute Christians in Japan. He ordered missionaries to leave the country or be killed. He had thousands of Japanese converts executed.

The Tokugawas also restricted the activities of foreign traders. By 1641, they had closed all but one port to outsiders. Only ten Chinese ships and one Dutch ship could land each year at the port of Nagasaki. Any Japanese who was away from the country at the time could not return. Japan isolated itself from the outside world for more than 200 years.

Cultural Achievements. Japan enjoyed a long period of peace and prosperity. During this time, its culture flourished. Art lovers still marvel at the beauty and craftsmanship of the wood-block prints made during the Tokugawa Shogunate. Japanese dramatists developed a new form of theater called *kabuki*. Kabuki theater included acting, dancing, music, and colorful costumes. Other writers produced novels and poetry.

A kind of poem called the *haiku* appeared at this time. The haiku must contain exactly 17 syllables divided into three lines. These poems are usually vivid descriptions of nature. The best of them suggest

Decorative Japanese screen showing Kyoto street scene, 1700

intense emotions and deep ideas. As these new forms of art developed, the number of people educated enough to appreciate them increased. Many new schools opened in the cities. Buddhist monks and Shinto priests ran schools for village children.

INFO CHECK

1. How did geography enable the ancient Japanese to develop their culture without outside interference?

2. List three ways China influenced Japan and one way Korea affected Japanese culture.

3. Define each of the following: shogun, daimyo, samurai, Bushido.

4. State some similarities between Japanese and European feudalism. How did the Tokugawa shoguns weaken feudalism?

5. Why do you think students of Japanese culture are attracted to *kabuki* and *haiku*?

THE SUNG DYNASTY (960–1279)

The Sung came to power as rulers of China in 960. Throughout the Sung period, tribes of fierce nomads continually threatened China. These warriors came from the deserts and plains beyond the Great Wall, which guarded China's northern border.

China: The Sung Empire

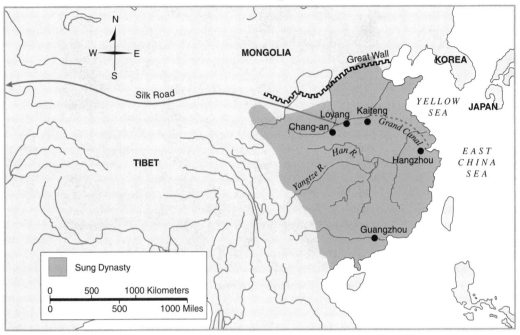

Two Empires

Early in the Sung period, nomads from Manchuria fought their way into northern China. The invaders captured the Sung emperor and began their own dynasty, the Chin Dynasty, in the north. Beijing became their capital city. The son of the captured emperor set up a new Sung capital at Hangzhou in southern China. By 1127, China split into the Chin Empire in the north and the Sung Empire in the south.

Science, Technology, and the Arts

Despite this division, advances in science, technology, and the arts continued under the Sung. Doctors developed an inoculation against smallpox. Mathematicians invented the abacus, the world's first adding machine. Soldiers began to use gunpowder as a weapon. Printers now used movable wooden type, which made it possible to produce more books in a shorter time.

Landscape painting reached its highest level during the Sung period. Potters became even more skilled in making porcelain objects. Unusual glazes gave the porcelain a rich color. The most used colors were greenish and lavender blues, transparent green, reddish brown, and whites.

Trade and Prosperity

Trade made the Sung Empire highly prosperous. Large ships carried cargoes of silk and porcelain to Korea and Japan. The ships also sailed to Southeast Asia, the Persian Gulf area, and Africa. Prosperity enabled the cities to become centers of learning and art. Hangzhou, the imperial capital, was larger than most European cities of the same period. Many streets in the capital were paved. An efficient garbage collection system kept the city clean.

Social Rights

By the 12th century, Sung China may have been the most advanced society in the world. But not everyone shared equally in its benefits. The peasants lived in poverty. The government taxed them heavily and forced them to labor on public works. The lives of Chinese peasants remained harsh until modern times.

Women in Sung China enjoyed few rights. In public, wives had to walk ten steps behind their husbands. Among the wealthy, it was fashionable to bind the feet of little girls to keep their feet small. The tight wrappings bent the toes toward the heel. This practice crippled many women. Some could not walk without support.

Military weakness and the corruption of government officials contributed to the downfall of the Sung. The problems of the Sung rulers continued until the Mongol invasion of 1279 ended their rule.

INFO CHECK

1. Explain how the Sung Empire prospered economically and culturally between A.D. 960 and 1279.

2. In what ways were women at a disadvantage in medieval China?

THE MONGOL EMPIRE

In the 13th century, nomadic Mongol horsemen in Central Asia united under a great leader named Genghiz Khan. He led his fierce warriors on a wave of conquest that lasted for 20 years. Russia and portions of the Muslim Empire fell to the Mongols. The conquests continued after Genghiz Khan died in 1227. Kublai Khan, grandson of Genghiz, became the Mongol emperor in 1260 and conquered the Sung in 1279.

The map on page 242 shows the vast size of the Mongol Empire. How did the Mongols, a relatively small group, manage to conquer such a large territory? Like other nomadic peoples, the Mongols were accomplished warriors with excellent survival skills. Herding sheep and horses on the dry, windswept steppes of their homeland had

The Mongol Empire   1300

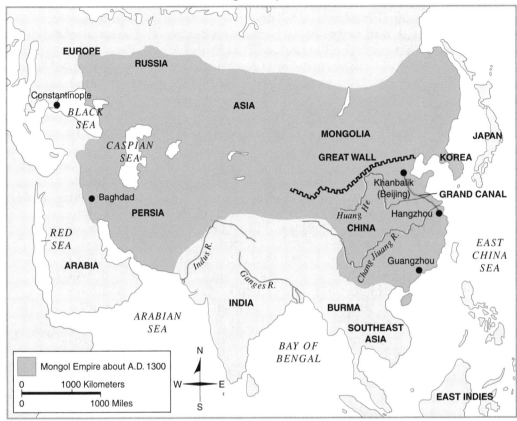

trained them to live for months with little food and rest. Hunting the small, swift animals of the steppes gave them practice in using weapons while on horseback. Then, too, Mongols were intensely loyal to their clan chiefs, men chosen for their leadership ability. The desire to win their leaders' approval made Mongol warriors courageous and well disciplined in battle.

Conquests by the Mongols

After Genghiz Khan united the Mongols, he sent elite officers to train the warriors in each tribe to be professional soldiers. Their skill in the arts of war was not the only reason for their success. They also conquered through cruelty and terror. When they took a city, they usually destroyed its buildings and killed all of its inhabitants.

Southwest Asia. Mongol soldiers destroyed Muslim cities and mosques in Southwestern Asia and Central Asia. Early Mongol rulers almost wiped out Muslim culture in these areas. In 1295, however, a Mongol ruler named Ghazan converted to Islam. Under Ghazan and his successors, Muslim culture became stronger than ever. The Mongols stimulated trade in Southwest Asia as well as in China. As long-distance trade increased, so did the flow of Western European goods and ideas to Asia.

Russia. The Mongols invaded Russia in 1237 and controlled it for about 200 years. Although the Mongols were exceptionally cruel soldiers, they were tolerant rulers. They demanded only tribute and soldiers from the Russians. The Mongol overlords did not interfere with the Russian government, religion, language, or customs.

Eastern Europe. Mongol armies swept through Hungary and Poland in 1241. This campaign might have brought large parts of central and western Europe into the Mongol Empire and changed the course of European history. But the Mongol khan (ruler) died before its completion, and the army had to return home to elect a new khan.

India. In 1398, Tamerlane, a descendant of Genghiz Khan, led his army into India. His forces destroyed the city of Delhi and slaughtered both Indian soldiers and civilians. The Mongols left India after a year. During this short time, they weakened the military power of the Delhi sultans. In 1526, India fell under the control of a new Muslim group called the Moguls.

The Yuan Dynasty (1279–1368)

In spite of their military skill, it took more than 45 years for the Mongols to conquer China. Kublai Khan completed the conquest and established the Yuan Dynasty.

Kublai Khan, ruler of the Mongol Empire, out hunting

Time Line

Year	Dates and Events

A.D.

250

250: Beginning of 450-year rule of Japan by Yamato clan; rise of Shinto as state religion

400s: Yamato attempt to conquer Korea; Japanese exposed to Chinese culture

699
604: Prince Shotoku writes constitution based on Buddhist and Confucian ideas

700
710: Beginning of Nara period in Japan; strong influence from China's Tang Dynasty

900s: Kyoto becomes new Japanese capital; emperors favor native culture

960–1279: Under Sung Dynasty, China becomes advanced but repressive society

999
1000–1871: Japan's feudal period

1000

1100s–1200s: Chinese Buddhist monks bring Zen to Japan

1127: Chin Dynasty begins rule of northern China; Sungs rule southern China

1200
1185–1333: Japanese emperor names as first shogun Minamoto clan leader Yorimoto; beginning of Kamakura Shogunate

1201
1237–1400s: Mongol invaders begin 200-year control of Russia

1244: Mongols invade Hungary and Poland; retreat after death of ruling khan

1260: Kublai Khan becomes first Mongol emperor of China

1274, 1281: Kublai Khan's two invasions of Japanese island of Kyushu turned back by typhoons ("Kamikaze")

1300
1279–1368: Kublai Khan establishes Yuan Dynasty in China

1301
1295: Ghazan, Mongol ruler of Persia, converts to Islam; stimulates flow of Muslim and western European culture to southwest Asia and China

1330s–1568: Ashikaga family control Japanese government; long period of civil wars

1368: Chu Yan-chang becomes first ruler of Ming Dynasty

1400
1398: Mongol Tamerlane invades India, destroys Delhi, retreats

1401

1500

1501
1526: India falls under control of Mogul invaders

1542: Portuguese traders arrive in Japan, introduce firearms

1550s: Jesuit and Franciscan missionaries arrive in Japan

1590–1598: Toyotomi Hideyoshi becomes ruler of unified Japan; invades Korea and China

1600
1600s: Japan forbids teaching of Christianity, expels missionaries, executes converts

1601
1600–1868: Tokugawa Ieyasu appointed shogun, moves capital to Edo (Tokyo), makes shogunate hereditary, centralizes Japanese government

1641: Shoguns initiate 200-year isolation of Japan from foreign trade and culture

1700

Restrictions and Good Works. As emperor, one of his main concerns was to prevent the Chinese from rebelling against his rule. To avoid this, he placed Mongols in all the important government positions and the Chinese in the lowest ones. He also limited the freedom of the Chinese. He made it illegal for them to own weapons, to meet in large groups, and to travel at night.

In spite of these harsh measures, Kublai Khan brought many advantages to China. He constructed roads and canals and rebuilt the city of Beijing. He gave aid to orphans and old people and provided hospitals for the sick. He also purchased food supplies in times of plenty to store away for use when famine struck.

Tolerance. Kublai Khan is famous for his tolerance. Most Mongols practiced Lamaism, the Tibetan form of Buddhism. But Kublai Khan did not force Lamaism on the lands he ruled. He allowed people in the different lands to worship in their own way. He appointed Muslims, Christians, Buddhists, and Taoists to minor posts in local governments. In China, he supported the concepts of Confucianism. Many Mongolians stationed in Persia converted to Islam. He allowed members of the Dominican and Franciscan Roman Catholic orders to set up missions in China.

Trade. Kublai Khan realized that he could obtain great wealth by developing Chinese trade. The new roads that were constructed during his rule allowed Chinese merchants to travel to Persia and Russia more easily and quickly. The Mongol policy of tolerance and good will toward different cultural groups also encouraged merchants of other countries to visit China. This policy brought a period of peace to Eurasia that is known as the "Pax Mongolia."

The increased trade resulted in more contact between China and distant lands. During this period, Marco Polo of Venice, Italy, went to China with his father and uncle, who were merchants. Polo, just 21 years old, became a favorite of Kublai Khan and remained in China for 18 years. He spent these years traveling through the empire, sometimes serving as a government official. After Polo returned to Italy in 1295, he wrote a book about what he had seen. Many of his readers refused to believe his descriptions of the size, wealth, and wonders of China. In time, however, Europeans came to accept what Polo had written as the truth. Some of the wonders he described were the burning of black stones (coal) as fuel, paper money (instead of metal coins), and an official postal system.

Other traders followed Polo's route to China. Marco Polo's book helped promote the exchange of goods and ideas between China and the West. It may have inspired later explorers to search for new lands.

A visitor from the Middle East also made his way to China. This famous Muslim traveler, Ibn Batutta, mentions China in his travel journal. He was in Beijing in the 1340s. Over a period of 30 years, Ibn Battuta traveled some 75,000 miles throughout the Middle East, southern and eastern Asia, and Africa.

Effect on China. Aside from promoting contact between China, Europe, and Southwest Asia, Mongol rule had surprisingly little effect on Chinese culture. The khans made no attempt to force Mongol culture on the Chinese. The Chinese, who looked down on the Mongols as barbarians, showed no interest in adopting any of their ways.

The Decline of the Mongol Empire

After the death of Kublai Khan in 1298, the Mongol Empire split into smaller empires. These were the Golden Horde in southern Russia and the Balkans, the Yuan Empire in China, and the Ilkhan Empire in western Asia.

The rulers who followed Kublai Khan lacked his strength and ability. As Mongol rule weakened, Chinese opposition increased. In 1368, Chu Yan-chang, who had studied to be a Buddhist monk and became a rebel leader, drove the Mongols out of Beijing. A new Chinese dynasty, the Ming, replaced Mongol rule.

Chapter 13 shows how the increased contact between East and West affected Europe's economy, politics, and culture.

INFO CHECK

1. Explain why you AGREE or DISAGREE with the following statement: Genghiz Khan was a great man and an admirable ruler.

2. List the changes brought to China by Kublai Khan. Indicate which of these you regard as most important or significant.

3. What did Marco Polo have in common with Ibn Batutta?

CHAPTER REVIEW

Multiple Choice

1. Before China heavily influenced Japan, one could describe the Japanese as

   1. writers and scholars
   2. farmers and warriors
   3. industrialists
   4. none of the above.

2. The Japanese religious belief in Shinto, or "the way of the gods," is most similar to

   1. Buddhism
   2. Hinduism
   3. Islam
   4. animism.

3. Cultural diffusion resulted in the Japanese adopting

   1. a class of warriors and a code of honor
   2. religious and bureaucratic practices

3. harmonious relations with their neighbors

4. nomadic and pastoral lifestyles.

4. Match the terms that represent social or political similarities between Japan and Europe.

1. A clan was to Japan as a dynasty was to Europe.

2. A king was to Japan as a vassal was to Europe.

3. A Zen master was to Japan as the patriarch was to Rome.

4. *The Tale of Genji* was to Japan as Homer's epics were to Greece.

5. The Tokugawas established a rigid social structure in Japan. Select the answer that correctly ranks the highest to the lowest social classes.

1. samurai, artisans, farmers, merchants

2. merchants, artisans, farmers, samurai

3. samurai, merchants, artisans, peasants

4. samurai, peasants, artisans, merchants

6. The Sung Empire became extremely wealthy because

1. it totally controlled all of the lands known as China

2. it gained great wealth from the nations it conquered

3. it discovered deposits of gold and oil in the north

4. it exported silks, porcelain, and other trade goods.

7. Women of noble families in China

1. were able to participate in social and political activities

2. were considered inferior to their husbands and suffered from footbinding practices

3. were often well educated and involved in trading ventures

4. none of the above.

8. The Mongols conquered other peoples and established several long-lasting dynasties because of their

1. vast armies and heavy cannons

2. use of secret police and repressive rule

3. hardy warriors and tolerant rule

4. hired mercenaries and religious beliefs.

9. The Yuan Dynasty is important because it

1. united the Chinese and Mongolian peoples forever

2. was the first time China was ruled by outsiders

3. encouraged religious tolerance and economic development

4. united the Chinese people to rise up and rebel against their ruler.

10. The causes leading to the decline of the Mongol and Sung empires were similar in that

1. weak leaders or conflict over who was to rule resulted in loss of power

2. natural disasters destroyed both empires' economies

3. new, more peaceful, religions destroyed the armies' spirit

4. nomadic warrior tribes from the north destroyed the empires.

11. The map on page 242 proves that

1. the Great Wall prevented Mongols from conquering China

2. Korea was not part of the Mongol Empire in A.D. 1300

3. Mongols captured Constantinople and A.D. 1300

4. The Mongol Empire included Russia and Persia.

12. Study the time line on page 244 and choose the most accurate statement.

    1. The beginning of Yamato rule of Japan and the rise of Shinto as the state religion occurred in A.D. 250.

    2. Buddhist and Confucian ideas influenced Japan's government during Japan's feudal period.

    3. Zen originated in Japan.

    4. The shoguns opened Japan to foreign trade during the 1600s.

Thematic Essays

1. Cultural diffusion influenced the development of Japan, China, and Mongolia. *Task:* Select ONE of these societies and give specific examples of the influence of cultural diffusion.

2. In East Asia, each society developed much that was unique to itself. *Task:* From among the societies presented in this chapter, select one important contribution made by each that is still valued today.

Document-Based Questions

Use your knowledge of Global History and Geography and the documents to answer the following questions.

1. From a book about Asian civilizations.

"Tea is the most wonderful medicine for nourishing one's health; it is the secret of long life. India and China both value it highly. . . . I wonder why the Japanese do not care for bitter things. In the great country of China they drink tea, as a result of which there is no heart trouble and people live long lives. Our country is full of sickly looking, skinny persons, simply because we do not drink tea."

Do you think the writer is Japanese or Chinese? Give reasons for your answer. How does this reading selection illustrate cultural diffusion?

2. Look at the illustration on page 234. How does the artist convey the function of the samurai?

3. From the Japanese government's Act of Seclusion (1636).

"1. Japanese ships shall by no means be sent abroad.

2. No Japanese shall be sent abroad. Anyone violating this prohibition shall suffer the penalty of death, and the shipowner and the crew shall be held together with the ship.

3. All Japanese residing abroad shall be put to death when they return home. . . .

11. The samurai shall not purchase goods on board foreign ships directly from foreigners."

What steps did Japan take to isolate itself from foreign influences? Why do you think this was done?

4. From a study of Asian civilizations.

"Buddhist learning is broader in scope than Confucian, but Japanese learning is even more embracing. All the various types of learning . . . are embraced in Japanese learning. . . . [The] Japanese should study all the different kinds of learning—even though they are foreign—so that they can choose the good features of each and place them at the service of the nation. . . . [The] Japanese differ from and are superior to the peoples of China, India, Russia, Holland, Siam, Cambodia, and all other countries of the world."

Describe the writer's view of Japanese culture as compared to other cultures.

Document-Based Essay

It has been said that Japanese foreign relations are like young trees that bend but do not break in a windstorm. *Task:* Using specific examples, comment on the accuracy of this statement.

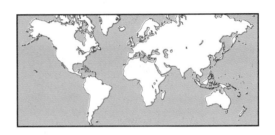

CHAPTER
13

Global Trade and Interactions

Clothilde unrolled the bolt of yellow silk in front of the window. How it glowed in the sunlight. Everything else in the room looked drab beside it. Even the colors in the tapestry hanging on the wall were gloomy compared to the shining cloth. Clothilde held a large swath of it against her face and looked into the mirror. When the seamstress made it into a gown, would it become her?

Clothilde's father had brought the cloth home from the Crusades. He had brought back so many wonderful things—spices, sugar, and perfumes. When she and her mother heard that the Muslims had captured Jerusalem and the Holy Land, they had prepared themselves to receive a broken and disappointed man. They were amazed at his enthusiasm and excitement. He even spoke admiringly of the Muslims. They had such wise doctors, such gifted musicians, such clever businesspeople. He seemed to have forgotten that they were not Christians.

He had lost a great deal of money financing his trip to the Holy Land. But even this did not seem to bother him. He would sell a part of his land and invest the money in a trading venture to Constantinople. "We will be richer than ever before," he promised.

Clothilde, a young girl of the 1300s, is living at the dawn of a new era. Her father has brought back more than luxury goods from the East. He has brought back ideas and economic practices that will drastically change European society. Chapter 12 pointed out that trade among Asia, North Africa, and Europe became more frequent during the Middle Ages. Contacts made during the Crusades—the wars between the Muslim Empire and Christian Western Europe—increased this commerce. Ideas as well as goods flowed freely between East and West. Some of the major trade centers at this time were the Chinese city of Canton, Cairo in Egypt, and the Italian port of Venice.

THE GROWTH OF EUROPEAN URBAN CENTERS

During the early Middle Ages, Europe was thinly settled and underdeveloped. Miles and miles of forest lay between the small communities that clustered around manors, forts, and monasteries. Here and there, hilltop cities with castles or cathedrals towered above the trees. Small, shabby port cities dotted Europe's coastline.

Reasons for Growth

As time passed, the landscape began to change. The forests decreased in size, and the cultivated fields of grain expanded. More roads began to wind through fields and forests. Wagons loaded with farm products creaked along the roads on their way to market villages. Cities spread down the sides of the hills on which they had been built. Fleets of ships anchored in the harbors of coastal cities. Warehouses to hold the spices and other goods brought by the ships sprang up around the harbors.

What brought about these changes? The success of European agriculture was one factor. Sturdier plows allowed farmers to ready larger fields for planting more quickly. Because farms were producing large quantities of crops, the food supply increased. With more food available, people lived longer and had more babies.

Then, too, this period was relatively peaceful. During the early Middle Ages, Muslim and Viking raids had reduced the population of most port cities. The return of peace and order made it safe for merchants to live near the sea and send their goods to faraway markets. Jobless laborers and poor nobles sought work and business opportunities in the towns.

As trade picked up, so did the demand for manufactured products. Craftspeople needed ready sources of raw materials for their products and a convenient means of transporting the finished goods. Therefore, they moved to cities near rivers and seas.

In Europe in the early 1300s, the cities with the largest populations were London, Paris, Venice, Florence, and Genoa. They were, however, far smaller than cities in the Middle East and China.

The Crusades, which began in the 11th century and ended in the

13th century, stimulated long-distance trade. Most of the Crusaders had never before been to the Byzantine Empire and the Middle East. They were amazed at the luxuries that came there from Asia. They brought silks, spices, sugar, and other goods home with them as well as new ideas about how to live. Soon more Europeans wanted to buy luxury items from the East. A brisk trade developed between Europe and the Middle East.

Italian City-States

Several city-states in northern Italy profited greatly from long-distance trade. During the early Middle Ages, many people moved away from coastal cities for fear of foreign raiders. The merchants in such cities as Genoa, Pisa, and Venice, however, continued to trade. In order to protect their harbors and their merchant ships, the leaders of these cities built up navies. These armed fleets protected trade and demonstrated the cities' power to rivals.

Even before the Crusades, Venice, which was officially part of the Byzantine Empire, had controlled trade with Constantinople. This commerce made other northern Italian cities wealthy as well. During the Crusades, the merchants of these cities found new ways of extending their influence. They provided the Crusaders with funds and transportation to the Holy Land. In exchange, the Crusaders gave

Polo expedition setting out from Venice in 1271 en route to China

European Trade Routes 1280–1500

them economic and political rights in port cities such as Acre and Tyre in the Holy Land.

As time went on, banking became a separate business. Italian bankers lent money to and invested money for other businesspeople, the nobility, and even royalty. By the 13th century, Italian banks had branches throughout the Mediterranean and Black Sea areas. They were also in Morocco, Armenia, Persia, London, Bruges, Ghent, and some Scandinavian cities.

The Hanseatic League

In the 14th century, political unrest weakened the power of the great Italian banking houses. Some of these houses had lent vast amounts of money to French and English kings. A war between France and England, called the Hundred Years' War (1337–1453), emptied the treasuries of these countries. The rulers could not pay their debts. As a result, many banks went out of business.

Because of the failure of these banks, the Italian city-states lost some of their hold on long-distance trade. A group of Scandinavian and German towns took over some of the northern markets no longer under the control of the city-states. This group, which included Lübeck, Lüneburg, Visby, Bremen, and Cologne, formed an alliance called the Hanseatic League. (*Hansa* means "company" in German.) By uniting, these cities gained control over the northern grain trade and Scandinavian fish exports. The members of this league had important business privileges all over Europe. The league remained strong from the 1100s to the 1400s.

INFO CHECK

1. Identify two causes of economic growth in Europe during the late Middle Ages.

2. Name the Italian city-states that prospered from trade in the Middle Ages. Explain how they lost power and wealth to the Hanseatic League in the 14th century.

THE EXPANSION OF CHINESE TRADE

During the 15th and 16th centuries, China enjoyed a period of stability and growth. Chu Yuan-Chang, who had studied to be a Buddhist monk, became a general. He led the Chinese in a successful revolt against Mongol rule. When he became emperor, he took the name T'ai Tsu. He was the first ruler of the Ming Dynasty (1368–1644).

T'ai Tsu, who ruled from 1368 to 1398, worked hard to rebuild China, which had been badly damaged by years of war. First he revived agriculture by organizing the peasants. He gave them seeds, tools, and animals. He made many promises. If they agreed to farm land that had been ruined by war, he promised to excuse them from paying taxes and laboring on public works for three years.

Ming Achievements

T'ai Tsu and the Ming emperors who followed him encouraged the use of new farming technology. Scientists developed a type of rice that could be harvested in 60 instead of 100 days. This meant that two plantings of rice could be made during the growing season. Thus more rice would be available to eat. Inventors designed an irrigation pump that could be worked by pedals. Farmers stocked their rice paddies with fish. (Rice is grown in fields covered by a few inches of water.) The paddies thus produced two kinds of food—rice and fish. Moreover, the fish fertilized the rice and ate malaria-bearing mosquitoes. Farmers also began to grow other crops besides rice for commercial purposes. Cotton and the indigo plant, which yields a blue dye, provided raw materials for China's textile industry.

The Ming emperors wanted to restore China's overcut forests. They required the peasants to plant millions of hardwood trees, fruit trees, and mulberry trees to feed silkworms.

The Chinese put more and more effort into producing cash crops for overseas trade. When the hardwood trees matured, carpenters used some of them to build ships for carrying fruit, spices, and textiles to foreign markets. In order to protect its merchant ships, China built up a strong navy.

Voyages of Zheng He

In the early 15th century, Ming emperors became interested in expanding Chinese trade even farther. One emperor sent a Muslim

Chinese Trade and Exploration   1400–1500

admiral named Zheng He on six expeditions between 1405 and 1433. Zheng He sailed to Sri Lanka, visited cities on the coasts of the Persian Gulf, and explored the east coast of Africa. His voyages spread Chinese influence throughout Asia and opened up new markets for Chinese goods. Zheng He also brought back a great deal of information about foreign lands. Learning about countries in Southeast Asia and about southern India encouraged some Chinese to move to these lands.

Not long after these voyages, the government ordered foreign voyages to stop. Officials apparently felt that they had learned all they needed to know about foreign lands. Perhaps, too, Ming rulers wanted to use their resources to keep out invaders from the north. Trade was confined to one or two ports.

By the late 16th century, Chinese merchants had connections with traders from all over the world. Japan traded silver for Chinese silks and porcelains. Traders in the Philippines exchanged sweet potatoes, tobacco, firearms, and silver for Chinese textiles, pottery, and paper. The Portuguese then carried the Chinese products from the Philippines to Europe. The Dutch sailed to China to buy tea, which they then traded all over Europe. Most Europeans paid for Chinese goods with silver from the Americas.

INFO CHECK

1. List the improvements brought to China by the Ming emperors.

2. What effect did the voyages of Zheng He have on China?

THE PORTUGUESE SPICE TRADE

During the early 15th century, the Portuguese led Europe in exploration of the seas. Their main objectives were the search for gold and the discovery of a sea route to the spice markets of India. The Ottoman Turks controlled the Silk Route. The Portuguese wanted to find a route they could control. Europeans valued spices because these items were unusual and scarce. Spices made food taste better and preserved it. They could also be used to produce scents that made people and homes smell better.

Prince Henry's Influence

Prince Henry of Portugal was responsible for many important advances in seamanship. His scientists improved the astrolabe and the magnetic compass. The astrolabe is an instrument used to determine

Pepper gathering in Ceylon, from an illustrated French manuscript

Model of a Portuguese caravel with its triangular sails furled

PRINCE HENRY THE NAVIGATOR

One of the people most responsible for beginning the great changes in the Age of Discovery was a member of the ruling family of Portugal—Prince Henry. He eventually came to be called "the Navigator." Born in 1394, the third son of King Joao, Henry grew to manhood in a country often at war. Like neighboring Spain, Portugal was engaged in the reconquest of lands held by Muslim forces. Henry was regarded by a historian of the time as a Crusader who wished to extend the Christian faith to Africa. At the age of 20, he persuaded his father to allow him and his brothers to attack the Muslim port of Cueta in Morocco.

In August 1415, the Portuguese fleet attacked and captured the Muslim port. In Cueta, Henry saw evidence of the riches to be obtained by trade with the African interior—spices, rugs, gold, silver, and much else. A growing desire to involve the Portuguese in this trade was the motivation for the voyages of exploration that Henry later organized.

After his victory at Cueta, Prince Henry took up residence at Sagres, a point of land on the Portuguese coast. There he established a base for sea exploration and a center for cartography (mapmaking), navigation, and shipbuilding. He was assisted by Jehuda Cresques, a Jewish cartographer from Spain. The base at Sagres also attracted Arabs, Italians from Genoa and Venice, Germans, and Scandinavians. This community developed navigational instruments and new mathematical tables for calculating a ship's location at sea. The caravel, a new type of ship, was developed at the port of Lagos.

Prince Henry's first success was the discovery of the Canary and Azores Islands in the Atlantic Ocean. His explorers were aided by Bartolemeu Perestrello, into whose family Christopher Columbus would later marry. Colonists sent to these islands returned substantial supplies of timber, sugar, and wheat to Portugal.

South of the Canary Islands lay Cape Bojador. Exploration of the African coast south of this cape was Henry's main objective. However, the reefs and difficult currents around Cape Bojador had convinced most seamen that the coast of Africa could not be navigated beyond this point. From 1424 to 1434, Henry sent out 15 expeditions. None of them dared to pass the cape, believing that the currents were too strong for their ships. Finally, a captain named Gil Eannes avoided the shallows near Cape Bojador. He sailed westward into the open sea before turning east again in order to round the cape. In the years that followed, Henry's ships explored farther and farther south along Africa's west coast. A supply of slaves and other African trade goods began to flow to Portugal.

By the time of Prince Henry's death in 1460, the Portuguese had reached Cape Palmas in Liberia. A trading post had also been established in the Cape Verde Islands, west of present-day Senegal. Henry's work inspired Portugal to search for an all-water route around Africa to the rich markets of Asia.

- PROVE or DISPROVE this statement: The Age of Exploration and Discovery was a direct result of the work of Prince Henry the Navigator.

the angle of the sun, stars, and planets above the horizon. It helps sailors know their location on the sea. The compass tells you where north is and helps you know in what direction you are traveling. The scientists worked with shipbuilders and ship captains to develop the light and speedy *caravel*. Compared with other ships of the time, the caravel was faster, sturdier, and easier to steer. It made use of a new type of rudder called the sternpost. Another of the caravel's advantages was its ability to maintain a high speed against the wind. Its triangular sails could be turned more easily than the rectangular ones used on earlier ships.

The Gold Trade

Portuguese explorers first sailed south along the western coast of Africa. The most important African gold markets were located in the Songhai Empire in western Africa west of the Niger River. Before the Portuguese expeditions to Africa, Europeans had to buy gold from Muslim traders. They carried it from Gao and Timbuktu across the Sahara to Mediterranean ports. The Muslims needed to pay for the expenses of their journey and make a profit. They therefore demanded a high price for the gold. By trading directly with the Africans, the Portuguese were able to buy gold more cheaply. Then, too, the trip by water was faster than the trip by land. By 1500, the Portuguese controlled the African gold trade.

Rounding Africa

Portuguese explorers next sought a water route to the spice markets of South Asia. In 1488, Bartolomeu Dias sailed around the Cape of Good Hope, the southern tip of Africa. Vasco da Gama followed Dias. His voyage, which lasted from 1497 to 1499, took him all the way to India. After da Gama returned to Portugal with spices and other luxury goods, the king sent trading ships to India. The traders established posts in India, as they had in Africa, and dealt directly with the Indians. The Portuguese now dominated the spice trade as well as the gold trade. (For more details, see Chapter 17.)

Securing the Trade Routes

Taking control of the spice trade was not as easy as taking control of the gold trade. Before the arrival of the Portuguese, the Muslims had been the chief carriers of spices from India to Europe. To protect this business, they had built forts along the coast of India. The Portuguese had to take the forts by force.

The Portuguese moved into these forts and used them as trading posts and military bases. Their foothold on the coast of India later helped them to take over the city of Goa on the west coast of India. They then extended their influence deeper into Asia. Their strong military presence in Africa enabled the Portuguese to colonize parts of that continent and to gain control of the slave trade there.

Other Europeans competed with the Portuguese in looking for sea routes to India. In 1492, five years before da Gama began his successful voyage to India, the monarchs of Spain (Ferdinand and Isabella) sent Christopher Columbus to find a westward sea route to Asia. When Columbus landed on an island in the Americas, he opened up entirely new areas of contact for Europe. As Europeans gained more knowledge about different parts of the world, they began to change many features of their society.

INFO CHECK

1. How did Prince Henry the Navigator help Portugal to become a maritime power?

2. What did Bartolomeu Dias and Vasco da Gama contribute to Portuguese control of the spice trade and the gold trade?

3. How did the voyage of Christopher Columbus in 1492 differ from the Portuguese voyages of exploration?

THE BUBONIC PLAGUE

Although European society made many important advances during the Middle Ages, its progress had serious setbacks. The 14th century was a particularly difficult time for Europeans. The increased contact with other areas of the world brought more than ideas and products to Mediterranean ports.

Causes of the Setbacks

In the early 1300s, grain, livestock, and dairy products became extremely expensive in the countries of northern Europe. Agriculture had expanded, but it could not meet the needs of the increased population.

A series of harsh winters made the situation worse. Because of the severe storms and low temperatures, historians call this period "the Little Ice Age." Rough and frigid weather ruined wheat, oat, and hay crops. As food for humans and animals became more scarce, prices rose. In 1318, European farmers suffered another blow when an epidemic killed much of their livestock. Great numbers of people starved to death because they could not find or pay for the food they needed. Those who survived the famine were undernourished and, therefore, more likely to get diseases.

A New Disease Arrives

In 1347, an even worse disaster struck the weakened European population. It began when a ship from Genoa in northern Italy docked in the Sicilian port city of Messina. The ship was returning from a trading post in the Black Sea port of Caffa. Many of its crew members and passengers had large black swellings in their armpits and groin. Sores called boils and dark bruises covered their bodies. Others, with more severe types of the illness, burned with fever, coughed, and spat up blood. Within a few days, the stricken people died. As the ship lay at anchor, some black rats scurried off it and ran into the city. In this way, the bubonic plague, known as the Black Death, entered Europe.

About a year before the arrival of the plague ship, travelers had returned from Asia with frightening news. A devastating disease was spreading from China to Central Asia, India, Persia, Mesopotamia, Syria, Egypt, and Asia Minor. According to these travelers, the disease was wiping out the populations of entire countries. After listening to many of these reports, Pope Clement VI estimated the death toll of the disease in Asia to be about 23,840,000. Having no knowledge of the ways in which diseases can move from place to place, Europeans did not expect it to infect them.

The Spread of the Black Death

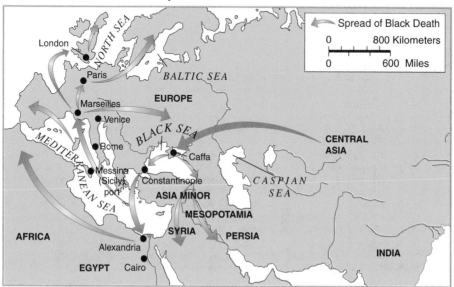

The people of Messina, therefore, did not prevent ships from the East from entering their harbor. Only when several citizens began to show symptoms like those of the dying passengers, did the city leaders force the plague ship back out to sea. Unfortunately, this measure was not in time to save Messina and the rest of Europe. The ship's rats, which were infested with fleas that carried the deadly bacillus, had already burrowed into people's homes.

Soon other infected ships arrived in Venice, Genoa, and Marseilles. From these ports, the plague spread deeper and deeper inland. In time, it made its way west to the British Isles, north to Scandinavia, and east to Hungary.

No one knows how many people the disease killed. Historians of today estimate that it killed about one-third of Europe's population. In Cairo, when the plague was at its worst, more than 7,000 people died each day. Modern scholars claim that the plague did not originate in China, as the rumors of the time stated. They believe that it started in central Asia and was carried through the East by traders.

Reaction of the People

Because medical knowledge was so limited, doctors could not cure the disease. Many blamed its spread on a strange and sinister property of the air. Bigoted people claimed that the Jews had joined in a conspiracy to kill Christians and, to accomplish this goal, had poisoned all the drinking water in Europe. Pope Clement VI tried to stop

Jews being burned alive by Christians, as fears of the Black Death spread

Time Line

Year	Dates and Events
A.D. **1001**	
1100	**1095–1291:** Crusades stimulate trade between Europe and Byzantium and the Middle East **1100s–1400s:** Hanseatic League of German and Scandinavian towns increasingly controls northern European grain and fish trade
1101	
1200	**1200s:** Feudal manors begin to break up as money is used to buy goods and services
1201	**1200s:** Italian banks set up branches in England, Belgium, Scandinavia, Mediterranean and Black Sea regions, North Africa, Middle East
	1294: Philip IV of France taxes Roman Catholic Church in France, imprisons Pope Boniface VIII, installs a French pope at Avignon; beginning of decline of Church's political power
1300	**1300s:** "Little Ice Age" and livestock epidemics bring famine to northern Europe
1301	**1337–1453:** Hundred Years' War between France and England **1347:** Bubonic plague (Black Death) spreads from Asia to Sicily, Europe, Britain **1368–1644:** Rule of China by Ming Dynasty; advances in agricultural technology, new cash crops for foreign trade with Asia, Philippines, Europe **1378:** Florentine wool workers rebel against city government **1378:** Elections of Avignon pope and Roman pope lead to Great Schism **1381:** English peasants rebel against high taxes
1400	**1394–1460:** Advances in navigation, spurred by Prince Henry the Navigator, enhance trade by sea
1401	**1405–1433:** Expeditions by Zheng He take Chinese culture and goods to new markets throughout Asia **1417:** Election of one Roman pope for all Europe; end of Great Schism **1488:** Portuguese explorer Bartolomeu Dias sails around Cape of Good Hope (Africa)
1500	**1492:** Christopher Columbus leads Spanish expedition in quest for westward sea route to Asia
1501	**1497–1499:** Expedition of Vasco da Gama begins Portuguese domination of spice trade with India **1500s:** Portuguese control of gold trade by sea with Africa; elimination of costly land routes **1500s:** Religious reformers begin to establish non-Catholic forms of Christianity
1600	

the resulting violence against the Jews. He pointed out that they, too, were dying of the plague. Nevertheless, mobs attacked Jews and burned their homes.

Some people believed that the sickness was a punishment from God. A number of these, called flagellants, tried to avoid divine wrath by forming processions and beating themselves. ("Flagellate" means to whip or punish by whipping.) Many people, who believed that the flagellants were sacrificing themselves to help others, revered and supported them. The flagellants felt that the Church was not doing enough to help people and criticized it severely. Although they were not priests, the leaders of the flagellants often listened to confessions and imposed penances. Some even attacked the clergy and took over churches. Because of the popularity of the flagellants, the leaders of the Catholic Church did not dare to put down the movement.

A few educated people noticed that the plague was worse in the crowded cities and moved to the country. A wealthy Moroccan called Ibn Abu Madyan successfully protected his family from the plague by isolating them on his country estate. While there, he made sure that the members of his household took no food and water from outside sources.

The Black Death preyed on the people of Europe, Asia, and North Africa for many years. After its initial attack in 1347, it struck again in the 1360s and the 1370s. A serious outbreak occurred as late as the 1700s. In later times, less severe episodes of the disease continued to crop up in cities all over the world. Not until the early 20th century did scientists develop effective methods of prevention and a cure.

Social and Economic Impact of the Plague

A period of social unrest followed the plague years. Many children had lost their parents. Appointed guardians often took advantage of their charges' youth and robbed them of their inheritance. Poor and homeless people banded together and raided farms and inadequately defended towns. Many monks and priests, who had cared for the sick, caught the disease from their patients and died. Since most educators of the time came from the clergy, illiteracy became a problem. With the reduction in population, cities declined. Manufacturing and trade fell off. As goods became scarce, prices rose.

The reduction in population at first benefited working people. There was now a shortage of laborers. Serfs, encouraged by the availability of jobs, fled to the towns. Peasants forced landlords to lower their rents by threatening to work on other manors. Artisans and craftspeople were in such great demand that they could now bargain for higher wages.

The shift in power between masters and servants made the upper classes uneasy. Rulers passed laws to fix all wages at the lower, pre-plague rates and to put stricter limits on the freedom of serfs. They

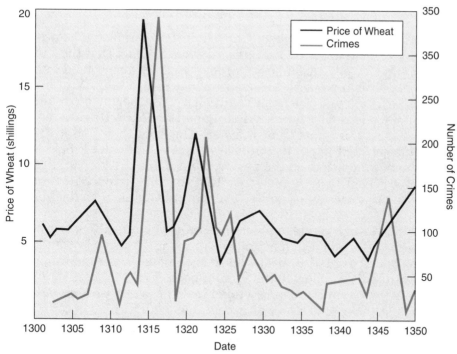

Wheat Prices and Crime in 14th-Century England

also raised the taxes of those workers who made more money than others.

The members of the working class were now aware of their own strength and did not submit to the new laws easily. Throughout Europe, peasants began to rebel against their oppressive masters. In 1358, a group of French peasants rose against their landlords. They burned castles and manors and killed the lords and their families. The revolt had not been organized very carefully. The lords called out their armies and easily overcame the peasants.

In 1381, English peasants, enraged by new and crushing taxes, burned tax records and attacked the homes of rich people. Their success in the country encouraged them to march on London. They killed two royal officials and threatened King Richard II. To secure his safety, the king made many promises to the peasants. He did not keep his promises and later ordered the leaders of the revolt to be killed.

Similar revolts took place in Germany and Italy. In Florence, a group of wool workers rebelled against the city leaders in 1378. The workers managed to take control of the government for six weeks before an army put them down. Although none of these uprisings was successful, they demonstrated that the social order was changing. The wealthy and powerful began to realize that they could no longer take the submissiveness of the poor and weak for granted.

Impact of the Plague on the Catholic Church

Conflicts existed between Church and rulers long before the plague. Medieval kings had always resented the fact that the Church did not have to pay taxes on its property. They also considered the Church's political power a threat. In 1294, King Philip IV of France decided to challenge the pope's authority. He began by requiring Church officials to pay taxes. When Pope Boniface VIII resisted this ruling, King Philip took him prisoner. The king then had a French clergyman elected pope in Boniface's place. Under the king's influence, the new pope moved the papacy from Rome to Avignon, France. (The popes lived in Avignon from 1309 to 1377.) By continuing to influence the selection of popes, French kings gained control of the Church.

The situation became more complicated when, in 1378, two popes were elected—one in Avignon and one in Rome. France, Scotland, and parts of Spain wanted to keep the French pope. The remaining European countries supported the Roman pope. This religious conflict is known as the Great Schism. It ended in 1417, when Church officials met and elected a pope who was acceptable to all European countries. Thereafter, the popes remained in Rome.

These political power struggles weakened people's respect for the Church. More people turned away from it when they witnessed its helplessness against the plague. Others felt contempt when they saw members of the clergy taking advantage of the sick and dying to enrich themselves. Among other greedy acts, many priests charged high prices for administering the last rites to victims of the plague.

People began to criticize the clergy for being grasping, corrupt, and ineffective. Leaders of the Church called these critics *heretics* and burned many of them at the stake. The Church could not entirely destroy this opposition. In the 1500s, a group of religious reformers managed to establish other forms of Christianity besides Catholicism.

Many historians consider the voyages of discovery and the plague to be two of the most important factors that shaped modern Western society. The next chapter introduces the development of other important features of this society. They are capitalism, humanism, and Protestantism.

INFO CHECK

1. Describe the difficulties encountered by Europeans in the 14th century.

2. If you had lived in Europe during the 14th century, what arguments would you have presented to those who blamed the Jews and criticized the Roman Catholic Church for the Black Death?

3. How did the plague lead to workers' revolts in France, England, Germany, and Italy?

CHAPTER REVIEW

Multiple Choice

1. Select the reasons for the growth of European urban centers.

    1. agriculture improved and population increased
    2. peace and order returned
    3. the demand for manufactured products increased
    4. all of the above.

2. Even before the Crusades, Italian bankers became wealthy because they controlled

    1. military arms development in Italy
    2. loans made to Arab merchants
    3. trade with Byzantium
    4. the treasury of the Holy Roman Emperor.

3. The name of the economic organization formed by German and Scandinavian cities to control trade was the

    1. Kroner League
    2. Alborg League
    3. Aachen League
    4. Hanseatic League.

4. The Ming Dynasty's expansion of Chinese influence and long-range trade resulted from

    1. the conquest of Japan
    2. the voyages of Admiral Zheng He's fleet
    3. the expulsion of foreigners
    4. all of the above.

5. The European desire for spices, silks, and gold encouraged the development or improvement of the

    1. magnetic compass
    2. astrolabe
    3. caravel
    4. all of the above.

6. As a result of the voyages of Bartolomeu Dias and Vasco da Gama

    1. Portugal gained control of the European spice and gold trade
    2. Italy gained control of the European spice trade
    3. trading posts were established in Canton
    4. trading posts were established in Kiev.

7. The bubonic plague came about because

    1. a famine forced people to eat unclean foods
    2. a minor earthquake destroyed the water and sewer treatment plants
    3. trading ships carrying infected rats docked at several European ports
    4. infected cows were sold in the European marketplaces.

8. The bubonic plague changed the economic relationship between the upper and lower classes of Europe. This occurred because

    1. jobs were plentiful and peasants and craftspeople were in scarce supply
    2. there were fewer jobs because of the population decline
    3. nobles paid less because they needed less
    4. nobles raised wages because the plague was a warning sign from God.

9. The Great Schism of 1378 refers to a

   1. power struggle between the emperors of Rome and Byzantium
   2. power struggle between the head of the Roman Catholic Church and the head of the Greek Orthodox Church
   3. power struggle between the French king and the pope
   4. debate over accepting icons and statues within the Muslim holy places.

10. After the bubonic plague ended, the European ruling class attempted to regain economic control of the people by taxes and regulations. The immediate results of these actions were

    1. workers boycotting and peacefully picketing their workplaces
    2. governments requiring the nobles to pay fair wages for an eight-hour workday
    3. workers accepting the return to lower wages
    4. attacks by peasants and workers against nobles and tax collectors.

11. Study the map on page 253 and decide which statement is correct.

    1. Antioch, Damascus, and Tyre were on the trade routes controlled by the Hanseatic League.
    2. Vienna and Kiev were not on major trade routes.
    3. The Italian city-states controlled the North Sea trade routes.
    4. Trade routes through the North and Baltic seas were controlled by the Hanseatic League.

12. The time line on page 263 indicates that

    1. the Ming Dynasty ruled China from 1368 to 1644
    2. feudal manors began to break up in the 1800s

    3. Portuguese and Spanish voyages of exploration began in 1294
    4. Europe experienced extreme cold and famine in the 1500s.

Thematic Essays

1. The development of global trade in the late Middle Ages increased contact between Europe and other lands. *Task:* Discuss the activities of the Italian city-states and the Hanseatic League.

2. Trade and banking made some peoples and nations wealthy and powerful. *Task:* Select one European and one Asian society or people. Describe the policies, actions, or practices that they used to become wealthy and powerful.

Document-Based Questions

1. Study the illustration on page 262. How do you think the townspeople justified their actions?

2. Study the chart on page 265. What relationship does the chart show? Give reasons to explain the relationship.

3. The following is from a book about Florence and Siena after the Black Death.

   "... men thought that, through the death of so many people, there would be an abundance of all produce of the land; yet, on the contrary ... most commodities were more costly, ... And the price of labor, and the products of every trade and craft rose in disorderly fashion. ..."

   Discuss the social and economic results of the Black Death.

4. The following is from a book about Florence and Siena after the Black Death.

   "In both Florence and Siena the laws controlling immigration were relaxed, and special privileges, and a rapid grant of citizenship, or exemption from taxes were offered to badly needed artisans or professional men, such as physicians. . . ."

What caused the governments of both Florence and Siena to alter their policies about immigration and skilled people?

Document-Based Essay

Task: Using specific examples, discuss positive and negative economic and social consequences related to the bubonic plague (Black Death).

CHAPTER
14

Major Developments in Europe: The Beginning of Modern Times

Otto had spent all day assisting his master, the blacksmith, at the forge. He was hot and covered with soot from the fire. One of the horses Otto had held for his master to shoe had repeatedly tried to bite him. Tonight, he would dream of the horse's great yellow teeth and rolling eyes. Otto was lucky that his father had taught him how to handle animals.

Otto would never be a peasant like his father. The old man had scraped together enough money to make him a blacksmith's apprentice. From the blacksmith, Otto would learn how to make metal shoes for horses, tools, weapons, and other items. He had to earn enough to pay the blacksmith back for his training. If he became really skilled, he might become an important person in this town and make his family proud.

He thought of Gretchen, the goldsmith's plump daughter. Ah, if only he could learn how to shape gold instead of iron. Gretchen would never look at a dirty blacksmith.

Otto is a young man living at the end of the Middle Ages. Had he been born a few centuries earlier, he could not have chosen his work or place of residence. He would probably have been a serf, bound to the land on which he worked. Now he has some freedom of choice. He has even learned to dream of greater opportunities. Perhaps he will make it possible for his sons to become prosperous businessmen.

Why were the people of this period, the 14th century, able to move up on the social scale? Many poor people died during the time of the Black Death. This meant that there were not enough people to work as farmers and artisans. To keep peasants working on their manors, many landlords reduced their rents. Some peasants, like Otto's father, could use the money they made from selling their produce for other purposes besides rent. They could help their children gain new skills. These skills would make it possible for the children to have a better life than their parents.

REVIVAL OF EUROPE

As people moved to the cities, they found new ways to become prosperous. Trade offered opportunities for making money. Trade opened up the world for Europeans of all classes. As a result, it transformed their culture. The wealth and ideas gained from new trading opportunities drastically changed the way that Europeans, such as Otto, lived, worked, and thought.

The Growth of Cities

Most people of the early Middle Ages lived on manors. These were self-sufficient communities. They produced all they needed to survive within the community. Serfs and peasants planted crops and raised livestock to produce food for everyone. Weavers, blacksmiths, and other craftspeople lived in the small villages that were part of the manor. They supplied all the clothing, tools, weapons, and other goods needed by the lords, their families, and their servants.

Trade. Gradually, agricultural methods improved. Crops gave greater yields. Manors produced more than could be used by the people who lived on them. The surplus was sold. Money could be used to buy other goods. The number of traders and merchants increased. They provided the services of buying, selling, and manufacturing goods. Workers were needed to make products. Traders, merchants, and workers came together in towns. As time passed, some towns grew larger and became cities.

Long-distance trade made cities more important than manors to the European economy. Cities served as ports to receive ships carrying products and as places where things could be manufactured to sell. People set up workshops, mills, and factories near cities to make simple items, such as soap, tile, varnish, and paper. Groups of people joined together to make more complex products, such as textiles, glass, and metal objects.

Effect on Serfs. The growth in industry created more jobs. Skilled and unskilled workers, such as Otto in the opening story, moved to cities to look for employment. Serfs ran away from manors to seek a better life. If serfs could avoid capture by their masters for a year and a day, they were legally free. As time passed, the lords began to free those serfs who remained on the land. They wanted money to buy the novelties and luxuries arriving from the Middle East and eastern Asia. One way to get money was to make their serfs pay rent.

Increase in Influence of Cities

As cities became larger and richer, they began to acquire more political influence. Kings turned to wealthy businesspeople to help them finance defense and public works, such as roads. Businesspeople realized that public works benefited them and their cities. Roads, for example, connected towns and helped trade. In exchange for their money, kings gave special rights and privileges to city dwellers.

One of the most important of these rights was the city charter. The charter made cities independent of the manorial system by allowing them to govern themselves. City leaders could set up their own law courts and make rules for conducting business. A mayor, who was

Leaders of a medieval town reading its new charter to the citizens

elected by the merchants, usually managed a city. Because it was to their advantage to keep the king in power, the townspeople usually sided with him in disputes with the lords.

The Guilds

Guilds had been especially active in obtaining many of the rights and privileges enjoyed by city dwellers. Medieval guilds were organizations that protected businesspeople and set good business practices. Merchants who were members of a town guild could trade in that town without buying a license. Guild regulations made sure that all guild members got a chance to sell goods that were limited in supply. This rule benefited buyers as well as merchants. If only one merchant controlled the entire stock of a desirable item, he or she could charge high prices for it.

Craft guilds set standards for the quality of the work produced by craftspeople. They regulated the number of products that could be made and the prices that could be charged. These rules helped the guild members by guaranteeing the high quality of their workmanship. They also protected customers from high prices and shoddy goods. Craftspeople often taught their craft to young people, called *apprentices*, who worked in the shops to pay for their education. By limiting the number of trainees a craftsperson could take on, craft guilds made sure that the young people received good training. (Otto, from the opening story, was an apprentice to a blacksmith.)

Guilds admitted women as members. Because more women worked at crafts than engaged in trade, most joined craft rather than merchant guilds. The craft guilds did not treat men and women equally, however. They often permitted craftsmasters to pay women less than men for doing the same work. Although many medieval women were the heads of households, the craft leaders claimed that they needed less money than men.

INFO CHECK

1. Describe the impact of the growth of trade on feudal life and the manorial system.

2. Explain how guilds benefited both workers and consumers.

THE COMMERCIAL REVOLUTION

As trade and shopkeeping became a more important part of the economy, new business practices came about. Merchants and traders looked for ways to get money to develop new businesses and trade routes. The change from feudalism and manorialism to business and trade is called the *Commercial Revolution*.

The Rise of Capitalism

A new economic system, called *capitalism*, developed. Merchants began to use the money they made from trade to build businesses. Money invested in a business is called *capital*, and the investors are called *capitalists*. The businesses set up by capitalists were not regulated by guilds. Under capitalism, merchants did not have to share supplies of desirable goods with other merchants. They did not have to control their prices.

One of the large European industries built by capitalists was cloth manufacturing. Merchant-capitalists paid weavers to make woolen cloth in their homes. Making goods in the home is the *domestic system* of manufacturing. The capitalists paid for the raw materials (wool, in this case) and labor and sold the finished goods at a profit.

Capitalists began to form *joint-stock companies*. Scholars point out that Muslims had been the first to develop this kind of organization. To raise large amounts of capital, merchants combined their funds. Each partner received shares, or stock, in the company in return for the money contributed. This money was then invested in a business project. The large investment made possible by the joint-stock company often led to large profits. The investors then shared the profits in the form of *dividends*. These are the total profit divided by the number of shares. The size of a partner's dividend depended on the amount of money invested in the company. If the company ran into problems, losses were spread among all stockholders, thus lowering the risk.

Role of the Middle Class

The businesspeople in the towns became the new middle class of Europe. Some of these now prosperous craftspeople and merchants were the children of serfs or had once been serfs themselves.

The nobility considered middle-class people to be inferior to them. They felt that only noble or high birth could determine a person's value. Church leaders also looked down on the merchants. The Church felt that businesspeople considered it more important to make money than to save their souls.

As the manorial system began to decline, more nobles needed money to maintain their lifestyle and political influence. They borrowed from businesspeople and even invested in commercial enterprises. The importance of the middle class to the monarch increased because of the taxes they paid. The nobility began to matter less to the monarch. There were fewer of them than the middle-class members, and they paid less in taxes.

Rise of the Atlantic Powers

The explorations described in Chapter 13 brought businesspeople even more wealth and influence. They also caused economic and political power to shift from the Italian city-states to countries along the Atlantic coast.

Spain, Portugal, England, the Netherlands, and France sent explorers to establish colonies in the Americas, Asia, and Africa. From these colonies, new products and riches flowed into Madrid, Lisbon, London, Amsterdam, and Paris. The dramatic increase in trade raised the standard of living of Europeans.

In the colonies, the reverse happened. The way of life of the local people (non-Europeans) was radically changed. Many were forced to do hard labor for long hours to provide riches for the new rulers. This type of work, such as mining for silver and gold, was not part of their traditional ways. The life of the local inhabitants did not usually improve with the coming of the Europeans. It got worse.

As trade increased, the economic well-being of Europe became more dependent on the economic growth of the colonies. Businesspeople in Europe invested money in sugar and tobacco plantations (large farms) in America and in coffee plantations in Asia. The profits of the investors depended on the success of their overseas business operations. A type of global economy began to develop.

From Spain's American colonies came large amounts of gold and silver. This helped the growth of businesses in Europe. More goods were made and sold. More money circulated. Workers received higher wages. With their wages, they could buy more goods.

European governments became stronger. Rulers were able to collect more taxes. Increased wealth enabled them to create larger armies and build more ships. By granting trading privileges and special licenses, rulers were able to strengthen the support given them by businesspeople.

Mercantilism

The increase in global trade led to the development of a new economic theory. It was called *mercantilism*. According to this theory, colonies existed only to enrich their founding, or home, country. The colonies sent to the home country raw materials needed for its industries. Products manufactured from the raw materials in the home country were sold back to the colonies at a profit. This kept more wealth flowing into the home country than leaving it. Most European mercantilists believed that such a favorable balance of trade would keep a nation prosperous. Colonies were not allowed to produce manufactured goods. They could sell their products only to the ruling country, not directly to any other country.

The wealth of a country was determined by how much gold or silver it held. These precious metals could come from mines the country owned or through trade. Colonies could be a controlled source of gold and silver.

The mercantilists also believed in the use of tariffs (taxes on imported goods) to protect home industries from competition. Taxes on

Trading Empires in the 1500s and 1600s

NORTH AMERICA
NEW SPAIN
Mexico City
Vera Cruz
Acapulco
FLORIDA
CUBA
HAITI
PUERTO RICO
CURACAO (Neth.)
Cartagena
Panama
SPANISH MAIN
NEW GRANADA
Quito
GUIANA
SOUTH AMERICA
Lima
PERU
Bahia
BRAZIL
Rio de Janeiro
Santiago
Buenos Aires
Cape Horn
Strait of Magellan
ATLANTIC OCEAN
PACIFIC OCEAN
NETHERLANDS
ENGLAND
PORTUGAL
Madrid
Lisbon
Cape Verde
GOLD COAST
N
W
E
S
Portuguese Control
Spanish Control
Portuguese Trade Routes
Spanish Trade Routes
Dutch Trade Routes
0 1500 3000 Kilometers
0 1500 3000 Miles

imported goods raised the prices of these goods. This encouraged people to buy the cheaper goods manufactured in their own country rather than foreign-made goods.

Mercantilism helped the industries of the Atlantic nations to grow. It also strengthened royal governments. Through taxation, rulers gained more control over the economies of their countries. This increased national unity. Mercantilism, therefore, made the Atlantic nations of Europe economically and politically strong.

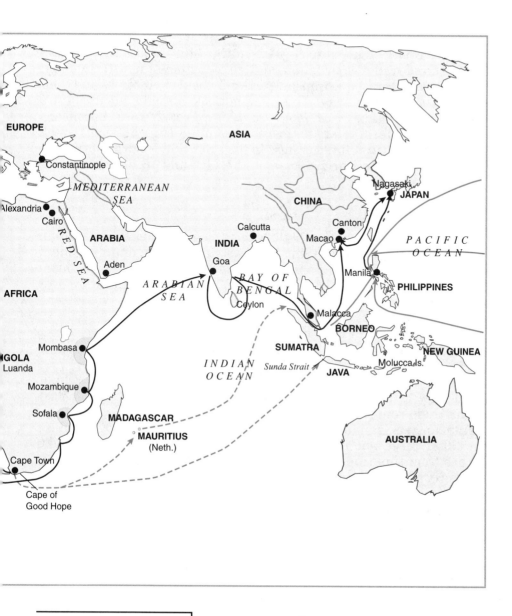

1. Summarize the role of each of the following in the Commercial Revolution: capitalism, domestic system, joint stock companies, dividends, the middle class.

2. List the Atlantic powers. How did they begin the development of a global economy?

3. Define mercantilism. How did it make the Atlantic powers economically and politically stronger?

THE RENAISSANCE AND HUMANISM

Many broad changes took place in the 1400s and early 1500s—expansion of trade, exploration, and introduction of new technology. These changes caused Europeans to think about themselves and their world in a different way. This new outlook brought about an era known as the *Renaissance*. *Renaissance* is a French word that means "rebirth." This term refers to the renewed interest in classical (Greek and Roman) culture. It also refers to the remarkable surge of creativity that occurred in Europe between the 14th and 16th centuries.

Beginnings in Italy

This intellectual and artistic rebirth began in northern Italy in the 15th century. At that time, Italy was a collection of independent city-states. The popes in Rome controlled the Papal States in central Italy. The Holy Roman Emperors of Germany had authority over northern Italy. Until the 19th century, no one ruler was strong enough to unify Italy.

The city-states of Italy during the Renaissance did not get along with one another. Wars, revolts, political plots, and assassinations occurred often.

Amid this unrest existed great wealth. Overseas trade brought fabulous wealth to Italy, particularly to the northern city-states. Most of the trade routes from the Middle East and Asia led to the Mediterranean Sea. Italian merchants sent ships to Arab ports to purchase the silks, spices, and jewels of China, India, and other Eastern lands. Riches from this trade poured into the city-states of Venice, Genoa, Florence, and Milan.

The rich merchants and bankers of these cities rivaled nobles in political influence. In order to keep their power, princes began to engage in business ventures. Instead of castles and manors in the country, princes and lords built elegant palaces in the cities.

The Medicis

Each of the city-states had its own government, which was usually run by the members of a prominent family. The Medicis, a family of bankers in Florence, Italy, were one of the most famous of these families. Although not the official rulers, they controlled the government of Florence from 1434 to 1737.

The Medicis and other ruling families used some of their wealth to encourage artists, scientists, and other creative thinkers. They hired the most creative people of the age to work on projects and rewarded their efforts magnificently. Because these powerful people helped artists and bought their productions, they were called *patrons* of the arts.

A Shift in Thinking

During the Middle Ages, artists and other creative people had worked for the Church. As a result, their creations were usually religious in nature. Even when medieval scholars studied and commented on the ideas of Greek philosophers, they gave Christian meanings to these ideas.

Under the patronage of princes and merchants, artists and philosophers became interested in worldly matters. This focus on things that can be experienced in the here-and-now is called *secularism*. Even when artists produced works with religious subjects, the works were done in a realistic style. Unlike most medieval artists, Renaissance artists usually emphasized the muscles and bone structures of their subjects' bodies—even when these subjects were angels and saints.

Explorers brought back new information about the world. The increase in knowledge made the people of the Renaissance more open to new ideas than the people of the Middle Ages had been. They enjoyed trying different ways of doing things. Some individuals developed great skill in many areas of learning and the arts. Even today, we call an individual with many talents and interests a "Renaissance person."

Art and Architecture

Many of the best-known and most talented of the Renaissance artists and writers were citizens of Florence. This city-state became Italy's great center of beauty, learning, and creativity. In some ways, it was like Athens, the leading city-state of ancient Greece.

Leonardo. Leonardo da Vinci (lived 1452–1519) was one of the geniuses who lived in Florence. He is regarded as the best example of a Renaissance person. In addition to being a great painter, he was a sculptor, an architect, a scientist, and an engineer. His paintings include *Mona Lisa* and *The Last Supper*, both masterpieces. In his sketchbooks there are designs for a flying machine, a bicycle, a machine gun, and a submarine. He planned a canal system and several buildings for the city of Milan. In addition, da Vinci studied botany, anatomy, and biology.

Michelangelo. Another citizen of Florence, Michelangelo Buonarroti (lived 1475–1564) was also a man with many talents. He was a painter, sculptor, architect, and poet. Lorenzo di Medici, ruler of Florence, hired Michelangelo to create many works of art for him.

Lorenzo di Medici, ruler of Florence and patron of the arts

Another famous patron was Pope Julius II. At his command, Michelangelo painted events from the Bible on the ceiling of the Sistine Chapel in Rome. When he was 45, Michelangelo took up architecture. His most famous works in this field are the dome on top of Saint Peter's Church in the Vatican and the square of buildings that form the civic center of Rome.

Palladio. Andrea Palladio (lived 1508–1580) was one of the most important architects of the Renaissance. He also wrote a book to explain his architectural theories. Many architects of the time studied the book and used Palladio's theories in their own building projects. When designing a building, Palladio was greatly influenced by ancient Roman architecture. He designed the Church of San Giorgio Maggiore in Venice, palaces, public buildings, private homes, and a theater near the city of Vicenza.

Literature

Humanism. *Humanism* was an important movement in Renaissance literature. Humanists wanted people to improve their lives through learning and new experiences. They urged people to study the literature of ancient Greece and Rome. The classical writers, they believed, could teach important ideas about life, love, and beauty. Humanists glorified the individual and world in which they lived. Religious topics did not interest them as much.

Dante. Dante Alighieri (lived 1265–1321) was one of the first writers considered by scholars to have Renaissance characteristics. He is best known for a long poem called the *Divine Comedy*. Although the highly religious theme of the poem was typical of the Middle Ages, Dante made many references to classical heroes, poets, and philosophers. Perhaps the most important reason for regarding this work as typical of the Renaissance, however, was that it was written in vernacular Italian, or the language spoken by ordinary Italians. During the Middle Ages, almost all books were written in Latin.

Petrarch. An early humanist writer was Francesco Petrarch (lived 1304–1374). He wrote poems called sonnets in Latin and Italian. Many of the sonnets express his love for a woman named Laura, who represented beauty and human hopes.

Petrarch was responsible for saving the works of many ancient Greek and Roman writers. He searched for them in the libraries of monasteries and brought the writings to the attention of his fellow scholars.

Boccaccio. Another humanist writer who became well known was Giovanni Boccaccio (lived 1313–1375). He wrote a book of short stories called *The Decameron* while the plague was devastating Italy. The stories are told by a group of ten young men and women, who have moved to a house in the country to escape the Black Death. The members of the group amuse each other by making fun of many customs of the Middle Ages.

Shakespeare. Later in the Renaissance, other countries beside Italy produced artists and writers that were typical of the age. In England, William Shakespeare (lived 1564–1616) wrote plays that are still performed today. This productive genius wrote historical plays such as *Richard III* and *Henry V*, tragedies such as *Hamlet* and *Romeo and Juliet*, and comedies such as *A Midsummer Night's Dream* and *The Taming of the Shrew*. Many modern writers have written plays, movies, and novels based on Shakespearean plots and themes. Shakespeare is also known for his sonnets and long, narrative poems.

Cervantes. The Renaissance reached Spain in the 16th century. Miguel de Cervantes (lived 1547–1616), one of the world's best-known writers, created the story of *Don Quixote*. In this humorous novel, a simple old man (Don Quixote) believes that he is a knight who must fight in defense of noble causes. His servant, Sancho Panza, accompanies him through all his absurd adventures. In the novel, Cervantes ridicules romantic ideas about medieval knights. At the same time, he arouses the reader's affection for the idealistic Don Quixote.

Political Science

Niccolo Machiavelli (lived 1460–1527) wrote about government and political power. As an official in the government of Florence, Machiavelli went on a diplomatic mission to Rome. There he was impressed by the leadership of Cesare Borgia. Later he based a guidebook for rulers, called *The Prince,* on Borgia's political practices.

Medieval political thinkers had based their ideas on religious principles. In contrast, Machiavelli looked at how real people thought and acted.

He urged rulers to give citizens only those rights that do not limit their power. Leaders should be strong and ruthless when necessary, kind and generous when possible. He said: ". . . it is far safer to be feared than loved!"

1. Why do you think the Renaissance began in Italy, in the 14th century, rather than in one of the other European countries?

2. Define secularism. How was Renaissance art influenced by both secularism and religion?

3. Why is Leonardo da Vinci regarded as the best example of a Renaissance person?

SCIENTIFIC AND TECHNOLOGICAL INNOVATIONS

During the Renaissance, scientists explored new areas of knowledge and began to think in new ways. Their many inventions and discoveries greatly changed the ways in which people lived.

Scientific Method

For many centuries, scientists had accepted the writings of ancient scholars and the teachings of religious leaders about science and nature. At the end of the Middle Ages, however, scientists began to use new methods to study nature. They began to apply what they learned to make life better and to conquer nature. Scientists also began to question old beliefs that could not be proved.

Conclusions based on observation and experimentation became the basis for scientific theories. Statements put forth as facts were accepted as true only after they had been tested in experiments. These tests and their results were written down so that other scientists could repeat them. Gradually, the *scientific method* of observation, experimentation, and drawing conclusions came into common use. It led to revolutionary advances in the fields of chemistry, physics, mathematics, astronomy, and medicine.

Galileo

Two of the most important men to use the scientific method were Galileo Galilei of Italy and Isaac Newton of England. Galileo (lived 1564–1642) built a telescope to study the planets. His observations led him to conclude that the Earth and all the other planets move around the sun. His theory conflicted with the beliefs of officials in the Roman Catholic Church. They taught that the Earth is the center of the universe. These officials persecuted Galileo and eventually forced him to deny what he had discovered. However, all scientists eventually accepted Galileo's ideas about the *solar system*.

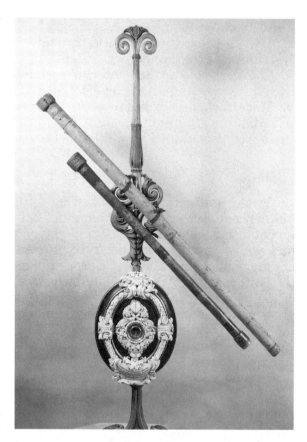

The elaborately mounted
telescope of Galileo Galilei

Newton

Isaac Newton (lived 1642–1727) taught mathematics. One of his early achievements was the creation of the system of advanced mathematics called calculus. Newton also developed the law of universal gravitation (often called the law of gravity). This law explained the operation of a force called gravity. On every planet, the force of gravity pulls objects toward the planet and keeps them from flying off into space. Newton also explained how gravity keeps planets in orbit around the sun. With this knowledge, Newton built the foundation of modern astronomy. He is regarded as one of the greatest of all scientists.

Anatomy and Chemistry

Medical scientists also made dramatic discoveries. In 1543, a doctor from Belgium, Andreas Vesalius, published the first accurate book on human anatomy. In studying the human body, Vesalius examined and dissected the bodies of dead people.

In 1628, William Harvey, an English doctor, wrote a book explaining how the heart pumps blood through the body. This was the first description of the circulatory system.

The works of Vesalius and Harvey have been rated by scholars as two of the most important medical discoveries since 1500.

Modern chemistry began with the work of Robert Boyle, an Irish scientist. His studies in the mid-1600s proved that air is a mixture of gases. He also studied how animals breathe.

Printing

Two inventions greatly helped the spread of ideas during the Renaissance. In the mid-1400s, Johannes Gutenberg, a German printer, invented movable metal type and the printing press. (The Chinese had earlier invented another type of printing press. Westerners did not know about it.) The first European book printed by machine was the Gutenberg Bible. It appeared around 1455. Before the invention of the printing press, books had to be copied by hand. The printing press produced books more cheaply, more accurately, and in greater numbers. The increased circulation of books by Italian and other European writers introduced more people to the ideas of the Renaissance.

Having more books available made it possible for more people

Book printing shop in the late 16th century

to learn to read. The next section points out the important role of the printing press in spreading a religious movement called Protestantism.

INFO CHECK

1. Why was the development of the scientific method so important to the expansion of human knowledge?

2. Which Renaissance scientist do you think made the most important discovery or contribution? Explain your choice.

THE REFORMATION AND COUNTER-REFORMATION

During the plague, many people lost confidence in the Catholic Church. Church leaders had been unable to protect people from this disaster. Some clerics had persuaded plague victims to leave their money to the Church rather than to their families. Others had charged high fees for giving last rites to the dying.

As a response to the Church's helplessness, various groups developed their own methods of dealing with the plague. The flagellants decided that the Black Death was a punishment from God. They believed that if they beat themselves in public, they could turn away God's wrath. The leaders of this group, which was not approved by the Church, criticized the Church for not doing enough to lead the people out of sin. They also took over many functions of the clergy, such as listening to confessions and giving out penances.

During the Renaissance, even more people began to question long-accepted religious beliefs and certain practices of the Roman Catholic Church. Those who challenged, or protested, against the ways of the Church were called *Protestants*. At first, Church leaders accused these people of *heresy* and burned them at the stake. (Heresy is holding an opinion on religion that goes against Church teachings.) In time, however, these critics gained power. Their demand for reform and religious changes in the Church was called the *Reformation*. This great movement led to the creation of a new branch of Christianity: *Protestantism*. The Reformation also caused terrible wars and major political changes in Europe.

The First Protestants

In 1517, a German monk named Martin Luther posted a document on the door of the church in Wittenberg, a university town. For the time, this was a common way to start a discussion among scholars.

The Ninety-five Theses. Luther's document is known as the "Ninety-five Theses." It stated Luther's criticisms of the Roman Cath-

Papal officials selling indulgences at a German country fair in the 1500s

olic Church for allowing the sale of *indulgences*. An indulgence was a promise by a Church leader to limit a person's stay in *purgatory*. According to Roman Catholic teachings, purgatory is the place where the souls of sinners who are sorry for their bad deeds go after death. There, suffering purifies the sinners and makes them worthy of heaven. In Luther's time, the Church issued indulgences in return for contributions for the building of St. Peter's Church in Rome. Luther condemned this practice. He claimed that indulgences could neither cancel nor reduce the punishment for sin.

Many Catholics agreed with Luther that selling indulgences was wrong. They also made other complaints against the Church, such as its practice of *nepotism*. Nepotism occurred when high-ranking clergymen appointed their relatives to important positions in the Church.

At the heart of Luther's plea for reform were three ideas that enraged Church officials. First, he believed that a person could be saved through "faith alone." Performing good works or buying indulgences would not guarantee salvation. Second, Luther argued that the Bible was the only guide to salvation that Christians needed. Third, Luther claimed that the leaders of the Catholic Church were not the only people who could interpret the Bible. All Christians should be able to read and interpret the Bible for themselves.

Reaction of the Church. In 1521, the pope excommunicated Luther as a heretic. In the next year, Charles V, the Holy Roman

Martin Luther, whose
teachings formed the basis
of Protestant belief

Emperor and ruler of most of the states of Germany, declared Luther an outlaw.

Luther continued to speak out for reform. Because of the invention of the printing press, his ideas spread rapidly throughout Germany. Knowing the power of the printed word, Luther translated the Bible into German so that more people could read it.

All of these actions touched off a long struggle between Luther's supporters and his Catholic opponents. Many German princes sided with Luther against the pope. When Charles V tried to force these princes to remain loyal to the Church, they resisted. They supported the establishment of Protestantism as a new branch of Christianity based on Luther's teachings. Protestant princes welcomed the opportunity to be independent of the pope and to rebel against the authority of the Holy Roman Emperor. Some princes seized Church lands and other properties.

In 1555, the Peace of Augsburg finally settled the long civil wars in Germany between Catholics and Protestants. It allowed each German prince to choose between the two faiths—Catholic or Protestant. The peace treaty required the subjects of each prince to follow the faith he chose.

Luther's ideas spread from Germany to many other parts of Europe. His ideas became popular in Norway, Sweden, and Denmark.

The Spread of the Reformation

The Reformation arrived in England in a rather roundabout way. The English king, Henry VIII, was a loyal Catholic. He very much wanted a son to insure the succession of the Tudor line of kings. His

Spanish wife, Catherine of Aragon, had given him a daughter but no son. Henry wanted the pope to annul (cancel) his marriage to Catherine so that he could marry someone else who might give birth to a son. The pope refused. (Catherine was a devout Catholic and the aunt of Charles V, the Holy Roman Emperor and a supporter of the pope.) Henry then appointed an English archbishop who granted the annulment.

In 1534, Henry broke completely with the Roman Catholic Church. He had Parliament issue the Act of Supremacy. This new law made Henry the leader of a separate church called the Church of England (also called the Anglican Church). Thus, Henry made himself more important than the pope in regulating religious matters in England. Henry closed down the monasteries and seized much of the land in England belonging to the Roman Catholic Church. King Henry VIII started the movement that made Protestantism the main faith authorized by the English government.

Between 1536 and 1541, a French lawyer named John Calvin organized Protestant churches in Switzerland. Many of Calvin's ideas were similar to those of Luther. Others were very different. Calvin believed that an all-powerful God determined which of the naturally sinful humans would go to heaven. This judgment was made before a person was born. Thus, a person was predestined to be saved or go to hell. A person would not know until death came whether he or she would go to heaven. But each individual should live a moral, upright life in order to show that he or she had been chosen. Calvin and his followers believed in a life of hard work and prayer. They denied themselves all but the simplest of pleasures.

Calvin's ideas spread to Holland, where the Dutch Reformed Church was established. In Scotland, a reformer named John Knox organized the Presbyterian Church in 1560 on the basis of Calvinist teachings.

French Calvinists were known as Huguenots. The followers of Calvin in England were called Puritans. Both the Huguenots and the Puritans were persecuted. Their religious ideas and strict way of life were quite different from the practices of most English and French people. Many Huguenots and Puritans eventually brought their Protestant faith and their belief in hard work to America. In America, the Puritans punished individuals and groups who held different religious ideas.

The Counter-Reformation

The spread of Protestantism throughout Europe in the 16th century threatened the power and authority of the Roman Catholic Church. Catholic leaders took several important steps to meet this challenge. Pope Paul III called Church officials to the Council of Trent. During three sessions held between 1545 and 1563, this council worked out ways to change Church policies. It ended the sale of indulgences and other practices that Protestants had criticized. It offered measures to improve the way in which priests were trained. The council also clearly restated the basic beliefs of the Church.

The Society of Jesus, whose members were known as Jesuits, was largely responsible for the success of the Counter-Reformation (also known as the Catholic Reformation). Ignatius Loyola founded the society in 1534 (the same year as King Henry's Act of Supremacy) to promote Catholicism. Sometimes called "soldiers of Christ," Jesuits acted as teachers and missionaries. They traveled to all parts of the world to win converts to the Catholic faith. The Jesuit missionary Francis Xavier went to Japan in 1549. Jesuits often accompanied Spanish and French explorers on voyages to the Americas.

The Counter-Reformation strengthened the Roman Catholic Church. Protestantism became less popular in Poland, Hungary, and other Eastern European nations. In Italy, France, Spain, and Portugal, Catholicism continued to be the main faith. The Catholic Church became a strong force in South and Central America and parts of North America.

Religious and Political Conflicts

When political ambitions became mixed up with religious differences, bloody wars often broke out. Hardly anyplace in Europe escaped conflict. England, Spain, France, and Germany were affected the most.

Philip II, the Catholic king of Spain, sent the Spanish Armada to attack Protestant England in 1588. The Armada consisted of 130 powerful fighting ships and thousands of sailors and soldiers. It was to prepare the way for an invasion of England by Spanish forces based in Holland. Philip regarded Protestant England, which was ruled by Elizabeth I, as the main enemy of Catholic Spain. (Elizabeth was a daughter of Henry VIII.) By defeating England, he hoped to strengthen both his country and his Church. Philip's plan failed when the small but strong English navy and severe winds defeated the Armada. England remained Protestant and free from Spanish rule.

Catholics and Huguenots (French Calvinists) fought a series of civil wars in France from 1562 to 1598. Powerful families of both religious groups wanted the crown. One of the worst incidents of the period was the St. Bartholomew's Day massacre on August 24, 1572. This was a general attack on Protestants in Paris and throughout France. All-out war followed. The conflicts ended when the Huguenot leader, Henry of Navarre, became King Henry IV of France.

The first of the Bourbon line, Henry reigned from 1589 to 1610. To be crowned, Henry needed Catholic support. He had to convert to Catholicism. (He is supposed to have said, "Paris [the capital] is well worth a mass [a Catholic religious service].") But as king, he issued

Time Line

Year	Dates and Events

A.D.
1

1300

1301

1265: Birth of Dante Alighieri, poet in Italian (not Latin)
1304: Birth of Petrarch, Italian poet, preserver of ancient Greek and Roman writings
1313: Birth of Giovanni Boccaccio, Italian author of *Decameron*

1300s–1500s: Renaissance

1400

1401

1434–1737: Control of Florence by Medicis
1450s: German printer Johannes Gutenberg invents moveable metal type, first European printing press
1452: Birth of Leonardo da Vinci of Florence, painter, sculptor, architect, scientist, engineer
1460: Birth of Niccolò Machiavelli, Florentine author of *The Prince*
1475: Birth of Michelangelo, of Florence and Rome, painter, sculptor, architect, poet
1478: Isabella and Ferdinand of Spain begin Spanish Inquisition
1492–1500: Isabella and Ferdinand expel from Spain all unconverted Jews (1492) and Muslims (1500)
1508: Birth of Andrea Palladio, Italian architect
1517: Martin Luther posts "Ninety-five Theses," beginning of Reformation

1500

1501

1521–1522: Luther excommunicated by Church, declared outlaw in Germany; German princes split into Protestant and Catholic factions; civil wars follow
1534: Henry VIII issues Act of Supremacy establishing Church of England
1534: Ignatius Loyola founds Society of Jesus (Jesuits)
1536–1541: John Calvin organizes Protestant churches in Switzerland; followers in France (Huguenots), England (Puritans), Scotland (Presbyterians), Holland (Dutch Reformed)
1543: Andreas Vesalius, Belgian doctor, publishes first accurate book of human anatomy
1545–1563: Council of Trent initiates Counter-Reformation

1600

1601

1547: Birth of Miguel de Cervantes, Spanish author of *Don Quixote*
1549: Jesuit Francis Xavier begins mission to Japan
1555: Peace of Augsburg ends German civil wars
1562–1598: Civil war in France between Catholics and Huguenots; Protestant Henry of Navarre becomes Catholic King Henry IV of France
1564: Birth of William Shakespeare, English poet and playwright
1564: Birth of Galileo Galilei, Italian astronomer
1598: Edict of Nantes protects French Huguenots from persecution
1618–1648: Thirty Years' War ended by Treaty of Westphalia
1628: William Harvey, English doctor, publishes first book explaining circulatory system

1700

1642: Birth of Isaac Newton, English mathematician, developer of calculus theory and law of gravity

Protestant and Catholic Europe in 1600

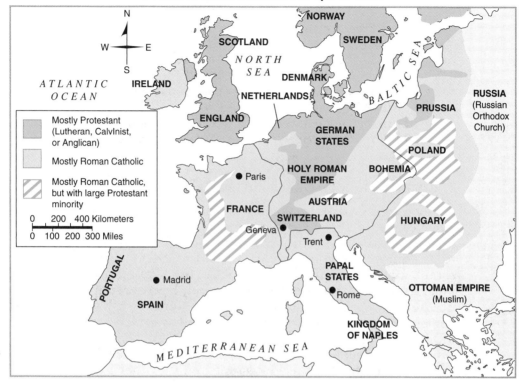

the Edict of Nantes in 1598. This law protected the Huguenots from persecution.

Perhaps the most destructive of the religious wars in Europe took place in Germany. Known as the Thirty Years' War, it lasted from 1618 to 1648. Almost every country in Europe joined the struggle between the Catholic and Protestant states of Germany. They all sent armies into Germany. As a result, a large portion of the population was killed and the economy nearly destroyed.

The Treaty of Westphalia ended the war in 1648. Germany remained a collection of independent Protestant and Catholic states. This division prevented Germany from uniting as one country under a national government until the 19th century.

INFO CHECK

1. State the causes of the Protestant Reformation. What changes were brought to Europe by this movement?

2. Summarize the role of each of the following in the Reformation: Martin Luther, Henry VIII, John Calvin, John Knox.

3. Explain how the Reformation led to the Counter-Reformation.

SOCIAL EFFECTS OF THE REFORMATION

The Reformation caused many changes in Europe's political and social structure. Religious differences between nations caused them to feel more hostile toward each other. The Protestant ideals of hard work and independent thought increased the prestige of the middle class. Some Protestant groups became suspicious of people who did not conform to the rest of society and persecuted them. In some cases, Protestantism worsened the social status of women. Catholic nations, threatened by the success of Protestantism, became less tolerant of minorities.

The Impact of Protestantism on the Roles of Men and Women

Although Catholic women could not become priests, they could enter convents. In convents, upper-class women could develop their talents for art, literature, medicine, and administration. The Protestant faiths offered no such opportunities. Society expected a Protestant woman, regardless of her class, to make marriage her most important occupation. Protestantism did, however, improve the education of lower-class women. Because Protestants believed that each person must interpret the Bible for himself or herself, women, as well as men, learned to read.

Catholics believed that marriage was a sacred bond, which could not be broken by divorce. Protestants, on the other hand, saw marriage as a contract that could be broken under certain circumstances. Both women and men could request divorces.

Religious leaders of the Reformation frequently wrote marriage manuals that described the different roles of husband and wife. According to the manuals, a man should earn a living for his wife and children and protect them. As the head of his household, he was expected to be just and self-controlled. The wife was supposed to take good care of the house, rear the children, and be obedient to her husband. Both partners were expected to be faithful to each other.

The Great Witch-Hunt

Historians are not sure why people became so preoccupied with witches during this period. Belief in witchcraft had always existed. According to this belief, witches are people who worship the devil and can cause harm by supernatural means. From the 15th century through the 18th century, a great witch-hunt took place throughout Europe. In southeastern Germany, between 1561 and 1670, 3,229 people were found guilty of witchcraft and executed. Between 1470 and 1700, the law courts of the Swiss Confederation killed 5,417 people for witchcraft. The English executed almost 1,000 so-called witches between 1559 and 1736.

The fear of people who are different or who hold different ideas

KING JAMES AND THE WITCHES

King James I, ruler of Scotland and England, was fascinated by witches. In fact, James believed so strongly in witchcraft that he spent much time having women arrested and tortured until they confessed to being witches. In 1606, James was eagerly anticipating a visit from his brother-in-law, King Christian of Denmark. As part of the celebration, James wanted a new play performed. Shakespeare wrote *Macbeth* to flatter the king. It was set in Scotland and had witches practicing black magic.

Persecutions of witches in Scotland increased in the 17th century as a result of James's beliefs. During her journey to Scotland, James's future bride, Princess Anne of Denmark, was detained in Norway by a violent storm. King James set sail to personally bring her to his country. The return voyage was troubled by an even worse storm. King James's ship was blown off course. After great difficulties, the couple finally reached Scotland. It was rumored that witches had caused the bad weather to kill the king.

King James was the target of assassination plots. Some of them were blamed on witches. In 1591, a woman named Geillis Duncan was arrested and tried for witchcraft. She confessed after being tortured. Duncan also named other possible witches—a Doctor Fian and three women. After severe torture, these people admitted to using spells, and even a dead cat thrown into the sea, in an effort to kill the king on his voyage to gain his bride. Dr. Fian named the king's half-cousin as leader of the *coven* (witches' group). King James personally attended. At the conclusion of the trial, three of those accused received the death sentence. The king's half-cousin was banished.

Regarding witchcraft as a political threat, James began an intensive study of the subject. He published the results in a book entitled *Daemonologie* in 1597. In it, he warned readers of the dangers presented by witches and spirits and attacked those who had publicly scoffed at their existence. The book became the manual for the conduct of witch-hunts in Scotland, and later in England. After gaining the throne of England, James took severe action against the practice of witchcraft. In 1604, he issued a law providing for the death penalty for a wide range of practices that James regarded as threats to public safety. These included communicating with evil spirits and removing a corpse from a grave.

The Statute of 1604 resulted in a mass witch-hunt. Although James truly believed in the power of witches, he was shocked by the vicious nature of the persecutions that his law provoked. He tried to improve the situation by persuading the public to stop the persecutions. Unfortunately, too many people refused to give up their prejudices and what they believed was their right to take violent action. It was not until the end of the 17th century, long after the death of King James, that the witch-hunts slowed down in Scotland and England.

1. Do the beliefs and actions of King James meet with your approval? Why or why not?

2. Why do you think so many people in the 16th and 17th centuries believed in witchcraft and magic?

A Jewish father's plea for his daughter, accused of witchcraft

may partially explain why people accused their neighbors of religious wrongdoing. Many people, Catholic and Protestant alike, suspected heretics of secretly worshiping the devil. The heretics, or witches, were said to be eager to help the devil snare the souls of the faithful and send them to hell.

Scholars disagree on why more women than men were accused of witchcraft. Some point out that the causes of sickness were mysterious to the people of the time. They frequently blamed illness and accidents on a neighbor's hostility. Country women often made mixtures of herbs from secret recipes and used them to treat illnesses. Their association with secret brews and illness made people see these women as having magical power. If their remedies did not work, the patients' relatives often expressed their anger by accusing the women of using witchcraft to cause the deaths of their kin.

The Status of the Jews

During the Reformation, great hostility often existed between people who belonged to different groups. In this climate of intolerance, some people turned against the Jews. In the early Middle Ages, Jews were well integrated into the economy of Europe. Some owned property and farmed. Most, however, lived in cities and engaged in such occupations as goldsmithing, medicine, trade, and moneylending.

As time went on, the status of European Jews became less comfortable. In 1215, the Catholic Church began to change its policies toward them. Previously, Church doctrine had forbidden the persecution of Jews. According to its teaching, the Jews would convert to Christianity shortly before the end of the world. Therefore, their conversion was in the hands of God, not of humans. In 1215, however, Church leaders held a meeting called the Fourth Lateran Council. Among other changes in policy, the council made a law requiring all Jews to wear a sign on their clothing to separate them from Christians. This sign was a constant reminder to people that Jews were different. Some people blamed the Jews for causing the plague and used violence against them.

In the 12th and 13th centuries, the governments of European countries became more centralized. Kings wanted to unify their subjects by imposing religious and national uniformity on them. Some kings began to expel Jews and other non-Christians from their kingdoms. In 1290, King Edward exiled all the Jews from England. In the late 1400s, Queen Isabella and King Ferdinand decided to make Catholicism the only religion in Spain. To accomplish this end, they passed laws that gave Jews and Muslims the choice of becoming Christians or leaving their kingdom. Jews who did not convert were expelled in 1492. (This was the year Columbus sailed west toward Asia and bumped into America.) Muslims who did not change were forced out after 1500.

In 1478, the pope had allowed Ferdinand and Isabella to establish the *Spanish Inquisition*. The Inquisition was a court that tried to determine whether or not Spanish subjects were good Catholics. Its main activity was the examination of converted Jews and Muslims to find out if they were secretly practicing their former religions. People feared being tortured by the Inquisition court until they could not resist confessing to heresy.

Chapter 15 covers powerful royal families and how they established absolute monarchies in European states. There is also a discussion of how various groups tried to limit royal power. Protestantism played an important role in one of these attempts to resist royal authority.

INFO CHECK

1. Explain why you AGREE or DISAGREE with each statement:

   • The lives of European women were improved by the Reformation.
   • The treatment of European Jews during the Reformation was an example of religious toleration.

2. Why did the rulers of Spain establish the Inquisition?

CHAPTER REVIEW

Multiple Choice

1. The shift from the manor to cities took place because

   1. serfs and peasants sought better lives
   2. fewer people died from the plague in the cities
   3. lords wanted their serfs to leave the manor
   4. nomadic invaders threatened, so people fled for safety.

2. Why did cities contribute more than manors to European economic growth?

   1. Manors were overcrowded, so people moved out.
   2. City status denoted nobility.
   3. Cities served both as ports where goods were received and as manufacturing centers.
   4. Cities were important gathering places in which to practice religion.

3. European nobles began freeing their serfs because they

   1. realized it was morally wrong to keep people bound to the land
   2. needed soldiers to fight the king's armies
   3. wanted to collect rents from their lands, and serfs did not pay rent
   4. hoped to earn salvation from the pope for good deeds.

4. In the struggle for political power between local nobles and the king, cities usually supported the

   1. king, because he was the leader of the nation
   2. king, who supported public works, such as road building

3. nobles, who allowed them to develop overseas trade
4. nobles, to whom they felt an allegiance.

5. The regulation of business, merchandise, and sales was done by the

   1. city charter
   2. guilds
   3. lord of the manor
   4. bishop of the Church.

6. Independent merchants, who were not part of the guilds, were called

   1. thieves
   2. vassals
   3. capitalists
   4. nomads.

7. European capitalists borrowed a method developed by the Muslims to raise large amounts of money. It was called a

   1. joint-stock company
   2. two-field system
   3. domestic system
   4. none of the above.

8. The rise of overseas colonies can be directly related to this economic system:

   1. domestic system
   2. manorial system
   3. feudalism
   4. mercantilism.

9. The Middle Ages was to Church-dominated religious themes as the

   1. Renaissance was to secular, worldly concerns
   2. Renaissance was to economic monetary organizations

3. Renaissance was to commercial banking syndicates

4. all of the above.

10. The Reformation and Counter-Reformation highlight the

1. political struggle between the pope and Holy Roman Emperor

2. political struggle between the pope and the German princes

3. religious and political struggle between the Protestants and the Catholics

4. religious struggle between the Catholic Church and the Jesuits.

11. According to the illustration on page 284, which statement about printing in the 16th century is correct?

1. Printing was done by hand.

2. Only one or two workers were required in a printing shop.

3. Workers operated printing presses.

4. Efforts to produce books in greater numbers failed.

12. According to the map on pages 276–277, the most powerful trading empires of the 16th and 17th centuries were

1. Spain and Portugal

2. China and Japan

3. Arabia and India

4. England and Australia.

Thematic Essays

1. *Task:* Discuss, using specific examples, how the worldly, secular concerns of the Renaissance clashed with the religious concerns of the Church. Consider in your answer world view, art, and science.

2. The Middle Ages was a period that changed social and economic practices. *Task:* Using specific examples, explain why the change in the economic order affected the social order.

Document-Based Questions

Use the documents and your knowledge of Global History and Geography to answer the questions.

1. Study the illustration on page 286. How does the artist of the woodcut show that he sides with Luther against the Catholic Church?

2. Study the illustration on page 284. What was the effect of the invention shown on the controversy between Luther and the Church?

3. Tetzel said the following in a sermon on indulgences.

"You may obtain letters of safe conduct from the vicar of our lord Jesus Christ, . . . and convey it from all pains of purgatory, into the happy kingdom . . . with these confessional letters you will be able at any time in life to obtain full indulgence for all penalties imposed upon you. . . ."

What is Tetzel offering? Why is he doing this? Why did Luther object to this?

4. Luther wrote the following.
". . . by faith alone in Christ without works, are we declared just and saved . . . they cannot produce a letter to prove that the interpretation of Scripture . . . belongs to the Pope alone. . . . But we are all priests before God if we are Christians . . ."

State the three issues Luther is presenting.

Document-Based Essay

Luther was able to spread his doctrines, while others who disagreed with the Church perished as heretics in the flames of the Inquisition. *Task:* Explain the reasons for Luther's success.

C H A P T E R
15

The Rise of European Nation-States

No one in London could talk of anything else. The new government had found King Charles guilty of treason and had beheaded him. Some people predicted that God would punish the English for executing the king He had chosen for them. But Katherine's father claimed that Charles had been a tyrant. English kings were supposed to obey laws just like other people. King Charles had taxed his subjects illegally and sent innocent men to prison. Some suspected that he had wanted to bring back Catholicism as the state-approved religion. As a Puritan, Katherine's father did not believe that God could possibly approve of such a king.

Katherine did not know what to think. She thought Oliver Cromwell, the man who would now rule England, looked very severe. Like her father, Cromwell did not approve of plays, dancing, drinking, and music in churches. Would life in London now be as dull as Katherine's home life sometimes seemed? Would people who were not Puritans be forbidden all their pleasures?

T his young Puritan girl lived during the English civil war that lasted from 1642 to 1649. The war ended with the execution of the English king. It drastically changed the way Katherine and other English people lived and thought. The ideas that came out of these events did much to shape the modern world. Therefore, it is important to understand both the causes and the effects of the events.

THE DECLINE OF FEUDALISM AND THE RISE OF ABSOLUTE MONARCHY

During the Middle Ages and the Renaissance, kings in Europe struggled to win more power. Gaining military strength helped them do this. The financial support they received from the growing middle class enabled them to build up armies, navies, and stockpiles of weapons. Trade, banking, and manufacturing of goods in Europe had made many members of the middle class very rich. Their money bought them influence and prestige.

Between the mid-1500s and the late 1600s, European nations fought a great many wars. Wealth from trade was not enough to pay for the wars. As a result, kings expected landowners and peasants to contribute more money to the royal treasury. But the landowners and peasants had little to give. They frequently rebelled against the rulers.

Divine Right

The problems of warfare, economic distress, and social disorder made kings determined to gain more control over their countries' governments. They wanted their wishes to be followed without opposition. Most European kings of the 17th century tried to exercise absolute, or complete, power. They believed that they had a *divine right*, a "God-given" right, to rule. (Recall the idea of the Mandate of Heaven in China.) God had chosen them as His representatives to rule over their subjects. Therefore, the kings did not have to answer to anyone but God. Because they represented God's will, the people had a religious duty to obey them. If the people rebelled against the monarch, they were rebelling against God's will.

Centralized Government

When one institution, such as the monarchy, controls a government, that government is centralized. As the governments of European countries became centralized, they developed into nation-states. These nation-states had definite boundaries, unified rule, and permanent armies loyal to the head of state. The people of these countries had national identities. This means that they spoke the same language, shared many cultural traits, and felt a strong sense of loyalty to and pride in their country. In some nation-states, most of the people followed the same religion.

Some absolute monarchs established dynasties. (Recall the dynasties in China and India.) Members of the same royal family maintained control of their country's government for several generations. These families played important roles in shaping European history.

INFO CHECK

1. Explain why the growth of the middle class was so important to the rise of European nation-states.

2. Why do you think absolutism and the theory of divine right of kings would not be popular today?

3. Can a nation-state exist without a centralized government? Explain your answer.

THE TUDORS OF ENGLAND

Since William the Conqueror, who ruled from 1066 to 1087, a strong central monarchy had existed in England. Some monarchs were stronger than others. William was from Normandy and ruled over a large part of western France. English kings held land in France for several hundred years. They fought many wars to keep control of the French holdings or to gain more land. One series of battles occurred off and on from 1337 to 1453. These battles are known as the Hundred Years' War. At its close, the English had been pushed out of France. English kings could devote their attention to England alone.

Within two years after the end of the Hundred Years' War, two powerful families began a 30-year fight for the English crown. They were the Lancasters and the Yorks. The Lancasters chose a red rose for their emblem, and the Yorks chose a white rose. Because of these emblems, the wars between the two families are known as the Wars of the Roses. Henry Tudor, a member of the Lancaster family, finally defeated Richard III of York at the Battle of Bosworth Field in 1485. He became King Henry VII (ruled 1485–1509). To gain the loyalty of the Yorks, Henry married Elizabeth of York. Henry was the first of the Tudor monarchs.

Henry VII

During his early years as king, Henry expended energy and funds to put down challenges to the throne. To prevent further revolts, he imposed heavy fines for illegally keeping private armies. Henry also opened up his advisory council to members of the middle class, the clergy, and low-level nobles. These individuals were loyal to Henry, not to his rivals. He set up an efficient tax collection system. Some fees and fines went directly into an account he controlled. He did not have to depend on Parliament to give him funds for his projects.

Henry VII made England prosperous by vigorously promoting trade at home. Trade agreements were signed with the Netherlands (Holland), Spain, Florence, and Denmark. To find new markets, Henry supported the exploratory voyages of John Cabot and his sons. He also kept England out of foreign wars.

Henry VIII

Henry VII's son, King Henry VIII (ruled 1509–1547), continued his father's policy of strengthening the monarchy. He appointed talented individuals to be his ministers. When they did not do as he wished, he got rid of them. These ministers helped influence Parliament to support Henry's policies.

In his early days as king, Henry tried to impress the English public by acting in "kingly" ways. He married an important princess— Catherine of Aragon, daughter of Ferdinand and Isabella of Spain. He entertained in a grand style. He went to war to win territory. The military adventures accomplished little except to spend money.

Henry replaced the Roman Catholic Church in England with the Anglican Church, which he could control. This move gave Henry more power and more money. He took over Church lands to further increase his wealth and to use to reward loyal nobles.

Elizabeth I

Henry's daughter Elizabeth I (ruled 1558–1603) was one of England's greatest monarchs. She, too, insisted on her own policies. With the help of her capable ministers, Elizabeth was able to persuade Parliament to do what she wanted.

She strengthened the Church of England and took decisive action against Catholic-sponsored plots against her. Her main aims were to keep England out of wars and to encourage trade. She did not shrink from fighting if she had to. The English navy defeated an effort by the Spanish Armada to invade England in 1588. (An armada is a large number of ships.) Voyages of exploration to find gold and sites for colonies were supported. Sir Walter Raleigh attempted to establish a colony in the Americas, in Roanoke in present-day North Carolina. This effort failed. Sir Francis Drake sailed around the world to find new trading partners for England and sites for colonies. With Elizabeth's approval, he raided Spanish ports and ships in the Americas and elsewhere.

Realizing that the public liked to see their monarch, Elizabeth often traveled about the country. During her 45-year reign, England had peace, prosperity, and prestige.

Queen Elizabeth I being carried in royal procession, from a contemporary painting

Both Henry VIII and Elizabeth encouraged writers, painters, and the theater. Many of William Shakespeare's great plays were written and performed while Elizabeth was queen.

Elizabeth was the last of the Tudors. Her successors, the Stuart kings, also considered themselves to be absolute monarchs who ruled by divine right. But Parliament was not willing to let the Stuarts have so much power. A great struggle between the lawmakers and the Stuart kings took place in the mid-1600s.

INFO CHECK

1. Summarize the role of the Hundred Years' War and the Wars of the Roses in England's development as a nation-state.

2. Which of the Tudor monarchs do you find most impressive? Explain your answer.

THE BOURBONS OF FRANCE

It took the work of many kings to centralize the French government. Not until the Bourbon line of kings took power did France become a true nation-state.

JOAN OF ARC—A HEROINE OF FRANCE

On May 30, 1431, a young woman was tied to a stake and burned alive by order of a French court. She was forced to wear a paper cap on which were written accusations of heresy. (*Heresy* is proclaiming ideas other than those approved by the Roman Catholic Church.) Her name was Joan of Arc. She was approximately 19 years old at the time of her death. She was also one of France's greatest heroines.

Joan was born a peasant in the village of Domremy in northern France. When she was 13 years old, she believed she heard heavenly voices belonging to Saints Michael, Margaret, and Catherine. In 1429, the voices urged her to assist the dauphin, the prince who was to become King Charles VII of France. At this time, France was fighting the bloody Hundred Years' War (1337–1453) against England. French armies were trying to expel English forces that were protecting their king's claim to portions of France. The dauphin, a sickly young man, was too weak to provide leadership. He seemed powerless to prevent the English from capturing Orleans, a key city in the area he controlled.

Joan persuaded her uncle to help her travel to the dauphin's court. He gave her a horse, a dagger, and an escort of six men. The young woman cut her hair short and put on male clothing.

After arriving at the dauphin's court, Joan was able to convince him that she had a divine mission to save France from the English invaders. She promised to win back Orleans if she were given soldiers to lead. The dauphin had armor and a banner made for her. Joan also carried a sword.

With 3,000 French soldiers and some of the best of the dauphin's knights, Joan attacked the English forces at Orleans. In the course of battle, the young woman was struck in the shoulder by an arrow. Her knights carried her from the field and cut the iron point from the arrow. Joan then pulled the shaft out of her shoulder herself, mounted her horse, and rejoined the fighting. The battle ended as a decisive victory for the French. Joan was known thereafter as the Maid of Orleans.

Joan's troops fought their way to Reims. In that city, the dauphin was crowned King Charles VII of France.

In May 1430, Joan was captured by Burgundian soldiers, who sold her to their English allies. (The Burgundians were rivals of Charles for ruling France.) The English arranged for her to be tried for heresy by a Church court. Church authorities accused Joan of the crimes of believing she was directly responsible to God, rather than to them, and of wrongdoing by wearing masculine clothes. Joan was sentenced to death. An appeal to the pope was denied, and Charles did nothing to help her. Although she was a hero to her soldiers and the people of France, both Church and French political leaders feared her. They regarded the Maid of Orleans as a threat to their authority. Joan was burned at the stake. In 1920, the authorities of the Church set aside Joan's conviction for heresy and granted her sainthood.

The Hundred Years' War resulted in the withdrawal of English forces from France and the surrender of English claims to French territory. This was an important step in the development of France as a modern nation.

- Compare Joan of Arc with other heroic figures you have read about. Given the time in which she lived, what made Joan especially remarkable?

Henry IV

Henry IV of Navarre (ruled 1589–1610) was the first of the Bourbons. Henry did his part in uniting France by ending the religious wars between the Catholics and the Huguenots. He reduced the power of the nobility and prevented their abuse of the peasants. Henry also helped the peasants by lowering their taxes. Production in the profitable textile industry was improved by Henry's ideas. His ministers promoted trade and rebuilt roads and bridges that had been damaged during wars over religion. The ministers also improved the way taxes were collected so that the government had more money.

Henry backed efforts to set up colonies in North America to gain wealth. He was particularly impressed by the adventures of Samuel de Champlain. Champlain explored areas of present-day eastern Canada and founded a permanent settlement at the site of the present-day city of Quebec.

Louis XIII

When Henry IV was murdered in 1610, his son, Louis XIII (ruled 1610–1643), was still a child. Louis's mother, Marie de Médicis, ruled for him. She appointed the Catholic leader Cardinal Richelieu as chief minister.

To strengthen the power of the monarchy, Cardinal Richelieu set up an effective administrative system. Under Richelieu's system, the ruler appointed a representative to govern each district in France. The royal representatives (*intendants*) controlled almost every aspect of life in their districts. Among other functions, they established armies, supervised tax collections, regulated businesses, and watched members of the nobility for signs of rebellion.

Richelieu took away privileges the Huguenots had gained under Henry IV. He also promoted the French textile industry and shipbuilding. Private trading companies were encouraged to set up colonies in Canada and the West Indies.

Richelieu and Louis increased French influence in European affairs by aiding Protestant princes in the Thirty Years' War (1618–1648) in Germany. The idea was to keep the Holy Roman Emperor (a Catholic) from gaining too much power over Germany and becoming more of a threat to France.

Louis XIV

Louis XIV became king in 1643, when he was only five years old, and ruled until 1715. His mother, Anne of Austria, and strong ministers directed the government until he was old enough to handle affairs himself.

Louis XIV's Palace of Versailles and surrounding park, in 1668

During Louis's reign, France became the greatest power in Europe. Called the "Sun King" and the "Grand Monarch," Louis is supposed to have said, "I am the state [the government]." He was called the Sun King because of the glitter of the lifestyle of the court and because Louis was the center of the French universe. He made France a center of learning and the arts. Louis also created the magnificent palace of Versailles outside Paris. Other countries imitated French culture. The French language was spoken by educated people throughout Europe.

Louis ruled through the administrative system set up by Richelieu. The intendants were even more strict under Louis XIV. One of Louis's great fears was the possibility of revolts against him. He put down any opposition. Huguenots were severely persecuted. Many left France to settle elsewhere, some in North America.

He kept control of the important nobles by requiring their presence at the court in Versailles. Lavish entertainments were staged to keep everyone amused. Honors and high offices were given to the most loyal.

One of Louis's most capable ministers, Jean Baptiste Colbert, promoted the policy of mercantalism. He encouraged the growth of colonies in New France (now Canada).

French industry prospered during this period. But constant wars to add more territory to France and protect French colonies overseas drained the royal treasury. It also took great amounts of money to maintain the grand style of living favored by Louis.

The Bourbon kings who followed Louis XIV were left with huge debts. Their efforts to find money through heavy taxation caused the French people to turn against the monarchy.

1. Describe the efforts of Cardinal Richelieu to strengthen Bourbon rule of France.

2. What mistakes do you think the Bourbon kings made?

THE HABSBURGS OF GERMANY, SPAIN, AND CENTRAL EUROPE

The Habsburgs were an old royal family in Europe. Members of the family sat on the thrones of various countries from the 1200s to the early 1900s. The men who held the title of Holy Roman Emperor during these years came from the House of Habsburg. In 1526, the dynasty split into two branches—one in Spain and one centered in Austria.

Charles V

Charles V, a member of the Habsburg family, inherited the Spanish throne in 1516 from his grandfather, Ferdinand II, the husband of Isabella. Charles also became Holy Roman Emperor in 1519. During his reign, Spain gained a huge colonial empire in Latin America and the Pacific and great wealth from it. Charles opposed the Reformation in Germany. He declared Martin Luther to be an outlaw and fought the Protestant princes in Germany. Efforts to reform the Catholic Church during the Counter Reformation received his support.

Charles also fought wars with the French over territory in Italy. His forces turned back attacks by the Ottoman Turks in eastern Europe (at Vienna in 1532) and around the Mediterranean. Suleiman the Magnificent was the best-known sultan, or leader, of the expanding Ottoman Empire.

Illness and weariness with his responsibilities caused Charles to step down as emperor and as king of Spain in 1556. He entered a monastery. Charles's brother, Ferdinand I, became the Holy Roman Emperor (ruled 1558–1564). Charles's son, Philip II, became king of Spain. He ruled from 1556 to 1598.

Philip II

Philip wanted to extend the influence of the Catholic Church in Europe and elsewhere. (The Spanish colony of the Philippine Islands in the Pacific was named for Philip II.) In the hope of restoring Catholicism in England—and gaining more territory for Spain—he married Queen Mary I, the daughter of Henry VIII, in 1554. (Her mother, Catherine of Aragon, was his great aunt.) Philip and Mary had no children. When Mary died in 1558, the English crown went to Elizabeth I.

Europe in 1648

Philip concentrated his attention on Spain and its interests. He was what would now be called a "hands-on" ruler. He expected written reports on all aspects of government. He read and made notes on the reports before making decisions.

The gold and silver that came into Spain from its Latin American colonies enriched the country. Philip used the wealth to build up his army and navy. Assisted by Italian forces, Spain turned back an invasion by the Ottoman navy in 1571 in the western Mediterranean. (Cervantes, the creator of *Don Quixote*, fought in this battle.)

One of his projects was the creation of the Spanish Armada, a fleet of ships sent to invade England in 1588. The English had been supporting Philip's enemies in the Netherlands (Holland). He also wanted to take over England to make it a Catholic country. The Armada was defeated.

Maria Theresa

Another strong Habsburg ruler was Maria Theresa of Austria and Hungary. She ruled from 1740 to 1780. Her husband, Francis I, was

Portrait of Empress Maria Theresa and her family in Schonbrunn Palace, Vienna

made the Holy Roman Emperor because women could not hold the title. Throughout Maria Theresa's reign, she had to fight to keep other monarchs from taking territory away from her. She succeeded more often than she failed. In 1772, she joined with Russia and Prussia in dividing Poland, a portion of which became part of Austria.

Maria Theresa made her own decisions and tried to rule wisely. She promoted reforms such as education for young children and tried to limit the power of the great landlords over the peasants. The Habsburgs ruled in Austria-Hungary until the end of World War I in 1918.

INFO CHECK

1. Why did the Habsburg family have such a strong influence on European history?

2. How did Philip II play an important role in the history of both Spain and England?

THE ROMANOVS OF RUSSIA

Russian rulers pushed out the Mongols in 1480. The new leaders, Ivan III and Ivan IV, took the title of *czar*. (It comes from "caesar," the head of the Roman Empire.) They worked hard to expand and unify their country and to strengthen the monarchy. Their methods were harsh and caused unrest. When Ivan IV, also known as Ivan the Terrible, died in 1584, no leader had enough power to take over the throne. Finally, in 1613, a group of clergy, nobles, and wealthy merchants chose a member of the Romanov family to be the czar. The Romanovs ruled Russia until overthrown in the Russian Revolution in 1917. They turned Russia into a powerful nation.

Peter the Great

The most influential of the early Romanovs was Peter I (Peter the Great), who was czar from 1682 to 1725. While a young boy, Peter became curious about other countries. He also grew fond of the craft of shipbuilding and of military tactics. He became unusually tall—nearly seven feet—and unusually strong. Peter wanted to make Russia more like the countries in Western Europe.

In 1697, Peter traveled to Western Europe. In disguise, he worked as a carpenter in shipyards in the Netherlands and England. During his travels, he tried to learn as much as he could about the more modern and technologically advanced way of life in Western Europe. He took his ideas back to Russia and imposed the new ways on his people. He brought teachers, engineers, and craftspeople from Western Europe to teach the Russians new skills. He brutally punished those who refused to follow his orders. Western European clothing had to be worn. No man could have a beard, unless given permission to do so. Women had to go against tradition and appear in public along with men.

In a series of wars with Sweden, Peter won territory along the Baltic Sea. The Baltic ports made it possible for the Russians to in-

Portrait of Peter the Great,
czar of Russia, 1717

crease their trade with Western Europe. The ports were called "windows on the West." One was the new capital city of St. Petersburg, which Peter had built on empty marshland.

Peter set up schools and centers for scientific research. He took away much of the nobles' power and put the Russian Orthodox Church under his control.

Catherine the Great

Catherine II (Catherine the Great) was the next strong Romanov ruler. She reigned from 1762 to 1796. Catherine continued to Westernize Russia. She encouraged Russian writers and artists and promoted educational reforms, some for women, and better health practices.

When Russia, Austria, and Prussia partitioned (divided) Poland in 1772, Russia received a large portion of the Polish territory. Catherine also added territory along the northern coast of the Black Sea. For the first time, Russia had a seaport that could be used year round. It was not ice-bound in the winter.

Unlike Maria Theresa of Austria, Catherine allowed large landholders to control local governmental affairs. During her rule, the upper classes gained more privileges. The peasants and serfs, however, lost many important rights.

Portrait of Catherine the Great, empress of Russia

At first, Catherine had wanted to help the peasants and serfs. When a large group of peasants rebelled, however, she changed her mind. After putting down the uprising, she gave the landlords more power than ever. Many landlords treated the serfs like slaves. Great discontent built up among the peasants, who made up 95 percent of the Russian population.

INFO CHECK

1. Why do you think it was important to the Romanovs to "Westernize" Russia?

2. Why were the Russian peasants unhappy under the rule of Catherine the Great?

EARLY EFFORTS TO LIMIT THE POWERS OF ABSOLUTE MONARCHS

The ideas of the Renaissance and the Reformation had an important effect on Europeans. More people believed that they had certain basic rights. Many started to question long-standing ideas about government. Inevitably, they began to challenge the total power of absolute monarchs and the theory of the divine right of monarchs.

Political struggles developed between monarchs who wished to keep their power and the common people who wanted their share of it. Often these struggles burst into violence. The use of violence or the threat of violence to bring about basic changes in the way a nation is governed is called a *revolution*.

Common Law and the Magna Carta

Many important institutions that benefited nobles and commoners had developed during the Middle Ages. At first, the increasing power of the kings brought about advances in liberty and justice for these groups. This was especially true in England.

After William of Normandy conquered England in 1066, one king ruled the whole country. The royal government collected taxes and decided important court cases. It won the support of the nobles by consulting them on important matters.

King Henry II, who ruled England from 1154 to 1189, strengthened the justice system. The judges he appointed traveled around the country deciding cases. Their decisions were written down and used as guides in future cases. These decisions formed the basis of the *common law*. Such law applied "in common" to all the people.

Often the pressure of money problems caused kings to break their own laws. In some cases, they ignored the rights of the Church and the nobility. John, one of Henry's sons, became king in 1199. England had heavy debts at that time. The economy had worsened because of a series of wars with France.

In order to finance these wars and ones he started, John raised his subjects' taxes. When the taxes did not provide enough money, he used various forms of pressure to fill the treasury. He threatened to force noble widows into marriages they did not want. To avoid this fate, they had to give him large sums of money. He married the orphaned daughters of nobles to anyone who would pay him the highest price. He forced the leaders in the towns and cities to give him money. When they objected, John threatened to take away the charters of self-government of the towns and cities.

At last the barons, who were important landholders, rebelled. Church leaders and other members of the nobility joined them. In 1215, these groups forced John to agree to the *Magna Carta*. This "great charter" set forth the rights of the barons. Over the following centuries, many of these rights were extended to the common people. One right said that a person could not be sent to prison without first receiving a jury trial. By agreeing to the Magna Carta, John accepted the idea that even a king's power is limited by laws. Many of the ideas in the Magna Carta continue to be a basic part of the justice system in Great Britain and the United States.

Parliament

During the 13th century, the English developed other important checks on the power of absolute monarchs. From early times, the kings of England had asked their chief vassals for advice about important matters. Edward I (ruled 1272–1307) was the first king to call on representatives from different groups to give him advice. These groups were the townspeople, knights, the clergy, and lords. In 1295, the representatives met together in the first *Parliament* to make laws for the country.

This Model Parliament, as it became known, was divided into two parts. The members of the House of Lords included the nobles and the church leaders. Their seats in this body were passed along to their sons or successors in office. In other words, the House of Lords was a hereditary body. The second part was the House of Commons, made up of wealthy merchants who were commoners. They were appointed or elected to their seats.

Edward I used this organization of Parliament to gain the support of the new middle class. He hoped that they would be more willing to pay taxes to support him if they helped pass the laws for the country. It would take until the 20th century before the elected House of Commons gained formal power over the hereditary House of Lords.

Throughout modern times, Parliament, rather than the monarch, has governed England. Thus, the English have had some say in their government for a long time. There was a tradition of limiting the power of the monarch.

INFO CHECK

1. State the importance of the Magna Carta in both British and U.S. history.

2. Did the establishment of the Model Parliament in 1295 strengthen or weaken absolutism in England? Explain your answer.

REVOLUTIONS IN 17TH-CENTURY ENGLAND

Although the Tudors ruled as absolute monarchs, they did try to give the appearance of governing through Parliament. In particular, Elizabeth I acted to win the support and love of her subjects. The people of England did not, however, approve of the Tudor successors, the Stuarts. In two revolutions, the English took steps to limit the power of their kings and make their government more democratic.

The Puritan Revolt

The death of Queen Elizabeth I in 1603 ended the rule of the Tudor family in England. Because she had no children, a cousin followed her on the throne. James I (ruled 1603–1625) was a member of the Stuart family, which had ruled Scotland for a long time. Tension quickly grew between James and Parliament.

James I. Members of Parliament resented James because he was a foreigner. They also disliked his many requests for money and his efforts to impose taxes without Parliament's consent. Parliament also distrusted James's desire for an alliance with Spain, which was a Catholic country. James and Parliament clashed many times throughout his 22-year reign.

Charles I. Under James's son, Charles I (ruled 1625–1649), relations between king and Parliament became worse. Like his father, Charles was a strong believer in absolutism and the divine right of kings.

Charles had little respect for Parliament. When Parliament refused to give him money to build up his military forces, he ordered knights and nobles to lend him money. Those who refused were sent to prison or drafted into the army.

Petition of Right. In 1628, Parliament agreed to give Charles the money he wanted if he signed the *Petition of Right*. This document prohibited the ruler from imposing taxes without the consent of Parliament. It also stated that no person could be sent to prison without having the charges against him or her made public. Charles at first

Time Line

Year	Dates and Events

A.D.
1101

1154–1189: Reign of Henry II, England; reform of justice system

1200

1201

1215: King John, England, signs Magna Carta
1295: First English Parliament

1300

1301

1337–1453: Hundred Years' War between France and England

1400

1401

1455–1485: English War of Roses; King Richard III (York) slain by Henry Tudor
(Lancaster)
1480–1584: Russians expel Mongols; harsh rule by early czars, ending with Ivan
("the Terrible")
1485–1509: Reign of Henry VII (Tudor), England
1500s–1600s: Rise of nation-states
1509–1547: Reign of Henry VIII, England; strong rule, costly wars
1519–1556: Reign of (Habsburg) Charles V, king of Spain, Holy Roman Emperor
1556–1598: Reign of Philip II, Spain

1500

1501

1558–1603: Reign of Elizabeth I, England
1589–1610: Reign of Henry IV, first Bourbon of France
1600s: Rise of absolute monarchs ruling by "divine right"
1603–1625: Reign of James I, England
1610–1643: Reign of Louis XIII, France; Cardinal Richelieu centralizes
government

1600

1601

1613–1917: Rule of Russia by Romanov Dynasty
1625–1649: Reign of Charles I, England; civil war between Royalists and
Puritans; Puritan victory, beheading of Charles I
1628: Petition of Right, England
1643–1715: Reign of Louis XIV ("Sun King"), France
1654–1658: English Commonwealth, repressive dictatorship under Oliver
Cromwell

1700

1701

1660–1685: English Restoration of Charles II
1679: Habeas Corpus Act, England
1682–1725: Reign of Czar Peter I ("the Great"), Russia
1685–1688: Reign of James II, England
1688: English "Glorious Revolution" with Protestants William III and Mary II
as joint rulers
1689: English Bill of Rights
1740–1780: Reign of (Habsburg) Maria Theresa, Austria-Hungary
1762–1796: Reign of Catherine II ("the Great"), Russia

1800

agreed to these provisions but later ignored them. He again raised taxes without the consent of Parliament. He also had people arrested and secretly tried in a special court called the Star Chamber. When Parliament objected, Charles dismissed it and ruled alone for 11 years, until 1640.

Tensions Build. Charles did not call Parliament into session again until he had exhausted every other way of raising money. Efforts by the new Parliament to restrict the power of the king led to more tension. In 1642, Charles attempted to arrest a few leading members of Parliament. This action touched off a civil war.

Civil War. Those who fought for the king were called Royalists or Cavaliers. They included the nobles, many Roman Catholics, and supporters of the Church of England.

Those who fought for Parliament were known as Roundheads because they wore their hair in a short, bowl-shaped style. Most of the Cavaliers wore their hair long. Many Roundheads were Puritans, followers of the ideas of John Calvin. Charles I had persecuted many Puritans for criticizing the practices of the Church of England. The Puritans controlled Parliament and led the effort to limit royal power. Small farmers, merchants, and others who had suffered from the king's policies also supported the Roundheads.

After 1643, Oliver Cromwell, a deeply religious Puritan, led the Roundhead forces. He trained and organized his men into a superior army, called the New Model Army. Cromwell's victory over the Royalists in 1648 left Parliament and the Puritans in control of England. Early in 1649, a special court tried Charles I, convicted him of treason, and had him beheaded. Absolutism and the monarchy had temporarily come to an end.

Eyewitness depiction of the execution of Charles I of England, 1649

Commonwealth and Protectorate

After Cromwell had won the civil war in 1649, he made England into a republic called the *Commonwealth*. In the new government, Cromwell and Parliament shared power. But tension soon developed between the two. After 1654, Cromwell ruled as a dictator. He took the title of Lord Protector of England. Cromwell dissolved (dismissed) Parliament twice.

During the period of the Commonwealth and Protectorate, England had its first, and only, written constitution. It was called the Instrument of Government. This document caused so much disagreement among all groups that Cromwell scrapped it in 1657.

Between 1649 and 1651, Cromwell put down royalist uprisings in Ireland and Scotland. He treated the Irish rebels in a particularly harsh and cruel manner, killing many. Cromwell thought the Irish had massacred English settlers in Ireland in 1641. Memories of these horrors persist to this day in Ireland.

In spite of his strong Puritan convictions, Cromwell allowed all Christians except Catholics to practice their own forms of worship. He encouraged the return of the Jews, a group who had been banned from England more than 300 years before under Edward I. Cromwell successfully fought a short war with England's commercial rivals, the Dutch. He also enforced laws that helped trade.

Cromwell did many things that offended the English. He closed

End of the Rump Parliament, which had unanimously favored Charles I's execution

all theaters and other places of public amusement. He did not permit the publication of newspaper articles that criticized his government. Katherine, the young woman in the opening story, thought that life was dull under Cromwell and the Puritans.

The Restoration

After Cromwell's death in 1658, Parliament again had the most power. But the majority of the English people wanted a king. In 1660, Parliament invited the oldest son of Charles I to return to England from his exile in Europe. Charles II, a Protestant, had fought against the Puritans to keep his father on the throne. He had been forced to flee England when Cromwell's forces won the civil war. The rule of Charles II (1660–1685) is called the *Restoration*. During the time of the restored monarchy, the king and Parliament shared power. Charles II reigned as a limited monarch.

Public life became less severe. The king supported the theater. He enjoyed having a good time. So the public could again attend places of amusement and openly enjoy themselves.

An important step to protect individual rights was taken during the Restoration period. In 1679, Parliament passed the *Habeas Corpus Act*. It stated that a person who was arrested could obtain a writ, or order, demanding to be taken before a judge within a certain period of time. The judge would then decide whether the person should be tried for a crime or released.

Habeas corpus is Latin for "you should have the body." The idea dates from the Middle Ages in England. The right is mentioned in the Magna Carta. It is an important part of the U.S. justice system.

Political parties began to develop during the Restoration. Supporters of the king came to be called Tories. Those who wanted Parliament to be stronger than the king were known as Whigs. Limited monarchy, habeas corpus, and the rise of political parties contributed to the growth of democracy in England.

The Glorious Revolution

James II became king of England in 1685. He was the younger brother of Charles II. Because he was Roman Catholic and a believer in absolute monarchy, Parliament disliked him. Nevertheless, Parliament was willing to support James. Since his daughters were married to Protestant princes, the members of Parliament felt secure that England would remain a Protestant country.

When James's second wife, a Catholic, gave birth to a son in 1688, Parliament became worried. A son, no matter what age, inherited the throne over a daughter. Parliament—and the public—greatly feared that James's son would reinstate Catholicism in England. It was agreed that the son had to be prevented from becoming king.

Parliament invited James's Protestant daughter Mary and her

Protestant husband, William, to rule England. William of Orange was of the royal house of the Netherlands. They accepted. William landed in England with an army and marched on London. James II fled to France. Because William and Mary won their victory without bloodshed, this event is called the *Glorious Revolution*. The joint monarchs (William III and Mary II) officially began their rule in 1689.

The Glorious Revolution of 1688 ended absolute monarchy in England. Limited monarchy became the permanent form of government. In 1689, the English *Bill of Rights* made it clear that Parliament would have more power than the kings and queens of England. The bill, also known as the Declaration of Rights, stated that taxes imposed without the consent of Parliament were illegal. A monarch could not suspend laws passed by Parliament. English courts could not impose cruel punishments. The bill further provided for frequent meetings of Parliament and gave all members of Parliament freedom of speech.

The English Bill of Rights was an important step toward democracy. It inspired people in other parts of the world to demand their rights and to eventually form democratic-style governments. The increase in the number of democratic governments is one important feature of the modern world.

This chapter has focused on Europe. Chapters 16 and 17 examine American and African civilizations, which Renaissance Europeans were just learning about.

INFO CHECK

1. State one cause and two results of the Puritan Revolt.

2. PROVE or DISPROVE the following statements:
   - The English had more rights under the Commonwealth than they did after the Restoration.
   - The Glorious Revolution did nothing to increase democratic government in England.

CHAPTER REVIEW

Multiple Choice

1. The monarchs of the 17th century justified their attempts to gain absolute power by claiming that

   1. they had a divine, or God-given, right to rule

   2. the threats of Mongol invasion justified their actions

   3. the Holy Roman Emperor had justified their actions

   4. the merchants were becoming too powerful.

2. An empire has many different peoples, cultures, and languages under one ruler. A nation-state has

1. people with different cultures but all speaking one language
2. people with a shared culture and a common language
3. people with distinctly different customs, religions, and languages
4. many groups of people, each seeking its own national identity.

3. Henry Tudor of the House of Lancaster sought to prevent another War of the Roses and ensure that his son would become the second Tudor king of England by

1. killing off all members of the York family
2. killing off all members of the Lancaster family
3. marrying a woman from the Lancaster family
4. marrying a woman from the York family.

4. Henry the VIII of England supported the Protestant Reformation because he was

1. a devoted follower of Martin Luther and the 95 Theses
2. able to take over Church property and get a needed divorce
3. angry at the wealth and lifestyle of the Catholic bishops
4. promised the support of the Holy Roman Emperor against the Spanish king.

5. Elizabeth I can be characterized as a leader who frequently

1. engaged in wars to protect her country

2. was a weak ruler who was resented by the people
3. promoted religious conflict
4. supported trade, exploration, and the arts and sciences.

6. English common law was the result of the

1. Twelve Tables of Roman Law being written down
2. writing down of King Henry's judges' decisions
3. translation of Hammurabi's Code
4. use of the Hebrews' moral code.

7. The major significance of the Magna Carta was that it limited the power of the

1. English kings
2. English nobles
3. Catholic Church
4. English merchant class.

8. Two of the causes of the English civil war of 1642 were

1. Charles I's religion, taxation, and foreign invasion
2. fear of a Catholic king and a Spanish invasion
3. Charles I's use of the Star Chamber and attempted arrest of members of Parliament
4. fear of Parliament passing new tax laws and imprisoning nobles.

9. The only period of time England did not have a king but had a written constitution was during the

1. Commonwealth
2. Glorious Revolution
3. Wars of the Roses
4. Restoration.

10. In France, Cardinal Richelieu's efforts

1. placed the Huguenots in power
2. set up an effective administrative system for all of France
3. extended French control over all of England, Scotland, and Wales
4. put Marie de Médicis on the French throne.

11. The map on page 307 shows that

1. city-states existed in Europe as late as 1648
2. the Habsburgs ruled a number of different European nations
3. Europeans were beginning to unite into a single nation
4. the Holy Roman Empire comprised most of Europe's territory.

12. According to the time line on page 314, between 1101 and 1800

1. freedom and democracy developed in most of the nations of Europe
2. dictators ruled with unlimited power and authority
3. most of Europe's royal families lost their thrones as a result of revolutions
4. monarchs ruled most nations in Europe, while some democratic foundations were being put in place in England.

Thematic Essays

1. *Task:* Compare the rule of the Tudors in England with the rule of the Bourbons in France.

2. How did the Puritan Revolt increase the rights of the English people? *Task:* Consider religious and legislative issues in your answer.

Document-Based Questions

Use the documents and your knowledge of Global History and Geography to answer the questions.

1. From writings by Frederick II.

"I repeat, then, the sovereign represents the state; he and his people form one single body which can only be happy in so far as it is harmoniously united. The prince stands in relation to the society over which he rules as the head stands to the body"

Explain the author's view of the relationship between the people and the ruler.

2. From a book about the reigns of Elizabeth I and James I.

"The state of monarchy is the supremest thing upon earth: for kings are not only God's lieutenants upon earth and sit upon God's throne, but even by God himself they are called gods. . . . In the scriptures kings are called gods and so their power [is] compared to the Divine power . . ."

Identify and explain the theory of government that is being defended here.

3. From the Magna Carta.

"39. No freeman shall be taken, or imprisoned, or disseized, or outlawed, or exiled, or in any way harmed—nor will we go upon or send upon him— save by the lawful judgment of his peers or by the law of the land."

Whose rights were protected in this document? Who was threatening these rights?

4. From *Two Treatises on Government* by John Locke.

"There is . . . another way whereby governments are dissolved and that is when the legislature or the prince, either of them acts contrary to the trust. . . . The end of government is the good of mankind. And which is best for mankind: that the people should be always exposed to the boundless will of tyranny, or that the rulers should be sometimes liable to be opposed when they grow exorbitant in the use of their power, and employ it for the destruction, and not the preservation of the properties of their people?

How does Locke's view of government differ from the views in the previous selections? What course of action is Locke attempting to justify?

Document-Based Essay

Task: Using specific examples from earlier readings and the chapter, describe how these documents mirror the political events that occurred in England.

UNIT REVIEW

Thematic Essays

1. Compare and contrast a day in the life of feudal England and feudal Japan. *Task:* Consider and cite political, social, and economic conditions in your answer.

2. Capitalism and the market economy arose out of the loss of life during the Crusades and the horrors of the Black Death. *Task:* Agree or disagree with this statement. Consider trade and the rise of merchants and a middle class in developing your answer.

Document-Based Questions

Use the documents and your knowledge of Global History and Geography to answer the questions

1. From the writings of Erasmus, a Renaissance philosopher.

"The world is waking out of a long deep sleep. The old ignorance is still defended with tooth and claw, but we have kings and nobles now on our side. . . . Time was when learning was only found in the religious orders. . . ."

What struggle is being referred to, and which side is it that the kings and nobles are supporting?

2. From the writings of Copernicus.

"I too began to reflect the earth's capacity for movement . . . that the earth turns from west to east, then, so far as pertains to the apparent rising and setting of the sun, moon, and stars. . . .

What revolutionary scientific theory is being described in this reading?

3. From the writings of Martin Luther.

"[Copernicus is the] new astronomer who wants to prove that the earth goes round, and not the heavens, the sun, and the moon. . . . But as the Holy Writ declares, it was the sun and not the earth that Joshua bade stand still."

Describe Luther's theory about the heavens and explain the reason he uses to support his views.

4. From a book about Galileo.

"I Galileo . . . kneeling before you Most Eminent and reverent Lord Cardinals, Inquisitors General . . . swear that I must abandon the false opinion that the Sun is the center of the world, and immovable and that the earth is not the center of the world and moves and that I must not hold defend or teach ... the said false doctrine."

Why would Galileo, a Renaissance man, give up his scientifically reached beliefs?

Document-Based Essay

Task: Describe the reasons for the conflict between the Renaissance thinker Galileo and the Catholic Church. Include the scientific theory and opposing religious doctrine to support your answer.

UNIT IV

The First
Global Age
(1450–1770)

The First Global Age
(1450–1770)

Year	Dates and Events
A.D. 1400	**1492:** Columbus discovers Americas for Spain
	1493–1528: Askia Muhammad rules Songhai Empire; Timbuktu becomes preeminent cultural center
	1494: Line of Demarcation gives Western Hemisphere to Spain except for Portuguese Brazil
	1497–1509: Portuguese expand trade from India to China, Japan, Southeast Asia
	1500s: Europeans introduce sheep, cattle, horses to Americas
1499	Spanish build forts in American Southwest, convert and dispossess Pueblos
1500	**1509:** Portuguese control Indian Ocean trade routes
	1519–1521: Magellan's Spanish expedition circumnavigates globe
	Cortés invades Mexico, defeats Aztecs, destroys Tenochtitlán
	1531–1533: Pizarro conquers Inca Empire, kills emperor
	1542: Spanish king bans enslavement of natives in New Spain; importation of African slaves increased
	1598–1640: Dutch build trading post on African Gold Coast, oust Portuguese, control European trade
1599	**1600s:** Native Americans tame wild horses for hunting, abandon farming culture
1600	**1600s–1700s:** Dutch in New Netherland, Indonesia, Sri Lanka, Caribbean, South Africa, South America
	1600s–1800s: Transport by Europeans of African slaves to Americas
	Slavery begins in Virginia, pervades South as cotton becomes major crop
	West Africa grows dependent on European goods, accepts European political control
1699	**1607:** Jamestown, Virginia, first permanent European (English) settlement in North America
1700	**1688:** French arrive in Cape Town; with Dutch, develop culture of Afrikaners
	1700s: France in eastern Canada, Mississippi Valley, Caribbean, India
	American, English, Dutch triangular slave trade—New York–Boston, West Africa, West Indies
	1756–1763: Seven Years' War involves most of Europe; Britain gains colonies in North America, India
1799	**1775–1783:** Iroquois-British alliance during American Revolution fatally weakens Iroquois League

CHAPTER
16

Empires Arise in the Americas Before 1500

By the time the hunters reached the grassy plain, they were so thin that their bones stuck out. Their band was only half the size it had been when they first started following the herds of great-tusked mammoths. Many had died while traveling the path that led past the frozen waters and the huge walls of ice. The old ones said that those who died had dreamed of the ice. It had gotten inside them and turned them stiff and cold.

When the band camped for the night, the old ones tried to ward off such dreams by telling stories. Everyone's favorite was about a warm land where great plants rose toward the sun and dropped delicious food on the earth. As they listened, the hunters thought of the lichen they had just eaten and laughed rather bitterly.

Now they stood and gazed at a vast green plain where herds of strange animals grazed. There in the distance was a clump of plants reaching toward the sky. The hunters wondered, were they dreaming? Would they wake once more to a world of ice and wind?

S cholars believe that the first immigrants to the Americas were bands of hunter-gatherers. They had crossed the Bering Strait from Siberia in eastern Asia into Alaska in North America. The first bands arrived during an Ice Age, perhaps as long as 40,000 years ago. At that time, much of the water of the Bering Strait was frozen into glaciers. Large areas of land, therefore, lay above water and served

Migration Routes From Asia Into the Americas

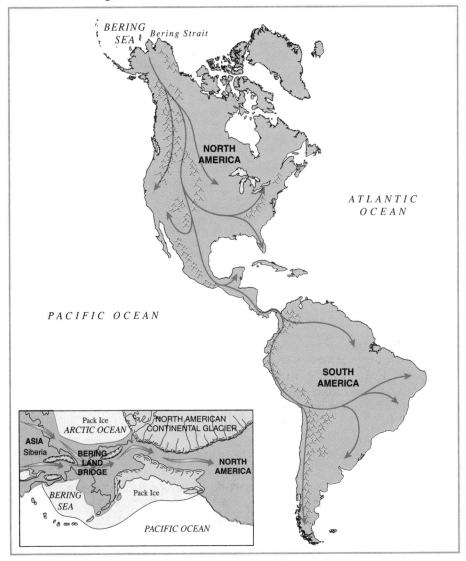

as a bridge between Siberia and Alaska. A long, ice-free corridor led the hunters into warmer parts of what is now North America.

HUMANS MOVE INTO THE AMERICAS

The hunters found areas along the way that provided animals and plants for food. Nonetheless, they must have had enormous courage and been unusually skilled at finding food and shelter to have endured such a journey. Scholars believe that the various groups of immigrants from Siberia came to North America during different periods of the Ice Age. Some of these groups became the ancestors of Native Americans. Recently discovered evidence suggests that some early immigrants to the Americas came by sea. They landed at various places along the Pacific Coast. The oldest remains of their campsites date to around 13,000 years ago.

Before the 15th century, most people of Europe, Asia, and Africa believed that their lands were the only ones on earth. Across the sea in the Western Hemisphere lay the continents now known as North America and South America. Living in these vast lands were people who knew nothing of the existence of Europeans, Africans, and Asians.

The cultural groups of the Western Hemisphere were strikingly different from those of the Eastern Hemisphere. They were also often strikingly different from one another. This is partly because the various societies of the Americas developed in environments that differed markedly from one another.

The Geography of the Americas

To understand the cultures of the Americas, therefore, it is helpful to look at the geography of the two continents. The map on page 328 illustrates the great diversity of their features.

The length of the two continents from the Bering Strait off present-day Alaska to Cape Horn at the southern tip of South America is about 11,000 miles. The extreme north of North America reaches into the Arctic Ocean. The extreme south of South America is about 600 miles from Antarctica. Along the western coast of both continents stretches a vast mountain range. The two landmasses are bounded by the Atlantic Ocean on the east and the Pacific Ocean on the west.

Both continents have a variety of geographical features. The tundra in the northernmost area of North America is a frozen plain where few plants can grow. The parts of North America now known as Canada and the United States once consisted mainly of forest and woodland. The central part of North America includes prairie and desert. There are rain forests in Central America. A long western mountain range extends from Alaska through North and Central America to the southern tip of South America. The range is known as the Rocky Mountains in North America and as the Andes in South America.

Besides the mountainous region it shares with North America, South America's main regions are rain forest, tropical scrub, and grassy plains. A strip of desert stretches between its mountains and western coast. A larger desert is located in its southern area.

The Early Americans

The hunter-gatherers from Siberia settled the Western Hemisphere later than similar groups settled the Eastern Hemisphere. When the resources of one place could no longer meet the needs of a

North and South America: Physical Map

group of hunter-gatherers, some of its members would leave to search for a new area. In time, Native Americans spread throughout North and South America. As they did, they became isolated from one another and developed many different ways of life. The climate and geography of the areas in which they settled affected the types of houses they built, the food they ate, and the clothing they wore.

The earliest evidence we have of human inhabitants in North America dates from about 11,200 years ago. The evidence is spear points found near Clovis, New Mexico, in the 1930s. Evidence of an earlier settlement was found in the 1990s in southern Chile in South America. This evidence—knotted strings, wood, mastodon meat—dates from about 12,500 years ago.

Many Native Americans remained hunters and gatherers. Some groups learned to farm and built permanent communities. All of the groups shaped stone, wood, and bone into tools and weapons. None used metal, except to make jewelry and ornaments. They did not know about firearms or how to use the wheel as a tool. Except for dogs and birds, they did not domesticate animals. Europeans introduced sheep, cattle, and horses into the Americas after 1500.

INFO CHECK

1. Describe how the first immigrants arrived in the Americas.

2. How did climate and geography influence early Americans?

ADVANCED CULTURES

In Mesoamerica, now southern Mexico, Guatemala, Belize, and Honduras, advanced cultures existed as early as 1100 B.C. Equally advanced cultures developed later in the Andes Mountains in western South America. These societies were much more complex than the more northern Native American societies. They were as advanced as any in early Mesopotamia and rivaled the one in ancient Egypt.

Geography

As in all early civilizations, geography influenced the growth of these societies. A warm, moist climate and fertile soil helped early Mesoamericans grow the surplus food necessary to support large populations. The few rivers provided water and transportation routes. Not all the environments of early Mesoamerican societies were ideal, however. In the central eastern coastal area, where the very first of these societies originated, thick rain forests and a hot, humid climate made life difficult. Later peoples founded civilizations in highland plains areas, which had cooler climates.

Agriculture

Corn was the most important crop grown by early Mesoamerican farmers. They also grew beans, cacao (or cocoa) beans, squash, chili peppers, some root crops, cotton, and fruit trees. They had no large domesticated animals, such as horses, sheep, or cattle. They kept flocks of turkeys and a small breed of dog, which they used for meat.

Trade

Although corn was their principal crop, Mesoamericans greatly valued the cacao bean. Along with cloth, beads made from seashells, and jade, they used cacao as money. They carried on long-distance trade by land and water routes. Besides wars of conquest, trade agreements with people in different places gave the strongest and wealthiest Mesoamerican societies political power over large territories.

Common Features

Because of frequent trade contacts, these early societies had many features in common. Through the process of *cultural diffusion*, their governments, farming techniques, social and religious systems, architecture, and city planning were very similar. Of course, the variety of environments and experiences gave rise to important differences. Then, too, as a younger civilization learned from an older one, it made discoveries of its own. Some developed beyond their teachers in science, art, and writing.

Early Mesoamerican cultures devised effective methods of farming. Intellectuals invented writing and number systems and studied the heavens. Artists and architects created beautiful pictures, sculptures, and buildings. Political and business leaders managed government and trade efficiently. Many features of early Mesoamerican culture were startlingly like those of early cultures in Asia, Europe, and Africa. Therefore, some scholars have wondered whether contact between Mesoamerica and cultures in the Eastern Hemisphere had occurred before Columbus landed in the Bahamas in 1492.

Technology

The technology in the Western Hemisphere was not as advanced as the technology of the Eastern Hemisphere. Early Mesoamericans did not make use of wheeled vehicles or plows. Mesoamericans knew about the wheel—archaeologists have found wheeled objects that might have been ornaments or toys. They did not use iron. They were skilled in preparing huge stones for building. They created rope bridges to cross narrow canyons. Terraces were constructed on steep hillsides for growing crops. All in all, Mesoamericans accomplished marvelous feats with the tools and skills available to them.

The Olmecs

The oldest great Mesoamerican civilization—that of the Olmecs—flourished from about 1200 B.C. to 400 B.C. It was at its height around the time the Egyptians were declining as a great power.

The birthplace of the Olmec culture was Mexico's Caribbean coast in the area where Tabasco and Veracruz are located today. Scholars do not know why Mesoamerica's first civilization originated in such a hot and swampy area. They often compare the Olmecs to the early Mesopotamians because both groups learned to drain marshy areas in order to farm and build on them.

Society. Also like the Mesopotamians, the Olmecs gradually united their small farming communities into a state and established a central government to rule it. Olmec society had a rigid class system headed by priest-kings. An elite group of warriors, administrators, and engineers managed important state functions for their rulers. The lower classes consisted of farmers and artisans. Below them were the slaves and serfs. They did such heavy labor as dragging huge blocks of stone from quarries from 40 to 50 miles away and building temples and creating sculptures for them.

Population Centers. Historians argue that the rulers must have had considerable power and wealth. They were able to organize the construction of the three major Olmec centers—San Lorenzo, La Venta, and Tres Zapotes. (They were given Spanish names because no record of their Olmec names exists.) They contained palaces, religious buildings, and marketplaces. The Olmecs built large, high earthen mounds. Religious ceremonies were held on the flat tops of the mounds.

Accomplishments. Like both the Mesopotamians and the Egyptians, the Olmecs had a writing system, a number system, and a calendar. The writing is called glyph writing. It is made up of symbols and pictures of real objects. The Olmecs devised mirrors of a metal called magnetite for personal decoration. Possibly, the mirrors were also used to light fires by reflecting the sun's rays onto flammable materials.

The Olmecs produced great works of art. The most impressive examples of their skill are massive heads carved from stone. Some are nine feet high and weigh 18 to 20 tons. Anthropologists assume these sculptures represented priest-rulers. Olmec artists also made sculptures of plumed serpents and a creature that was half-jaguar and half-human. The jaguar was the Olmecs' rain god. Both the plumed serpent and the jaguar were powerful spirits in the religions of later Mesoamerican societies.

Influence on Others. So many features of the Olmec civilization recurred in later cultures that scholars call it the "mother" civilization of Mesoamerica. It also had a strong influence on other societies that existed at the same time. This influence was probably not the result of military conquest. The Olmecs were too few in number to have conquered other groups. Then, too, there is little evidence that the Olmecs occupied other people's lands.

Trade. The Olmecs spread their culture through trade. In fact, they were responsible for most of the cultural exchange that took place between other groups as well. They created the trade networks

Massive stone head of the Olmec culture, probably representing a sky god

through which various groups exchanged such luxury items as jewels for such necessities as corn. As trade items moved from place to place, so too did ideas, customs, and myths. Cultural diffusion occurred.

Collapse. Scholars do not know why the Olmec civilization ended. Around 900 B.C., some unknown group destroyed the ceremonial center called San Lorenzo. Scholars have various theories about what happened. A rival leader may have tried to drive out the Olmec ruler. A peasant group might have rebelled against harsh usage by their overlords. After the fall of San Lorenzo, La Venta began to decline. The Olmec state collapsed in about 600 B.C. Olmec culture lived on, however, and developed into new forms.

The People of Teotihuacán

In about A.D. 300, a city called Teotihuacán appeared northeast of what is now Mexico City. The people who built it shared many elements of Olmec culture. Their social scale ranged from priest-kings and their administrators through craftspeople and farmers down to slaves and serfs. They built pyramids and worshiped the plumed serpent and a rain god. Like the Olmecs, they had calendars, a number system, and a writing system.

The City. City planners had laid out Teotihuacán's streets in a grid pattern. The east-west streets are at right angles to the north-south streets. Some dwellings were like large apartment houses. Craftsworkers and artisans lived in them and worked in shops that had been built close by. The homes of wealthier people were airy and spacious. The walls of some of the buildings were decorated with beautiful murals. In the ruins of Teotihuacán, archaeologists have found workshops for many crafts. There are places for tanning leather, making pottery, and carving blades from obsidian to make weapons and tools. (Obsidian is hardened glass from the lava of volcanoes. The edges of thin pieces can be sharpened by chipping and polishing.)

Some 100,000 to 200,000 people lived in Teotihuacán during its most prosperous period. It was larger than most European or Asian cities of the time. At one end of a two-mile-long avenue was the gigantic Pyramid of the Sun. It stood 200 feet high and measured 700 feet long on each side. At the other end of the avenue as the smaller Pyramid of the Moon. The ruins of these structures can be seen today.

Empire. The people of Teotihuacán established an empire throughout Mesoamerica by means of trade rather than war. Archaeologists have found evidence that these people colonized small areas where important resources, such as obsidian, were found. Having control of the source of obsidian made the people of Teotihuacán the major manufacturers of weapons and tools. Having the main supply of such necessities gave them great control over other Mesoamerican societies. As the master traders of the area, they, like the Olmecs, spread their own culture and learned new ways from other groups.

As with the decline of the Olmecs, the reasons for the end of the Teotihuacán civilization are a mystery. Between A.D. 600 and 650, the great city was burned. Possibly an enemy force destroyed it. Nonetheless, its culture survived to be adopted and developed by other peoples.

The Mayas

The Mayas built the first centers of their culture in what is now northern Guatemala. Later they spread to areas that are now Belize, Honduras, and the Yucatan in Mexico. The Mayas shared many cultural features with the people of Teotihuacán. Building on earlier traditions and technologies, they created the greatest early civilization in the Americas.

Class Structure and Religion. The Mayas' class structure was organized like those of the Olmecs and the people of Teotihuacán. As did other Mesoamericans, the Mayas believed the jaguar and the plumed serpent to be powerful spirits. They also worshiped gods connected with nature, such as the rain god Chac and a corn god. Human blood and human sacrifices were needed in the ceremonies to honor some gods.

THE DARK SIDE OF MAYAN HISTORY

In 1996, a startling discovery was made by a team of archaeologists working in northern Yucatán. While excavating a 1,700-year-old pyramid in Yaxuna, a Classic Mayan city, they noticed a small hole near one of the trenches. Peering in, they found a large chamber. It was a sealed tomb.

The tomb chamber was approximately six feet long and five feet wide. A stairway at one end led to its entrance. A member of the team carefully cleared away the dirt at the entrance. He uncovered a pile of human bones and ceramic pots. The archaeologists suspected that the bones were the remains of human sacrifices. The bones of the tomb's principal occupant was found at the bottom of the pile. He was a male, more than 55 years old. His head had been placed on top of the other bodies. Near the headless man's shoulders was an obsidian blade, used for ritual bloodletting. The remains of a polished white shell crown were near his feet. It was a type of royal headdress familiar to the archaeologists. Near the crown was a small jade carving of a quetzal bird, probably part of a royal headband.

The bones of a young woman and a teenage girl were on either side of the man's skeleton. Each wore a royal headdress. The young woman cradled in her left arm a doll representing a goddess. Other artifacts in the tomb included jade jewelry, carved bones, small mosaic pieces, and small pots and pitchers.

The tomb contained the remains of a total of 11 murdered men, women, and children. The archaeologists concluded that the royal family of Yaxuna had been sacrificed at the time of a violent change of rulers in the late 4th or early 5th century. The excavation team had stumbled on the dark side of the Mayan history.

Located ten miles south of Chichen Itza, a powerful Mayan city, Yaxuna was built around 500 B.C. The site had natural wells for water, level ground for crops, and abundant stone for construction. It occupied a strategic location on an overland trade route through the Yucatán, linking other Mayan cities with salt deposits on the north coast. Stronger neighbors fought to control it.

Archaeological investigation of Yaxuna revealed evidence of six deliberate destruction events between the 4th and 13th centuries A.D. The evidence indicated that warriors from Chichen Itza had destroyed the city's palace and the royal tomb in the late 4th or early 5th century. Possibly, the murder of the royal family was an act of war, rather than a ritual sacrifice. It may have signaled the beginning of a new ruling dynasty in Yaxuna. Future investigation will enable archaeologists and historians to gain a clearer picture of the urban warfare that caused so much violence and destruction in the Mayan world.

1. Does the urban warfare that took place among the Mayas between the 4th and 13th centuries indicate that their civilization was inferior to those of Egypt or Mesopotamia? Explain your answer.

2. What does "The Dark Side of Mayan History" tell you about the work of archaeologists?

Agriculture. Like most early civilizations, Mayan society was based on farming. Mayan farmers cleared small plots of land out of the rain forest. In the hot, humid climate, they grew mainly corn, beans, peppers, and tomatoes. They also raised sweet potatoes, tobacco, cotton, fruits, and cacao (its seeds are made into chocolate).

Trade. The Mayas carried on a widespread trade with peoples in other parts of Central America. For cloth, craft items, and other products, they received such items as obsidian, jade, and feathers of exotic birds. From their contacts with other cultures, they learned new ideas and ways of doing things.

Building. As early as 600 B.C., the Mayas started building cities in northern Guatemala. But the period of their highest level of development occurred between A.D. 250 and 900. These centuries are called the Classic Period. During this time, the Mayas built many cities, such as Tikal in Guatemala and Copán in Honduras. They were ceremonial and religious centers. Only priests and royalty lived in them. The common people lived on small farms around the centers. The cities are characterized by tall, flat-topped stone pyramids. These structures served as stages for ceremonies and as royal tombs.

Some buildings were astronomical observatories. From them, priests studied the stars and the movements of the planets. The priests used this information to predict eclipses of the sun and the moon. The information also guided the Mayas in the planting of their crops and in planning ceremonies.

Achievements. In mathematics, the Mayas used the zero and created a number system based on 20. (Our number system is based on 10 and comes from India through the Muslims.) They had a calendar of 365 days that was as accurate as the one we use today. The Mayas also had a highly developed writing system that has not yet

Maya Temple of the Sun,
Palenque, Mexico

been completely deciphered. Mayan writing used hieroglyphs, or symbols, that stood for ideas, dates, numbers, and sounds. They carved glyphs on tall stone monuments called stelae. These glyphs record the events in the lives of their rulers.

Skilled workers created pottery in many shapes and painted beautiful designs on it. Other workers made objects out of jade. On the inner walls of buildings in religious centers, artists painted colorful murals. Sculptors made intricate stone carvings and modeled figurines from clay.

Decline. In the 800s, the Mayas began to leave their cities in Guatemala. They may have done so to escape victorious enemies or contagious diseases. Perhaps the population had become so large that the amount of food grown in the area could no longer support it.

Groups moved north to the Yucatán and created cities there. One, Chichén Itzá, became powerful and dominated a wide area. It was like the city-states of ancient Greece and eastern Africa.

About the year 1200, invaders from other parts of Mesoamerica moved into Mayan territory. Wars broke out among the city-states. The civilization was in disarray. Spanish explorers conquered the remaining Mayas in the early 1500s. By then most of the great cities had been abandoned. Descendants of the Mayas continue to live in the areas of their once-great civilization. They speak a form of the ancient Mayan language.

The Toltecs and the Aztecs

The Toltecs were a confederation of many groups that had banded together in order to defend themselves and to make conquests. They were more warlike than the earlier peoples had been. Admiring the culture of Teotihuacán, they intermarried with its inhabitants and adopted their religion and other traditions. The Toltecs soon dominated the area known today as the Valley of Mexico. Toltec influence also spread to the Mayas in the Yucatan.

Rise of the Aztecs. The Aztecs first entered the Toltec realm in the 1200s. A poor, weak people, they were forced to live on some marshy islands in the middle of Lake Texcoco (near present-day Mexico City).

In spite of these disadvantages, the Aztecs quickly advanced. They absorbed both Toltec warrior skills and the cultural legacy of Teotihuacán. During the next 200 years, the Aztecs built an empire by conquering most of central Mexico. The Aztecs kept a full-time army of warriors. Aztec power reached its peak in the 1400s. From the conquered peoples, the Aztecs demanded a yearly tax and took slaves and victims to sacrifice in ceremonies.

A Great City. The center of the Aztec Empire was Tenochtitlán. The Aztecs built this large city in about 1325 on one of the swampy islands in Lake Texcoco. Long stone causeways and bridges connected

Mesoamerican Civilizations

the city with the mainland. By the late 1400s, more than 100,000 people lived in Tenochtitlán. Food for the people of the city was grown on islands in the lake. Aztec workers created the garden islands by piling up mud from the lake bottom.

Aztec craftspeople made beautiful objects out of gold, silver, and precious stones. They wove fine cotton cloth. The system of picture writing they used resembles Mayan glyphs.

Religion. The Aztecs worshiped many gods, including Quetzal-coatl, the feathered serpent that originated with the Olmecs. They believed that this god and the gods of the sun, the rain, the wind, and war required human blood to keep the world alive. To obtain sacrificial victims, the Aztecs constantly fought wars with other Indian peoples. On certain days of the year, the priests laid the prisoners on a temple altar. Then they used a sharp stone knife to cut out the heart of each living victim. The Aztecs believed that the person whose heart they offered to the gods became a messenger to the gods. They expected the victim to plead with the gods for the well-being of the Aztecs.

Society. There were four main classes of people in the Aztec culture: nobles (including priests), commoners, serfs, and slaves. Most commoners were farmers. Some became skilled in various crafts. Some became soldiers. Serfs worked the nobles' land. They remained with the land when its was acquired by another noble. (Recall the manorial system in medieval Europe.) Slaves were property who had been captured in war or bought. They became the sacrificial victims in ceremonies honoring the gods.

The emperor had great power and was considered to be a god. He did, however, consult a council of nobles.

There were schools for boys over the age of ten. Girls were generally taught household skills at home.

Spanish Invaders. In 1519, a few Spanish soldiers led by Hernando Cortés arrived in Mexico. They came in search of land and gold. By then, revolts of subject peoples had weakened Aztec rule. Many of the rebelling people helped the Spaniards conquer the Aztec Empire. By 1522, the Spaniards had destroyed Tenochtitlán and built Mexico City on its ruins.

The Incas of South America

The most powerful of the early American civilizations developed in the Andes Mountains of South America. By the 16th century, the Incas ruled an empire of 12 million people in what are today the countries of Ecuador, Peru, Bolivia, Chile, and Argentina. The people in the Inca Empire belonged to 100 different cultural groups and spoke 20 different languages.

Way of Life. The Incas worshiped their emperor as a representative of the sun god. He had total power over everyone and everything in his empire. The government owned and controlled all land and most businesses. In addition to farming, men served in the army and worked on government construction projects or in the gold and silver mines. Some young women received special training in religion so that they could take part in sacred ceremonies.

Farmers had to take care of the land belonging to the temples first. Then they worked on the government's land. Finally, they could take care of their own fields. Women had to weave a certain amount of cloth for the government. To take care of the needy or to give aid when times were bad, the government kept storehouses full of foodstuffs in all parts of the empire.

Rule of the Empire. The Incas ruled their empire more successfully than the Aztecs ruled theirs. The different peoples of the empire had to learn about the Inca language, religion, and way of life. The Incas had no alphabet and so could not spread their culture by the written word. Therefore, the government sent colonists into conquered lands to serve as teachers.

The Incas brought the sons of conquered rulers to Cuzco, the Inca capital, for education and to serve as hostages. With their sons in the power of the Inca rulers, conquered kings would be less likely to rebel. After being educated by Inca teachers, the sons returned home to rule their people.

Government officials closely watched all activities in the conquered lands. Those who were disloyal or who did not pay their taxes were severely punished. The emperor ruled by fear.

Agriculture. Inca farmers in the Andes Mountains planted crops, particularly potatoes, on terraces. These were flat areas dug into the side of a mountain and kept in place by a stone framework.

South America: The Inca Empire

The Andean climate is cold and very dry. Inca farmers used a highly efficient irrigation system to water their crops.

Skills. Incas were expert builders of roads and bridges. The vast network of roads connected all parts of the empire. Messengers and the army could move quickly over them.

Inca doctors performed many types of operations, including opening up the skull to treat growths on the brain or relieve headaches. They also discovered quinine, a medicine for malaria.

Craftsworkers made beautiful gold and silver objects. Weavers created fine cotton and woolen cloth. Inca workers built stone structures so carefully that no mortar was needed to hold them together.

Ruins of the Inca city of Machu Picchu, high in the Andes Mountains of Peru

In the buildings that still stand, the stones fit together so tightly that a thin knife cannot be pushed between them.

Spanish Invaders. In 1532, Spanish soldiers led by Francisco Pizarro marched into the Inca Empire. (They numbered about 170 individuals.) They seized the emperor and demanded that he pay a huge ransom in gold and silver. Although the emperor's subjects paid the ransom, the Spaniards killed him anyway. By 1572, the Spaniards had completed their conquest of the entire Inca Empire.

INFO CHECK

1. Define the term "Mesoamerica."

2. List the advanced cultures of Mesoamerica and indicate the dates during which each flourished.

3. What did these cultures have in common with Egypt and Mesopotamia? What possibility is indicated by those common features?

4. Why do you think the Spanish wanted to conquer the Mesoamerican cultures? How might the Americas be different today if the Spanish had never arrived?

NORTH AMERICAN CULTURES

Native American tribes developed a wide variety of cultures in what are today Canada and the United States. None created the advanced civilizations that the Mesoamericans and Incas did. Many groups lived by hunting and gathering. Some farmed and lived in villages. Similar ways of life developed in each particular geographical area. Four major cultural groups are the Native Americans of the Eastern Woodlands, the Southwest, the Plains, and the Northwest Coast.

The Iroquois

The forests of southeastern Canada and the eastern United States were rich in game animals. The soil of the region is fertile and its

North American Indian Cultures

Village of Eastern
Woodlands people

climate is moist and *temperate* (with no extremes of heat or cold). The
Native Americans of the Eastern Woodlands area lived as hunters,
farmers, and traders. The trees from the vast forests provided material for building houses and canoes. The people fashioned farm
tools, hunting weapons, and ornaments from stone, bone, and wood.
A network of rivers provided them with transportation routes to other
regions where they traded their craftwork.

One of the largest groups of Native Americans in the Eastern
Woodlands area were the Iroquois. Five tribes formed the Iroquois
League of Five Nations: Seneca, Cayuga, Mohawk, Onondaga, and
Oneida. (Later the Tuscaroras joined the league.) The purpose of the
league was to keep peace among the member tribes and unite them
against hostile outsiders. The unity and fighting ability of the Iroquois made them very powerful.

Government. In their tribal councils, the Iroquois practiced a
type of representative democracy. The leading women of the tribes
chose the chiefs, who were called *sachems*. These sachems represented the people in their tribe. Each sachem attended the Council of
the League, which was the governing body of the Five Nations.

Anyone could attend meetings of the council. At these meetings,
people presented proposals for acceptance or rejection. After a great
deal of discussion and speechmaking, the sachems would reach a
decision about each proposal. Some historians believe that Council
of the League influenced the men who planned the government
of the United States. Others point out that Greek and Roman
forms of democracy were stronger influences on the United States
government.

Women had a great deal of authority among the Iroquois. A
woman headed each clan, or group of related families. The head
woman owned all of the family goods. No one could inherit anything

except from his or her mother. Mothers arranged all marriages between young men and women.

Society. When a man married, he went to live with his wife's clan. At the same time, he remained a member of his mother's clan. As such, he had no responsibility for raising or teaching his children. His wife's brothers brought them up. Children, in turn, had no responsibility for taking care of aged fathers. When men got old, they went back to their mothers' clan.

The Iroquois called themselves the "People of the Long House." They lived in houses made of bark attached to wooden pole frames. Most of the houses measured about 60 feet long, 18 feet wide, and 18 feet high. Some were as long as 150 feet. Several related families shared each house. A number of houses, arranged in rows, made up a village. A stockade (a high fence made of poles) surrounded the village. Outside the stockade were fields where the women raised corn, squash, and beans. The men hunted, fished, and sometimes raided the villages of other Indian tribes.

During the American Revolution (1775–1783), some of the Iroquois tribes sided with the British. After the Americans won the war, they sent troops to punish the Iroquois. This action weakened the league forever.

Anasazi of the Southwest

In 1888, at a place called Mesa Verde, a pair of ranchers found a deserted village. It had been built on a ledge of a cliff wall of a canyon in southwestern Colorado. The dwellings in this village were like modern apartment houses. They were three or four stories tall. Here and there, towers rose above the houses. So impressive was this stone and adobe structure that the ranchers named it the Cliff Palace.

Since the discovery of the Cliff Palace, more ancient villages have been found. Most of these are located in an area called the Four Corners, where the borders of Colorado, New Mexico, Arizona, and Utah meet. The dry Southwestern climate preserved the bones of the former inhabitants as well their belongings.

From fossils and artifacts, anthropologists have pieced together information about these people. Most scholars believe that they are the ancestors of the Pueblo and the Hopi who now live in this area. These Native Americans call their ancestors the Anasazi (the ancient ones).

Way of Life. Originally, the Anasazi were hunters and gatherers. About A.D. 100, they began to cultivate corn. To be near their crops, they settled in permanent communities. Lacking a large supply of trees for building material, they made adobe bricks from the desert soil. As communities grew larger and natural water supplies became inadequate for their populations, the Anasazi built simple irrigation systems.

Cliff dwelling from the 1200s, in Mesa Verde National Park, Colorado

The artifacts the Anasazi left behind show that they were skilled craftspeople. They wove their baskets so tightly that they could carry water and cook in them. They were clever at making nets for snaring animals. One kind of net had a large, black spot painted in the middle. Anthropologists believe that the Anasazi stretched it across a dry stream bed and then beat the bushes to scare out the rabbits. The frightened rabbits would mistake the black spot for a hole and ensnare themselves as they tried to escape through it. Judging from their pottery and fabrics, the Anasazi had a keen sense of beauty.

Religion. Anthropologists believe that these people had a complex religion. In the deserted Anasazi villages, they have found structures called *kivas*. On the walls of some of these underground rooms, artists have painted supernatural figures bestowing rain, seeds, fish, and other good things on the earth. Priests once used the altars and firepits, which were also found in the kivas, for performing sacred rites.

Abandonment of the Area. Historians do not know what disaster struck the Anasazi to make them leave the area within a short period of time. They only know that these ancient people began deserting their cities in the late 1200s. A combination of problems may have caused them to look for new homes—a prolonged period of drought, attacks by fierce newcomers, and a dwindling supply of wood for fuel and construction.

The Pueblo of the Southwest

Scholars assume that the Anasazi did not die out. They most likely became the ancestors of various groups of Native Americans now living in the Southwest. Among these groups are the Pueblo. Anthropologists believe that the lifestyle of the Pueblo is very similar to that of the Anasazi. Like the Anasazi, the Pueblo live in multistoried adobe houses that are clustered together to form villages. Spanish explorers gave them the name Pueblo, which is the Spanish word for "town."

Way of Life. Before the Spanish came to their area, the Pueblo lived as peaceful farmers. The men grew corn, beans, squash, and cotton. The women cooked, wove cloth, made pottery, and helped build the houses.

A council of religious leaders and clan chiefs governed each Pueblo town. In order to survive in the arid environment of the Southwest, the Pueblo had learned to cooperate with each other. Their society needed little law enforcement. Community members ridiculed or ignored troublemakers until they behaved properly.

Religion. Religion was very important to the Pueblo. Each community had a kiva, like those found in Anasazi ruins. This underground room served as a religious center and meeting place for men only. Women were not allowed to enter. The Pueblo held many different ceremonies throughout the year. Using special costumes and rituals, the Pueblo hoped to persuade the gods to give them rain and good fortune. They also believed in spirits called *kachinas*. The Pueblo believed that these messengers from the gods lived with them for six months of the year. During the other six months, the kachinas lived with the gods in the mountains. The Pueblo had the most elaborate religion of all the tribes in the area north of Mexico.

Apache and Navajo

Sometime after A.D. 1000, invaders from the north threatened the peaceful existence of the Pueblo. These invaders, the Apaches and the Navajos, were hunters. They brought to the Southwest more powerful bows and arrows than the Pueblo possessed. The Apaches and Navajos often attacked Pueblo towns to take food and slaves. The Pueblo were good farmers, traders, and craftsworkers but not warriors. They fought only to protect their homes.

Way of Life. The Apaches long remained hunters and raiders. Over time, contact with the Pueblo gradually changed the Navajos. They abandoned the ways of the warrior and became farmers and herders. Some Navajo men developed great skill as silversmiths, learning the art from Mexicans. Navajo women made beautiful rugs and blankets out of the wool from their sheep. They had originally learned weaving from the Pueblo. The Navajo people make up the largest group of Native Americans in the United States today.

Government. Groups of Apache families were headed by a chief. Some inherited the role. Others were chosen for their ability as a hunter, warrior, or speaker. If a family did not respect the leader, the family could leave the group and join another. The leader could not force a decision on his followers. They all had to agree to support his ideas.

Navajo family groups chose a leader to give advice. Policy decisions were made in public meetings. Both men and women took part in the process. All had to agree to a decision before it could be carried out.

Arrival of the Spanish

When the Spanish came to the Southwest in the mid-1500s, they drastically changed the lives of the people living there. Each group reacted to the newcomers in its own characteristic way. The Pueblo tried to live peacefully with the Spanish. At first they submitted when the Spanish forced them to become Christians and to work at the missions and forts. After the Spanish punished them for secretly practicing their own religion and treated them harshly, the Indians rebelled in 1680. Although the Spanish still ruled, the Pueblo were able to live and work in their own communities and to worship in their own way.

Since the Navajo lived in scattered groups on land with few resources, the Spanish tended to leave them alone. The Navajo, however, learned much from the Spanish. On observing that the Spanish raised sheep for wool, milk, and meat, they acquired some of these animals and became herders.

The Apaches resisted the invaders. They specialized in sudden attacks and swift retreats into their mountain strongholds. Later, they used the same tactics against the pioneers and soldiers of the United States. The Apaches were never defeated by military forces. They eventually agreed to a treaty of peace with the United States government.

The Peoples of the Great Plains

The grasslands stretching from the Missouri River in the east to the Rocky Mountains in the west are known as the Great Plains. The area extends from Canada in the north to Texas in the south. Before the coming of the Europeans, most of the Native Americans who lived on the western plains spent part of the year hunting buffalo and the rest of the year farming. During the hunting season, they followed the buffalo herds, carrying their goods with them and sleeping in temporary camps. When they farmed, they lived in villages. Among the best-known Plains tribes were the Sioux, Cheyenne, and Comanche.

Way of Life. Hunting was far more important than farming. The lives of the Plains people depended mainly on the buffalo. From the buffalo, they obtained meat and the skins they needed for their clothes and tepees. (Tepees are the cone-shaped tents in which the Plains people camped during hunts.) They made most of their tools and weapons from buffalo bones. Dried buffalo dung (droppings) provided fuel for campfires.

The leader of the hunting band was chosen for qualities of courage or wisdom. He served as an adviser to the council of the adult male warriors. Any decisions made by the council had to be unanimous.

Their religion had few large ceremonies. An important one was the sun dance. Individuals looked for guidance from a personal guardian—a spirit power.

The Effect of Horses. Until the Spaniards brought the horse to North America, hunting buffalo was difficult. Before the late 1600s, the Indians hunted on foot. They often killed buffalo by driving them over a cliff. As more Spanish came to America, some of the horses they brought with them escaped. These animals formed wild herds that gradually made their way to the Great Plains. The Plains people soon learned to tame these new creatures and to ride them. On horseback, the hunters could easily run down the buffalo herds and shoot arrows into the big animals. Once they tamed the horse, the Plains people devoted all their time to hunting and no longer farmed.

Warriors. Their skill in handling horses and the discipline and organization they developed hunting buffalo helped make the Plains people great warriors. Tribes generally fought to avenge a wrong or to get more horses. Gallant behavior during battle was highly valued. A warrior won great honor if he touched an armed enemy with a hand or a special stick. Another act admired by the Plains people was the stealing of horses from the middle of an enemy camp. They called such acts "counting coup."

Settlers and Change. Settlers who moved into the Great Plains after the mid-1800s destroyed the way of life of the Plains people. Farmers, miners, and cattle ranchers pushed the tribes out of their hunting grounds. People who did not need the buffalo for food hunted them for sport. Soon almost none of the great animals were left. The disappearance of the buffalo weakened the Plains tribes. Little by little, the United States Army forced the tribes to move onto *reservations*. The United States government had set aside these areas of land for the use of the Native Americans. On the reservations, the Plains people could no longer follow their old ways of life. They came to depend on the government to provide their food, clothing, and shelter. (In time, almost all Native American groups were forced to live on reservations.)

The Northwest Coast Peoples

On the northwest coast of North America, the mild, wet climate and abundant natural resources made possible the development of a complex Native American culture. The people who inhabited what are today British Columbia, Washington, and Oregon were able to obtain a good living without much effort. They could spend their time and energy making beautiful objects and performing religious and social ceremonies. Among the most prosperous of the Northwest Coast peoples were the Haida and the Tlingit.

Villages. The peoples of the Northwest Coast lived in villages built along the seashore or the edge of a bay or river. A typical village consisted of eight or more large wooden houses. Each house held 30 to 40 related people and had its own chief. One house chief also served as the village chief. This was a hereditary position passed on from one male relative to another. Being chief gave a person wealth and prestige.

The construction of the houses reflected the woodworking skill of

Ornately carved totem pole of the Northwest Coast people, British Columbia, Canada

the Northwest Coast people. So did the tall, elaborately carved totem poles set up in front of each house. Some totem poles were memorials to dead chiefs. The carvings on these poles represented their deeds. Other poles held the bones of dead chiefs. Still others showed that some families had special privileges.

Trade. The only crop that the Northwest Coast people grew was tobacco, which they used as a trade item. Trade with other tribes was an important activity among these people. They also exchanged their beautiful craftwork for farm products.

Fishing. The Northwest Coast people got most of their food from the rivers and the sea. In their great canoes, some 60 feet long and 8 feet wide, they pursued whales, seals, sea otters, and fish. They made harpoons and other fishing tools of wood and bone and attached shell points. They also built traps in the rivers to catch salmon and other fish.

Conflicts. Despite the wealth of the Northwest Coast people, they were not always peaceful. Tribal conflicts over village sites or fishing places sometimes set off wars. The raiders took the heads of enemies and mounted them on poles in the village or on their canoes. The Northwest Coast people also fought wars to capture slaves and goods or to avenge a murder. Sometimes one group went out to kill people to accompany a dead chief on his journey to the next world.

Social Classes. Most Northwest Coast groups were divided into four social classes: chiefs, nobles, commoners, and slaves. Each person was born into a class. An individual could advance to a higher class, however, by showing a certain skill or by acquiring wealth. To demonstrate the possession of wealth, important members of the community gave away their belongings at a community feast called a *potlatch*. Potlatch ceremonies were held to legalize changes in rank, marriages, and the inheritance of a title. By striving to gain honor and high standing at a potlatch, chiefs and even whole families sometimes made themselves poor by giving away all they owned.

Diseases. Sickness, not war, ended the complex culture of the Northwest Coast tribes. The Native Americans caught diseases from European explorers and traders. Eventually, the few survivors left their coastal villages to live on reservations provided by the United States government.

The Inuit of the Far North

The Inuit lived in the northernmost region of North America. Named Eskimos by outsiders, they called themselves the Inuit, which means "the people." (Most Native American groups called themselves by a name meaning "the people.") Many scholars believe the Inuit originally came from northern Asia. But they crossed into North America long after the Native Americans who settled the more southern regions.

Time Line

Year	Dates and Events
B.C. **40M**	**38,000 B.C.:** Arrival of first Asian nomads into North America
	10,000 B.C.: Artifacts of human settlement in Chile
	9000 B.C.: Artifacts of human settlement at Clovis, New Mexico
	1800 B.C.: Earliest migrations of Inuit from Asia to Arctic North America, Greenland
	1200 B.C.: Earliest advanced cultures in Mesoamerica
	1200–600 B.C.: Olmec civilization flourishes near Mexico's Caribbean coast
1M	**900 B.C.:** Destruction by unknown forces of Olmec center, San Lorenzo
A.D. **101**	**A.D. 100:** Anasazi of Southwest begin cultivation of corn, settle in permanent villages
	A.D. 250–900: Highest development of Maya civilization in Central America and Yucatán Peninsula
500	**A.D. 300:** Rise of city and civilization of Teotihuacán
	A.D. 600–650: Teotihuacán destroyed by fire
501	**A.D. 1000:** Navajos and Apaches invade Pueblo settlements in Southwest
	A.D. 1000–1500: Inuit absorb Viking settlers on Greenland
	A.D. 1200–1400: Aztecs move into Valley of Mexico, subdue Toltecs, build empire with huge capital at Tenochtitlán
	A.D. 1200–1500s: Breakup of Maya civilization, first by Mesoamerican invaders, then by Spanish explorers
900	**A.D. 1250–1400s:** Incas build and rule huge empire along Andes Mountains, South America
901	**A.D. 1500s:** Europeans bring sheep, cattle, horses to Americas
	A.D. 1500s: Spaniards reach Southwest
	A.D. 1519–1522: Cortés and small Spanish force invade, conquer Aztec Empire
1300	**A.D. 1532–1572:** Pizarro's Spanish forces invade, conquer Inca Empire
1301	**A.D. 1600s:** Wild horses reach Great Plains, Native Americans tame them, use them in buffalo hunts, give up farming culture; Iroquois League of Nations formed
	A.D. 1680: Pueblo rebellion against harsh treatment by Spanish
1700	

Family Groups. The frozen lands of the Arctic could not support large numbers of people settled in one place. The Inuit, therefore, lived in small family groups. They frequently traveled from place to place in search of animals and fish. They had no need for a central government or a complex economy. The Inuit became highly skilled at living a satisfactory life in an extremely harsh environment.

Hunting. From caribou (North American reindeer), polar bears, whales, seals, and smaller game and fish, the Inuit obtained food and skins for clothing and tents. They fashioned bones into harpoons, spears, and fishhooks. On hunting trips, the Inuit generally camped in tents. Hunters who ventured farther north built igloos, or temporary shelters made of blocks of hard-packed snow. When not hunting, the Inuit lived in dome-shaped houses of sod and wood built partially underground for warmth.

When the Inuit moved to a new area in the winter, they packed their possessions on sleds pulled by dogs. To hunt sea animals, the Inuit used *kayaks*. These small, one- or two-person boats are made of waterproof skins stretched over a wooden frame. The Inuit also used larger open boats for long voyages and to carry goods.

Religion. For the Inuit, as well as for most Native American groups, the world was full of spirits. The Inuit believed that special people called *shamans* could influence the spirits. They believed the shamans used magic to heal sick or wounded people and could summon animals to be killed by hunters. Inuit legends include many stories about the most skilled shamans.

Contact With Europeans. Long hunting trips sometimes took the Inuit as far east as Greenland. There they made contact with Norse colonists (Vikings) who had settled in western Greenland in the 10th century. Historians believe that between A.D. 1000 and 1500, the Inuit absorbed these Norse people by intermarriage. Eventually, the Norse colony disappeared. Some Greenland Inuit today are somewhat European in appearance. They may be the descendants of Norse people who lived in Greenland long ago.

As happened to other Native American groups, vast numbers of the Inuit died from diseases brought by the Europeans. The Inuit came to depend on goods such as guns and metal knives and cooking utensils traded by the Europeans. As a result, they lost many of their old skills.

Permanent Change

Contact with Europeans greatly affected the cultures of Native American groups. Settlers took over hunting lands. Prejudice and fear caused the settlers, backed by the military, to kill Indians. Native Americans were pushed onto government-regulated reservations. Usually, these places were in undesirable areas of the United States and Canada. Indians were urged to develop farming skills, which went against the hunting tradition of many groups. In these groups, farming was done by women, not men. The new ways broke down ancient relationship patterns.

Native American languages and religious practices were discouraged. Missionaries and government agents urged Indians to take up the ways of the white, European-style culture. Consequently, old ways were forgotten. Not until the mid-20th century did it become popular to preserve old ways and teach the traditions to the children.

Chapter 17 describes early African civilizations south of the Sahara. Chapter 18 deals with the encounter between Europeans and the peoples of America and Africa. The results of these encounters have profoundly affected the world we know today.

INFO CHECK

1. Identify an interesting or important feature of each of the following North American cultures: Iroquois, Anasazi, Apache, Plains tribes, Northwest Coast peoples, Inuit.

2. Which European groups most affected the North American cultures? Was contact with Europeans helpful or harmful to Native Americans? Support your answer with examples from the chapter.

CHAPTER REVIEW

Multiple Choice

1. The first humans to come to America were probably

   1. nomadic warriors seeking riches
   2. sheepherders looking for pasture land
   3. hunter-gatherers seeking food
   4. European sailors seeking a short route to India.

2. Some of the major cultural differences between the societies of the Western and Eastern hemispheres were caused by the

   1. different religious practices of these societies
   2. different geographic environments of these societies

   3. arrival of the last Ice Age
   4. different patterns of war and conquest.

3. The Olmecs and Mesopotamians were similar to the Egyptians in that they had

   1. a writing system
   2. a numbering system
   3. a calendar
   4. all of the above.

4. Which listing gives the correct chronological development of the civilizations named?

   1. Olmec, Inca, Maya
   2. Inca, Teotihuacán, Aztec
   3. Olmec, Teotihuacán, Aztec
   4. Aztec, Maya, Inca.

5. Significant Mayan accomplishments are:

   1. great buildings and art, an accurate calendar, and a complex writing system
   2. a number system based on ten, an educational system, and a complex transportation system
   3. a large empire
   4. great buildings, colorful murals, and recordkeeping devices made of knotted strings.

6. The aim of the Incas in ruling their empire was to

   1. allow each group of conquered people to keep their own way of life
   2. control most aspects of everyone's life and make all groups follow one culture
   3. make everyone into skilled road builders and potato growers
   4. develop a form of representative government in which conquered kings would have a voice.

7. Among the Iroquois tribes, inheritance, family property, and clan leadership were decided by

   1. women
   2. warriors
   3. village elders
   4. sachems.

8. The Pueblo Indians lived in the southwestern United States. Their ancestors belonged to which tribal group?

   1. Iroquois
   2. Comanche
   3. Anasazi
   4. Inuit.

9. The survival of the Great Plains Indians was dependent on

   1. adequate rainfall to nourish their crops
   2. fresh fish to supply them with protein and bones for needles
   3. tobacco that was exchanged for food and needed clothing
   4. buffalo herds that provided food, clothing, and bones for needles.

10. The Haida and Tlingit tribes of the Northwest adapted to their environments by

    1. becoming nomadic warriors
    2. becoming sheep and cattle herders
    3. growing tobacco and fishing
    4. carving wood and farming vegetables.

11. The map on page 341 shows that

    1. few tribes settled in the Eastern Woodlands
    2. cultures existed in many parts of North America
    3. Native American tribes consisted of a single cultural group
    4. most North American tribes were located in California

12. According to the time line on page 350,

    1. the earliest peoples to populate North America were nomads
    2. North America was populated before 38,000 B.C.
    3. Europeans were among the first peoples to arrive in the Americas
    4. the Olmec civilization developed after the Inca.

Thematic Essays

1. The Olmec civilization has been called the "mother civilization of Mesoamerica." *Task:* Using specific examples from their culture, describe how the Olmec affected future civilizations in the region.

2. *Task:* Explain why the period of time from A.D. 250–900 is known as the Mayas' Classical Period.

Document-Based Questions

Use the illustrations, the documents, and your knowledge of Global History and Geography to answer the questions.

1. According to the map on page 339, the Inca civilization extended through which countries and what major geographic feature?

2. Look at the photo on page 340. What is geographically significant about the location of Machu Picchu?

3. From an account of the Spanish conquest of Mexico.

   "Here we had a clear prospect [view] of the three causeways by which Mexico communicated with the land, and of the aqueduct . . . which supplied the city with the finest water. . . . The noise and bustle of the market-place below us could be heard almost a league off, and those who had been at Rome and Constantinople said, that for convenience, regularity, and population they had never seen the like . . ."

3. What city is the writer describing? To what Mesoamerican culture does it belong? Why is the 16th-century Spanish writer impressed by this city?

4. What does the illustration on page 344 tell you about Native American life in the Southwest? How is this lifestyle different from or similar to your own?

Document-Based Essay

Compare and contrast one Mesoamerican empire with any one European or Asian society that you have studied. *Task:* In your answer, cite examples from their cultures and governing practices that describe how they controlled their empires.

CHAPTER
17

The Rise and Fall of African Civilizations

On the way to Timbuktu with her father, Wututu sometimes walked and sometimes rode the oxen. She was so excited that she never felt tired, just impatient to arrive. Wututu's aunt had invited Wututu to come and live with her. She needed help in the market, where she had a stall. There she sold the elephant tusks and lion skins that Wututu's father and brother brought her after their hunts.

Wututu did not think that she would be homesick. She would see so many new things. Her father had told her about foreign people with pale skin who came to Timbuktu from across the great desert. They rode ugly beasts with humps on their backs and spoke a strange tongue. They brought shining cloth and delicate cups to trade.

Still, she would miss her family and the other villagers. Of course, she would come back home for visits. Then she would astonish everyone with her tales about the great city. How her friends would envy her.

Wututu is a young African girl of the 14th century. She is on her way to one of the great centers of African civilization. There she will experience a way of life quite different from the one she knew in her village. She will see the great wealth of the Mali emperor, come in contact with scholars from the Middle East, and learn about business and a formal legal system. As her aunt's helper, she will also be a small part of the great world-trade network that was beginning to include Africa south of the Sahara, the great desert. At this time, Muslims and Europeans were becoming aware of the rich resources in West Africa.

GEOGRAPHICAL SETTING

Africa is the second largest continent in the world. (Asia is the largest.) It is surrounded by the Atlantic Ocean on the south and west, the Indian Ocean on the southeast, the Mediterranean Sea on the

Africa: Physical Map

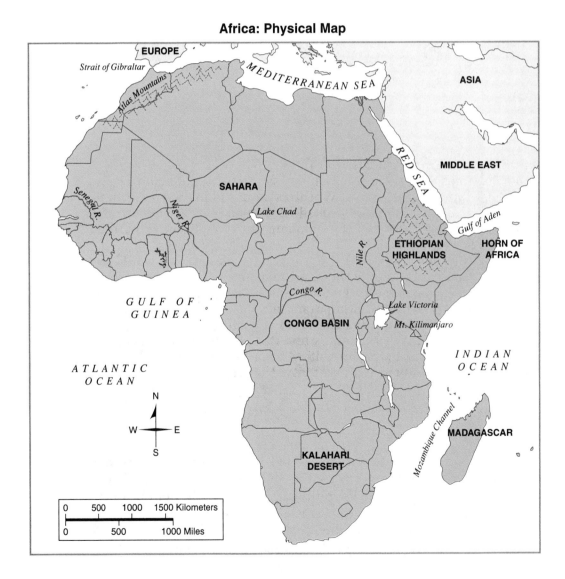

north, and the Red Sea on the northeast. The Mediterranean Sea makes travel easy between North Africa and Europe, and the Red Sea aids travel between North Africa and the Middle East.

The part of Africa that lies south of the Sahara is known as sub-Saharan Africa. The geography of sub-Saharan Africa is more varied than that of North Africa. It includes rain forests, deserts, great rivers, grassy plains called savannas, mountains, basins, and deep valleys. The rain forests, deserts, and mountains are natural barriers to easy land travel. Powerful rapids and steep waterfalls make it difficult to navigate the rivers. Because of the diversity of environments and the natural barriers that separate one region from one other, the cultures of sub-Saharan Africa are very different.

Starting in the 4th century A.D., powerful empires developed in western and eastern Africa. Scholars have few written records describing these civilizations. Most of the written information about them comes from the reports of Muslim travelers. Oral history hands down additional information that adds to our knowledge about the greatness of these peoples.

INFO CHECK

1. What major bodies of water are near Africa?

2. How did the geography of Africa affect the cultures of the sub-Saharan area?

THE EMPIRES OF GHANA, MALI, AND SONGHAI

Between A.D. 300 and 1500, three large empires arose in western Africa. They carried on a brisk trade with the Romans and later with the Muslims and medieval Europeans. The wealth of these African empires amazed traders from the north.

The Empire of Ghana

The first western African empire was Ghana. It developed from a large farming community in the area north and east of the Senegal River. (Present-day Ghana is in a different location in West Africa.) As early as A.D. 300, the people of this empire had mastered the art of ironworking. By then, according to ancient legends, 44 kings had ruled the empire.

The early Ghanaians were militaristic. The name of their empire comes from their word for ruler—*ghana*, or war chief. In the 10th century, the Ghanaians conquered the town of Audagost, which put them in control of an important caravan route. Gaining control of this trade route gave Ghanaians the power and wealth to continue their

Early African Kingdoms, City-States, and Trade Routes

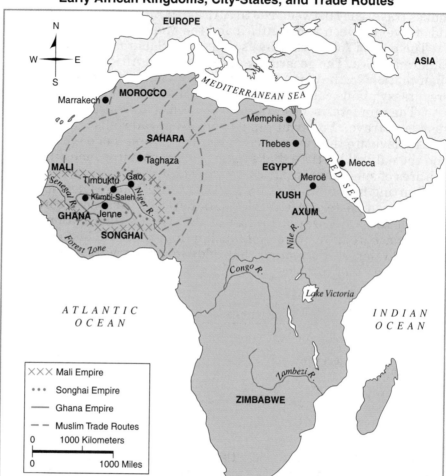

expansion. By A.D. 1000, they had built an empire about the size of Texas. As the Ghanaians expanded their empire, they increased their trade with the Muslims.

Riches. The areas owned by Ghana's rulers were rich in gold mines. Ghanaian gold, ivory, and slaves attracted Muslim traders. To exchange for these items, the Muslims brought salt, cloth, tools, and copper from northern Africa. Salt was especially important to the Ghanaians. Most modern people think of salt as just a seasoning that makes food taste better. Before the invention of refrigerators, however, salt was essential for preserving food. It is also a necessary ingredient of the body. Since people living in hot climates lose large amounts of salt when they sweat, they must replace it by adding salt to their food.

Commerce with the Muslims made the kings of Ghana so rich that they armed their personal guards with gold-mounted swords. The kings even covered their horses with blankets made of gold cloth.

Kumbi-Saleh. Kumbi-Saleh, a city of about 15,000 people, was the capital of the Ghana Empire. Aided by his nobles, the king headed a strong centralized government. A large, powerful army backed up his commands. The soldiers carried weapons made of iron.

In the mid-11th century, North African Berber warriors, called Almoravids, conquered Ghana and most of western Africa. Under Almoravid rule, many members of the royal family of Ghana became Muslims. The Almoravids destroyed the capital city of Kumbi-Saleh in 1076. This badly weakened the power of the kings. Eventually, the Ghana Empire broke up. The Mali Empire absorbed it.

The Riches of Mali

In 1235, a warrior-chief named Sundiata conquered large areas along the Niger River. (He ruled until about 1255.) These conquests laid the foundation of the empire of Mali. Malian kings now ruled land that had been part of the Ghanian Empire. This area included the gold mines of western Africa. The mines made Mali so prosperous that its wealth became famous throughout Africa and the Middle East. Before the Europeans reached America, much of Europe's gold came from Mali. Ivory, cotton, and herds of cattle also contributed to Mali's wealth. By the beginning of the 14th century, Mali had grown into an empire about twice as large as Ghana had been at its peak.

Mansa Musa. The greatest Malian king, Mansa Musa, was a grandson of King Sundiata. Mansa Musa ruled from 1312 to 1337. He was devoted to the Muslim religion. Largely through his influence, Islam spread throughout his empire.

In 1324, Mansa Musa made a pilgrimage to the holy city of Mecca. (He was fulfilling one of the Five Pillars of obligation of the faithful.) An enormous caravan loaded with 24,000 pounds of gold accompanied him on the journey. Among his followers were 500 servants, each carrying a six-pound staff made of gold. Few kings anywhere could display such wealth. In the words of an Arab historian, these treasures "almost put Africa's sun to shame." Mansa Musa spent and gave away so much gold on this trip that he affected the economy of the areas he visited. Some scholars estimate that the price of gold in Egypt went down. The resulting inflation (general rise in prices of goods) did not correct itself for ten years.

On his return from Mecca, Mansa Musa brought back many talented people to Timbuktu, his capital city. They included teachers, scholars, artists, engineers, and architects. These talented people made Timbuktu's university a famous center for learning and the arts.

Way of Life. Travelers to Timbuktu were impressed by Mali's many commercial activities, fair legal system, and law-abiding citi-

THE GRIOTS OF THE MANDINGO

Since ancient times, *griots* have been oral historians, praise singers, and musical entertainers. During the great days of the Malian Empire of western Africa (mid-1200s to mid-1400s), griots tutored princes and gave advice to kings. The griots had a reputation for being educated and wise. They used their detailed knowledge of history to shed light on complex problems. Long after the fall of the Malian Empire in 1468, the griots remained an important part of the Mandingo society of western Africa. A prosperous family would have its own griot to advise it and help it negotiate important matters with other families. Griots arranged the terms of marriages and aided in the settlement of disputes. In doing these things, they relied on their understanding of each family's history. Such knowledge had been transmitted orally by griots through the generations.

In time, the griots, also called *jelis*, also became the official musicians of Mandingo society. Playing instruments such as the *balafon* (a wooden xylophone), the *ngoni* (a small lute), and the 21-stringed harp known as a *kora*, the jelis have sung the history of the Mandingo people. Today, there are both male and female griot singers. The majority of these respected musicians, however, are women.

Most modern Mandingo families cannot afford their own private griot. Instead, the musicians perform at weddings, baptisms, and other functions. Their songs entertain and praise the guests. Those concerned with maintaining the purity of this ancient art form complain that modern griots are forced to learn a little about each family's history. They are prevented from knowing the rich detail of one family's heritage because they do not have a long association with only one family.

Nevertheless, *jelia* music remains very popular in contemporary Africa. Some of the most famous pop music stars of Mali, Guinea, Senegal, and Gambia are griots who have transformed traditional compositions into modern music. Their recordings are widely sold in music stores and other local outlets. Griot music is also heard on radio and television and at music festivals.

One of West Africa's most celebrated singers is Salif Keita, of Mali. He does not have griot ancestry. As his name indicates, however, he is a descendant of King Sundiata Keita, the founder of the Malian Empire. Salif draws heavily from griot tradition in his own music.

1. What comparisons can you draw between *jelia* and the pop music of your own society? What similarities and differences can you find?

2. Why is *jelia* an example of cultural continuity in West African society?

zens. (Ibn Battuta, the famous Muslim traveler, visited Mali and wrote about his impressions in the mid-1300s.) They claimed that there were few incidents of robbery or violence in Mali. Some visiting Muslims disapproved of the great freedom exercised by the women of Mali. Unlike women in other Muslim lands, Mali women were free to take an active part in the social and cultural life of the empire.

Mansa Musa, from a manuscript celebrating his extravagant pilgrimage to Mecca

After the death of Mansa Musa, the power of Mali declined. Another great empire that arose in western Africa, the Songhai, replaced Mali.

The Songhai Empire

Songhai grew into the most powerful of the western African empires. Songhai's wealth came from its gold trade. Within Songhai's many towns lived craftsworkers, businesspeople, judges, doctors, and religious leaders.

The Songhai Empire reached its greatest extent at the end of the 15th century. By then Sunni Ali, a warrior king of the Songhai Empire, had conquered large amounts of territory along the Niger River. He ruled from 1464 to 1492. In 1468, he captured Timbuktu from desert tribal rulers.

Center of Learning. Askia Muhammad, the most powerful king of the Songhai Empire, ruled from 1493 to 1528. He was a nephew of Sunni Ali. A devout Muslim, he based his laws on the teachings of the Quran. Askia set up a fair system of taxation and encouraged the establishment of Muslim schools.

Under Askia's rule, philosophers, scholars, and teachers increased the reputation of Timbuktu as a center of learning. The people of Timbuktu put such value on learning, that they spent more on books than on any other merchandise. Another great Songhai city, Jenne, was known for its skilled doctors. Surgeons there were able to operate on the delicate human eye. Jenne's medical researchers discovered that the bite of a mosquito causes malaria.

The kings who followed Askia Muhammad were not as capable as he. They could not defend the empire against its enemies, who had guns against their spears and bows. The sultan of Morocco conquered the Songhai Empire in 1591.

INFO CHECK

1. Explain the importance of the gold trade to the empires of western Africa.

2. Identify each of the following: Kumbi-Saleh, Sundiata, Mansa Musa, Timbuktu, Askia Muhammad, Jenne.

THE CITY-STATES OF EAST AFRICA

Starting in the 700s, Arab traders explored the east coast of Africa. They found bustling seaports. The markets in these ports offered such goods as ivory, iron, and gold for sale. The Arabs had discovered a new source of trade items to exchange for Eastern goods. Asians purchased ivory to carve into art objects, chess pieces, and furniture. The Indians, Chinese, and Muslims needed iron for swords, spears, and daggers.

In return for their products, Africans wanted cotton cloth, glass beads, and porcelain (fine chinaware). African merchants highly prized the delicate cups, bowls, and vases from China.

As commerce developed among the peoples of India, Arabia, and Africa, the East African merchants became wealthy. The coastal towns where they settled grew into great cities. The map on page 365 shows how it was easy to establish water routes among these lands.

The Trading Cities

The East African coastal cities of Mogadishu, Malindi, Mombasa, and Kilwa developed into city-states. Each city controlled land outside its walls. Each had its own ruler, made its own laws, and had a small army. The rulers obtained money by taxing trade goods.

Control of the gold trade made the city-state of Kilwa rich. In the 13th and 14th centuries, the rulers and merchants of Kilwa built fine stone palaces and homes. One palace contained 100 rooms, interior courtyards, and an eight-sided swimming pool. It was the largest building in East Africa. Mosques, parks, and fountains added to the beauty of the city. The ruins of Kilwa can be seen today.

The Swahili Culture

Most East Africans spoke the Swahili language. As they came in contact with Arabic and Asian languages, they added words from these tongues to Swahili. The language was written in Arabic script.

Ruins of a great mosque on the island city-state of Kilwa, in present-day Tanzania

Over time, the many different peoples of the coastal cities adopted customs from one another. The blending of languages and customs produced a new culture called Swahili. Many Swahili people accepted Islam as their religion. Others clung to the old African religions.

Swahili artists, craftspeople, poets, storytellers, traders, and others created a sophisticated culture in East Africa. When the Portuguese arrived in the late 1400s, they were amazed by the cities there. They were particularly impressed by the fine quality of the Swahili people's clothing and furniture and the cleanliness and comfort of their way of life.

The Swahili were suspicious of the Portuguese. After the Swahili rejected demands for trading rights, the Portuguese attacked the city-states and destroyed them. The trade was taken over by the Portuguese and the Arabs.

Great Zimbabwe

In the southeastern part of South Africa lie the ruins of a great city and fort that had been constructed in the 11th century. The remains of a thick wall, 30 feet high, surround what were once palaces and temples. Both the wall and buildings were made of fine stonework laid in a variety of patterns. The builders of Great Zimbabwe, as the city was called, were masters of construction. They were also active in the gold and ivory trade of eastern Africa.

This great city began in about the 9th century as a community of cattle herders. As the settlement's wealth increased, so did its population. To grow more food, farmers dug terraces into the hillsides and supported them with stones.

The area around Zimbabwe was rich in gold. In the 10th century, the leaders of this community began to trade with the Swahili. In time, they traded their gold with China, Persia, and India in exchange for cotton cloth, porcelain, and other Eastern goods. As the community grew powerful and wealthy from trade, it developed into the city of Great Zimbabwe.

The Zimbabwe Way of Life. The people of Zimbabwe considered their kings to be gods. According to tradition, the prosperity of the kingdom depended on the strength and good health of the ruler. If the king became ill or physically weak, disaster might come to the people. Zimbabwean tradition required a king who became sick to kill himself so that a healthier ruler could take his place.

Among the privileged people who lived in the palace with the king were his wives and royal advisers. Only these people were allowed to see the king. Ordinary people, such as farmers and soldiers, could not look at the king. The common people lived in small stone houses outside the city wall.

Many of the people of Zimbabwe worked as gold miners. They sifted through the dirt in streams and dug pits in search of the metal that was so important to the region's trade. Others hunted elephants for their ivory tusks.

Change and Decline. By the 15th century, Zimbabwe had reached its peak of prosperity and power. Eventually, word of its great wealth reached the Portuguese, who were exploring Africa's eastern coast. In the 16th century, these traders tried to gain control of the goldfields around Zimbabwe. But the Portuguese were not successful and no European ever saw the great city. The destruction of the coastal cities disrupted trade with Zimbabwe.

Great Zimbabwe continued as a city until the 19th century. The decline of trade and conflict within the ruling family weakened it. In 1830, Zulu tribes attacked Zimbabwe. The Zulus had migrated from farther south in search of new land. The people of Zimbabwe fled from the invaders, abandoning their great walled city.

INFO CHECK

1. Describe the relationship between the Swahili culture and the coastal cities of East Africa.

2. How did Great Zimbabwe become wealthy? What caused the decline of this kingdom?

THE ARRIVAL OF THE EUROPEANS

The Portuguese were the first Europeans to sail along the western African coast south of the Sahara. The Dutch and the French soon followed. At first, the Europeans came to trade for gold and ivory.

Then they began to buy slaves in Africa. They soon set up trading posts and, eventually, established colonies along the coast of Africa. The arrival of the Europeans brought profit to some Africans, misery and ruin to others.

The Portuguese

In the 1400s, the Portuguese began to look for an all-water route to India and East Asia. They wanted to trade with these areas and to spread Christianity among the inhabitants. It was expensive to use the land routes to Asia, most of which were controlled by the Muslims

Voyages of Dias and Da Gama Around Africa

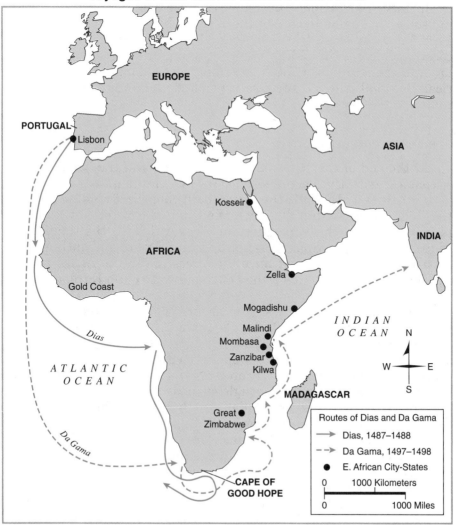

and Italian trading cities, such as Venice. Therefore, the Portuguese sailed along the western coast of Africa looking for a new route to Asia. When they stopped in African seaports to stock up on fresh food and water, they discovered that Africa was a rich source of gold and ivory.

Trade. In 1471, the Portuguese began to trade with people in what is present-day Ghana. This is a gold-rich area about midway along the western African coast. The trade was so profitable that this section of western Africa came to be called the Gold Coast. To protect their trade from other Europeans, the Portuguese built a series of forts. At the same time, they established contact with the Congo Empire along the Congo River farther to the south. By converting the ruler of this empire to Christianity, the Portuguese gained his favor and were able to expand their trade in this region.

In 1488, Bartolomeu Dias, a Portuguese explorer, continued sailing south and came to the southern tip of Africa. Between 1497 and 1498, Vasco da Gama traveled around the tip of Africa, up the eastern coast, and across the Indian Ocean to India. The Portuguese who followed these trailblazers set up trading posts along the coasts of Africa. By 1509, the Portuguese controlled the Indian Ocean trade routes.

The Dutch and the French

At the end of the 16th century, the Dutch and the French began to compete with the Portuguese for trading rights in western Africa.

The Dutch. In 1598, the Dutch built their first trading posts on the Gold Coast. Within 40 years, they gained control of most of the territory held by the Portuguese in West Africa. At the time, Spain controlled Portugal. Spain was fighting with France and putting down internal revolts. It did not have the forces to send to Africa to keep the Dutch away. After 1640, the Dutch were the main European traders in the area.

The Dutch took their first step toward colonizing southern Africa in 1652. The Dutch East India Company, a private company with government backing, established a settlement called Cape Town. In 1688, Huguenots (Protestant groups) from France arrived in the Cape Town area. The Dutch (also Protestants) and French settlers intermarried, and a new culture soon developed. The settlers of European descent called themselves Afrikaners. Because of their hard work, their farms and businesses prospered. Cape Town grew and the population spread inland. The Africans were friendly toward the settlers. Their African population was not large, and it had been weakened by the Europeans' diseases. Thus, Africans were not strong enough to keep the new settlers out.

The French. In the early 17th century, the French also moved into West Africa. In 1658, they built a settlement called St. Louis at the mouth of the Senegal River. Further exploration of the lands along this river led the French to build several trading posts. They began a gradual conquest of the Senegal region.

In 1643, the French built their first settlements on Madagascar. This is a large island in the Indian Ocean off the east coast of Africa.

These early efforts at colonization gave Europeans control of some land along Africa's coasts. For the most part, the Europeans did not move very far into the interior of the continent. Strong African rulers, a hot, humid climate, and killing diseases confined most Europeans to the coastal areas. The real conquest of Africa did not begin until the 19th century. Europeans tended to be more interested in making money from trade than in settling large land areas in Africa.

INFO CHECK

1. How did the Portuguese protect their interests in Africa from rivals?

2. Why was western Africa the first area of the continent to experience European trade and colonization?

THE RISE OF THE SLAVE TRADE

The desire for gold and ivory first brought Europeans to Africa. In the 17th and 18th centuries, however, they came to buy captive human beings for the slave trade. The slave trade developed into a rich business for Africans, Europeans, and Americans. Earlier, Muslims from North Africa and the Middle East had traded in slaves. The number involved, though, was much smaller than the number involved in the later trade.

Slavery in Africa

Slavery had existed for centuries in the African kingdoms. As did the governments of many other civilizations, African governments enslaved criminals, people who could not pay their debts, and prisoners captured in wars. Some rulers had thousands of slaves. Merchants bought and sold slaves in the markets of many cities, especially in Muslim North Africa.

Occasionally, the families the slaves served adopted them. Some masters gave their slaves the opportunity to earn their freedom. Those who earned their freedom had the same social status as people who had never been slaves. The children of free men and slave women were born free. Africans expected their slaves to work hard. But the owners often worked alongside their slaves at the same tasks.

In many of the African kingdoms, slaves were sold to Arab traders. The Arabs then sold the Africans in Arabia, Persia, and India. Both Africans and Asians profited from the Indian Ocean slave trade. The

Berbers of North Africa also purchased slaves from African rulers. Berber traders took slaves across the Sahara to sell in Mediterranean countries, particularly Spain and Portugal. In these countries, long wars between Christians and Muslims had resulted in a shortage of men. The Spanish and Portuguese purchased Africans to work as farmhands, as household servants, and as common laborers in the cities.

Europeans and the Slave Trade

In the 17th century, the trade in slaves changed drastically. Europeans wanted workers for their colonies in North and South America and the West Indian islands in the Caribbean Sea. On plantations (large farms) in the colonies, Europeans grew crops to sell in Europe and elsewhere. The main crops were sugarcane, rice, tobacco, and cotton. Planting, tilling, and harvesting these crops required many workers.

At first, Europeans forced American Indians to work on the plantations. But there were not enough Indians to do the work, and many died from mistreatment and diseases. The Spanish, Portuguese, British, Dutch, and French owners of the plantations then sought workers from West Africa. West Africans were used to a hot, humid climate like that of the Caribbean. Many were used to laboring in the fields. Indians from the warrior classes and the hunter-gatherer societies were not used to field labor.

From the 17th to the 19th centuries, traders sold an enormous number of West Africans to Europeans—possibly as many as 10 million individuals, mainly men. The area between the Gold Coast and the mouth of the Niger River came to be called the Slave Coast. The Portuguese were the first Europeans to buy slaves in large numbers. They sent the slaves to Portuguese plantations in Brazil. By the

Nineteenth-century engraving of African slaves being marched to a coastal market

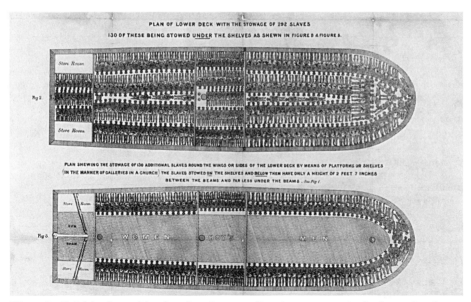

Plan of a British slave ship showing the crowding in steerage on the lower levels

1650s, the Dutch, British, and French also controlled slave-trading areas along the west coast of Africa. Arabs and, later, Americans also took an active part in the slave trade.

European slave traders depended on the cooperation of African kings and chiefs. These rulers raided villages in the interior and kidnapped healthy young people to sell to the traders. They sent these captives to slave-holding areas on the coast, where they were loaded onto ships.

The voyage across the Atlantic Ocean killed many Africans. During most of the trip, they were chained below deck in spaces too small to allow them to stand erect. They had very little to eat and frequently died of starvation. Because their captors did not allow them to clean and take care of themselves, many died of diseases. Some, to avoid spending their lives as slaves, threw themselves overboard when they were brought on deck for exercise. When the ships reached the Americas, traders sold the captive Africans in public marketplaces.

Evils of the Slave Trade

The slave trade was *racist*. European and American slave owners regarded both Africans and American Indians as inferior. They were different in skin color. They were not Christian. Also, the Europeans thought that African and American Indian cultures were primitive. Then, too, laws in Europe and the Americas did not protect Africans and American Indians. Slave traders justified their actions. They

Time Line

Year	Dates and Events

A.D.
301

300s–1050s: Ghana Empire flourishes

700s: Arab traders establish seaports in East Africa to trade with India, China, Middle East

900

800s–1000s: Rise of great African city-state of Zimbabwe

901

900s: Ghana conquers Audagost, controls important caravan route, increases trade with Muslims

1075: Destruction of Ghana capital Kumbi-Saleh by Almoravids (Berbers); decline of Ghana Empire

1200s–1300s: City-state of Kilwa (East Africa) grows rich by controlling gold trade

1235–1255: Rule of Sundiata, foundation of Mali Empire, absorption of Ghana Empire

1300s: Peak of Mali Empire, center of prosperous gold mining

1200

1300s–1400s: Portuguese explorers and traders arrive in East Africa, destroy Swahili city-states, take over (with Arabs) Swahili trade

1201

1312–1337: Reign of Mali king Mansa Musa; makes capital Timbuktu center of learning and arts; makes pilgrimage to Mecca (1324); spreads Islam throughout empire

1493–1528: Reign of Askia Muhammad, greatest king of Songhai Empire, which replaces Mali

1500s: Zimbabwe trade disrupted by Portuguese destruction of Swahili city-states; Portuguese fail to win control of Zimbabwe

1509: Portuguese control India Ocean trade routes

1500

1591: Songhai Empire conquered by sultan of Morocco

1501

1598–1640: Dutch build trading post on Africa's Gold Coast, oust Portuguese, control its European trade

1600s–1800s: Duration of African slave trade by which Portuguese, Dutch, British, French transport West Africans to Americas

1643: French build first settlement on Madagascar

1652: Dutch East India Company establishes Cape Town in southern Africa

1658: French establish St. Louis at mouth of Senegal River (West Africa)

1688: French Huguenots arrive in Cape Town; with Dutch, develop new European culture of Afrikaners

1800

1830s: Zulus attack weakened Zimbabwe; inhabitants abandon the city

considered their captives to be less than human. The profits the traders made were more important than any question of morals.

Having convinced themselves that Africans were not like themselves, European slave traders treated them as pieces of property that they could buy and sell. They often sold children and parents, husbands and wives to different masters.

One of the worst evils of the slave trade was its destruction of the captive Africans' language, customs, and religion. The traders often separated members of the same tribe or village. Plantation owners did not want their slaves to have family or community feelings. They feared that if the slaves had close ties with one another, they would join together and revolt. Therefore, the slaves on plantations were a mixed group of strangers, with different languages and beliefs. They had to learn the language and culture of the slave owners. Because of this, many lost their African heritage.

The trade in slaves also changed West Africa, where most of the slave trade occurred. The people of West Africa came to depend on the metal tools, cloth, and guns that the traders exchanged for slaves. The possession of guns made the wars among the tribes more violent and deadly. Dependency on Western goods put them under the control of the Europeans. In addition, the slave trade took away young, healthy men and women who might have contributed a great deal to their tribes.

Other Nations' Racism. Europeans were not the only people to exhibit racist attributes. The Chinese regarded Europeans and all other foreigners as barbarians (inferior peoples with little to offer of cultural value). For this reason, European merchants were confined to certain coastal cities and were otherwise restricted in their activities in China.

The Japanese also regarded Europeans and, later, Americans as barbarians. Japan's rulers periodically closed their country to foreigners. To avoid "contamination" by cultures considered to be inferior, Japanese outside of Japan were prevented from returning to their homeland. In addition, Japanese treatment of the Ainu, in northern Japan, was marked by the same lack of acceptance of people who were "different."

In Europe, racism was mainly practiced in the form of anti-Semitism, or intolerance toward Jews. In several European countries, Jews were persecuted in a variety of ways. They were barred from certain occupations, forced to wear clothing different from other Europeans, and confined to enclosed areas of cities, called ghettos. Periodically, Jews were expelled from countries. In some places, they were sometimes tortured and killed because of their religious beliefs and identity.

Chapter 18 expands on the reasons why Europeans explored Africa and the Americas. It also describes early interactions between

Europeans, the native peoples of America, and the Africans who worked in the colonies as slaves.

INFO CHECK

1. Explain why you would AGREE or DISAGREE with the following statements:

   • The slave trade was a global business.

   • People of many nationalities profited from the slave trade.

2. Which of the evils of the slave trade do you consider to be the most damaging or destructive to Africans? Give reasons for your answer.

CHAPTER REVIEW

Multiple Choice

1. A result of the diversity of environments in sub-Saharan Africa is

   1. uniform cultures and life-styles
   2. a variety of differing cultures
   3. frequent merging of tribes and kingdoms
   4. limited military and political conflict.

2. The early West African kingdoms of Ghana, Mali, and Songhai all grew wealthy and powerful because of their

   1. military technology and use of steel weapons
   2. control of the caravan routes and goldmines
   3. wars of religious conquests that spread Islam throughout West Africa
   4. sale of fellow Africans to Arab and European slave traders.

3. The Malian king Mansa Musa traveled to the Middle East to make a pilgrimage to Mecca in 1324. The fact that his trip was recorded and he was honored in all the lands he traveled through tells us that

   1. he was a fierce warrior who had a large army
   2. he was a deeply religious and respected person
   3. he impressed the leaders with his wealth and the size of his group
   4. the Holy Roman Emperor and the pope wanted to make a military alliance with him against the Muslims.

4. Select the best example of cultural diffusion in Africa.

   1. archaeologist finding the ruins of a Portuguese fort
   2. European trading posts are preserved as museums
   3. South African whites attending Calvinist church services
   4. the Swahili language containing Asian and Arabic words.

5. The Kingdom of Zimbabwe had the same belief regarding their ruler as

the Japanese. This belief was that the ruler

1. had limited powers
2. shared power with his nobles
3. was a god
4. was selected by God.

6. The first European power to explore the coast of West Africa was

1. Portugal
2. England
3. Holland
4. France.

7. The delayed penetration of Europeans into the interior of sub-Saharan Africa was mainly due to

1. powerful African armies all united against the Europeans
2. Europeans' lack of desire for African products or minerals
3. ships and instruments, which were not advanced enough to reach the African continent
4. the geography and climate of sub-Saharan Africa, which made trade and travel into the interior very difficult.

8. The intermarriage of French Huguenots and Dutch Protestants formed the basis of a new South African culture and people. They were the

1. Afrikaners
2. Senegali
3. Gold Coasters
4. Biafrans.

9. African kingdoms sold slaves to traders, who then sold the slaves to Spanish and Portuguese buyers. The slaves were needed because

1. cotton plantations in both nations needed farmhands

2. the African slaves were valued as warriors
3. the African slaves were skilled metal workers
4. wars between Christians and Muslims had killed many men, causing a shortage of workers in Spain and Portugal.

10. The African region where most of the slaves were taken to and transported from was

1. the east coast of Africa
2. the west coast of Africa
3. North Africa
4. sub-Saharan Africa.

11. The map on page 358 illustrates that

1. Timbuktu, Memphis, and Thebes were important cities located along Muslim trade routes
2. Muslim trade routes connected West Africa and the Mediterranean coast
3. the Nile River was an important means of transportation for the Muslim traders
4. Europeans played a major role in early African trade.

12. The map on page 365 shows that both Dias and Da Gama

1. reached the southern tip of Africa
2. successfully sailed around Africa to India
3. sailed from east to west
4. began their voyages on the Gold Coast

13. According to the time line on page 370,

1. the slave trade from West Africa to America took place between the 1600s and 1800s
2. a number of great African empires and civilizations existed from 300 to the 1500s

3. African contact with the Portuguese took place prior to African contact with the British, French, or Dutch

4. All of the above are true.

Thematic Essays

1. *Task:* Compare and contrast the reasons for the rise and fall of any two of the three African empires of Ghana, Mali, and Songhai. Consider in your answer such factors as religion, geography, natural resources, and family or governmental organization.

2. *Task:* Using historical examples from the empires of Mali, Songhai, or Ghana, discuss whether there was a relationship between trade and the spread of religion.

Document-Based Questions

Use your knowledge of Global History and Geography and the documents to answer the questions.

1. Using specific examples from the map on page 356, explain how the geographic environment of Africa divided the continent and hindered early exploration.

2. From a history of sub-Saharan Africa:

   "Muhammad bin Ebrahim al-Fazari, an eighth-century Arab astronomer, provides the first written mention of Ghana—what he calls the land of gold."

   What information does this reading provide in addition to Ghana being called a "land of gold"?

3. From the writings of al-Omari, one of the Egyptian sultan's officials:

   "This man Mansa Musa spread upon Cairo the flood of his generosity: there was no person, officer of the court, or holder of any office of the Sultanate who did not receive a sum of gold from him. . . . So much gold was current in Cairo that it ruined the value of money. . . . Let me add that gold in Egypt had enjoyed a high rate of exchange up to the moment of his arrival."

   What does al-Omari's report tell us about the economic effects of Mansa Musa's visit to Egypt?

Document-Based Essay

Early European historians believed Africans to be uncivilized barbarians. *Task:* Support or refute this view, citing specific historical and cultural evidence.

C H A P T E R

18

The Peoples of Asia, the Americas, and Africa Encounter Europeans

On his way to school, Itzcoátl stopped in the marketplace to watch the pale strangers enter Tenochtitlán. He was both frightened and delighted. All week long rumors had been flying that gods were approaching the city. It was said that one of them was Quetzelcoatl himself. The feathered serpent had taken on the form of a man and had come to rule the Aztecs.

Itzcoátl wished he could get closer to the procession. He might never see such a sight again. And there was so much about these strangers that puzzled him. What were their bodies made of? Was it silver or some magical substance only gods could own? And what were those long tubes that they carried? Itzcoátl had heard that the strangers had sticks that thundered and flashed lightning. Perhaps they had come to make rain.

This young Aztec boy did not realize that the men who were entering his city would change the world as he knew it. The meeting between the Aztecs and Hernan Cortés and his soldiers was just one of many encounters between Europeans and native peoples in the Americas. The contact with the Aztecs ended violently. Other Europeans had friendlier relations with the people whose land they colonized. Nonetheless, all the encounters eventually destroyed native societies.

The Aztec boy had never seen horses, metal armor, or guns. Bearded men were unusual. The Spaniards, in turn, had never seen such a grand city as Tenochtitlán. There were so many people, so many goods for sale in the market. The huge, tall pyramids may have seemed as grand as the great churches at home. Even if the Spaniards had come in peace, would they have gotten along with the Aztecs? No one knows, of course, but peoples of vastly different cultures often find it difficult to accept each other's differences.

What caused Europeans to make long and dangerous voyages to unknown lands? Once they got to these lands, how were they able to disrupt long-established societies? Why did they want to do so?

THE AGE OF EXPLORATION AND DISCOVERY

Influence of the Renaissance and the Scientific Revolution

During the Renaissance, Europeans became more interested in the world around them than they had been during the Middle Ages. They were especially curious about Asia. Many Europeans were fascinated by Marco Polo's book on China. They longed to see for themselves if the wonders he had described in it were true. They also wanted to go to the lands that produced so many useful and beautiful trade goods. Although Europeans desired such luxuries as silks and jewels, they needed Asian spices. Since refrigerators had not been invented, one of the few ways that they could preserve their food was by treating it with spices and salt.

Trade. The merchants of the Italian city-states of Venice and Genoa had grown rich buying and selling the silks, spices, and jewels of Asia. They controlled the trade routes across the Mediterranean Sea to Byzantium. They did not, however, control the overland trade routes to Asia. These routes were in the hands of Muslim and Asian merchants, who carried goods from India and China over them.

The overland trade routes were long, difficult, and dangerous. The entire trip to Asia and back might take an individual or a group a year or more to complete. Goods were passed along the trade routes from merchant to merchant. Each time the goods were traded, their prices went up. By the time they arrived in Europe, they were extremely expensive.

Water Route. European merchants felt that a water route to Asia would make their fortunes. If they traded directly with Asian merchants, they could buy their goods at very low prices. They could then sell them more cheaply and still make enormous profits.

In 1453, the Ottoman Turks conquered Constantinople. Fearing that the Turks' victory would completely disrupt the Mediterranean trade routes to Byzantium, Europeans became more eager than ever to find a direct water route to the East.

Explorers from several European countries sailed south along the African coast and west across the Atlantic Ocean, looking for such a route. Technological innovations, such as the astrolabe, the compass, and the caravel, made long sea voyages easier and safer. As Europeans sailed more frequently along what had once been unfamiliar coasts, they drew more accurate maps. They learned the latitude of important geographical features and marked the location on the maps, or sea charts. Having reliable maps increased the navigators' confidence and encouraged them to venture still farther into the unknown.

Exploration and Discovery

The nations facing the Atlantic—Portugal, France, Spain, the Netherlands, and England—sent out expeditions to look for new and convenient trade routes.

Portugal. Portugal began these explorations in the 15th century. Prince Henry the Navigator, a member of the Portuguese ruling family, used his wealth to send expeditions to explore the west coast of Africa and find a way to India. These expeditions led to the growth of the Portuguese trade in African gold and slaves and Indian spices and silks. Eventually, Portuguese ships reached Indonesia, China, and Japan. (About 100 years before the Portuguese voyages to India, Zheng He of China explored the same areas.)

Prince Henry had another reason for wanting to make contact with the peoples of Africa and Asia. He intended to send missionaries to teach them about Christianity. Many other European rulers and explorers had the same goal.

Spain. The other Atlantic nations quickly followed the lead of Portugal. In 1492, Christopher Columbus began the first of his westward voyages under Spain's flag. (This was the same year that Ferdinand and Isabella expelled from Spain the Jews who had not converted to Christianity.) Columbus believed that he had reached Asia or the "Indies." Instead, he found lands previously unknown to Europe that became known as the Americas. Because he thought he had landed in the Indies, Columbus called the people he met "Indians."

Ferdinand Magellan also sailed from Spain for King Charles V of Spain. In a voyage that took three years (1519–1521), his expedition became the first to travel completely around the world. Magellan was looking for and found a way around the Americas to Eastern markets.

England. An Italian named John Cabot explored the parts of Canada known as Nova Scotia and Newfoundland for England in 1497 and 1498. (King Henry VII authorized the voyages.) In 1576, Martin Frobisher explored the Labrador coast of Canada for England. (Queen Elizabeth I backed the voyage.) Both Cabot and Frobisher were looking for a Northwest Passage that would take them around or through North America to Asia. They did not find it. Explorers

Voyages of Exploration to North and South America

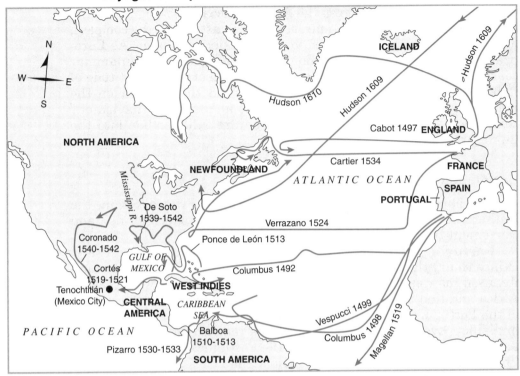

hoped that a Northwest Passage would shorten the trip to the East. The English were the first to establish a permanent European settlement in North America—at Jamestown, Virginia, in 1607.

The Netherlands. (The Netherlands is also referred to as Holland. The people of this country are called the Dutch.) An Englishman named Henry Hudson sailed from the Netherlands for North America in 1609. He traveled along the east coast of what is now the United States. The greatest amount of time was spent exploring the area along what is now the Hudson River in New York State. He claimed the area for the Netherlands. Earlier, Hudson had failed in his search for a Northwest Passage through the Arctic Ocean.

France. Between 1534 and 1541, Jacques Cartier, a Frenchman, explored the St. Lawrence River and eastern Canada. Another Frenchman, Samuel de Champlain, also explored the St. Lawrence area for King Henry IV in 1603. In 1608, Champlain established a fur-trading post at what is now Quebec in Canada. It was the first permanent French settlement in North America.

The French explorers were looking for gold and markets for French goods. They also tried to find a Northwest Passage.

Eventually, English, Dutch, and French explorers also reached

India and other parts of East Asia. They established trading posts and colonies wherever they went.

The Columbian Exchange

Contact between the Atlantic nations and the Americas brought great changes to both the Eastern and Western hemispheres. With the voyages of Columbus, people, animals, plants, and ideas began to move eastward across the Atlantic. This movement is known as the *Columbian exchange*.

On his trips to America, Columbus brought horses, cattle, sheep, sugarcane, and seeds for growing wheat, onions, and other plants. Returning to Spain, he carried back turkeys, corn, potatoes, tomatoes, chili peppers, pumpkins, beans, peanuts, avocados, tobacco, and pineapples. The Europeans who followed Columbus brought more plants and animals from the Eastern Hemisphere. They also brought their languages, religion, and cultures.

Contact between the peoples of Europe and the Americas often caused conflicts and bloody wars. This contact also caused Native Americans to die from European diseases to which they had no resistance, or immunity. Smallpox, measles, and influenza killed more Indians than the violent conflicts with the Europeans did. Some scholars estimate that the population of Latin America in 1650 was one-tenth of what it was in 1500. The same diseases affected Africans in the same way.

Plants from Africa, such as coffee and bananas, were taken to Latin America. The sweet potato became a popular food source in China.

The lives of Europeans who remained at home were also affected. From the Americas came new wealth, often in the form of gold and silver. Trade expanded, and European cities grew larger and more prosperous. New foods, such as potatoes, beans, and corn, improved the diet of Europeans. This brought about a population increase. Opportunities for obtaining land in the colonies gave poor Europeans a chance to improve their lives.

The Rise of Empires

The age of exploration and discovery was followed by an age of colonization and empire building. The Atlantic nations quickly sent government officials, missionaries, and colonists to the lands claimed by their explorers. Great empires began to grow in the New World, Africa, and the western Pacific during the 16th and 17th centuries. Some nations, such as Portugal and the Netherlands, controlled territories through forts or trading posts at strategic spots on the coasts. Until the 1800s, the colonial powers rarely occupied large interior areas in Africa and India. The main areas of settlement by large num-

European Land Claims in the Americas in 1700

bers of Europeans were in North and South America and the Caribbean islands.

Spain. Spain's empire was huge. By the end of the 16th century, its American colony, New Spain, included Mexico, Central America, most of South America, a large part of what is now the western United

States, Florida, and a number of Caribbean islands. Spain also colonized the Philippine Islands in the Pacific Ocean.

France. France took control of eastern Canada and the Mississippi Valley in what is now the United States. This large territory was called New France. The French also established trading colonies in the Caribbean and in India.

The Netherlands. The Dutch empire included New Netherland in what is now New York State, a few islands in the Caribbean, and parts of South Africa and South America. It also claimed Asian areas known today as Indonesia and Sri Lanka.

Portugal. The richest colony in the Portuguese empire was Brazil in South America. Portugal also controlled trading areas on the coasts of Africa, India, and China.

Great Britain. By 1750, Great Britain had the largest empire. The British established 13 colonies on the Atlantic coast of North America. While doing this, Britain fought a series of wars against the Netherlands, Spain, and France to expand its empire. Victories on land and sea gave the British control of Canada, India, New Netherland, and several islands in the Caribbean Sea.

Competition. In 1494, not long after Columbus returned from his first voyage to the Americas, Spain and Portugal reached an agreement. They asked the pope to draw an imaginary line around the world from north to south. This Line of Demarcation ran through the eastern part of South America. Spain could claim rights to land west of the line and Portugal to the east. This agreement gave Portugal what is now Brazil. Spain could claim the rest of the Western Hemisphere. A similar agreement in 1529 in the Pacific area gave Spain the Philippine Islands.

Each exploring nation wanted a large empire and the wealth it could bring. Such rivalries resulted in wars for the control of colonies and trading posts. The most widespread of these conflicts was the Seven Years' War, which lasted from 1756 to 1763. (It was known in the American colonies as the French and Indian War.) Britain, aided by Prussia, fought France and its allies, Austria and Russia. Their armies and navies battled all over the world—in Europe, North America, and India. Britain won and gained a great deal more territory.

Case Study—The Dutch in Indonesia

During the 17th century, the Dutch competed with the Portuguese and British for control of the Spice Islands in the Indian Ocean. This island group came to be called the Dutch East Indies. (The main islands are Sumatra, Borneo, Java, Celebes, and New Guinea.)

The Dutch East India Company, formed in 1602, dominated the trade of the islands and made strong efforts to exclude other Europeans from the trade. As a result, the company became a major power in the Indies. It traded across a huge area and was able to use its large bureaucracy and superior military power to impose its will on East Indian rulers. Local leaders and traders were forced to accept Dutch trading conditions.

In 1641, the Dutch East India Company captured Malacca, a city in Malaya, from the Portuguese. It also confined British trading activity to a small section of the island of Sumatra. The company was drawn into island politics, settling conflicts between rival rulers. Eventually, the company became the main political power in the East Indies. As a result, local rulers were forced to do business only with the company. The company also told farmers what spices to raise for trade. For a time, the company made a great deal of money. But costs rose, and the company went out of business in 1799. The Dutch government took over the East Indies.

Not until the 19th century was Dutch control extended through all of the East Indies. Conflict with the French and British continued during this time. For a brief period, Java was under British rule. When the Dutch returned, they strengthened their political and economic control. This was a major change for the East Indians, who had never before experienced centralized administrative government. The East Indians resisted, but the Dutch military forces kept rebellions from spreading. Dutch rule of the East Indies continued until the mid-20th century, when the islands became the independent nation of Indonesia.

INFO CHECK

1. Explain the connection between European trade with Asia and the voyages of exploration and discovery of the 15th to 17th centuries.

2. Define the terms "northwest passage" and "Columbian exchange."

3. Why do you think the empire building of the Atlantic nations led to more conflict than cooperation?

THE ENCOUNTER IN SOUTH AMERICA

Political and economic conditions in their home countries strongly affected the way Europeans treated the people who already lived in the lands they colonized. Spain was one of the first countries to send settlers to the Americas. Political events in Spain at the time Columbus landed in America may help us to understand the behavior of Spanish colonists there.

Ferdinand and Isabella

In 1492, King Ferdinand and Queen Isabella succeeded in driving the Muslims out of their last stronghold in Granada, a city in southern

Spain. Their triumph is known as the *reconquista*, which is Spanish for "reconquest."

Ferdinand and Isabella spurred their soldiers on to victory by reminding them of the Crusaders' struggle to drive non-Christians out of the Holy Land. Ferdinand and Isabella also set their subjects against the Jews, who had been living peacefully in Spain for many centuries.

Ferdinand and Isabella wanted to unify Spain by making all members of its population Spanish and Christian. They felt they could more easily control a country in which all the inhabitants shared the same ideas and beliefs. Therefore, they forced Spanish Jews and Muslims to choose between exile and conversion to Christianity. Once they converted, however, they were not left in peace. Ferdinand and Isabella established the Spanish Inquisition and authorized it to examine converted Jews and Muslims to make sure that they were not secretly practicing Judaism and Islam. The inquisitors frequently obtained confessions by torture. Such policies encouraged Spaniards to feel suspicious of people who were not of "sangre pura," or of pure blood. Only Christian Spaniards, they thought, met this standard.

To further strengthen their monarchy, Ferdinand and Isabella turned to the Catholic Church. They easily persuaded the current pope, who was a Spaniard, to allow them to appoint bishops in Spain. This gave them great control over the Spanish Catholic Church and its policies.

The Sword and the Cross

The Spaniards who came to the Americas from this background believed they had a duty to save souls as well as to find treasure. The leaders of the soldiers, called conquistadors, believed that God wanted them to carry Christianity to the Indians. They were proud of their Spanish blood and their religion.

Many of the conquistadors were poor, however, and had no land at home. They and the soldiers they led were ready to plunder the Americas to obtain wealth for themselves and their king. As a result, Native Americans were killed, robbed, tortured, and enslaved. The conquistadors justified their actions by claiming that they were bringing the benefits of Christianity to Native Americans. They felt that the Indians were worshiping false gods. Only by becoming Christian would they be able to go to heaven.

The Conquest of Mexico

When he was 19 years old, Hernando Cortés (lived 1485–1547) went from Spain to Hispaniola, an island in the Caribbean (now the Dominican Republic and Haiti). He aided the Spanish officials in subduing the Indians there and in Cuba, another island. For his services, he was granted land for a plantation. He wanted to get rich quickly, however. He had heard that the mainland contained great quantities of gold. Therefore, when the governor of Cuba asked him to lead an expedition against the Aztecs in Mexico, he willingly accepted.

In February 1519, Cortés sailed to Mexico with only 600 soldiers, 16 horses, and a few cannons. So determined was he to conquer the Aztec Empire that he ordered his soldiers to burn the ships that brought them. Cortés believed his men would fight harder without ships to take them to safety. Within two years, Cortés had defeated the entire Aztec army and destroyed Tenochtitlán, its capital city.

Reasons for Victory. Cortés was able to achieve this victory by a combination of superior weaponry, chance, cleverness, and ruthlessness. The Spanish fought with guns and steel swords and wore metal armor. The Aztecs had only spears, swords with obsidian blades, and armor made of padded cloth.

A strange coincidence added to this advantage. The Spanish had arrived in Mexico just at the time when, according to an ancient legend, the god Quetzalcoatl would return from his long exile across the eastern sea. Quetzalcoatl was supposed to take the form of a pale-skinned, bearded man. When the Aztecs saw the pale, bearded Spaniards on horseback, they were stricken with awe. (Remember the rumors Itzcoátl, in the opening story, had heard.) The Aztec emperor Moctezuma sent Cortés gifts of gold and silver and invited the supposed god into Tenochtitlán.

In spite of these advantages, the Spaniards still might have lost. But they had cleverly enlisted the aid of other Indian groups. The Spaniards found it easy to make allies. Neighboring Indian groups hated the Aztecs, who took their people as slaves and sacrificial victims to the Aztec gods. The Spaniards were also helped by a captive woman who served as a translator. Called Doña Marina by the Span-

Moctezuma meeting Cortés in Tenochtitlán, from an 1892 Mexican painting

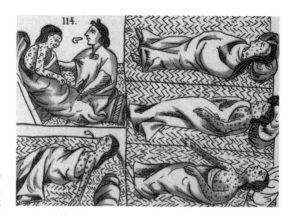

Native American suffering the
stages of smallpox, as shown in
a Florentine codex

iards, she was named Malinche by the Aztecs. When the Spaniards attacked Tenochtitlán, their Indian recruits helped them block all entrances to the city. Because of this help, the siege was a success. In 75 days, the conquistadors captured Tenochtitlán.

Destruction of Aztec Culture. After their victory over Tenochtitlán, the conquistadors went on to conquer the whole empire. They struck at the roots of Aztec culture by shattering temples and statues and burning Aztec books. Countless Aztecs died at the hands of the conquistadors. Germs carried by the soldiers infected other Indians. They died from diseases such as smallpox and measles because they had no natural defense or immunity against them. To show that Spaniards would now shape Mexican culture, the conquistadors destroyed Tenochtitlán and built Mexico City on its ruins. Christian missionaries started to convert the Aztecs. The missionaries also tried to stamp out any effort to practice old forms of worship.

Overcoming the Mayas

About five years after destroying the Aztec Empire, the Spaniards marched against the Mayas. Conquest of these people proved more difficult. The Mayas hid in the rain forests and fought from the cover of thick foliage. It took the Spaniards about 20 years to defeat the Mayas. European diseases killed great numbers. As with the Aztecs, missionaries tried to Christianize the Mayas.

The Fall of the Incas

About the same time that Cortés was attacking the Aztecs, Francisco Pizarro (lived 1478–1541) was leading an expedition against the Incas. From Panama in 1531, he sailed south along the west coast of South America with only 180 men. Pizarro was looking for the rich Inca Empire.

Like Cortés, Pizarro was exceedingly fortunate. He struck at the

Incas just when a civil war had broken out between their ruler, Atahualpa, and his brother. Superior weapons and treachery also helped the conquistadors. Pizarro kidnapped Atahualpa and demanded a fabulous ransom of gold and silver for freeing him. Once the Incas had paid the ransom, the conquistadors killed Atahualpa. With one stroke in 1533, Pizarro acquired an enormous fortune for himself and won an empire for Spain.

New Spain

Lured by treasure and land, Spanish settlers flocked to the colony of New Spain. There they obtained mines and large farms, or plantations. Running the mines and plantations required many workers. In order to make a profit, the colonists had to find a source of cheap labor.

To solve this problem, the colonists turned to the *encomienda system*. Under the encomienda system in Spain, the owner of a large piece of land, called an encomienda, could tax the peasants who lived on the land. The landlords in New Spain felt that this system gave them the right to force the Indians to work without wages instead of paying taxes. New Spain's distance from the home country made it easy for the colonists to interpret Spanish laws as they pleased. Before long, colonists were enslaving Indians to work their plantations and mines.

Many of the colonists were harsh masters. They had little respect for people who were neither Christian nor Spanish. Those who had been soldiers had learned to behave cruelly. Few hesitated to work the Indians to death. The colonists often claimed that they were abusing the Indian bodies to save their souls. Cruel treatment and diseases caused the Indian population in Latin America to decline rapidly. From about 25 million in 1519, it fell to about 1 million in 1605.

Although Spanish rulers were mainly interested in the wealth that New Spain provided, they were also eager to convert the Indians to Christianity. Therefore, they sent missionaries to their new territory. One of these, Bartolomé de Las Casas, wanted to help the enslaved people. Because he tried to persuade the owners of the encomiendas to treat their workers better, he became known as the "Protector of the Indians." When the landowners ignored his pleas, Las Casas complained to the Spanish government. In 1542, the king prohibited enslavement of the Indians. Unfortunately, this law was largely ignored. The encomienda system did not die out until the end of the 18th century.

The concern of Las Casas for the Indians turned out to be a disaster for Africans. He encouraged the importation of African slaves to replace Indians as workers. No one took up the cause of the black slaves.

MACHU PICCHU: CITY OF THE INCAS

The Incas built a mighty empire in South America. The city of Cusco was the Inca capital. It and other Inca sites were seized and plundered by the Spanish conquistadors, who destroyed the Inca Empire in the 16th century. One Inca city, however, was never found by the Spanish. Until its discovery in 1911, Machu Picchu, in what is today Peru, remained forgotten for 400 years.

It is believed today that Machu Picchu was not actually a city or place where people lived and worked. It was probably built by an Inca ruler named Pachacuti as a royal estate and religious retreat between 1460 and 1470. Its location, in rugged terrain high above the Urubamba River canyon cloud forest, was remote even to the Incas. As a result, Machu Picchu had no administrative, commercial, or military functions. Travel on the roads leading to the site was restricted to those with royal authority.

After Pachacuti's death, Machu Picchu remained the property of his family. It was responsible for the maintenance and administration of the site and for continued building. Other Inca rulers visited Machu Picchu and built their own palaces and temples there. However, despite the presence of builders, farmworkers, and servants and the flow of goods from outside, Machu Picchu remained a secret.

The Inca government moved around large numbers of people who were required to work on state projects. Once at a location, however, those people did not depart without permission. The royal roads were reserved for official travel. Control of this system depended on a tightly structured hierarchy. Information and direction from the royal government flowed down through ten high-level administrators to 100 others, to 1,000, and so on. When instructions reached the lower level officials, they conveyed the rulings to the ordinary people. Although the Incas did not have a written language, it is believed that they used symbols and diagrams. They also used *quipus*, or groupings of colored strings and knots, for accounting and recordkeeping. However, only trained specialists could read the quipus.

It was easy for the rulers of so controlled a society to keep secret the location of their royal estates at Machu Picchu. The conquistadors, who arrived in 1532, did not learn very much about the Incas. They could not find anyone who would translate the quipus records for them. By the mid-1500s, smallpox had killed an estimated 50 percent of the population, and civil war had caused more deaths and disorder. Machu Picchu was abandoned around this time. The labor force needed to maintain the royal estates was no longer available to work there.

Today, Machu Picchu is one of the most popular tourist sites in South America. Each day, hundreds of visitors explore the ruins of this sacred city of the Incas.

- Pretend you are a 16th-century scholar or treasure hunter who has heard about Machu Picchu. How would you obtain information about the site? What questions would you ask? What sources would you seek?

The Portuguese in Brazil

The Portuguese began to settle Brazil in the 1530s. The Portuguese government granted huge tracts of lands to noblemen. At first, the main resource of the colony was a tree that yielded a red and purple dye. Called brazilwood, the tree gave the colony its name. To obtain this wood, Portuguese settlers traded with the Indians.

Later, the Portuguese learned that the soil and climate of Brazil was good for growing sugar cane. Then they discovered gold and diamonds. New resources gave rise to new enterprises that changed the colonists' relationship with the Indians. The Portuguese began to view them as a source of cheap labor. Bands of raiders roamed through the tropical forests to capture Indians to work on plantations and in mines as slaves.

The exhausting work and diseases killed the enslaved Indians at a rapid rate. Also, the Indians ran away when they could. The Portuguese found it difficult to capture enough people to perform all the work that had to be done. Many plantation and mine owners began to use Africans as slave workers. The colonists easily obtained Africans from West Africa, where Portugal controlled the slave trade.

Portuguese slave masters convinced themselves that Africans were stronger than Indians and lived longer. But tens of thousands Africans also died from overwork and other harsh treatment.

As in New Spain, missionaries worked to convert the Indians. They also tried to improve conditions for the Indians. The plight of the black slaves did not receive much attention.

INFO CHECK

1. How did the *reconquista* influence the attitudes of the Spanish conquistadors and colonizers in the Americas?

2. Do you think that Hernan Cortés and Francisco Pizarro should be regarded as military heroes? Why or why not?

3. State your opinion of the *encomienda* system. What do you think was right or wrong about it?

THE ENCOUNTER IN NORTH AMERICA

The English

The English were the second group of Europeans to establish a permanent colony in the Americas. The first English attempt to colonize was made in 1585. A group sponsored by Sir Walter Raleigh landed on Roanoke Island in what is now the state of North Carolina. Queen Elizabeth I had approved of the enterprise.

The Indians of that region had no great empires. Their culture was that of the Eastern Woodland peoples—hunting and gathering.

They felt that land could not be owned by one person or one group. Having no sense of land ownership, they did not at first understand that the newcomers intended to take land for their own exclusive use. Therefore, the Indians attempted to help the colonists, who were having difficulty surviving in the new land. When one of the colonists killed their chief, however, they stopped giving aid. Without the help of the Indians, the English had to return to England.

A second attempt to settle Roanoke Island also failed. The English persisted, however. In 1607, a new group of settlers, led by John Smith, landed in present-day Virginia along the James River. This settlement, called Jamestown, survived. (King James I was the ruler of England at the time.)

The English went on to establish 13 colonies along the east coast of North America. The English colonists came to farm the land. Crops rather than treasure were the basis of their economy. Although the English Protestants did try to convert the Indians, they did not make the effort their major focus.

In almost every colony, similar interactions between settlers and Indians occurred. The Indians usually began by trying to help the settlers and, at first, both parties were cooperative with one another. Sooner or later, however, the settlers took too much of the Indians' land. Realizing that their way of life was being threatened, the Indians tried to drive the settlers away.

The French

The French claimed eastern Canada and the Mississippi Valley in what is now the United States. In 1608, Samuel de Champlain established Quebec, which became France's first settlement. Quebec played two important roles for the French. It was a station where explorers searching for a Northwest Passage to Asia could stop for supplies. It also served as a trading post. The Indians of the region were expert trappers and supplied the French with furs. Soon trade with the Indians became more important than the search for a Northwest Passage.

Most French settlers came to America to trade for furs rather than to farm. They did not see the Indians as rivals for land but as trading partners. The Indians liked the knives, tools, and guns the French exchanged for furs. From the Indians, the French learned how to trap animals for furs and how to survive in the forest. They also learned how to handle the light canoes used for transporting furs to the trading posts. Many French colonists married Indian women and became part of their wives' communities. They showed respect for the way the Indians lived.

Although Catholic missionaries came to convert the Indians to Christianity, these missionaries lived in Indian villages and adopted some Indian ways. Relations between French settlers and Indians were not perfect—the Iroquois were very hostile to the French. The Algonquian allies of the French had attacked the Iroquois in 1609 to take over fur-trapping areas. Hurons and Algonquians preferred the French over the English. When conflicts arose between the French and the English in North America, these Indian groups sided with the French.

The Dutch

Like the French, the Dutch traded furs with the Indians. In 1624, a group of merchants called the Dutch West India Company financed an expedition to set up colonies in New Netherland. In return, the merchants expected to make huge profits from the fur trade.

Thirty families sailed to the area that is now New York State. The families broke up into three groups, each founding a settlement—one on the Hudson River, one on the Delaware River, and one on the Connecticut River. The trading post on the Hudson River eventually developed into the city of Albany.

Sixty families followed the first group of colonists. In 1625, this second group founded a permanent settlement consisting of a town and a fort on Manhattan Island. First called New Amsterdam, this town eventually grew into New York City.

Dutch fur traders had good trade relations with the Iroquois. The Iroquois were glad to befriend a group that competed with the French. Dutch settlers who came to farm, however, had problems with the Algonquians. The Algonquians were suspicious of the Dutch because

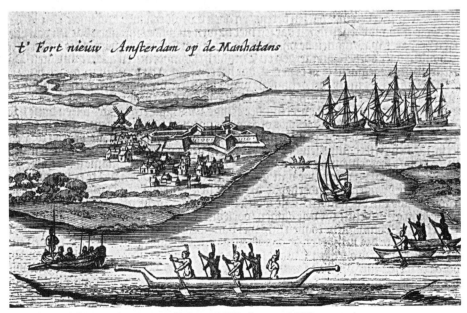

New Amsterdam as it appeared about 1626, from a 1657 engraving

of their friendship with the Iroquois, who were their rivals. When the Dutch began turning their hunting grounds into farms, the Algonquians became openly hostile. The Dutch felt that the Algonquians were treacherous. They had, after all, sold the land to the Dutch. But the Algonquians did not understand that land could be bought and sold. They believed that the payments for the land were gifts that the Dutch gave the Algonquians for being allowed to share it.

Inability to understand one another's cultures caused the Dutch and the Algonquians to look down on each other. When Algonquian men went off to hunt and fish and left their wives to tend the farms, the Dutch felt that the men were lazy. The Algonquians scorned Dutch farmers for doing women's work. Many Dutch settlers showed no understanding or respect for the Algonquians' religion.

More and more settlers came to New Netherland and took Algonquian land for farms. Dutch colonial leaders made things worse by requiring the Algonquians to pay taxes. The resentful Algonquians began to raid isolated Dutch farms.

Open warfare broke out when a Dutch leader ordered the massacre of a group of Algonquians. The Indians had come to a Dutch village for refuge from an enemy tribe. The government in the Netherlands recalled the leader. The Dutch and Indians made a peace agreement in 1645 that lasted for 10 years. War broke out again in 1655. It ended in 1663 with the defeat of the Algonquians and the loss of their homeland.

The English and Dutch had long been trading rivals. Both had strong navies and private merchant fleets. In 1664, the English, directed by King Charles II, sent warships to New Amsterdam. They claimed that New Netherland belonged to the English because of the explorations of John Cabot. The English also wanted to be part of the profitable fur trade. At first, the Dutch leader, Peter Stuyvesant, wanted to fight the English. Dutch merchants persuaded him to surrender without fighting. The English took over and renamed the area New York.

INFO CHECK

1. Compare English, French, and Dutch interactions with the Indian tribes of North America. What was similar? What was different?

2. How did rivalries between the European colonizers affect the Indians?

SLAVERY AND THE SLAVE TRADE

The desire for wealth strongly influences the way people treat each other. Of course, other factors certainly play a large part. Individual efforts to help the Indians of New Spain demonstrate that humane feelings can have a powerful effect on how people behave toward others.

In the case of the slave trade, financial interests played a greater role than morality. Some people did protest against the evils of slavery. But they were outnumbered. African kings and traders, Muslim traders, European and American businesspeople, colonial plantation and mine owners all profited from the buying and selling of human beings. Therefore, it continued.

The Triangular Trade

During the 1700s, the slave ships traveled a triangular route. On the first leg of the triangle, ships loaded with rum, iron goods, and guns left Boston or New York for the coast of West Africa. In Africa, the ships' captains traded their cargoes for gold, ivory, and slaves. Some 6 million Africans were brought to the Americas in the 1700s.

The second leg of the triangle was called the Middle Passage. It brought the enslaved Africans to the West Indies, islands in the Caribbean, where they were exchanged for molasses. The time of the Middle Passage was the cruelest for the Africans. Chained in place, poorly fed, and roughly treated, many died. Undoubtedly they were

African Destinations in the Western Hemisphere

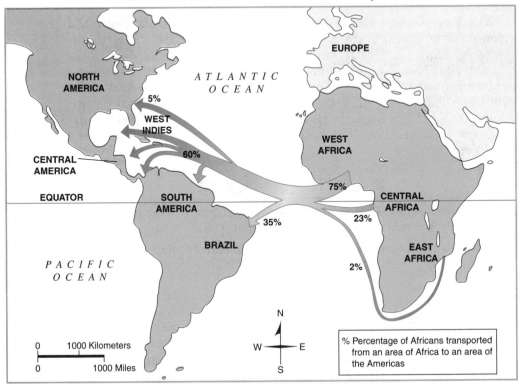

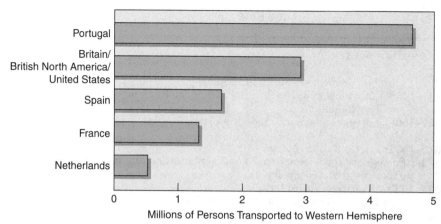

Leading Slave-Trading Nations 1520–1867

afraid and confused. Few were shipped with people they knew or who could speak the same language.

On the third and last leg of the triangle, ships carried the molasses to Boston and New York, where it was made into rum. The business-people of Boston and New York grew rich on this trade.

The English and the Dutch were also heavily involved in the slave trade. A great many slaves worked on the sugar plantations in the Caribbean islands and Brazil.

Slavery in the West Indies

The Africans who survived the misery of the Middle Passage were sold in the West Indies. There they were put to work on the sugar plantations. Many died from overwork in the hot, humid climate. Conditions on the sugar plantations were so harsh that only the strongest, healthiest people could live through them. When traders resold these survivors, they emphasized their value by advertising them as having been "seasoned" in the Caribbean.

Gradually, more people learned about the cruelties committed by slave-ship captains and by plantation owners. In the 1700s, a religious group called the Quakers began to petition the British government to outlaw slavery. In 1789, a freed African slave named Olaudoh Equiano wrote a book that described the horrors of the Middle Passage. (He was from Nigeria.) Many readers of this book joined the Quakers in protesting against the slave trade.

An event in Haiti caused the British government to refuse these petitions. In 1791, a freed slave named Toussaint L'Ouverture led a successful uprising against French slaveowners in Haiti. British leaders feared that Africans enslaved on other islands in the West Indies might also commit acts of violence against British plantation owners.

Time Line

Year	Dates and Events
A.D. **1401**	**1492:** Columbus discovers Americas for Spain
	1497–1498: Cabot looks for Northwest Passage for England; finds Nova Scotia, Newfoundland
	1497–1509: Portuguese expand trade from India to China, Japan, Southeast Asia
	1519–1521: Cortés defeats Aztecs
	1530s: Portuguese settle Brazil; natives flee plantation and mine work; big importation of African slaves
	1531–1533: Pizarro conquers Inca
1500	**1534–1541:** Cartier explores eastern Canada and St. Lawrence River for France
1501	**1542:** Spanish king bans enslavement of natives in New Spain; big importation of African slaves
	1576: Frobisher looks for Northwest Passage for England; finds Labrador
	1585: First English attempt to establish colony on Roanoke island (North Carolina)
	1600s–1700s: Dutch in New Netherland, Indonesia, Sri Lanka, Caribbean, South Africa, South America
	1603: Champlain explores St. Lawrence River for France
1600	**1607:** Jamestown, Virginia, first permanent European (English) settlement in North America
1601	**1608:** Champlain establishes fur trading post at Quebec
	1609: Hudson explores east coast of North America for the Netherlands
	1619: Africans arrive in Virginia
	1624: Dutch found New Netherland along the Hudson, Delaware, Connecticut rivers
	1643–1663: Dutch defeat and expel Algonquians from New Netherland
	1664: Dutch surrender New Netherland to English
1700	**1700:** Spanish in Mexico, Central America, South and North America, Caribbean, Philippines
1701	**1700s:** France in New France (eastern Canada, Mississippi Valley), Caribbean, India
	1700s: American, English, Dutch triangular slave trade
	1750: Britain's huge colonial empire in North America, India, Caribbean
	1756–1763: Seven Years' War involves most of Europe (French and Indian War in America); Britain adds colonies in North America, India
	1767: Quakers urge Northern slaveholders to free slaves; call for boycott of slave-made goods
1800	**1789:** Freed slave Equiano writes about miseries aboard slave ships
1801	**1791:** L'Ouverture leads successful uprising against French slaveowners in Haiti
	1807: British outlaw slave trade; ban applies to entire empire by 1834
	1808: Importation of slaves into United States prohibited (by Constitution)
	1820s: Slaves in Spanish Latin America gain freedom through independence movements
	1848: France frees colonial slaves
	1865: Slavery ends in United States (13th Amendment to Constitution)
1900	**1888:** Brazil frees slaves

Therefore, they felt it was best to keep the social order as it was. Not until 1807 did the British government outlaw the slave trade. In 1834, slavery was outlawed throughout the British empire.

France freed the slaves in its colonies in 1848. Slaves became free in Latin America when the countries in this area gained their independence from Spain in the 1820s. Brazil did not free the slaves there until 1888. Spain waited until 1873 to free slaves in its colony of Puerto Rico in the Caribbean. Slaves in the Spanish colony of Cuba had to wait even longer, until 1886, to receive their freedom.

Slavery in North America

In 1619, a small group of Africans arrived in Virginia. They were hired labor obligated to work for their master for a certain number of years. Later, Africans were brought in as slaves to work on the rice, tobacco, and sugarcane plantations. Not until the early 1800s did cotton become a major crop. The economy of the South became more and more dependent on the cheap labor of slaves.

Most slaves lived in the South and worked as field laborers. Some became skilled craftsworkers. Northern slaves tended to be laborers and factory workers. The smaller farms in the North did not require as many workers as the plantations of the South.

The white masters in the South were outnumbered by the slave population. Fear of revolts caused them to pass laws known as slave codes. The codes prohibited slaves from owning weapons, learning to read, meeting in groups except at church, and going from place to place without permission.

From the 1790s on, more and more Americans criticized the slave system. The U.S. Constitution prohibited the importation of slaves after 1808. But it took the Civil War (1861–1865) to destroy the institution of slavery. Officially, the 13th Amendment to the Constitution ended slavery in 1865.

Chapters 16, 17, and 18 have described the civilizations that the Europeans encountered in the 1400s and 1500s in Africa and the Americas. There was discussion of how the encounter changed everyone. In most cases, the changes were disastrous for the colonized peoples. Europeans tended to believe that the local people could improve themselves by accepting European ways and the Christian religion.

Chapter 19 sets forth new ideas about rights and freedoms. These ideas had a profound effect on governments and social systems in Europe and the Americas.

INFO CHECK

- For each date, state an event or development related to the slave trade: 1619, 1789, 1791, 1807, 1808, 1834, 1848, 1873.

CHAPTER REVIEW

Multiple Choice

1. The Europeans purchased many products from Asia. Select the item that was needed for health reasons.

   1. silk
   2. spices
   3. natural or carved precious stones
   4. porcelain and jade.

2. The search for an all-water route to Asia and India was undertaken by five European nations. They included

   1. Portugal and the Netherlands
   2. France and Spain
   3. England and the Netherlands
   4. all of the above.

3. The voyages around the Cape of Good Hope proved that

   1. the world was flat and one could sail off the edge of it
   2. a ship could sail around the southern tip of Africa
   3. a sea route to the Indian Ocean and India did not exist
   4. an all-water route to North America could not be found.

4. The Columbian exchange refers to the movement of what across the Atlantic Ocean?

   1. people, animals, plants, and ideas
   2. precious minerals and slaves
   3. gold and feathers
   4. all of the above.

5. As a result of the *reconquista* in Spain, the following event(s) happened:

   1. expulsion of all Muslims
   2. expulsion or religious conversion for all Jewish people

3. establishment of the Spanish Inquisition
   4. all of the above.

6. Cortés and Pizarro were able to defeat the Aztecs and Incas because of steel weapons, guns, Indian allies, and

   1. the corruption and cowardice of the Indian governments
   2. Indian warriors' surprise at by the tactics of the Spanish
   3. superstition and/or disunity among the Aztecs and Incas
   4. excellent intelligence and maps of the Indian strongholds.

7. The *encomienda* system in Spain allowed large landholders to tax the peasants who lived on their land. In New Spain the landholders

   1. taxed the Indians living on their lands
   2. forced the Indians to leave their lands since they had no money to pay taxes
   3. made the Indians work without wages instead of paying taxes
   4. none of the above.

8. New France's colonists had better relations with the Indian tribes than the Dutch or English settlers did. This was because the Frenchmen

   1. were not interested in acquiring the land, only in trading or trapping for furs
   2. did not try to convert the Indians to Catholicism
   3. refused to marry Indian women
   4. were all Huguenots fleeing religious abuse, so they treated the Indians fairly.

9. Cultural differences have often led to misunderstandings and anger between groups. The Dutch and Algonquians are an example. Select the correct examples that illustrate those differences.

1. The Algonquians had no religious beliefs, while the Dutch were deeply religious.
2. The Dutch thought the Algonquians lazy for allowing their women to farm the land.
3. The Algonquians valued their land and thought the Dutch foolish for selling off shares of theirs.
4. The Dutch wanted to buy furs, but the Algonquians sold only to the French fur traders.

10. The decline of Spain, Portugal, and the Netherlands left England and France to struggle for colonial empires and power. The worldwide struggle that left England as the greatest colonial power was the

1. Hundred Years' War
2. Mayan 20-year struggle
3. Crusades
4. Seven Years' War.

11. The chart on page 393 shows that

1. Spain engaged in a smaller slave trade than the Netherlands
2. France and the Netherlands traded a larger combined total of slaves than Portugal
3. all European nations were involved in the African slave trade
4. nearly 3 million slaves were traded by Britain, Britsh North America, and the United States.

12. According to the time line on page 394

1. the French were the first Europeans to outlaw slavery
2. Brazil freed its slaves after slavery ended in the United States
3. the British were the last Europeans to outlaw slavery
4. slavery in America began in 1492.

Thematic Essays

1. *Task:* Select one area and discuss who benefited the most and who the least from the initial encounters between the Europeans and the peoples of Africa, Asia, or the Americas. Include specific historical examples to support your answer. Benefits may include natural resources, location, land, and markets.

2. The colonizers of the Americas and Asia developed large empires. *Task:* Compare and contrast the causes for the rise and fall of those empires. Factors to consider in your answer include: political and social organization, location and geography.

Document-Based Questions

1. Study the illustration on page 385. Why were the Europeans' diseases so deadly to the Native Americans?

2. Study the map on page 380. Which nations gained immediate wealth from their colonies, and at whose expense?

3. From the writings of Bartolomé de Las Casas.

"That which led the Spaniards to these [terrible deeds] was the desire of gold, to make themselves suddenly rich . . . for the Spaniards so little regarded the health of their souls that they [allowed] this great [number] to die without the least light of religion. . . . The Indians never gave them the least cause to offer them violence. . . ."

Whose souls is Las Casas concerned about, and why?

4. From the writings of John Winthrop.

"It will be a service to the Church of great consequence to carry the Gospell into those parts of the world. . . . This land grows weary of her inhabitants . . . all towns complain of the burden of their poore . . ."

Explain the three reasons Winthrop gives for leaving his homeland.

Document-Based Essay

Using specific social and economic examples from the encounters between Europeans and Mesoamerican or African cultures, agree or disagree with the statement: "What is beneficial to one person or culture, another finds harmful and destructive."

UNIT REVIEW

Thematic Essays

1. Prior to European discovery, the peoples of Mesoamerica had developed advanced societies. *Task:* Using social, economic, and governmental examples, compare and contrast the Mesoamerican societies with any one African, Asian, or North American civilization.

2. "Technology enabled the Europeans to overcome geographic barriers and establish trading relations with China and Africa. Later, European technology was used to dominate those African and Chinese peoples." *Task:* Comment on the accuracy of this statement, using specific historical and geographic examples to explain the changing nature of the encounters between European, Africans, and Asians.

Document-Based Questions

Use your knowledge of Global History and Geography and the documents to answer the questions.

1. From a letter by King Louis XIV about France's commercial policy.

"All merchants and traders by sea who buy ships or build new ones for trade or commerce will receive subsidies from us to help them. . . . Those who undertake long voyages will receive from us . . . subsidies for each ton of merchandise that they carry or bring back from the voyage. . . ."

How and why do you think Louis XIV is encouraging overseas trade?

2. An account of Vasco da Gama's meeting with the king of Calcutta in India.

"Vasco da Gama said to the King: 'Sire, you are powerful and very great, above all the kings and rulers of India. The great King of Portugal, my sovereign, having heard of your grandeur . . . had a great longing . . . to send his ships with much merchandise to trade and buy your merchandise, and above all pepper and spices, of which there are none in Portugal . . .'

Describe who has the power in this meeting, da Gama or the king of Calcutta, and tell why you made that decision.

3. A letter from the Chinese emperor to King George III of England.

"You, O King, live beyond the confines of many seas. Nevertheless, impelled by your humble desire to partake of the benefits of our civilization, you have dispatched a mission respectfully bearing your memorial. . . . Our dynasty's majestic virtue has penetrated into every country under heaven . . . we possess all things. I see no value on objects strange or ingenious and have no use for your countries' manufactures."

What is the Chinese emperor's message to the king of England?

4. Antonio de Montesinos preached this sermon to Spanish colonists on the island of Hispaniola in 1511.

"Why do you keep them [Native Indians] so oppressed and fatigued, neither giving them enough to eat nor taking care of them in their illness, for with the . . . work you demand of them they become ill and die, or rather you kill them with your desire to extract gold every day. . . . Be certain that, in the state in which you are, you can no more be saved than the Moors or Turks who lack and do not believe in the Christian faith."

If you had been present, how would you have reacted to what Father Montesinos was saying? In your answer consider the history of the period.

5. Study the illustration on page 368. How does this illustration depict what occurred when Africans and Mesoamericans encountered European societies?

Document-Based Essay

Task: Use economic, scientific, and cultural examples either to agree or disagree with this statement: "Non-Western societies gave much to the Europeans and received little in return."

UNIT V
An Age of Revolutions (1750–1914)

An Age of Revolutions (1750–1914)

Year	Dates and Events
A.D. 1700	**1762–1796:** Catherine the Great of Russia exercises absolute power over peasants and serfs
	1774–1792: Reign of Louis XVI; National Assembly limits king's power, widens commoners' rights
	1775–1783: American Revolution—colonists win independence from Britain
	1789–1799: French Revolution—end of absolute monarchy; Napoleon ends Directory, takes control of French government
	1791–1804: L'Ouverture leads Haitian slave uprising; Dessaline wins independence from France
	1810–1841: Many Latin American colonies win independence from Spain, Portugal, France
	1814: Congress of Vienna sets up balance of power among European monarchies; suppresses nationalism
1799	**1825–1855:** Nicholas I of Russia crushes liberal movement
1800	**1830:** Belgians oust Dutch, set up constitutional monarchy
	1830–1848: French oust Charles X in favor of Louis Philippe; rise of French middle class
	1848: French oust Louis Philippe, set up Second Republic under Louis Napoleon
	1848: Unsuccessful revolutions in Germany, Austria, Hungary, Italy; peasants gain basic rights
	1848: Marx and Engels publish *Communist Manifesto*—class struggle, coming revolution
	1852: Beginning of risorgimento; Cavour tries to unite northern Italian states against Austria
	1852–1870: Louis Napoleon as Emperor Napoleon III sets up Second Empire
	1855–1881: Alexander II of Russia frees serfs, institutes social and legal reforms
1899	**1857–1859:** Sepoy Mutiny; British government rules India directly as colony
1900	**1861:** Victor Emmanuel II named king of unified Italy
	1881–1894: Assassination of Alexander II by Russian terrorists; Alexander III suppresses all opposition
	1897: First Zionist congress meets in Switzerland to promote Jewish state in Palestine
	1899: Boers revolt against British rule in South Africa
	1908: Belgian government takes control of Congo from King Leopold
	1910–1914: Madero, Villa, Zapata force dictator Díaz to flee Mexico; Huerta takes over government; revolutionists, with U.S. aid, force Huerta to resign
	1911: Revolution led by Sun Yixian overthrows Manchus, declares China a republic
1999	**1917–1922:** Russian Revolution brings Communist leaders to power; Soviet Union created

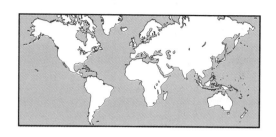

C H A P T E R

19

Revolutions in Science and Philosophy

Gabrielle woke up early, eager to begin the day. At the convent school where she had spent the last six years, she had never wanted to get up. She had felt hemmed in by all the rules. The lessons on how to conduct herself in society and how to manage a household bored her. Why couldn't she have been taught about science, mathematics, and philosophy? But school was behind her. Now that she was back home in Paris, each day brought something new. She wondered if she would have a chance to talk to Monsieur Hervé, her brother's tutor, as she had last evening.

What wonderful ideas he had. Gabrielle especially agreed that human nature was basically good. All one needed was liberty to develop into a kind and generous person. She remembered how spiteful some of the girls at the school had been. The strict rules at the school had doubtless warped their spirits. Gabrielle had never been ill-natured. She had been disobedient toward the school authorities instead. Now she felt quite proud of her defiance. Monsieur Hervé said that people had a right to rebel against tyranny.

This young woman of the 18th century is just becoming aware of new ideas about human nature and society. These new ideas clashed with what was taught in traditional schools. People now began to question established forms of government. As the century wore

403

on, some groups joined together to overthrow restrictive governments. They hoped to replace the governments with ideal societies. These ideas and political movements developed from a new way of studying nature.

THE SCIENTIFIC REVOLUTION

For many centuries, scientists had accepted the writings of ancient scholars and the teachings of religious leaders about science and nature. Early in the Renaissance, scientists began to use new methods to study nature. Conclusions based on observation and experimentation became the basis for scientific theories.

Statements put forth as facts were accepted as truth only after they had been tested in experiments. These tests and their results were written down so that other scientists could repeat them. Gradually, the *scientific method* of observation, experimentation, and drawing conclusions came into common use. It led to advances in the fields of chemistry, physics, mathematics, astronomy, and medicine. This method made such major changes in the study and understanding of nature that it is said to have caused a *scientific revolution*.

The Renaissance and the Scientific Method

Renaissance explorers, such as Columbus and Magellan, had demonstrated that the earth is larger and more varied than Europeans had previously thought. Similarly, Renaissance scientists changed their ideas of what the heavens were like. The new understanding of the universe came about as the result of applying the scientific method to observations and theories.

People of the Middle Ages acquired concepts of the everyday world from Christian teachings. Ideas also came from the philosophic and scientific theories of the Greek philosopher Aristotle. Christian theologians believed that the biblical account of creation was literally true. God's realm was, of course, the most important part of the universe. But it was somewhere beyond and above the solar system. Earth, being the home of human beings created by God, was the focus of God's attention. Therefore, the religious leaders and scientists of the Middle Ages thought that the earth was the center of the solar system. Aristotle's theory that the solar system is *geocentric* supported this belief. A geocentric solar system is one in which the sun and all the planets revolve around earth, which does not move.

Copernicus. Interestingly enough, the first person who challenged this view of the solar system was a devout clergyman from Poland called Nicolaus Copernicus (lived 1473–1543). Copernicus was an astronomer as well as an authority on church law. In his astronomical studies, he had read the theories of the astronomer

Diagram of the pre-
Copernican, earth-centered
universe, published in 1539

Ptolemy, who lived during the 2nd century A.D. in Alexandria, Egypt.
Ptolemy had developed rules based on the geocentric model of the
solar system. The rules helped other astronomers follow the paths of
the planets in their revolutions around the earth.

These rules were so complicated and sometimes so inaccurate that

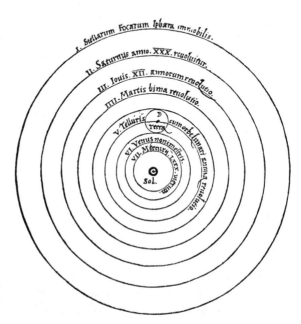

Diagram of the Copernican,
sun-centered universe,
published in 1543

Copernicus began to feel that God could not have made a geocentric solar system. If God had done so, Copernicus thought, He would not have been perfect. Copernicus turned to a model of the solar system that had been proposed by Aristarchus, a Greek astronomer who lived in the 200s B.C. This was a *heliocentric* model in which the earth and all the other planets revolved around the sun. Copernicus found that the heliocentric model explained the pathways of the planets better than the geocentric model. For nearly 40 years, Copernicus studied and tested Aristarchus's assertion that the solar system is heliocentric. Finally, he wrote a book, *On the Revolutions of Heavenly Bodies*, that discussed the theory. It was published in 1543, the year Copernicus died.

Although Copernicus had written his book to demonstrate the perfection of God's creation, it outraged religious leaders. Not only did it contradict the Bible, it gave human beings an insignificant place in the universe. Most scientists of the time complained that Copernicus's theory lacked common sense. "If the earth is spinning around the sun," they asked, "why doesn't everything fall off it?" A century passed before scientists began to consider the heliocentric solar system a possibility.

Kepler. One of the first astronomers to accept Copernicus's theory was Johannes Kepler (lived 1571–1630) of Germany. In the early 1600s, he began work that supported Copernicus's mathematical reasoning.

Kepler studied a table on the movement of the stars and planets drawn up by the Danish astronomer Tycho Brahe. Brahe had observed the heavens without the use of a telescope, which had not yet been invented. Applying the table to the heliocentric model of the solar system, Kepler formulated three laws of planetary motion. The planets follow elliptical (oval-shaped) paths around the sun. (Earlier it had been thought that the paths were circles.) They revolve at different speeds from one another. The speed of each planet's revolution around the sun depends on its distance from the sun. Kepler was the first scientist to demonstrate that carefully recorded observations about the pathways of the planets were consistent with the heliocentric theory.

Galileo. Galileo Galilei (lived 1564–1642), a professor of mathematics at the universities of Pisa and Padua in Italy, also accepted the heliocentric theory. He, too, realized that only the heliocentric model could answer such questions as: Why do the planets appear to be different distances from earth at different times of the year? A newly invented device, the forerunner of the modern telescope, provided Galileo with visual evidence that supported Copernicus and Kepler.

After hearing a description of the new instrument, Galileo made one of his own. His telescope was much more powerful than the original. It revealed heavenly bodies as distant as the moons of Jupiter.

Galileo's experiment on the Leaning Tower of Pisa, proving that objects of different mass fall at the same rate

For the first time, there was proof that all heavenly bodies do not revolve around earth. In 1610, Galileo started to publish his findings. They did not, of course, support the Church's teachings that the earth does not move and is the center of the universe.

The Catholic Church warned Galileo that his theories were heretical (contrary to the teachings of the Church). Galileo felt that he was not a heretic. He believed that the heliocentric solar system expressed God's perfection better than did the geocentric solar system. Although he submitted his writing to the Church for censorship, his ideas continued to stir up controversy. Church officials had told Galileo not to defend the heliocentric theory of Copernicus. Galileo continued to write favorably about Copernicus's ideas. In 1633, exasperated Church officials ordered him to appear before the Inquisition. When the inquisitors threatened to burn him at the stake, Galileo took back, or recanted, his assertion that the earth moves around the sun. He was sentenced to life imprisonment in the form of house arrest. (In 1983, a special Church commission ruled that Galileo was not guilty.)

VESALIUS: FOUNDER OF SCIENTIFIC ANATOMY

Between 1536 and 1562, Andreas Vesalius, a Belgian-born physician, wrote six medical works. His fame is based mainly on his book titled *On the Structure of the Human Body*. Published in 1543, this 700-page book, with more than 300 illustrations, established the foundations of the modern science of anatomy. It contained Vesalius' firsthand observations of the structure and operation of the human body. This application of the scientific method of investigation would not have been possible had not Vesalius dared to dissect human bodies.

In the mid-1500s, medical knowledge of the workings of the human body was limited mainly to the writings of Galen, a physician who lived during the period of the Roman Empire. Galen's work was not very accurate, because he never studied a corpse. Not until the 15th century did European universities permit occasional public dissections of the bodies of executed criminals. Because most people were horrified by such studies, only the boldest doctors attempted such demonstrations. Vesalius, however, was determined to learn by firsthand investigation and observation. As a 20-year-old medical student in Paris, he took the risk of doing two public dissections before large audiences.

At age 23, Vesalius became professor of anatomy at the University of Padua in Italy. His anatomy demonstrations became popular events that attracted observers from all over Italy. He also gained a reputation as an expert medical doctor. This resulted in his appointment as court physician to the Holy Roman Emperor and King of Spain, Charles V, and to Philip II, Charles's successor as King of Spain.

At the time of the publication of *On the Structure of the Human Body*, Vesalius was 29 years old. The young doctor's views and methods came under attack by the authorities of the Roman Catholic Church, his medical colleagues, and society at large. Angered by the criticism, Vesalius burned his notes. For 20 years, while he was the physician to Charles V and Philip II, he did not perform any dissections. Eventually, Vesalius resumed his investigations into the workings of the human body.

He left the service of Philip II in 1564. While returning from a pilgrimage to the Holy Land, he was shipwrecked and died of disease or starvation on a Mediterranean island. His work lived on. The science of anatomy, which he pioneered, became one of the great achievements of the scientific revolution.

- Write a letter to Vesalius in which you comment on his reaction to criticism. Advise him as to how and why he might have responded differently.

In spite of Galileo's recantation, scholars could not dismiss his ideas as they had Copernicus's and Kepler's. His ideas were based on solid reasoning and careful analysis of recorded data. They were also backed up by visual evidence.

Galileo provided evidence for other theories about the physical world. Instead of relying on Aristotle's scientific writings, Galileo studied natural forces by experimentation. He was particularly interested in the motion of objects. By rolling brass balls down a slanted surface, he found that they speeded up at a uniform rate. This and other experiments on motion led to his formulation of the law of inertia. The law of inertia states that an object in motion tends to keep moving unless stopped by an outside force. Galileo also expressed the law of falling objects. They fall at the same speed regardless of mass. He showed that scholars and others did not need to accept what some

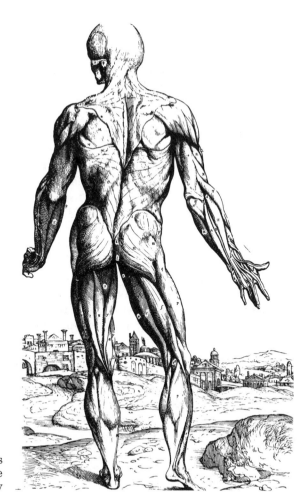

Woodcut of a Vesalius diagram showing the muscles of a male body

authority told them was true about nature. They could draw their own conclusions through observations and experimentation.

Bacon. Sir Francis Bacon, an English philosopher, writer, and public official, lived from 1561 to 1626. He promoted the scientific method. In his book *The Advancement of Learning*, Bacon described how scientists such as Galileo used the method to study the world around them. As they worked, they wrote down what they did. Other scientists could use these records to check the validity of a theory by repeating the process that led to it. Bacon felt that scientists should also use *inductive reasoning*. In inductive reasoning, the thinker develops general ideas after making specific observations about one or two events or things. This type of reasoning suggests conclusions that may or may not be true.

Descartes. René Descartes (lived 1596–1650) was a French mathematician, scientist, and philosopher. He added important ideas to Bacon's conception of the scientific method. Descartes felt that deductive reasoning was more effective in establishing natural laws than drawing conclusions from observation.

Descartes knew that reasoning from a commonly accepted generalization could result in serious errors. One could not draw true conclusions from a faulty generalization. Scientists had made that mistake when they explained the pathway of heavenly bodies in terms of a geocentric solar system. Therefore, Descartes strongly disapproved of the medieval reliance on traditional knowledge. More than any other thinker of his time, he emphasized the importance of questioning all established ideas. He made it clear that only the most self-evident principles, such as those used in geometry, should serve as the basis for deductive reasoning.

Newton. The scientist who made some of the most important discoveries was a mathematics teacher in England named Isaac Newton (lived 1642–1727). As a young man, Newton created the system of advanced mathematics called calculus. Newton also developed the law of universal gravitation, which law explained the operation of a force called gravity. On every planet, the force of gravity pulls objects toward the planet and keeps them from flying off into space. Newton further explained how gravity keeps planets in orbit around the sun.

Newton's identification of the laws that govern natural forces gave rise to the *mechanistic world view*. Since the universe obeys consistent laws, people began to picture it as a great machine. They began to believe that human intelligence is capable of discovering all the laws that govern the universe.

Leeuwenhoek. A Dutch scientist named Anton van Leeuwenhoek (lived 1632–1723) helped to develop the microscope. Through it he discovered creatures too small to be seen by the naked eye. On studying them, he found that each was made up of a tiny unit he called an "animacule." We now know them as bacteria and protozoa.

Leeuwenhoek's work disproved the idea of spontaneous generation. This is the notion that tiny living things, such as lice or fleas, come from nonliving matter. They actually come from eggs.

Influence of the Scientific Revolution

The scientific method did more than revolutionize how people studied the physical world. Scholars began to apply the scientific method to history, government, and economics. Historians studied documents from the past with a more critical eye. They no longer placed the classical ages of Greece and Rome above their own. The new methods of observation and experimentation helped them advance beyond the views of ancient philosophers. They saw no reason people in the future should not improve even more. Such ideas gave rise to the concept of *progress*.

Political thinkers and economists began to feel that reason or *rationality*, as it was called, could solve many social problems. When rulers abused their power and rich people oppressed the poor, they were behaving irrationally. Proper education could train both political leaders and ordinary citizens to act humanely. (Gabrielle, in the opening story, was becoming exposed to this way of thinking.) Because of these beliefs, people became more concerned about the education of children.

During the 17th and 18th centuries, scholars had such confidence in rationality that they believed that they could use it to free people from superstition, poverty, and oppression. The importance of rationality to this period has caused it to become known as the *Enlightenment* and *The Age of Reason*.

INFO CHECK

1. Define the terms scientific method and scientific revolution.

2. Explain the connection between the Renaissance and the scientific revolution. How did the work of Galileo illustrate this connection?

3. Why did the discoveries of Isaac Newton result in a mechanistic world view?

4. Why were the 17th and 18th centuries known as the Enlightenment, or Age of Reason?

THE ENLIGHTENMENT IN EUROPE

In the late Renaissance, scientists began to realize the importance of communicating with each other. Learning from one another became more important than reading the works of ancient scientists and philosophers. Progress in unraveling the secrets of the natural world depended on learning about each other's discoveries and ideas. Therefore, scientists in different nations formed an international community. Intellectuals in other fields also began to apply the scientific method to their interests. They, too, formed societies that did not recognize national boundaries. Because these people were always eager to learn each other's thoughts, ideas spread quickly throughout Europe. Particularly influential were the new ideas about power, authority, governance, and law.

Hobbes

Thomas Hobbes (lived 1588–1679) was an English political philosopher who defended royal absolutism. While living in France, he became tutor to the exiled prince who would one day become King Charles II of England. During this period, he also completed the most important of his many books. *Leviathan*, published in 1651, was given the name of an all-powerful sea monster in the Bible. The name emphasized Hobbes's belief that government must be all-powerful and absolute.

Hobbes believed that people are constantly in conflict with each other, have difficult lives, and fear a violent death. These conditions cause them to surrender their freedom to a ruler. To enable the ruler to maintain law and order, people grant him or her absolute power. Thus, people enter into a *social contract* in which they exchange freedom for security. Hobbes also wrote that once people enter into such a social contract, they have no right to criticize, or seek to change, the ruler's policies.

Hobbes's ideas were not popular. Although he supported royal absolutism, Hobbes claimed that power comes from the people. This challenged belief in the divine right of kings. Such a point of view annoyed the Stuart monarchs of England and Scotland. Hobbes also irritated religious officials. He stated that temporal, or civil, authority was always superior to ecclesiastical, or religious, authority. Finally, popular thought in England favored more democratic ideas. As a result, Hobbes was overshadowed by another political philosopher of the 17th century—John Locke.

Locke

An English philosopher named John Locke (lived 1632–1704) strongly influenced the thinking of Europeans about how institutions shape human personality. In his 1610 work *An Essay Concerning Human Understanding*, Locke stated that individuals are born with no basic ideas or ways of thinking. A newborn baby's mind is a *tabula rasa*, or a blank tablet. The way the baby is treated and educated determines what kind of personality he or she will have. Therefore, the family, school, and other institutions that constitute a child's environment form his or her personality. Locke felt that political freedom is one of the most important factors in producing a good and productive person.

Like the universe, Locke argued, human nature is governed by natural laws. These laws are the pursuit of good and the avoidance of pain. Reason enables humans to recognize which desirable things are truly good for them. Although Locke thought that newborn babies have no specific personality traits, he did believe that they have the power to reason. Institutions, therefore, must help a person develop reasoning powers. They should not foster blind acceptance of regulation.

In order to obey natural laws, all humans must exercise certain natural rights—the rights to life, liberty, and property. In his *Two Treatises of Government* (1690), Locke argues that the function of government is to protect these rights. If a government does not do this, the citizens then have the natural right to change it for one that does. Locke's ideas on government and natural rights spread through Europe and across the Atlantic Ocean to America. The colonists who rebelled against England and set up their own government were inspired by Locke's political philosophy.

Montesquieu

Another important political thinker of the period was the French philosopher, the Baron de Montesquieu (lived 1689–1755). Disapproving of the absolute monarchy of Louis XIV, Montesquieu studied ways to prevent despotism (the exercise of unlimited power). He admired the English method of dividing political power among the monarch, Parliament, and the English courts. He suggested that all governments should provide for the separation of powers among the executive, legislative, and judicial parts. No one part should be able to become more powerful than the others. Like Locke, Montesquieu influenced the American revolutionists, who included his ideas about checks and balances of power in the United States Constitution.

Voltaire

Under the pen name Voltaire, François Marie Arouet (lived 1694–1778) of France wrote books and essays about government, religion, and philosophy. He was also known for his plays. In his writings on government, Voltaire supported Locke's ideas that people have natural rights. He was not optimistic about human nature, however. He felt that few people were capable of governing themselves. Therefore, he thought that the best government was one that was ruled by a good king. He particularly admired the monarchy of England.

As were many Enlightenment thinkers, Voltaire was a *deist*. Deists believed that there was a planned order to the universe and thought that using reason was the only way to find truth. They saw God as the master mechanic or divine clockmaker. After creating the universe, He wound it up like a clock and left it to operate on its own. Voltaire frequently wrote against religious intolerance and criticized governments that persecuted people for following their own faith.

Rousseau

A major philosopher of the Enlightenment was Jean-Jacques Rousseau of France (lived 1712–1778). He felt that both reason and civilization destroyed the best in human beings. Therefore, he did not believe that society was improving. On the contrary, people had been better off when they had lived in a state of nature alone or in small, agricultural communities. In these surroundings, their true goodness would not be spoiled. He described precivilized people as "noble savages." The noble savage had been generous, free, spontaneous, and sincere.

Although Rousseau felt that people could not return to a state of nature, he believed that the basic goodness of the noble savage survives in children. Therefore, it was important to educate children in such a way as to preserve their unspoiled state.

Since modern society cannot function without some government, Rousseau thought that people should develop one that would not be too oppressive. In his book *The Social Contract* (1762), Rousseau described an ideal society. The members of this society would make a contract to give up some of their freedom in order to serve the common interests of all the people in the society. The general will would determine the common interest. It is not necessarily the majority of people, however, that expresses the general will. The majority might be mistaken. Sometimes a small group can have a better sense of the common good. Even those who disagree with the general will must obey it so that society will not be disrupted.

All kinds of political leaders found Rousseau's theories attractive. Those who wanted to set up democracies readily adopted his ideas. Society should be ruled by a social contract rather than by a monarch, they said. Political decisions should reflect the general will. Despots took up the notion that the majority is not always right. They defended their right to absolute rule by insisting that they were in a better position to know what was best for the nation than were the uneducated masses.

The Physiocrats

The economists of the Enlightenment in France were known as *physiocrats*. Many of these thinkers were influenced by the ideas of natural law and individual freedom. In their view, the wealth of a nation was based on agriculture. Manufacturing and trade did not add to wealth. A nation's economy should not be regulated by the government but should be left to follow its own natural laws. For example, they argued that the government should not set restrictions on trade as was done under the mercantalist theory of economics. If farmers were able to sell their goods at the best prices, trade would increase and make the entire nation richer. In other words, the physiocrats supported the idea of *laissez faire*—being free from government regulation.

Enlightened Despots

Some political thinkers of the Enlightenment believed that the ruler of a nation, rather than its citizens, should bring about political change. Those who held this point of view had little faith that the common people of the time could govern themselves. Most, however, simply realized that the strong monarchs of Europe had no intention of allowing themselves to be replaced by democratic leaders. Political philosophers, therefore, hoped to persuade monarchs to adopt enlightened policies.

Several absolute rulers were ready to take their advice. These rulers were educated, cultured people who wished to live by the most advanced ideas of their time. They were also shrewd politicians who realized that some of the reforms promoted by philosophers would strengthen their states.

Frederick the Great of Prussia. Frederick II (ruled 1740–1786) was strongly influenced by Voltaire. The two men carried on a

Frederick the Great of Prussia astride his horse, in a contemporary engraving

long-term correspondence. Frederick even invited Voltaire to be a member of his court. (Prussia was a large, powerful state in what is now Germany.) Frederick was called "the Great" for his victories in war. For much of his reign, he fought for territory against Austria, France, and other German states.

Frederick the Great made many reforms that reflected Enlightenment ideals. Describing himself as "only the first servant of the state," he took many measures to make his subjects happy and well educated. Adopting Voltaire's principle of tolerance, he allowed his subjects to worship as they saw fit. He also improved Prussian schools, made the law system fairer and easier to understand, and outlawed the practice of torture.

Many historians point out that Frederick's reforms did little to change the structure of Prussian society. Although Frederick expressed disapproval of serfdom, he did not abolish it.

Catherine the Great of Russia. Catherine the Great (ruled 1762–1796) also corresponded with Voltaire. Influenced by him and by other thinkers of the time, she made several attempts at reform. One of her main concerns was to systematize Russia's laws. She was unable to complete this task, but she did make Russia's legal system more just and merciful. She prohibited torture and religious persecution. (These laws were frequently broken.) She also made some improvements in Russian schools.

At the beginning of her reign, she had wanted to free the serfs. Unfortunately, Russian serfs joined together in a violent uprising shortly after she came to power. Although the royal army easily subdued the rebels, Catherine began to regard the serfs as dangerous. Then, too, her power depended largely on the goodwill of the nobility. She acted to reassure the nobility that she would not allow the serfs to threaten their lives and property again. She gave the landlords absolute power over them. In the end, Catherine came to be known more for adding territory to Russia than for reform.

Maria Theresa and Joseph II of Austria. Maria Theresa (ruled 1740–1780) and her son, Joseph II (ruled 1780–1790), made more sweeping reforms than did Frederick and Catherine. Maria Theresa began by weakening the control that the Catholic Church had over her subjects, making Austria's tax system more just, and giving the serfs more freedom.

Joseph, who was also the Holy Roman Emperor (ruled 1765–1790), tried to carry these reforms further. He gave Protestants and Jews civil rights and passed laws against their persecution. He abolished serfdom entirely. He also tried to pass a law requiring landlords to pay the peasants cash in exchange for their labor.

This reform turned out to be a disaster. Because the peasants bought and sold items through the barter system, money was useless to them. Both peasants and landlords protested violently. Joseph's successor, Leopold II (ruled 1790–1792), had to reverse this and other

Time Line

Year	Dates and Events
A.D. **1401**	**1473–1543:** Life of Copernicus; Polish astronomer believes Aristarcus's theory that planets orbit sun
	1561–1626: Life of Bacon; English philosopher promotes scientific method and inductive reasoning
	1564–1642: Life of Galileo; Italian astronomer uses telescope to verify heliocentric theories of Copernicus and Kepler
	1571–1630: Life of Kepler; German astronomer devises mathematics to support Copernicus's heliocentric theory
1500	**1588–1679:** Life of Hobbes; English political theorist of materialism and selfishness
1501	**1596–1650:** Life of Descartes; French scientist-philosopher promotes deductive reasoning
	1600s–1700s: Age of Reason
	1632–1704: Life of Locke; English philosopher stresses importance of environment on personality, natural laws, natural rights including right to change bad governments
	1632–1723: Life of Leeuwenhoek; Dutch scientist improves microscope and studies bacteria and protozoa
1600	**1633:** Church officials force Galileo to recant heliocentric theory of planetary movement
1601	
	1642–1727: Life of Newton; English scientist-mathematician formulates calculus system, laws of gravity
	1689–1755: Life of Montesquieu; French philosopher disapproves of absolute monarchy, promotes separation of governmental powers
	1694–1778: Life of Voltaire; French writer-philosopher endorses Locke's natural rights, favors enlightened monarchy over self-government, promotes religious tolerance
1700	**1712–1778:** Life of Rousseau; French philosopher promotes return to state of nature or small farms unspoiled by civilization, social contract
1701	**1740–1780:** Reign of Maria Theresa of Austria; weakens internal power of Catholic Church, improves tax system, improves life of serfs
	1740–1786: Reign of Frederick the Great of Prussia; influenced by Voltaire—religious tolerance, good schools, fair legal system
	1762–1796: Reign of Catherine the Great of Russia; at first, influenced by Voltaire—religious tolerance, good schools, improved legal system; later, gives nobility absolute power over peasants and serfs
1800	**1765–1790:** Reign of Joseph II of Austria; extends rights and tolerance to Protestants and Jews, abolishes serfdom
1801	**1775–1783:** American Revolution—American colonists win independence from Britain
	1789–1799: French Revolution—French overthrow absolute monarchy, try to establish republic
	1790–1792: Reign of Leopold II of Austria; reverses reforms of Joseph II to restore public order
1900	**1810–1841:** Many Latin American colonies win independence from Spain, Portugal, France

reforms in order to restore order. Landlords could once more force their peasants to work for them.

Nationalism and Democracy

Many of the ideas about government and human nature that arose during the Enlightenment profoundly affected people's nationalistic feelings. People who speak the same language and share a common culture tend to feel a sense of unity. If they live in one general area, they may have a strong desire to unite under one government. These feelings of cultural pride, loyalty, and patriotism are called *nationalism*.

There are many ways in which to express nationalism. In times of war, people may express their nationalism as hatred of the enemy. In times of colonial expansion, they may express it as pride that their nation is growing more powerful. During the 17th and 18th centuries, many people longed for their nations to have governments such as those envisioned by the political thinkers of the Enlightenment. Many expressed their love of country by resisting the rule of absolute monarchs and foreign tyrants.

Nationalism inspired revolutions in British colonial America, France, and Latin America. In the late 1770s, the revolutionists of colonial America shook off British control and established a form of democracy to take its place. They incorporated many Enlightenment ideas on government in their Declaration of Independence and their Constitution. The French rebelled against an absolute monarchy in 1789 and tried to replace it with a republic. In the early 1800s, Spain's colonies in Latin America won their independence. They, too, attempted to set up democratic-style governments.

Chapter 20 describes how the ideas of the Enlightenment encouraged people to defy tyrannical rulers. It answers the question of why these small groups of patriots were able to defeat the armies of powerful governments.

INFO CHECK

1. Select the Enlightenment political philosopher whose ideas you believe have had the greatest influence on government and society today. Give reasons for your choice.

2. Which Enlightenment philosopher do you disagree with? Why do you dislike his ideas?

3. Why do you think so many political leaders have found Rousseau's ideas attractive?

4. How did Enlightenment ideas stimulate nationalism and democracy?

CHAPTER REVIEW

Multiple Choice

1. The Renaissance brought a renewed confidence in the intellectual abilities of human beings. This meant that

   1. ancient writings on scientific theories and nature were no longer accepted without question
   2. religion was no longer accepted by the masses of people
   3. humans no longer needed to worry about anything, since they controlled nature and science
   4. witches were now accepted, since they controlled nature and the supernatural.

2. The term *scientific method* refers to the practice of scientists

   1. accepting as fact theories that justified a person's actions
   2. observing, experimenting, and drawing conclusions
   3. accepting statements that were Church doctrines
   4. accepting nothing as fact unless one could see it for oneself.

3. The geocentric theory, devised by Aristotle, stated that

   1. astronomers can predict the motions of the planets
   2. the heavens were created from a frozen ice mass
   3. the earth revolves around the sun like the rest of the planets
   4. the earth is the center of the solar system, and the sun and planets revolve around it.

4. Copernicus's book *On the Revolutions of Heavenly Bodies* was not accepted by the Catholic Church because it

   1. was written by a Muslim infidel
   2. stated that the Greek god of war ruled the universe
   3. presented the heliocentric theory of the solar system
   4. was supported by the Protestants.

5. Galileo used a telescope to see Jupiter's moons circling around that planet. This observation disproved what theory of planetary movement?

   1. Newton's gravitational theory
   2. Aristotle's geocentric theory
   3. Einstein's relativity theory
   4. Aristarchus's heliocentric theory.

6. The Renaissance scientist who was forced to recant his theories was

   1. Copernicus
   2. Kepler
   3. Galileo
   4. Newton.

7. Newton's Law of Universal Gravitation explained that

   1. gravity causes all items to fly off at different speeds away from the center of the planet
   2. the gravity of a planet pulls all items toward the center of the planet
   3. the moons of Jupiter revolve around the earth because earth is the center of the universe
   4. none of the above.

8. The scientific revolution gave human society great hope for the future. This was because

1. people were living longer and had more money to spend
2. people were freed from their dependence on the Church
3. people believed that the new way of thinking could enable them to solve problems and end superstitious beliefs
4. people no longer relied on Greek or Roman philosophies.

9. During the American Revolution, political thinkers got the idea for a division of powers to prevent one branch of government from overpowering the others from the French philosopher

1. Descartes
2. Locke
3. Cartier
4. Montesquieu.

10. The French physiocrats believed in economic development through

1. manufacturing and trade
2. mercantilism
3. laissez faire
4. price regulation.

11. What conclusion can be reached after studying the two diagrams on page 405?

1. In 1539, many scientists believed that the planets revolved around the sun.
2. After Copernicus published his findings, everyone agreed that earth revolved around the sun.
3. There was disagreement about the structure of the solar system during the middle 1500s.
4. An accurate explanation of the phases of the moon was discovered between 1539 and 1543.

12. According to the time line on page 402,

1. the French Revolution took place about six yeas after the end of the American Revolution
2. revolutions in Russia began between 1825 and 1855
3. all revolutions took place between 1750 and 1914 were successful
4. Communists took control of Russia immediately after Marx and Engels published the *Communist Manifesto.*

Thematic Essays

1. Francis Bacon and René Descartes used different scientific methods. *Task:* Contrast the ideas of these scholars. With whose method do you agree? Why?

2. Identify any one of the Enlightenment rulers. *Task:* For the ruler you have selected, discuss whether he (or she) was able to rule his (or her) subjects using the beliefs of the Enlightenment. Describe specific Enlightenment social or political theories to support your position.

Document-Based Questions

Use the documents and your knowledge of Global History and Geography to answer the questions.

1. Study the text on page 412–413. Explain the difference between Hobbes's, Locke's, and Rousseau's views of the "state of nature."

2. Use facts from the text to describe what type of government each of the above writers would support.

3. The German philosopher Immanuel Kant wrote about the Enlightenment:

"What is Enlightenment? . . . Dare to know! Have the courage to use your own intelligence! [This is] the motto of the Enlightenment. . . . Which restriction is hampering Enlightenment and which does not, or even promote it? I answer: the *public use* of a man's reason must be free at all times, and this alone can bring Enlightenment among men."

If you were an absolute monarch, how would you view the meaning and intent of this writing?

4. The Italian writer Niccolo Machiavelli wrote an essay on government entitled *The Prince*. It was a guide for rulers on how to maintain their powers.

"And in the actions of men, and especially princes from which there is no appeal, the end justifies the means. Let a prince aim at conquering and maintaining the state, and the means will always be judged honorable and praised by everyone. . . . A certain prince of the present time, . . . preach[es] peace and good faith, but he is really a great enemy to both, and either of them, had he observed them, would have cost him his state or reputation on more than one occasion."

Explain what Machiavelli is telling the prince to do in order to maintain power.

Document-Based Essay

Using specific examples, explain why the ideas of the Enlightenment were used by some to support absolute monarchy and by others to challenge this form of government.

C H A P T E R

20

Political Revolutions

The dust of the road felt soft and warm under Edgár's bare feet. The moon was so bright that he could see quite clearly the little shack where he lived with his family at the bottom of the hill. Everything in his world looked the same and yet everything had changed

He had spent the evening with Father Emilio, as he did at the end of every workday. Father Emilio had taught Edgár how to read when he was a little boy. Now he gave him books and discussed them with him. His mother thought that the good father was encouraging Edgár to be a priest. Edgár tried to tell her that Father Emilio said little about religion. Just the same, she bragged to the neighbors that one day Edgár would be hearing all the villagers' confessions. Edgár sighed. What would his mother say when he told her what Father Emilio had in mind for him?

Edgár had always thought it strange that a priest should encourage him to question the way that Mexico was governed. He had not puzzled over it much though. Evenings with Father Emilio were the only brightness in his life. Their discussions lifted the fog that always settled in Edgár's mind after his day of repetitive field work. But he had never imagined that someone as poor and insignificant as he could act on the ideas they talked about.

Tonight everything had become clear. Father Emilio wanted Edgár to join a revolution. Father Emilio's friend, Father Miguel Hidalgo, would lead him and other Indians out of poverty and servitude. They had the same rights, Father Emilio said, as Señor Hernandez, the owner of the plantation where Edgár worked. They must fight for their rights, though. Edgár was afraid. But what would his life be without the ideas he had learned from Father Emilio? He shrugged. Of course, he would fight.

T his young Mexican has just joined a movement that will not only change his life but the lives of all Latin Americans. The revolution led by Father Miguel Hidalgo in Mexico in the early 1800s would encourage the leaders of other Latin American countries to break away from Spain. Inspired by the political ideas of the Enlightenment and by each other's daring, oppressed people in Europe and the Americas were beginning to assert their rights.

The "oppressed" came from all walks of life. But the better educated middle class tended to be the leaders of rebellions and the creators of new governments. The people of Edgár's class were the followers. They provided the bodies for the armies and the mass demonstrations. But without the support of the more numerous lower classes, the revolutions could not have succeeded.

An important revolutionary goal was independence from foreign rulers. Colonial North Americans fought for independence from Britain. Latin Americans fought for independence from Spain.

THE AMERICAN REVOLUTION

Historical and Philosophical Background

The two English revolutions of the 1600s prepared the ground for the American Revolution. The English civil war, known as the Puritan Revolt, struck an effective blow at absolute monarchy in England. The Glorious Revolution of 1688 ended that form of government there. In its place, the English established a limited monarchy whose power was held in check by a strong Parliament.

Neither the Puritan Revolt nor the Glorious Revolution brought about full democracy in England. Although Cromwell set up a republic, he soon changed it into a dictatorship. Instead of establishing another republic, the leaders of the Glorious Revolution of 1688 invited the monarchs William and Mary to rule England.

Nevertheless, the two English revolutions launched powerful new ideas about government. The English revolutionists believed that a government should serve the interests of the governed not those of the ruler.

Ideas in the American Colonies

By 1750, the 13 English colonies in America along the Atlantic coast were thriving. Their populations were increasing, and their

English Colonies in North America   1750

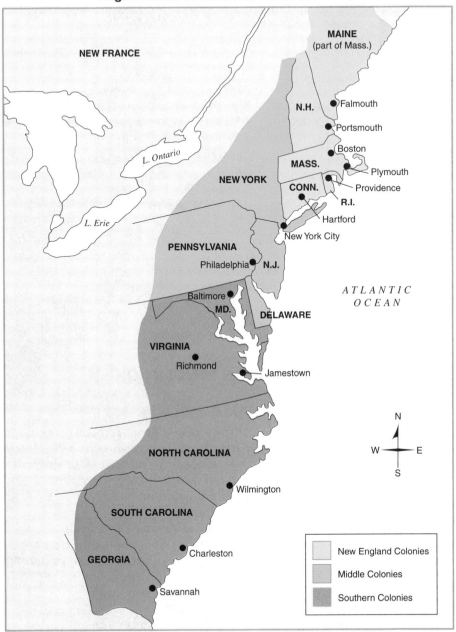

economies were doing well. Almost anyone who wanted land could have it. In general, the people felt secure and contented. They were part of a great empire and were protected by the army and navy of Great Britain. (In 1707, England and Scotland merged to become Great Britain.)

Not everyone in the colonies was given the same rights. White adult males who owned property had more rights than others. Women had few legal rights. Slaves and Native Americans had none. The rights of the followers of Catholicism and Judaism were restricted.

Under the mercantilist economic policy, colonists could legally trade only with Great Britain. The development of colonial manufacturing was discouraged.

Government. In the mid-1700s, each colony had a governor appointed by the king of England or the private developer of the colony. A legislature made the laws. White male colonists who owned a certain amount of property could be elected to seats in the legislatures (often called assemblies). The governor held the most power. But his actions could be curbed by the legislatures through the "power of the purse." The legislature voted on taxes and how money could be spent.

Rights. The majority of people in colonial America were from England. They spoke the English language, followed English ways, and viewed themselves as English citizens. They felt entitled to exercise the rights set forth in the English Bill of Rights of 1689.

It was difficult for the British government to oversee closely the details of life in the colonies across the Atlantic Ocean. Ships took a month or more to travel from Great Britain to the colonies and a month to return. From the late 1600s until the mid-1760s, Britain followed a policy of *salutary neglect* toward the colonies. It let the colonies govern themselves with little regulation. The colonists got used to feeling independent. Then, after 1763, the British government acted to curb this independence. The colonists resented this outside interference. Resentment built up and finally led to open conflict with Britain.

The Road to War

From the late 1600s through the mid-1700s, England and France fought a number of wars to see who would be the greatest power in Europe. At stake, too, was control of their worldwide colonies, a source of wealth and prestige. Occasionally, Spain also became involved in the wars. One of the conflicts, called the French and Indian War, was fought mainly in North America between 1756 and 1763. It was known in Europe as the Seven Years' War. Great Britain finally won the wars and gained the largest empire. But the victories left the British with many debts. To solve their financial problems, King George III (ruled 1760–1820) and his ministers decided to collect more taxes from the American colonies.

Unpopular Taxes. Many Americans objected to Britain's new colonial policy. They particularly disliked the Stamp Act passed in 1765. It required people to pay taxes on newspapers, pamphlets, legal documents, playing cards, and other items. A stamp was put on the items to show that the tax had been paid. Because they were not represented in the lawmaking body, the Americans felt that Parliament had no right to tax them. "Taxation without representation is tyranny" became the American rallying cry.

The Americans openly refused to obey the tax laws. They stopped buying British products and called a *congress*, or meeting, to protest the Stamp Act. Because British merchants were hurt by the boycott of their goods, some members of Parliament asked that the Stamp Act be repealed. George III and his ministers finally agreed.

In 1767, Britain passed a new set of tax laws called the Townshend Acts. Colonial protests and a boycott of British goods again forced a repeal. All taxes except for those on tea were ended in 1770.

Colonial Response. Colonial leaders, such as Sam Adams in Massachusetts and Patrick Henry in Virginia, worked to stir up anti-British feeling. They and others wanted the American colonies to govern themselves. When a new British law increased the tax on tea in 1773, more colonists joined these leaders. The demonstrations reached a peak in December 1773. A British ship carrying a cargo of tea arrived in Boston harbor. A group of Americans dumped the tea into the harbor. Groups of colonists in other colonial seaports followed their lead and destroyed cargoes of tea during the next few months.

The king and his ministers reacted with great anger and took steps to punish Boston. They closed Boston harbor and suspended the government of Massachusetts. They also moved a large number of British troops into the Boston area. The colonists called the response the Intolerable Acts.

Bostonians paying the British tax collector—with tar, feathers, and scalding hot tea

Some leaders in Virginia felt that the rest of the colonies should show support for Massachusetts. They called for a meeting of delegates from each colony. The First Continental Congress met in Philadelphia in the fall of 1774. The Congress asked all colonists not to buy British goods. It urged Parliament and the king to stop punishing Boston and recognize the basic rights of the colonists. Parliament's reply did not satisfy the Americans. The Americans began to train military groups called Minutemen and store weapons and ammunition in secret locations.

In April 1775, British troops marched out of Boston toward Lexington and Concord. They intended to arrest the leaders of the protesters in Massachusetts and seize the stockpiles of hidden weapons. Colonial forces resisted the British at Lexington and Concord and shot at the royal troops all along the route back to Boston. The American Revolution had begun.

The Beginning of a New Nation

In May 1775, the Second Continental Congress met to discuss the procedure that the American colonies should follow now that war had begun. Its most important decision was its approval of the Declaration of Independence on July 4, 1776. This famous document explained why the American colonies should no longer be part of the British Empire. It also made clear the high value placed by Americans on liberty and individual rights. Many of the ideas it expressed were based on those of John Locke and other political philosophers of the Enlightenment.

In the Declaration of Independence, Thomas Jefferson wrote "We hold these truths to be self-evident, that all men are created equal, that they are endowed by their Creator with certain unalienable rights, that among these are life, liberty, and the pursuit of happiness." These ideas and the idea that governments that take away these rights should be replaced are based on Locke's writings. The Declaration of Independence influenced revolutionaries in France and Latin America. It continues to inspire freedom seekers to this day.

The American Revolution lasted for eight years. In spite of many setbacks, the ragged American soldiers finally overcame the well-equipped British army. France aided the Americans with money and naval support. The loans drained the French treasury and, within a few years, created great problems for the French king.

The Peace of Paris formally ended the war in 1783. The treaty recognized the United States of America as a fully independent nation stretching from the Atlantic Ocean to the Mississippi River and from Canada to Florida.

When the leaders of the new country wrote the U.S. Constitution in 1787, they borrowed ideas from the philosophers of the Enlightenment. The division of the government into three separate branches (legislative, executive, judicial) came from Montesquieu. So did the idea that each branch should be given powers to check the others. Spelling out the rights of individuals and the limits of government came from Locke's writings, the Magna Carta, and the English Bill of Rights.

INFO CHECK

1. Explain why you AGREE or DISAGREE with those who argue that the American Revolution was a direct result of the Puritan Revolt and the Glorious Revolution.

2. State your opinion of the American refusal to pay British taxes. Were the colonists justified? Why or why not?

3. How did the Declaration of Independence and the Constitution reflect the ideas of the Enlightenment?

THE FRENCH REVOLUTION AND THE NAPOLEONIC ERA

In the late 1700s, France was going through difficult times. It had lost a war and colonies to England. It had economic problems and a huge debt. In short, the king needed more money. The only way to obtain it seemed to be through increasing taxes. This has never been a popular idea.

Background of the Revolution

Inequality. The major problem in France during the 1700s was inequality. French society was divided into three groups called *estates*. The high-ranking clergy and nobles made up the First and Second Estates. Most of these people lived in luxury, held the most important government jobs, and paid very little in taxes.

The Third Estate (professional people, peasants, and laborers) made up 98 percent of the French population. The members of this group paid more than their share of the taxes and did the work that made it possible for the nobles and high church officials to live well. (Of course, many of the clergy were poor and had very little influence on religious or government affairs.)

The lawmaking body of France, the Estates General, represented all three estates. But this body rarely met. As a result, the majority of French people had almost no voice in government.

The Economy. Economic problems mounted during the 18th century. The many wars fought by Louis XIV against Great Britain and other nations had drained the treasury. France's support of the American revolutionary cause had also been costly. The nobles and

First Estate .5% Second Estate 1.5%

First Estate 10%

Second estate 20%

Third estate 98%

Third estate 70%

Population by estate

Population by land ownership

First Estate (Clergy)

Second Estate (Nobles)

Third Estate (Middle Class; City Workers; Peasants)

France: Population and Land Ownership Before the Revolution

The First and Second Estates supported by heavy taxes imposed on the Third Estate

clergy refused to pay higher taxes or to give up any of their privileges. Consequently, the government was almost bankrupt.

Unjust Legal System. A third serious problem was an unjust legal system. France did not have one set of courts and laws that applied to everyone. The king or his representative could imprison anyone for any reason for any period of time. A person might remain in jail all his or her life without ever being tried for a crime.

The Beginning of the Revolution

When King Louis XVI (ruled 1774–1792) could not raise more money to finance the government, he called the Estates General into session. He wanted to discuss imposing a tax on landed property. It met in 1789 for the first time in 175 years. At this meeting, the Estates disagreed about the way in which votes were distributed. The Third Estate had 600 representatives, the Second, 300, and the First, 300. Nonetheless, each Estate had only one vote. This meant that the Third Estate, which had the greatest number of representatives, could be outvoted by the First and Second Estates by a margin of two to one.

The National Assembly. The Third Estate felt that each representative should be given a vote. When the First and Second Estates disagreed, the Third Estate withdrew from the Estates General and formed the National Assembly. The representatives from the Third Estate took an oath to provide France with a constitution that would limit the power of the king and give more rights to the common people.

One of the influential individuals who spoke out in favor of the National Assembly was the Marquis de Lafayette. He had fought in the American Revolution and helped influence France to aid the American revolutionary cause.

Most French people enthusiastically supported the aims of the National Assembly. Threats by the king to arrest the leaders of the Assembly caused riots all over France. On July 14, 1789, an angry crowd captured a fortress called the Bastille in Paris. The Bastille was a prison for political prisoners, those who opposed the government. But the mob was more interested in finding arms than in freeing prisoners. At the same time, leaders of the revolutionary movement set up a government. July 14 is celebrated in France today as the beginning of the revolution and independence from an absolute monarch. It is called Bastille Day.

In the countryside, the peasants rose up against the nobles and burned manor houses on some feudal estates. Peasants sought to find and destroy the grain and tax records. These records determined how much money or grain the peasants owed the Church or the landowning noble. When the people stopped paying taxes and the royal officials fled France to keep from being killed, the government broke down. The king was forced to accept the revolutionary government led by the National Assembly.

New Rights and a Constitution. The National Assembly changed France in many ways. In August 1789, it adopted the Declaration of the Rights of Man and of the Citizen. Its first article declares that "all men are born free and equal in rights." The declaration provided the people of France with such basic rights as freedom of speech, religion, and the press. It also guaranteed the right of the people to participate in the government of France. The French Declaration was greatly influenced by the words of the American Declaration of Independence.

The National Assembly reformed the legal system. It provided for elected judges, trial by jury, and an end to brutal punishments. Nobles could no longer purchase judicial and high military positions.

Perhaps the Assembly's most important work was the Constitution of 1791. It reformed the government by establishing a limited monarchy. (The king's powers could be checked by the legislature.) The constitution also put the land of the Catholic Church under the control of the national government. After Louis XVI accepted the new constitution, the National Assembly was dissolved. A Legislative Assembly was then elected to make laws for France.

The Republic

In 1792, the new lawmakers faced threats from outside France. Prussia and Austria went to war with France to aid the royal family. Later, Britain, Spain, and the Netherlands joined the fight against France.

Jacobins. A powerful extremist group called the Jacobins convinced the French people that King Louis XVI had plotted with Austria and Prussia. Their aim was to overthrow the revolutionaries and restore the king's rule. The Jacobins forced the Assembly to arrest the king and queen. (The queen was Marie Antoinette, the daughter of Maria Theresa of Austria and the sister of Emperor Joseph II.) Then the Assembly called for new elections to choose representatives for a National Convention. (Almost all males over 21 were allowed to vote.) The Convention drew up a new constitution and created the First French Republic.

Patriotism. Although the Jacobins created a dictatorship and fostered great fear among the people, they did stimulate patriotism. The majority of people at last felt that the privileges of the aristocracy had ended. They were inspired by the ideals of liberty, equality, and fraternity. Pride was stirred by a song called "The Marseillaise," which became the French national anthem. The people stood together to save France from its enemies. By 1795, French armies had not only defended the nation but had also conquered parts of the Netherlands, Belgium, and Germany.

ROBESPIERRE: ARCHITECT OF TERROR

On July 27, 1794, Maximilien Robespierre, leader of France's Committee of Public Safety, was arrested by order of his political opponents. Together with other extremists, Robespierre was executed. His death ended the Reign of Terror that he had begun ten months before.

During this period, special courts ordered the execution of many thousands whom Robespierre and his associates considered "enemies of the republic." His victims included aristocrats, clergy, and ordinary people suspected of treason, even if no actual proof existed. At their trials, they were given no chance to defend themselves. Their deaths at the guillotine were public spectacles.

For Robespierre and other members of the 12-man Committee of Public Safety, the Reign of Terror was necessary. They believed they had to defend the gains made by the French Revolution by eliminating all those who might oppose or even criticize the National Convention. (It governed France during this stage of the revolution.) Today, the Reign of Terror is regarded as a grim chapter in French history, one dominated by fanatics and extremists.

Robespierre was a highly educated lawyer who joined the revolutionary government after a brilliant legal career. Elected to the Estates General in 1789, he became known as a skillful public speaker. His passionate protests against royal absolutism and his demands for reform of French government and society made many enemies. In 1792, Robespierre was elected by the citizens of Paris to head their delegation to the National Convention. He was also president of the Jacobin Club, the most extreme of the revolutionary groups. Execution of King Louis XVI and replacement of the monarchy with a republic were two of his strongest demands. Robespierre forced the Girondists to be expelled from the National Assembly. Moderates, they were attempting to save the life of the ex-king.

In July 1793, Robespierre became leader of the Committee of Public Safety. This enabled him to control the French government. It was a time of disorder in which the revolution was threatened by a range of military and financial problems. The committee rapidly put into effect policies that stabilized the economy. It began the formation of a successful army to oppose the foreign powers attacking the borders of France. Counterrevolutionary uprisings, especially in the south and west of the country, also had to be put down. This action began the Reign of Terror.

Robespierre would not tolerate disagreement with his policies. As the Terror claimed more victims and Robespierre's speeches became more aggressive, members of the National Convention began to fear for their lives. Both moderates and extremists formed a conspiracy to overthrow him. Robespierre was barred from speaking in the National Convention and was arrested in July 1794. After a rescue attempt by some of his Paris supporters failed, Robespierre attempted to commit suicide. Badly wounded, he and some of his followers were taken to the guillotine to which he had sent so many others.

- Argue for or against the description of Robespierre as a dictator. Why do you think many regarded him as a great leader? Had you lived in France in 1793, would you have supported Robespierre? Explain your answer.

The Directory. In 1795, another constitution placed France under the control of the Directory, a five-member committee. The Directory proved to be corrupt and inefficient. It could not solve the serious financial problems of the country. Furthermore, in 1798, the enemies of France gained new strength. Britain, in control of the seas, persuaded other countries to join the fight against France. In 1799, French armies lost land battles in Italy, Switzerland, and the Netherlands. The future looked dark.

The Napoleonic Era

In 1799, an able 30-year-old general named Napoleon Bonaparte forced the Directory to resign. He had just returned to France after a victory in Egypt. The French people backed his move against the Directory. Napoleon then took over the government and brought the French Revolution to an end.

Background. Napoleon was a "son of the Revolution." If it had not been for the Revolution, he could not have risen from poverty in Corsica, an island south of France, to the throne of France. After 1789, France tended to choose leaders for their talent and energy rather than for their noble birth. The qualities that made Napoleon the youngest and most popular general in France also made him the first French emperor in 1804. Under Napoleon's military dictatorship, France became the most powerful nation in Europe.

General Bonaparte crossing the Alps to victory over Austria, while the Directory back in France grows powerless

Napoleon's rapid rise to power was due to a number of personal qualities. He had a brilliant mind, limitless energy, and great ambition. Believing himself to be a man with a special destiny, he was able to convince others to follow him.

As a young artillery officer, Napoleon first came to the notice of his superiors when he helped drive British troops from the French seaport of Toulon. In 1795, he saved the National Convention in Paris from rioters by firing artillery shells over the heads of the mob. Napoleon was given command of the French army in Italy during the campaign of 1796–1797. Although outnumbered by Austrian forces, he won important victories. As a result, he became a national hero.

In 1798, troops led by Napoleon invaded Egypt in order to establish a base for an attack on British India. Although the young general's reports of great military achievements were exaggerated, his popularity in France increased. The British navy, however, gave Napoleon his first defeat. Napoleon managed to avoid capture and returned to France in 1799.

Although Napoleon had abandoned many of his troops in Egypt, his popularity did not suffer. There were few objections when Napoleon moved quickly to replace the corrupt and inefficient Directory with his own government. The voters approved a new constitution that gave Napoleon ruling power as First Consul. He had made himself military dictator of France.

In 1804, Napoleon proclaimed the republic to be at an end. France became an empire ruled by Emperor Napoleon I. In a *plebescite* (yes or no) vote, the French people again gave Napoleon overwhelming approval.

Changes. Between 1802 and 1805, Napoleon increased the efficiency of the French government. He had a new law code prepared. The Code Napoleon made all citizens equal before the law. It provided for trial by jury and religious freedom. The Code Napoleon is still the basis of the French legal system. It has also served as a model for the legal systems of several countries in Europe and Latin America.

Napoleon organized a public school system run by a committee called the University of France. He established the Legion of Honor, an honorary society for people who had performed important services for France.

Napoleon gave France a fairer taxation system and set up the Bank of France. This organization coined money and kept the currency stable. It also made sure that economic conditions favored business activity. As a result, France stayed reasonably prosperous.

Because of these reforms, the people of France approved of Napoleon even though he was a dictator. He gave them order, stability, and the kind of equality that the Revolution had called for. But Napoleon did not give them peace.

Napoleonic Wars. Shortly after Napoleon took control of the government, he defeated the Austrians and made peace with Great Britain. But in 1803, the treaty with Britain fell apart. Britain persuaded Austria, Russia, Sweden, and Naples to renew the fight against France. The resulting battles are known as the Napoleonic Wars. They lasted from 1805 to 1815. Napoleon showed his military genius by leading his armies to victories over Austria, Russia, and Prussia. He also invaded Portugal and Spain. Russia became an ally of France in 1807. All of Italy, except for areas ruled by the pope, came under Napoleon's control. So did the Netherlands. He abolished the Holy Roman Empire. In its place, he grouped most of the German states together in the Confederation of the Rhine.

By 1807, Napoleon controlled most of the European continent. He had given France an empire. Only Britain, with its powerful navy, was able to continue fighting Napoleon.

Actions Against Britain. To weaken Britain, Napoleon took steps to cut off its trade. Through laws called the *Continental System*, he ordered European countries not to buy goods from or sell to Britain. He even tried to prevent ships from British colonies from trading with their home country. Many countries in Europe, such as Russia and Portugal, did not want to follow Napoleon's orders. France took over parts of Portugal and invaded Spain. Napoleon appointed his brother Joseph to be king of Spain. The Spanish and Portuguese turned against France and started the Peninsular War, which lasted from

Napoleon's Empire   1812

1808 to 1813. By then, Spanish, Portuguese, and British troops had pushed Napoleon's forces back into France.

Invasion of Russia. Partly to punish Russia for not going along with the Continental System, Napoleon invaded that country in 1812. Some 600,000 French troops started out on the march to Moscow in June. The French forces occupied Moscow in September. They were far from reliable sources of supplies and could not easily get food, ammunition, and other essentials. In October, the Russians counter-attacked. The French retreated, and in November, winter set in. The fighting and the cold took their toll. Only some 100,000 of the French forces survived.

The setback in Russia encouraged all parts of the empire in Europe to rebel against French military rule. In 1813, the armies of Prussia, Austria, and Russia decisively defeated Napoleon at Leipzig, Germany, in the "Battle of Nations." Early in 1814, even the French people turned against the emperor. Finally, in April, Napoleon was captured and exiled to Elba, an island in the Mediterranean.

Final Defeat. In March 1815, Napoleon saw a chance to regain power. He escaped from Elba and marched through France. Loyal French soldiers joined his cause. Troops from all over Europe and Britain rushed to stop Napoleon. Led by the British Duke of Wellington, the allies defeated Napoleon in June 1815 at Waterloo in Belgium. Napoleon was then exiled to the island of St. Helena in the South Atlantic Ocean. He died there in 1821.

The Napoleonic Era was over. The long wars had caused great bloodshed and destruction throughout Europe. Yet Napoleon's armies had also spread the revolutionary ideals of liberty, equality, and fraternity. Napoleon unleashed the forces of nationalism, reform, and revolution, which changed Europe dramatically in the 19th century.

INFO CHECK

1. Identify the problems that caused the French Revolution. Which do you regard as the most difficult for 18th-century French people to endure?

2. How did the Declaration of the Rights of Man and the Constitution of 1791 respond to the problems that had caused the French Revolution?

3. Under Jacobin rule, did the French government put into practice the ideals of liberty, equality, and fraternity? Explain your answer.

4. If you had lived in France in the early 19th century, would you have regarded Napoleon Bonaparte as an admirable leader? Why or why not?

THE LATIN AMERICAN REVOLUTIONS

While the Napoleonic Wars raged in Europe, great changes were occurring elsewhere. The people in the Spanish colonies of the Western Hemisphere did not like the way they were ruled. They wanted to break Spain's control over them. The successful revolutions in the 13 colonies in North America and in France gave hope to Latin Americans.

Toussaint L'Ouverture

The Spanish colonists were also inspired by the victory of the forces of Toussaint L'Ouverture. Toussaint led a slave uprising in the French colony of Saint Domingue on the western part of the island of Hispaniola. The island contains the present-day countries of Haiti and the Dominican Republic.

The sugar plantations in Saint Domingue provided France with great wealth. The slaves brought from Africa to work on the plantations outnumbered the French colonists. The colonists lived comfortably while they worked the slaves to exhaustion. As the slaves' anger at their harsh treatment built up, some began to look for opportunities to revolt.

When the slaves heard of the French Revolution, they felt that the French government would be too busy dealing with the turmoil in France to send help across the sea. In 1791, Toussaint L'Ouverture, a freed slave, led an uprising against the colonists. He and his follow-

Portrait of Touissant l'Ouverture, ruler of Saint Domingue, present-day Haiti

ers defeated the colonial army and gained control of Saint Domingue. He remained in control until Napoleon sent an army to retake the island in 1802. As Toussaint resisted this attack, he was captured and put in prison, where he died in 1803.

Toussaint's successor, Jean-Jacques Dessalines, was able to drive off the French. A great many of the French soldiers had come down with yellow fever and died. Saint Domingue became independent from France in 1804, when it was renamed Haiti.

Causes of Discontent Against Spain

The colonists in the Spanish Empire had many reasons to resent Spanish rule. The Spanish government controlled trade for the benefit of Spain. The colonies had to buy manufactured goods from the home country and sell their products to Spain only. This mercantilist policy kept wealth flowing into Spain. It did little to help the colonists.

The unequal distribution of wealth and power among the Latin Americans created another source of resentment. Spain gave important political and military jobs only to *peninsulares*. These people had been born in Spain, which with Portugal, is part of the Iberian Peninsula. *Creoles*, colonists born in Latin America to Spanish parents, wanted more power for themselves. They tended to be wealthy landowners, mine owners, and businesspeople. *Mestizos*, children of Spanish and Indian parents, also wanted a share of the political power. They tended to work in towns or be overseers on estates. The *peons*, who made up the largest part of the population, were Indians and people of mixed and African heritage. Most peons worked on the great estates and in the mines. They had no land of their own and lived in poverty. They had little hope of achieving wealth or power.

The desire for revolution was strongest among the Creoles. They were well educated and aware of the Enlightenment ideas behind the revolutions in North America and Europe. In 1808 the discontented Creoles got their opportunity to begin a revolt. In that year, the armies of Napoleon Bonaparte conquered Spain. His brother, Joseph Bonaparte, became king of Spain. The Latin American colonists refused to accept French rule. Revolutions broke out in many parts of Latin America. Even after the Spanish king was restored to the throne in 1814, the revolutions continued. The colonists did not want to return to the old ways. They wanted independence.

The Great Liberators

A number of gifted military and political leaders arose in Latin America to organize the revolutions. They directed the separate struggles for independence in different parts of the Spanish Empire.

Hidalgo. In Mexico, a village priest named Miguel Hidalgo led his Indian followers in an uprising against Spanish rule in 1810. (Re-

In this painting, Father Hidalgo proclaims Mexico's freedom from Spain

call Edgár in the opening story. His priest had been influenced by Hidalgo's ideas and had persuaded Edgár to join the cause.) Hidalgo and his army won a few battles. When they reached Mexico City, the capital, Spanish forces stopped them. Hidalgo and some of his followers were captured and executed in 1811. Other revolutionaries continued to fight.

Iturbide. Agustín de Iturbide, a Creole leader, finally won freedom for Mexico in 1821. Well supported by the Creoles and the Roman Catholic Church, he united most of Mexico against Spain. Soon after his victory, Iturbide proclaimed himself emperor of Mexico. He was overthrown, and Mexico became a republic in 1824.

Miranda. The struggle to free Venezuela began about 1808 under the leadership of Francisco de Miranda and Simon Bolívar. Miranda had fought in the French Revolution. He had also tried to get help for his revolutionary causes from the English government and Catherine the Great of Russia. The Venezuelans won their independence in 1811. But a year later, Spanish forces retook the country. Bolívar escaped to Colombia, and Miranda died in prison.

Bolívar. During the next few years, Bolívar unsuccessfully tried to invade Venezuela and to widen the revolution in Colombia. Finally, he gathered enough support to drive the Spaniards out of Colombia in 1819. "The Liberator," as people called Bolívar, became president of Colombia. He then turned his attention back to Venezuela. This new war for independence was won in 1821. Bolívar also aided the struggle against Spanish rule in Ecuador. This war was won in 1822. Ecuador, Venezuela, and Colombia joined together in one nation called Gran (Great) Colombia. It was governed by Bolívar. He hoped that the nation would be the beginning of a union of all Latin American states. Gran Colombia broke up in 1830. After that each nation went its own way.

San Martín. José de San Martín, another great revolutionary leader, was born in Argentina. He became an army officer in Spain and fought Napoleon's invading army from 1808 to 1811. Returning to Argentina, he joined with the revolutionary forces. They won Argentina's independence in 1816. San Martin then organized an army in western Argentina to free Chile. San Martín marched over the Andes Mountains and defeated the Spaniards. In 1818, he declared Chile's independence. Two years later, he went on to free northern Peru, which became independent in 1824.

San Martín met with Bolívar in 1822 to determine how best to win control of southern Peru. When the two leaders disagreed on

Latin America: Dates of Colonial Independence

strategy, San Martín left northern Peru. Bolívar took over the government of northern Peru and sent forces to drive the Spaniards out of the south. After this part became independent in 1825, it was renamed Bolivia in honor of Bolívar.

Brazil

When Napoleon's soldiers invaded Portugal in 1807, the ruler, John VI, fled to Brazil. The presence of John VI made the huge Portuguese colony in eastern South America a kingdom. John considered himself to be the head of both Portugal and Brazil. Even after the French were driven out of Portugal, John stayed in Brazil. In 1820, his advisers persuaded him to return to Portugal as a constitutional monarch. John left the Brazilian government in the hands of his son, Pedro.

When the Cortes, the Portuguese lawmaking body, tried to make Brazil a colony once more, the Brazilian Creoles resisted. They persuaded Pedro to become the ruler of an independent Brazil. He agreed and became Pedro I. In 1822, he proclaimed Brazil to be free from Portugal. Since the Portuguese government did not wish to fight a war to keep Brazil, the Cortes recognized its independence. Brazil remained a monarchy until 1889, when its ruler, Pedro II, was overthrown. The nation then became a republic.

Achievements and Problems

Independence brought the Creoles some of the benefits they wanted. They gained political power for themselves and freedom from Spanish economic control. They could now trade with all nations. But Bolívar's dream of a united Latin America was not realized. Nationalism, ambitious leaders of individual states, and rugged terrain all prevented the people of the various nations from uniting.

Furthermore, the Creole leaders in individual nations were unable to establish governments that attracted the loyalty of all citizens. As a result, revolutions and dictatorships became common in Latin America. Often the military would take over an unpopular government by declaring a state of emergency. The military leader would then govern as a *caudillo*, a dictator. Today, almost all of the governments in Latin America are popularly elected democracies.

Independence did little to help the peons. Most of them continued to be poor and without legal political power. Members of this disadvantaged group often turned to violence to bring about change. Their main goal was a fairer distribution of land.

Conflicts also arose over the position of the Roman Catholic Church in Latin America. Many Latin Americans wanted their government to take over Church lands and wealth and to distribute them to the poor. Almost all ideas about land reform were resisted by

Time Line

Year	Dates and Events
A.D. **1601**	**1600s–1763:** "Salutary neglect" of American colonies by Britain; increased self-government
	1688: Glorious Revolution ends absolute monarchy in England; joint rule by William III, Mary II
	1756–1763: Seven Years' War (French and Indian War in Americas) increases British debt; 13 colonies more highly taxed
	1765: Stamp Act causes American boycott of British goods; act repealed
	1767: Townshend Acts (new taxes) cause American boycott of British goods; repealed except for tea
	1773: Boston Tea Party (dumping of tea); British close Boston harbor, send troops
	1774: First Continental Congress, Philadelphia
	1774–1792: Reign of Louis XVI; National Assembly limits king's power, widens commoners' rights
1700 **1701**	**1775:** American Revolution begins at Lexington and Concord
	1775: Second Continental Congress; Declaration of Independence
	1783: Peace of Paris ends American Revolution, recognizes independent United States
	1787: U.S. Constitution—separation of powers, checks and balances, individual rights
	1789: Storming of Bastille; French Revolution; Declaration of Rights of Man
	1791: First French constitution; limits powers of monarchy, Catholic Church; election of lawmakers
	1791–1804: L'Ouverture leads Haitian slave uprising; Dessaline wins independence from France
	1793: Louis XVI beheaded; Robespierre heads Reign of Terror
	1794: Robespierre beheaded; Reign of Terror ends
	1795: New French constitution creates corrupt and inefficient Directory
	1798–1799: European powers defeat French in Italy, Switzerland, Netherlands
	1799: Napoleon Bonaparte ends Directory, takes control of French government
1800 **1801**	**1802–1805:** New Napoleonic law code
	1805–1814: Most of Europe at war with France; trade blockades, invasion of Russia (French disaster)
	1813–1814: France defeated at Leipzig; Napoleon exiled to Elba
	1815: Napoleon escapes Elba; rallies French; defeated at Waterloo by British; exiled to St. Helena
	1816–1821: San Martín wins independence from Spain for Argentina (1816), Chile (1818), Peru (1821)
	1819: Bolívar ("The Liberator") drives Spain from Colombia
	1821: Iturbide wins Mexico independence from Spain; Bolívar wins independence for Venezuela
	1822: Ecuador wins independence from Spain
	1822: Pedro I becomes king of Brazilian monarchy, independent from Portugal
	1823: Monroe Doctrine declares the Americas no longer open for colonization
	1825: Independent Bolivia created
1900	**1889:** Brazil becomes republic

wealthy landowners and the military leaders. These powerful groups continued to control most Latin American nations.

The Role of the United States

The United States supported the revolutions in Latin America. In 1822, the United States and Britain became concerned that other European nations might help Spain win back its colonies. Latin America had become a profitable trading market, and Britain and the United States did not want the market shut off by Spain. British leaders wanted the United States to join them in warning European powers to keep out of Latin America. The United States decided to issue a declaration of its own, knowing that Britain's naval power would enforce it.

In December 1823, President James Monroe included in his yearly address to Congress several points that have become known as the *Monroe Doctrine*. Monroe stated that the Americas were no longer open for colonization. He also said that any attempt by the European powers to interfere in the affairs of the Americas would be considered "as dangerous to our peace and safety."

The revolutions discussed in this chapter changed many attitudes about the power structure. Disadvantaged people began to realize that it was possible to demand a voice in their country's government. As a result, powerful people began to feel less secure in their privileged places. In defense, some tried to tighten their control of the

Cartoon of European rulers observing American naval power guarding the Americas

government and the economy, while others tried to work gradually toward sharing their power with the disadvantaged. Chapter 21 describes the steps that the established powers took to maintain their positions. It also discusses new conflicts between revolutionary groups and the ruling classes.

INFO CHECK

1. What did Toussaint L'Ouverture and Jean-Jacques Dessalines contribute to the birth of Haiti?

2. Define: peninsulares, Creoles, mestizos, and peons. How did the interaction of these groups lead to revolutions in Latin America?

3. Which of the great liberators do you most admire? Give reasons for your selection.

4. Is it correct to argue that the revolutions in Latin America brought independence to the countries there, but not democracy? Why or why not?

CHAPTER REVIEW

Multiple Choice

1. In his writings on government, John Locke wrote that the purpose of government is to protect its

   1. citizens' religious and political freedoms
   2. citizens' life, liberty, and property
   3. citizens from the abuses of the peasants
   4. citizens from the tyranny of the Church.

2. Thomas Jefferson and the other American political leaders were influenced by the

   1. French Revolution and writings of Baron de Montesquieu
   2. English Bill of Rights and writings of John Locke
   3. Russian Revolution and the writings of Karl Marx
   4. 95 theses and other writings of Martin Luther.

3. Prior to the French Revolution, French society was divided into three groups, or estates. The Third Estate complained that

   1. the peasants were lazy and not tending the fields
   2. the Church was supporting the merchants against the nobility
   3. the lawyers and other professionals were not paying their fair share of taxes
   4. they paid most of taxes and had almost no say in government.

4. The king called the Estates General into session because he

   1. was an enlightened despot
   2. wanted all classes to be involved in governmental decision making
   3. was out of money and wanted the legislature to approve a tax on property
   4. needed approval to call out the army to deal with the military crisis.

5. The breakup of the Estates General and the formation of the National Assembly occurred because the

   1. nobles and clergy refused to pay taxes or share political power
   2. Third Estate wanted voting power equal to their number
   3. lawyers, merchants, and professionals refused to keep paying the bills while they had no political power
   4. all answers are correct.

6. The French people supported Napoleon because

   1. he restored order and granted some of the equality promised in the revolution
   2. they liked being under a dictatorship and not having to make any political decisions
   3. he alone defeated their worst enemy, the English navy
   4. he ruled by fear and terror with the help of the courts and the guillotine.

7. Spanish colonial society was organized into four social classes, *a.* Creoles, *b.* Peons, *c.* Mestizos, and *d.* Peninsulares. Select the answer that places the classes in the social order that existed in New Spain.

   1. *a, c, d, b*
   2. *c, a, d, b*
   3. *d, a, c, b*
   4. *b, d, a, c.*

8. Simon Bolívar's dream of a unified Latin America never happened because

   1. of power-hungry local rulers, nationalism, and rugged terrain
   2. Spain, France, and England developed colonies in Latin America
   3. the United States intervened, using the Monroe Doctrine

   4. Bolívar lost power and was captured and imprisoned by the Spanish authorities.

9. The United States issued the Monroe Doctrine, but it was the British navy that enforced it. However, the real reason behind the American and British actions was

   1. conflict over who would control Latin America
   2. British and American merchants found a rich market in Latin America
   3. Britain and America were against the Spanish king
   4. Britain and America wanted to set up their own colonies in Latin America.

10. The Code Napoleon is important because it

    1. made all citizens equal before the law
    2. provided for a trial by jury
    3. is the basis for the French legal system
    4. all answers are correct.

11. The illustration on page 426 shows that

    1. agents of the British crown were greatly feared in the 13 American colonies
    2. boycotts were the colonists' only effective protest against taxation
    3. anger over British taxation sometimes led to violence
    4. American colonists did not like to drink tea.

12. Which statement is supported by the time line on page 442?

    1. Napoleon dominated France and Europe from 1799 through 1825.
    2. Haitian slaves revolted and won their independence in the period 1791–1804.

3. Napoleon ruled France prior to the French Revolution.

4. The Monroe Doctrine encouraged San Martín and Bolívar to fight for the independence of various Latin American nations.

Thematic Essays

1. Events such as the Crusades and the Industrial Revolution changed the social structure of European society. *Task:* Assess the amount of political and social change brought to the Americas by the revolutions of the 18th and 19th centuries. Which groups of people benefited? Which did not?

2. *Task:* Discuss the influence of the Church on the social and political power structures in Western Europe or the Americas. Include historical information to describe whether the Church supported democracy or the power of monarchs.

Document-Based Questions

Use the documents and your knowledge of Global History and Geography to answer the questions.

1. Study the map on page 435. Identify any nations that were not allied with, or part of, Napoleon's empire. How did geography limit Napoleon's conquests?

2. From a selection by the German poet Ernst Moritz Arndt:

"Fired with enthusiasm the people rose with God for King and Fatherland. . . . to save the Fatherland and free Germany. The Prussians wanted war; war and death they wanted; peace they feared because they could hope for no honorable peace from Na-

poleon. . . . The most beautiful thing . . . was that all differences of position, class, and age were forgotten . . . that the one great feeling for the Fatherland, its freedom, its honor, swallowed all other feeling. . . . "

What emotion is the poet describing, and why is it happening?

3. From the decree of *levée en masse* (nation in arms), August 23, 1793.

"1. From this moment until that in which the enemy shall have been driven from the soil of the republic, all Frenchmen are [required] for the service of the armies.

The young men shall go to battle; the married men shall forge arms and transport provisions; the women shall make tents and clothing and serve in the hospitals; the children shall turn old linen into lint; the aged shall betake themselves to the public place in order to arouse the courage of the warriors and preach the hatred of kings and the unity of the Republic."

Who is involved in defending France and the Republic against its enemies? How is this different from what happened in the past?

4. Study the map on page 440. How do you explain the fact that so many of the nations shown on the map achieved their independence within a few years of each other?

Document-Based Essay

"Napoleon's armies overthrew the old ruling monarchies of Europe. His armies spread the ideals of liberty and equality. Yet his empire was destroyed by his actions and the ideals that his armies spread."

Task: Using specific historical examples, explain this statement.

C H A P T E R
21

The Reaction to Revolutionary Ideas

The well-dressed young man in the carriage spoke a quiet word to his uniformed driver. Responding to light pressure on the reins, the perfectly matched horses came to a halt a short distance from the Speakers' Corner in London's Hyde Park. The man waited until his driver had leaped from his perch and opened the carriage door before descending. The crowd was already forming around the speaker, a hungry-looking radical with burning eyes in a lean face. The crowd was made up mainly of working-class people. A few from the middle and upper classes watched from the edges. Although they made way for the man from the carriage, he found the close presence of so many laborers and shop clerks to be unpleasant. Pulling a perfumed lace handkerchief from his sleeve, he held it to his nose rather than inhale the aroma of so many of his social inferiors.

The radical speaker was in full flow. In a voice ringing with passion, he denounced the evils of industrialism and the factory system. He shouted the need for reform of government and society in order to bring about a better world. In such a world, wealth would be shared equally. Poverty and disease would be no more. As he denounced those who resisted change in order to preserve their own power and privilege, glances were directed at the gentlemen in the crowd. Faces expressionless, they ignored the looks and maintained their apparent lack of concern.

The young man turned away before the speech had ended. Seething with anger, he returned to his carriage. Men like this firebrand speaker threatened the stability of the entire British nation and, indeed, of the world. This insane desire for reform had to be stopped before it led to more revolutions. Tersely, he ordered his driver to take him to the Conservative Club.

Europe did not achieve peace after the defeat of Napoleon. The French Revolution and the wars arising from it had been brought to a conclusion, but the desire for the improvement of society through political, social, and economic reforms continued. A new kind of struggle began between those who demanded change and those who resisted it.

EUROPE AFTER NAPOLEON

Struggles between absolutist rulers and revolutionaries took place all over the world during the 1800s and early 1900s. This conflict had its roots in the ideas of the Enlightenment and was nourished by the American and French revolutions.

Three Different Viewpoints

The French Revolution and the Napoleonic Era stirred up different kinds of feelings in Europeans. Some people welcomed the changes in government and social structure that took place. These *liberals* were usually professional and businesspeople who made up a rapidly increasing middle class. They tended to support efforts to make governments more democratic.

Later in the 1800s, *radicals* argued that democratic reforms did not improve society enough. Many radicals wanted a new system of government called *socialism*. Socialists believed that society should be more cooperative than competitive. They felt that governments should regulate the nations' economies to bring about a more even distribution of wealth among the population. They wanted to restrict or even to do away with private property. Socialists and other radical groups were usually led by intellectuals and consisted mainly of workers and other disadvantaged people.

Aristocrats and other people who benefited from the old forms of government and society wanted to stop or slow the rate of changes. Because they wanted to conserve an already existing way of life, these people were called *conservatives*.

The Congress of Vienna

After the fall of Napoleon, a group of aristocratic leaders from various European countries met together to make decisions about how to govern Europe. The members of this group preferred the old power structure to democracy. Because of their efforts, conservatism enjoyed a temporary triumph over liberalism in Europe.

Europe's conservative leaders held a conference in Vienna, Austria, in September 1814, to discuss ways to prevent more political and social unrest. Representatives came from most European countries. Even France was allowed to send a delegate. Lord Castlereagh represented Great Britain; King Frederick William III, Prussia; Prince Talleyrand, France; and Czar Alexander I, Russia. Officials from Great Britain, Russia, Prussia, and Austria (the Quadruple Alliance) made most of the decisions at the conference. These countries had been the winners in the wars with Napoleon.

Aims of the Congress. Prince Klemens von Metternich, a brilliant Austrian diplomat, dominated the conference. Metternich's ideas greatly influenced European affairs for 30 years.

The Congress of Vienna wanted to establish a *balance of power* among the nations. Its leaders hoped that the rules they made would prevent any one nation from becoming militarily stronger than its neighbors. If successful, the rules would keep Europe at peace. The

Europe After the Congress of Vienna   1815

general agreement among the leading powers about the aims of the congress has been labeled the Concert of Europe.

The decision makers at the congress also supported the principle of *legitimacy*. They felt that absolute monarchy was the most stable form of government. Wherever possible, they restored power to royal families who had ruled before the French Revolution and the Napoleonic Era.

The Bourbon king, Louis XVIII, had been placed on the French throne before the congress met. Former ruling families returned to Austria, Prussia, Spain, and the many states of Italy. Any demand for limiting royal power or granting political rights to the common people was rejected. Such ideas were considered to be revolutionary and dangerous.

The leaders of the congress also believed in the principle of compensation. They supported the idea of giving land or colonies to nations that had lost the most in the Napoleonic Wars. Nations that had done the most to defeat Napoleon were also entitled to compensation.

Nationalism. The congress opposed the efforts of the Poles, Belgians, and other national groups to govern themselves. The homelands of these people had been divided among their more powerful neighbors. The more these groups were deprived of political power and the freedom to express their native cultures, the more strongly nationalistic they became.

The Austrian Empire, which Metternich represented at the Congress of Vienna, consisted of several European countries. Metternich feared that nationalism would destroy his own and similar states and make Europe more vulnerable to war. If the different groups split off into small, weak countries, they would be in constant danger of attack. The older, stronger powers might seek to expand control over weaker neighbors. Consequently, Metternich and the other decision makers repressed nationalistic groups. Nonetheless, nationalism grew into a powerful force. Not only did it influence events throughout the 19th century, it continues to do so today. In the 20th century, nationalism has caused frequent conflicts in Europe, Africa, and Asia.

Effect on France. The decision makers at Vienna did not force France to sign a harsh peace treaty. They wanted the French people to accept the government of Louis XVIII. France lost all the territory it had taken in Europe during the Napoleonic Wars. Its boundaries were to be the same as they had been in 1792, and it could keep most of its overseas possessions. France was made to pay for damages it had done to other nations during the wars. This kind of payment is known as *reparations*. France also had to pay to keep troops of the victorious nations stationed along French borders. The victors wanted to confine France within its traditional boundaries.

The Congress of Vienna ended the era of the French Revolution and Napoleonic rule. Yet the revolutionary spirit did not die.

Throughout the 19th century, demands for political change led to violence in France and elsewhere in Europe.

INFO CHECK

1. Define the terms liberals, radicals, and conservatives. Which group dominated the Congress of Vienna? Why was this so?

2. Explain how the desire for a balance of power and legitimacy influenced the decisions reached by the Congress of Vienna.

3. Why do you think Prince Metternich opposed the nationalism of less powerful ethnic groups?

LIBERALS FIGHT FOR DEMOCRACY AND NATIONALISM

In the early 19th century, the theories of Enlightenment thinkers, such as Rousseau, had a major influence on both liberalism and nationalism. The roots of the liberal idea of democracy lay in Rousseau's theory that a good government expresses the general will of the ruled. His belief that people are basically good promoted the nationalistic idea that each ethnic group is best qualified to shape its own destiny. Many people of the time believed that a peaceful and united Europe would result if each major ethnic group had its own country and was free to develop its own ethnic character.

The Revolutions of 1830

France had fought hard to gain democratic rights. Under Louis XVIII's Constitutional Charter of 1814, the French continued to enjoy such rights as freedom of the press and parliamentary representation. When Louis XVIII died in 1824, his brother, Charles X, came to the throne. Charles wanted to restore the absolute monarchy of prerevolutionary France. This angered French liberals, as did Charles's support of some very unpopular laws. One of these laws ordered payments to be made to nobles who had lost lands during the revolution. The money for the nobles came mainly from the middle class. Another law restricted freedom of the press.

In 1830, Charles X and his ministers issued the July Ordinances. These laws dismissed the legally elected lawmaking body. They also took the right to vote from most of the eligible French voters. They placed the press under government control.

A revolution broke out. In Paris, the people set up barricades (roadblocks) in the streets and fought the king's soldiers. After three days, the government collapsed, and Charles gave up the throne. Although many in France wanted a republic, a committee of liberals chose Louis Philippe, the Duke of Orleans, to be the new king. A new

Louis Philippe entering Paris during the July Revolution, 1830

constitution limited the power of the king and gave the vote to more of the middle class in France. As a result, the middle class became the dominant group within France.

The Belgians also revolted in 1830. They succeeded in winning their independence from the Dutch and establishing a constitutional monarchy. The Poles attempted to gain freedom from Russia. Some Italian states revolted against Austrian rule. These last two revolutions failed.

The Revolutions of 1848

In France. Trouble came again to France in 1848. A poor economy and reports of government corruption caused unrest among liberals. They were also disappointed that restrictions on voting continued. Although most wealthy men had gained the right to vote, most doctors, lawyers, teachers, artists, and workers could not. Dissatisfaction with the government of King Louis Philippe grew.

In February 1848, the government ordered reformers to cancel a political meeting. Protesters gathered in the streets of Paris. Riots broke out. Unwilling to use the army to restore order, Louis Philippe abdicated (resigned) and fled to Great Britain. The revolutionaries set up the Second Republic. (The first was set up during the French Revolution in the 1790s.)

Under a new constitution, an elected president and legislature governed the Second Republic. In December 1848, Louis Napoleon, a nephew of Napoleon Bonaparte, was elected president. He wanted to follow in his uncle's footsteps as a glorious ruler of France. In 1852, he turned the Second Republic into the Second Empire. President Louis Napoleon became Emperor Napoleon III. He ruled until 1870.

In Germany, Italy, and Austria. In 1848, revolutions also took place in Germany, Italy, and Austria. German revolutionaries called for more political rights guaranteed by new constitutions. They also wanted to unify the many German states into one nation. Their efforts failed because of the opposition of Frederick William IV, king of Prussia, the largest German state. Elected representatives of the German states met in the Frankfurt Assembly. They tried to unite Germany by offering to make Frederick William emperor. He refused on the grounds that, if he were elected by the people, he could not be a king by "divine right."

Conservative forces in the Austrian Empire beat down revolutions attempting to establish republics in Italy and Hungary. Russia helped crush the Hungarian uprisings. Conservatives also defeated demands for democracy from the citizens of Austria. The unpopular Prince Metternich was forced to flee Austria.

The peasants of Europe (but not in Russia) gained rights during this troubled period. They could now own land themselves and no longer owed labor to landlords. The old manorial system ended.

Reforms in Britain

No revolution took place in Britain in the 1800s. A series of compromises between liberals and conservatives made gradual reform possible without bloodshed. The Reform Bill of 1832 was the first of these compromises. By lowering the property requirements for voting, the new law doubled the number of British voters. At that time, only males could vote. Most of the new voters were members of the middle class.

In 1867, another reform bill lowered the property requirements

The Frankfurt National Assembly, 1848, tries but fails to unite the German states

THE ANTISLAVERY CRUSADE OF WILLIAM WILBERFORCE

On July 31, 1834, 800,000 slaves, chiefly in the British West Indies, were set free. Slavery had been abolished throughout the British Empire. The person most responsible for this historic action was William Wilberforce, member of Parliament and one of the great British reformers.

From an early age, Wilberforce desired a career in politics. He was elected to the House of Commons in 1780, at the age of 21. Although young, he was a superb parliamentary speaker. He had a powerful voice that thrilled audiences. A deeply religious man, Wilberforce was a major supporter of programs for public education, parliamentary reform, and religious freedom. He is best known, however, for his untiring dedication to the abolition of the slave trade and slavery.

Wilberforce introduced his first antislavery motion in the House of Commons in 1788. Despite his passionate three-hour speech, the motion was defeated. He reintroduced the motion every year for the next 18 years. Finally, on March 25, 1807, the slave trade was abolished. Although ownership of slaves remained legal, the importation and sale of slaves in British territories was outlawed. Abolition of the slave trade resulted in the assignment of the Royal Navy to the task of intercepting slave ships attempting to smuggle slaves for illegal sale. The British warships were eventually joined in this effort by the U.S. Navy's African Slave Trade Patrol, established in 1819 when Congress declared the slave trade to be a form of piracy. Piracy was punishable by death. The British and American warships searched the seas off West Africa, South America, and Cuba for the fast, elusive slavers. By 1861, one of the last years of the slave trade by any nation, more than 100 suspected slavers had been captured.

Wilberforce's triumph in Parliament brought him great prestige. Stopping the slave trade enabled him to pursue other goals—improving the quality and morality of life in Great Britain. He continued the campaign against slavery itself and achieved victory shortly before his death.

- Compare the British and American efforts to abolish slavery. Why do you think the British were able to accomplish this without a civil war such as occurred in the United States?

still further and gave the vote to working-class men. Conservatives accepted these reforms because they wanted to ensure that change would come to Britain peacefully. As a result of these reforms, more people could have a say in government.

Another important reform made by the British was the abolition (elimination) of slavery. Ideas of the Enlightenment had sparked a growing movement against slavery. Many people began to point out that Africans, too, had natural rights that entitled them to freedom and equal opportunities. Religious groups declared that holding people in slavery was a sin.

In 1807, the efforts of two abolitionist leaders, William Wilberforce and Thomas Clarkson, caused Parliament to outlaw the British slave trade. Parliament gave the British navy authority to search and seize ships suspected of carrying slaves. If the ships contained slaves, the British government paid for their release and return to western Africa. In 1833, Parliament abolished slavery in the British colonies.

Absolutism and Reform In Russia

Compared with other European countries in the 1800s, Russia was both politically and economically backward. The czars, who were absolute monarchs, completely controlled Russia's lawmaking body. Serfs, or farm laborers, made up more than 75 percent of the population. Most of them were tied to the land, much as the serfs of the Middle Ages had been. The landowning nobles had almost complete power over them.

Alexander I. Like his grandmother Catherine the Great, Alexander I of Russia (ruled 1801–1825) was strongly influenced by the political philosophy of the Enlightenment. He wished to avoid a major upheaval, such as the French Revolution had been. In order to achieve gradual and moderate change, Alexander tried to reform some of the social injustices that existed in Russia. He also wished to modernize his state and make it more like those of Western Europe.

Alexander improved the bureaucracy that helped run the government by appointing better trained officials. Unfortunately, he did not carry out more extensive reforms. Scholars feel that Alexander's weak and indecisive character was partly responsible for this failure. Then, too, the effort to drive Napoleon's army from Russia in 1812 had left the country economically and politically weak.

Many young people from the educated classes wanted Russia to be more democratic. They formed secret societies to develop and promote their aims. When Alexander I died in December 1825, some of these groups, called the Decembrists, staged an unsuccessful revolt.

Alexander II. To discourage a repetition of the Decembrist revolt, the next czar, Nicholas I (ruled 1825–1855), discouraged all liberal tendencies. No significant reforms were made until Nicholas's son, Alexander II (ruled 1855–1881), came to the throne.

Alexander II did what other czars had failed to do. He freed the serfs in 1861. Although the emancipation of the serfs was an important step forward for Russia, the method by which it was done had drawbacks. The serfs had to pay high prices for the land they were allotted. Since the villages in which the serfs lived were held responsible for this payment, the villages rather than individuals owned the land. Consequently, serfs found it difficult to better themselves by

Peasant faces reflecting the hardships of rural life in Russia in the late 1800s

trying new farming techniques or moving to villages that offered them more opportunities. They were still, to a large extent, tied to one place.

Alexander II made other changes as well. In 1864, he established local governments called *zemstvos*. These were elected bodies that made decisions on how to manage a district's education, health, and welfare. However, the zemstvos were largely controlled by local landowners. They did not have the power to collect taxes for carrying out improvements agreed upon by the members.

Alexander also freed Russia's legal system from domination by the czar. Russians who were accused of most kinds of crimes now had a right to trial by jury with independent judges and professional lawyers. Alexander still retained the czar's power to judge political cases.

Reaction to Reforms. Many Russians felt that these reforms were inadequate. Students formed groups to spread socialist ideas among the poor. When the government cracked down on these associations, the young radicals adopted terrorist tactics. One of the groups assassinated Alexander II on March 13, 1881. The new czar, Alexander III (ruled 1881–1894), used harsh measures to stamp out any suspected opposition. He persecuted liberals and minority groups, targeting Jews in particular.

Expansion and Russian Nationalism

During the 19th century, nationalism played as important a role in Russia as it had in Western Europe. Russian nationalism took sev-

The Growth of Russia to 1900

eral forms. One sprang from the desire to see one's country become powerful by controlling other nations. This is called *imperialism*. Russian leaders often stirred up nationalistic feelings in their subjects to distract them from their dissatisfaction with czarist rule.

Expansion. During the 19th century, several czars waged wars of expansion. Nicholas I fought a long and difficult war to win the Caucasus. (This is the area between the Black and Caspian seas.) During Alexander II's reign, Russia took control of Muslim areas in Central Asia and made them colonies. In 1858, the governor-general of Siberia signed a treaty with China giving Russia an area along the Amur River. This extended Russia's borders even farther east.

Crimean War

In 1853, the desire for expansion also led Russia into conflict with Turkey. Russia wanted to control the water route connecting the Black Sea with the Mediterrean Sea. This water route was the straits known as the Dardanelles and the Bosporus. To accomplish its goal, Russia demanded the right to protect Eastern Orthodox Christians living in the Ottoman Empire. When Turkey refused, Russia sent troops into the Crimean peninsula, which juts into the Black Sea.

Britain and France opposed Russian expansion into the Black Sea region and sent troops to the Crimea to support the Turkish forces. In fighting that followed, Russia's lack of supplies, railroads, and reinforcements led to its defeat. The Treaty of Paris, signed on March 30, 1856, ended the Crimean War. It forced Russia to give up some territory it had taken from the Ottoman Empire and barred Russia from placing warships and fortifications around the Black Sea.

The English poet Alfred, Lord Tennyson, wrote "The Charge of the Light Brigade" about the Battle of Balaklava, one of the major engagements of the Crimean War. This famous poem paid tribute to the courage of the British cavalry's charge against a position heavily fortified by Russian artillery. Many regarded the poem as an indictment of the stupidity of the commander who had ordered the suicidal charge.

The Crimean War also made Florence Nightingale, an English nurse, famous. Her care of the wounded was widely reported by newspaper journalists. This humanitarian work later helped bring about improvements in hospital and nursing care.

Pan-Slavism. Another expression of nationalism is the feeling of identity and sympathy among the members of the same ethnic group. Influenced by this form of nationalism, Russian leaders claimed the right to protect Slavic peoples living anywhere in Europe. (Slavs are people who speak the Slavic language. They are centered in Eastern Europe, including Russia.) This support of Slavic unity was called *Pan-Slavism*. It led Russia to help Slavic Serbia in its conflicts with Austria-Hungary.

A strong element of imperialism was mixed with Pan-Slavism. The Russians felt that their own Slavic heritage gave them the right to take over parts of the territories inhabited by other Slavs. When Slavs in the Balkan states of Montenegro and Serbia revolted against the Ottoman Turks in 1875, Russia helped them win their independence. The peace treaty gave Russia access to Bulgaria's seaport on the Aegean Sea. Other European countries felt threatened by Russia's expansion into the Balkans. At the Congress of Berlin in 1878, they forced Russian leaders to make another peace treaty. It took away Russia's right to use the Bulgarian seaport. Russia resented this humiliation.

Discrimination Against Non-Russians. Influenced by Pan-Slavism, Russians began to look down on people of other ethnic backgrounds. Russian leaders tried to force non-Russian inhabitants of the Russian Empire to replace their own cultures with Russian culture. The Russian government forbade Ukrainians to speak or write their own language. When the Poles revolted in 1863, Russia banned all public expression of Polish culture.

Anti-Jewish Actions. In the 1890s, the Russian government reinforced discriminatory laws against Jews. These laws limited the places where Jews could live and took away their freedom to attend schools. The laws also required compulsory military service for a long period of time. The Russian government also failed to protect Jews against violent attacks on them. (These attacks, called *pogroms*, were sanctioned by government officials.) Many Jews left Russia for Western Europe and the United States. Those who stayed joined radical political movements in an effort to defend themselves against persecution.

| **INFO CHECK** |

1. List the causes and major results of the revolutions of 1830 and 1848. Which revolution do you think accomplished more? Explain your answer.

2. In 1848, revolutions occurred in nearly every European country, except Britain and Russia. Why was this so?

3. How did the struggle between liberalism and conservatism affect events in 19th-century Russia?

4. Explain how Pan-Slavism and persecution of Jews were related to Russian nationalism.

SOUTH AMERICA AFTER THE WARS OF INDEPENDENCE

When Simon Bolívar fought to free South America from Spain, he dreamed of uniting the entire continent under a democratic government similar to that of the United States. Many factors worked against his dream.

Factors Influencing Unification

Before air travel, South America's geographical features—high mountains, dense rain forests, few natural harbors—made travel from one area to another difficult. The map in Chapter 16 shows some of the obstacles to easy travel in South America.

Because people in different regions could not communicate easily with one another, they developed their own ways of life. Isolation and nationalistic pride in their own cultural groups brought them under the influence of local leaders. Many local leaders discouraged their followers from uniting with other people under a central government.

Some of the local leaders had led armies during the revolutions. After the wars, they retained control of the armies. They won support from some by using their armies to police their regions and keep order. A few leaders used their military power to discourage opposition and became dictators.

Religious Issues

Religious and social issues also kept Latin Americans apart. One was the status of the Catholic Church. Catholicism is the major religion in Latin America. During colonial days, the Church had been a strong unifying force. Many revolutionary leaders, however, felt that it took money that might be better used to help the poor. They weakened the Church economically by not permitting the collection of tithes. These are taxes paid by the congregation of a church to help maintain it. Part of the money was sent to Rome for the work of the international Church.

Different political factions disagreed about whether to let the Church or the state appoint Church officials. Consequently, many Church offices were left unfilled. Without enough leaders, the Church lost some of its political power.

Class System

Just as geographical features and social issues hindered unity in South America, so too did the class system prevent true democracy. Latin Americans had no tradition of equality such as people in the North American colonies had. Once the peninsulares were gone, the Creoles, who were the main landowners and businesspeople, took political power. Next in the social hierarchy came the *mestizos* (people who were part Spanish and part Indian). Indians, and people who were a mixture of African, Indian, and Spanish, followed the mestizos. Slaves made up the lowest class. In some South American countries, such as Brazil, slavery lasted until the late 1800s.

Immediately after the revolutions, members of some lower classes had an opportunity to move up the social scale. Free Africans, for example, enjoyed more social mobility than free Africans in the United States. South American revolutionary leaders had offered freedom to slaves who would help them fight for independence. Many former slaves distinguished themselves in battle. After the wars, the leaders rewarded them with land and political power.

In general, however, it was more difficult for Latin Americans than for the people of the United States to improve their social position. Only people the wealthier classes could afford a good education. Resentment built up among the disadvantaged people, who sometimes protested angrily against their circumstances. In response, the ruling classes passed repressive laws against the disadvantaged. Frequent conflicts among different social classes contributed to the instability of South American governments.

Economics

The economic structure of Latin America was largely responsible for the uneven distribution of wealth there. Most Latin American wealth came from the big plantations and mines. Even after the revolutions, they remained in the hands of only a few people. The landowners and mine owners led lives of luxury and ease while their farmworkers and miners were little better off than slaves. Many poor people had to resort to robbery to get enough to live on. Some banded

Time Line

Year	Dates and Events
A.D. **1801**	**1800s:** Rise of liberalism and nationalism based on principles of Enlightenment **1801–1825:** Czar Alexander I, Russia, attempts reform of social ills, government inefficiency **1807:** Britain abolishes slave trade **1814:** Congress of Vienna ensures European balance of power, legitimacy of monarchies; suppresses nationalism **1824:** Charles X, France, tries to restore absolute monarchy **1825:** Decembrist revolution by young Russian intellectuals fails **1825–1855:** Nicholas I of Russia crushes liberal movement **1830:** July Ordinances in France dismiss legislature, restrict voting, control the press **1830:** Revolution in France ousts Charles X in favor of Louis Philippe **1830:** Belgian revolt ousts Dutch rule, sets up constitutional monarchy **1832:** Reform Bill in Britain doubles number of (male) voters **1833:** Britain abolishes slavery by Act of Parliament **1848:** French revolution ousts Louis Philippe, sets up Second Republic under President Louis Napoleon
1850 **1851**	**1848:** Revolutions in Germany, Austria, Hungary, Italy are unsuccessful; peasants gain basic rights **1852–1870:** Louis Napoleon sets up Second Empire, becomes Emperor Napoleon III **1853–1856:** Russian expansion into Black Sea region; Crimean War erupts between Britain, France, Ottomans against Russia, the loser **1855–1881:** Alexander II of Russia frees serfs (1861), sets up local government to manage education, health, welfare (1864), institutes trial by jury, independent judges **1858:** Siberian-Chinese treaty extends Russia's borders to Pacific coast **1863:** After Polish revolution, Russia suppresses Polish culture **1867:** Reform Bill in Britain extends vote to working-class males **1875:** Russia pursues Pan-Slavism by aiding Montenegro and Serbia against Ottomans **1876:** Díaz establishes order in Mexico by killing opponents, tightening police control
1900 **1901**	**1878:** At Congress of Berlin, European powers force Russia to give up Bulgarian port on Aegean Sea **1881:** Assassination of Alexander II by radical Russian terrorists **1881–1894:** Alexander III suppresses all opposition, persecutes Jews **1910–1911:** Mexican rebellion spread by Madero, Villa, Zapata forces Díaz to flee **1913:** Huerta, backed by Mexican landowners, kills Madero, takes over government **1914:** Mexican revolutionists, aided by U.S. troops, force Huerta to resign
1925	**1917:** New Mexican constitution breaks up plantations, grants free public education, ousts foreign business interests

together to ambush travelers as they passed through wild and remote country. Hazardous travel conditions became another reason for slow political and economic progress in Latin America.

Because so many Latin Americans were poor, there were only a few local buyers for the products of the mines and plantations. The land and mine owners had to go to foreign markets to sell their goods. Each Latin American country became dependent on just a few sources of wealth. For instance, Bolivia depended on the sale of tin; Chile on copper. The plantations in each region produced one or two major *cash crops*. A cash crop is raised to be sold on the world market. Brazil, for example, exported mainly sugar and coffee. When the world demand for either of these goods decreased, the Brazilian economy suffered.

The Mexican Revolution

To improve the local economies in Latin America, leaders of several nations tried to persuade outsiders to invest in their countries. Foreigners, however, thought that frequent political turnover and social unrest made it risky to invest too heavily in Latin America. Mexico, for example, was rich in oil and minerals, but outside investors were reluctant to develop its resources.

Díaz. After Porfirio Díaz became dictator of Mexico in 1876, he set about establishing order. He did this by having all his political opponents killed and directing his police force to clear the roads of bandits. Surprisingly, Díaz did keep constitutional forms of government in place. However, he made all decisions himself.

When foreigners saw that Díaz had established order, they decided to develop businesses in Mexico. Foreign money, however, did not solve Mexico's problems. It simply made the rich richer and the poor poorer. The rich did not share the wealth by paying higher wages or making land available at reasonable prices. The new wealth enabled a few thousand landowning families to acquire almost half of Mexico's land. This left almost all of the country's farmers with no land of their own. Mexico was ripe for revolution.

Many Mexicans began to protest against Díaz's repressive government. Nationalistic feelings also played a part in the political unrest. Protesters felt that foreign investors had too much control over the Mexican economy and were dictating Mexico's social and political policies.

Madero. Leaders soon arose to organize the protest movement. A reformer named Francisco Madero urged the middle class to help him replace the Díaz dictatorship with a democratic government. In November 1910, small groups of poor farmers raided the properties of large landowners. They hoped to get free land. The rebellion spread, and the rebels gradually started winning battles against government troops. Some farmers became leaders themselves. Francisco "Pancho" Villa led revolutionists in the northern part of Mexico.

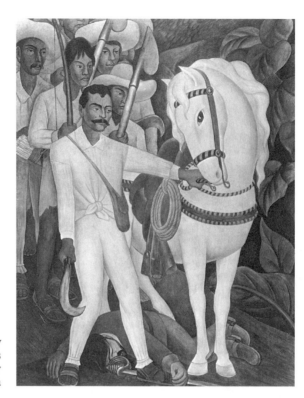

Mexican revolutionary
Emiliano Zapata, as
depicted in a 1931 fresco by
Diego Rivera

Emiliano Zapata led an army in the south. Defeated by the revolutionary forces, Díaz fled to France in 1911.

Madero hoped that the establishment of a democracy would end the revolution. But the farmers, who wanted land reform, continued to fight the landowners.

Huerta. General Victoriano Huerta sided with the landowners. With the support of his army, he had Madero killed and took over the Mexican government himself in 1913. But the revolutionaries did not give up. With the help of American troops sent by President Woodrow Wilson, they forced Huerta to resign in 1914.

A New Constitution. In 1917, a constitution for a new democratic government was drawn up. Under this constitution, the government was able to take over huge plantations and mines and divide them among the poor. A plan for free public education was set up. Control of Mexico's resources was given to Mexicans rather than to foreigners.

Elusive Democracy. In spite of victories such as the Mexican Revolution, large gaps between rich and poor in most Latin American countries remained. Such differences made true democracy there difficult to achieve. Many of these countries were unable to shake off their dependency on foreign investors. Economic dependency caused leaders to support policies that brought in foreign wealth rather than taking action to help their people. Nationalists complained that their countries might just as well have remained colonies.

Nationalism also became a powerful force in Europe and Asia. Chapter 22 describes how nationalist movements helped shape many modern states in both the Western and Eastern hemispheres. National groups continue to struggle for the right to direct the development of their states.

INFO CHECK

1. Explain how each of the following prevented the unification of Latin America in the 19th century: geography, religion, and the class system.

2. Who were Pancho Villa and Emiliano Zapata? Why do you think they were heroes to some Mexicans but not to others?

3. Why was it so difficult to achieve democracy in 19th-century Mexico?

CHAPTER REVIEW

Multiple Choice

1. The revolutions that took place in Europe during the 19th century arose from the ideas and actions of

   1. the Renaissance and the Protestant and Catholic reformations
   2. the Middle Ages, the Crusades, and international trade
   3. the reconquest, and the expulsion of Muslim and Jewish people from Spain
   4. the Enlightenment and the American and French revolutions.

2. Much social and political change occurred in middle to late 19th-century European society. Select the choice that correctly links the group's social class with their political view.

   1. Workers and other lower-class people usually favored a radical or Socialist form of government.
   2. Upper-class aristocrats usually favored a republican form of government.

   3. Middle-class businesspeople usually favored a conservative dictatorship government.
   4. Clergy and religious individuals usually favored a liberal democratic form of government.

3. The aim of the Congress of Vienna was to

   1. create an economic union that would rebuild the war-torn European states
   2. restore the European monarchies that Napoleon had overthrown and establish a balance of power
   3. assist the nationalistic desires of people to establish their own countries
   4. prevent the former monarchs from retaking their thrones and overseas colonies.

4. Identify the political philosophy and goal that Prince Metternich of the

Austrian Empire had for the Congress of Vienna.

1. liberal—wanted to spread democratic principles throughout Europe
2. socialist—wanted governments to regulate the economy, ending business competition
3. conservative—wanted to preserve the Austrian Empire by preventing the spread of nationalism
4. radical—wanted to completely overthrow the old monarchies and put Napoleon back on the throne.

5. Rousseau's political philosophy was used by both liberals and conservatives to justify their type of government. This was because he believed that good government

1. is an expression of the citizens' general will
2. is a gift from the gods
3. is a peaceful and stable process
4. comes from the goodness of people.

6. Based on the 1830 July Ordinances, Charles X wanted to be what type of ruler?

1. president
2. absolute monarch
3. limited monarch
4. Holy Roman Emperor.

7. England, unlike continental Europe, did not suffer any revolutions in the 1800s. This was because

1. the English king granted freedom to all serfs
2. Parliament passed two voting reform bills
3. England was not influenced by the Enlightenment's political philosophy

4. England was ruled by an absolute monarch who used the army and secret police to prevent revolutions.

8. Nationalism can be a force for good or evil. When it results in one nation dominating another it is called

1. mercantilism
2. socialism
3. capitalism
4. imperialism.

9. The Russian government supported the Balkan states against the Ottoman Turks because of

1. its concern over the treatment of their fellow Slavic rulers
2. its financial investments in Rumania and Serbia
3. its Pan-Slavic belief that Russia was the protector of all Slavic peoples anywhere in Europe
4. the opportunity to control the vital Panama Canal and its ice-free waterway.

10. One of the causes for Latin America's economic problems has been its reliance on one or two cash crops. This means that

1. the economy relied on the world market to sell its goods at fair market value
2. the exchange of money for goods occurs at inflationary rates
3. Brazil exchanged oil and gold for beef and vegetables
4. when worldwide demand for the cash crops decreases, the entire economy is in trouble.

11. Studying the photograph on page 456 reveals that

1. the lives of Russian peasants improved as a result of reforms of the czars

2. technology had recently been introduced into Russia's rural areas

3. the ideas of the American and French revolutions as well as the Enlightenment had little impact on rural life in Russia

4. peasants and serfs had reason to hope for improved living conditions

12. The painting on page 463 depicts Emiliano Zapata as

1. a tyrant

2. a monarch

3. a hero

4. a frustrated loser.

Thematic Essays

1. Democratic beliefs and ideals shook the old ruling classes of Western Europe. However, the peoples of Russia and Latin America seem to have been less successful in establishing democratic governments. *Task:* Analyze the reasons for the authoritarian nature of governments in Russia and Latin America. Consider geographic, economic, and social factors.

2. Metternich and the Congress of Vienna attempted to turn the clock back and restore deposed monarchs to their thrones. *Task:* Identify and explain two reasons why these efforts failed. Include specific examples for at least one nation in Europe in your answer.

Document-Based Questions

1. Study the map on page 457. Identify the geographic factors that would hinder the spread of information to the Russian people about events such as the American and French revolutions and the ideas of the Enlightenment.

2. It was not until 1861 that Russian serfs were emancipated [freed]. This is a description of a Russian village community.

" . . . the villages are bound together by ties quite unknown to the rural English population. . . . they cannot begin to mow or plow the fallow [unplanted] field until the village assembly has passed a resolution on the subject. . . . No peasant can permanently leave the village without the consent of the community, and this consent will not be granted until the applicant gives satisfactory security for his actual and future liabilities [taxes]."

How did Russian society bind the peasant to the village and prevent individual action?

3. A young idealist wrote about village life in Russia:

"Everyone who settles there, whether as artisan, or as communal teacher, or clerk is immediately under the eye of all. He is observed and his every movement is watched as though he was a bird in a glass cage. . . . The peasant is absolutely incapable of keeping secret the propaganda in his midst. . . . Thus, whenever a propagandist visits any of his friends, the news immediately spreads throughout the village."

Why was it easy for the government to identify the propagandist, and difficult for the propagandist to hide among the people?

4. Russian revolutionaries wrote a letter to the new czar Alexander III after the assassination of his father, Alexander II.

"For this reason, your majesty: that a just government, in the true sense of the word, does not exist among us. A government should, in conformity with its essential principle of its existence, be the expression of the aspirations [goals] of the people, [it] should carry out only the will of the people."

What are the justifications used by the revolutionaries for their actions? What are the sources of their political ideas?

Document-Based Essay

Task: Discuss the reasons why the peasants and serfs of Latin America and Russia were so slow to react to the ideas of the Enlightenment and the revolutions in America and France.

C H A P T E R
22

Global Nationalism

Lurking in the small kitchen garden, Aldo eavesdropped on his father and uncles as they sat laughing and talking over their wine. There was no need for him to strain his ears—they were certainly loud enough. But no wonder. They had had a marvelous week. Before they left, they had told Aldo that they were going on a long hunting trip. He had been hurt and angry when his father had not let him go along. But now it turned out that he had missed even greater sport. All the men in his family but himself had been at war.

They had been helping the great Garibaldi to free Sicily. *Why, why* had his father not allowed Aldo to fight for his country? What did his age matter? Every Italian was old enough to die for his country. Ever since Garibaldi had returned to Italy, Aldo had been longing to join the Red Shirts. In his dreams, he had command of his own troop. For a signal, his men would have whistled one of the patriotic melodies from Verdi's opera *Nabucco*. What a touch that would have been! His cousin from Rome had told him that the name "Verdi" was a code word for "Victor Emmanuel, king of Italy." The signal would have given courage to the soldiers. It would have reminded them that one day Italy would be united under its own king. Now Aldo's dream would remain only a dream and would never become a glorious memory.

Aldo, a young Italian living in Sicily during the mid-1800s, was strongly influenced by the spirit of *nationalism*. Various parts of his country were ruled by more powerful states. Like the citizens of other fragmented countries, Aldo longed for Italy to unite under its own government. Much music, art, and literature of the time expressed and encouraged this longing.

HISTORIANS' VIEW OF NATIONALISM

Nationalism, along with other forces, has shaped the modern world. It has fueled the wars, revolutions, and imperial expansions that have determined modern political boundaries. National heroes have performed deeds that stand out as historical landmarks. Others, in the name of nationalism, have committed crimes against people and nations. The consequences of these crimes still cause problems today. Artists and engineers have been inspired to create great public works that form a part of the cultural heritage of many countries. Ordinary people have sacrificed their own needs in order to help their nation survive.

Power of Nationalism

Why is nationalism so powerful? Some of its strength comes from its practical value. Most people realize that supporting their country during a crisis is the best way to get through the crisis themselves. They know that they and their families need the protection and services provided by their government. But, to a large extent, nationalism is an emotional force that sweeps aside concern for safety and other practical matters.

Patriotism. Nationalism is closely related to patriotism, or love of one's country. Patriotic people feel the kind of affection and gratitude to their country that they feel toward their families. They believe that it is their duty to repay their country for protecting them and giving them opportunities for self-fulfillment. Nonetheless, patriotic people often claim the right to question the aims of their country's actions. They feel that they can best serve their country by making sure that it's leaders behave morally and humanely. During times when their country is in trouble, however, the patriotism of many people develops into intense nationalism. They believe leaders who claim that it is disloyal to find fault with their country.

Inspiration. Many national groups that were ruled by foreign states longed for the old days and their traditional lands. Nationalism fed their desire to restore their own governments. The leaders of these groups knew that they would have to inspire others with the same fervor. To do so, they did everything they could to heighten the people's love of country. Nationalistic artists painted pictures, wrote poems, and composed music that aroused national love and pride. Leaders used their countries' flags and anthems as rallying points. They spoke as fondly of national traits as the members of a family sometimes speak of their inherited characteristics.

Misuse of Emotion. Unscrupulous leaders often take advantage of this uncritical attitude in nationalistic people. In order to persuade their followers to support aggressive policies, they boost national pride with propaganda, slogans, and spectacles that exhibit their nation's strength. They bolster individual pride by presenting characteristics shared by the people of the country as superior to those shared by people in other countries. Such leaders then arouse the people's fear of and contempt for other groups.

Influence Through the Ages

Although the term nationalism is associated with patriotic movements of the 18th, 19th, and 20th centuries, the emotions and attitudes it represents have influenced people through the ages. Recent history provides many examples of how nationalism affects world events. Nationalism motivated some events that set off the first and second world wars. It has caused terrible genocides, attempts to eliminate certain ethnic groups. However, it has helped oppressed people, such as the black South Africans, to gain a voice in their country's government.

Nationalism has also made people of prosperous countries turn against immigrants from less fortunate countries. In the 1990s, for example, extreme nationalist groups in Germany bombed the homes of Turks who had come to Germany to find work. The German government condemned these acts. But at the same time, it passed laws limiting the number of people that could come there in search of asylum. (Most other countries also have laws restricting immigration.)

Nationalism made it possible for divided and oppressed countries to unite. Nationalism also caused severe problems in the 20th century.

INFO CHECK

1. Explain the difference between nationalism and patriotism. Which force do you think is more beneficial? Which is more destructive? Give reasons for your answers.

2. Identify one or two late-20th-century crises caused by nationalist feelings and ambitions.

WESTERN NATIONALISM

Nationalistic feelings became very strong among 19th-century Germans and Italians. These feelings led to a struggle to unify the separate states into which each country was divided. By 1871, strong nationalist leaders in both Germany and Italy succeeded in their aim of unification. Each became a country united by a central government headed by one person.

The Unification of Germany

Before 1848, Germany was a confederation of 38 states ruled by princes or kings. Prussia was the largest and most powerful of the states. During the Napoleonic Wars, 16 states grouped together as the Confederation of the Rhine. The Congress of Vienna turned the Rhine grouping into the German Confederation. But the ties were loose and no central government developed.

A tariff union or free trade association called the Zollverein was set up in 1834. It united many German states economically.

Many Germans believed that unity could be gained only under Prussian leadership. In 1848, the Frankfurt Assembly had attempted to unify Germany. It had offered to make King Frederick William IV of Prussia emperor of all of Germany. He had refused the offer. He said he did not want to take a crown from the hands of revolutionaries and liberals.

Blood and Iron. Frederick William did, however, want Prussia to head a unified country. His successor, Wilhelm I, shared this goal. To help him achieve it, he appointed Otto von Bismarck as his chief minister in 1862. Bismarck set forth a policy called "blood and iron." The phrase meant that he intended to use war to achieve his aims of unifying Germany and expanding its power.

The major obstacles to German unity were Austria, France, and the princes who ruled the German states. Austria and France opposed the unification of Germany because they feared having a large, strong nation on their borders. The German princes did not want to give up their power to a national government. To remove these three obstacles, Bismarck started three wars.

Schleswig-Holstein. In 1864, Danish forces took over an area called Schleswig that is located between Denmark and Prussia. (Many Germans lived in Schleswig.) Bismarck and Austria objected and invaded Schleswig to free it from the Danes. The defeated Danes turned over Schleswig and Holstein, the province just to the south of Schleswig, to Prussia and Austria. Bismarck persuaded Austria to govern Holstein while Prussia ruled Schleswig.

The two powers quarreled over the administration of the provinces. The disagreement led to the Austro-Prussian War in 1866. Bismarck persuaded France and Russia not to aid Austria. Prussia won the conflict, which is often called the Seven Weeks' War. The easy defeat of Austria demonstrated Prussia's military strength. It also ended Austria's influence over the future of Germany.

North German Confederation. To extend Prussia's political power, Bismarck organized the North German Confederation in 1867.

It brought together many small north German states under Prussia's leadership. The princes of the lesser states joined because they were impressed by the Prussian army's ability to win victories. Four major states in southern Germany chose not to be part of the confederation. Mainly Roman Catholic, the south Germans feared domination by the Protestant north Germans. The south Germans also did not want to upset France by joining with Prussia. The new confederation set up a legislature with two houses. The members of the upper house, the Bundesrat, were appointed. The members of the lower house, the Reichstag, were elected. Bismarck was the chief officer of the Reichstag. The executive post, the presidency, was held by a Prussian.

Franco-Prussian War. To encourage the southern states to join with the north, Bismarck started a third war—this time with France. He stirred up anti-French feeling in both northern and southern Germany.

Emperor Napoleon III of France was also eager for a war. He wanted to stop Prussia from gaining more power. In addition, the emperor hoped that a military victory over Prussia would make him more popular with the French.

The issue that set off the war was a dispute between France and Prussia over the selection of a Prussian prince to be king of Spain. Bismarck stirred up hostile feelings between the French and the Prussians by playing on their national pride. By trickery, Bismarck made it seem as if the two countries had insulted each other.

Napoleon III had sent an ambassador to talk to King William I while the king was on vacation in Ems, Germany. The king refused to announce publicly that no Prussian prince would become king of Spain, which was what Napoleon wanted. William sent a telegram to Bismarck reporting the conversation. Bismarck changed the Ems Telegram to make it seem as if the king had insulted the French ambassador. He made the telegram public. Newspapers in France and Prussia demanded war.

France declared war in July 1870. The south German states blamed France for the situation and came to the aid of the North German Confederation. The Franco-Prussian War, therefore, was really a war between France and all of Germany.

German armies invaded France. They defeated a large French army under the personal command of Napoleon III and took the emperor prisoner in September 1870. The Germans moved on to Paris. In January 1871, Paris surrendered. The Germans had won a quick and total victory.

Unification. The Treaty of Frankfurt (May 1871) ended the war. Under its terms, France gave Germany the border province of Alsace and part of Lorraine. Both were rich in coal and iron. France also had to pay a large sum of money to Germany. German troops remained in France until the money was collected.

Following the great victory of 1871, Bismarck met with the lead-

The Unification of Germany   1871

ers of all the German states at Louis XIV's Palace of Versailles outside Paris. There, with much ceremony, the south German states joined with the North German Confederation to form the German Empire (Reich). King Wilhelm I of Prussia became the kaiser (emperor) of all Germany. Bismarck was named the chancellor, or prime minister.

A constitution was written. It created a two-house legislature consisting of the Bundesrat and Reichstag. All men over 25 could vote for members of the Reichstag.

Bismarck had succeeded in his plan to unify Germany and turn it into a powerful nation. The policy of "blood and iron" had worked.

The Unification of Italy

Since the Middle Ages, Italy had been a collection of provinces, small kingdoms, and city-states rather than one nation. From the early to the mid-1800s, much of Italy was ruled by Austria. The pope controlled the portion of central Italy in which Rome is located.

Mazzini. In the 1830s, the voice of a young nationalist leader began to be heard. Giuseppe Mazzini founded Young Italy. It was a secret society that called for the unification of Italy under a representative government. Mazzini stirred up revolts in several cities. They were quickly put down by the authorities. Mazzini fled to France. He continued to promote unification efforts with his writings from Switzer-

Giuseppe Garibaldi, Italian patriot, in a photograph taken during the fight for Italy's unification

land and England. Mazzini has been called the "soul" of Italian unification.

Garibaldi. A second great figure who fought to unify Italy was Giuseppe Garibaldi. He had worked with Mazzini in the revolts of the 1830s. When they failed, he fled to France and then to Latin America. In 1848, Garibaldi returned to Italy. He led troops in the states of northern Italy in their unsuccessful revolt against Austrian rule. The following year, he led an effort to replace the pope's rule over Rome with a more liberal government. The effort failed when French troops sent by Napoleon III arrived in Rome to back the pope. On their retreat through central Italy, Garibaldi and his troops gathered many supporters. But he had to go into exile to keep his freedom.

Cavour. In 1852, the unification movement gained new life. This dramatic period was called the *risorgimento*, or reawakening, from the name of a newspaper founded by Camillo di Cavour. Through the newspaper, Cavour stirred up anti-Austrian feeling and pushed for

Count Cavour, Italian statesman who spearheaded the *risorgimento* and unification of Italy

the northern Italian states to join together to overcome Austrian rule. In 1852, King Victor Emmanuel II of Sardinia and Piedmont made Cavour prime minister. Cavour believed in constitutional monarchy and in industrial growth. He strengthened the economy of Piedmont by encouraging the building of factories and railroads and by increasing trade with other countries. Piedmont had to be built up so that it could win Italian territory from Austria.

Overcoming Obstacles. The major obstacles to Italian unification were Austria and the pope. Austria controlled portions of northern Italy and had no wish to give them up. The pope ruled the Papal States in central Italy. A strong national government would threaten Church ownership of these lands.

Cavour moved first against the Austrians. He arranged a secret alliance with France and then provoked a war with Austria. (France was to receive the western part of Piedmont, Savoy, and Nice for help against Austria.) When Austrian troops invaded Piedmont, the French aided the Italians. The war ended with a treaty signed by France and Austria in July 1859. Piedmont received the northern Italian state of Lombardy, previously controlled by Austria.

The Austrian invasion of Piedmont had increased nationalistic feelings in the Austrian-controlled areas of northern Italy. Rebellions broke out in Tuscany, Parma, and Modena. The people of these states demanded to be joined with Piedmont. Knowing that France supported Piedmont, Austria agreed. By 1860, Piedmont controlled all of Italy except the Kingdom of the Two Sicilies in the south, the Papal

States in the center, and Venetia in the northeast. The foundation for an Italian nation had been built.

The Return of Garibaldi. In May 1860, Giuseppe Garibaldi landed in Sicily with an army of about 1,000 soldiers called Red Shirts, from the color of their clothing. His nationalistic soldiers de-

The Unification of Italy   1859–1870

FRANCE

SWITZ.

LOMBARDY
(1859)

AUSTRIAN
EMPIRE

VENETIA
(1866)

Venice

HUNGARY

PIEDMONT

Milan

Genoa

MODENA
(1860)

OTTOMAN
EMPIRE

PARMA
(1860)

TUSCANY
(1860)

PAPAL
STATES
(1860)

KINGDOM
OF
SARDINIA

CORSICA
(Fr.)

ADRIATIC SEA

(1870)
Rome

KINGDOM
OF THE
TWO
SICILIES
(1860)

Naples

SARDINIA

TYRRHENIAN SEA

MEDITERRANEAN SEA

Palermo

SICILY

N
W ⊕ E
S

0   75   150 Kilometers

0   50   100 Miles

AFRICA

feated the larger professional army of the island's Bourbon rulers. Then, Garibaldi's troops crossed to the Italian mainland and captured southern Italy and the city of Naples. These victories gave Garibaldi control of the entire Kingdom of the Two Sicilies. Cavour sent the Piedmont army to aid Garibaldi's forces and capture the Papal States. Rome, however, was left untouched. The French army that occupied the city protected the pope. Garibaldi, called the "sword" of unification, then transferred control of the areas taken by his Red Shirts to the king of Piedmont. Victor Emmanuel II became king of Italy in March 1861. Cavour, the brain or mind of unification, died in June before his dream of a fully unified Italy was realized.

Italy became Prussia's ally in 1866 before the Seven Weeks' War with Austria. The Prussian victory ended Austrian rule of Venetia, and the province was taken over by Italy. During the Franco-Prussian War in 1870, the French withdrew their troops from Rome, and Italian troops moved in. The pope's territory was reduced to the Vatican and Lateran palaces and the papal villa at Castel Gandolfo. Rome became the capital city of the Kingdom of Italy in 1871. Unification of the entire peninsula was complete.

Germany and Italy After Unification

In the years following unification, Germany and Italy developed quite differently.

Germany. Bismarck made Germany into one of the strongest nations of Europe. He increased German military and naval power. Germany's many natural resources, especially coal and iron, aided the growth of industries. Productive farms and factories and a good school system gave Germans a high standard of living and a high rate of literacy.

Bismarck had no use for democracy. A legislature existed in Germany, but the kaiser held supreme authority in the government. Labor unions and political parties had little power. Bismarck weakened the influence of unions on workers by giving the workers social insurance benefits, such as old-age pensions and compensation payments for injury or illness. The German social insurance laws were the first passed by any country.

Italy. Italy faced many problems. Because the country had few natural resources, Italian industry developed slowly. The economy remained weak. Many Italians were poor and illiterate.

Italy was organized as a democracy. A constitution limited the power of the king and provided for an elected parliament to make laws. Only a small number of wealthy males had the right to vote. This changed in 1912 when all Italian men were given the right to vote. Many poor Italians traded their votes for money. This behavior led to widespread corruption in the government. An additional problem was the refusal of the Roman Catholic Church to recognize the national government. The pope resented the seizure of the Papal States. Until 1904, the Church forbade devout Catholics to vote or hold government office.

Similarities. Both Germany and Italy shared strong nationalist emotions. This led to the desire to gain glory by competing with other nations for colonies overseas. Between 1871 and 1914, the German Empire and the Kingdom of Italy spent large amounts of money and sacrificed many lives in the race for colonies.

Italy acquired Eritrea and Somalia in eastern Africa and Libya in North Africa. Germany took over the sections of Africa that are the present-day countries of The Gambia, Togo, Cameroon, Namibia, and Tanzania. It also controlled a few islands in the South Pacific.

INFO CHECK

1. Describe Otto von Bismarck's policy of "blood and iron." Did the formation of the Reich in 1871 signify the success or failure of this policy?

2. Which 19th-century leader best fits each of the following descriptions?

   - the soul of Italian unification
   - the sword of Italian unification
   - the mind of Italian unification

3. After German unification, what steps did Bismarck take to limit the power of political parties and labor unions? How did these measures affect the development of democracy in Germany?

SECTIONALISM VERSUS NATIONALISM IN THE UNITED STATES

In the 19th century, the United States became a powerful, prosperous nation. Americans believed in Manifest Destiny, their right to settle the continent from the Atlantic Ocean to the Pacific Ocean and from Canada to the Gulf of Mexico. It seemed only right to them that they should win a large area of land from Mexico in the Mexican War (1846–1848). But by midcentury, nationalism was weakened by a force called *sectionalism*.

The Rise of Sectionalism

By 1850, the various parts of the United States had developed different ways of life. Industries and cities had grown up mainly in the northeastern states. The South and West were primarily agricultural. Western farms tended to be small enough to be handled by a single family. Southern agriculture was dominated by landowners with large plantations that were worked by slaves.

Slavery. Many people, especially Northerners, regarded the slave system as a great evil. One small but influential group called abolitionists demanded the immediate end to slavery and the freeing of all slaves. Although few northerners became abolitionists, most believed that slavery should not spread outside the Southern states. In particular, Northerners wanted slavery to be kept out of the lands taken from Mexico in the Southwest and West as a result of the Mexican War.

Tariffs. Slavery was not the only issue that divided the North and South. The tariff policy of the United States government also caused conflict between the two sections. (A *tariff* is a tax on goods imported from other countries.) Northern businesspeople wanted to protect their growing industries from foreign competition. They demanded that Congress pass laws that created high tariffs. Southerners opposed such laws. High tariffs increased the cost of imported goods because the amount of the tariff was added to the price of the goods. Southerners traded mainly with Britain and Europe, not with businesses in the U.S. North. Cotton, tobacco, and other agricultural products were exchanged for manufactured goods.

Tensions Increase. Tension between North and South greatly increased between 1850 and 1861. Sectional differences caused many Southerners to feel more loyalty to their states and the South than to the United States as a whole. Political differences deepened between the proslavery, low-tariff Democrats and the antislavery, high-tariff Republicans.

By 1860, many Southerners felt that they had little future under a national government dominated by the more heavily populated Northern states. Southerners threatened to *secede*, or withdraw, from the United States and establish a country of their own.

The Civil War

In November 1860, Abraham Lincoln, a pro-Union, antislavery Republican, became president of the United States. The South feared that the new president would end slavery and destroy the southern economy. Within three months, six southern states seceded from the United States, which then became known as the Union. South Carolina, Mississippi, Louisiana, Florida, Alabama, and Georgia united to form the Confederate States of America. By May 1861, Texas, North Carolina, Virginia, Tennessee, and Arkansas also joined the Confederacy. Fighting between the Confederate States and the Union broke out on April 12, 1861, in South Carolina.

The Civil War, which lasted until 1865, was a terrible struggle, marked by great bloodshed and destruction. (Almost as many soldiers died as the combined number in all the wars the United States has fought.) The southern states, where most of the fighting took place, suffered the most damage. The northern victory in April 1865 forced the Southern states to rejoin the Union. It ended slavery and the prewar way of life in the South. Nationalism triumphed over sectionalism. No state would again consider secession.

INFO CHECK

1. Explain the difference between nationalism and sectionalism in 19th-century America.

2. Complete the following sentences:

   • The two great sectional issues that divided 19th-century Americans were _____ .

   • In 1860, many Southerners wished to secede from the United States because _____ .

   • The northern victory in the Civil War resulted in _____ .

NATIONALISM IN ASIA

Throughout the 19th and 20th centuries, intense conflicts arose in countries in Asia. Some were nationalistic responses to European imperialism. Others were clashes between groups that had conflicting nationalistic goals. The focus here is on India, Turkey, and Israel.

Nationalism in India

Effect of British Rule. From the 1600s to the mid-1900s, Britain ruled India. The British developed India's economy to the benefit of British industry and to a lesser extent the Indian colony. They built telegraph, railroad, and irrigation systems and created new industries. Industrial progress did not help most of the Indian people. Their living standard remained low. The British seldom treated the Indians as equals. They showed little respect for their religions or their way of life.

The British brought their governmental and legal systems to India. They made the central government more important than the governments of the individual states. Many well-to-do Indians went to colleges in England and learned British ways. They learned about civil rights and having a say in government. It seemed to those with British educations that Indians should have a right to run their own country.

Sepoy Mutiny. In 1600, the English government gave a trade monopoly in India to the East India Company. It represented English interest in India and, in many ways, acted as a government until 1858. That year marked the beginning of Indian resistance to English rule. The key event was the Sepoy Mutiny of 1857. Sepoys were Indian soldiers hired by the East India Company. British army officers commanded the sepoys. Through the years, British forces fought the French and various local princes for trading rights and territory.

In the spring of 1857, sepoys were issued new ammunition for their rifles. The cartridges were greased with a mixture of beef and pork fat. The end of each had to be bitten off before it could be inserted into the rifle. Indian soldiers refused to handle the cartridges. Hindus could not touch beef products. Muslims could not eat pork products.

A number of soldiers were jailed for not using the cartridges. In response, thousands of sepoys rebelled against British authority. They released the prisoners, killed their British officers, and headed for the city of Delhi to set up a new government. Civilians and princes joined the revolt. Regular army forces from Britain arrived in 1858 and cruelly put down the revolutionaries. Fighting lasted into 1859.

After the mutiny, the government of Great Britain took over the administration of India from the East India Company. Britain promised not to interfere with local religious practices.

Nationalist Reaction. Those who wanted to get the British out of India kept alive nationalistic feelings after the rebellion. There was no national organization until the Indian National Congress was founded in 1885, mainly by middle-class Hindu professionals and scholars. Muslims set up their own organization, the Muslim League, in 1906.

Some Indians tried to change British rule from within the government. Others actively opposed anything British. Writers criticized British practices. Calls went out to stop buying British goods. But the main demand was for self-rule by Indians.

Clashes Continue. The British gradually allowed limited Indian participation in governing India. But they did not encourage public education. They still looked down on Indians. Some Indians responded by using terrorist tactics (bombings and shootings) against officials.

Indian troops fought for the British in World War I (1914–1918). When they returned to India, many demanded more respect from British authorities. Protests against British rule became more widespread after the war. Authorities tried to contain them without resorting to violence.

This aim was not realized in 1919 in Amritsar. Protests had turned violent. A crowd of some 10,000 peaceful men, women, and children gathered in a public garden for a festival. British military authorities became nervous about its intentions and ordered soldiers to fire at the crowd. Some 400 civilians were killed and 1,200 were wounded.

Gandhi. The Amritsar Massacre stirred up strong nationalist feelings. Demands for self rule became louder. Mohandas K. Gandhi (lived 1869–1948) a lawyer, became head of the Indian National Congress. Gandhi persuaded many Indians to practice *passive* (nonviolent) *resistance* to British rule. Indians refused to buy or use British goods, serve in the armed forces, pay taxes, or obey British law. Anyone who protested British rule faced arrest. Great numbers of Indians went to jail.

In 1930, Gandhi led a massive demonstration against the tax on salt. Hundreds of his followers marched long distances to the sea to collect their own salt. They filled containers with sea water, set them in the sun, and let the water evaporate. Salt was left behind in the containers. Many were arrested and jailed for this protest.

Gandhi was revered by his followers. They called him "Mahatma," the great one. His resistance activities landed him in jail on many occasions. He also used the tactic of fasting to get his way. He would go without food for weeks until his demands were met.

Jinnah. Muhammad Ali Jinnah (lived 1876–1948) was active in the Muslim League in the 1920s and became president in 1934. He cooperated with the Indian National Congress at times. At other times, he worked with the British to get protection for Muslims from the Hindu majority. During the 1940s, Jinnah called for a separate Muslim state.

Nehru. Jawaharlal Nehru (lived 1889–1964) became a strong Hindu nationalist leader in the 1930s. He, too, was put into prison by the British for his activities.

Mahatma Gandhi (right), advocate of nonviolence, with Jawaharlal Nehru in 1946

India and Pakistan

Independence. Any attempts by the British to share power did not seem to go far enough. Full independence was the goal of the Indians. It might have happened more quickly if the Hindus and Muslims could have agreed on how to govern the country. World War II (1939–1945) also put off any plans for a British pullout.

In 1947, independence seemed near. But Jinnah, Gandhi, and Nehru could still not agree on the details of government. Bloody riots between Hindus and Muslims broke out throughout India. Finally, to prevent further bloodshed, the British and the Indians agreed to create a Muslim country out of Indian territory. It became Pakistan. The greater portion of the subcontinent became the newly independent Republic of India. Some 10 million people moved between the two new countries. Many Hindus left Pakistan, and many Muslims left India.

Nehru became the first prime minister of India under the new constitution adopted in 1948. Jinnah headed the government in Pakistan. Gandhi was assassinated in 1948 by a Hindu extremist who objected to his call for fair treatment of Muslims. This event caused worldwide outrage and plunged India into mourning.

Nationalism in the Middle East

From the 1500s until the 1920s, the Ottoman, or Turkish, Empire unified the Middle East politically. The empire covered Turkey, parts of the Balkan states, the eastern Mediterranean area, and parts of North Africa. Over the years, the central government in Constantinople (now Istanbul) grew weaker. It gradually lost the respect and loyalty of the various ethnic and national groups within the empire.

Groups calling for reform of the Ottoman government emerged in the late 1860s. A new constitution was created in 1876. The sultan (ruler) refused to abide by it and dissolved the lawmaking body by 1878.

In 1908, a group of army officers, called the Young Turks, staged a revolution. They wanted to restore the constitution of 1876. Because

The Middle East   1919–1939

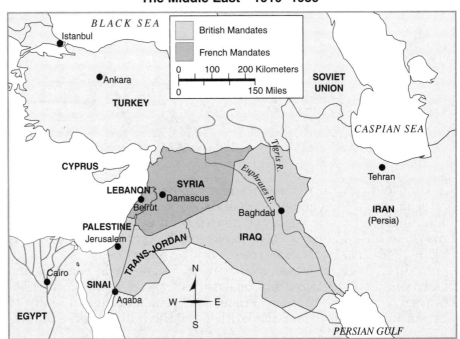

they had the support of other sections of the army, the sultan agreed to their demand.

The reformers also wanted to open the empire to Western European ideas. They promoted the development of industries. A number of nationalist groups began to call for the organization of the Turkish nation as a modern republic.

When World War I broke out in 1914, the Ottoman Empire sided with Germany. Their opponents were Britain, France, and Russia. In 1916, the British and French secretly agreed to divide up the Ottoman Empire after the war. Russia went along with the agreement, but did not sign it. The peace treaty in 1919 acknowledged the terms of the secret agreement. France gained control of Lebanon and Syria. Great Britain received Iraq, Jordan, and the Holy Land (then called Palestine, now Israel). Britain wanted to protect the routes to India and its interests in the developing petroleum industry in the Middle East. The areas controlled by France and Britain were called *mandates.*

During the war, Arabia had been encouraged by the British to revolt against the Ottomans. Fighting among tribal groups delayed the unification of Arabia until 1932. The Kingdom of Saudi Arabia under Ibn Saud came into being in that year.

The Founding of Turkey

After World War I, the victorious European countries wanted to divide Turkey among themselves. The Young Turks united under General Mustafa Kemal against the outsiders. Led by Kemal, the Young Turks successfully resisted the invasion of the Europeans and captured Constantinople. In 1923, the Turks signed a peace treaty that gave them Asia Minor and a strip of European land between the Black Sea and the Aegean Sea. Kemal became president of the new government of Turkey.

The Call for a Jewish Homeland

The strong sense of cultural identity held by the Jewish people had helped them survive centuries of persecution. From their locations around the world, they longed for a homeland where they could enjoy their culture unmolested. In the late 1800s, an Austrian Jew named Theodore Herzl became the leader of a nationalist movement called Zionism. (Zion is a biblical term for an ideal nation.) The members of this movement wanted to establish a Jewish state in Palestine. Then part of the Ottoman Empire, the area was thinly settled by Muslim Arabs.

Persecution in Russia in the late 1800s led many Russian Jews to settle in Palestine. The situation of Jews in Russia gave strength to the Zionist movement. Its supporters believed that persecuted Jews around the world had to have a safe place to live. The Zionists held their first general meeting in Switzerland in 1897.

Herzl and other leading Zionists tried to persuade European leaders to support the Jewish claim to Palestine. Finally, during World War I, Great Britain agreed to help. It issued the Balfour Declaration of 1917. The British promised to support the establishment of a Jewish national homeland in Palestine. The Arabs were insulted. How could the British give away their land to non-Muslims? In 1917, about 600,000 Arabs and 80,000 Jews lived in Palestine. Emigration of Jews to Palestine increased in the 1920s and 1930s. They tended to develop agricultural communities. The British continued to supervise the area and attempted to keep peace between the Arabs and Jewish settlers.

After the Nazis came to power in Germany in 1933, they began a systematic policy of eliminating Jews from Germany. German Jews emigrated to safer locations. A great many went to Palestine. Britain, fearful of the reaction of the Arabs, limited Jewish immigration to Palestine in 1939.

World War II broke out in 1939. During the war, Nazis killed some 6 million Jews from Germany, Poland, and other countries they controlled. After the war ended in 1945, demands for a Jewish state in Palestine intensified. Great Britain resisted and continued to limit Jewish immigration. Jews in Palestine fought against the British policies and tried to undermine British authority. Finally, Britain asked the newly organized United Nations to handle the problem. The UN, in 1947, decided to divide (partition) Palestine into a Jewish state and an Arab state. (Jerusalem was to be under international control.)

The Jewish inhabitants of Palestine accepted, but the Arabs did not. When the British pulled out in 1948, the Jewish settlers, or Zionists, declared the birth of the State of Israel. The surrounding Arab states (mainly Egypt, Syria, Lebanon, Iraq, and Jordan) attacked the new state. The Arabs refused to recognize Israel as a legal country. The aim of the Palestinian Arabs and other Arabs was to drive the Jews out of Palestine. In 1949, after a year of fighting the Arab powers, Israel survived and gained new territory. Peace did not come, however. More wars followed.

INFO CHECK

1. How did British rule benefit India?

2. Why did Indian nationalists want independence from Britain?

3. Summarize the contributions to Indian independence of each of the following individuals: Mohandas K. Gandhi, Jawaharlal Nehru, Muhammed Ali Jinnah.

4. Who were the Young Turks? What did they contribute to the formation of the modern Republic of Turkey?

5. Define Zionism. Why has it been supported by Jews but opposed by Arab nationalists? How did this difference lead to conflict in the Middle East?

Time Line

Year	Dates and Events

A.D.
1801

1830s: Mazzini founds Young Italy, secret society to unify Italy under representative government

1852: Beginning of risorgimento; Cavour tries to unite northern Italian states

1857–1859: British army puts down Sepoy Mutiny; Britain takes control of Indian government

1859: Franco-Italian war against Austria; Austrian Lombardy ceded to Piedmont

1860: Piedmont controls all of Italy but Two Sicilies, Papal States, Venetia

1861: Garibaldi's Red Shirts and Piedmont army capture Two Sicilies, Papal States; Victor Emmanuel II named king of unified Italy

1861: Southern U.S. states secede; Civil War erupts at Fort Sumter

1864: Prussia wins Schleswig and Holstein from Denmark

1866: Seven Weeks' War ends Austrian influence over Germany, gives Italy control of Venetia

1867: Bismarck's North German Confederation

1870–1871: Franco-Prussian War: Germany defeats France

1871: German Reich proclaimed; Wilhelm I, Prussia, as emperor; Bismarck as prime minister

1871: Treaty of Frankfurt gives Alsace-Lorraine to Germany

1897: First Zionist congress organized by Herzl, meets in Switzerland

1906: Muslim League organized; political rival of Indian National Congress

1908: Young Turks win sultan's recognition of 1876 constitution

1917: Balfour Declaration

1919: Treaty of Versailles gives Ottoman lands to France (Lebanon, Syria), Britain (Iraq, Jordan)

1900
1901

1921: New Irish Free State in Roman Catholic Southern Ireland; Ulster remains united with Britain

1923: Kemal becomes president of Turkey

1932: Arabian tribes unite as Saudi Arabia under Ibn Saud

1939–1945: World War II and Holocaust intensify Jewish demand for Palestinian homeland

1947: UN divides Palestine into Jewish and Arab sectors

1947: India becomes independent; creation of Muslim Pakistan

1948: Jews declare State of Israel, initiating years of war with Egypt, Syria, Lebanon, Iraq, Jordan

1949: Irish Free State becomes Republic of Ireland

1964: Organization of PLO by displaced Palestinian Arabs

1967: Israel wins war with Arabs, occupies Sinai, Golan Heights, West Bank

1978: Camp David Accords; Israel evacuates Sinai, Egypt recognizes Israel

1990s: PLO and Arafat renounce terrorism, recognize Israel, continue talks about independent Palestine

1991–1992: Yugoslavian break-up; Croatia, Slovenia, Bosnia-Herzegovina, Macedonia declare independence; Serbian objections lead to civil war and "ethnic cleansing" of Bosnian Muslims

1995: Dayton Accords; cease-fire in Bosnia

1998: Peace agreement calls for Northern Ireland assembly, future vote on union

1998–1999: War in Yugoslavia's Kosovo province; peace plan ousts Serbs, restores some self-rule to Kosovars

2000

THE ROLE OF NATIONALISM IN CONTEMPORARY STRUGGLES

As the world's population grows, political boundaries shift and governments change. Different groups contend with one another for land and leadership. The members of these groups often band together in nationalist movements. In some cases, dictators use nationalism to provoke conflicts among ethnic groups. In others, patriots form nationalist organizations to resist outside interference in the governing of their country. In still other cases, people who live in different countries but share a cultural identity unite against other cultural groups.

The Bosnian War

In 1990, as Communist control of Eastern Europe collapsed, Yugoslavia's parliament set about creating a multiparty system.

Yugoslavia was a union of six republics occupying part of the Balkan Peninsula. Yugoslavia had a population of mostly Eastern Orthodox Christians, with a large Muslim minority.

In 1991, Croatia and Slovenia declared independence. Serbia, largest of the republics, objected, and its leaders revived old hostilities between groups in the region. Fighting among Serbs, Croats, and other ethnic groups exploded into civil war. In 1992, Bosnia-Herzegovina and Macedonia also declared independence. Yugoslavia now consisted of only Serbia and Montenegro.

Croats and Serbs fought each other. Both groups inflicted damage on Bosnia's Muslims. To wipe out the Muslims, the Serbs adopted a policy of *ethnic cleansing*—of forcibly expelling a population from their homeland because of their religion and national origin. The UN failed to make peace. But as 1994 ended, the Croats agreed to stop fighting. Some NATO bombings of Bonsnian Serb positions began to turn the tide. In November 1995, leaders of Croatia, Bosnia, and Yugoslavia, on behalf of the Bosnian Serbs, signed a peace agreement after talks in Dayton, Ohio. U.S. and European troops worked with UN peacekeepers to maintain the shaky cease-fire.

Kosovo

Meanwhile, the violence spread to Yugoslavia's Kosovo province. There, the vast majority of inhabitants, ethnic Albanians of the Muslim faith—Kosovars—were under the political control of the Serb Orthodox Catholic minority. The Kosovars' demand for self-rule within Yugoslavia provoked a Serbian military crackdown. The Kosovars retaliated with a demand for full independence and backed it up with *guerrilla warfare* (suprise raids by small bands of fighters).

In 1999, the Serbs refused to comply with a peace plan worked out by NATO countries along with Russia. NATO forces initiated a series of bombings. The Serbs, in turn, began a campaign against the Kosovars, most of whom fled to Albania and elsewhere. Accelerated bombing attacks eventually forced the Serbs from the region. Gradually, many Kosovar refugees returned to their ruined province, hoping to eventually gain full independence.

The Crisis in Northern Ireland

In 1921, southern Ireland became a self-governing country with close ties to Great Britain. It was called the Irish Free State. In 1949, it declared itself an independent state, the Republic of Ireland. The population is mainly Roman Catholic. Northern Ireland, in which Protestants make up the majority, chose to retain its close relationship with Great Britain. (Another name for Northern Ireland is Ulster.) Most Protestants of Northern Ireland are descended from Scottish and English people who settled there in the 1600s. These people do not share the nationalist feelings that led the people of southern Ireland to free themselves from Britain.

Catholics are a large minority in Northern Ireland. Many of them have strong ties to the people in the Republic of Ireland. They never accepted the separation of Northern Ireland from southern Ireland. Protestants own most of the industries in Northern Ireland and outnumber Catholics in the legislature. They, therefore, have great control over Northern Ireland's government policy. Catholics complain of being second-class citizens in their own country.

Catholics in Northern Ireland began to hold civil rights demonstrations in 1969 to call attention to the discrimination they felt. The demonstrators were physically attacked by Protestants. Britain sent troops to restore order. The Irish Republican Army (IRA), based in southern Ireland, used violence against the British in the fight for independence. The IRA, feeling that the British troops favored the Protestants, demanded that Britain allow Northern Ireland to join the Republic of Ireland.

The Ulster Defense Association (UDA), a Protestant group, terrorized Catholics with bombings and killings. The IRA bombed sites in London and other cities in England. Hostility between the Protestants and Catholics intensified over time.

In April 1998, the British and Irish governments and all the political parties in Northern Ireland signed the Good Friday Peace Accord. It gave authority for governing the province to an elected assembly and created a North-South Council and a British-Irish Intergovernmental Council. Majority votes in Ireland and Ulster were to decide whether Ulster would become part of the Republic of Ireland or remain part of Britain. Unfortunately, the issue of the IRA's sur-

GERRY ADAMS—IRISH NATIONALIST

For the British province of Northern Ireland (Ulster), the Multiparty Agreement of 1998 offered an opportunity to end peacefully a long-standing dispute. The often violent dispute is between those who desire separation from Britain (Nationalists) and those who prefer to remain part of the United Kingdom (Loyalists). A key figure in the negotiations that led to the agreement was Gerry Adams. He is the president of Sinn Fein, the political wing of the Irish Republican Army. Many have regarded the IRA as a terrorist organization. Although Adams has denied involvement of Sinn Fein, or himself, in violence, Ulster Loyalists regard him as a terrorist. Others have hailed him as a statesman.

The oldest of ten children, Gerry Adams was born in the working-class area of West Belfast in Northern Ireland. After finishing school in the 1960s, he became involved in the Ulster civil rights movement. It worked to end discrimination against the Catholics of Northern Ireland in the areas of voting rights, housing, employment, and education. Demonstrations for these rights often turned violent.

Starting in 1971, those arrested for suspected involvement in the violence were imprisoned without trial. Gerry Adams was one of those arrested. Following his release, Adams participated in peace talks. These resulted in a truce, which later broke down. As violence continued, Adams was again arrested and detained without trial from 1973 to 1977.

Adams and his family have suffered from the bloodshed in Northern Ireland. His brother-in-law was killed and his brother was shot. Several family members have been imprisoned. His wife and son narrowly escaped injury in a bomb attack on their home. Adams himself was nearly killed in a murder attempt.

In 1983, Adams was elected president of Sinn Fein and a member of Parliament from West Belfast. In London, he was not permitted to take his seat in Parliament when he refused to take the compulsory oath of allegiance to Queen Elizabeth II. Instead, he continued to campaign for the rights of Irish nationalists in Ulster.

In September 1993, Adams worked with the leader of the Socialist Democratic Labor Party to revive the peace process. As the British government began to respond favorably, the Irish Republican Army was persuaded to support the peace effort by announcing a complete halt to its military operations in August 1994. Six weeks later, a similar announcement was made by the Loyalist paramilitary organizations.

Adams was involved in discussions on the future of Ulster with the government of the Irish Republic and with most of the Irish political parties. He was a member of the Sinn Fein delegation to the Forum for Peace and Reconciliation. Adams regained his seat in the British Parliament in 1997 and was elected to the newly created Northern Ireland Assembly in June 1998.

Adams has written several books. Among them are *A Pathway to Peace* and *Cage Eleven*, stories related to prison experiences, and *Before the Dawn*, an autobiography. Adams is also a fluent speaker of Gaelic, the ancient Irish language.

- Respond to those who describe Gerry Adams as a terrorist and one of those responsible for the long history of violence in Northern Ireland by giving your own analysis of the situation and Adams's role.

render of weapons (called "decommissioning") stalled the peace process. Although a compromise allowed the Northern Irish government to take office in November 1999, decommissioning continued to delay the achievement of the Good Friday Accord in the spring of 2000.

Palestinians on the West Bank and Gaza

Although, in 1949, the Jews and Arabs signed an armistice, they did not agree on the boundaries of Israel. Israel claimed most of Palestine. The West Bank was to be joined to Jordan to form a Palestinian state. (This never happened, which angered the Palestinians and caused even greater hatred of Israel.) The city of Jerusalem was split between the Israelis and the Palestinians.

Arab nationalism increased in Palestine and surrounding countries. Displaced Palestinian Arabs sought refuge in Jordan, Syria, Lebanon, and parts of Egypt. These refugees formed the Palestine Liberation Organization (the PLO) in 1964. The PLO engaged in acts of terrorism against Israel and countries such as the United States that sympathize with Israel. The PLO and the Arab leaders of the countries that border Israel launched four more wars against Israel. After winning the 1967 war, Israel occupied the Sinai Peninsula, the Golan Heights, and the West Bank.

After 1977, the Egyptian president, Anwar Sadat, visited Israel in order to ease tensions. President Jimmy Carter hosted peace talks between Sadat and Israeli leader Menachem Begin, in 1978. These

President Clinton fostering a diplomatic breakthrough between Yitzhak Rabin (left) and Yasir Arafat in Washington, D.C., 1993

resulted in the Camp David Accords. Israel left the Sinai Peninsula in 1983 and Egypt recognized Israel's right to exist.

In 1993, Israeli leader Yitzhak Rabin promised to return Gaza and the West Bank to the Palestinians. Under the leadership of Yasir Arafat, the Palestinians assumed more control over their own affairs. The PLO renounced terrorism and recognized Israel's right to exist.

In November 1995, a Jewish extremist assassinated Rabin. The next prime minister, Benjamin Netanyahu, determined to slow the peace process and resumed construction of Israeli settlements on the West Bank.

Netanyahu also delayed implementing the agreement which he had negotiated with Arafat in 1998. In 1999, a Labor Party leader, Ehud Barak, replaced him as prime minister and revived the peace efforts with the Palestinians.

Other movements besides nationalism shaped world history during the 19th and 20th centuries. Combined with nationalism, imperialism led the Western nations to expand into Africa and various regions in Asia. Chapter 23 explains how revolutions in agriculture and industry brought great wealth and power to the West. Chapter 24 describes how several Western nations won and lost great empires.

INFO CHECK

1. Identify the nationalist and ethnic groups that clashed in the Bosnian war of 1991–1995.

2. What issues have divided Catholics and Protestants in Northern Ireland? How did nationalism influence both groups?

3. How has nationalism divided Israelis and Palestinians in the 1990s?

CHAPTER REVIEW

Multiple Choice

1. The first attempt to unify the 38 German states failed because the

    1. Frankfurt Assembly voted to form a confederation of 38 German states

    2. Prussian king refused to accept power from the liberals and revolutionaries of the Frankfurt Assembly

    3. rulers of the 38 German states refused to give up their powers

    4. German people felt loyalty to their local princes and did not want to unify into one nation.

2. The individual and the policy that succeeded in unifying Germany were

    1. Frederick William IV of Prussia and his policy of "Divine Right"

    2. Emperor Napoleon III of France and his rebuilt Third Empire

    3. Otto von Bismarck and his policy of "blood and iron"

4. Garibaldi and his "Red Shirt" policy.

3. As a result of the Franco-Prussian War, Bismarck achieved his goal to
   1. conquer all of France
   2. defeat Spain
   3. capture the British fleet
   4. unify all the German states under Prussian leadership.

4. Austria and the pope both opposed the unification of Italy. This was because
   1. they both controlled lands that were part of the Italian peninsula
   2. the pope supported Prussia
   3. the leaders of the Italian unification movement were against the Catholic Church
   4. Austria refused to give up its claim to the city of Rome.

5. Both the Indian National Congress and the Muslim League wanted to end British rule of India. The policy and practice that was adopted by many Indians to accomplish this goal was
   1. boycott of British products
   2. urban terrorism
   3. nonviolent, passive resistance
   4. all of the above.

6. Which did most to cause the collapse of the Ottoman Empire?
   1. birth of the State of Israel
   2. formation of the Arab League
   3. formation of Palestine under joint Arab and Jewish leadership
   4. revolt of the "Young Turks" under Kemal's leadership

7. The number of Jewish immigrants to Palestine in the late 1920s increased because
   1. the government promised new

settlers 40 acres of land and a mule for plowing
2. anti-Semitism in Europe was increasing
3. the British government needed settlers in the colony
4. the discovery of oil brought immigrants seeking employment.

8. Northern Ireland, Bosnia, the West Bank, and Gaza have all been
   1. newly independent developing nations
   2. areas of United Nations peacekeeping efforts
   3. World Bank economic development zones
   4. sites of nationalistic conflicts.

9. Theodore Herzl and Mustafa Kemal were nationalistic leaders whose efforts resulted in the
   1. Seven Years' War
   2. founding of the states of Israel and Turkey
   3. founding of the states of Iran and Bangladesh
   4. Declaration of International Human Rights.

10. What was the reaction to the 1947 decision by the UN about Palestine?
    1. The British refused to enforce it.
    2. The Jewish inhabitants accepted it and the Arabs did not.
    3. The Arab inhabitants accepted it and the Jews did not.
    4. The neighboring Arab states offered to enforce it.

11. A comparison of the maps on pages 473 and 476 shows that
    1. both Germany and Italy had strong traditions of unity
    2. German and Italian unification were both accomplished by the early 1870s

3. the Germans and Italians were once divided into a variety of states or kingdoms
4. both statements 2 and 3 are accurate.

12. The photograph on page 482 shows that two leaders appealed to Indian nationalism by promoting

1. equality for untouchables
2. voting rights for women
3. traditional Indian culture and values
4. separation of India into Muslim and Hindu states.

Thematic Essays

1. "Blood and iron," "passive resistance," "Young Turks," "IRA," "Zionism," and "PLO" all represent a policy or group related to nationalism. *Task:* Select *two*, each from a different region of the world, and compare and contrast their policies and the results they achieved.

2. Peoples, nations, and empires can be united or torn apart by the forces of nationalism. *Task:* Using historical examples, describe *one* situation that resulted in unification and *one* that ended in division.

Document-Based Questions

1. Study the photos on pages 474 and 482. Explain the similarities and dif-ferences in the practices of these leaders.

2. From "The Oath of Young Italy":

"By the blush that rises to my brow when I stand before the citizens of other lands; to know that I have no rights of citizenship, no country, no flag. . . . By the memory of our former greatness. . . . Convinced that God has ordained that a nation shall be. . . . "

How did this oath appeal to Italians' pride and sense of nationalism?

3. From a speech by Otto von Bismarck:

"The great questions of the time will not be decided by speeches and reso-lutions of majorities—that was the mistake of 1848 and 1849—but by iron and blood."

Describe Bismarck's attitude toward the German parliament and its liberal democratic practices.

4. Study the photo on page 491. Explain the importance for the Middle East of the handshake between these men.

Document-Based Essay

Task: Using historical examples from the 19th and 20th centuries, answer the fol-lowing question: Can nationalism be a force for peace?

C H A P T E R

23

Economic and Social Revolutions

Maggie's head ached and her throat felt scratchy. It was 10:00 P.M. She should have gone straight home from work and gone to bed. If she felt sick tomorrow, she would slow down, and they would cut her pay. Then what would she do for rent money?

She looked around the crowded hall. Perhaps it was the hot, stuffy air that made her feel so bad. Why had she promised her friend Lewis to come to this lecture anyway? She was so drowsy, she could barely take in what the speaker, Mr. Harris, was saying. Only a few words and phrases penetrated through the thick atmosphere of the hall— Socialism. Workers' rights. Strike. "Oh yes, strike," she thought, "and get beaten for my pains and lose the money I need to eat and pay my rent."

Maggie began to cough. Pains cramped her chest. What if she couldn't leave her bed tomorrow? She wouldn't lose just pay. She'd lose her job. Well, why not strike then? Better to fight on the picket line than slowly starve to death in the streets. Maggie straightened her back and began to listen to the man's speech. Lewis was right, she decided. Mr. Harris did want to help. She looked around at all the pale, strained faces turned toward the speaker. Could such exhausted people really stand up against their sleek, well-fed bosses?

aggie represents many of the young factory workers living in British manufacturing towns during the mid-1800s. A century or so earlier, she would probably have been part of a farming household. Her father might even have owned a small amount of land. As a farm girl, Maggie would have done her share of the chores—spun thread, milked the cow, minded her younger sisters and brothers. The work might have been hard, but she would have been with her family. They would have cared for her when she became ill and made sure that she had food and shelter.

As one of many factory workers, however, Maggie is no longer a member of a close community. To the owner of the factory where she works, she is just another machine that helps him make money.

The change in the lives of workers such as Maggie was partly caused by a rise in the number of people who needed work. It was also caused by a change in the methods of manufacturing. The shift from producing goods by hand in the home to manufacturing them by machine is known as the *Industrial Revolution*. The Industrial Revolution affected poor workers and spurred them to join together to improve their situation. Their struggle inspired new ideas about society and brought about political and social reforms.

THE AGRARIAN REVOLUTION

New approaches to agriculture began to be practiced by landowners in such Western European countries as the Netherlands, England, and France. By the early 1700s, landowners needed to find ways to increase the production of food for Europe's expanding population. Western European inventors designed machines that increased the productivity of land and reduced the number of people needed to work on it. This meant that many laborers had to find other work.

Enclosure System

One new approach to agriculture, the *enclosure system*, brought about some of the earliest and most drastic changes. It was first widely practiced in the Netherlands during the 1600s. When English and French farmers heard about the benefits of the system, they too adopted it.

Open-Field System. Under the previous system, called the open-field system, landowners allowed small farmers to plant crops in a part of the owners' fields. The small farmers grew a variety of crops on the strips of land set aside for them. The landlords also let the local farmers graze their livestock in meadows and other pieces of land that were not good for cultivation. Such communal, or jointly used, pastures were called "commons."

Specializing. As Europe's trade expanded, the number of people in European cities increased. The open-field system did not produce enough food to feed them. It did not supply the surplus of goods necessary to meet the demands of the world market. Landowners realized that they could make more money if they grew produce and raw materials for city and foreign markets. Small farmers could no longer use the large landowners' land. Fields were enclosed, or fenced off, and planted with crops that could be sold for large profits. The Dutch, for example, planted flax (the plant from which linen is made), which they sold to cloth manufacturers. Where flax was grown, food could no longer be planted.

Crop Rotation. Once farming became a business, landowners began to look for ways to increase their profits. To do so, they needed to make the available land more productive. Under the old open-field system, small farmers had at least three fields on which to grow crops. They planted two of the fields each year and rested the third (kept it fallow) in order to restore its fertility.

In the 1730s, Charles Townshend, an English nobleman, presented a new idea. He argued that none of the fields had to be kept fallow. They could be planted with turnips and clover. These plants return to the soil the nutrients that wheat and barley take from it. The turnips and clover could then be used for animal feed during the winter. Instead of killing many of their lambs and calves in the autumn, farmers could keep them to provide milk and wool year round.

Landowners who used the enclosure system no longer grew a variety of crops to meet the needs of their workers. They could, therefore, respond more easily to changes in the market. They were able to plant all their fields with grain when prices for grain were high or use their fields as pastures when animal products brought better prices.

Inventions

Landowners seeking greater profits from their land were eager to try new techniques and machinery. In 1701, Jethro Tull, an English farmer, invented the seed drill. This machine planted seeds in rows. Before its use became common, farmers had scattered seeds by hand across their fields. By using Tull's machine, a farmer could save seeds and produce more crops while using the same amount of land. Tull also invented the horse-drawn hoe to break up the soil between the rows of plants.

In the mid-1800s, new inventions speeded up the harvesting of grain. The reaper, invented by Cyrus McCormick, an American, was one of the most important of the laborsaving devices. The reaper was pulled through a field of grain by horses. In one operation, it cut the grain stalks and separated the heads with seeds from the stalks. With the new machines, fewer workers could now take care of larger farms and produce more grain.

Effect on Small Farmers. While the enclosure system and new machines were profitable for landowners, they were a misfortune for the small farmers. This group of farmers often could not make a living on the land left to them. Most had to move to towns and cities to find work. They, thus, were available to work in the factories that were being built.

1. Describe the changes brought to European farming by the Agrarian Revolution of the 18th century. Why do you think these changes occurred in the nations of Western Europe?

2. If you were a small farmer in Western Europe, in the 18th century, why might you object to the enclosure system?

THE INDUSTRIAL REVOLUTION

The Industrial Revolution began in Great Britain. That country contained just the right mix of raw materials, laborers, and people with money to make the development of the factory system possible. The advances in agriculture made it possible to grow more food to feed the factory workers.

Great Britain had a government that supported business and commercial interests. Many members of Parliament were involved in business. Britain also had colonies to supply raw materials and markets. British capitalists invested in new practical inventions for speeding up production in factories and mines.

Great Britain had long been a center for the weaving of wool cloth. Until the 17th century, weavers in India supplied most of Europe's cotton cloth. When Britain acquired India as a colony in the 1700s, it took over the cotton textile industry.

Inventions

As the production of cloth became more important to Britain's economy, manufacturers began to look for machines that would speed up the process of weaving.

Flying Shuttle. In 1733, John Kay invented the flying shuttle. The shuttle made it possible for one person, instead of two, to operate a weaving loom. More cloth could be woven in less time. This caused a demand for more thread.

Spinning Jenny and Power Loom. In 1764, James Hargreaves invented the spinning jenny. This machine spun thread eight times faster than the old spinning wheel. A water-powered spinning machine was created in 1769. By that time, looms could not weave fast enough to use all of the available thread. Then, in 1784, Edmund Cartwright invented a more effective power loom. All of these developments created a demand for more and more raw cotton.

Cotton Gin. The major supplier of raw cotton for Britain's weavers was the United States. After the invention of the cotton gin by Eli Whitney in 1793, cotton became the leading export of the Southern states. The gin made it possible to separate the seeds from cotton fibers much faster than the process could be done by hand. As more fields were planted in cotton, more workers were needed. Southern plantation owners imported more slaves to fill the need.

Home to Factory

Before the new machines were invented, people had done weaving and other forms of manufacturing at home. Home-based manufacturing was called the *domestic*, or cottage, *system*. With advances in technology, weaving looms and other manufacturing machines became too large to fit in houses. They were also too expensive for the average weaver to own. Therefore, factories were built. Weavers came to work in factories that housed many looms.

Power Sources. At first, factories were built beside fast-running rivers or waterfalls. The movement of the water powered the machines. After James Watt of Scotland improved the steam engine in the late 1700s, power came from burning coal. The coal heated water to produce steam. Steam drove the engine. The steam engine made it possible for factories to be located anywhere. Usually, they were built near towns close to supplies of coal. Coal mining became an important industry in Britain.

Use of Iron. Ironmaking also developed rapidly. Iron parts replaced wooden parts in machines. New processes were invented to

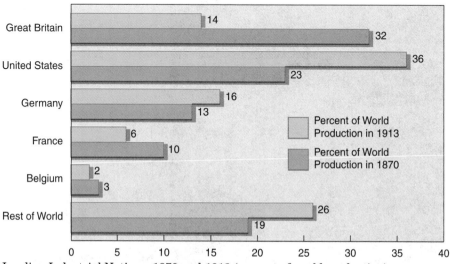

Leading Industrial Nations, 1870 and 1913 (percent of world production)

produce better quality iron for tools, machines, bridges, and other structures.

Industrialization and Wealth. Invention followed invention in rapid succession. More and more products were made in factories. By the mid-1800s, Britain had become an industrialized nation. By the late 1800s, France, Germany, and the United States had also become industrialized.

Machines produced goods more rapidly and cheaply and in greater quantities than they could be produced by hand. Because more people received a steady income, they could afford to buy more things. Increased sales made factory owners wealthy. As methods of transportation improved, markets for goods opened up around the world. Traders and shippers became wealthy. The new wealth was used to build more factories, create more goods, and open up more markets.

The Factory System

Men, women, and children—some as young as five—worked in factories. They generally worked during daylight hours, six days a week. They had only a short time off for lunch during the day. There were no safety devices on the machines to keep the workers from getting hurt.

When workers did not work, their employers did not pay them.

Nineteenth-century mill workers in Lancashire, England

There were no government agencies that helped during times of unemployment. Wages were low.

As more factories were built in an area, more workers came to live near the factories. Towns quickly grew into cities.

Interchangeable Parts. To turn out products that contained many parts faster, manufacturers decided that the same parts should all be alike. Eli Whitney introduced the idea of standardized, or interchangeable, parts in 1800. Before this, weapons and tools were made by hand. The size and shapes of the parts could not be standardized. When the trigger of a gun, for example, wore out another trigger had to be made to fit that particular gun. Whitney invented a device that made all triggers and other such parts the same size and shape. Such interchangeable parts made repairing broken weapons and tools cheaper and faster.

Mass Production. Machine-made parts gave rise to the *mass-production* system. When a group of workers used this system to make a wagon, for example, each worker made only one part of it. To put the wagon together, other workers each took a particular part and put it in place. Because the workers repeated a few simple tasks over and over again, they became very fast. By using the mass-production system, a factory could turn out great quantities of an item in a very short time. The items were inexpensive to produce and could be sold at a low price.

In the 20th century, the automobile industry altered the mass-production system through the introduction of the *assembly line*. Workers stood alongside a wide, moving belt. The belt carried the product to each worker in turn. Each worker put a standardized part on the car being assembled. At the end of the line, a completed car rolled out of the factory. Henry Ford introduced the assembly line in the United States.

Economic Theory

In the 17th and 18th centuries, economists began to criticize mercantilism. Mercantilism was the system under which a country's government strictly regulated its economy.

Adam Smith. In 1776, Adam Smith, a major economist of the Enlightenment, published a book entitled *Inquiry Into the Nature and Causes of the Wealth of Nations*. Instead of regulating economic activity, Smith believed that a country's government should allow its businesspeople to compete freely with one another. He pointed out that business is affected by two natural laws: the law of supply and demand and the law of competition.

Supply and Demand. Smith's theory can be summarized as follows: Supply and demand regulate prices. Demand for a product rises when it is very popular. If the supply is low, people may be willing to pay a high price for a popular item. Manufacturers who make the product decide that they can make large profits if they produce more of it. Once the supply of the product increases, however, the price for it drops. The manufacturers then compete for customers by lowering their prices even more or improving the product. Manufacturers who are unable to compete lose profits and may have to close down. When fewer manufacturers are making the product, the price for it again increases.

Laissez-faire. Smith felt that markets regulate themselves through competition. Competition motivates people to work more efficiently and make better products. If freely competitive private enterprise is encouraged, more people will have a chance to make more money. Consumers (buyers) would get better goods at the lowest possible prices. This economic theory promoting unregulated competition became known as the doctrine of *laissez-faire.* (*Laissez-faire* is a French phrase that means "leave it alone.")

Smith also warned that businesspeople try to limit competition in a market. An individual business may try to create a monopoly, or be the only one to manufacture a particular product. If this happens, Smith believed that that government should step in and restore competition to the market.

The doctrine of laissez-faire was popular with the businesspeople of the Industrial Revolution. The owners of factories felt that the government had no right to interfere with the way they ran their businesses. They believed that the government should allow them to do whatever they needed to do to compete with other manufacturers.

Social Changes

As manufacturers and other businesspeople became wealthier and more influential, they changed the character of the middle class.

Power. Their wealth and their control over their countries' economies gave the middle class more political power. The new businesspeople (entrepreneurs) also brought diversity to the middle class. Formerly, most upper-middle-class people had been well-educated professionals or owners of long-established businesses. Many of the new industrialists had started out as skilled workers. Others, such as Quakers and Jews, were members of groups that had long been discriminated against.

Attitudes and Values. The new members of the middle class developed their own set of attitudes and values. Although some imitated the tastes and adopted the pastimes of the aristocracy, most knew they owed their success to hard work and thrift. Although they lived lives of solid comfort, they remained disciplined and careful in their habits. They disapproved of both the aristocracy and the poor because they believed that neither group worked hard enough.

White-Collar Workers. Before the Industrial Revolution, the lower middle class had consisted largely of shopkeepers and school teachers. A small number of people worked as clerks for merchants and lawyers. With the growth of industry, more jobs became available for people who could read, write, and do arithmetic. This need gave rise to a rapid increase in *white-collar workers*—traveling salesmen, bookkeepers, store managers, and office clerks. The term comes from the white shirts they wore to the office. These people owned no property and were paid only a little more than factory and mine workers. They did not do physical work, however, and took pride in their skills. They also felt that they had a good chance of getting richer. The demand for this group of workers contributed to the increase in literacy that took place during the Industrial Revolution.

Laborers. The quality of life changed drastically for laborers. Before the Industrial Revolution, most people who worked with their hands and used physical strength to perform their tasks had been tenant farmers and peasants. Some were carpenters, blacksmiths, bricklayers, or stone masons. Under the agricultural-based system, they lived in small communities where they could rely on the help of neighbors and the local landowner. As factory workers in cities, they were on their own. Rents and food prices were high compared to wages. Their neighbors were usually as poor as themselves.

Factory workers and other laborers are often called *blue-collar workers*. The term comes from the color of the shirts they often wore. Laborers tended to wear colored, rather than white, shirts.

Education. Factory laborers had to work long hours to make enough money just to survive. They had no time for educating themselves or their children. Consequently, they were unable to improve their position in society. Their children had to contribute to the upkeep of the family, and so they too seldom learned to read and write. Children were usually sent off as early as possible to work in factories at wages even lower than their parents'. As factory owners controlled more and more of their lives, members of the working class became increasingly powerless.

Changing Household Roles. In farm households, both husbands and wives had shared the economic responsibility for the family. Each sex usually did different jobs. Women and girls tended to do the milking and spinning. Men and boys did the plowing and weaving. In spite of these differences, men and women were equally important as family providers. Once people started working in factories, men became the primary wage earners. They were given the better paid, more highly skilled work. Women were expected to do the more routine, poorly paid tasks. Even when they did the same jobs, women earned less than men. Married women generally took care of the homes, where they supplemented the family income by doing craftwork.

Married women accepted this new status for several reasons. Before such conveniences as running water, refrigerators, and washing machines became common, housework took the entire day. The rigid routine of the factory did not allow women the time to care for infants and toddlers. Since the wife's confinement to the home made the husband's wage the sole source of income, married women did not challenge the practice of giving the better jobs to men.

Often the man's paycheck was not enough to support the family. As many members of the family as possible had to work to meet their needs. Even children spent all day operating dangerous machines. In coal mines, they dragged carts filled with coal through dark, narrow tunnels. Many grew up stunted and sickly. Illiteracy prevented them from improving their lives.

Factory Towns. In spite of long hours, unhealthy conditions, and low wages, people flocked to the factories to get the only work available. As factories were built near sources of power and raw materials, cities formed around them. The populations of these and already existing cities increased so rapidly that proper housing could not be built for newcomers. The poorly paid factory workers were forced into cheap housing. Whole families lived in one or two tiny rooms. Slums developed in these neighborhoods. Apartment buildings, or tenements, were badly built, poorly ventilated, and damp. Open sewers bordered the streets of the slums, and factory smoke polluted the city's air. Epidemics of cholera, typhoid, and tuberculosis broke out, increasing the already high death rate among slum dwellers.

Improvements in Transportation and Communication

As manufacturing and mining centers grew up, better means of transportation and communication were developed. Raw materials needed to be taken to the factories. Products needed to be moved to the markets where they could be sold. The new steam power provided factories with energy to run the machines. Inventors also used the steam engine to run vehicles.

Steamships. Robert Fulton, an American, applied the principle of steam power to boats. In 1807, he ran his steamboat, the *Clermont*, up the Hudson River from New York to Albany. It took 32 hours instead of the 96 required by sailboats. Industrialists could now speed up the transportation of raw materials to their factories and the finished goods to markets.

By the mid-1800s, oceangoing steamships began to replace sailing ships. Steamships used coal to produce the steam needed to power the engines that moved the ships. On long voyages, the ships needed to stop periodically to take on more coal. Ship companies looked to find locations that could serve as coaling stations. This need spurred the new drive for colonies.

Railroads. In 1814, George Stephenson of England demonstrated the first successful steam-powered railroad locomotive. In 1825, he opened the first public railroad. The tracks covered a distance of 20 miles. Soon railroad tracks crisscrossed Europe and the

AUTOMOBILES: THE WORLD ON WHEELS

Few inventions have revolutionized the ways people live and work as the automobile has. Its development is one of the great technological achievements of human history.

The first successful, self-propelled road vehicle was a steam automobile demonstrated in 1769 by Nicholas-Joseph Cugnot, a French engineer. It had no room for passengers and was never put into mass production. The first automobile to carry passengers was built by the British inventor Richard Trevithick in 1801–1803. His power unit was the first to have a piston moved by steam. However, further development of the automobile depended on the invention of the internal combustion engine.

The first practical internal combustion engine was patented by Etienne Lenoir in 1860. But it was the high-speed motor of German engineer Gottlieb Daimler that gave birth to the automobile industry. His four-cycle, four-cylinder motor, patented in 1887, achieved speeds many times greater than those of any previous engine. Another German engineer, Karl Benz, also pioneered the gasoline-powered engine. Eventually, Daimler and Benz combined their efforts.

In the United States, Henry Ford acted to meet the growing demand for automobiles. He greatly speeded up production in 1913 by introducing a moving assembly line. American inventions such as the electric self-starter in 1912 and balloon tires in 1921 made the automobile easier to operate and more comfortable to ride in.

The greater efficiencies of the mass-production process made it possible for Ford to reduce the price of the Model T Ford auto. In 1909, it sold for $950, in 1916, for $360, and in 1926, for $290. In the late 1920s, Ford produced about half of the automobiles made in the world. Great Britain, France, and Germany were also automobile manufacturing centers. Japan did not become a major center until the 1950s.

The automobile has changed the look of both urban and rural areas. Highways and narrower roads crisscross the countryside. Cities have to plan for traffic flow and parking. Automobiles give a feeling of independence. People can travel almost anywhere with speed and comfort in an automobile. Without the automobile it is likely that suburbs, motels, and shopping malls would not exist. The petroleum industry has grown into a major economic force largely because gasoline is the power source of automobiles. The technology of the internal combustion engine also made possible tractors, buses, and trucks.

As automobiles became more widely used, problems arose. One is air pollution caused by substances released into the air by the burning of gasoline in automobile engines. A second is traffic congestion. A third is accidents, injuries, and loss of life.

1. Explain why development of the automobile was a global effort rather than the achievement of any single nation.

2. Describe the global impact and significance of the automobile.

United States. Trains proved to be an efficient way to move heavy materials and large numbers of people long distances. Railroads quickly became major businesses. In wartime, troops and equipment could be moved quickly from one area of fighting to another.

Automobiles. About 1885, Karl Benz of Germany created the first automobile powered by an internal-combustion engine. The same year, Gottlieb Daimler, also of Germany, introduced a gasoline-powered engine. It was eventually used to run automobiles.

Airplanes. In 1903, two Americans, Orville and Wilbur Wright, made the first successful flight in a heavier-than-air plane. Charles Lindbergh's 1927 solo, nonstop flight from New York to Paris altered ideas about distance. In one sense, the airplane brought the countries of the world closer together.

Telegraph. Technology also improved the ability of people to communicate rapidly over long distances. In the 1830s, Charles Wheatstone and William Cooke of Britain and Samuel F. B. Morse of the United States developed the telegraph. The telegraph is a machine that sends messages in the form of sound codes over electrical wires. In 1866, U.S. businessman Cyrus Field linked North America and Europe through a transatlantic cable.

Telephone. Alexander Graham Bell of Canada and the United States successfully developed a telephone in 1876. Using this device, businesspeople could conduct their affairs more quickly over longer distances. Private individuals could stay in touch with friends and loved ones in faraway places.

Radio. The wireless telegraph, invented by Italian scientist Guglielmo Marconi in 1895, further speeded up communications. He sent a message by radio waves across the Atlantic in 1901.

Between 1904 and 1912, John Fleming of Britain and Lee De Forest of the United States developed the radio. Radio broadcasts were first offered on a regular basis in 1920. The use of the radio quickly spread everywhere.

Television. Vladimir Zworykin, a Russian-born American, gave another important communication device to the world. In 1923, he invented tubes for broadcasting and receiving pictures through radio waves. Six years later, he demonstrated the first practical television system. But television would not be readily available to the average person until the 1950s.

Changes in Power Sources

During the 19th century, people found other sources of power besides steam. In the early 1800s, natural gas began to be used to provide factories with light and heat. Much later it was piped into homes. After 1859, petroleum, or oil, became an important source of power and fuel. In that year, Edwin Drake drilled the first oil well. He tapped into sources in western Pennsylvania.

In the late 1790s, Alessandro Volta, an Italian, created the first electric battery. The first electric generator was put into operation in 1832. In 1882, electric generators, developed by Thomas Edison of the United States, began to light city streets in London and New York.

INFO CHECK

1. Define the following terms: Industrial Revolution, mass production, assembly line.

2. Describe the role of new inventions in 18th-century Britain. Why did so many relate to the production of cloth?

3. Explain why you would approve or disapprove of Adam Smith's ideas if you were a businessperson during the Industrial Revolution.

4. Identify the social change that you believe did most to change lifestyles in Europe in the 1800s.

SCIENTIFIC AND MEDICAL ADVANCES

Along with the practical inventions of the Industrial Revolution came advances in science and medicine. Scientists developed explanations for the workings of the natural world. Medical specialists found cures for certain illnesses and helped people live longer, healthier lives.

Scientific Knowledge

Dalton. A British school teacher named John Dalton contributed many new ideas to the field of chemistry. In 1803, he stated that atoms are the smallest parts of elements and that each element is made up of one kind of atom. Dalton also said that the atoms of one element are different from the atoms of all other elements. He devised a system of atomic weights. Hydrogen, the lightest element, was the standard to which all other elements were compared. Dalton's theories were not entirely correct. But his work laid the foundation for modern atomic theory.

Faraday. Scientists in the 19th century also contributed to the field of physics. In the early 1800s, Michael Faraday of England demonstrated that magnetism can produce electricity. His work made it possible to turn mechanical power into electrical power and to create electric generators.

Roentgen. Wilhelm Roentgen of Germany announced the discovery of X-rays in 1895. They particularly aided the medical profession. Now doctors could "see" into the body to find broken bones or growths in the lungs or other parts of the body.

Curie. Marie Curie discovered two radioactive chemical elements, radium and polonium, in 1898. Marie was born in Poland, but

Marie Curie, photographed
at work in her laboratory,
1905

worked in France with her husband, Pierre. Pierre also contributed
to the detection of the new elements. Until the 1950s, radium was
used to treat certain cancers. Exposure to large amounts of radium
can cause cancer. Polonium is used in nuclear research.

Darwin. Charles Darwin (lived 1809–1882), a British naturalist,
changed many people's ideas about how new forms of plants and animals have come into being. He said that they develop from earlier
forms over a long period of time. This process is called *evolution*. Darwin set forth his basic ideas in his book *On the Origin of Species by
Means of Natural Selection*, published in 1859. In the never-ending
struggle for food, Darwin said, the plants and animals that are best
suited to obtain food survive and reproduce. Those that have difficulty
finding enough to eat eventually die out. Through "natural selection,"
animal and plant forms change over long periods of time. Others
called this idea "the survival of the fittest."

Many scholars in the 19th century did not agree with Darwin's
ideas. Some people still do not think his theories can be proved.

Mendel. An Austrian monk, Gregor Mendel, experimented with
pea plants. He wanted to find out how certain characteristics, such
as color, are passed on to new generations. His work on inheritance,
published in 1866, greatly influenced the field of genetics in the 20th
century.

Medical Advances

Throughout the 19th century, many discoveries in the field of
medicine improved the health and well-being of the masses of people.

Jenner. Edward Jenner (lived 1749–1823), a British doctor, introduced the practice of vaccination to prevent smallpox in 1796. Before vaccination, this disease killed most people who contracted it and left ugly scars on those who survived.

Pasteur. The work of Louis Pasteur (lived 1822–1895), a French scientist, explained why the vaccination procedure works. Pasteur's experiments proved that some microorganisms known as bacteria, or germs, cause diseases. If a weak solution of disease-causing germs, a vaccine, is injected into an individual, the body will produce chemicals called antibodies to resist the germs. These antibodies remain in the individual's system and protect the person when he or she is exposed again to the germs. Pasteur developed vaccines to treat rabies and anthrax in humans and animals.

Bacteria also cause milk to sour. Pasteur discovered that heating milk kills the bacteria. This heating process is called *pasteurization*. It is commonly used today to keep milk and other liquids and some foods from spoiling quickly.

Koch. A German doctor, Robert Koch, expanded the knowledge of how germs cause diseases. In 1882, he identified the germ that causes tuberculosis. He developed a method of isolating and growing (culturing) bacteria. This aids the work of scientists studying bacteria in laboratories. In addition, Koch found that cholera can be transmitted by bacteria in drinking water and food. Keeping water and food free from these bacteria prevents the disease.

Lister. Pasteur's ideas about germs influenced Joseph Lister, a British surgeon. In 1865, Lister began to use strong chemicals (antiseptics) to kill bacteria in operating rooms. This practice prevented infection in patients during and after surgery.

Morton. William T. G. Morton, an American dentist, developed a way of making surgery safer and easier for patients. In 1846, Morton gave the first demonstration of the use of ether as an anesthetic, or painkiller, in surgery. He proved that the reduction of pain during surgery prevented shock and speeded the recovery of patients.

The advance of scientific knowledge in the 19th century revolutionized the practice of medicine. The treatment of patients improved. Many diseases could now be prevented, made less severe, or cured.

INFO CHECK

1. Why do you think the Industrial Revolution gave rise to so many scientific and medical advances?

2. Which 19th-century scientist best fits the following description: developed new ideas about the origins of plants and animals; regarded as the founder of the study of evolution.

3. Identify the 19th-century scientists who discovered the most about the connection between germs and disease.

CULTURAL ADVANCES

During the 19th century, painters, musicians, and writers created new and different forms of expression. These forms reflected the changes in lifestyle and attitudes brought about by the political revolutions of the period and the Industrial Revolution.

Painting

Romantic Style. Many artists in the late 18th and early 19th centuries painted in the *romantic style*. Romantic paintings were dramatic, emotional, and sometimes fantastic. The beauty of nature was a favorite theme. John Constable (lived 1776–1837) and Joseph Turner (lived 1775–1851) of Great Britain painted beautiful landscapes. Jean-François Millet (lived 1814–1875) of France created idealized pictures of peasant life.

Effect on Nationalism. Romanticism is closely linked to nationalism. The great Spanish painter Francisco Goya (lived 1746–1828), for example, portrayed the struggle of the Spanish people against the armies of Napoleon. The political events of the day also inspired Eugène Delacroix (lived 1798–1863), the greatest of the French Romanticists. In the *Massacre at Chios*, he expressed his sympathy for the Greeks' fight for independence from the Ottoman Empire in the 1820s.

Realism. During the second half of the 19th century, romanticism gave way to a style of painting called *realism*. Artists such as Gustave Courbet (lived 1819–1877) of France tried to show life as it

Goya's *The 3rd of May*, showing Spanish patriots executed by Napoleon's troops

The working people of Paris, in Daumier's realistic *Third-Class Carriage*

really was. Courbet's *Woman with a Parrot* and *The Stone Breakers* shocked some people who thought the works were too realistic. Honoré Daumier (lived 1808–1879), another French realist, drew social criticism and political cartoons. He attacked corruption in politics and spent six months in prison for drawing a caricature of King Louis Philippe. (A caricature is an exaggerated picture that usually shows a subject's faults or unusual features.)

Realism reached a peak in the works of Édouard Manet (lived 1832–1883) of France. Manet's *Death of Maximilian* shows the French emperor of Mexico being executed by rebels.

Impressionism. In the 1860s and the 1870s, a completely different style of painting began in France. It was called *impressionism*. Impressionists wanted to show the effect of light on the objects or scenes they painted. They generally used much brighter colors than the romanticists and realists. Scenes of everyday life indoors and outdoors captured their interest. Leading impressionists were Claude Monet (lived 1840–1926), Pierre-Auguste Renoir (lived 1841–1919), and Edgar Degas (lived 1834–1917).

Postimpressionism. The impressionists were followed by the postimpressionists. These artists concerned themselves with form, space, and blocks of colors rather than with the actual appearance of a subject. Paul Cézanne (lived 1839–1906), Vincent van Gogh (lived 1853–1890), Paul Gauguin (lived 1848–1903), and Georges Seurat (lived 1859–1891) were among the most important postimpressionistic painters.

Music

Romanticism and nationalism also affected the music of the 19th century.

Beethoven. The greatest romantic composer was Ludwig van Beethoven (lived 1770–1827), a German. He created idealistic, emotional works for individual musical instruments as well as for full orchestras. Most of Beethoven's compositions have numbers rather than names: for example, the Fifth Symphony. The Third Symphony is also called *Eroica*. It idealizes Napoleon's heroism.

Wagner. Another German, Richard Wagner (lived 1813–1883), composed operas featuring heroes and gods from German folklore. He made Germans proud of their history and legends. The *Ring of the Nibelung*, a cycle of four operas, is one of Wagner's most famous works. The Ring cycle is based on Norse myths.

Verdi. In Italy, Giuseppe Verdi (lived 1813–1901) created great operas. Among his masterpieces are *Rigoletto, La Traviata*, and *Aida*. A strong nationalist, he supported the Italian struggle for unification under a central government.

Tchaikovsky. Nationalism also inspired Peter Ilich Tchaikovsky (lived 1840–1893), a great Russian composer. His *1812 Overture* is a musical description of Napoleon's retreat from Moscow, which led to the Russian victory over the French invaders.

Sibelius and Grieg. Jean Sibelius (lived 1865–1957) of Finland and Edvard Grieg (lived 1843–1907) of Norway also wrote important nationalistic music. Sibelius's main works were symphonic poems for orchestras. They give his impressions of the beauty of Finland's natural landscape and summers and winters. Grieg's music featured compositions based on folk songs and dances. His most famous work for an orchestra is the *Peer Gynt* suite.

Debussy. Impressionism was reflected in music as well as in painting. French composer Claude Debussy (lived 1862–1918) wanted his listeners to react to his compositions as if they were poems without words. He tried to describe scenes and images with his music. *Prelude to the Afternoon of a Faun* and *La Mer* (The Sea) are two of his best-known impressionistic works.

Literature

Romantic literature focused on life in the past, folklore, or the beauty of nature. It stirred the emotions and stimulated the imagination. One of its main themes was freedom.

Realistic literature focused on everyday life and its problems. Strongly influenced by science, realists believed that human life is determined by society and by physical needs.

Shelley and Keats. Romanticists such as the British poets Percy Bysshe Shelley (lived 1792–1822) and John Keats (lived 1795–1821) wanted their work to liberate the human spirit and make it brave, generous, and creative. Shelley's long poem *Prometheus Unbound* envisions a world free from tyranny and hatred. Keats explored the themes of beauty and the relationship between dreams and the everyday world. One of Keats's opening lines is frequently quoted: "A thing of beauty is a joy forever."

Coleridge and Wordsworth. Samuel Taylor Coleridge (lived 1772–1834) and William Wordsworth (lived 1770–1850) were also leading British Romanticists. Coleridge's "Rime of the Ancient Mariner" deals with a man's voyage into the realm of the supernatural and his return to the human world. Wordsworth's poetry celebrated simple people and the beauty of nature.

Scott and Tennyson. Sir Walter Scott (lived 1771–1832) of Scotland wrote historical adventure novels. Books such as *Ivanhoe, The Talisman*, and *Quentin Durward* took readers to the Middle Ages where they experienced battles fought by knights in shining armor. Alfred, Lord Tennyson (lived 1809–1892) of England also wrote about the Middle Ages. *Idylls of the King* is a collection of poems about King Arthur and his knights.

Dumas. The French writer Alexandre Dumas (lived 1802–1870) created exciting and popular adventure novels. Two of his most famous works are *The Three Musketeers* and *The Count of Monte Cristo.*

Cooper. An American, James Fenimore Cooper (lived 1789–1851), wrote novels about the relations between frontier settlers and Indians. *The Deerslayer* and *The Last of the Mohicans* are among his most famous works.

French Realism. Realistic writing began in France. Honoré de Balzac (lived 1799–1850) applied Darwin's ideas to his study of human society. In his series of novels called *The Human Comedy*, he shows people competing for wealth and power with the same savagery that wild animals compete for food and dominance. *Madame Bovary* by Gustave Flaubert (lived 1821–1880) gives a detailed picture of a dissatisfied housewife who feels trapped in a stuffy middle-class town. Émile Zola (lived 1840–1902) attacked social conditions in 19th-century France in *Nana* and *Germinal.*

Dickens. The British writer Charles Dickens (1812–1870) was also interested in social problems. He described conditions in debtors' prisons, poorhouses, and law courts. *Oliver Twist* and *David Copperfield* are two of his novels about poor people.

Evans. Other English novelists of the time were even more influenced by the French Realists. Mary Ann Evans (lived 1819–1880) wrote under the name of George Eliot. She felt it was just as important to describe a character's environment as it was to analyze his or her personality. Her novel *Middlemarch: A Study of Provincial Life* shows how the society of a small town can affect people's moral choices.

Shaw. The plays of the Irish dramatist, George Bernard Shaw, (lived 1856–1950) criticized the social attitudes and customs of his day. Two of his well-known works are *Major Barbara* and *Pygmalion*.

Ibsen. Another dramatist, Henrik Ibsen (lived 1828–1906) of Norway, challenged 19th-century ideas about how people should behave. *A Doll's House* and *An Enemy of the People* are two of his best-known plays.

Tolstoy. Russia produced a number of realist writers. Leo Tolstoy (lived 1828–1910) is one of Russia's most famous authors. His best-known work is *War and Peace*, a long novel about the effect of Napoleon's campaign on five families. He also tried to demonstrate that humans, even such great leaders as Napoleon, are not really free but act according to a force called "historical necessity." Historical necessity is closely related to the nationalistic belief in the general will.

Twain. Mark Twain (lived 1835–1910), whose real name was Samuel Clemens, used humor to poke fun at American society. His best-known novels are *The Adventures of Tom Sawyer* and *The Adventures of Huckleberry Finn*.

INFO CHECK

1. Explain the difference between romanticism and realism. How were they used to reflect political ideas?

2. Would you describe Goya, Wagner, and Dumas as romanticists or realists? Give reasons for your response.

RESPONSES TO INDUSTRIALISM

The Industrial Revolution brought many new problems to the nations of Western Europe and the United States. The most outstanding of these problems was the extreme poverty of factory workers and rural workers. The plight of the poor caused people to question old ideas about societies, economic systems, and governments. How could these be changed to make life better for everyone?

Competing Solutions

Different groups of people came up with different answers to this question. Some were against making changes. Those who did want changes often disagreed about what the changes should be.

The members of the aristocracy tended to be conservative. They wanted to maintain the kind of power structure in which they were dominant and their rights were preserved. Businesspeople such as bankers and merchants whose families had enjoyed wealth and prestige for many generations or who had only recently become wealthy sided with the aristocrats.

Many members of the middle class, though, were liberals. They thought freedom and equality should be expanded. In the 19th century, most liberals believed in *laissez-faire* economics. Therefore, while many wanted to help the poor, they did not feel that the government should regulate businesses in order to do so.

The Socialist Movement

Socialists believed that setting up a new form of government and economic system was the best solution to the problems caused by the Industrial Revolution. They wanted the people as a whole, rather than single individuals, to own factories, mines, and farms. Socialists attacked the practice of producing goods for profit. Instead, they wanted the goods everyone needed to be produced at prices everyone could afford. Most important, socialists demanded that governments serve the needs of all the people and not just the wealthy landowners and industrialists.

Utopianism. In spite of being a wealthy businessman, Robert Owen (lived 1771–1858) had radical ideas about how to make life better for working people. He became one of the best-known socialists in Britain. To show how society could be reorganized, Owen conducted a practical experiment. He bought a cotton mill in Scotland and provided safe, healthy working conditions for his employees. Owen also turned the nearby town of New Lanark into a model community with good schools and a high standard of living.

An exercise class in Robert Owen's model community at New Lanark, Scotland

Owen and other 19th-century socialists who shared his beliefs were called *utopians*. They tried to establish ideal communities in which the residents contributed to and shared in the economic success equally. Owen succeeded in doing this in New Lanark. But other utopian communities he tried to set up in Britain and the United States failed. Most people could not cooperate and work together for the common good to the degree required to make the communities successful.

Blanc. Louis Blanc (lived 1811–1882), a French utopian socialist, owned a newspaper. In his writings, he attacked the French government for giving the industrialists, or capitalists, too much freedom. Blanc believed that the government should set up workshops to provide all workers with employment. Eventually, the workers would take over the workshops and run them. Blanc also had the idea that workers should produce according to their ability and be paid according to their needs. National workshops were set up in France in 1848, but they failed.

Not all socialist ideas proved to be successful or even practical. By the 20th century, however, socialist ideas had become powerful in European politics. Socialist-led governments have been elected many times in Britain, Germany, Norway, Sweden, Denmark, and France.

The Communist Movement

Marx and Engels. Karl Marx was a 19th-century German revolutionary who lived much of his life in London. His solutions to the problems of industrialization were more radical than those proposed by most other socialists. In 1848, Marx and a friend named Friedrich Engels published a pamphlet titled the *Communist Manifesto*. The ideas discussed in it came to be called scientific socialism, or *communism*.

Class Struggle. Marx blamed the problems faced by workers on capitalism. Under the capitalistic system, business owners put up the money, or capital, needed to bring workers, machines, and raw materials together to produce goods. Workers receive wages for their labor. Capitalists gain profits on their investments. Marx claimed that it was unfair for workers who produce goods to get less for their labor than the capitalists get for their investments. According to Marx, workers and capitalists were enemies locked in an endless conflict. He referred to this conflict as a "class struggle." It would take place between the *proletariat*, the working class, and the *bourgeoisie*, the owners of businesses.

Revolution. For Marx, the solution to the problems caused by capitalism was revolution. He urged the workers of every nation to rise up and smash the capitalistic system. The workers would then own all the sources of wealth. Since everything would be shared and businesses would be cooperative instead of competitive, the state would no longer be necessary. People would be truly free.

Limited Acceptance. The theories developed by Marx and Engels appealed to many. They were especially attractive to those who saw no other solution to problems such as poverty and unemployment. But the worldwide revolution Marx predicted never occurred. Instead, conditions for workers gradually improved. By the beginning of the 20th century, the standard of living for most people in the Western world had begun to rise higher than ever before.

Communist Governments. Russia and China adopted Communist governments. A great revolution in 1917 gave Communist leaders control over Russia. This revolution was caused by the inability of the czar's government to stop the terrible suffering and problems brought about by World War I. Communists took over the government of China in 1949 after a long civil war. Neither Russia nor China had gone through the Industrial Revolution at the time of the Communist takeovers. Workers never directed the government in either country. The government in China remains a dictatorship. Russia was a dictatorship until late 1991, when the Communist system collapsed. Vietnam, North Korea, and Cuba continue to have Communist governments.

The Labor Union Movement

While utopians and other thinkers tried to design the perfect society, workers sought more immediate solutions to their problems. The eventual success of their attempts was one of the reasons that communism did not replace capitalism throughout Europe.

Organizing. People who worked in the same occupation or industry joined together in organizations called *unions* to improve their wages and working and living conditions. They realized that, as a group, they could put more pressure on employers to raise wages or improve safety measures than they could as individuals.

Tactics. Union members elected representatives to present their requests or demands to an employer. This process is called *collective bargaining*. If an employer did not grant their requests or demands, the workers might strike. They would stop working until they got what they wanted. Sometimes unions organized a *boycott* of an employer's product. They refused to buy the product and urged others not to buy it until the employer came to an agreement with the union.

To stop a strike, an employer might hire strikebreakers to replace the striking workers. Police or military troops might be called in to end a strike. Some employers tried to weaken union causes by *blacklisting* outspoken members. This list, which was sent to other employers, branded selected workers as undesirable employees. Blacklisting meant that the selected workers could not get jobs in their usual line of work.

History. British workers could not legally organize unions until 1824. Efforts to form a national union in the 1830s had only short periods of success. Until 1871, the government and the factory owners forcefully discouraged attempts to form unions.

Unions in France did not become strong until the 1880s. The German labor movement gained power in the 1890s. The Industrial Revolution did not take hold in Russia until the late 1800s. As a result, labor unions did not become important there until shortly before the revolution of 1917.

In the United States, the labor movement followed a course similar to that in Great Britain. Early efforts at unionizing specific types of workers succeeded for only a short time. Unions did not become legal in the United States until 1842.

In 1869, a union called the Knights of Labor was formed in the United States. Its members included skilled and unskilled workers, women, and African Americans. The Knights called for an eight-hour working day and the banning of child labor as well as other reforms. After a few unsuccessful strikes and some violent incidents, the Knights declined in power. The American Federation of Labor (AFL), officially founded in 1886, became the most important national labor union. It joined with the Congress of Industrial Organizations (CIO) in 1955. The AFL-CIO continues to be the most powerful labor organization in the United States. About 75 percent of all unionized laborers belong to the AFL-CIO.

Political Influence. In Britain in 1900, liberals and trade unionists joined forces to form the Labour Party. It won a number of seats in Parliament in the 1906 elections. The Labour Party became a major force in British politics in the 1920s and remains so today. Labor unions on the European continent also developed political parties that elected representatives to legislative bodies.

After the 1920s, unions and other reform groups influenced their governments to pass laws that benefited workers. Child labor laws protected children. Standards for maximum hours of work and minimum wages were established. Sanitary and safety conditions in factories were improved. Compensation payments for on-the-job injuries, old-age pensions, and unemployment insurance lessened workers' financial worries.

Reforms Made by Existing Governments

Another reason communism did not replace capitalism was that existing governments responded to the demands of the workers and made changes to reduce social injustice.

Political Reforms. In Great Britain, reformers pressured Parliament to pass laws that established several important reforms. The Reform Bill of 1832 gave suffrage, or the right to vote, to all males who owned a certain amount of property. As a result, middle-class males had the vote and the right to hold public office. This victory encouraged people to demand suffrage for all men with or without property and the right to vote by secret ballot. By 1885, Parliament had passed laws that met these demands. Working-class males now also had the right to vote. Women, however, did not win suffrage until 1918.

As the right to vote was extended to poor, uneducated people, reformist leaders realized how important it was that the new voters be able to make responsible political decisions. Consequently, reformers urged the passing of the Elementary Education Act of 1880 that made it possible for all children in Great Britain to get an elementary-school education. Parliament also passed laws giving Catholics and non-Anglican Protestants the right to engage in political activity.

Labor Reforms. In the early 1800s, religious and political groups started concerning themselves with the abuses of factory workers. One reformer, Michael Sadler, set up a Select Committee on Child Labor in Parliament. The reports made by this committee resulted in a law (1833) limiting the working day of children aged 9 to 12 to 8 hours and those 13 to 17 to 12 hours. So many children worked in manufacturing that the mills and factories could not function without them. When the children left work for the day, the factories had to close. Therefore, a bill that reduced the length of the children's workday also reduced the number of hours that adults had to work.

Legislative activity led to the establishment of a minimum wage. A minimum wage is the lowest amount that employers are allowed to pay their workers. The new laws also forced factory owners to provide safer working conditions and to reduce the length of the workweek.

Suffrage in the United States. As in Great Britain, social reform in the United States came about peacefully. By 1850, the constitutions of most states gave all white men the right to vote. In 1865, the 13th Amendment outlawed slavery. In 1870, the 15th Amendment extended suffrage to all men regardless of their race or national origin. Women did not gain the vote until 1920.

Progressives. American social reformers in the early 1900s were known as Progressives. Newspaper reporters called "Muckrakers" helped reformers win public support for changes. They wrote articles that described unhealthy working conditions, slum life, and government corruption. The Progressives eventually brought about reforms that protected child workers, established social security benefits for all workers, and gave voters the power to remove crooked politicians from office.

Changes in France. The French people had to fight for social change. Recurring conflicts between French aristocrats, peasants, and members of the middle class prevented lasting reform until the end of the 19th century.

The dictatorship of Napoleon Bonaparte replaced the republic established by the French Revolution. Napoleon allowed the French little or no political freedom. He did, however, bring about many reforms. He created a new law code, organized a public school system, and set up a fair taxation system. He also gave peasants land of their own.

Paris Commune. Napoleon Bonaparte's nephew, Louis Napoleon, was a more repressive dictator. When his government collapsed in 1870 after the Franco-Prussian War, the National Assembly wanted to bring back the monarchy. This outraged the workers of Paris. They set up their own government in 1871, which they called the Paris Commune. The leaders of the Paris Commune demanded, among other reforms, that workers be given higher wages and a shorter workday. Although their rebellion was harshly put down, the French government eventually passed many of the reforms the Communards had fought for.

Global Migrations

During the 19th century, more Europeans than ever before in history began to emigrate from their native countries. Since most of these emigrants went to the United States, their movement is called the Atlantic Migration. Some left Europe to find work in U.S. cities. Others wanted to escape bloody revolutions or religious persecution. Still others fled from devastating famines.

In previous centuries, people had been unable to get away from bad conditions in their own countries. But in the 19th century, improved transportation helped them to find refuge in distant lands. Better means of communication informed them about the countries that provided the best opportunities. Want ads and public posters encouraged them to go to industrialized countries, which needed more workers for their factories.

The Great Famine

Between 1845 and 1851, some one million Irish flocked to the United States. These people left their country to escape a great famine.

At this time, Ireland was a part of Great Britain. A few wealthy Protestant Irish families owned the country's great estates. The poor Catholic Irish worked on the estates for little or no wages. The wealthy landowners wanted to use their land to grow cash crops, or crops that they could sell for large profits. They gave their tenant farmers only small amounts of land on which to plant food crops.

The Irish peasants discovered that the best crop to plant in a small space was the potato. Potatoes are easy to plant, take up little room, need little care while growing, and thrive in moist climates such as Ireland's. This vegetable is also extremely nourishing. Because the potato took so little of their time and soil, the Irish planted no other major food crop.

Time Line

Year	Dates and Events
A.D. 1701	**1700s–1840:** Industrial Revolution: inventions and innovations in agriculture, manufacture, transportation, communications
	1770s–1900: Period of realism and nationalism in painting, music, and literature
	1776: Smith advocates free enterprise, laws of supply and demand and of competition
	1780s–1880s: Period of romanticism in music, painting, literature
	1796: Jenner introduces vaccination against smallpox
	1798: Malthus formulates theory that only population control can prevent widespread starvation
	1817: Ricardo formulates theory that population growth causes unemployment, low wages
	1830s: Telegraph developed
	1832: Britain's Reform Bill grants suffrage to male property holders
1800	**1833:** British Parliament limits work hours of children
	1845–1851: Irish famine brings one million immigrants to United States
1801	**1848:** Marx and Engels publish *Communist Manifesto*
	1855: British Parliament grants suffrage to all males, authorizes secret ballot
	1859: Darwin publishes theory of evolution and natural selection
	1859: Drake drills first oil well (western Pennsylvania); rise of petroleum for power and fuel
	1860s–1880s: Pasteurization against food spoilage; vaccinations against anthrax and rabies
	1865: Lister initiates use of antiseptics to kill bacteria during and after surgery
	1866: Field links North America and Europe by transatlantic cable
	1869: Founding of Knights of Labor, union of skilled and unskilled workers
	1870: 15th Amendment extends suffrage to all U.S. males
	1870–1910: Period of French impressionism in painting and music
	1876: Bell develops telephone
	1879–1893: Spencer formulates theory of Social Darwinism
1900	**1880:** Britain makes elementary education available to all children
1901	**1880s–1890s:** Period of French postimpressionism
	1882: Edison's electric generators light New York and London
	1885: Benz invents first auto with internal-combustion engine; Daimler introduces a gas-powered engine
	1886: Founding of American Federation of Labor
	1895: Roentgen discovers X rays as aid to medical examination of body's interior
	1895–1901: Marconi's wireless telegraph accelerates transatlantic communication
	1903: Wright Brothers successfully fly heavier-than-air plane
	1904–1920: Fleming (Britain) and De Forest (U.S.) develop radio; regular broadcasts become common
	1908: Ford uses interchangeable parts and assembly line to manufacture affordable autos
2000	**1920:** 19th Amendment extends suffrage to all U.S. women
	1929: Zworykin demonstrates first practical television system

From 1845 to 1851, a fungus carried over from America destroyed the yearly potato crops. The Irish were so dependent on the potato that almost 25 percent of the population (between 500,000 and 750,000) starved to death or died from diseases caused by malnutrition.

The British government, which ruled Ireland, was not prepared to handle this disaster. When the famine first started, charitable organizations opened soup kitchens in Ireland. But when British banks experienced a financial crisis, the government stopped the charitable aid. British leaders then turned the problem over to the Irish Poor Law system, established in 1838. Under this law, the government was authorized only to set up workhouses where poor people could live and work. There were no facilities for sick and dying people who were too weak to work.

The British were not only incompetent at handling the problem, they were also unfeeling. The government did not prevent the wealthy estate owners from demanding that the tenants pay their rents. When the starving tenants were unable to come up with the money or to do their farm work, the landlords evicted them. British troops often forced the tenants to leave their homes.

It is hard to understand how a country as wealthy as industrialized Great Britain could let the Irish die from hunger. Many at that time believed that poverty was a moral failing. But many people were outraged. They joined groups that sought to eliminate the kind of poverty experienced by the Irish. Others, however, argued that, according to the science of economics, poverty was simply a fact of life.

Malthusian Economics

Many European economists of the time accepted extreme poverty as unavoidable. They based their beliefs on the theories of Thomas Malthus (lived 1766–1834) and David Ricardo (lived 1772–1823). In his *Essay on the Principle of Population*, Malthus had pointed out that human populations would always increase faster than the amount of food necessary to feed them. He felt that the only way to prevent famine was for people to have fewer children.

Ricardo used Malthus's ideas to formulate his own theory about what he called "the iron law of wages." He stated that as the population got larger, more and more people would need work. To get the comparatively few jobs available, they would accept very low wages. Ricardo did not think that they would starve to death. They would, however, have to work long and hard and accept whatever terms their employers wished to give them.

Social Darwinism

Industrialists and others who benefited from free competition accepted the theories of Malthus and Ricardo. The theories seemed to clear them of blame for the poverty of the working classes. Most ignored the possibility that if the world's wealth were shared more equally, large groups of people might not have to starve. When reformers pointed this out to them, they replied by quoting the ideas of Herbert Spencer, an English philosopher who lived from 1820 to 1903.

Spencer was influenced by Darwin's theories about evolution. He felt that society progressed the same way that animals had developed—from primitive into more complex beings. He argued that economic competition stimulated society to make advances, thus reforms should not be made. By weeding out the weak and inefficient, economic competition promoted the "survival of the fittest." It ensured that society would eventually consist of only the strongest and most productive people. Spencer's ideas also appealed to leaders who wanted to take over weaker foreign countries and exploit their resources. The application of the idea of natural selection to society is called *Social Darwinism*.

The Movement Toward a Global Economy

One of the most important results of the Industrial Revolution is the *global economy* that exists today. Today almost all the countries of the modern world are interdependent. They rely on each other for goods and services. Russia, for example, relies on the United States for wheat, while the United States depends on the countries of the Middle East for fuel oil. Then, too, a financial crisis in Asia can affect stock markets all over the world.

The expansion of Western nations into the less industrialized regions of the world during the 19th century set the stage for our global economy. Western European countries, Japan, and the United States took control of areas of Asia, Africa, and the South Pacific and used them as both sources of raw materials and markets for manufactured goods. This is called *imperialism*.

The improvements in transportation and communication made worldwide trade possible. Trains and ships moved goods quickly over vast distances. In the late 19th century, new methods of refrigeration made it possible to carry such perishable goods as meat and milk and deliver them unspoiled to markets. The telegraphs and telephone enabled businesspeople to conduct their affairs in several countries at once.

European and American capitalists invested heavily in colonial railroads, bridges, plantations, and mines. Latin American countries sought foreign money to build their own industries. As the 19th century wore on, events in places whose names most Europeans had never heard had profound effects on their lives.

Chapter 24 explains more about the expansion of Western nations during the 19th century. Imperialism spread Western culture and technology all over the globe and contributed to many problems of the modern world.

INFO CHECK

1. How did socialism, communism, and the labor union movement each seek to respond to the problems arising from the Industrial Revolution? Why was communism regarded as the most revolutionary and potentially violent solution?

2. Why do you think the process of reform was more violent in France than it was in Britain and the United States?

3. Explain why you AGREE or DISAGREE with the ideas of Thomas Malthus and David Ricardo.

4. How did the Industrial Revolution lead to the growth of a global economy?

CHAPTER REVIEW

Multiple Choice

1. With regard to agriculture, the beginning of which practice ended the other?

    1. technology—crop rotation
    2. open-field system—animal grazing
    3. enclosure movement—open-field system
    4. crop specialization—seed drill.

2. The people who were negatively affected by the agricultural revolution were

    1. small farmers
    2. farmers having no land
    3. poor landowners
    4. wealthy landowners.

3. In *An Inquiry Into the Nature and Causes of the Wealth of Nations*, Adam Smith presented the idea that government should

    1. not regulate or attempt to control business activity
    2. regulate or attempt to control business activity

    3. run all business
    4. run only "heavy-metal" industries.

4. Fulton is to steamboats as

    1. Benz is to airplanes
    2. Daimler is to steam engines
    3. Bell is to oil wells
    4. Morse is to the telegraph.

5. Charles Darwin's concept of evolution states that plants and animals that survive

    1. have naturally changed or adapted to their environment
    2. do so because the environment changes to suit their needs
    3. are developed by scientists to fit the environment
    4. evolve from lab tests.

6. Pasteur, Koch, and Lister all developed methods to use, prevent, or destroy

    1. the common cold
    2. bacteria
    3. diseases
    4. allergies.

7. The style of painting used by Goya and Delacroix to support nationalistic themes was

   1. realism
   2. impressionism
   3. romanticism
   4. postimpressionism.

8. Wagner, Verdi, Sibelius, and Tchaikovsky all were

   1. painters of romantic themes
   2. musical composers of nationalistic themes
   3. writers of folklore and fairy tales
   4. military leaders of different nations.

9. The economic theory that government should not regulate the marketplace or businesspersons is

   1. laissez-faire
   2. mercantilism
   3. capitalism
   4. socialism.

10. An individual who believed that the people as a whole should own businesses and not produce for others' profit was called a

    1. reactionary
    2. liberal
    3. radical
    4. Socialist.

11. The photograph on page 500 illustrates that

    1. British children were given opportunity to work after school
    2. British factories during the 19th century were often cramped and unsafe
    3. more males than females worked in 19th-century British factories
    4. working conditions had improved by the 19th century.

12. The painting on page 510 shows a style of art know as

    1. romantic
    2. abstract
    3. realistic
    4. impressionistic.

13. The painting on page 511 strongly suggests that

    1. railroad travel in 19th-century France provided luxury accommodations for everyone
    2. public transportation in 19th-century France was free but very crowded
    3. few people traveled by railroad in the 19th century
    4. some artists used their work to protest abuses of the Industrial Revolution.

Thematic Essays

1. The Communists and the Utopians both developed plans to deal with the social and economic problems of the working class. *Task:* Using historical examples, compare and contrast the methods proposed or adopted by each group to help the workers. Include in your answer, economic, social, and political examples.

2. In the 18th and 19th centuries, science and technology developed methods, materials, and inventions to make life and work easier, safer, and healthier for the common person. *Task:* Select and describe two examples that support this statement.

Document-Based Questions

Use the documents and your knowledge of Global History and Geography to answer the questions.

1. Study the painting on page 511. The painting's title is *Third-Class Carriage*. Describe the feelings of the people shown in this picture. Do you think they are happy or sad? Why?

2. Adam Smith wrote in the *Wealth of Nations*:

   "By pursuing his own interest, he frequently promotes that of the society more effectually [better] than when he intends to promote it. I have never known much good done by those who affected to trade for the public good ... Every individual can in his local situation judge much better than any statesman or lawgiver can do for him."

   Give two reasons, according to Adam Smith, why government should not regulate business and business activities.

3. From a report to the House of Commons:

   "Were the children [beaten]?—Yes. With what?—A strap; ... sometimes he got a chain and chained them, and strapped them all down the room. ... Were the children excessively fatigued at the time?—Yes, it was in the afternoon. ... You dragged the baskets?—Yes: down the rooms to where they worked. ... It has had the effect of pulling your shoulders out?—Yes. ... Were you heated with your employment. . . ?—No, it was not so very hot as in the summertime; in the wintertime they were obliged to have the windows open, it made no matter what the weather was, and sometimes we got very severe colds in frost and snow. ... Suppose you had not been on time in the morning at these mills, what would have been the consequences?—We should have been quartered. What do you mean by that? If we were a quarter hour late, they would take off a half an hour. ..."

   Select and describe any *three* examples of how child workers were abused.

Document-Based Essay

Task: Using economic, political, and social examples, explain why the workers were treated so poorly in the early factories and mines.

C H A P T E R

24

The Growth of Imperialism

Sabata wished he was back on the veld (grasslands) herding cattle with the other village boys. He had been working in the mine for only a few months, and he had spent all of his 15 years on the veld. Yet now his life there seemed as unreal as a bright and airy dream. Here in the mine shaft there was nothing but darkness, choking dust, and cramped limbs.

Sabata sighed. He himself had chosen to leave his village. He had wanted to become a miner so that he could live in this other world. How fascinated he had been when he listened to his uncle describe it. Johannesburg, uncle had said, was full of wonderful machines, buildings that rose into the sky, and new, mouth-watering food.

Sabata smiled sourly. Oh yes, Johannesburg was full of marvels. But not for him. His wages were very low. After he had paid his rent, he had just enough to buy a little food. He often went to bed hungry, longing for his mother's plain stew.

Ah, but worse than his homesickness was his new feeling of shame. Mr. Barton, the white overseer, never neglected an opportunity to make him feel stupid and clumsy. He, Sabata, who had been the leader of the village boys.

Far from being clumsy, he had been the best at every sport. He could hit a bird on the wing with a stone from a slingshot, catch fish with twine and a bit of twisted wire, and beat any opponent at stick-fencing. As the leader, he had never humiliated his followers. How had Mr. Barton been brought up?

This was not the place for Sabata. He would have to leave. Even

Johannesburg's streets were like mine shafts. For all the treasure hidden within them, they were narrow, dark, and stifling.

Sabata is a young South African boy who is experiencing what it means to be an inhabitant of a colonized country. People who lived under colonial rule saw their natural resources being used to enrich the ruling nation. The foreign administrators often treated them as inferior. Although colonialism brought technological and industrial advances to their countries, it destroyed the people's traditional culture and their pride in themselves. But not everyone lost hope. Native peoples resisted their colonial rulers and eventually took back control of their countries.

CAUSES OF MODERN IMPERIALISM

The major industrial countries of Europe, the United States, and Japan all acquired colonies in the 19th century. The areas they took over were in Asia, Africa, the South Pacific, and Latin America. Some

Colonial Empires in 1914

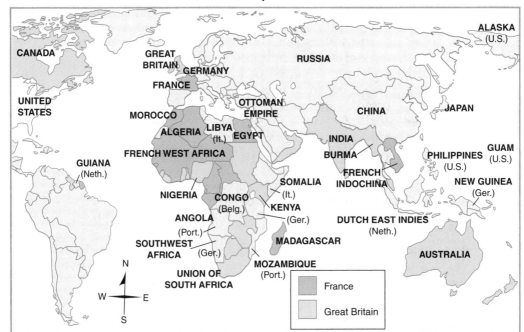

nations, such as Great Britain, already controlled large areas of the world. Others, such as Germany, did not enter the race for possessions until after 1870.

The period from the 1850s until about 1910 is called the Age of Imperialism. *Imperialism* is the policy of extending a nation's political and economic dominance or control over another territory or country.

The Industrial Revolution increased the wealth of many nations. To keep their countries prosperous, the leaders wanted to be sure that they had readily available supplies of raw materials for their factories. They also looked for new markets for the products that their industries turned out. In addition, businesspeople sought places where they could invest their profits and make even more money. All these needs were met by acquiring colonies.

Imperialism was important to the political power of many nations—Western and Eastern. Not only did the possession of colonies add to the wealth and prestige of these nations, it also increased their military strength. They could maintain their authority all over the world by using their colonies as supply bases and fortifications.

The strong sense of nationalism in most European and North American countries in the 1800s put their leaders in competition with each other. Acquiring colonies was one way for a nation to surpass the others in strength, wealth, and prestige.

Many people in Western countries believed that their civilization was superior to that of non-Western peoples. Westerners wanted to bring the benefits of their culture to others. They also wanted to teach non-Christians about Christianity. For many Europeans and North Americans, such goals helped to justify imperialism.

INFO CHECK

1. Define imperialism.

2. State one economic and one political reason for imperialism.

3. Do you agree with the Western nations' justification for imperialism? Why or why not?

EMPIRE BUILDING IN THE 19TH CENTURY

During the Age of Discovery in the 1500s and 1600s, Spain, Portugal, Great Britain, the Netherlands, and France colonized parts of Africa, Asia, and the Americas. As Europeans moved into these new regions, they brought their goods and ideas with them. During the "new imperialism" of the late 1800s, European expansion reached its peak. Industrialization, technology, and military might gave European nations enormous power and influence in the world.

John Bull, symbol of Britain, here caricatured as "Greedy Johnnie," jealously holding on to his colonies

Nations That Held Colonies

In the early 1800s, Great Britain had more colonies than any other Western nation. It controlled Canada, part of India, Australia, New Zealand, British Honduras (now Belize) in Central America, British Guiana (now Guyana) in South America, and islands in the Caribbean. Much of the eastern half of Africa was also under British influence. By 1900, it also controlled much of Southeast Asia, Hong Kong, and islands in the Mediterranean and the Pacific.

It was said that "the sun never sets on the British Empire." At the peak of its time as a colonial power, Britain controlled colonies around the world. Thus, as the earth turned on its axis, some part of the British Empire was always in daylight.

By the late 1800s, France also had a sizable empire. It controlled much of northern and western Africa, Indochina, islands in the Caribbean, and French Guiana in South America. Germany entered the race for colonies after 1870. It took sections of east and southwestern Africa and several islands in the Pacific. After 1871, Italy also acquired pieces of northeastern Africa.

Belgium, the Netherlands, Portugal, and Spain each had a few colonies scattered throughout the world. The United States acquired territory in the late 1800s and early 1900s. From the 1890s to the 1940s, Japan asserted its authority in East Asia.

The British in India

During the 1700s, the Mogul Empire in India became weaker and weaker. At the same time, the British and the French East India trading companies gained strength. They competed for control of India.

The British East India Company. The major aim of Britain's East India Company was to profit from selling Indian cotton cloth, silk, and sugar to other countries. Victory over France in the Seven Years' War (1756–1763) left Britain the major power in India. (This was called the French and Indian War in North America.) The portions of India not governed directly by Britain were ruled by Indian princes. These local leaders eventually signed treaties that placed their states under British protection.

With some restrictions placed on it by the British government, the East India Company ruled India until 1857. The company built telegraph, railroad, and irrigation systems there. In addition, it set up a postal service and a number of schools. The company also organized a large army of Indian soldiers, called *sepoys*, to defend its interests and India's borders. The sepoys were commanded by British officers and were supported by units of the British Army. Missionaries arrived to teach Hindus and Muslims about Christianity.

Reaction of Indians. Although the Indian people benefited from some of the changes, many resented British rule. The East India Company officials made sure that British colonists received most of the advantages from the new technology and industrialization. Indian factory workers and servants received very low wages. Farmers got very little for their produce. Indians could not hold high-level positions in the East India Company. Schools taught English and Western ideas and paid little attention to the long history and advanced culture of India. The British too often treated Indians as inferiors.

Sepoy Mutiny and After. Resentment turned into revolt. In 1857, some sepoys touched off a widespread rebellion that was not put down fully for two years. (See Chapter 22 for more details.)

After the Sepoy Mutiny, the East India Company lost its power. The British government ruled India directly as a colony. It appointed a viceroy (governor) to head the Indian government. Local civil and police officers were trained in Britain. An Indian civil service was established by the British. Its ranks were filled mainly by young Englishmen seeking careers in India. Few Indians qualified for government service because of the strict rules set up by the British. Then, in 1876, Queen Victoria became Empress of India.

Imperialism in Africa

Ever since the days of the Portuguese explorers in the late 1400s, Europeans had taken African land for colonies. But they made no strong efforts to add to their holdings until the early 1800s. By 1900, almost all of Africa was in European hands

The French. The French took over Algeria in northern Africa in 1830. They said they wanted to stop pirate raids in the Mediterranean. In 1878, with the approval of Great Britain, which had interests in Tunisia, France gained control of Tunisia. This country is also in northern Africa, to the east of Algeria. When French leaders showed interest in owning Morocco as well, the Germans opposed them. The dispute was finally settled in France's favor in 1911. France also acquired vast areas of West and Central Africa.

British Holdings. Great Britain took the largest portion of Africa. It had scattered holdings in western Africa—Nigeria, the Gold Coast, Sierra Leone, and Gambia. Most of its possessions were in the eastern half of Africa. They stretched in an almost unbroken line from Egypt in the north to the Cape of Good Hope in the south.

The Suez Canal. The British were very interested in the Suez Canal, which opened in 1869. It had been built through Egypt to link the Mediterranean and Red seas. British ships used the waterway to shorten the voyage between Britain and India. The Turkish ruler of Egypt owned the largest number of shares in the French-Ottoman company that built the canal. In 1875, Britain gained control of the canal by buying his shares. Seven years later, Britain stepped in to settle a rebellion in Egypt and stayed on to rule the country. Part of the reason was to protect the canal, a vital link to British territories in Asia.

Central and East Africa. Just to the south of Egypt is the Sudan. Although France had wanted to add this area to its empire, Britain colonized it in 1898. Britain also gained control of British East Africa (now Kenya) in the 1880s and Uganda in the 1890s.

South Africa. Britain's richest African colonies were in the south. It had acquired South Africa from the Dutch in the early 1800s during the Napoleonic wars. The Dutch farmers, called Boers, resented British rule. They moved north in the hope of escaping the British.

When trying to settle the new territory, however, the Boers met the resistance of a group of African people called the Zulu. They had invaded an empire created by the great Zulu leader, Shaka. The Boers, backed up by rifles and British troops, defeated the Zulu, who had only spears. The Boers then set up the independent republics of the Transvaal and the Orange Free State. (They are now part of the Republic of South Africa.)

In 1867, diamonds were found near the Boer territory. The area became the richest source of diamonds in the world. Gold was discovered in a nearby area in 1886. A leading developer of the gold and diamond industries in southern Africa was Cecil Rhodes, an Englishman. He promoted British interests in Africa and dreamed of a "Cape to Cairo" railroad to link all of Britain's territories from the south to the north. The railroad was never built, but Rhodes expanded British rule into what are now Zimbabwe and Zambia.

The Boers revolted against British rule in 1899. It took British forces three years to defeat the guerrilla fighters. In the hope of preventing future uprisings, the British gave the Boers more political

SHAKA: FOUNDER OF THE ZULU EMPIRE

In the 19th century, a Zulu king named Shaka became known as Africa's military genius. His conquests dazzled Africans and Europeans alike and made the Zulus rulers of an empire in southern Africa.

In the early 1800s, the Zulus were a small tribe in what is today the Republic of South Africa. They numbered approximately 2,000 to 3,000 people. By 1820, the Zulus could put 100,000 warriors into battle. Their fighting skills and ferocity in battle terrorized British and Boer settlers. One man was responsible for the change in status of the Zulu—Shaka.

Born in 1787, Shaka was the son of the Zulu king. But he was forced to spend his youth in exile after his father rejected his mother. In his 20s, Shaka distinguished himself as a warrior in the service of a chief named Dingiswayo. When Shaka's father died in 1816, Dingiswayo seized the political opportunity and assisted Shaka to become the new ruler of the Zulu.

The young king quickly reorganized the Zulu fighting force into a formidable military machine. He introduced military discipline by organizing warriors into *impis*, or regiments, under carefully selected officers. He also taught coordinated tactical movements in response to strategic plans. Supported by the troops of Chief Dingiswayo, Shaka began the conquest of neighboring tribes. The young men of the defeated tribes were incorporated into the Zulu army, swelling the number of warriors available to fight.

By 1818, the Zulu conquerors had killed or brought under their rule all their neighbors, except the Umdwandwe. This large tribe was ruled by a king named Zuidi. After Zuidi captured and executed Chief Dingiswayo, Shaka began the *mfecane*. This was a period of forced migrations among the southern African peoples. After his defeat of King Zuidi, Shaka's power was unchallenged. By 1820, his empire extended over much of southern Africa.

Shaka had introduced to southern Africa the practice of total war. He created a highly centralized military kingdom, which ruled the Zulu and their conquered neighbors. To the south of that kingdom, his policy of forced migrations created a devasted buffer zone. Founded on massacre, destruction, and unquestioning loyalty, Shaka's empire could not last. In 1824, he came into contact with British settlers and officials from Capetown. In return for assistance in some military operations, Shaka granted the British trading facilities and ceded Port Natal to them.

Eventually, Shaka became mentally ill. His half-brother, Dingaan, murdered Shaka in 1828. Dingaan then became ruler of the Zulu Empire. The empire lasted until 1879, when the British defeated it.

- Evaluate the accomplishments of Shaka. Do you find him an admirable historical figure? Why or why not?

rights. Boer areas were joined with British areas in 1910 to become the Union of South Africa.

Germany and Italy. Germany and Italy came late to the race for colonies in Africa. In the 1880s, Germany claimed German East Africa (now Tanzania). At about the same time, Germany acquired Togo and the Cameroons in West Africa. In 1898, Portugal gave Germany a part of Angola (South West Africa, now called Namibia) in payment for a loan it had received from Germany. Italy acquired Libya in North Africa and part of Somalia in the northeast.

Portugal and Spain. Portugal and Spain also held pieces of Africa. Spain's possessions included Cuba and Puerto Rico in the Carib-

Africa: European Imperialism in 1914

bean, the Philippines and Guam in the Pacific, and a few territories in northwest Africa. Portugal's colonies were scattered: islands in the east Atlantic; Guinea-Bissau, Angola, and Mozambique in Africa; Goa in India; Macau in China; and Timor in Indonesia.

Belgium. King Leopold of Belgium owned a large portion of central Africa, the Congo, as his personal colony. In 1908, the Belgian government forced the king to give up the colony because he allowed his representatives to treat the Africans there in an extremely cruel way. The Belgian government then ruled the area.

Independent Countries. Two African countries remained independent throughout the colonial period. They are Liberia in the west and Ethiopia in the east. Liberia had been founded by former slaves from the United States in the 1820s.

The Berlin Conference

In 1884–1885, the European countries, Turkey, and the United States held the Berlin Conference to set rules for dividing Africa. (No Africans were present.) They decided to recognize a nation's right to a colony if that nation first made a formal announcement of its claim and then occupied the claimed territory. Before this decision, a nation could gain legal right to a colony by establishing that it had historical claims to it. For example, a nation might assert ownership of an area by providing evidence that, in the past, the area had been inhabited and governed by the first nation's citizens.

The new procedure intensified the competition among Western powers. They all rushed to send troops, officials, and settlers to the lands they felt they had a right to own or influence.

The Berlin Conference recognized three kinds of imperial control. Western nations could establish colonies that they owned and governed directly. They could mark an area as a *sphere of influence* in which they had sole investment or trading rights. They could turn a weak country into a *protectorate*. This means that the country could keep its ruler, but the imperial power would set the policy for that ruler to follow. Boundaries rarely respected tribal locations or rivalries. Tensions built up that still cause problems today.

Through this conference, the major Western nations gave each other the right to take parts of Africa. It also set a precedent for similar activity in Asia and the Pacific.

Spheres of Influence in China

Although ancient China was known for its learning and art, it had not begun to industrialize by the 19th century. The Ch'ing, or Manchu, emperors were not interested in learning about Western technology. They felt that the European "barbarians" could not teach them anything worth knowing. Such an attitude is called *ethnocentrism*. As a result, the Chinese lacked modern weapons. This left them unable to resist the demands of Western nations for more trading privileges in China.

Europeans were attracted to China by the rich profits they hoped to make there. The huge Chinese population offered a supply of cheap workers and a market for European goods. Also, European business-people (capitalists) hoped to develop China's natural resources, such as coal and iron.

Opium War. Economic exploitation of China began with the Opium War (1839–1842). The British were looking for a product to sell to the Chinese. Britain bought more from China than it sold to that country. The British wanted to change the unfavorable balance of trade. Opium seemed like a product that would accomplish this aim. Opium, a habit-forming drug, was produced in India. British traders sold great quantities of it in China, and many Chinese became addicted. Large amounts of money flowed out of China into British hands. In 1839, Chinese officials tried to stop the opium trade. They destroyed 20,000 chests of the drug and imprisoned the British traders who were selling it. The British responded by sending a fleet of ships to invade China. Without a navy and modern weapons, the Chinese could not defend themselves against the British military power. The British forced the Chinese government to sign the Treaty of Nanjing in 1842.

Additional Rights. As a result of the 1842 treaty, the British and other foreigners gained new privileges in China. Prior to the treaty, foreign traders had the right to live and work only in the port of Canton. The treaty forced the Chinese to open five more ports to Westerners and to pay a large sum of money to Britain. China gave the island of Hong Kong to the British and reduced tariffs. It also granted *extraterritorial rights* to foreigners living in the treaty ports. This meant that foreigners accused of crimes would be tried in their own courts and by their own laws rather than by those of China.

After the Taiping Rebellion. China's troubles did not end with the 1842 treaty. In 1850, the Taiping Rebellion broke out. The rebels wanted to overthrow the Manchu Dynasty because it had allowed China to become weak. To overcome the rebels, the Chinese government had to ask the Western nations for help. Even with Western aid, it took 14 years to crush the rebellion.

In the midst of the civil war, in 1856, the British and French attacked China. Both countries wanted additional trading rights. The two countries easily defeated the Chinese. The Treaty of Tientsin (1858) made the Chinese open 11 more ports to Westerners. It allowed foreign traders and Christian missionaries to move into the Chinese interior. In addition, the treaty made it legal for traders to import opium into China.

Loss of Territory. During the second half of the 19th century, China lost colonial states all around its borders. Britain took Burma, and France assumed control of Cambodia, Laos, and Vietnam (to-

China: Spheres of Influence in the 19th Century

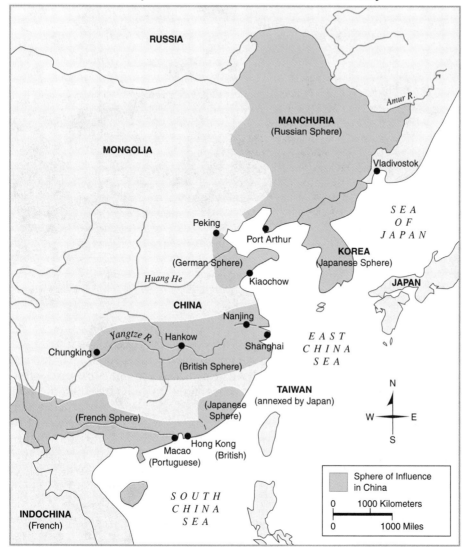

gether known as Indochina). Russia gained territory in the north and the right to run a railroad through Manchuria.

In 1894, China and Japan clashed over Korea in the Sino-Japanese War. (Sino is another word for China.) Japan won. The 1895 peace treaty awarded Taiwan and some nearby islands to Japan. Korea's independence was recognized, but Japan retained its influence over that country.

Open Door Policy. The United States did not take direct control of any portion of China, but Americans did a great deal of business there. The United States government wanted to protect its trade.

Cartoon showing Western imperialists pulling at China from all directions—
for China's own good!

Therefore, in 1899, Secretary of State John Hay asked the European
nations and Japan to agree to respect each other's trading rights in
China. The U.S. proposal that all nations interested in commerce with
China be given equal trading rights was called the "Open Door
Policy."

Boxer Rebellion. Many Chinese hated the foreigners who humiliated their country. A number of nationalists formed a group
called the "Righteous and Harmonious Fists" to drive all "foreign dev-
ils" out of China. Westerners called the members of this group "Boxers." In 1900, the Boxers set out to eliminate foreign influence in
China. They killed Chinese who supported Western ideas as well as
some Europeans and Americans. Their attacks on Western embassies
in Beijing were resisted for eight weeks. Finally, an international
force of American, British, French, German, Russian, and Japanese
troops marched on Beijing. They saved the embassies and crushed
the Boxer Rebellion. To make peace, the Chinese government agreed
to pay a huge sum of money, an indemnity, to the foreign nations and
to give them additional privileges in China.

Dr. Sun Yixian. Patriotic Chinese blamed the Manchu ruler for
China's troubles and demanded reforms. They wanted China to industrialize and to have a government more responsive to the wishes
of the people. In 1911, a revolution led by Dr. Sun Yixian (old spelling
Yat-sen) overthrew the Manchus and made China a republic. The son
of a poor family, Sun was educated in Hong Kong and Hawaii. He

became a medical doctor and then traveled in Europe, the United States, and Japan to get support for his movement.

The Kuomintang, or Nationalist Party, tried to follow Sun Yixian's "Three Principles of the People" as it set up the new government. The principles called for freeing China from foreign control, establishing a democratic government, and improving the economy through the application of Socialist ideas. The Chinese had a difficult time putting these ideas into effect.

U.S. Imperialism

The United States started its empire in 1867 when it purchased Alaska from Russia. Americans had wanted Hawaii since the 1820s. A revolt there, led by American planters in 1893, brought the islands under United States control five years later.

Victory over Spain in the Spanish-American War (1898) gave the United States control of the Philippine Islands and Guam in the Pacific Ocean and of Puerto Rico in the Caribbean. The United States had entered the war to help Cuba gain its independence from Spain. But for years afterward, the United States government dominated Cuban affairs.

Panama Canal. For many years, the United States had wanted to build a canal across Central America. Panama seemed to be a good choice because the distance across it was shorter than in any other location. A French company had started to dig a canal in 1882, but the company went out of business in 1889. The Spanish-American War of 1898 convinced the United States that it needed a canal for national defense. It took too long for warships stationed in the Atlantic to reach the Pacific. The United States needed to protect its interests in the Philippines and other parts of East Asia.

In 1903, U.S. Secretary of State John Hay negotiated an agreement with Colombia to allow the United States to build a canal across Panama. Panama was part of Colombia at that time. The Colombian legislature refused to approve the agreement. In November 1903, Panama revolted against Colombia. U.S. President Theodore Roosevelt supported this action and quickly recognized Panama's independence. The United States was given the right to build and operate a canal and govern an area around it called the Panama Canal Zone. In return, Panama received an annual payment. The canal officially opened in 1920. Panama is to take over operation of the canal on the last day of 1999. Ships of all nations use the canal to move cargo between the Atlantic and Pacific.

Dollar Diplomacy. The United States also dominated the governments and economies of other Latin American countries through a policy called *Dollar Diplomacy*. This policy encouraged United States' businesses to invest in the development of countries and to

T. Roosevelt, watchdog of economic welfare in the Americas—and debt collector

build factories in them. Then, if one of these countries threatened or harmed U.S. business interests, the United States government would send troops to protect American lives and property. The United States also tried to regulate events in the Caribbean and Latin America to protect the Panama Canal.

Between about 1912 and 1934, the United States used the policy of Dollar Diplomacy as an excuse to interfere in the affairs of several Latin American countries. Chief among them were Nicaragua, Haiti, the Dominican Republic, and Mexico.

Virgin Islands. In 1917, The United States purchased the Virgin Islands from Denmark. This purchase completed the building of the American Empire.

Multiple Perspectives on Imperialism

Imposing Foreign Ways. European nations reshaped the countries they colonized. The industrialization imposed on these countries caused some of the most profound changes. Although industries modernized, strengthened, and enriched the countries, they disrupted traditional economies, cultures, and social organizations. Before industrialization, most of the inhabitants of the colonized countries lived in villages where they earned their living by farming and craftwork.

Suddenly, many of these people had to perform different kinds of work and sometimes live in areas away from their families. (Sabata in the story at the beginning of the chapter had this experience.)

New Governments and Religions. European officials took the place of traditional rulers. The wealth and technology of the new rulers challenged the natives' code of values and their sense of self-worth. The Europeans taught them that their own country's welfare was not as important as the welfare of the colonizing country. European missionaries preached against local religions. They encouraged the people to dress, talk, and behave like Europeans. Some native people, though, did enjoy more money and a better lifestyle than they had before colonial rule.

Discrimination and Resentment. But no matter how comfortable the native people became or how European they seemed, most Europeans never fully accepted them. The colonized people seldom had the same opportunities to obtain wealth and power and often faced severe discrimination.

Eventually, most people in colonized countries began to resent their foreign rulers. Some demanded equal rights with Europeans. Others became strongly nationalistic and wanted their countries to regain independence. Often, it was the Western-educated natives who led the movements for independence.

Effect on Colonial Powers. Imperialism altered life in the home countries as well. Raw materials and new products from the colonies brought great wealth to some. The home countries' economies improved and their standards of living rose. Colonies provided places for educated and skilled Europeans to build careers in business or government. Such careers often gave them greater prestige than they might have achieved at home. Different forms of music, art, and literature enriched Western culture. The remains of ancient civilizations that were discovered in Asia, Africa, and Latin America advanced Western learning.

Perhaps the most important effect of imperialism in Europe was on the relationships among the Western nations. Although Britain continued to be a leader in Europe, it withdrew its attention from that continent in order to govern its colonies. In the process of unifying, Germany had gained a great deal of strength. Its only rival on the European continent was France.

Russia took over territory along its borders. The Western powers tried to keep Russia from gaining too much power in South Asia.

Triple Alliance. Bismarck, Germany's chancellor, saw France as a threat. In order to weaken it, he set up the Triple Alliance in 1882. The Triple Alliance was an agreement among Germany, Italy, and Austria to separate France from the other major European powers. Bismarck believed that isolation would prevent France from starting a war. For a while, the Triple Alliance brought peace to Europe.

Aggressive Tactics. When Wilhelm II became the new German kaiser in 1889, he upset this balance of power. Wanting Germany to become an imperialist power, he took several measures to strengthen it as a military force. Dismissing Bismarck, Wilhelm II began to change the Triple Alliance into an aggressive rather than a peaceful force. He also began to build up the German navy. Britain saw this as a threat to its control of the seas and, in turn, began to construct more and bigger ships.

Reaction. France also felt alarmed by Germany's increased militarization and entered an arms race with that country. As small neighboring nations watched Germany develop its military and industrial power, they also began to feel unsafe. Europe's delicate balance of power was now in danger.

INFO CHECK

1. Select one Western European nation that engaged in imperialism in the 19th and 20th centuries. Describe how that nation built an empire.

2. Define or identify each of the following: Sepoy Mutiny, Boer War, Opium War, Open Door Policy, Boxer Rebellion.

3. Explain the difference between a colony, a sphere of influence, and a protectorate.

4. Explain the role of Dollar Diplomacy in the building of the American Empire.

JAPAN'S RESPONSE TO WESTERN IMPERIALISM

Starting in 1603, a series of shoguns from the Tokugawa family ruled Japan. They encouraged trade and industry. However, in the early 1600s, they became suspicious of the influence of Christians and European traders. In 1612, the shogun began to persecute Christians and European traders. He drove out the missionaries and restricted the activities of foreign traders. By 1641, only one port was open to outsiders—traders from the Netherlands. Any Japanese person who was away from the country at the time could not return. Japan isolated itself from the outside world for more than 200 years.

Although Japan prospered under the Tokugawa Shogunate, the Japanese began to desire change. The one Dutch trading ship that arrived each year brought European books. From these books, scholars learned about Western ideas. They were particularly interested in geography, medicine, and military tactics.

In the 19th century, new ideas and financial problems weakened the Tokugawa shoguns. They could not resist a new effort by Western nations to trade with Japan.

Opening Up Trade

Starting in the late 1700s, Russian, British, French, and American officials tried unsuccessfully to establish relations with Japan. In 1853, Commodore Matthew Perry of the United States sailed into Tokyo Bay with four ships. Perry presented Japanese officials with a letter from President Millard Fillmore asking for trading privileges. Perry left and the following year returned with more ships. Without modern weapons, the shogun could not resist. He signed an agreement opening Japan to trade with the United States.

Under this treaty, Japan agreed to allow American traders to come to two ports. An official, called a consul, was allowed to live in Japan to take care of American citizens and businesses. In 1858, the U.S. consul made another treaty with Japan. This opened more ports to U.S. ships and set tariffs. It also permitted Americans to live in Japan under U.S. laws rather than under Japanese laws. In return, the United States promised to help the Japanese build up and modernize its army and navy. The Japanese then negotiated similar treaties with Great Britain, Russia, France, and the Netherlands.

Increased contacts with the West made the Japanese aware of the wealth and military power of Europe and the United States. Japan appeared backward by comparison. As a result, discontent with Tokugawa rule increased.

The Meiji Restoration

In 1867, some of Japan's most powerful nobles forced the shogun to resign. The Emperor Meiji took power the following year, thus restoring the position of emperor as the actual head of government. The rule of shoguns had ended. During the Meiji reign (1868–1912), Japan developed into a strong modern nation.

Rapid and dramatic changes transformed almost every aspect of life in Japan. Businesses imported new machinery to manufacture textiles and other goods. New systems of communication were established. A modern school system gave more Japanese children an opportunity to obtain an education. A national army and navy were created. No other nation achieved the goal of modernization in so short a time.

Japan's first constitution went into effect in 1889. It created a *Diet*, or parliament, and recognized the emperor as a god. The emperor had certain powers, but a small group of officials exercised the real authority. Although they set up a strong central government, they included some democratic features, such as political parties.

To increase national loyalty, Japanese leaders revived the ancient code of Bushido, the "path of the warrior." It stressed honor, loyalty, fearlessness, and absolute obedience to the emperor.

Time Line

Year	Dates and Events
A.D.	
1500	**1500s–1800s:** Spain, Portugal, Britain, France colonize parts of Africa, Asia, Americas
	1641: Shoguns of Japan initiate 200-year ban on foreign trade and culture
	1756–1763: Britain defeats France in Seven Years' War; becomes major power in India
1800	**1820:** Liberia founded by former U.S. slaves
1801	**1839–1842:** China loses Opium War to Britain, cedes Hong Kong; Westerners gain new trading ports
	1853–1854: Commodore Perry opens Japan to U.S. trade
	1857–1859: Sepoy Mutiny; British government rules India directly as colony
	1858: U.S.-Japanese treaty opens up more Japanese trading ports, wins rights for foreign residents
	1858: China opens additional ports
	1867: U.S. purchases Alaska from Russia
	1867–1886: Discovery of diamonds in Boer South Africa
	1868–1912: Meiji Dynasty reclaims imperial power from shoguns; Japan industrializes
	1869: Suez Canal linking Mediterranean and Red seas is opened
	1882: Britain takes political control of Egypt and Suez Canal
	1882: Germany, Austria, Italy form Triple Alliance to limit French influence in Europe
	1884–1885: Berlin Conference sets rules for European control of African territories
	1889: Wilhelm II becomes kaiser of Germany; rise of German militarism
	1889: Japan's first constitution—limited monarchy, strong official class, some democratic features
1900	**1893–1898:** Revolt by American planters in Hawaii brings islands under U.S. control
1901	**1895:** Japan wins Sino-Japanese War, gains Taiwan, controls independent Korea
	1898: U.S. wins Spanish-American War, gains control of Philippines, Guam, Puerto Rico
	1899: U.S. "Open Door Policy" calls for equal rights for all nations trading in China
	1899: Boers revolt against British rule in South Africa
	1900: International force crushes Boxer Rebellion in China
	1904–1905: Russo-Japanese War weakens Russia, expands Japan's influence in Asia
	1908: Belgian government takes control of Congo
	1910: Creation of (Boer-British) Union of South Africa
	1911: Revolution led by Sun Yixian overthrows Manchus, declares China a republic
	1912–1934: U.S. intervenes in affairs of Nicaragua, Haiti, Dominican Republic, Mexico
	1917: U.S. purchases Virgin Islands from Denmark
	1920: Panama Canal opens; U.S. controls Canal Zone
	1941–1945: Japan loses World War II and its empire
2000	**1999:** Panama takes over control of canal

By the beginning of the 20th century, Japan had become a modern industrial and military power. Government leaders felt ready to compete with Western nations for colonies in Asia.

Japan as a Global Power

The Japanese believed that they needed to expand in order to build up their country's economy. Japan had few natural resources. It was dependent on the world market for the raw materials that kept its industries going.

To gain new markets and sources of raw materials, Japan began colonizing nearby countries. At the end of the 19th century, Japan used its increased military power and industrial strength to take over

Japanese Imperialism   1875–1910

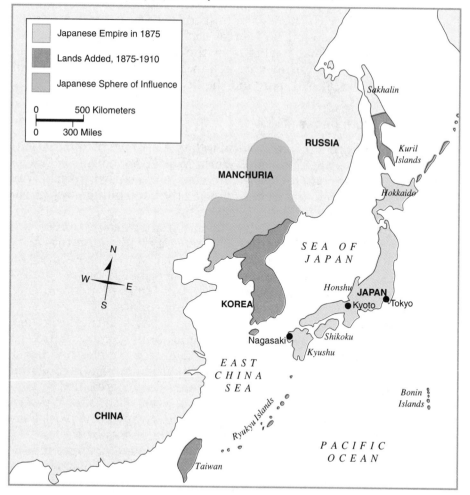

parts of East Asia. It fought the Sino-Japanese War over Korea from 1894 to 1895. Victory over China gave Japan control of Taiwan until the end of World War II in 1945. Korea officially kept its independence, but Japan actually controlled it until 1945.

In the late 1800s, disputes arose between Russia and Japan over interests in Korea and Manchuria. They went to war. The Russo-Japanese War (1904–1905) also ended in a Japanese victory. President Theodore Roosevelt took a part in ending the fighting and negotiating the peace treaty. The war weakened Russia but strengthened Japan. Japan's military and naval power impressed the West. It received Russian-controlled territory in China, the southern half of Sakhalin Island, and rights to build a railroad in Manchuria. Russia recognized Japan's influence in Korea. (Japan made Korea a colony in 1910.) Participation on the winning side in World War I (1914–1918) enabled Japan to acquire German-owned islands in the Pacific Ocean.

The Japanese Empire reached its peak in the early 1940s. During the 1930s and 1940s, the government built the Greater East Asia Co-Prosperity Sphere with the idea of uniting eastern Asia under Japanese control. Japanese military forces conquered much of China and Southeast Asia and many islands in the Pacific. Conflict with the United States and its European allies in World War II (1941–1945) resulted in the defeat of Japan and the loss of its empire.

The Retreat From Imperialism

Few colonies are left in the world today. A strong spirit of nationalism arose in the colonies when World War II ended in 1945. The swift defeat of European forces by Japanese forces early in World War II affected the way colonial nations viewed the controlling powers. No longer did the Europeans seem so powerful.

By various tactics, the leaders of nationalist groups forced the imperialist nations to realize that the colonies had rights too. Also, the war badly weakened Great Britain and France. They could no longer afford to administer and defend their colonies. Some colonies had to fight wars to win their freedom. Others achieved independence through peaceful agreements with the ruling country.

The imperialist nations did bring some benefits to their colonies. They introduced modern technology and built roads, railroads, bridges, schools, and hospitals. But the colonized peoples had fewer rights in their own lands than did their imperialist masters. Colonial people were treated as second-class citizens. They were ruled by governments they did not choose and laws they did not make. Western ways disrupted their traditional ways of life. Eventually, most Europeans and Americans came to regard imperialism as evil.

Unit V covered a time of revolutions, of profound changes in philosophy, education, governments, economies, work, and non-Western cultures. Unit VI shows how the pace of change increased even more. It describes an era of terrible crises and great achievements. Chapter 25 discusses some of the scientific and medical advances that took place during the early 20th century.

INFO CHECK

1. How did Commodore Perry's visit to Japan in 1853 lead to the Meiji Restoration?

2. Explain the role of the Sino-Japanese War (1894–1895) and the Russo-Japanese War (1904–1905) in the rise of the Japanese Empire.

3. How was the Japanese Empire affected by World War I (1914–1918) and World War II (1939–1945)?

CHAPTER REVIEW

Multiple Choice

1. The Industrial Revolution encouraged the policy of imperialism because industrialized nations needed

    1. raw materials and markets
    2. investment opportunities for surplus funds
    3. military bases to expand their areas of conquest
    4. all of the above.

2. Until 1857, the private stock company that ruled India for profit was the

    1. Dutch West India Company
    2. Hanseatic League
    3. East India Company
    4. Merchants of Venice.

3. Native Indian soldiers revolted against their British officers because they

    1. wanted better wages and working conditions
    2. believed that the use of new ammunition violated their Hindu and Muslim beliefs
    3. had not been paid for over three months

    4. thought mercenary soldiers were going to take over their jobs.

4. The Suez Canal was a vital waterway because it

    1. shortened the sailing distance between the east and west coasts of America
    2. controlled all sea travel between the Mediterranean Sea and Atlantic Ocean
    3. was the only ice-free waterway from Eastern Europe to the Atlantic Ocean
    4. shortened the sailing time from England to India.

5. South Africa was the location of many battles because

    1. imperialistic European powers sought control of the region
    2. European powers fought over natural resources
    3. native peoples, European immigrants, and imperialistic powers fought for control of the area and its natural resources
    4. its oilfields were necessary for industrial growth.

6. The Berlin Conference clearly illustrated that

   1. Germany dominated all other Western European nations
   2. Africans' nationalistic desires were to be recognized by the European nations
   3. the nations of the world were anxious to preserve world peace
   4. Africa was to be controlled by the imperialistic European nations.

7. The superiority of Western military technology was demonstrated by the

   1. rapid defeat of the Chinese forces in the Opium War
   2. Taiping Rebellion in Japan
   3. granting of extraterritorial rights only to European nations
   4. privileges given to European merchants to trade in the city of Canton.

8. Examples of Chinese nationalism would be

   1. the Taiping Rebellion and the Open Door Policy
   2. the granting of extraterritorial rights and tariff reductions
   3. formation of the Nationalist Party and the Boxer Rebellion
   4. none of the above.

9. The nations of Latin America were dominated by

   1. Germany and its policy of expansionism
   2. Russia and its policy of Pan-Slavism
   3. America and its policy of Dollar Diplomacy
   4. Britain and its policy of mercantilism.

10. Japanese nobles reacted to the growth of Western imperialism and the opening of China by

    1. shutting out all foreign traders
    2. supporting the shogun and his military advisers
    3. forcing the Meiji Restoration
    4. taking over Chinese and Korean territory.

11. Study the map on page 528 and choose the most accurate statement.

    1. By 1914, colonies no longer existed in America.
    2. The United States and Japan had no colonies in 1914.
    3. By 1914, imperialism had an impact on areas in both Africa and Asia.
    4. France and England continued to fight each other over possession of colonies.

12. Which conclusion about spheres of influence in China can be reached by studying the map on page 537?

    1. Industrial areas were usually included within spheres of influence.
    2. Most spheres of influence were in southern China.
    3. Spheres of influence tended to include coastal areas, rivers, and ports.
    4. The government of China had lost control of most of its territory.

13. The artist who drew the cartoon on page 538 believed that

    1. other nations were acting in China's best interests
    2. the Chinese government was in complete control of its affairs
    3. the nations of the world fought one another for preferential trade agreements
    4. the way in which imperialist nations divided China and controlled it was not in China's best interests.

Thematic Essays

1. Ethnocentrism is an attitude common to all societies. *Task:* Describe how this attitude affected relations between the imperialistic nations of Europe and the peoples of China, Japan, and India. Take into consideration religious, social, and political factors.

2. Technology can have beneficial or harmful effects. *Task:* What would be the Chinese and Japanese views of the effects of Western technology on their cultures?

Document-Based Questions

Use the documents and your knowledge of Global History and Geography to answer the questions.

1. Study the cartoon on page 540. Why does the artist show Theodore Roosevelt as being able to pull ships and walk through oceans?

2. Japanese Prince Ito Hirobumi wrote, regarding the modernization of Japan:

"... We realized fully how necessary it was that the Japanese people should not only adopt Western methods but should also speedily become competent to do without the aid of foreign instruction and supervision. ... I have always recognized the vital importance of a supremely efficient navy and army. ..."

List the goals the prince wants to pursue. Why is he urging this course of action?

3. From a Chinese leader's view of Japanese activities, December 10, 1874:

"Japan recently has changed to the practice of Western military methods, has imitated the West in building railways, setting up telegraph lines, opening coal and iron mines. ... She has also sent many students to foreign countries to acquire learning and practice in the use of machinery and technology."

Describe two methods this Chinese observer says Japan is using to modernize without being controlled by Europeans.

Document-Based Essay

Task: Using historical examples, explain why Japan, which was smaller than China, became an imperialistic nation while the larger China was dominated by imperialists.

UNIT REVIEW

Thematic Essays

1. Refer to the description of the Irish potato famine on pages 520–522 and the following quote by Thomas Malthus to answer the question.

"I say that the power of population is indefinitely greater than the power in the earth to produce subsistence for man ... Population, when unchecked, increases in a geometric ratio. Subsistence only increases in an arithmetic ratio."

Task: In the case of the Irish potato famine, discuss whether Malthus's gloomy predictions were correct or whether other factors (social, political, economic, or cultural) contributed more to the famine.

2. New ideas, technologies, and inventions changed the lives of the people in the Industrial Age. AGREE or DISAGREE: The majority of the people worldwide at that time benefited from these changes. *Task:* Include social and economic factors in your answer.

Document-Based Questions

Use your knowledge of Global History and Geography and the documents to answer the questions.

1. Samuel Smiles in his book *Self-Help* (1859) wrote:

   "The spirit of self-help is the root of all genuine growth in the individual ... it constitutes the true source of national vigor and strength."

   Why would this writer be opposed to labor unions?

2. Adam Smith in *The Wealth of Nations* wrote:

   "Every man, as long as he does not violate the laws of justice, is left perfectly free to pursue his own interest his own way, and to bring both his industry [efforts] and capital [money] into competition with those of any other men or order of men."

   According to Smith, how will wealth be achieved? By whose efforts will wealth be achieved?

3. Adam Smith in *The Division of Labour* wrote:

   "The greatest improvement in the productive powers of labour ... seems to have been the effect of the division of labour. This great increase of the quantity of work is owing to three different circumstances ... lastly to the invention of a great number of machines which facilitate [aid] labour and enable one man to do the work of many."

   Describe two things that Adam Smith believed had increased the productivity of each laborer.

4. Frederick Engels in *Conditions of the Working Class in England* (1844) wrote:

   "It is only when [a person] has visited the slums of this great city, that it dawns upon him that the inhabitants of modern London have had to sacrifice so much that is best in human nature in order to create those wonders of civilization with which their city teems. ... Everyone exploits his neighbor with the result that the stronger tramples the weaker underfoot. The strongest of all, a tiny group of capitalists, monopolize everything while the weakest, who are in the vast majority, succumb [fall] to the most abject [deepest] poverty."

   What is the human cost of the advances of the Industrial Age and who is paying the price, according to Engels?

Document-Based Essay

Task: Using social and economic examples, explain why the capitalists were able to control the lives of the majority of the people in England in the mid-1800s.

UNIT VI

A Half-Century of Crisis and Achievement (1900–1945)

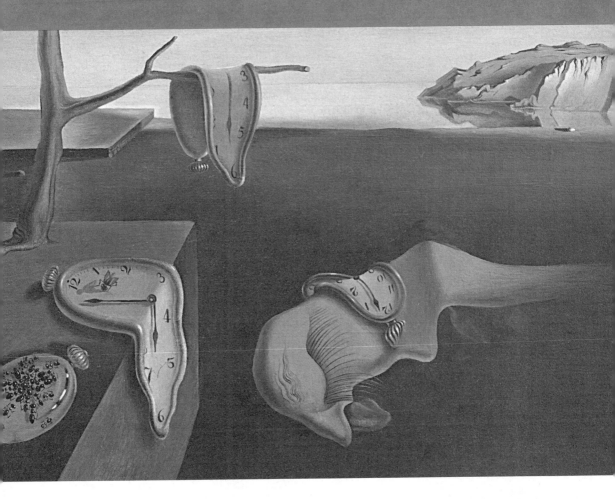

A Half-Century of Crisis and Achievement (1900–1945)

Year	Dates and Events
A.D. **1900**	**1905–1915:** Einstein's theories equating matter and energy—first step in development of nuclear power
	1914: Archduke Franz Ferdinand and wife assassinated; Central and Allied powers drawn into war
	1917: Germany renews U-boat raids on Allied (and U.S.) shipping; Zimmermann Note seeks Mexican-German alliance against U.S.; U.S. Congress declares war on Germany
	1917–1922: Russian Revolution; Communists in power; peace with Germany; creation of Soviet Union
1909	**1918:** Germans oust Kaiser Wilhelm II, ask Allies for peace
1910	**1919:** Treaty of Versailles humiliates Germany; sets up new nations based on nationalism
	1919–1922: Mussolini founds Italy's Fascist party; becomes prime minister and absolute dictator
	1920s–1940s: Culture of anxiety, disillusionment ("Lost Generation," dada, cubism, surrealism)
1919	**1928:** Fleming discovers penicillin
1920	**1930s:** Great Depression causes worldwide economic disaster
	1931: Japan seizes Manchuria
	1933: As German chancellor, Hitler initiates systematic killing of Jews, other minorities, political enemies
	1934–1935: Chinese Communists' "Long March"
	1936: Formation of Rome-Berlin Axis
	1937–1945: Jian and Mao join forces to resist Japanese in China
	1938: At Munich, Britain and France appease Hitler by ceding Sudentenland to Germany
1929	**1939:** German invasion of Czechoslovakia; German-Soviet nonaggression pact; German blitzkrieg in Poland; Britain and France declare war on Germany
1930	
	1941: Japan bombs Pearl Harbor; U.S. declares war on Japan; Germany and Italy declare war on U.S.
	1942–1943: Soviets defeat Germans at Stalingrad; push them west toward Germany
	1943: Italy signs armistice with Allies
1939	**1944:** D-Day; Allies invade Normandy, push Germans from France, Belgium, Netherlands
1940	**1945:** Mussolini executed; Russians enter Berlin, Hitler commits suicide, Germans surrender, war in Europe ends
	At Yalta Conference Allies plan German occupation, war crimes trials, United Nations
	U.S. drops atomic bombs on Hiroshima, Nagasaki; Japan surrenders
	50 nations meet in San Francisco to organize UN; U.S. Senate approves U.S. membership
1949	**1945–1946:** Cold war begins

CHAPTER

25

Medical, Scientific, and Technological Advances of the Early 20th Century

Catherine sighed and glanced out the window. Good heavens, dusk was falling. She had spent the whole day reading H. G. Wells's new novel, *The Time Machine* (1895). She was sorry she had finished—partly because it had been so exciting and partly because the ending had disappointed her. Why had Wells painted such a gloomy picture of the future? She, for one, believed that the world was getting better and better.

Here they were on the brink of a new century. Her parents were always saying how things had improved since they were young. Medical advances now were curing people of diseases that had once almost always been fatal. New inventions were making life easier and more fun. Surely in the 20th century, the problem of poverty would be solved. Crime would diminish. War would be eliminated.

Catherine wished her father would let her go to the university. She would become a scientist and help make at least some of these things come true.

L ike Catherine, many people at the end of the 19th century were optimistic about future progress. In the 20th century, scientists built on the advances made in the 1800s. New products improved the quality of life for great numbers of people. In the field of medicine, especially, scientists made such great strides forward that the optimism of the 19th century was almost justified. Expectations about progress in other areas were not met, however. War, disease, and poverty continued to plague the world.

MEDICAL ADVANCES

By the end of the 19th century, scientists had identified the causes of tuberculosis, typhoid fever, leprosy, malaria, cholera, diphtheria, and pneumonia. Chemists had developed new medications or more effective forms of old ones. Improvements in nutrition, personal hygiene, and public-health policies also contributed to a lower rate of deaths from infectious diseases.

Infection Fighters

Penicillin. Perhaps the most important medical advance was the discovery of the so-called wonder drugs. Penicillin, one of the earliest of these discoveries, was found by accident. In 1928, a Scottish microbiologist, Alexander Fleming, noticed that a culture of bacteria that he had been preparing had stopped growing. Contamination by a rare form of mold, called penicillin, had killed it. Fleming reasoned that if this mold could kill disease bacteria in the laboratory, it might also destroy them in the human body. Unfortunately, the mold was difficult to grow in large amounts, so Fleming lost interest in the experiment.

Several chemists at Oxford University in England in the late 1930s were intrigued by the possibilities of penicillin. Among them were Ernst Chain (originally from Austria) and Howard Florey. They finally produced enough of the substance in a pure form to prove that it was a powerful *antibiotic*. An antibiotic is a substance produced by one microorganism that can destroy another microorganism.

Because Great Britain was in the midst of World War II at the time, the drug companies there did not have the money and resources to manufacture the antibiotic. Chain and Florey brought their techniques to the United States. Drug companies there had sufficient resources to produce large amounts of penicillin. By 1944, enough was being made to help the wounded soldiers of World War II fight off infections.

Sulfa. In 1932, a German bacteriologist named Gerhard Domagk announced that a red dye, Prontosil, could cure infections in mice. Chemists soon realized that a simpler form of Prontosil, called sulfanilamide, was the agent that enabled the dye to destroy germs. The drugs derived from sulfanilamide were extremely effective in killing streptococci, germs that cause a serious and painful throat infection and other illnesses. Sulfa drugs saved many lives during World War II (1939–1945).

Since the discovery of penicillin and the sulfa drugs, many different types of "miracle drugs" have been made. Doctors prescribe them for a variety of problems, such as boils, wound infections, ear infections, tuberculosis, influenza, and bacterial meningitis. Unfortunately, overuse of these medicines has caused germs to build up resistance against them. As a result, they are no longer effective against some forms of infections. Today, scientists are searching for new antibiotics to treat the drug-resistant infections.

The Conquest of Polio

One of the most important medical victories of the 20th century was the development of a vaccine against poliomyelitis. Also known as infantile paralysis, this disease is caused by a virus to which young children are especially susceptible. In its most serious forms, it attacks the nervous system and sometimes paralyzes its victim. Franklin Delano Roosevelt, the U.S. president who held office during the Great Depression and World War II (1932–1945), had been crippled by polio.

No prevention existed for this disease until the 1950s when an American microbiologist named Jonas Salk developed a vaccine that protects people against it. By 1955, the vaccine had dramatically reduced the number of polio cases. An oral vaccine produced by Albert Sabin in 1960 was even more effective against the disease. In 1994, the nations of the Western Hemisphere were declared polio-free zones.

Conquering Diseases

As the 20th century progressed, medical researchers produced vaccines that prevented other childhood diseases, such as measles and whooping cough. Organizations, such as the World Health Organization (WHO) and United Nations Children's Fund (UNICEF), set up programs to immunize the world's children against diseases. By 1980, smallpox had been wiped out.

Advances in Surgery

In the first half of the 20th century, surgical techniques and procedures made spectacular advances. By 1912, neurosurgery was possible. This is surgery on the nerves, brain, and spinal cord. During World War I, surgeons improved methods of treating wounds and performing amputations. They also became interested in reconstructive surgery and learned to correct severe disfigurements caused by war wounds. During the Spanish Civil War (1936–1939), new techniques of blood transfusion enabled surgeons to save more lives than ever before.

As more antibiotics became available in the 1950s, surgery became even safer. Surgeons no longer limited themselves to removing tumors and damaged organs but began to restore the functions of damaged parts and to replace those that could not be fixed. In 1959, Dr. Åke Senning in Sweden implanted the first heart pacemaker. Doctors then began to work on methods of replacing hearts and other organs with those of animals and other humans as well as with artificial organs. The first human heart transplant was accomplished by Dr. Christiaan Barnard of South Africa in 1967.

The Importance of Mental Health

During the late 1800s and early 1900s, many people began to turn to medicine rather than religion and education to solve emotional and behavioral problems. Medical science, however, could not explain certain unusual workings of the mind. Troubling dreams and impulses to perform strange, even harmful acts, for example, could not be blamed on germs or other outside agents.

Freud. Doctors often could not find medical causes for some physical symptoms, such as certain kinds of paralysis. An Austrian neurologist named Sigmund Freud (lived 1856–1939) was intrigued by patients with such symptoms. Another doctor, Josef Breuer, had demonstrated that hypnotic suggestion could relieve many physical problems not caused by infection or damage to the nervous system. Pa-

Sigmund Freud, founder of psychoanalysis, photographed in 1921

tients who had such symptoms were said to be suffering from *neuroses*. At first, Freud tried different methods of hypnosis to treat neurotics. From his experiments with hypnosis, he developed what he called the "talking cure."

The "talking cure" evolved into *psychoanalysis*. In this method patients sit or lie down in a relaxed position and free associate, or say whatever comes into their minds. Freud found that during psychoanalysis, patients would often recall troubling experiences that they had totally forgotten. A discussion of their dreams, for example, frequently led people to remember material that they had stored in an area of the mind that Freud called the *unconscious*. When patients recovered these experiences, they usually felt the emotions the experiences had originally aroused. After reliving these memories, some patients lost their disturbing symptoms.

As Freud used psychoanalysis to study his patients, he formed theories about the human personality. One of Freud's most important concepts was that of the unconscious. He believed that the memories and desires hidden in this part of the mind have great influence on people's behavior. Because the memories are charged with strong feelings of guilt and desire, they often cause people to behave self-destructively or unethically. Therefore, education and punishment alone are not always able to bring about productive and moral behavior. Freud hoped that psychoanalysis would free people from the damage caused by painful experiences and allow them to make better use of the rational part of their minds. He claimed that he wanted his therapy to free people so that they could love and work.

Jung. One of Freud's colleagues, a Swiss doctor named Carl Gustav Jung (lived 1875–1961), also believed that the unconscious controls people's lives. He, however, felt that it could have a creative and healing influence. According to Jung's theories, part of a person's unconscious is linked to the collective unconscious. The collective unconscious is a pool of symbols and patterns called *archetypes* that are common to the whole human race. He felt that symbols and myths that deal with rebirth and salvation are evidence that the human mind has a natural tendency to seek a condition of wholeness and balance. Art, he argued, owes much of its power to its expression of this tendency. Jung encouraged his patients to draw and write their dreams and fantasies as a method of enlisting the aid of the collective unconscious against neuroses and other forms of mental illness.

Adler. Besides Jungian therapy, many other psychological theories and treatments arose from Freud's basic theories. Alfred Adler (lived 1870–1937), also of Austria, focused on what he called the "inferiority complex." He felt that people who have extremely poor opinions of themselves cannot adjust properly to society. The goal of his therapy was to help people gain better self-images so that they could function well with others. Adler's ideas have influenced many mental health professionals who deal with criminals, drug addicts, and people who have trouble holding a job.

Value of Therapy. While they have not transformed society, the various psychotherapies have relieved the loneliness and despair of many unhappy and confused people. The theories on which psychotherapies are based have given rise to important studies of human behavior. The results of these studies have proven valuable in child rearing, education, and the management of groups of people. Social scientists continue to look to psychology for methods of preventing and responding to crime and drug addiction. Interest in psychology has also led to the establishment of mental health services that deal with acute family problems, such as child abuse.

Many governments have established agencies that seek to promote mental health. In the United States, for example, the National Institute of Mental Health is dedicated to curing mental illness. It concerns itself with the training of psychologists and social workers and the construction of clinics and other facilities. It also provides leadership, technical assistance, and financial aid to more local mental-health agencies.

Results of Medical Advances

The effects of medical science are easier to measure than those of the psychotherapies. For the most part, the former have been positive. Improved diet, drugs, medical techniques, and personal hygiene have extended the life spans of people throughout the world. In North America and Western Europe, life expectancy has increased from an average of 50 years in the 1800s to an average of 75 years in the 1900s. Medical advances have reduced the number of infant and child deaths.

Scientists are presently working on ways to prevent global epidemics. Public health officials throughout the world are constantly on the watch for viruses that might cause widespread health problems. By recognizing such viruses in time, officials hope to limit their effects. AIDS (Acquired Immune Deficiency Syndrome) affected some 30.6 million people worldwide in 1997. Scientists are working to find effective ways to prevent and treat this destructive illness. They are also concerned about potential outbreaks of the Ebola virus. No one knows what causes people to acquire this fatal infection. Nor do they know how to treat it.

INFO CHECK

1. Why do you think "wonder drugs" were not made before the 20th century?

2. Define psychoanalysis and list the three pioneers in this field. Whose theories of treatment make the most sense to you? Give reasons for your choice.

3. Evaluate the medical advances. To what extent have they helped people?

PURE SCIENCE AND TECHNOLOGY

Advances in the field of physics have had a greater impact on 20th-century history than advances in any other science. Discoveries in this field have given us an awesome new source of power—nuclear energy.

Atomic Energy

In the late 19th century, physicists made discoveries that led them to question established ideas about physical reality. Prior to these discoveries, they had thought that atoms, the so-called building blocks of matter, were tiny, solid balls. Marie and Pierre Curie provided the first contradiction to this idea. In 1899, when they discovered the new element radium, they observed that its atoms do not have a constant atomic weight. (This is the average mass of an atom of an element.) The atoms constantly give off tiny particles of matter called electrons and protons.

Planck. The German physicist Max Planck (lived 1858–1947) took up the study of subatomic energy. He discovered in 1900 that an atom releases its particles in uneven spurts, which he called *quanta*. His ideas are called the quantum theory. Quantum mechanics is part of this theory. Planck's studies of subatomic energy suggested that there is no sharp division between matter and energy.

Einstein. Albert Einstein (lived 1879–1955) did more than anyone else to challenge traditional ideas about physical reality. He is considered to be one of the greatest scientists ever. Einstein was driven out of Germany in 1933 by the Nazi government. The rest of his life was spent in the United States.

Einstein's theory of relativity corrected Newtonian concepts of

Einstein baffles an audience of scientists with this chalk equation, 1931

time and space. Newton had believed the concepts to be constant. In a universe where space and time are constant, speed and distance can be measured. Einstein pointed out that space and time are not constant. Because everything is in motion, there is no fixed point from which to measure it.

To illustrate his ideas, Einstein gave various everyday examples involving trains and elevators. Suppose that a person walked from the center of a moving train to the front of it. The distance that the person travels and the speed of his or her motion will be different if measured from inside the train than if measured from a point outside it. This means that measurements of speed and distance are relative to the frame of reference from which they are measured. The speed of light is an exception to this theory, however. No matter from which frame of reference it is measured, the speed of light is constant.

Einstein also disproved the belief that atoms are tiny balls of matter that cannot be reduced into other forms. He stated that matter and energy are basically the same thing. His equation $E = mc^2$ expressed the fact that a tiny particle of matter is capable of releasing vast amounts of energy. This equation, by unlocking the potential energy of the atom, was the first major step in the development of atomic and nuclear weapons.

Rutherford. A New Zealand physicist, Ernest Rutherford (lived 1871–1937), described the structure of the atom in 1911. As though they were planets in a tiny solar system, units of electrical energy, called protons, orbit around a central particle, called the nucleus. In 1917, Rutherford split the atom by artificial means, an achievement that made the development of atomic weapons and nuclear power plants a practical reality.

Meitner. The work of Lise Meitner (lived 1878–1968) of Germany and Sweden also contributed to current uses of nuclear power. In 1939, she and her colleague Otto Frisch (of Austria) identified nuclear fission—the process by which a heavy nucleus combines with another particle and then divides into two other, lighter nuclei. They also realized that because this process would occur in a chain reaction, the energy it released would be enormous.

Nuclear Fission. World War II increased efforts to produce the superweapons promised by the process of nuclear fission. Danish physicist Niels Bohr was working on a theory of nuclear fission when the Germans invaded Denmark in 1940. Learning that the Germans planned to force him to produce an atomic bomb for their war effort, he escaped to the United States in 1943. Bohr joined British and American scientists working on the atomic bomb project at Los Alamos, New Mexico.

The Bomb. The project to develop the atomic bomb was called the Manhattan Project to keep it a secret. Among the other physicists who contributed to the development of the atomic bomb were Enrico

Lise Meitner, scientist credited with valuable early work on the development of the atomic bomb

Fermi, J. Robert Oppenheimer, and Edward Teller. Fermi's experiments with nuclear fission had resulted in the first sustained nuclear reaction in 1942. Oppenheimer was director of the weapons laboratory that produced the bombs in 1945. Teller later used his experience on the Manhattan Project to formulate theories that led to the production of the much more powerful thermonuclear, or hydrogen, bomb. Oppenheimer and Teller disagreed about the future of nuclear weapons. When Oppenheimer opposed further development, Teller publicly criticized his judgment. Many scientists of the time felt that Teller's criticism heightened suspicions of Oppenheimer's loyalty to the United States and hurt his career.

INFO CHECK

1. Complete the following sentences:
   a. $E = mc^2$ is the formula that expresses Albert Einstein's _____ of _____.
   b. The development of atomic weapons and nuclear power plants was made possible when Ernest Rutherford _____.
   c. Niels Bohr worked on the theory of _____.
2. Explain why you AGREE or DISAGREE with J. Robert Oppenheimer's opposition to the further development of nuclear weapons.

IMPROVEMENTS IN THE STANDARD OF LIVING— EARLY 20TH CENTURY

In the early 20th century, daily life for people of the industrialized nations changed dramatically. Science, technology, and industry worked together to produce extraordinary new tools, weapons, and luxury goods.

Electricity

In the early 20th century, more and more people began to wire their homes for electricity. This enabled them to use appliances that made it easier and faster to do household chores. The use of electric refrigerators, washing machines, and vacuum cleaners gave people more time for leisure activities. City dwellers could use elevators instead of stairs to reach their apartments on the upper floors. Elevators also allowed architects to design skyscrapers, which created more space in crowded urban areas for housing and offices.

Farmers especially benefited from the new conveniences. Refrigerators and freezers kept meat fresh longer. Electrically heated hatcheries and barns saved the lives of baby chicks and newly born calves and lambs. Telephones brought help to isolated farmers in

American magazine advertisement for an electric stove, 1927

times of crisis. Electrically powered machines made it possible to run larger, more profitable farms. Today some farms are so heavily automated that they resemble factories.

Electricity now came into use to power machinery in factories and equipment in offices. It made possible other means of communication besides the telephone.

Entertainment and Propaganda

New forms of public entertainment became popular in the early 1900s. Motion pictures attracted audiences to movie theaters. Entertainment and news reached into individual homes via the radio.

Movies. In the 1890s Thomas Edison created a device to show moving pictures. He went on to develop the early motion picture industry in the United States.

The first movie theaters appeared in Los Angeles in 1902. People flocked to them to see short silent films, such as *The Great Train Robbery*. (As the term implies, silent films had no sound. Viewers read the dialogue, which was projected onto the screen.) Encouraged by the success of these films, directors began to make longer, more serious ones. The Italian film *Quo Vadis* and the American film *Birth of a Nation* appeared during this era. Some famous names from the silent films of the 1920s are Mack Sennett, who created the Keystone

Charlie Chaplin and four-year-old Jackie Coogan as they appeared in the movie classic *The Kid*, 1920

LENI RIEFENSTAHL'S OLYMPIA

At the end of World War II in 1945, one of the most talented filmmakers of the early 20th century was blacklisted and shunned by the motion picture industry. Although her films were regarded as masterpieces, they had been used as propaganda by Nazi dicatator Adolf Hitler in the 1930s. Despite being cleared of any wrongdoing by a special court, Leni Riefenstahl's career had come to an end.

Born in Germany in 1902, Riefenstahl studied painting and ballet in Berlin. From 1923 to 1926, she performed in dance programs throughout Europe. Riefenstahl began her motion picture career as an actress in German "mountain films." In such films, landscapes, especially mountain scenes, were featured. Leni eventually became a film director and, in 1931, formed her own production company.

With the support of the Nazi party in the 1930s, Riefenstahl directed films that glorified the German ideal of physical beauty and the belief in the superiority of the "Aryan race." (This referred to Germans and people of German descent.) Although she made several films, she became best known for *Triumph of the Will*. This was a documentary study of the 1934 Nazi party convention at Nuremberg. It demonstrated to the world the unity and power of the dictatorship of Hitler and introduced Nazi leaders to the German people. Like all of Riefenstahl's films, it featured a rich musical score, scenic beauty, and brilliant editing.

Despite Leni's association with the Nazi party, one of her best films had no propaganda value to it. *Olympia* was a two-part record of the 1936 Olympic games, which were held in Germany. The film was praised for the effectiveness of its music and sound effects. The film was commissioned by Hitler, who is seen briefly in the ceremonies opening the games. However, *Olympia* does not glorify Nazi achievements. Instead, it documents the athletic skills of men and women of all races and nationalities and even records the German teams losing events.

Olympia showcases the legendary track and field achievements of Jesse Owens, an African American. Owens shattered sports records and Hitler's myth of Aryan supremacy. Other memorable scenes include the equestrian events in which several horses threw their riders before reaching the toughest hurdles. Also featured is a pole vault competition that lasted well into the night, with athletes charging out of the darkness and soaring through the sky.

Film critics have praised Riefenstahl's superb direction, enhanced by slow-motion photography, low-angle camera placement, and ingenious tracking shots. *Olympia* has been called a brilliant film record of the human spirit and athletic excellence. It is not about politics and was an embarrassment to the Nazis. Nevertheless, Riefenstahl's other films reflected the Nazi ideology of the 1930s, and served their propaganda purposes. As a result, she made few films after World War II.

1. How would you respond to those who argue that Riefenstahl should have been allowed to keep making films after World War II, despite her association with a brutal and racist dictatorship?

2. What does Riefenstahl's career tell us about the role of technology in filmmaking in the early part of the 20th century?

Cops, Mary Pickford, Lillian Gish, and Rudolph Valentino. Charlie Chaplin became famous for his portrayal of a touching and hilarious little tramp.

In the 1930s, a severe economic depression struck Europe and the United States. Movies were now equipped with sound tracks. Moviegoers could hear their favorite stars sing and engage in witty conversations. Hollywood began turning out musical comedies that gave the broke and jobless a chance to escape into a glittering, lighthearted world.

Use as Propaganda. As the 1930s wore on, movies began to serve another purpose—to promote a point of view. They were developed as *propaganda* pieces. The term propaganda refers to ideas that are deliberately spread to benefit a particular cause or to damage an opposing one. The silent American film *Birth of a Nation* influenced what many Americans thought about the Civil War. The film represents the view of the Confederate side and the Ku Klux Klan. It gives a racist interpretation of the war and the Reconstruction period afterward.

Political leaders began to use the movies to stir up nationalistic feelings. In Russia, a director named Sergei Eisenstein made films that presented the history of Russia from a Communist point of view. One was *Ten Days That Shook the World* (1928). The Nazi dictator in Germany, Adolf Hitler, commissioned Leni Riefenstahl to make *The Triumph of the Will*, a documentary film that glorified the Nazi party.

Radio. The first European and American radio stations began broadcasting in the 1920s. The coverage of a concert by the famous Australian soprano Nellie Melba aroused the public's interest in the new medium. Soon, many people in Western nations had cheap, mass-produced radios. In America, anyone who had a radio could tune into music, soap operas, news broadcasts, and ball games.

Politicians used the radio as well as the movies to influence public opinion. Hitler and the Italian dictator Mussolini allowed no other point of view but their own to be expressed on the airwaves of their countries. Both British Prime Minister Stanley Baldwin and U.S. President Franklin Roosevelt gave informal talks over the radio. (Roosevelt's were called fireside chats.) While listening to the broadcasts, many people felt that the great leaders were their personal friends.

Commercials. In the United States, radio had another important effect on the listening public. In this country, the networks were owned by private companies. They paid for broadcasts by selling airtime to advertisers who wanted to promote products or services. During brief *commercials*, announcers advertised laundry soap, cigarettes, and other goods by giving little sales pitches and singing jingles. Listeners tended to buy brands that they had heard mentioned on their favorite shows.

The largest audiences tuned in to programs that presented comfortable and familiar ideas. Therefore, advertisers seldom sponsored

Time Line

Year	Dates and Events
A.D. **1801**	

1856–1939: Life of Freud; developed psychological therapy based on theories of unconscious and human personality

1870–1937: Life of Adler; developed psychological therapy based on theory of inferiority complex

1875–1961: Life of Jung; developed psychological therapy based on theory of collective unconscious

1879–1955: Life of Einstein; theory of relativity (space and time are in motion, not measurable); formulas equating matter and energy

1890s: Edison invents device to show moving pictures

1899: Pierre and Marie Curie discover radium and its particle-emitting properties

1900: Planck develops quantum theory linking matter and energy

1902: First movie theaters open in Los Angeles

1911: Rutherford splits atom

1912: Neurosurgery made possible

1914–1918: Development of reconstructive surgery

1920s: First American and European radio broadcasts

1928: Fleming discovers penicillin

1930s: Rise of movies with sound tracks; increased use of movies for propaganda

1930s–1940s: Chain and Florey refine technique for mass production of penicillin

1930s–1940s: Domagk's sulfa drugs prove effective against bacterial infections

1936–1939: New techniques of blood transfusion save many lives

1939: Meitner and Frisch identify nuclear fission

1942: Fermi produces first sustained nuclear reaction

1945: Oppenheimer directs laboratory that produces first atomic bombs

1950s: Salk develops first vaccine effective against poliomyelitis

1952: Teller's theories, based on nuclear fission, produce hydrogen bomb

1959: Senning implants first heart pacemaker

1960: Sabin develops more effective oral vaccine against poliomyelitis

1967: Barnard performs first human heart transplant

1980s–1990s: Rise and spread of AIDS

1994: Western Hemisphere declared polio-free

1900

1901

2000

shows that offered challenging or controversial material. Cultural critics feared that narrow, commercial interests were shaping the American mentality. Some feared that advertisers might also control which political opinions were broadcast and which events were reported on news programs.

Television. Television has followed much the same path as movies and radio. It can be an effective vehicle of propaganda and is largely controlled by commercial interests. All three media, however, have brought cultural events and information to a wide audience. The media also unite people in times of tragedy—when a public figure dies—or joy—when ceremonies or worldwide sporting events take place. News pictures showing the effects of wars and disasters have sometimes inspired viewers to send help to the victims. Some fear that frequent exposure to the misery of others will make people turn away from bad news or become hardened to it.

Contrast in Ways of Living

At the beginning of the 20th century, the standard of living in industrialized countries contrasted sharply with the standard of living in nonindustrialized countries. Many of the latter were either still colonized by greater powers or had just won their independence. These countries were located mainly in Asia, Africa, and Latin America. Having few industries, these countries relied heavily on farming, which was carried on in simple, traditional ways. Typically, their populations were divided into the very rich and the very poor. The poorer classes seldom had access to health facilities and schools.

Although the imperialistic Western nations did little to improve daily life for the greater number of their colonial subjects, they laid the foundations for later improvement. The colonizers built railroads, canals, bridges, and modern communication systems in the countries that they ruled. They also gave a small minority of their subjects Western educations. Once the colonized peoples threw off imperial rule, they used the structures and ideas left by their former masters to bring their countries into the modern world.

This chapter has provided a general introduction to the 20th century. Chapter 26 discusses the first global war, World War I, which took place early in the 1900s.

INFO CHECK

1. Which 20th-century invention do you think did most to improve the standard of living in the 20th century? Give reasons for your choice.

2. How were new inventions used for political propaganda purposes?

3. What great difference developed between industrialized and nonindustrialized countries in the 20th century?

CHAPTER REVIEW

Multiple Choice

1. In addition to new drugs, what other factors helped people live longer?

   1. improved diet and hygiene
   2. radio and television
   3. longer workweek
   4. a change in climate.

2. An antibiotic is a microorganism that can kill another microorganism. An example of an antibiotic is

   1. penicillin
   2. salt cube
   3. sugar cube
   4. anthrax.

3. Why were the vaccines developed by Jonas Salk and Albert Sabin so welcomed in the 1950s and 1960s?

   1. They made penicillin more effective.
   2. They gave protection against malaria.
   3. They protected children against the virus that causes poliomyelitis.
   4. They protected people against mental illness.

4. The United Nations Children's Fund and the World Health Organization are similar in that they both

   1. protect the world's environment
   2. operate only in developed nations
   3. have programs to prevent early-childhood diseases
   4. have both been thrown out of Pacific Rim nations.

5. The major theories of men such as Adler, Freud, and Jung attempted to prove that

   1. physical illness has nothing to do with one's self-image

2. the mind and the memories it holds can affect people's behavior
3. hypnosis can assist in treating certain types of burn patients
4. psychoanalysis is a waste of the patient's money.

6. Select the choice that correctly places the events in their order of occurrence:

   1. atomic bomb, $E = mc^2$, Manhattan Project, study of subatomic energy
   2. study of subatomic energy, atomic bomb, $E = mc^2$, Manhattan Project
   3. $E = mc^2$, study of subatomic energy, atomic bomb, Manhattan Project
   4. study of subatomic energy, $E = mc^2$, Manhattan Project, atomic bomb.

7. The person who might be called "the father of the hydrogen bomb" is

   1. Enrico Fermi
   2. Robert Oppenheimer
   3. Niels Bohr
   4. Edward Teller.

8. The German film *Triumph of the Will* and the American film *Birth of a Nation* were similiar in that they were

   1. both pieces of propaganda
   2. both box office failures
   3. the first films produced in color
   4. the first films having music and dialog sound tracks.

9. Advertisers quickly saw the value of radio and television because they

   1. influence people's political ideas
   2. reached a large number of people

3. made large profits from the ownership of radio and television stations

4. had stock shares in both the products and the film studios.

10. How did electricity change farming?

1. Made it harder to raise animals.

2. Made it possible to run larger, more profitable operations.

3. Made it necessary to decrease the size of farms.

4. Made it necessary for farmers to earn college degrees to run their farms.

11. According to the time line on page 552, which group of events is in the correct chronological order?

1. U.S. drops atomic bombs
   Russian Revolution
   Great Depression
   Hitler initiates systematic killing of Jews

2. Great Depression
   Hitler initiates systematic killing of Jews
   U.S. drops atomic bombs
   Russian Revolution

3. Hitler initiates systematic killing of Jews
   U.S. drops atomic bombs
   Great Depression
   Russian Revolution

4. Russian Revolution
   Great Depression
   Hitler initiates systematic killing of Jews
   U.S. drops atomic bombs

12. Study the movie still on page 563 and select the statement that best describes the situation depicted.

1. I'm okay, you're okay.

2. Want to hear another joke?

3. It's you and me against the world.

4. Happy New Year!

Thematic Essay

As a result of World War I, many advances in medical science and mental health came about. *Task:* Identify and describe any two examples of such advances. Make sure to show how their development and use are linked to World War I.

Document-Based Questions

The scientific and technological advances of the period were to influence the lives of the world's people. Use the documents and your knowledge of Global History to answer the questions.

1. Review "Leni Riefenstahl's Olympia" on page 564. Using specific examples, explain how the radio and movies were used to entertain as well as influence people's ideas.

2. The following is from the letter of a German soldier, written in November of 1940 to his family in Germany:

   "The last words of the Fuhrer's radio address are over and a new strength streams through our veins. It is as if he spoke to each individually, to everyone of us, as if he wanted to give everyone new strength. With loyalty and a sense of duty, we must fight for our principles and endure to the end. . . ."

   Based on the reading, for what purpose was technology used, and was this purpose achieved?

3. Study the photos on pages 559 and 561. In what scientific developments did these scientists play a role? What positive and negative effects did their work have on society?

4. The atomic age began with the first successful test of an atomic bomb in the New Mexican desert on July 16, 1945. Here are the impressions of Brigadier General Thomas F. Farrell, who viewed the test from the test control center.

"... Atomic fission would no longer be hidden in the cloisters [shelter] of the theoretical physicists' dream. ... It was a great new force to be used for good or for evil. All seemed to feel that they had been present at the birth of a new age—the Age of Atomic Energy ... As to the present war ... we now had the means to insure its speedy conclusion and save thousands of American lives. ..."

Describe what General Farrell's feelings were regarding the results of the test. What did he think should be a future use for the bomb?

5. In 1949, William Faulkner received the Nobel Prize for Literature. Here are a few lines from his acceptance speech:

"Our tragedy is a general and universal physical fear so long sustained by now that we can hear it. There are no longer problems of the spirit. There is only the question of when will I be blown up? Because of this, the young man or woman writing today has forgotten the problems of the human heart in conflict with itself which alone can make good writing because only that is worth writing about ..."

Discuss what Faulkner said people were thinking and writing about, as opposed to what he believed they should be writing about.

Document-Based Essay

"The century began with the belief that science and technology could heal the sick and improve the lives of the world's peoples. Unfortunately, those high hopes were to be lost in the hot and cold wars of the 1900s." *Task:* Write an essay that either agrees with, or disagrees with, this statement. Include and describe specific examples of scientific and technological developments to support your essay.

CHAPTER
26

World War I

Max did not want to wake up. He had been so exhausted that he had fallen asleep despite the lice in his clothes and the rats that swarmed all over the trench. But Karl was shaking him. The bombardment had started, and he had to get up and man his machine gun. He stood up stiffly. At the age of 20, he felt like an arthritic old man. It was the damp, he supposed.

He looked at Karl. How pale he was. His lips were pulled back in a savage grin. Max knew that Karl was terrified—not so much of dying but of injuring his hands. Karl had been a pianist before the war. Max had been at the university studying philosophy. Would either of them ever return to their old lives? Would their old lives be there waiting for them when the war was over?

This young soldier is a German fighting in World War I (1914–1918). He and his friend are assigned to positions in a trench facing the enemy. He is beginning to realize the profound changes that war can bring about. It causes death and the destruction of cities and towns. Even more serious, war undermines the ideas and values on which human culture is based. The soldiers who survived the war returned to a world that seemed to have lost its meaning.

As the 20th century began, Europeans had reason to be hopeful. They felt powerful and in control of the economy of the world. Their colonies were giving them wealth and prestige. Factories turned out a wide variety of products. New inventions kept improving the way people lived. All seemed well until Europe stumbled into war in 1914.

This Great War, as it was called, involved most of the major countries of the world. Some leaders, such as President Woodrow Wilson of the United States, hoped that the war would make the world "safe for democracy." Others feared that the world would be changed for the worse.

The pessimists were right; the war changed the world drastically. Its battles maimed and killed a great many young men in the European population. The treaty that ended the fighting made Europe less stable than before. It formed new countries and altered relationships between the leading powers of Europe. The people of Russia, Italy, Germany, Spain, and Japan turned to dictators to solve the problems brought about by the war and the peace settlement. The remainder of the 20th century became a time of struggle between democracies and dictatorships and between the richer, developed nations and the poorer, less-developed countries.

EUROPE: THE PHYSICAL SETTING

The geography of Europe had an important influence on the relationships between its nations. Friction is bound to occur when several ambitious and powerful nations are located very close to each other. If these nations are not equally endowed with resources, conflict is likely to erupt. The probability that one nation will engage in armed aggression is increased when the geography of that nation gives it advantages in conducting war or surviving it. These advantages might be abundant raw materials with which to manufacture weapons or a natural barrier against invasion.

France and Germany had long been enemies. At the end of the Franco-Prussian War (1870–1871), Germany outraged the French by taking the province of Alsace and part of the province of Lorraine. Both are in eastern France on the German border. Although Germany as a whole was rich in natural resources, its leaders desired more raw materials for its growing industries. Alsace and Lorraine had large deposits of coal and iron ore.

Great Britain's position as an island nation was both a strength and a weakness. Britons had made good use of the natural barrier provided by the Atlantic Ocean and the English Channel by building up the greatest navy in the world. This navy helped them win a worldwide empire. Resources from their many colonies supplemented Britain's own raw materials. When the German navy began to rival theirs, however, British leaders worried that their island fortress would be vulnerable to siege. If the German navy became too powerful, it could easily cut off supplies of raw materials and ruin their economy.

Italy had few natural resources to help it develop industries. Expansion would help the country keep pace with its more industrialized neighbors. Although Italy had already acquired colonies in Africa, it wanted to add some Italian-speaking areas in Austria-Hungary.

The lack of a warm-water port limited Russian economic growth. Russian leaders, therefore, looked longingly at the passageway that joins the Black Sea with the Mediterranean Sea. But it was controlled by Turkey, an ally of Germany. War would give Russia an opportunity to win rights to this passageway. The Russians felt that they had less to fear from war than the smaller, more western European countries did. In the event of an invasion, Russian troops had plenty of space in which to retreat and recover their strength.

INFO CHECK

1. PROVE or DISPROVE: Prior to World War I, European leaders were strongly concerned about the geographic advantages and disadvantages of their countries.

2. State the geographic reason Britain feared Germany's expansion of its navy before World War I.

CAUSES OF THE GREAT WAR

For any event, there are old causes that have developed over time. There are also new happenings that trigger an event. These causes and happenings are known as *long-term* or *underlying causes* and *immediate causes*.

Long-Term Causes

In the early 1900s, geographical factors fostered some important movements in the European countries. These movements were imperialism, nationalism, militarism, a system of entangling alliances, and international anarchy. Over time, these movements built up tensions that threatened to erupt into violence. In 1914, a tragic act in an out-of-the-way city in southeastern Europe set in motion events that sparked a world war.

Nationalism. The tension created in the world by imperialism was strongly linked to nationalism. Many people in each nation of Europe felt themselves to be superior to the peoples of other nations. This attitude convinced the leaders of various nations that their country had the right to rule territory beyond their own borders and on different continents. For example, Russia and Austria-Hungary competed for control of the Balkan nations of southeastern Europe. Germany and France nearly went to war over the right to claim Morocco in North Africa. Russia and Japan fought over Korea.

Pan-Slavism and Pan-Germanism. Nationalism also led to the rise of *Pan-Slavism* and *Pan-Germanism*. Pan-Slavism was the name given to a movement in Russia. The people who belonged to this movement felt that it was Russia's right and duty to protect Slavic people living anywhere in Europe. The supporters of the Pan-Germanism movement sought the protection of all German-speaking people in Europe. Russia, therefore, supported Serbia, a Slavic nation, in conflicts with Austria-Hungary. Germany backed Austria-Hungary against Russia. On occasion, these movements conflicted, resulting in strained relations between the different countries.

Militarism. A policy of militarism caused the governments of larger European countries to build up their armies and navies. These countries believed that having a large military force gave them prestige and power. Many also acted as if the best way to solve problems between nations was by the use of military force. Militarism created fear and distrust in Europe. Militarism also resulted in professional military leaders having increasing influence over civilian leaders and their nation's policy decisions.

The British had the best and biggest navy, but they became alarmed when Germany began building more and better ships. Ger-

European Political Alliances in 1914

many was suspicious of Russia's plans to modernize its army. Fear and distrust led to an *arms race*—the desire to have a bigger military force than a rival had.

Entangling Alliances. The tensions created by imperialism, nationalism, and militarism led to a system of entangling alliances. To be safe from their rivals, European nations entered into agreements to help their allies in the event of war.

By 1914, two major alliance systems had been put together. Pan-Germanism had led Germany to form the *Dual Alliance* with Austria-Hungary. The Dual Alliance developed into the *Triple Alliance*, which included Italy. Eventually, it also took in the Ottoman Empire (Turkey) and Bulgaria. Together, these nations were known as the *Central Powers*. The opposing system was the *Triple Entente*. This agreement had begun as the *Entente Cordiale*, formed by France and Great Britain as a response to Germany's growing militarism. It became the Triple Entente when Russia entered the pact against Germany. Later, Japan and many other nations also joined. Collectively, these nations were called the *Allied Powers*. Instead of increasing security, the alliance systems made it almost certain that a clash between any two nations would draw others into a conflict. The opposing alliances made a widespread war more likely.

Immediate Causes

Serbian Aims. On June 28, 1914, Archduke Franz Ferdinand and his wife, Sophie, visited the Balkan city of Sarajevo to inspect military training sessions. He was the heir to the throne of the Austro-Hungarian Empire. Sarajevo was the capital of Bosnia, an area populated by South Slavs. The language and culture of the South Slavs

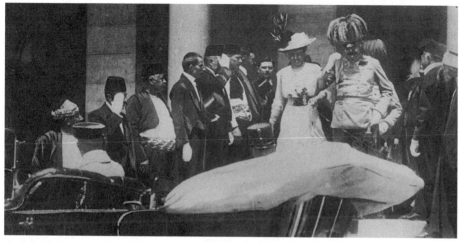

Archduke Franz Ferdinand and wife Sophie minutes before their assassination, 1914

were similar to those of the Serbs. Also, the South Slav lands bordered Serbia. The Serbs wanted to acquire these lands in order to enlarge Serbia and gain a port on the Adriatic Sea. Some Serbian officials urged the South Slavs to revolt against Austria-Hungary.

A Shooting Brings Demands. During the royal couple's visit to Sarajevo, a member of a Serbian nationalist group shot and killed them. The government of Austria-Hungary blamed the government of Serbia for the murders. Backed by Germany's offer of unlimited support, Austria-Hungary presented a set of demands to Serbia. One called for the dismissal from the Serbian government of officials opposed to Austria-Hungary. Serbia rejected the demands.

Declaration of War. On July 28, 1914, Austria-Hungary declared war on Serbia. The system of entangling alliances quickly brought other nations into the conflict. Russia came to the aid of Serbia on July 30. This caused Germany to declare war on both Russia and France. When German forces moved through neutral Belgium to reach France, Britain declared war on Germany on August 4, 1914. Although it had been part of the Triple Alliance, Italy did not support Germany in the war. Germany thought Italy was an aggressor and did not deserve support. Italy remained neutral until 1915. It then joined the Allied Powers, in hopes of obtaining the Italian-speaking areas in Austria-Hungary. What had started as a limited conflict in the Balkans quickly exploded into World War I.

Old Aims Reappear. Serbian nationalism continued to generate violence throughout the 20th century. In the 1990s, the re-emergence of Serbian nationalism caused a violent conflict that devastated large

U.S. cartoon: Blame placing among European nations as World War I breaks out

parts of Croatia and Bosnia-Herzogovina. By disrupting peaceful relations among the three major ethnic groups—the Catholic Croats, the Orthodox Serbs, and the Muslim Bosnians—Serbia has made the area a breeding ground for even more dangerous conflicts.

INFO CHECK

1. List the long-term causes of World War I. Which of these made a conflict between any two nations the trigger for a larger war that would involve many European nations? Why was this so?

2. Explain the relationship among Pan-Slavism, Pan-Germanism, and nationalism.

3. What role has Serbia played in European conflicts, both in the early 1900s and in the 1990s?

GLOBAL CONFLICT AND GLOBAL CHANGE

World War I involved most major nations of the world and lasted four years. The battles took place in Europe, Africa, the Middle East, and on both the Atlantic and Pacific oceans. The war changed the world. Europeans lost their optimism about progress. The technology that was to have improved life for all had created weapons of mass destruction.

World War I: Battlefronts and Areas Controlled by Each Side

Trench warfare: Allied troops going "over the top" in World War I

The Western Front

The most important battles of the war were fought in Europe, primarily in France. German armies struck through Belgium and invaded France. Their attempt to capture Paris was stopped at the Marne River in September 1914. From 1915 to 1917, the British and French fought the Germans in one bloody battle after another. Even though tens of thousands were killed, very little territory changed hands.

Both sides dug trenches that stretched for miles. Troops shot at each other across the "no-man's-land" in between. Soldiers lived and fought in the deep ditches. They endured the miseries of filth, dampness, lice, and disease. Added to these awful conditions was the constant danger of being killed by machine gun, rifle, or artillery fire. If a shell did not kill the men, poison gas might. By 1917, the British, French, and German armies were exhausted, but no one was willing to give up.

The Eastern Front

The Central Powers won many victories in Eastern Europe. The forces of Austria-Hungary and Bulgaria defeated Serbia and occupied that country in 1915. In the same year, the Ottoman Turks stopped a British attempt to capture the Dardanelles.

German and Austrian armies invaded Russia in late 1914. Russian suffering was so great that the Russian people lost their will to fight. In 1917, a revolution overthrew the czar. The new government kept Russia in the war. This action proved to be unpopular, and another set of leaders—the Communists—gained power. In March 1918, they signed the Treaty of Brest-Litovsk with Germany and withdrew Russia from the war. Germany gained a great deal of Russian territory and valuable natural resources. (About one third of the population of Russia came under German control.) Even more important, it no longer had to fight on two fronts.

Africa and the Middle East

During the first year of the war, the Allies occupied most of the German colonies in Africa. Only in German East Africa (now Tanzania) did a German force hold out against British troops.

In Egypt, British forces successfully defended the Suez Canal from attacks by the Turks. But British efforts to liberate Syria and Iraq from the Ottoman Empire failed. Not until 1917 were Arab nationalist forces able to weaken Ottoman control of the Middle East. Arabs, with British support, attacked Turkish forts in what are today Saudi Arabia, Syria, and Israel. The Arab actions helped the British take over the cities of Jerusalem, Baghdad, and Damascus.

The War at Sea

To cripple Germany economically, the British blockaded the German coast. They seized all ships carrying goods to German ports. This caused a great shortage of food in Germany. In the Battle of Jutland (off Denmark) in 1916, the German fleet attempted to break the North Sea blockade. They were defeated by British ships, which continued to control the seas until the end of the war. The Germans did, however, slip many light cruisers and submarines (U-boats) past the blockade to raid Allied shipping. Attacks by German submarines proved to be especially damaging. By 1917, Britain also suffered from food shortages.

U.S. Entry Into the War

At the beginning of the war, the United States tried to stay neutral and trade with both Britain and Germany. It did not officially take sides, but it sympathized with the Allies. As the war continued, attacks by German submarines on U.S. ships caused the loss of many American lives. Americans were particularly angered by a German submarine attack on the British passenger ship *Lusitania* in May 1915. It occurred with no warning off the coast of Ireland. Of the 1,198 who were killed, 128 were Americans. U.S. President Woodrow Wilson told the Germans to stop unrestricted submarine warfare. Four months later, the Germans said they would not attack neutral or passenger ships. In spite of their agreement, Germany again began a policy of unrestricted submarine warfare in February 1917. It was a desperate effort to cripple the Allies and risked bringing the United States into the war. The new German policy caused the loss of many more U.S. ships and naval personnel. Anti-German feeling increased.

Another action by Germany deepened American anger. In January 1917, the German foreign secretary, Arthur Zimmermann, sent a telegram to the government of Mexico. Called the Zimmermann Note, it asked for Mexican help if Germany and the United States went to war. In return, Germany offered to help Mexico conquer the states of Texas, Arizona, and New Mexico, areas that had once belonged to Mexico. The British found out about the note and told the Americans. Newspapers printed it in March 1917. Americans were furious. Some may have remembered the Ems Dispatch created by Bismarck to draw France into a war with Prussia.

A major concern of many Americans was whether democracy could survive in Europe if Britain and France lost the war. Americans considered the Central Powers to be undemocratic and militaristic. This idea was promoted by Allied propaganda. President Wilson believed that helping the Allies to win would make the world "safe for democracy." At Wilson's urging, Congress declared war on Germany on April 6, 1917.

The End of the War

In late June 1917, the American Expeditionary Force started arriving in France. For a number of months, the American soldiers completed their training and occasionally served as replacements in the

CASUALTIES IN WORLD WAR I

	Dead in Battle	Wounded in Battle
Allies		
France	1,358,000	4,266,000
British Empire	908,000	2,090,000
Russia	1,700,000	4,950,000
Italy	462,000	954,000
United States	50,000	206,000
Other	502,000	342,000
Central Powers		
Germany	1,808,000	4,247,000
Austria-Hungary	922,500	3,620,000
Ottoman Empire	325,000	400,000

THE HUNT FOR A DEADLY VIRUS

Some 9.2 million people died during World War I (1914–1918). Toward the end of the war, 20 to 40 million more people died from an epidemic of influenza that swept the world from 1918 to 1919. Because of the global nature of this illness and the number of people it killed, historians and medical researchers now refer to it as a *pandemic*. At the time it occurred, doctors did not know that flu is caused by a virus. Also, they had no antibiotics to treat bacterial infections such as pneumonia that often attacked already weakened bodies and caused death. Without these medical weapons, little could be done to help victims of the pandemic.

Until the 1990s, the causes of the pandemic of 1918–1919 remained a mystery. However, medical investigators now have technology that aids their search for answers. To learn why this particular flu was so powerful is one of the key objectives of their search. Researchers have focused on determining the composition, nature, and genetic structure of the 1918 virus. Such knowledge could lead to the development of a vaccine against this acute form of influenza. Improvement of current anti-viral drugs for treating flu is also a possibility.

The secret of one of the most deadly viruses the world has ever known may lie in the preserved tissues of some of the victims of the pandemic. In 1997, a biologist at the Armed Forces Institute of Pathology in Washington, D.C., reported finding viral fragments in preserved lung tissue of two American soldiers who died of flu during World War I. The analysis of this material enabled the scientists to map one of the virus's protein-making genes. In the same

year, another investigator went to the tundra of Alaska to exhume the well-preserved body of an Eskimo woman who had died of the 1918 flu. Lung tissue samples were sent to the Armed Forces Institute laboratory. More viral traces were isolated. And in 1998, other researchers set up an investigation site on Spitsbergen, an island in the Arctic Ocean between Norway and Greenland. With a team of British gravediggers, they uncovered the bodies of six young men buried in a mass grave in the frozen ground. The young Norwegians had died of the pandemic in October 1918.

The international team assembled for the investigation in Spitsbergen included pathologists, virologists, molecular biologists, geologists, and medical archaeologists. Scientists who come into direct contact with the bodies of pandemic victims must take precautions against the spread of any infectious material that may have survived. They wear modified space suits with self-contained breathing apparatus and work inside a tent with a special airlock. Tissue samples from the victims' lungs, intestines, and other organs were sent to laboratories in Norway, Britain, Canada, and the United States. In time, the results of these investigations will be published. It is possible that the findings will help develop new defenses against deadly diseases.

1. Why do you think the search for the causes of the 1918 pandemic did not begin immediately after World War I?

2. Compare the benefits and risks of this investigation. Would you like to participate? Why or why not?

front lines. The presence of fresh fighting men and the increased quantities of supplies lifted the spirits of the French and British troops. Then, in June 1918, the Americans saw heavy action in the battles of Château-Thierry and Belleau Wood. They helped the British and French stop the last great German offensive of the war. A few months later, American troops pushed the Germans out of St. Mihiel, which the Germans had held since 1914.

Discouraged by the continuing military reverses, the German people revolted against their government. Kaiser Wilhelm II resigned and fled to the Netherlands. Germany became a republic, and its new leaders asked for peace. The armistice (agreement to stop fighting) of November 11, 1918, ended World War I.

The Peace Conference

In January 1919, the Allied leaders met in France to draw up the official peace treaty. The resulting Treaty of Versailles, signed in June, set forth the conditions for peace between the Allies and Germany. Regarded as unfair by most people, its terms came to be hated by Germans.

World Leaders. The most important leaders at the peace conference were President Woodrow Wilson of the United States, Prime

OVERWEIGHTED.

PRESIDENT WILSON. "HERE'S YOUR OLIVE BRANCH. NOW GET BUSY."
DOVE OF PEACE. "OF COURSE I WANT TO PLEASE EVERYBODY; BUT ISN'T THIS A BIT THICK?"

Lampoon of Woodrow Wilson's over-optimistic view of the post–World War I world

Minister David Lloyd George of Britain, Premier Georges Clemenceau of France, and Premier Vittorio Orlando of Italy.

This conference marks the entry of the United States into the circle of world leaders. President Wilson presented several important proposals. He wanted the Allies to treat the Germans fairly. His ideas, publicized in January 1918, were known as the Fourteen Points. They called for a "peace without victory." Wilson also wanted an end to secret treaties, freedom of the seas for all nations, and the reduction of weapons. The other Allied leaders wanted revenge and as much territory and wealth as they could force Germany to give them. The French, in particular, wanted to make sure that Germany would never again be strong enough to invade France.

Treaty Terms. The Treaty of Versailles included a war guilt clause, which Germany had to accept. This clause made Germany responsible for starting World War I. Historians regard the war-guilt clause as especially unfair. All the nations involved in the war participated in the rivalries that led to conflict. The treaty also punished Germany in other ways. It had to pay huge *reparations* (money for damage done during the war) to the Allied nations. The Allies not only divided all of Germany's overseas colonies among themselves but also took portions of Germany itself. France took back Alsace and Lorraine. Poland received part of northeast Germany (the Polish Corridor). The Allies took control of important industrial areas and mineral resources in western Germany. To lessen the threat of German aggression, they greatly reduced the size of German military forces. The terms of the Treaty of Versailles crippled Germany economically. For years afterward, Germany experienced severe recession, inflation, and unemployment.

Side Agreements. Agreements with other Central Powers broke up the empires that Germany, Austria-Hungary, and Russia had amassed. Various nationalist groups located in the former empires persuaded the peacemakers to let them become independent countries. Minority groups from Germany, Russia, and Austria-Hungary united to form Czechoslovakia. Bosnia, Herzegovina, and Montenegro joined Serbia to become Yugoslavia. Four groups separated from the Russian Empire and created the new nations of Finland, Estonia, Latvia, and Lithuania.

Effect on Europe. Germany and several of the new countries became republics. (Germany was called the Wiemar Republic.) This choice of government made the Allies feel that their victory had strengthened democracy in Europe. They did not anticipate that their punishment of Germany would cause that country to abandon democracy. Twenty years later, a rearmed Germany would threaten the world.

Break-up of Empires. The Allied nations also did not foresee another consequence of their peace settlement—the rise of nationalistic movements in their own colonies. Watching the subjects of once-

Europe After the Treaty of Versailles

powerful empires gain independence encouraged other colonized peoples to seek their freedom.

The peace treaties of World War I also broke up the Ottoman Empire. Turkey, Arabia, and Iran emerged from its collapse as independent nations. Palestine, Jordan, and Iraq came under the control of Great Britain. France took over Syria and Lebanon.

League of Nations. The Allied leaders accepted Wilson's proposal for the establishment of a League of Nations. Its purpose was to prevent future wars by finding peaceful solutions to international problems. Unfortunately, it had no way to enforce its decisions. All nations of the world were invited to join. The original members numbered 42.

The United States Senate rejected the Treaty of Versailles and the League of Nations. (The Senate must approve all treaties before they are binding on the United States.) The senators who opposed the treaty feared that membership in the league might involve the United

States too deeply and easily in European problems. The U.S. decision weakened the power and prestige of the league.

In general, the peace agreements did little to solve the problems that had caused World War I. Instead, they created new tensions.

INFO CHECK

1. If you were a World War I solider, why might you prefer service on the Eastern Front or in Africa to the trench warfare of the Western Front?

2. Why do you think the German navy relied so heavily on U-boats during World War I?

3. Explain why you AGREE or DISAGREE: The entry of the United States in World War I ensured Allied victory.

4. World War I was regarded by many as the "war to end all wars." Why was this hope not fulfilled?

AFTER THE FALL OF THE OTTOMAN EMPIRE

The collapse of the Ottoman Empire had consequences that still trouble the world today. It had started to decline as early as 1699, when Austria took Hungary from it. Russia was the next to gain an important part of the empire—a large area north of the Black Sea. The Greeks broke free from it in 1829.

Protecting the Turks

During the mid-1800s, Western European leaders began to fear that the complete breakdown of the Ottoman Empire would upset the balance of power in Europe. Therefore, they protected the Turks when Russia attempted to seize the straits (passageways) that connect the Black Sea with the Mediterranean Sea. (They were also protecting their own interests in the area.) Western Europe sided with the Turks against Russia during the Crimean War in 1854 and during the Russo-Turkish War of 1877–1878. As a result of this war, however, the Turks lost a great deal of territory to Russia. Britain also gained a piece of territory—the island of Cyprus.

Civil Conflicts in Turkey

Besides having to defend themselves from foreign aggression, the Turks had to deal with civil conflicts. Their empire included many different ethnic groups and several different religions. In 1876, the sultan put into effect reforms to satisfy the conflicting demands of these groups. But his efforts succeeded only in encouraging the various factions to make more and greater demands. Two years later, the sultan abolished all liberal reforms and crushed resistance to his rule. The Young Turks, a nationalist group, successfully revolted against his repressive government in 1908. They hoped that the government they supported would preserve what was left of the Ottoman Empire in Asia.

Arab Reaction

The Arabs in the areas of the Ottoman Empire that are now Lebanon, Syria, Israel, Jordan, and Iraq had long resented Turkish control. During World War I, the Ottoman Empire sided with the Central Powers. The British and French decided to make allies of the empire's dissatisfied subjects. They promised to help the Arab leader, Hussein ibn-Ali found an independent Arab state. Arab nationalists wanted their new state to include much of the Middle East. When Hussein revolted against the Ottoman Empire, T. E. Lawrence, a British officer, led the Arabs in a successful guerrilla war against the Turks. By 1918, Arab and British troops had conquered Iraq and Syria. The Ottoman Empire had collapsed.

The Arab dream of a large unified Arab state faded at the end of the war, however. Britain and France bitterly disappointed the Arabs by their plans to divide the Ottoman Empire between them. They had made these plans in the secret Sykes-Picot Agreement of 1916. This agreement gave Syria, Lebanon, and a large portion of southern Turkey to France. England received Palestine, Jordan, and Iraq. When Britain and France began to take over these countries, Arab nationalist resentment of Western countries deepened. This attitude has affected relations between the Middle East and the West to the present day.

Jewish Homeland

Britain had also promised to establish a Jewish homeland in Palestine. When it issued the Balfour Declaration of 1917, Britain made conflicting promises to the Arabs and the Jews. The British kept their promise to the Jews. (See Chapter 22.) When the Arabs tried to set up their own government, however, British and French troops moved in and took the territories that the Sykes-Picot Agreement had assigned to them. Arab nationalists regarded these actions as a betrayal by the West.

Mustafa Kemal

Britain and France also tried to take over Turkey. The sultan was helpless to stop them. Greece joined Britain and France and began invading Turkey in 1919. Mustafa Kemal and the Young Turks resisted. Kemal's troops fought on for over a year. Finally, in 1920, when the Greeks were threatening their stronghold in central Turkey, the Young Turks won a decisive victory. The Greeks and British gave up their claims on Turkey. In 1923, the Treaty of Lausanne recognized it as an independent state. Mustafa Kemal pushed aside the sultan and became president of a republican Turkey.

INFO CHECK

1. Summarize the role of each of the following in the fall of the Ottoman Empire: (a) Russo-Turkish War (1877–1878), (b) Arab Revolt (1914–1918), (c) Sykes-Picot Agreement (1916), (d) Balfour Declaration (1917).

2. How did the Young Turks and Mustafa Kemal make the Ottoman Empire into the modern nation of Turkey?

SCIENTIFIC, LITERARY, ARTISTIC, AND CULTURAL CHANGES

Scientific and Technological Advances

Weapons. The soldiers of World War I fought with more sophisticated weapons than had ever been used before. Both the Allies and the Central Powers used the Maxim machine gun. This gun, which could kill so many so quickly, made cavalry charges suicidal. Because most of the soldiers on both sides fought from the protection of trenches, the war became largely a defensive war. Instead of fighting decisive battles, the enemies tried to wear each other down. This strategy helped to prolong World War I.

Seeking to break the deadlock of trench warfare, war leaders demanded newer and deadlier weapons. In response to this demand, technology produced poison gas, the flame thrower, the tank, and the airplane. Inventors on each side then came up with protective measures against the new dangers, such as gas masks. Barbed wire, an American invention, marked off the no-man's-land and prevented the combatants from making surprise attacks on one another. Both the Allies and the Central Powers kept pace with one another in finding new methods of killing and in counteracting those methods. Consequently, the deadlock continued until fresh soldiers arrived from America.

Medicine. During World War I, new medical and surgical techniques appeared. At that time, surgeons introduced the procedure of grafting healthy skin on burned areas of the body. This procedure paved the way for the development of plastic and reconstructive surgery. Efforts made to transfuse blood into wounded soldiers led to the establishment of blood and plasma banks.

Psychology. Advances in psychology were also made during this time. Psychotherapists became interested in emotional problems caused by horrifying experiences in battle. Soldiers who had returned home complained of nightmares, irritability, and feelings of depression and guilt. They often had vivid flashbacks, during which they

Time Line

Year	Dates and Events
A.D. **1870**	**1870–1871:** Franco-Prussian War; Germany takes Alsace-Lorraine from France
	1882: Austria-Hungary, Germany, Italy form Triple Alliance; with Ottoman Empire and Bulgaria (but not Italy) become World War I's Central Powers
1910	
1911	**1912–1914:** Britain, France, Russia formalize Triple Entente; with Japan and other nations, become World War I's Allied Powers
	1914: Archduke Franz Ferdinand and wife assassinated by Serb in Sarajevo, Bosnia
	1914: Austria-Hungary declares war on Serbia; Central Powers (with Ottoman Empire and Bulgaria, but not Italy) and Allied Powers (with Japan and other nations) drawn into war
	1914: Germans invade Belgium and France, fail to capture Paris
	1914: Central Powers (Germany and Austria) invade Russia
	1915: Italy enters World War I as member of Allied Powers
	1915: Central Powers defeat and occupy Serbia; turn back British attempt to capture Dardanelles
	1915: German U-boat sinks British *Lusitania*
	1915–1917: British-French forces face Germans in ongoing trench warfare
	1916: Battle of Jutland: British ships defeat German attempt to break North Sea blockade
	1916: Sykes-Picot Agreement, secret Franco-British pact to break up Ottoman Empire and take over its territories
	1917: Germany renews U-boat raids on Allied (and U.S.) shipping
	1917: Germany sends Zimmermann Note to Mexico; asks for Mexican alliance, promises restoration of U.S. Southwest to Mexico
	1917: U.S. Congress declares war on Germany
	1917: Arab nationalists and British attack Ottoman forts in Middle East; British occupy Jerusalem, Baghdad, Damascus
	1917: Balfour Declaration: Britain promises to set up Jewish homeland in Palestine (it does), set up Arab homeland in Palestine (it does not)
	1917–1918: Russians revolt, overthrow czar; Russian Communists gain power, sign peace treaty with Germany, cede much Russian territory and natural resources
1920	**1918:** U.S. forces help British and French turn back Germans at Château-Thierry, Bellau Wood
1921	**1918:** Germans revolt against kaiser, set up Weimar Republic, ask Allies for armistice
	1918: Wilson's Fourteen Points published
1930	**1919:** Treaty of Versailles humiliates Germany: war guilt clause, huge reparations, dismantling of German overseas colonies, award of German territory to France and Poland, reduction of German military power; sets up many new nations based on nationalism; sets up League of Nations (U.S. does not join)
1931	
	1920s: "Jazz Age" highlighted by new music of African Americans
	1920s–1940s: Rise of culture of anxiety, disillusionment (writings of Hemingway, Stein, Joyce, Malraux, Brecht; art by Duchamp, Picasso, Dali, Diego Rivera, Orozco)
1940	**1923:** Treaty of Lausanne: Greeks, British give up claims to Turkey; recognize its independence

relived terrible war events. At times, while under the influence of a flashback, they lashed out as though threatened by some danger.

During World War I, this condition was called "shell shock." Later, it became known as "battle fatigue." Today, psychologists know that any stressful experience can cause the condition. It is now called *post-traumatic stress disorder* (PTSD). Doctors and therapists use a variety of treatments, such as drug therapy, group therapy, and individual therapy to treat PTSD.

Literature in the Early 20th Century

Art and literature of the 1920s and 1930s reflected the anxiety and disillusionment that followed World War I. Shocked by the deadly new weapons and the suffering war had caused, many people lost their belief that society was improving. Writers, especially, expressed disillusionment with the world.

Hemingway. The American writer Ernest Hemingway (lived 1899–1961) had served with the ambulance corps during World War I. While performing his duties, he was badly wounded and almost lost the use of his legs. After the war, he moved to Paris and became a member of what is called the "lost generation." The writers who lived in Paris after World War I felt that the old ideals had failed them. They tried to create their own values. Hemingway adopted a code of personal courage and stoicism. He expressed these values in such novels as *The Sun Also Rises, A Farewell to Arms*, and *For Whom the Bell Tolls*. His use of short sentences and avoidance of unnecessary adjectives gives his prose a spare, energetic quality. This type of writing style was revolutionary at the time and attracted many imitators.

Stein. Gertrude Stein (lived 1874–1946) was another American writer who lived and worked in Paris. Her experimental writing style reflects a world that has lost its clarity and order. She used simple words and repeated them even in one sentence. Using the same word over and over got across the feelings she wanted to express. Some of her most famous works are *Three Lives, The Making of Americans*, and *The Autobiography of Alice B. Toklas*. She gave much emotional and professional support to the other artists in her circle, especially Hemingway.

Joyce. Another experimental writer was the Irishman, James Joyce (lived 1882–1941). His prose style, called "stream of consciousness," was inspired by the technique of "free association" that Freud used in psychoanalysis. As did Freud's patients, Joyce reveals the subconscious ideas and feelings of his characters by means of dream imagery, slips of tongue, and run-on thoughts and conversation. Although Joyce's work expresses dissatisfaction with Western culture, its humor and enthusiasm show his affection and hope for humanity. His most famous works are *A Portrait of the Artist as a Young Man, Ulysses*, and *Finnegan's Wake*.

Malraux. The French writer André Malraux (lived 1901–1976), was concerned about political problems all over the world. His subjects include French imperialism in Indochina and civil war in Spain. The novel *Man's Fate* is about the Chinese revolution of 1911.

Brecht. Most European writers of the time focused on political and social problems. Bertholt Brecht (lived 1898–1956), a German, wrote poems and plays that expose the greed and corruption pervading political and social systems. His musical play *The Threepenny Opera* is one of his best-known works. Brecht also wrote a play about Galileo.

Art in the Early 20th Century

The artists of the early 20th century were influenced by the exciting and sometimes threatening productions of technology. They

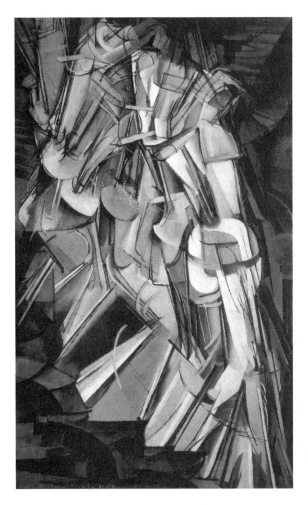

Marcel Duchamp's *Nude Descending a Staircase, No. 2:* motion shown as a series of movements in one painting

also used their creations to express their sense that World War I had made the world meaningless and absurd.

Duchamp. Marcel Duchamp (lived 1887–1968), a French painter, began as an impressionist. He later contributed to the dada movement. The French word *dada* means "hobbyhorse." The artists chose this name to show that art no longer reflected the old ideals of beauty, truth, and order. Duchamp commented on the effect that technological productions have on people's tastes and values. He did this by presenting manufactured objects, such as a bicycle wheel, as art. Duchamp also painted cubist pictures, such as *Nude Descending a Staircase.*

Picasso. Cubism is a style of painting and sculpture that breaks objects into their geometric components and gives the viewer the impression that the objects can be seen from several angles at once. This style was strongly influenced by motion picture techniques and by African art. The Spanish artist Pablo Picasso (lived 1881–1973), who worked in many different styles, created a number of cubist masterpieces, such as *Les Demoiselles d'Avignon* (1907). In *Guernica* (1937), one of his most famous paintings, Picasso also used surrealist techniques to present a horrifying image of war.

Surrealism. Surrealism developed from dadaism and was strongly influenced by psychoanalytic theory. This movement began about 1924. It focused on mysterious images such as those that occur

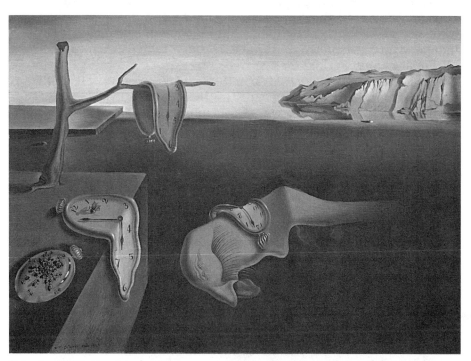

Salvator Dali's *Persistence of Memory*—photolike painting of an extreme fantasy

in dreams and hallucinations. One of the best-known examples of surrealism is *The Persistence of Memory* (1931) by Salvador Dali (lived 1904–1989), which shows a large watch melting on a broken tree branch in a barren landscape.

Rivera and Orozco. Artists in Latin America began to take pride in their pre-Columbian roots. Diego Rivera (lived 1886–1957) and José Orozco (lived 1883–1949) are two important mural painters of Mexico. They adopted techniques and images found in Mayan and Aztec murals. Rivera and Orozco created paintings showing scenes from contemporary Mexican life and from Mexican history.

Popular Culture After World War I

The end of the war brought prosperity to the victorious nations. The people of the United States, who had suffered least from the war, adopted an exuberant lifestyle. They flocked to the movies and imitated the behavior of the film personalities. Inexpensive cars gave them a freedom of movement that only the very rich had previously experienced.

Role of Women. During the war, when most young men served in the army, employers hired women for jobs that had once been exclusively given to men. Doing men's work and getting good wages boosted their confidence. They bobbed their hair (cut it short), shortened their skirts, and adopted manners that women of an older generation considered shocking. (Some smoked and drank in public and went out alone with young men.) Not all women expressed their new independence frivolously, however. Many joined woman suffrage movements and worked for the right to vote.

African Americans. African Americans made great contributions to popular culture, especially in the field of music. The jazz that black musicians played became so popular that the 1920s became known as the Jazz Age. African Americans also invented the favorite dances of the period—the Charleston and the Lindy Hop.

A New Leader. At this time, the United States became a world cultural leader as well as a world political leader. Movies and radio introduced American culture to Europe. Europeans were especially enthusiastic about African-American entertainers. Jazz and American dance tunes became the rage among the younger sets.

The good times for Western European nations and the United States did not last. The Great Depression of the 1930s brought an end to the fun. The rising power of dictators in Europe began to threaten freedom all over the world. Chapter 27 shows how World War I and the peace treaty that ended it contributed to these problems.

INFO CHECK

1. Identify the World War I-era medical advances that you regard as most beneficial. State reasons for your selection(s).

2. Which of the post-World War I writers was most inspired by the teachings of Sigmund Freud? How did his books differ from those of other writers of the 1920s and 1930s?

3. Define the term "lost generation."

4. How did cubism differ from surrealism? For each, name an artist whose work reflected the style.

CHAPTER REVIEW

Multiple Choice

1. An immediate cause of World War I was the assassination of the Archduke Franz Ferdinand and his wife. A long-range cause would be

   1. militarism
   2. nationalism
   3. entangling alliances
   4. all of the above.

2. Austria-Hungary, with German support, presented a series of demands to Serbia. The nation that supported the Serbian government in its refusal to meet those demands because of Pan-Slavism was

   1. Great Britain
   2. Italy
   3. France
   4. Russia.

3. A member of the Triple Alliance that remained neutral until 1915 and then joined the Allies was

   1. Japan
   2. Serbia
   3. Italy
   4. Russia.

4. The 1918 Treaty of Brest-Litovsk was important to Germany because

   1. Germany no longer was fighting a two-front war
   2. Germany gained military assistance from Russia

   3. Russia came under German rule
   4. Russia reentered the war based on a military assistance pact.

5. Two German actions that greatly angered President Wilson and the American people were

   1. attacking Italy and France
   2. unrestricted submarine warfare and the Zimmermann Note
   3. joining with Austria-Hungary and attacking Belgium
   4. spreading the German measles and sauerkraut.

6. The Allied leaders who met to decide on the terms of the peace treaty represented the nations of

   1. France, Russia, the United States, and Great Britain
   2. Italy, Serbia, the United States, and Great Britain
   3. the United States, Great Britain, Italy, and France
   4. Japan, Serbia, Russia, and Italy.

7. The Treaty of Versailles was particularly harsh toward Germany because it required Germany to

   1. accept responsibility for starting the war
   2. pay huge reparations to the Allies for war damages
   3. lose all overseas colonies and Alsace and Lorraine
   4. all of above.

8. As a result of World War I, the map of Europe changed as old empires disappeared and new nations formed. Select one former empire and a nation that arose out of its collapse:

   1. Russian Empire—Finland
   2. German Empire—Iran
   3. Ottoman Empire—Estonia
   4. Austro-Hungarian Empire—Turkey

9. The Sykes-Picot Agreement and the Balfour Declaration ignored the nationalistic feelings of the

   1. African people
   2. Arabic people
   3. Italian people
   4. Turkish people.

10. After World War I, artists' disillusionment with the old order and lack of faith in the future was clearly expressed by

    1. Picasso's painting *Guernica*
    2. Hemingway's novel *A Farewell to Arms*
    3. the dada movement in painting
    4. African Americans' introduction of jazz.

11. A comparison of the maps on pages 574 and 584 shows that, as a result of World War I,

    1. the former Balkan states were unified as Yugoslavia
    2. Spain was punished for its membership in the Triple Alliance
    3. the border between Norway and Sweden was altered
    4. independent new nations were created in Africa.

12. The cartoon on page 582 refers to

    1. the warlike nature of Europeans
    2. the expected survival of colonialism after World War I
    3. President Wilson's efforts to restore the forests and wildlife of a devastated Europe
    4. the over-optimistic expectations for a League of Nations.

Thematic Essays

1. If World War I had not occurred, is it likely that the Austro-Hungarian Empire would have lasted longer? *Task:* Give reasons for your answer.

2. World War I altered the map of Europe, destroying the Austro-Hungarian Empire, the German Empire, and the Russian Empire. *Task:* Discuss the role of nationalism in the creation of new nations in Europe.

Document-Based Questions

Use your knowledge of Global History and Geography and the documents to answer the questions.

1. Study the map on page 577.
   Identify the nations known as the Central Powers and explain how they received that name.

2. From a statement by a British official before the war:

   "It is clear that France and Russia are decided to accept the challenge thrown out to them. Whatever we may think of the merits of the Austrian charges against Serbia, France, and Russia, consider these are pretexts and that the bigger cause of Triple Alliance versus Triple Entente is definitely engaged. . . . Our interests are tied up with those of France and Russia in this struggle. . . ."

   How does this reading reveal entangling alliances as a cause of World War I?

3. Study the table on page 580. Which nations had the largest number of dead or wounded soldiers? Why do you think this was so?

4. From an American newspaper reporter's account of the German army's destruction of Louvain, a town in Belgium:

"The Germans sentenced Louvain to become a wilderness. . . . Money can never restore Louvain. Great architects and artists, dead these six hundred years made it beautiful, and their handiwork belonged to the world. At Louvain it was war upon the defenseless, war on churches, colleges, shops of milliners and lacemakers; war brought to the bedside and fireside; against women harvesting in the fields against children in wooden shoes playing in the street. . . ."

Is the reporter stating fact, opinion, or both? Is he pro-German or anti-German? Give reasons for your answers.

5. From President Wilson's war message to Congress on April 2, 1917:

". . . announcement of the Imperial German Government that on and after the first day of February it was its purpose to put aside all restraints [controls] of law and humanity and use its submarines to sink every vessel that sought to approach the ports of Great Britain. . . . I was for a little while unable to believe that such would in fact be done by any government that had hitherto [previously] subscribed [followed] the humane practices of civilized nations. . . ."

What actions of the German government is President Wilson referring to? After reading President Wilson's words, how do you think he feels about the actions of the German government? Use the document to support your answer.

Document-Based Essay

Referring to World War I: Entangling alliances and modern technology resulted in a most expensive and deadly war. It killed millions of soldiers and civilians and altered the map of Europe. *Task:* Using historical information, PROVE or DISPROVE the accuracy of this statement.

CHAPTER
27

The Post-World War I Era

Frau Bildner took the groceries out of her string bag and laid them on the kitchen table—five potatoes and a loaf of bread. No butter, no meat, no green vegetables. The rate of inflation was incredible. She had left the house with a purse full of marks, and this is all she had been able to buy. A few potatoes to feed a man and a 16-year-old boy.

Ernst and Franz would be home soon. These days, Ernst, her husband, was often too depressed to eat. Ernst taught mathematics in the local high school. The Nazis had threatened to beat Herr Stoltz, the history teacher, if he didn't use the textbook they had recommended. Frau Bildner thanked God that Ernst taught math. "Just stay out of it," she had told him.

Franz would be starving, of course. What a bad mood he would be in when he saw his supper. If only he wouldn't quarrel with his father. Lately, he had taken to praising the Nazis, boasting how they would soon lead Germany out of all this poverty and shame. Ernst flew into such rages when Franz talked like that. Mealtime had become a nightmare.

T his housewife in Germany is experiencing some of the misery caused by World War I. Other European countries also suffered from severe social and economic problems. Most governments of the time adjusted in some way to meet these problems. In Russia, Italy, and Germany, postwar difficulties led to the rise of dictatorships.

REVOLUTION AND CHANGE IN RUSSIA

In the early 1900s, Russia was rapidly becoming industrialized. Russian leaders also wanted their country to be one of the great imperialist powers of the world. Having set up a sphere of influence in Chinese Manchuria, they next sought to gain control of northern Korea. Japan also had claims on northern Korea. After protesting unsuccessfully against Russia's presence there, Japan declared war on Russia in 1904. The European countries had not realized the extent to which Japan had modernized its army and navy and were surprised when it won the Russo-Japanese War in 1905.

The Revolution of 1905

The humiliating defeat in the Russo-Japanese War increased political and social unrest in Russia. Businesspeople, professionals, and intellectuals resented Czar Nicholas II's autocratic government. They felt that political reforms were as necessary to the modernization of Russia as industrialization. Factory workers stepped up their demands for better wages and hours by forming labor unions and supporting some Socialist reformers.

Russia's population consisted of large groups of minorities, such as Poles and Ukrainians. They wanted to create their own independent states. The workers, minorities, and reformers felt that the opportunity had come to take action. The army would not be able to react quickly. Part of the forces had been weakened by the Russo-Japanese War. The other part was protecting Russian interest in Manchuria.

At first, the dissidents expressed their demands by peaceful demonstrations. A group of workers headed by a priest marched to the Winter Palace in St. Petersburg to present a petition to Nicholas. When the palace guards fired on the crowd, killing hundreds, dissatisfaction flared into revolutionary rage throughout the country. Unable to control the disorder that followed the massacre, Nicholas agreed to allow his subjects to elect a duma, or parliament. The czar took control of the duma and prevented it from representing the general will. Czarist absolutism seemed to have been restored. Nonetheless, radical movements continued to gain support in Russia.

The Effect of World War I on Russia

World War I seemed at first to unify Russia. Expansionists saw the war as an opportunity to gain territory in the Balkans. Liberals and Socialists hoped that Russia's alliance with France and Britain would cause it to adopt more democratic policies. All Russians drew together to defend their country. Their unity was short-lived, however. Defeats in battle, the loss of millions of men at the front, and food shortages made the Russian people desperate. They demanded an end to Russia's participation in the war. Czar Nicholas II did not agree and continued to prosecute the war. He also did nothing about the starvation and poverty caused by the war.

Russian Revolution. In March 1917, the Russian Revolution began. Nicholas II was driven from his throne. Moderate leaders—Prince George Lvov and Alexander Kerensky—took control of Russia through a provisional government. They spoke to the people about constitutions, democracy, and reforms. However, they, too, refused to take Russia out of the war. The hunger and misery continued. Finally, in November 1917, a second revolution occurred. It was led by Vladimir I. Lenin. He promised the Russian people what they wanted most—peace, bread, and land.

Lenin. A follower of the theories of Karl Marx, Lenin believed socialism must replace capitalism through violent revolution. Marx had thought that the first Socialist revolution would occur in an industrialized country. In spite of its industrial advances, Russia's economy was still based on agriculture. Lenin realized, however, that after centuries of poverty and abuse, Russian peasants were ready to revolt. Showing no respect for the new, moderate regime, many of the peasants had started to seize the estates of the nobility. Lenin's promise of land really meant that if the peasants followed him, he would allow them to keep what they had taken.

Bolsheviks. Lenin's party, the Bolshevik (later called Communist), took over the government. One of its first acts in 1918 was to

Lenin addressing troops of the Red Army in Moscow, 1919

take Russia out of World War I by signing the Treaty of Brest-Litovsk with Germany. This action cost the Russians dearly. They gave up rights to land that held a third of the population of Russia, a third of its agriculture, and half of its industry. Eventually, Russia won back much of this territory.

Meanwhile, the Communists fought various groups of anti-Communists in a bloody civil war. The Communists became known as the Reds and their opponents as the Whites. As the fighting continued, Lenin reorganized the government and economy of Russia into what he called "war communism." Under war communism, the government owned most industries, banks, and railroads. Although it did not at this point take away the peasants' land, it seized large portions of their crops. Lenin claimed this policy would make it easier for the government to use Russia's resources, industries, and communication systems to win the civil war.

A New Government. Under Lenin's regime, workers and peasants were permitted to elect representatives to a lawmaking body. But this congress was really controlled by Lenin and a few advisers. The new Communist government discouraged religious worship and adopted *atheism* (the belief that God does not exist) as official government policy. It also forbade Russians to recognize class distinctions, encouraging them to address one another as "comrade."

One Party. The Communist party was the only political party allowed to exist. In order to prevent criticism of communism, the government censored newspapers and other forms of communication. In 1918, to make sure that the Whites would not rescue the royal family, the Communists executed the czar, his wife, and children. The government's secret police, the Cheka, stalked political opponents and killed them. By 1921, the Communists (Reds) had defeated the Whites.

Economic Changes. Once victory had been won, Lenin eased the hardship caused by the civil war by instituting the New Economic Policy (NEP). This program made some compromises with Marxist doctrine. Peasants were allowed to sell their surplus grain for a profit. Although the government still owned banks, railroads, and major industries, NEP allowed small manufacturers to resume control over their businesses. Under NEP, the Russian economy improved. In 1922, Russia changed its name to the Union of Soviet Socialist Republics (USSR)—the Soviet Union.

Stalin and the Rise of a Modern Totalitarian State

After Lenin died in 1924, Joseph Stalin took control of the Soviet Union. He remained in control until he died in 1953. Stalin abolished NEP and replaced it with a command economy.

A Command Economy. A command economy is one in which the state has complete control of industry. It determines what is to be produced, how much is to be produced, and the price. Lenin's NEP had brought the Soviet economy out of the disastrous state it had been in during World War I and the civil war. In 1927, however, the economy showed signs of slowing down. Ideological reasons played a part in Stalin's new economic policy. NEP included too many capitalistic elements. As did Lenin, Stalin wanted to make the Soviet Union a Socialist state. It was to be totally controlled by the Communists with himself as head of the Communist Party of the USSR.

First Five-Year Plan. Stalin also wanted the Soviet Union to avoid being destroyed economically by the more industrialized nations. To accomplish this, he said, the Soviet Union would have to catch up to the industrialized nations within ten years. Thus, Stalin put forth two programs for socializing and industrializing his country. They were called the *Five-Year Plans*. The first called for the total industrial output to increase by 250 percent in just five years. Agricultural production was to increase by 150 percent.

In order to bring about these increases, the government took over all the industries. It also took the peasants' land away. Some peasants were forced to work on big, government-owned farms called collective farms. Others were relocated to cities and mining towns where they labored in factories, mines, and on construction sites. They worked long hours and received very low wages in return.

Collectivization of Farms. Many peasants resisted the collectivization of the farms that they had fought so long and so hard to obtain. They burned their crops and killed their livestock rather than give them up to the government. Those who submitted to the governments' order that they work on collective farms often labored halfheartedly. Consequently, grain production did not increase. This caused a famine. Between 1932 and 1933, millions of people died of starvation and diseases caused by malnutrition.

In the end, however, the government succeeded in collectivizing agriculture. Because it had stripped the peasants of their political power, it could force them to produce food for industrial workers. In three years, Stalin declared that his first Five-Year Plan was a success. Although this was an exaggeration, he had succeeded in setting the basis for the Soviet planned economy.

Second Five-Year Plan. The second Five-Year Plan was put into effect in 1933. This plan was designed to make the Soviet Union economically independent of the West. It reduced the manufacture of consumer goods in favor of encouraging heavy industry, such as the production of steel. In 1938, the Soviet Union was able to take its place among the major industrial powers. The only two countries that outranked it in industrial production were Germany and the United States.

Education. Perhaps the one solid social achievement of the Soviet Union was providing its people with free public education. This raised the rate of literacy and helped people move into managerial and professional work. The standard of living did not improve for ordinary people, however. They had to pay high sales taxes. Even when their wages went up, the money did not buy as much as it had before the introduction of the Five-Year Plans. Then, too, fewer consumer goods were produced, and there was less to buy.

Repression. Stalin was able to meet his goals by using harsh and repressive measures. He ruled both Russians and the ethnic minorities in the Soviet Union by means of terror. His secret police tracked down all dissidents. He first turned the secret police on the peasants who resisted collectivization. Later, he set them on anyone who opposed or might oppose him, whether in the government, the military, or industry. Not only did he target important Communists who were in positions to harm him politically, he also harassed ordinary people for no apparent reason.

To elicit confessions, the police tortured prisoners who had been accused of political crimes. They threatened to harm the families and friends of those that did not give in under torture. No one knew when he or she might become the next victim to be punished. The accused might be given a mock trial. When found guilty (hardly anyone was found innocent), the person would be killed, imprisoned, or exiled to labor camps (gulags) in Siberia. The worst of these persecutions occurred in the mid-1930s. In the great purges, millions were arrested, imprisoned, and killed.

The Soviet Union   1917–1938

Non-Russian Republics. Stalin also kept a tight grip on the non-Russian republics included in the Soviet Union. All of these countries were occupied by the Red army. Stalin made their regimes replicas of the Soviet government. He repressed their cultures and insisted that they follow Russian culture.

INFO CHECK

1. Explain the connection between World War I (1914–1918) and the Russian Revolution (1917).

2. Identify or define: (a) Vladimir I. Lenin, (b) Joseph Stalin, (c) war communism, (d) New Economic Policy, (e) Five-Year Plans.

3. Describe the most significant political changes brought to Russia and the non-Russian republics by the 1930s.

BETWEEN THE WORLD WARS: 1919–1939

The Treaty of Versailles had a great influence on the course that European history took after World War I. Unfortunately, when the Allies wrote the treaty, they did not focus sufficiently on making terms that would keep peace in Europe. They were more interested in punishing and weakening Germany and in enlarging their own empires.

League of Nations

The Allies did, it is true, establish the League of Nations. They intended to use the league as a forum. In it, nations could discuss their differences and resolve them without resorting to war. The nations that belonged to the league were supposed to work together to prevent aggression. They were to submit disputes to a neutral group to resolve and to abide by that decision. If disputing nations went to war, the other members of the league were supposed to stop trading with the warring nations. The league, however, had no power to enforce these requirements. Many members ignored them when it suited their national aims. Japan and Italy, for instance, violated league principles by aggression in Asia and Africa.

One of the League of Nations' weaknesses was its indirect support of imperialism. It gave France, Great Britain, and a few other nations mandates over the territories of the Ottoman Empire and over Germany's old colonies. It was understood that the nations that had received these territories would help the inhabitants develop their own governments. Because it allowed the "protector" nations to assume control of the process, the league, in effect, legalized the colonization of the territories.

THE MASSACRE OF THE ARMENIANS

For centuries, the Armenian people lived as a minority in the northeast section of the Ottoman Empire. As Christians, they did not enjoy equality with the Muslim Turks, but they were able to live in relative harmony with neighbors. In the late 19th and early 20th centuries, their situation worsened. Fearful of the growing nationalism of the Young Turk movement and distrustful of Christian minorities, the Ottoman sultan ordered persecutions. Hundreds of thousands of Armenians were killed between 1894 and 1897. The victory of the Young Turks in 1908 ended the oppressive rule of the sultans in Turkey. Many Armenians had supported the Young Turks in the hope that political reform and modernization would improve their lives. But the new nationalist government regarded the Armenians as an obstacle to Turkish unity and expansion. The decision was made to eliminate the Armenian community.

Turkey's participation in World War I provided government officials the opportunity to treat the Armenians as "subversives" who threatened national security. New massacres began on April 24, 1915. Hundreds of leaders of the Armenian community were summoned to Istanbul, the Turkish capital, and murdered. This was followed by systematic, government-planned massacres until 1917.

Armenian men were drafted into the Turkish army and put to work at hard labor. Many were killed. Others were worked to death. Deportations followed. Women, children, and the elderly were driven from their villages into the deserts of Syria and Iraq. Turkish police herded the helpless Armenians in forced marches across Turkey. Along the way, they were beaten, robbed, raped, and murdered by the police, or by others who were not stopped by the police. Many of the death march survivors were killed on arrival in the deserts where they were to be "resettled." Some Armenians were helped by humane Turks, Arabs, and foreign missionaries to make their way to safe havens beyond the Turkish borders.

As a result of the massacres of 1915–1917, more than one million Armenians lost their lives. Another wave of persecutions took place in 1923, the year Turkey became a republic under the presidency of Mustafa Kemal. Some 2 million Armenians lived in Turkey in 1915. By the 1990s, fewer than 60,000 people of this 3,000-year-old community remained.

Much of what we know of the Armenian crisis comes from eyewitness accounts by foreign missionaries present in Turkey at the time. Many of these people helped survivors of the massacres to escape and later organized refugee assistance committees. However, it was the book *The Forty Days of Musa Dagh* by Austrian writer Franz Werfel, published in 1933, that brought world attention to the plight of the Armenians. In addition to describing the suffering caused by Turkish brutality, the novel also tells about heroism of the Armenian fight for survival.

1. Explain why you AGREE or DISAGREE with those who regard the Turkish 1915–1917 campaign against the Armenians as genocide.

2. The Armenians still do not trust Turks. Why do you think they still feel this way? What can be done to change this attitude?

The Westernization of a Secular Turkey

Atatürk. After Mustafa Kemal took over Turkey in 1923, he was called "Atatürk," meaning "father of the Turks." Although Atatürk called himself the president of Turkey and proclaimed it a republic, he was actually a dictator. He set up a one-party system and made reforms without putting them to the vote. He refused to allow such ethnic minorities as the Kurds and the Armenians to set up their own states.

New Government. Nonetheless, Atatürk established a solid framework for a future democratic-style government. He achieved this by separating religion and the state. This meant that the legal system was based on European rather than on Islamic law. The state took over the schools and allowed them to teach the same subjects that were taught in modern European schools. Women no longer had to stay in the seclusion imposed on them by Islamic law. They could now vote. European civil law rather than the Islamic code governed marriage. Men could have only one wife. Women could sue for divorce.

Cultural Changes. Atatürk also brought Turkey nearer to the West in other ways. He ordered his people to wear Western-style clothes. Instead of the Arabic script, he introduced a new Turkish alphabet based on Roman letters. Most important, his government sponsored industrialization, which brought higher employment, larger cities, and a new spirit of progress and independence to Turkey.

Kemal Atatürk ("Father of the Turks"), introducing language reform

Opposition. Not all Turks approved of Atatürk's efforts to secularize Turkey (or reduce the influence of religion on daily life there). Many Muslims wanted their country to be ruled by Islamic tradition and law. They formed the Islamic party and worked against secularization.

The Women's Suffrage Movement

Beginnings. European and American women had been demanding equal rights at least as early as the 18th century. In 1792, an Englishwoman, Mary Wollstonecraft, wrote *A Vindication of the Rights of Women*. In it, she called for women and men to be educated together. She argued that if women were as well educated as men were, they would be able to support themselves and to make good political decisions. Her book marked the beginning of the women's movement.

In Britain. British and American women struggled for their rights throughout the 19th century. In 1867, John Stuart Mill, a philosopher and economist, petitioned Parliament to give women the right to vote. That same year, Mill, Emily Davies, an educator, and others founded the first women's suffrage society. It became the National Union of Women's Suffrage Societies. But it was Emmeline Pankhurst's Women's Social and Political Union, founded 1903, that was most active publicly. The "suffragettes," as the members of this group were called, began to practice civil disobedience. They were often arrested (Pankhurst 12 times in one year) for causing public disturbances. The contributions of British women to the war effort during World War I gave them more support in their struggle to win the vote. British women were granted suffrage in early 1918.

In the United States. American women who worked for the abolition of slavery in the 1800s also demanded their own freedom and equality. The Seneca Falls Convention, held in 1848, was their first attempt at organizing. The American women's movement split after the Civil War. When the 15th Amendment gave African Americans the right to vote in 1870, such leaders as Susan B. Anthony and Elizabeth Cady Stanton objected. They wanted women to have the vote, too. Another group, headed by Lucy Stone and Julia Ward Howe, felt optimistic about the 15th Amendment. They believed that its passage ensured that women would also win their rights.

Anthony and Stanton organized the National Woman Suffrage Association. It pressured the federal government to make such changes as granting married women the right to own property. Stone formed the American Woman Suffrage Association, which worked for suffrage on the state level. In 1869, Wyoming, a territory, gave women the right to vote. The two organizations united in 1890.

In the early 1900s, the younger leaders of the American women's movement, like those of the British movement, began to practice civil disobedience. Alice Paul of the National Woman's Party organized mass marches and hunger strikes. These demonstrations, along with other political activity, died down during World War I. Women then put all their energy into supporting the war effort.

After World War I, women increased their demand for the vote. Filling in at the workplace for the young men at the front gave them a taste of real independence. Finally, in August 1920, American women won the right to vote in national elections through the 19th Amendment to the Constitution.

The Rise of Fascism in Italy

Many Italians felt that the peace agreements that ended World War I had not treated them fairly. They believed that they should have received more territory in return for the large number of Italian soldiers killed in the war. Italians, for example, resented the treaty arrangements that gave the city of Fiume (now Rijeka) to newly established Yugoslavia. Also, Italy faced severe economic problems in the 1920s. Unemployment and high prices caused great hardship.

Mussolini. The democratic Italian government found it difficult to solve these problems. The political parties in the parliament would

Dictator Benito Mussolini declaiming to Italian troops from atop a tank

not work together for the good of Italy. No leader had the strength and prestige to make the system work. Italians began to lose faith in democracy. One man, Benito Mussolini, leader of the Fascist party, appeared to have solutions to the problems facing Italy. As a result, many Italians began to support his policies.

Fascists. The Fascist Party, founded by Mussolini in 1919, was composed mainly of unemployed former soldiers. The party believed in nationalism and militarism. Most important, the Fascists were determined to replace the democratic government of Italy with a dictatorship. To achieve their goals, the Fascists beat up and sometimes killed those who opposed them.

In October 1922, Mussolini and 10,000 armed Fascists marched on Rome. They hoped to force the premier to resign. The king feared that a civil war would break out if he attempted to stop the march. He asked Mussolini to become prime minister.

Dictatorship. As head of the Italian government, Mussolini remade Italy into a Fascist dictatorship. He outlawed all other political parties. Under his orders, secret police arrested critics of the government. New laws forbade strikes. The government regulated all economic activities. Newspapers and radio stations operated under strict censorship. The Fascists also took complete control of the schools. Teachers now taught children that the individual existed to serve the state. Boys trained to be good soldiers. Girls were expected to become mothers of large families.

Mussolini did strengthen Italian industry and agriculture. But wages fell, hours of work increased, and taxes rose. Although most Italians benefited from the order and stability Mussolini provided, they lost many of their personal freedoms.

INFO CHECK

1. State the reason for the establishment of the League of Nations. Why do you think the league was unsuccessful?

2. Why do some Turks regard Mustafa Kemal as a great leader, while others do not?

3. Compare the women's suffrage movements in Britain and the United States. What were the most important similarities?

4. Define *fascism*. Why do you think so many Italians accepted the leadership of Benito Mussolini in 1922?

THE WORLDWIDE DEPRESSION

During the 1930s, an economic disaster hit the world. It was so devastating that it has become known as the Great Depression. In the late 1920s, the economies of many countries had started to decline. Financial leaders apparently did not realize that this decline came about because of serious problems in their economies. They felt optimistic because, in the past, recovery had always followed similar slumps.

U.S. Economy

In the United States, a booming stock market throughout the 1920s disguised many important problems. Vital industries, such as agriculture, were in trouble. Farmers were receiving such low prices for their crops that many could not pay the mortgages on their farms. Banks that relied on mortgage payments for their income failed.

Another weakness in the U.S. economy was the growing trend among Americans to buy things on credit. Many people were unable to keep up their payments. Less and less money began to circulate. Manufacturers as well as banks went out of business.

The crash of the New York stock market in October 1929 speeded up the economic decline. Many investors had bought stocks "on margin." This meant that they had paid a large part of the price of the stock by borrowing from their stockbrokers. When the stock prices began to fall, investors were terrified not only of losing large sums of money but also of being saddled by huge debts. By rushing to sell, they started a panic. Other investors followed suit. Millions were ruined as they found themselves the owners of worthless stock. Fortunes were wiped out.

Effect on Other Parts of the World

The depression in the United States affected economies all over the world. American investors who had lent money to businesspeople in Europe began to demand payment. This drew capital from countries that had not yet recovered from the expenses of World War I. Manufacturers everywhere tried frantically to sell their products in order to raise money to repay loans. Few people were able to buy these goods, and world prices collapsed. With the loss of markets, production fell.

Loss of Jobs and Hope. The Great Depression caused millions of people all over the world to lose their jobs. In 1932, unemployment in Great Britain was about 17 percent of the workforce. In 1933 in the United States, it was almost 25 percent. Germany was the hardest hit of all. In causing unemployment, the Great Depression caused many social problems as well. Unable to earn money, people felt worthless as well as hopeless. Families broke up. People left their communities to find work in unfamiliar environments. Angry and fearful, people made unwise choices.

Reaction in the United States. Different governments tried different ways to end the depression. President Franklin Delano

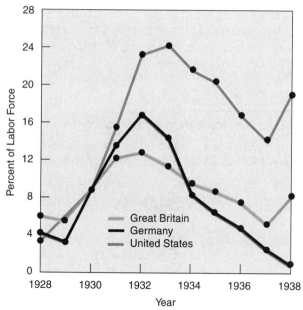

Unemployment During the Great Depression (1928–1938)

Roosevelt of the United States introduced a program called the New Deal. He tried a direct means of reducing unemployment by setting up agencies to manage new public works projects. (These are government-financed programs that benefit the general public.) The best known of the agencies was the Works Progress Administration (WPA). The WPA constructed bridges, highways, and public buildings. By giving jobs to desperate people, the agency did much to prevent the outbreak of revolution in the United States. Roosevelt also established a national social security system and, by passing the National Labor Relations Act of 1935, made collective bargaining by unions legal.

Roosevelt's reforms had a long-range effect on the economic policies of the U.S. government, but they did not end the depression. The unemployment problem did not go away until after the United States entered World War II.

British Actions. British leaders did not make major changes in their government's economic policies. They balanced the country's budget and provided subsistence welfare for the unemployed. After 1932, the economy recovered by itself.

French Solutions. French leaders were never able to solve the social and political problems caused by the depression. Conflicts broke out among various political factions. Fascist organizations rioted and spread propaganda. Socialists, Radicals, and Communists joined together in the Popular Front party. Léon Blum, the leader of the Popular Front, was elected to office in 1936. When this party tried to pass reforms similar to the ones Roosevelt had made in the United States, conservatives and Fascists threatened a revolution. Blum resigned in June 1937. Divided and impoverished at this time, France also had to face the renewed threat of German aggression.

INFO CHECK

1. Define the term *Great Depression*. How and when did it begin?

2. Which government do you believe responded most successfully to the problems caused by the Great Depression? Give reasons for your answer.

THE RISE OF TOTALITARIANISM

Dictatorships have existed in many countries and in many eras. In the 20th century, however, a new form of dictatorship arose. These *totalitarian* governments seek to establish centralized control of all aspects of political, economic, and social life. Individual citizens have few political or legal rights. The needs of the people are considered to be less important than the needs of the nation. Police and security forces are used to maintain the government's control of the people. Those who disagree with or criticize government policies are arrested and imprisoned, or executed. Schools are required to teach children to obey the government and its leaders without question. In the post-World War I era, totalitarian governments were established in Russia, Italy, Germany, and Japan.

The Weimar Republic and the Rise of Nazism

After World War I, many Germans made a strong attempt to establish a democratic government in Germany. But the Weimar Republic, as the new government was called, faced great problems. Many Germans blamed the Weimar leaders for agreeing to the terms of the hated Treaty of Versailles. Also, widespread unemployment, rapidly rising prices, and the burden of the huge war debt (reparations payments) made the German people resentful. Just as the economy improved, the Great Depression of 1929 brought new hardships. Businesses failed, and more people lost their jobs. (Recall the story at the beginning of the chapter. The Bildners were facing serious economic and political problems.)

Extremist groups in Germany opposed the Weimar Republic. To many, communism seemed to offer a better way of life. Those who disliked both communism and democracy were often drawn to the Nazi Party, led by Adolf Hitler.

Hitler. Hitler, originally from Austria, had served in the German army during the war. He had been wounded and decorated for brav-

Berlin housewife, 1923, lighting her stove with nearly worthless currency—cheaper than kindling wood

ery on the Western Front. The defeat of Germany filled Hitler with shame and bitterness. He hated the democratic leaders of postwar Germany for surrendering to the Allies.

Hitler was a highly skilled politician. A brilliant public speaker, he easily won support from German audiences. The program of the Nazi Party was based on nationalism, militarism, and racism. Hitler told the Germans they were a superior race, destined to rule the world. He assured his listeners that they were not responsible for Germany's defeat in the war or its economic problems. He claimed that Communists, Socialists, and democrats had betrayed Germany. Hitler singled out Jews for special hatred. He blamed them for all the problems existing in Germany and the world. The Jews thus became scapegoats.

In 1923, Hitler's attempt to seize the government of the German state of Bavaria failed. He was sent to prison. While there, he wrote the book *Mein Kampf* (My Struggle). It set forth Hitler's racist ideas and his plans for world domination.

Third Reich. The Nazis became more popular in the early 1930s because they seemed to offer solutions to the severe economic problems brought on by the Great Depression. The Nazis gained a large number of seats in the legislature. Then in January 1933, Hitler became chancellor of Germany. He quickly ended democratic government and turned Germany into a dictatorship known as the Third Reich. As *führer* (leader), Hitler had unlimited power. He controlled everything: industrial and agricultural production, education, newspapers, and radio broadcasts. Children had to join the Hitler Youth organization to learn to be "good Nazis."

The Third Reich became one of the most brutal dictatorships in the history of the world. The Nazis crushed all opposition. They sent political enemies and millions of Jews to concentration (prison) camps. These eventually became death camps where people were murdered on arrival or were worked, starved, or tortured to death.

Under Hitler, Germany gained power but at a great cost to the German people. They had most of their rights and freedoms stripped from them. The country also lost the talents of intellectuals, artists, writers, and scientists who fled from Germany to escape persecution. Many, such as Einstein and Meitner, were Jewish.

Nazi propaganda poster of Hitler receiving a pledge from the German people: Führer, we follow your lead!

Jewish family in flight from
Nazi Germany, 1933

Japanese Militarism and Expansion

Japan has few natural resources. To run its industries, it must
obtain raw materials from other countries. In the 1920s and 1930s,
the industrial and military leaders of Japan developed a long-range
plan to acquire sources of raw materials. The plan called for conquering East Asia. Control of China was the most important aim of
Japan's East Asia Co-Prosperity Sphere.

In Manchuria. In September 1931, the Japanese seized Manchuria, a region of northeast China. Renamed Manchukuo, it was
given its independence in 1932. But, in fact, Japan actually controlled
the government. Few objected when the Japanese began to use the
rich natural resources of their new colony.

In China. In 1937, Japan opened a full-scale attack on China.
Japanese forces quickly overran much of the northern part of the
country. They captured the capital, Nanking (now Nanjing), committing horrible atrocities on the citizens of that city. But General Jiang
Jieshi (old spelling Chiang Kai-shek), head of the Chinese government, refused to surrender. He moved the Nationalist government
forces into western China and set up a new capital. The Japanese
then realized that the war in China would be long one. It lasted from
1937 to 1945, until Japan was defeated in World War II.

Reaction of the West. The League of Nations condemned Japan's aggression. The United States, the Soviet Union, and other

nations also protested Japan's actions and gave aid to China. Because no one was willing to use military force against Japan, the Japanese continued their conquests in China. In 1940, they moved into northern Indochina (now Vietnam).

China After World War I

During World War I, China had joined the Allies, expecting to gain some Russian territory in the north in exchange for its help. The peace treaty, however, did not recognize China's claims to this territory. Chinese nationalists were especially angered. On May 4, 1919, nationalist student groups demonstrated against the Western powers in what has become known as the "May Fourth Movement." It backed additional political reforms and formed the basis of the Communist party in China.

Jiang Jieshi and Mao Zedong. Impressed by the success of the Bolshevik Revolution in Russia, some Chinese became Communists. Among them was Mao Zedong, a supporter of the May Fourth Movement. The Communists opposed the Nationalist government set up by Dr. Sun Yixian. When Jiang Jieshi took over from Sun Yixian in 1925, he attacked the Communists. A civil war between the Nationalists and the Communists began in 1927. For a time, the Nationalists seemed to be winning the fight. But Jiang's control of China was never as solid as it appeared. Even so, the Nationalist forces succeeded in driving the Communists into the interior of China. In early 1934, some 100,000 Communists started the "Long March" from the south to northwestern China. It took until 1935 and cost the lives of more than 50,000 people. They died from exhaustion and in battles with the Nationalists.

When the Japanese invaded China in 1937, Jiang and Mao joined forces against their common enemy. They temporarily set aside the civil war.

INFO CHECK

1. Define *totalitarianism*. Was the Third Reich a totalitarian state? Why or why not?

2. Why did Adolf Hitler and the Nazi Party become popular with so many Germans in the 1930s? What do you find attractive or objectionable about Hitler's ideas?

3. Describe the impact of Japanese militarism on China. Why was the League of Nations unable to help China and other Asian nations?

COLONIAL RESPONSE TO EUROPEAN IMPERIALISM

In the Treaty of Versailles, Allied leaders allowed groups whose homelands were part of the former German and Austro-Hungarian empires to set up independent states. The victors, primarily Britain and France, clung to the colonies they owned. They also divided up most of the Ottoman Empire among themselves. Colonized people had become increasingly nationalistic during the later 1800s and had begun to work for their freedom. The Allies gained the support of some of these peoples, such as the Arabs, against the Central Powers by promising them independence after the war. When the Allies did not keep their promises, the subject peoples increased their struggles for independence.

The Indian Response to World War I

Chapters 22 and 24 described how the Indian people struggled against British domination during the second half of the 19th century. Although British troops put down the rebellion, Indian nationalism remained a strong force. When World War I started, the British were afraid that the Indians would use it as an opportunity to start another revolt.

Support of Britain. Contrary to expectations, the Indians rallied behind the British during the first years of the war. About 1.2 million Indians served as soldiers and laborers in Europe, Africa, and the Middle East. The British repaid their help by hiring more Indians for the better government jobs. These new opportunities did not, however, make a significant difference to the majority of the Indian people. When the long war brought hardships to India, the native people suffered the most.

Problems at Home. Discontent increased as inflation, high taxes, food shortages, and an outbreak of influenza devastated Indian lives. Nationalist groups began to work to improve the status of all Indians. In order to act more effectively, the moderate and radical factions of the Indian National Congress united. The All-Indian Congress Party was established with mainly Hindu leaders.

Muslim View. To promote their own interests, Muslims in India had founded the Muslim League. To avoid internal conflict, the Congress party persuaded the Muslim League to join in the Lucknow Pact of 1916. United in this pact, the Muslims and Hindus now jointly demanded that Britain make India a self-governing dominion, similar to Canada.

Rowlatt Acts. India had aided Britain during World War I with men and supplies. When the soldiers came back home, they were still not treated with respect. The economy was going through a difficult time, so jobs were hard to find. Rallies were held to protest conditions and British rule. In order to assert their authority, the British forced the passage of the Rowlatt Acts of 1919 through the legislature. These acts were designed to subdue unrest and prevent conspiracies against the British government.

Nationalist Indian groups all over India rioted in protest against

Time Line

Year	Dates and Events
A.D. 1916	**1916:** Indian Muslim-Hindu Lucknow Pact, demands status as British commonwealth
	1917: March and November revolutions; czar overthrown, Lenin becomes Russian leader
	1918: British women granted the vote
	1918: Bolsheviks withdraw Russia from war, cede territory, population, resources to Germany; Communists (Reds) execute czar and family
1920	**1919:** Rowlatt Acts end unrest and conspiracies in India; British massacre protesters at Amritsar
1921	**1919:** India Act defines British and Indian governing powers
	1919: Mussolini founds Italy's Fascist party
	1919: Chinese students demonstrate against Western influence; beginning of Chinese Communist party
	1920: American women granted the vote (19th Amendment)
1925	**1920s–1930s:** German Weimar Republic faces unemployment, inflation, debt, threat from Communists, Fascists
1926	**1920s–1930s:** Japan seeks to control East Asia, acquire needed raw materials
	1921: Russian Communists defeat opposition (Whites)
	1921–1933: British-appointed Arab, Faisal, rules Iraq; wins Iraqi independence
	1922: Russia renamed Union of Soviet Socialist Republics: Soviet Union
	1922: Fascists march on Rome; Mussolini becomes Italy's dictator
	1922: Egypt becomes constitutional monarchy
1930	**1923:** Kemal Atatürk becomes Turkish dictator; separates religion, state; liberates women; industrializes
1931	**1923:** Hitler imprisoned after attempt to seize Bavarian government
	1924–1953: Stalin controls Soviet government
	1925: Reza Khan ends British control of Iran
	1925–1927: Jiang Jieshi begins Chinese civil war against Mao Zedong
1935	**1927–1932:** Soviet's first Five-Year Plan (takeover of industry, collectivization of farms); millions starve
1936	**1929:** New York stock market crashes; widespread hardship, poverty
	1930s: Stalin's great purges: arrests, imprisonments, execution of millions
	1930s: Great Depression causes worldwide economic disaster
	1931: Japan seizes China's Manchuria for needed resources
1940	**1933:** Second Five-Year Plan (few goods, much heavy industry); Soviet Union becomes industrial power
1941	**1933:** Hitler appointed German chancellor; as absolute dictator, initiates system to persecute, kill Jews, other minorities, political enemies
	1933–1938: Franklin Roosevelt's New Deal program: public works to reduce unemployment, social security system, legalized collective bargaining
1945	**1934–1935:** Chinese Communists' "Long March" to northwestern China
	1935: New Indian constitution gives Indians real power in government
1946	**1937–1945:** Japan at war with China; Jiang's Nationalist government flees to western China; Mao and Jiang join forces against Japanese
	1940: Japan's forces move into northern Indochina (Vietnam)
	1941: British, Soviets invade Iran, depose Nazi-supporting shah, install son
	1943: French-controlled Lebanon becomes independent republic
1950	**1946:** France grants Syria independence
	1947: Hindus and Muslims control independent India; independent Pakistan

the Rowlatt Acts. In Amritsar, British troops ended a peaceful gathering by killing and wounding hundreds. The Amritsar Massacre caused even moderates to turn against the British. Mohandas Gandhi intensified his efforts to bring about independence through passive resistance and nonviolence. He urged Indians to disobey British laws, stop buying British goods, and end payment of taxes imposed by the British. Great numbers followed his ideas.

The India Act. To win support among the Indians, the British hastily promised to help the Indians develop their own government. The India Act of 1919 stated that during the transition between India's status as a colony and its independence, the administration of India's government would be split between British and native officials. This arrangement empowered the British officials to make all decisions on such important matters as taxes, police, and the law courts. The Indians were put in charge of agriculture, health, and education. Millions of Indians were given the right to vote for various levels of officials.

A New Constitution. Finally, in 1935, a new constitution gave Indians a real voice in their government. After World War II, in 1947, they gained complete control over their country. Unfortunately, Gandhi was unable to effect a lasting union between Hindus and Muslims. The religions of both peoples strongly influenced their cultures. The Muslims resented living in a state shaped by a culture not their own. The leaders of the Muslim League set up Pakistan as a separate Islamic nation within India. Today, India is still torn by conflicts between Muslims and Hindus.

Arab Nationalism

The British and the French broke their promise to the Arabs to help them set up their own state. The Arabs were in no position to resist these powerful nations. Nonetheless, they gradually obtained some degree of independence in all the mandated territories except Palestine.

Iraq. The British appointed an Arab prince, Faisal of Syria, to be king of Iraq. Faisal (ruled 1921–1933) worked hard for his people. He persuaded Britain to give Iraq its independence in 1932 in exchange for Iraqi military support of Britain.

Egypt. Egypt also managed to reduce British rule. A surge of Egyptian nationalism after World War I convinced the British that it was time to leave that country. In 1922, Britain allowed Egypt to have its own government but continued to occupy it militarily. Egypt's form of government was a constitutional monarchy. In 1936, British troops were restricted to the Suez Canal zone.

Syria and Lebanon. Unlike the British, the French held onto their mandate in Syria and even managed to acquire Lebanon as well. The French prevented revolt by setting the different ethnic groups that lived in the areas against each other. Lebanon eventually became a republic but remained under French protection. In 1943, it became independent. Syria signed a treaty of friendship with France in exchange for a promise that France would grant Syria independence. It finally came in 1946.

Oil and Power. Western influence remained strong in the Middle East. Arab landowners and merchants gained many financial benefits from supporting Britain and France. Most Arab leaders realized that their armies were not capable of facing Western military forces. Then, too, Western companies owned the oil fields that were just being discovered in the Middle East. This gave Western nations a great deal of power over the Arab economies. Arab rulers also received huge amounts of money for allowing Western companies to explore and drill for oil.

Iran Under Reza Shah

Influence of Britain and Russia. During the 19th century, Iran was under pressure from the British in the south and the Russians in the north. The shah (ruler) of Iran kept his country independent by granting economic privileges to both nations. Nationalists resented this concession to foreign powers. The movement aimed at restoring Islamic civilization and independence. In 1906, a group of merchants, religious leaders, and intellectuals forced the shah to set up a national assembly and to put a constitution into effect.

Iran was not allowed to benefit by these reforms. Russia and Britain simply took over the country, dividing it between them into spheres of influence. Britain took the region around the Persian Gulf, which had oil fields. Russia's sphere of influence included the northern half of Iran. By 1912, Russia virtually ruled Iran.

Then, during the Bolshevik Revolution, Russia lost its hold in Iran. In 1919, Britain tried to bribe Iranian officials to agree to a treaty appointing British advisers in every level of the Iranian government. The Iranian national assembly refused to accept this treaty. Nationalist movements rose up to oppose Britain's takeover. The British left.

Reza Shah Pahlavi. In 1925, a strong military leader, Reza Khan, overthrew the government and became shah. He took the name Reza Shah Pahlavi and modeled himself on Atatürk. Like the Turkish leader, he intended to free Iran of foreign influence and to modernize it. To realize his goals, Reza Shah created a modern army, constructed railroads, and began to industrialize Iran. He gave women more rights. To rid the country of foreign domination and to gain money for the Iranian treasury, he raised taxes on foreign businesses. In particular, he targeted the oil companies.

Reza Shah believed in separating religion and state. This policy offended the Muslim leaders in Iran, who were more powerful than their counterparts in Turkey. Loss of the support of the religious leaders was a serious blow to the shah's rule. In an effort to re-establish his authority, Reza Shah became increasingly cruel, grasping, and repressive. He ordered the deaths of his opponents and increased his personal wealth at public expense. When Hitler rose to power in Germany, Reza Shah supported his government. British and Soviet troops invaded Iran in 1941 and forced Reza Shah to leave. His son Mohammad Reza took over.

World War I left the world unstable and ripe for conflict. The Communist leaders of the Soviet Union had put into effect a new form of government and transformed the country's economy. They suspected that Western powers wanted to destroy their new state and kept their industries ready to produce war materials. Colonized peoples grew more resentful of the countries that ruled them. Arabs of the Middle East and the Indians were poised to revolt. The terms of the Treaty of Versailles had humiliated Germany and harmed its economy. The treaty had also ignored the claims of Italy. The frustrated Italians and Germans turned to military dictators to solve their problems. The Great Depression that gripped most of the world during the 1930s intensified the general unrest. Chapter 28 discusses the war that all this unrest produced.

INFO CHECK

1. List the colonized countries in which demands for independence grew stronger after World War I.

2. Identify each of the following nationalist leaders:(a) Mohandas Gandhi, (b) King Faisal, (c) Reza Shah Pahlavi.

3. Describe the roles of the Indian National Congress and the Muslim League in the achievement of independence for India by 1947.

4. How did Iran gain independence from Britain and Russia?

CHAPTER REVIEW

Multiple Choice

1. Czar Nicholas II allowed his subjects to elect a governing body. It was called the

   1. Diet
   2. Congress
   3. Duma
   4. Reichstag.

2. Russia's participation in World War I hastened the fall of the czar because it resulted in

   1. high casualty rates
   2. military defeats
   3. massive food shortages
   4. all of the above.

3. Lenin's government succeeded after the moderates, Kerensky and Prince Lvov, failed because

    1. Lenin followed through on his pledge of "peace, bread, and land"

    2. Lenin had the support of the Russian army for his renewed war effort

    3. the Allied forces supported Lenin's government

    4. Lenin was a brilliant general who defeated the German armies.

4. Lenin's New Economic Policy was closer to Socialist than Communist economic practices because

    1. the government controlled all the business and agricultural decision making

    2. the economy had a mixture of government and private ownership of business and agriculture

    3. it was a command economy

    4. the government allowed private individuals to make all economic decisions for the state.

5. Under Stalin, the change from farmers working their own land to forced labor on government-owned farms was known as

    1. blitzkrieg

    2. socialism

    3. collectivization

    4. capitalism.

6. The League of Nations was supposed to provide a place for nations to resolve differences peacefully. However, if the nations did go to war, then the league

    1. would stop trade with the warring countries

    2. would send a peacekeeping force

    3. dismiss the warring countries from the league

    4. would use the massive military forces loaned to it by the United States.

7. Under the League of Nations, the former colonies of the Ottoman and German empires were to be assisted in forming their own governments. The result of this new mandate system was to

    1. establish dictatorships

    2. put the former colonial peoples on the road to self-government

    3. prohibit the colonization of the territories

    4. take economic advantage of the former colonies.

8. After World War I, Turkey and Iran had to deal with major conflicts over

    1. women's rights

    2. industrialization

    3. military commanders who refused to support the popularly elected government

    4. secular vs. religious government.

9. The purpose of the suffrage movement was to

    1. help African Americans win the right to vote

    2. achieve voting rights for all women

    3. protest the suffering of the migratory farm workers

    4. protest the suffering of the enslaved peoples of the world.

10. The Depression and the failure of many governments to achieve order and stability in their nations led to the

    1. spread of Communist governments in Western Europe

    2. spread of democratic governments in Western Europe

3. rise of parliamentary governments in Western Europe

4. rise of military dictatorships in Western Europe.

11. Examine the map on page 601. Which is the most accurate conclusion about the Soviet Union between 1917 and 1938?

1. Japan, China, and India joined the Soviet Union.

2. The Soviet Union extended approximately 1,000 miles from east to west.

3. The Soviet Union comprised a number of republics.

4. The official title of the Soviet Union was Russia.

12. The most accurate conclusion to be drawn from the line graph on page 609 is that

1. the Nazis in Germany had eliminated unemployment by 1934

2. during the worldwide depression, Britain had higher unemployment than Germany

3. the worldwide depression had a less severe impact in the United States than in Britain or Germany

4. Hitler probably owed much of his public support to his success in combating unemployment between 1933 and 1938.

13. The propaganda poster on page 612 attempted to convince people that

1. Hitler was supported by the vast majority of German people

2. the Nazis could not govern without the public support of the German people

3. Jews were fearful of Hitler's growing power in Germany

4. most of the people of Europe were sympathetic to the Nazi cause.

Thematic Essays

1. The governmental and economic practices of Communist Russia, Fascist Italy, and Nazi Germany differed greatly from those of the democracies of Europe and the United States. *Task:* Using examples from the areas of economics and government, compare and contrast the practices of any two of the dictatorships with the practices of a democracy, such as Great Britain or France.

2. The Treaty of Versailles was intended (1) to punish the German nation for causing World War I and (2) to prevent Germany from ever regaining its military power. The League of Nations was intended to preserve the peace of Europe. Those three goals were not reached. *Task:* Using specific historical examples, explain why none of those goals was achieved.

Document-Based Questions

Use the documents and your knowledge of Global History and Geography to answer the questions.

1. Study the photos on pages 606 and 612. What does each photo tell you about each leader?

2. From Benito Mussolini:

". . . The Fascist conception of life stresses the importance of the State. . . . The State became the conscience and will of the people . . . Fascism is totalitarian . . . It discards pacifism [anti-war beliefs]. . . ."

How do you think he would react to demands for individual rights and freedoms?

3. Adolf Hitler, while in jail for attempting to overthrow the government, wrote in *Mein Kampf:*

"There must be no majority decisions, but only responsible persons. . . .

Surely every man will have his advisors by his side, but the decision will be made by one man . . . responsibility can and may be borne by only one man, and therefore only he alone may possess the authority and right to command . . ."

Discuss how this quote reflects the ideology of dictatorship. How did the Third Reich reflect this ideology?

4. A description of Kemal Atatürk:

"When he came there was a dynasty, the Ottomans, and he needed a nation, Turkey. . . . Mustafa Kemal knew . . . that you cannot have a strong nation composed of weak individuals, and that a country cannot be strong if it is ridden with disease, ignorance, and poverty. . . . The foe was the turban and the fez, the women's veil and the peasants' ignorance, the illiteracy of the shepherd and the people's indifference. . . . The nation was mightier than Allah. . . . The good Turk wore European dress and the fez belonged to a dead era. . . . The state was secularized and Turkey was no longer wedded to Islam."

Who and what was Kemal attacking, and what did he wish to achieve?

5. Study the photo on page 604. Discuss what the photo tells about cultural changes in Turkey. Why do you think some Turks opposed these changes?

6. Study the photo on page 611. What does this tell you about the value of the money and the post-World War I German economy?

7. In Chapter 28, you will learn that Italy attacked Ethiopia. The League of Nations voted to use economic sanctions against Italy but was not supported by the non-League nations of the world. The emperor of Ethiopia appeared before the League of Nations and appealed for aid:

"In October 1935 Italian troops invaded my territory . . . I assert [state] that the problem . . . is much wider than merely a question of . . . Italian aggression, it is collective security, it is the very existence of the League. It is the value of promises to small states that their integrity and independence shall be respected and assured. . . . What undertakings can be of any value if the will to keep them is lacking?"

Discuss the emperor's sentiments toward the League. Why does he use the term "collective security" to describe the league?

Document-Based Essay

Leaders such as Stalin, Hitler, and Atatürk claimed to have the solutions to their nation's problems after World War I. They were willing to take drastic measures to change the conditions of their countries. *Task:* For any *two* such leaders, list the economic and political problems of their nations and then describe the effect their solutions had on these nations.

C H A P T E R
28

World War II

Startled, Colin sat upright in bed. As he did, the shrill whining noise that awakened him expanded into a boom. The Germans were bombing London again. Here, in the country, with his grandparents, Colin was safe. But that thought didn't reassure him. His parents were still in the city. It didn't help to bury his head under the covers. In his mind, Colin could see his house smashed and burning. And his parents? But they had made it safely to the shelter in the underground (subway) station. There was always plenty of warning. They would be all right. They *had* to be all right.

Colin could hear sobbing from the room next to his. It was Miriam, the German-Jewish girl his grandparents had taken in. Her parents had sent her to England at the start of the war. Colin didn't want to think about what might have happened to her family.

T he hope that the League of Nations could keep the peace after World War I faded rapidly. The dictators who came to power in Europe and the militarists in Japan refused to be stopped by words. The league had little except words to use as weapons.

Finally, at the end of the 1930s, England and France took a stand against Nazi Germany. World War II broke out. It lasted for six years and was the most terrible war the world had yet seen. The conflict featured large-scale air, land, and sea battles. It was also characterized by atrocities, such as deliberately bombing civilians and trying to exterminate entire religious and ethnic groups.

From the beginning of the war in 1939 to the end in 1945, men, women, and children worried about death and destruction and about being homeless. Even if they were not in the war zones, they worried about relatives or friends who were soldiers or who were imprisoned by the warring nations.

After the war, most of the nations of the world again tried to find a way to keep peace. They established the United Nations.

THE NAZI STATE, 1933–1945

The difficult economic conditions in Germany in the 1930s brought the Nazi Party and Adolf Hitler to power. He became head of the German government in 1933. Hitler's government caused profound changes to Germany. By naming his government the Third Reich, Hitler announced his intention of ruling a vast empire. *Reich* is the German word for "empire."

Taking Total Control

Like the emperors of ancient times, Hitler expected his subjects to follow his direction without question. He was determined to control the thoughts, feelings, and acts of the German people.

Hitler revived old German myths, legends, and imagery. He promoted the music of Richard Wagner, who had written operas about ancient German gods and heroes. Art, literature, and music that contradicted Nazi values were banned. Young people formed mobs and burned books containing some of the most brilliant ideas of the time. The works of such geniuses as Sigmund Freud, Albert Einstein, and Marcel Proust (a French writer) went up in smoke.

Economy. Various factors enabled Hitler to persuade many Germans to accept his leadership. The improvement of the economy was one of the more important factors. During his first year as chancellor, Hitler reduced unemployment by starting public works programs, such as the construction of superhighways and public housing. He set aside the Treaty of Versailles and began to rearm Germany. The military buildup created even more jobs than did public works. Many industrialists profited from the policies and became Hitler's supporters. Business leaders were also won over by Hitler's anti-Communist attitude. Communist policy called for the government to take over private businesses.

National Pride. Not only did the new prosperity make people more comfortable, it also restored their self-esteem, which had been badly damaged by the consequences of the Versailles peace treaty. It had saddled them with the war-guilt clause and heavy debts. All Hitler's propaganda was designed to stimulate German national pride. According to Hitler, Germans were not inferior to people of other nationalities but superior to them. They were, in fact, the master race, destined to rule the world. If Germans were the master race, it followed that other races existed to serve them.

Methods. Hitler was a powerful orator and had a genius for staging grand spectacles. He held huge rallies, at which he made impassioned and hypnotic speeches. Crowds cheered wildly as he described the treachery of Jews and Communists. He blamed them for Germany's defeat in the war. Germany's need to expand into other countries for *lebensraum* (living space) was a feature of many speeches. To make sure that the German people would not be influenced by anti-Nazi ideas, the party took complete control of the media. Germans had access only to state-approved radio broadcasts, movies, and publications.

Youth. Perhaps Hitler's most powerful method of indoctrination was his education of young people. The Nazi Party took control of all schools and universities. It weakened parental influence by requiring children from the ages of 6 to 18 to join groups run by the Nazis. If parents objected to letting their children become members of these organizations, Nazi officials threatened to take the children away from them.

At age six, boys began training to join the Hitler Youth. They participated in athletics and camping and learned the Nazi version of history. At ten, they were allowed to join the Jungvolk ("Young Folk"). From the Jungvolk, 14-year-old boys graduated into Hitler Youth. Military training was added to camping, athletics, and indoctrination in Nazi ideology. At age 18, they entered the army.

The Hitler Youth movement also included girls. As did the boys' organization, the League of German Girls offered training in sports, camping, and soldiering. Nazi leaders prescribed vigorous exercise for girls so that they would grow up to be healthy mothers of future soldiers.

Suppression. The super-nationalism Hitler preached glorified his own need for power. He made all the decisions in the government and military. Germans had to subordinate their individual needs and goals to serve his ends. Although Hitler was a compelling leader, he could not persuade all Germans to cooperate with his plans. Those who opposed him were killed or imprisoned in death camps.

INFO CHECK

1. Give at least one reason for the acceptance of Hitler and nazism by each of these groups: (a) workers, (b) business leaders and industrialists, (c) veterans, (d) supernationalists and racists.

2. Evaluate the Nazi educational program. Why do you approve or disapprove of it?

3. What happened to Germans who opposed nazism?

THE ROAD TO WAR

German Aggression in Europe

Hitler had promised the Germans that he would tear up the hated Treaty of Versailles. In 1935, he started a series of actions that violated the terms of the treaty. He began to draft men into the German army to increase its size. He also organized an air force. No one took steps to stop the illegal German rearmament—not the League of Nations, Britain, France, nor the United States.

Rhineland. In 1936, Hitler again violated the Treaty of Versailles. He sent German troops into the Rhineland. This border area between France and Germany was supposed to be demilitarized (free of all armed forces). Hitler had ordered his military commanders to withdraw their troops if the French showed any signs of opposition. Although the French considered taking action, they could not get the British to support them. Consequently, nothing was done. Hitler controlled the Rhineland, an area rich in coal and iron, resources needed by German industries.

Neither France nor Britain wanted to go to war again so soon after the end of World War I. Their economies were weak, and they had not rebuilt their military forces.

Austria. In 1938, after having expanded German war industries and military forces, Hitler annexed Austria. This German-speaking country increased Germany's size and power considerably. Although the Treaty of Versailles prohibited the union of Germany and Austria, no one took any action against Nazi Germany.

Czechoslovakia. Czechoslovakia was a small democratic nation that had emerged from the break-up of the Austro-Hungarian Empire. More than 3 million Germans lived among 15 million Czechs. The German-speaking population was centered mainly in the Sudetenland in western Czechoslovakia on the German border. In 1933, Hitler sent Nazi agents into the Sudetenland to stir up riots against the Czech government. Unrest continued for several years. Then, in 1938, Hitler demanded that the Sudetenland Germans be given the right to decide whether they would remain part of Czechoslovakia or unite with Germany. He backed up his demands with the threat of invasion.

Appeasement. To prevent war, a conference was held in the German city of Munich in September 1938. Prime Minister Neville Chamberlain of Britain and Premier Edouard Daladier of France met with Hitler and Mussolini. Czech government officials were not allowed to attend the meeting, and were forced to accept the results. The participants in the Munich Conference decided to give the Sudetenland to Germany. In return, Hitler promised that he would not attempt to take over any more territory in Europe.

During the 1930s, British and French leaders often followed the policy, called *appeasement*, of giving in to Hitler and Mussolini in

Chamberlain (center) escorted by Nazi officers to the Munich Conference, 1938

order to avoid war. Instead of preventing World War II, appeasement made it more probable. It confirmed the dictators' belief that the democratic nations were too weak and frightened to stop them.

Italian Aggression in Africa

Benito Mussolini's great dream was to rebuild the Roman Empire. As a first step toward achieving this goal, he ordered the invasion of Ethiopia in October 1935. An independent nation, Ethiopia bordered Italian Somaliland in eastern Africa. Ethiopia had few modern weapons to use against the well-equipped Italian army and air force.

Emperor Haile Selassie of Ethiopia pleaded with the League of Nations for help. The league asked member nations not to sell food and war materials to Italy until it withdrew from Ethiopia. But many nations ignored the league, and the attempt at economic pressure failed. Italy continued the war against Ethiopia, which fell in May 1936.

The Spanish Civil War

A violent struggle between democracy and dictatorship took place in Spain. In 1936, General Francisco Franco, a Spanish military officer, began a revolt against the democratically elected government of Spain. While this Loyalist government received some aid from the Soviet Union, Franco was heavily supported by military advisers,

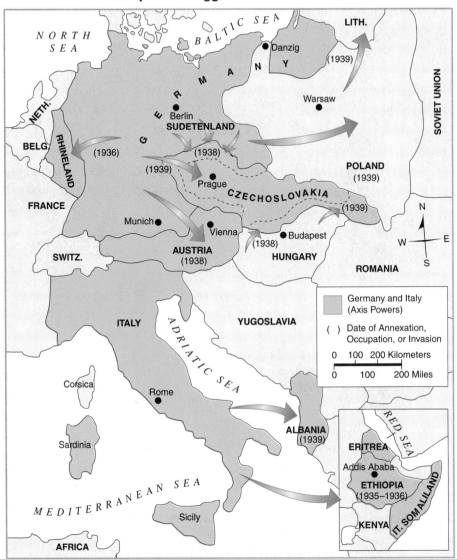

Europe: Axis Aggression   1930–1940

troops, weapons, and aircraft from Fascist Italy and Nazi Germany. For Hitler and Mussolini, Spain became a testing ground for their new weapons and military tactics. From other European nations and the United States, volunteers came to Spain to fight for democracy. Forming military units such as the Abraham Lincoln Brigade and the International Brigade, they supported the Loyalist government.

The people of Spain suffered greatly during the bloody three-year civil war. The destruction was most graphically portrayed by Pablo Picasso's famous painting *Guernica*. The city of Guernica was heavily damaged, and many civilians were killed in a raid by the Condor Legion, a German Air Force unit.

In 1939, Franco's forces won complete control of Spain and established a Fascist dictatorship friendly to Germany and Italy. Many regarded the Spanish Civil War as a prelude to World War II.

INFO CHECK

1. List Hitler's violations of the Treaty of Versailles. Why did the United States and other nations fail to stop these actions?

2. Name the leaders who attended the Munich Conference of 1938. How did the decisions reached reflect the policy of appeasement?

3. How did the Italian invasion of Ethiopia and the Spanish Civil War bring the world closer to World War II?

GLOBAL CONFLICT

In March 1939, Hitler broke the promise he had made at the Munich conference. He took over the remainder of Czechoslovakia. Britain and France finally realized that Hitler intended to dominate Europe. They abandoned the policy of appeasement and decided to resist any further Nazi aggression. War seemed ready to break out at any moment. The world waited to see what Hitler, Mussolini, and the Japanese would do next. Everyone hoped that if conflicts did break out, they would be brief and localized. A few experts feared that the only way to stop the dictators would be to wage a general war.

War Breaks Out

Nonaggression Pacts. To make sure that he had support for his war plans, Hitler allied Germany with Italy and Japan. In 1936, he formed the Rome-Berlin Axis and made an informal agreement with Japan. The three nations signed the formal military and economic alliance, creating the Rome-Berlin-Tokyo Axis in 1940.

The anti-Communist Hitler unexpectedly signed a nonaggression pact with the anti-Fascist Stalin in 1939. Both countries pledged not to attack the other. Temporarily secure from attack from the east, Hitler took new aggressive actions.

Invasion of Poland. Now Hitler felt that he could carry out his plans to conquer Europe. On September 1, 1939, German forces poured into Poland using what were called *blitzkrieg* (lightning war) tactics. Troops and artillery in motorized vehicles quickly overran defenses. Aided by planes and tanks, they crushed the opposing forces and moved on. Speed and mobility characterized blitzkrieg tactics.

Britain had signed a mutual assistance treaty with Poland in late

August. Along with its ally France, Britain demanded that the attack be called off. Hitler refused. On September 3, Britain and France declared war on Germany. World War II had begun—just 25 years after the start of World War I.

The Soviet Union took advantage of the turmoil, and in mid-September, attacked Poland from the east. The Soviets also seized Latvia, Lithuania, and Estonia on the Baltic Sea. These three small countries became part of the Soviet Union. The Soviet Union also advanced into Finland. Although it fought hard, Finland lost territory to the Soviet Union in the "Winter War" (1939–1941).

Poland fell in less than a month. Germany and the Soviet Union divided the country between them. Hitler then turned his attention north and west.

Moves North and West. Throughout the winter of 1939–1940, Hitler built up German strength. Then, in April 1940, German forces took over Norway and Denmark. A month later, they conquered Belgium and Holland. Hitler then ordered the invasion of France. The French surrendered in June 1940. At this point, Italy entered the war against the democracies.

Occupying France. Under the surrender agreement, the Germans divided France into two parts. The north, Occupied France, was directly controlled by German forces. Pro-German French officials administered the south, which was named Vichy France after its capital city.

Most French people regarded those who cooperated with the Vichy government as traitors. Some French leaders escaped to North Africa and Britain. General Charles de Gaulle collected the French in Britain into an organization called the "Free French." He urged all French people to resist the Germans in any way they could.

Attacking Britain. After the fall of France, Britain stood alone against the dictators. The United States continued to be neutral. It did, however, send food and arms to the British. Britain was also aided by its colonies and those former colonies that had kept close ties with it.

Winston Churchill had succeeded Chamberlain as prime minister. Churchill had a strong personality and was anti-Nazi. He did not shrink from a battle. A forceful speaker, Churchill inspired the British people to resist any German attack. "Victory at all costs," he said, "victory in spite of all terror, victory however long and hard the road may be; for without victory there is no survival."

Hitler stepped up preparations to invade Britain. In August 1940, the German air force started its mass bombings of British cities, industrial areas, seaports, and military installations. The bombings caused many deaths and great destruction. Fierce air battles were fought over Britain for a period of ten months. During the Battle of Britain, the Royal Air Force destroyed large numbers of German

American cartoon depicting
the Nazi menace, 1940

planes. By June 1941, the German air raids eased off. Britain seemed safe from a land invasion. Churchill paid tribute to the contribution of the Royal Air Force with these words: "Never in the field of human conflict was so much owed by so many to so few."

Eastern Europe. Hungary and Rumania joined the Berlin-Rome-Tokyo Axis in late 1940. Bulgaria followed in 1941. Italian forces had conquered Albania in 1939. They began to move into neighboring Greece in October 1940. By May 1941, Yugoslavia and Greece had been crushed. Hitler and his allies now controlled the whole of the Balkans. Only small bands of resistance fighters continued to oppose them.

Invading the Soviet Union. In June 1941, Hitler tossed aside the nonaggression pact with Stalin and invaded the Soviet Union. The Germans wanted the large grain-producing areas and oil resources of the Soviets. German forces advanced almost to Moscow. Britain and the United States quickly came to the aid of the Soviets, sending arms and food. In December 1941, the Soviet Army counterattacked. Their action and the harsh winter weather temporarily halted the German forces.

The Holocaust

Hitler's victories allowed him to establish a "New Order" in Europe. He planned to colonize Eastern Europe by Germans. Deserving members of the German "master race" were to be given farms, factories, and businesses. The original owners—Russians, Poles, and other "inferiors"—were to work as slave laborers to produce food and goods for Germany. Millions of Europeans of all nationalities and culture groups met such a fate. Most were transported to factories inside the dreaded concentration camps. Besides Slavs, such as the Russians and Poles, Hitler wished to eliminate Jews, Gypsies, and people with disabilities.

Anti-Semitism. Hitler had especially marked the Jews for destruction. The Nuremberg Laws of 1935 took away the citizenship rights of German Jews. During the "Night of Broken Glass," or *Kristallnacht* (November 9–10, 1938), Nazis killed and beat Jews throughout Germany and Austria. Their homes, shops, and places of worship were looted and smashed.

Many Jews then fled to other parts of Europe to escape the misery of life in the Third Reich. Some also went to Britain and North and South America. Many more would have left but could not find anywhere to go. Most countries, including the United States, limited the number of Jews they would take in. Families did try to send children, such as Miriam in the opening story, to safe places.

As the Nazis overran Europe, the Jews who had moved to other European countries once again found themselves at Hitler's mercy. The Nazis referred to the continued presence of Jews in Europe as "the Jewish problem." In 1942, Nazi leaders officially decided to murder all the Jews in Europe. At the Wannsee Conference in January of that year, they worked out their plans for carrying out this "final solution."

Death Camps. In every country they conquered, the Nazis rounded up Jews and sent them to death camps. Some resisted, of course, but the Nazi might was too great for small groups to overcome. One of the largest and best-known camps was Auschwitz in Poland. In this place alone, some 3 million Jews were murdered. In all, the Nazis killed at least 6 million Jews and an equal number of Poles, Russians, Gypsies, homosexuals, and others.

The Nazi plan to kill all of the Jews of Europe is an example of *genocide*. Genocide is the deliberate destruction of an entire cultural or religious group. The *Holocaust* is the term people now apply to this terrible event in history.

The United States in the Early War Years

Throughout the 1920s and the 1930s, the United States tried to keep out of international disputes. It did, however, participate in sev-

THE NIGHT OF BROKEN GLASS

As soon as he became chancellor of Germany, Adolf Hitler began a series of legal actions against Germany's Jews. In 1933, he proclaimed a one-day boycott of Jewish shops. Jews were dismissed from government service and universities and were forbidden to enter the professions. The Nuremburg Laws of 1935 forbade marriages between Jews and "pure" Germans and deprived Jews of their civil rights. In 1936, Jews were barred from voting in parliamentary elections. Signs stating "Jews Not Welcome" appeared in many German cities.

In July 1938, all Jews were required to carry identification cards. On October 28, 1938, 17,000 Jews who were Polish citizens living in Germany were arrested. Although many had been living in Germany for decades, they were forcibly deported to Poland. When the Polish government refused to admit them, the Jews were held in "relocation camps" on the Polish frontier.

Among the deportees was Zindel Grynszpan, who had been born in western Poland and had moved to Germany in 1911. He owned a small store in the city of Hanover. He and his family were forced out of their home by German police, and they were made to move over the Polish border.

Grynszpan's 17-year-old son, Herschel, was living with an uncle in Paris. When he learned of his family's deportation, Herschel went to the German Embassy in Paris armed with a pistol. It was November 7, 1938. The young man shot and critically wounded Third Secretary Ernst von Rath. Rath died of his wounds on November 9.

The assassination gave Nazi Minister of Propaganda Joseph Goebbels an excuse to launch a nationwide attack on German Jews. Goebbels considered the shooting in Paris to be part of a global conspiracy by "International Jewry" against the German nation and Hitler. The anti-Jewish brutality organized by Goebbels in response came to be called *Kristallnacht*—the Night of Broken Glass.

On the nights of November 9 and 10, 1938, gangs of young Nazis all over Germany roamed through Jewish neighborhoods breaking windows of Jewish homes and businesses, burning synagogues, and looting. Physical assaults on Jews caused 91 deaths. Some 26,000 Jews were arrested and sent to concentration camps. More than 100 synagogues and several thousand businesses were destroyed.

Shortly after Kristallnacht, Nazi leaders decided to place the blame for Kristallnacht on the Jews themselves. New laws aimed to remove Jews from participation in German economic life. Germany's Jews were fined for the death of the German Embassy official in Paris. Money paid by insurance companies to Jews for damages to their homes and businesses was confiscated by the German government.

Life became even more difficult for German Jews, especially young people. Already barred from entering museums, playgrounds, and swimming pools, Jewish youngsters were expelled from the public schools after Kristallnacht. The Holocaust had begun.

1. Respond to Joseph Goebbels' argument that Kristallnacht was a necessary and justified action.

2. To what extent did Nazi laws constitute a policy of segregation of German Jews? Could such laws exist in the United States today? Why or why not?

eral weapons-reduction conferences. When Hitler and Mussolini started on their aggressive paths, the United States declared its neutrality and its wish not to be involved in overseas conflicts.

Aid to Britain. After World War II began in 1939, the United States took steps to help Britain hold off Hitler's forces. In spite of strong antiwar groups in the country, President Franklin Roosevelt persuaded Congress to pass the Lend-Lease Act in March 1941. It permitted the United States to sell, lend, or lease military equipment to the Allies. The United States also offered to sell arms if Britain would transport the weapons in its own ships and pay cash for them. Throughout 1940 and 1941, the United States found a variety of ways to maintain its neutrality and still send aid to Britain. After the Soviet Union was attacked in 1941, the United States also sent aid there.

Japanese Tactics in Asia

Japanese aggression against China in the 1930s called forth strong protests from U.S. officials. The Allied nations were particularly shocked by the brutality with which Japanese soldiers treated Chinese civilians. When they conquered the Nationalist Party's capital city, Nanjing, in December 1937, the Japanese killed some 40,000 and abused thousands of others.

After France and the Netherlands fell to the Nazis, Japan made plans to take over their colonies in Indochina and the Dutch East Indies. (The East Indies are now Indonesia.) To stop such action by the Japanese, U.S. President Franklin Roosevelt banned the export of materials vital to Japanese industry. The ban went into effect in July 1941 and covered such materials as petroleum, petroleum products, and scrap metal.

As Japan's oil reserves dropped, the country became more and more desperate for supplies of fuel. Japan tried to persuade the United States to change its policies. The United States refused. In early December 1941, Japanese military leaders ordered a force of ships and planes to attack an American base in the Pacific.

The United States Enters the War

During the early morning hours of December 7, 1941, Japanese planes bombed the American naval base at Pearl Harbor in Hawaii. Most of the U.S. Pacific fleet was destroyed or severely damaged, as were most of the planes on the base. The United States could not now stop the Japanese from taking over East Asia and key islands in the Pacific. (At about the same time, Japan attacked the Philippines, Hong Kong, and Thailand. They pushed on to the Netherlands East Indies and its resources of oil.)

Asia: Axis Aggression   1930–1940

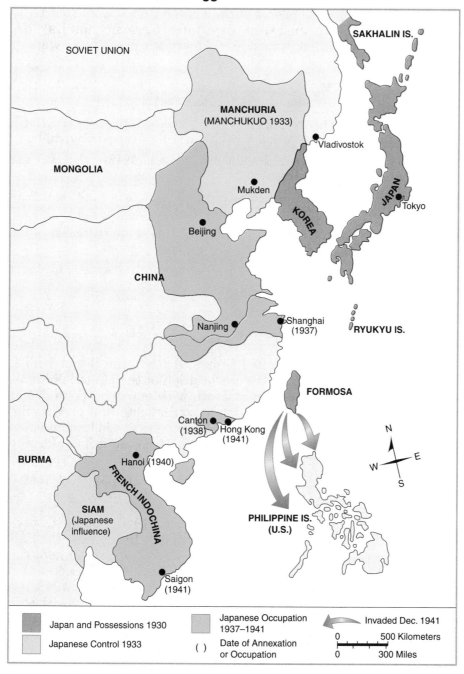

SOVIET UNION

SAKHALIN IS.

MANCHURIA
(MANCHUKUO 1933)

MONGOLIA

Vladivostok

Mukden

JAPAN

KOREA

Tokyo

Beijing

CHINA

Nanjing   Shanghai
(1937)

RYUKYU IS.

FORMOSA

Canton
(1938)   Hong Kong
(1941)

BURMA

Hanoi (1940)

FRENCH INDOCHINA

SIAM
(Japanese
influence)

N

W   E

S

PHILIPPINE IS.
(U.S.)

Saigon
(1941)

Japan and Possessions 1930

Japanese Control 1933

Japanese Occupation
1937–1941

( )   Date of Annexation
or Occupation

Invaded Dec. 1941

0   500 Kilometers

0   300 Miles

On December 8, President Roosevelt requested Congress to declare war on Japan. The people of the United States wholeheartedly supported his decision. Just three days later, Germany and Italy declared war on the United States. Now Americans faced major wars in both Europe and Asia.

INFO CHECK

1. Identify or define: (a) Rome-Berlin-Tokyo Axis, (b) blitzkrieg, (c) Winter War, (d) Occupied France and Vichy France, (e) Winston Churchill.

2. Explain the importance of the Battle of Britain (1940). What was the United States doing at this time?

3. How did Hitler change German policy toward Russia in June 1941? Why did he do this?

4. Define the term New Order. What was the role of the Holocaust in the New Order? Why was the Holocaust a policy of genocide?

5. How did Japanese actions in Asia bring the United States into World War II?

THE FIGHTING IN WORLD WAR II

In January 1942, the United States, Britain, the Soviet Union, and 23 other nations signed the Declaration of the United Nations. The Allied Powers pledged to cooperate with one another to defeat the Axis Powers. The Allies decided to concentrate first on winning the war in Europe. Enough supplies and soldiers would be channeled to the Pacific command to try to keep the Japanese from enlarging their empire.

Allied Strategy in Europe

The Italians moved into North Africa in 1940, hoping to take Egypt from Britain. Germany sent help in 1941. By winning the Battle of El Alamein in Egypt in November 1942, the British kept the Italians and Germans from taking over the Suez Canal. Soon afterward, Allied forces landed in Algeria and Morocco. By May 1943, the whole of North Africa was in Allied hands. From their position in North Africa, the Allies moved into Sicily and then on into Italy.

Stalingrad. In late 1942, the Soviets stopped the German advance in Russia. The Germans suffered a major defeat at Stalingrad (now Volgograd) in February 1943. But the Germans held on in western USSR throughout most of 1943. In the fall, the Soviets began pushing west toward Germany and south into the Balkans. They did not stop until they reached Berlin in April 1945.

The Allies invaded Sicily in July 1943. Late in July, Mussolini

World War II in Europe   1943–1945

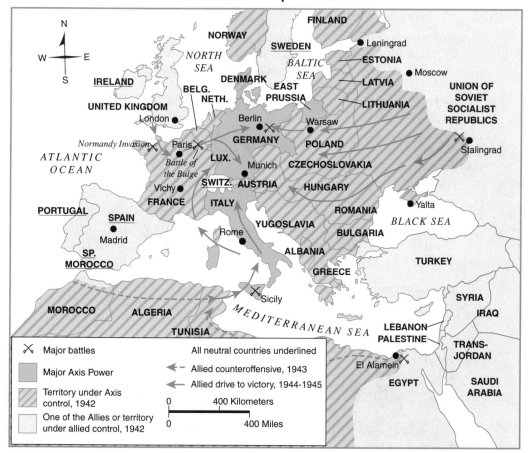

was forced out of office and imprisoned. He was later shot by anti-Fascists. A new Italian government signed an armistice with the Allies in September. German forces continued to fight. Rome fell to the Allies in June 1944. Nonetheless, the Germans occupied northern Italy until May 1945.

D-Day. The greatest seaborne invasion of modern times was launched on June 6, 1944 (D-Day). Under the command of U.S. General Dwight D. Eisenhower, Allied troops crossed the English Channel and landed in Normandy, France. They relentlessly pushed the German forces out of France, Belgium, and Holland. In December 1944, the Germans won the Battle of the Bulge in Belgium. But the Allied forces counterattacked and broke the German attack.

V-E Day. In March 1945, the Allies moved into Germany. As the Russians entered Berlin, Hitler committed suicide. On May 7, the new German leaders surrendered. The next day, the end of the war in Europe—V-E Day—was officially declared.

Allied Strategy in the Pacific

At first, the Japanese held the Pacific area in a firm grip. They had a strong navy and talented fighter pilots. They also had been able to build strong defenses on the territories they conquered.

Fall of the Philippines. Although the American and Filipino armies fought hard for control of the Philippines, they were forced to retreat from Manila to the Bataan Peninsula. There they resisted the Japanese for three months. When they surrendered on April 9, 1942, the Japanese forced the starving soldiers to march to a distant prison camp. When the prisoners were too weak to walk any farther, the Japanese shot them. Ten thousand soldiers died as a result of the Bataan Death March, as it came to be called.

Sea Battles. After the defeat in the Philippines, the Allied Powers began to make significant gains in the Pacific. In May of 1942, the Allies won their first victory there. The Battle of the Coral Sea kept the Japanese from invading Australia. It was fought entirely by air-

United States Marine Corps Memorial to the heroes of Iwo Jima, Washington, D.C.

craft based on U.S. and Japanese aircraft carriers. The second naval victory in 1942, the Battle of Midway, stopped the eastward advance of Japan.

Island Hopping. In the Pacific, the Allies followed a strategy termed "island hopping." They chose key islands to attack. When the attacks were successful, they used them as bases to invade other islands. Enemy forces on bypassed islands were cut off from supplies and support. Names such as Guadalcanal, Tarawa, Kwajalein, and Iwo Jima became familiar as places where bloody battles were fought.

In the fall of 1944, American forces commanded by General Douglas MacArthur landed in the Philippines. Shortly afterward, the U.S. Navy destroyed the main strength of the Japanese Navy in the Battle of Leyte Gulf.

China and India. Chinese forces, with American aid, kept the Japanese from overrunning all of China. British and Indian troops pushed the Japanese out of eastern India and Burma. Nonetheless, almost all of Southeast Asia remained under Japanese control throughout the war.

Closing in on Japan. In early 1945, U.S. bombers began regular runs over Japan. They caused great destruction in Tokyo and other

World War II in the Pacific   1941–1945

CASUALTIES IN WORLD WAR II

	Dead in Battle	Wounded in Battle
Allies		
Britain	389,000	475,000
France	211,000	400,000
Soviet Union	7,500,000	14,102,000
United States	292,000	671,000
Axis		
Germany	2,850,000	7,250,000
Italy	77,500	120,000
Japan	1,576,000	500,000

major cities. In April 1945, U.S. troops landed on the island of Okinawa, just 350 miles from Japan.

Atomic Bomb. To avoid the horrible losses predicted when the Allies invaded Japan, the United States tried to persuade the Japanese government to surrender. When Japan refused, an American plane dropped an atomic bomb on the city of Hiroshima on August 6, 1945. This one bomb leveled between 4 and 5 square miles of the city and killed more than 80,000 people. On August 8, the Soviet Union declared war on Japan. The Japanese still refused to end the war. On August 9, a second atomic bomb was dropped, this time on Nagasaki. The Japanese now realized that the Allies had the power to destroy their homeland. They signed documents of surrender on September 2, 1945—V-J Day.

Technology and World War II

As shown by the atomic bomb's destruction of two Japanese cities, technology played an even larger part in World War II than it had in World War I. Throughout the war, conventional bombs destroyed civilians, their homes, architectural masterpieces, museums, and social institutions, such as schools and hospitals. Airplanes vastly superior to those used during the World War I made such mass destruction possible.

Giant aircraft carriers brought fighter planes close to their targets. The carriers were vital to the success of the strategy in the Pacific. The United States had no land bases between Hawaii and Australia and New Zealand. The Japanese controlled the islands in between.

The invention of radar provided a means both to detect approaching enemies and to pinpoint targets for attack. Armored tanks bull-dozed their way into cities and across enemy lines. Weapons and war machines had never been so elaborate and so lethal.

INFO CHECK

1. Who were the Allied Powers?

2. How did each of the following lead to Allied victory in World War II? (a) El Alamein (1942), (b) Stalingrad (1943), (c) Sicily (1943), (d) D-Day (1944), (e) V-E Day (1945).

3. Explain how island hopping and the atomic bomb led to Allied victory in the Pacific.

PLANNING FOR THE POSTWAR WORLD

Throughout the war, President Franklin D. Roosevelt and Prime Minister Winston Churchill of Great Britain met frequently. They cooperated in making plans for conducting the war. Premier Joseph

"The Big Three"—Churchill, Roosevelt, and Stalin—meeting at Yalta, 1945

Stalin of the Soviet Union was kept informed of Allied strategy. General Jiang Jieshi, the head of China, also met with the Allied leaders.

Yalta

One of the most important meetings of the war took place at Yalta, a city on the Black Sea in the Soviet Union, in February 1945. Stalin, Churchill, and Roosevelt worked out the peace terms for Germany. They agreed to divide Germany into four occupation zones. Britain, France, the United States, and the Soviet Union would each administer a zone. This decision divided Germany into eastern and western parts. Germany was to be disarmed and its war criminals punished. War crimes included participation in the mass murder of Jews and other peoples. Since Stalin agreed to enter the war with Japan after Germany was defeated, Soviet domination of Poland and other Eastern European countries was allowed.

Another agreement of long-lasting importance was the pledge to establish the United Nations. This world peace organization would replace the League of Nations.

The United Nations

In April 1945, delegates from 50 nations met in San Francisco to organize the United Nations. The U.S. Senate approved the charter in July 1945, ensuring U.S. membership in the organization.

The purpose of the UN is to work for world peace and security and to improve the lives of the people of the world. The charter of the United Nations calls for six major parts to the organization: the General Assembly, the Security Council, the Secretariat, the Economic and Social Council, the International Court of Justice, and the Trusteeship Council. There are also specialized agencies that carry out specific functions of the UN.

The *General Assembly* is open to all independent countries of the world. Currently, there are 185 members. Each member nation has one vote. The General Assembly oversees the operation of the UN and discusses questions the members bring before the body.

The *Security Council* is charged with keeping the peace. It has 15 members, five permanent ones and ten seated on a rotating basis. The five permanent members are the United States, Russia (originally the Soviet Union), Great Britain, China, and France. Each of the five has a veto over the actions of the Security Council.

The *Secretariat* manages the day-to-day operations of the UN. It is headed by the *Secretary General*. This individual is the spokesperson for the UN and uses the moral authority of the office to help settle disputes among nations.

The *Economic and Social Council* takes on projects to improve the standard of living and health conditions throughout the world. It also promotes human rights and educational and cultural cooperation.

The *International Court of Justice* hears disputes that countries bring to it. The parties that ask for an opinion from the court agree to abide by the court's decision.

The *Trusteeship Council* was set up to oversee colonies and territories of Japan, Germany, and Italy. The council helped the trust territories to develop self-government and independence. There are no more such territories to oversee, so the work of this council has been suspended.

After the War

General Douglas MacArthur and U.S. troops directed the postwar occupation of Japan. A new constitution turned Japan into a democracy and stripped the emperor of his divinity (godlike status). Japan was not allowed to have military forces except for defensive purposes. The Allies tried Japanese war criminals, executing some and imprisoning others.

Nazi war criminals were also made to answer for the horrors of the Holocaust. At Nuremberg, Germany, an International Military Tribunal met in 1945 and 1946. Nazi leaders were charged with crimes against humanity, violations of international law, and waging aggressive warfare. Of the 22 defendants, 19 were found guilty. Twelve of these were sentenced to death. The others went to prison.

Many war criminals, however, escaped capture and assumed new identities in a variety of countries. Government and private organizations in the United States, Israel, and other nations spent years tracking down and bringing to trial S.S. officers, concentration camp guards, and Gestapo (secret police) members who were accused of committing atrocities. The most famous of these trials was that of Adolf Eichmann. He had been the Gestapo officer most responsible for planning the arrest and deportation to death camps of millions of Jews. Found living in Argentina, Eichmann was captured by Israeli commandos in 1960. He was brought to Jerusalem, tried, and executed for crimes against humanity.

Soviet troops, which had liberated the countries of Eastern Europe from Nazi rule, stayed in these countries. Most of Eastern Europe turned Communist. These countries usually followed Soviet leadership in economic and political matters. Because of this, they were called satellite nations. Soviet control of East Germany and Eastern Europe was to have serious consequences in the decades that followed the war. Winston Churchill said that the satellites were cut off from Western influence by "an *iron curtain*."

The Soviet Union and the United States had the largest military

Time Line

Year	Dates and Events
A.D.	**1933:** Hitler named German chancellor; ultranationalism, Hitler Youth
	1935: Germans violate Versailles Treaty: military draft, air force, rearmament
1933	**1935:** Nuremberg Laws strip German Jews of citizenship
	1935–1936: Italy conquers Ethiopia
	1936: Formation of Rome-Berlin Axis (alliance of Italy and Germany)
	1936: German troops take over demilitarized Rhineland, mineral resources
1934	**1938:** Germany annexes Austria, threatens Sudentenland (Czechoslovakia)
	1938: Munich Conference: Britain and France appease Hitler and Mussolini by ceding Sudentenland
1935	**1939:** Italy conquers Albania; Germany takes rest of Czechoslovakia
	1939: Nonaggression pact between Germany and Soviet Union
	1939: German blitzkrieg overpowers Poland
1936	**1939:** Britain and France declare war on Germany; World War II begins
	1939: U.S. Lend-Lease Act provides Britain with military equipment
	1939–1940: Soviet Union seizes eastern Poland, Latvia, Lithuania, Estonia, eastern Finland
1937	**1940:** Japan, Hungary, Romania join Axis Powers
	1940: Germany conquers Norway, Denmark, Belgium, Netherlands, France
	1940–1941: Battle of Britain (German bombings of British cities)
1938	**1940–1941:** Italy takes control of Greece, Yugoslavia; Italy and Germany invade North Africa
	1941: Germany invades Soviet Union for grain, petroleum
	1941: U.S. ban on petroleum and metal exports to Japan
1939	**1941:** Japan bombs U.S. naval base at Pearl Harbor, Hawaii; invades Philippines
	1941: U.S. declares war on Japan; Germany, Italy declare war on U.S.
1940	**1942:** Nazis plan genocide of European Jews (Holocaust)
	1942: Battle of El Alamein, Egypt: British protect Suez Canal
	1942: U.S. and Filipino armies surrender to Japan at Bataan
	1942: Allied naval victories against Japan in Pacific: Coral Sea, Midway
1941	**1942–1943:** Soviets defeat Germans at Stalingrad
	1943: Allies control North Africa; move into Sicily, Italy; Italy signs armistice
	1944: D-Day (June 6): Allies invade Normandy; push Germans from France, Belgium, Netherlands
1942	**1944:** U.S. forces under General MacArthur retake Philippines; destroy Japanese Navy in Leyte Gulf
	1944–1945: Allies push Germans out of Italy
1943	**1945:** Russians enter Berlin; Hitler a suicide; Germans surrender; war in Europe ends
	1945: U.S. saturation bombing of Japanese cities; occupation of Okinawa
	1945: Yalta Conference: Allies plan German occupation, war crimes trials; United Nations
1944	**1945:** U.S. drops atomic bombs on Hiroshima, Nagasaki; Japan surrenders
	1945: 50 nations meet in San Francisco to organize UN; U.S. Senate approves U.S. membership
1945	**1945–1952:** U.S. occupation of Japan: democratic constitution, war crimes trials, economic reforms
1946	**1945–1946:** Cold war begins: nations of Eastern Europe are economic, political satellites of Soviet Union

forces left after the war. Because it had not suffered any damages during the war, the United States had the strongest economy. Relations between the great democracy of the West and the Communist dictatorship of the East would have a great effect on the entire world throughout the rest of the century.

INFO CHECK

1. Explain why you AGREE or DISAGREE with this statement: The Yalta Conference had little influence on post-war Germany.

2. How does the U.N. General Assembly differ in composition and duties from the Security Council?

3. Define the terms *satellite nations* and *iron curtain*. What do they indicate about Eastern Europe after World War II?

LITERATURE AND ART

The years of World War II were troubled times for artists and writers. Nazi-occupied countries were dangerous for creative people who refused to cooperate with the conquerors.

Literature

Mann. One of the most notable writers who left Germany was Thomas Mann (lived 1875–1955), already known for his novels *Buddenbrooks* (1901), *Death in Venice* (1912), and *Magic Mountain* (1924). He was in danger in Germany because of his severe criticism of the Nazi government and because he had married a Jewish woman. In 1933, he moved to Switzerland and later to the United States. In the United States, he wrote many important novels. One, *Doctor Faustus*, sets the story of a composer who has made a pact with the devil against the rise and fall of Nazi Germany.

Remarque. The Nazis also persecuted Erich Maria Remarque (lived 1898–1970), who had written about World War I in the novel *All Quiet on the Western Front* (1929). After they revoked his citizenship, Remarque took refuge in the United States, where he wrote several novels dealing with war and exile.

Céline. French writers had a variety of reactions to the European political climate of the 30s and 40s. The early novels of Louis-Ferdinand Céline (lived 1894–1961) reflected the pessimism and anxiety that gripped European thinkers after the First World War. His two most famous novels are *Journey to the End of Night* (1932) and *Death on the Installment Plan* (1936). As time went on, his despair developed into madness. His writing became incoherent and filled with rage. In 1944, Céline, accused of collaborating with the Nazis, fled to Denmark, where he was put into prison.

Sartre. Jean-Paul Sartre (lived 1905–1980) of France was also concerned with politics. His main interest was philosophy, however. He belonged to a school of philosophy called existentialism. One important principle of *existentialism* is the freedom of human consciousness. Individuals must continually make decisions about life and right and wrong. But they have no overall standard on which to base their decisions. They never know if they are correct. Because most humans find this freedom frightening, they turn away from it. In Sartre's short story "The Childhood of a Leader," a young man tries to escape his existential freedom by becoming anti-Semitic. As an anti-Semite, he has given up the freedom to choose his associates and his acts. His prejudice chooses for him.

The hero of Sartre's play *Dirty Hands* (1948) struggles to accept his freedom. In the end, he refuses to be used by a corrupt political group even though his refusal to do so leads to his death. Sartre, himself, knew what it was like to act freely and courageously. During World War II, he was a member of a group of intellectuals who resisted Nazi occupation.

English Writers. In England, the works of three poets exemplify the impact that World War I, the Great Depression, and the rise of fascism had on British intellectuals. These poets were Wystan Hugh (W. H.) Auden, Cecil Day-Lewis, and Stephen Spender. They felt that poetry should come to terms with political and social conditions. Unlike the novelists of the times, they did not expose social problems or offer solutions for them. Instead they wrote poetry that reflects the anxiety and confusion created by modern life.

Lewis published several collections of poems. Among those published after World War II are *The Room and Other Poems* (1965) and *The Whispering Roots* (1970). In 1968, he became poet laureate of England.

Stephen Spender published several collections of poetry between 1933 and 1971. His autobiography, *World Within World* (1951), documents the important intellectual trends of the 1930s and 1940s.

Auden is the best known of these poets. He experimented with many different poetic forms and published numerous volumes of poetry. His long poem *The Age of Anxiety* (1948) expressed the depression, confusion, and aimlessness that people felt during World War II.

U.S. Writers. In the late 1930s, American writers, many of whom were already focused on social problems, began to deal with the subject of fascism. In the novel *Dragon's Teeth* (1942), Upton Sinclair turned from exposing corruption and hypocrisy in the United States to chronicling Hitler's rise to power. Sinclair Lewis, famous for satirizing the narrowness and mediocrity of middle-class Americans, wrote *It Can't Happen Here* (1935). In this novel, Lewis showed how certain moral weaknesses characteristic of Americans might make them susceptible to the manipulations of a fascist dictator.

Art

The Nazis not only burned books, they destroyed and banned modern art as well. So many artists took refuge in the United States that the center of artistic activity shifted from Europe to New York. The schools of art, including surrealism and cubism, continued to be prominent during World War II.

Kandinsky. *Expressionism* originated in the early 1900s with the Russian painter Wassily Kandinsky (lived 1866–1944). Kandinsky felt that ideas for pictures should arise from intensely personal experiences, but the finished products should present these experiences as universal, able to be understood by everyone. To do this, they must be abstract—pure line and color used with mathematical precision. He pointed out that the art of music, which relies a great deal on mathematics, can effect such a transformation. Just as the carefully ordered tones of music evoke emotional responses in the listener, so do the carefully ordered shapes and colors of a painting stir the observer.

Kandinsky's influence on the artistic world continued after his death in 1944. When painters, such as Max Ernst (German), Fernand Léger (French), André Masson (French), and Piet Mondrian (Dutch), fled from Europe to New York, they brought Kandinsky's ideas with them. American artists, who were dissatisfied with the styles in which they had been working, readily adopted new European trends.

Abstract Expressionism. In the United States, the kinds of painting inspired by Kandinsky's theories became known as *abstract expressionism*. By the 1940s, it was the most important influence on both American painters and the European painters who had settled in the United States. Those artists who had lived under Fascist regimes needed to find new ways to respond to events that had destroyed their faith in human nature. Some of the abstract expressionists painting at this time were Willem de Kooning, Clyfford Still, Mark Rothko, Jackson Pollock, and Robert Motherwell.

De Kooning. Willem de Kooning (lived 1904–1997) was originally from the Netherlands. He was best known for his pictures that present women in an abstract style. Their faces and bodies seem as vast and sprawling as landscapes.

Still. Clyfford Still (lived 1904–1980), a westerner from North Dakota, began his career by painting scenes of prairies. Once under the influence of abstract expressionism, he began producing canvases with upright, jagged shapes against dark backgrounds.

Rothko. Mark Rothko (lived 1903–1970) created compositions of colored rectangles against a glowing background. He intended his uncluttered, vibrant paintings to produce a meditative state in the viewer.

Pollock. Perhaps more than the other abstract expressionists, Jackson Pollock (lived 1912–1956) felt that artistic creation should be directed by the unconscious mind. He expressed strong, sometimes violent emotions by hurling paint or dripping it onto his canvases. This technique is called "action painting."

Motherwell. Robert Motherwell (lived 1915–1991) was strongly affected by the threat of fascism. He painted more than 100 pictures expressing his horror over the Spanish Civil War.

After the Holocaust and other atrocities of the 20th century, many people began to question basic assumptions about the decency of human nature and its ability to progress ethically.

With the invention of nuclear weapons, world leaders feared that human beings might destroy the earth. Having witnessed the excesses of Hitler, they knew that power-hungry dictators might do anything to control the world.

The chapters in Unit VII concern postwar developments all over the world. Chapter 29 discusses the Cold War between the United States and the Soviet Union and the rise of Communist China.

INFO CHECK

1. Select one writer and one artist of the World War II era and describe the work of each.

2. Define the terms *existentialism* and *expressionism*. What do you like or dislike about each art form?

CHAPTER REVIEW

Multiple Choice

1. The Jungvolk and Youth Movement in Germany were organized for the purpose of

   1. learning Nazi ideology
   2. sports training
   3. military basic training
   4. all of the above.

2. Increasing the size of the German army, organizing an air force, and reoccupying the Rhineland are all examples of Hitler's

   1. violating the Treaty of Versailles
   2. policy of nonalignment
   3. demilitarized policy
   4. pacifist policy.

3. The agreement of the British and French governments to turn over the Sudetenland, a part of Czechoslovakia, to Hitler's Germany is an example of their policy of

1. neutrality
2. nonalignment
3. appeasement
4. blitzkrieg.

4. This treaty paved the way for the German invasion of Poland and support of Hitler's future war plans:
   1. Berlin Conference
   2. Rome-Berlin-Tokyo Axis
   3. Kellogg-Briand Pact
   4. Treaty of Portsmouth.

5. Before the establishment of concentration camps, one Nazi action that showed anti-Semitic beliefs was
   1. their attempt to control the German churches
   2. passage of the Nuremberg Laws
   3. the drafting of Jewish youths into work battalions
   4. the removal of all travel restrictions for Jews.

6. The term that came out of World War II that refers to the planned destruction of an any culture or religious group is known as
   1. anti-Semitism
   2. Kristallnacht
   3. serial murder
   4. genocide.

7. The Lend-Lease Act enabled the United States to
   1. sell munitions to either Germany or the Allies
   2. allow the purchase of war materials by any combatants
   3. sell, loan, or lease war materials to the Allies
   4. sell, loan, or lease war materials to the Axis.

8. The technological development that ended World War II and dominated postwar foreign policy was the development of
   1. atomic weapons
   2. radar
   3. jet airplanes
   4. attack-class submarines.

9. The Yalta conference was important because
   1. Roosevelt did not attend
   2. the terms for peace and the division of Germany into four zones was agreed to
   3. Stalin and Churchill lost their elections and were replaced by other politicians
   4. German representatives signed the agreement ending the war.

10. The purpose of the formation of the United Nations was to
    1. separate Germany from the rest of the world
    2. raise money for countries in need of assistance
    3. form a military stronghold against Hitler
    4. work for world peace.

11. The maps on pages 628 and 635 show that
    1. Germany, Italy, and Japan were unsuccessful at keeping peace with their neighbors
    2. Germany, Italy, and Japan invaded, attacked, or occupied many neighboring nations
    3. Japan was less aggressive against its neighbors than were Italy and Germany
    4. Italy and Germany invaded nations to their west while Japan invaded its eastern neighbors.

12. The photograph on page 641 shows that

1. there was little concern about the world's future after the defeat of the Axis Powers
2. the Allied leaders met for the purpose of structuring the postwar world
3. there were few disagreements between Stalin, Churchill, and Roosevelt
4. plans for creating the UN were made at Yalta.

Thematic Essays

1. *Task:* Explain how nationalism and propaganda aided Hitler's domination of the German people and set off World War II.

2. Many Germans willingly followed nazism. *Task:* Describe which Nazi practices would appeal to each of the following: a business owner, a factory worker, and a teenager. Explain how these practices would cause each of these people to support nazism.

Document-Based Questions

Use the documents and your knowledge of Global History and Geography to answer the questions.

1. Study the map on page 637. Explain whether Germany's position in Europe was an advantage or disadvantage in a general war. Use the map to support your answer.

2. After British Prime Minister Chamberlain agreed to Hitler's demand for the part of Czechoslovakia known as the Sudetenland, he returned from Munich and defended his actions in the House of Commons:

   "Ever since I assumed my present office my main pupose has been to work for the pacification of Europe. . . . The path that leads to appeasement is long and bristles with obstacles. The question of Czechoslovakia is the lat-est and perhaps the most dangerous. Now that we have got past it, I feel that it may be possible to make further progress along the road to sanity. In our relations with other countries everything depends upon there being sincerity and good will on both sides. I believe that there are sincerity and good will on both sides of this declaration."

   What policy is Chamberlain following and what has he received from Hitler in return for signing away a piece of the Czechoslovakian nation?

3. Chamberlain explaining his views on war and the Sudetenland:

   "However much we may sympathize with a small nation confronted by a big and powerful neighbor, we cannot in all circumstances undertake to involve the whole British Empire simply on her account. If we have to fight, it must be on larger issues than that. . . . I am myself a man of peace to the very depths of my soul. Armed conflict between nations is a nightmare to me. . . ."

   What is Chamberlain's attitude to giving small nations help when they are threatened? Do you AGREE or DISAGREE with his views?

4. Study the map on page 628. Explain the Axis powers' strategy to gain mastery of Europe. Why was their success only temporary?

5. On May 11, 1940, Chamberlain resigned and the new prime minister, Winston Churchill, took office. Here are Churchill's responses in the House of Commons to questions about his government's policy and aim:

   "You ask, what is our policy? I will say it is to wage war, by sea, land, and air, with all our might and with all the strength that God can give us. . . . You ask what is our aim? I can answer in one word: It is victory, victory at all costs, victory in spite of all terror, victory however long and hard the way may be. . . ."

Compare Churchill's policy with that of Chamberlain.

6. A few days before the surrender of France in June 1940 and the defeat and forced evacuation of British troops at Dunkirk, Churchill addressed the House of Commons:

"Even though large tracts of Europe and many old and famous states have fallen or may fall . . . we shall fight on the seas and oceans. . . .

"We shall defend our Island, whatever the cost may be . . . we shall never surrender. . . ."

If you were a British citizen at this time, how would you react to this speech? If you were a German general, why would you be discouraged by this speech?

Document-Based Essay

Task: Compare and contrast the attitudes and actions of the two British prime ministers and discuss the value of Churchill's wartime leadership to Great Britain.

UNIT REVIEW

Thematic Essays

1. How did technology affect the lives of the people and the politics of nations in the 20th century? *Task:* Include military and industrial advances as well as communication and transportation advances in your answer.

2. At the beginning of World War II, it appeared that the dictatorships and military aggression of Italy, Germany, and Japan could not be stopped. Why were they initially so successful and the democratic responses so weak? *Task:* Consider the types of government, world economic conditions, experiences in World War I, and people's attitudes in your answer.

Document-Based Questions

Using your reading of the chapters and the documents to answer the questions that follow.

1. In 1792, two years after the French issued their "Declaration of the Rights of Man," Mary Wollstonecraft published "Vindication of the Rights of Woman."

". . . My main argument is built on the . . . principle that if she [woman] is not prepared by education to become the companion of man, she will stop the progress of knowledge and virtue. . . . Let woman share the rights, and she will emulate [copy] the virtues of man; for she must grow more perfect when emancipated [freed]. . . .

What does Wollstonecraft want for woman and why?

2. John Stuart Mill (English philosopher and member of Parliament) in 1869 argued for women's rights in his work "The Subjection of Women."

". . . To have a voice in choosing those by whom one is to be governed, is a means of self-protection due to everyone. . . . The majority of the women of any class are not likely to differ in political opinion from the majority of men of the same class, unless the question be one in which the interests of women, as such, are in some way involved; and if they are so, women require the suffrage as a guarantee of just and equal consideration. . . ."

Identify three reasons Mill gives for granting [voting rights] to women.

3. In 1883 Susan B. Anthony spoke about American women's right to vote.

"It was we the people; not we, the white male citizens; nor yet we, the male citizens; but we, the whole people, who formed the union. And we formed it, not to give the blessings of liberty, but to secure them; not to the half of ourselves and the half of posterity, but to the whole people—women as well as men."

How and in what ways do Anthony's views agree or disagree with arguments presented in the previous documents?

4. From a speech given by Emmeline Pankhurst in 1913:

". . . The only justification for violence, the only justification for damage to property, the only justification for risk to comfort of other human beings is . . . that you have tried all other . . . means and failed to secure justice. . . . Our marriage and divorce laws are a disgrace to civilization. . . . After she has risked her life to bring a child into the world [a woman] has absolutely no . . . rights over the future of that child. . . . [A man can] bring his mistress into the house to live and she can not get legal relief from such a marriage. . . . Take the industrial side of the question; have men's wages for a hard day's work ever been so low and inadequate as are women's wages today?"

What sort of actions is Pankhurst willing to take for her cause, and how does she justify them?

5. How does the poster show the changing role of women brought about by factory work and the world wars?

Document-Based Essay

Task: Discuss how gaining financial independence and influence in matters outside the home during the world wars helped women solve some of the problems described in the documents.

UNIT VII
The 20th Century
Since 1945

The 20th Century Since 1945

Year	Dates and Events
A.D. **1940**	**1945:** Potsdam Conference: Allied leaders recognize Soviet control of Eastern Europe
	1948–1949: Berlin Airlift: U.S. flies in food, fuel, machinery to Berliners; Soviets end blockade
	1948–1952: Marshall Plan: U.S. economic aid to European nations recovering from war
1949	**1949:** Organization of NATO, defense pact of Western nations
	1950–1953: Korean War: South (with U.S. aid) against North (with Chinese aid)
1950	**1955:** Warsaw Pact of Soviet Union and satellites in Eastern Europe
	1959: Castro leads Cuban revolt; sets up Communist state allied to Soviets
	1960: Iran, Kuwait, Saudi Arabia, Venezuela organize OPEC to regulate production and price of oil
	1961: East Germans build Berlin Wall
1959	**1962:** Cuban Missile Crisis: Soviets remove missiles, U.S. pledges nonintervention in Cuba
1960	**1966–1968:** "Great Cultural Revolution," in China
	1967: Six-Day War: Israel occupies East Jerusalem, parts of Syria, Jordan, Egypt
	1971–1973: East Pakistan rebels against West Pakistan; becomes nation of Bangladesh
1969	**1973–1975:** U.S.–North Vietnam peace; North Vietnam defeats the South
1970	**1977:** U.S. and Communist China establish diplomatic relations
	1979–1981: Shah of Iran ousted; Iranian militants occupy U.S. embassy, hold 53 hostages for 444 days
	1980s: U.S. aids Nicaraguan Contras against Marxist Sandanistas
	1985: Gorbachev becomes Soviet leader; perestroika (economic reforms), glasnost (openness)
1979	**1986:** Nuclear accident in Chernobyl, Ukraine, spreads radiation across Europe
1980	**1989:** Massacre in Beijing's Tiananmen Square
	1989–1991: Poland, Hungary, Czechoslovakia, Albania, Bulgaria, East Germany hold free elections, turn out Communists
	1990: Reunification of East and West Germany
	1990: Yelstin elected president of Russia
	1991: Operation Desert Storm drives Iraq from Kuwait
1989	**1991:** End of apartheid in South Africa
1990	**1991:** Collapse of Soviet Union and end of cold war; Soviet republics form CIS
	1993: PLO signs peace accord with Israel
	1994: Multiracial government rules South Africa for first time, with Mandela as president
	1997: Britain returns Hong Kong to China
	1999: Czech Republic, Hungary, Poland become members of NATO
1999	**1999:** Yeltsin resigns as president of Russia, is succeeded by Putin

C H A P T E R

29

The Cold War

Jodie found it hard to believe that her brother would have to fight in Korea. She didn't want to believe it. Just five years ago, when he was 14 and she was 11, World War II had ended. She remembered how glad her parents were that their boy had been too young to fight. They hadn't expected another war so soon. Who would dare to challenge the United States when it had the atomic bomb?

But now the Soviet Union had one too. And it was friends with the North Koreans. Jodie thought of the pictures she had seen of the people in Hiroshima who had been burned by the bomb. Could such things happen to Americans? The government thought so. Schools and communities were required to conduct air-raid drills on a regular basis. Some people had even built shelters to keep themselves safe during a nuclear bomb attack. Some of the fear that Jodie had felt as a little girl during the dark war years came back.

Peace did not come easily to the world after World War II ended in 1945. Almost immediately, tension developed between the United States and the Soviet Union. The Communist and democratic nations had different aims for the future of the world. For a while, communism seemed to be fulfilling its goal of taking over the world. This political system spread from Eastern Europe to China. The efforts of democratic nations to halt its spread led to crises in Europe and wars in Asia.

The existence of nuclear weapons caused fears that any conflict might touch off a nuclear war. In an effort to prevent global destruction, the major powers engaged in an *arms race*. They competed to build more nuclear weapons with greater destructive power. The second half of the 20th century was a time of great insecurity. It was also a time of great progress.

THE SEARCH FOR A GLOBAL BALANCE OF POWER

At the end of World War II, much of Europe lay in ruins. People faced the tremendous task of reconstructing their lives. Homes had to be built. Crops for food had to be grown. Factories had to start manufacturing civilian goods.

Almost every country was exhausted from its war efforts. Although the Soviet Union had suffered severe losses, it still retained great military strength. The Soviet Union and the United States were the major powers in the world. As *superpowers*, or nations with powerful military forces, they began to compete for world leadership.

The Soviet Union's Control of Eastern Europe

One of the Soviet Union's advantages over the United States was its control of a large bloc of Eastern European countries. It had begun to move into these countries early in World War II. When Hitler invaded Poland in 1939, the Soviet Union seized Latvia, Lithuania, and Estonia in addition to eastern Poland. In 1940, it also took parts of Finland.

Meeting at Teheran. At the 1943 conference in the Iranian capital of Teheran, Stalin persuaded Roosevelt to support his plan for the final assault on Germany. He wanted the Americans and British to attack Germany from France while the Soviets struck from the east. This plan was accepted. As they pushed toward Germany, the Soviets drove the Axis forces from Poland, Bulgaria, Romania, Hungary, parts of Yugoslavia, and much of Czechoslovakia. They did not liberate these countries, however, but simply replaced the previous occupiers.

Meeting at Yalta. At the Yalta meeting in February 1945, Stalin tried to make Soviet control of the Eastern European countries official. Churchill and Roosevelt insisted that these countries be allowed to choose their own governments. As a compromise, the three leaders agreed that the Eastern European countries could have free elections. But the new governments had to follow policies friendly to the Soviet Union.

Meeting at Potsdam. Unfortunately, Stalin refused to hold to the compromise negotiated at Yalta. He feared the rebirth of a militant Germany and insisted on having a buffer zone of Communist allies between Germany and the Soviet Union. At the Potsdam Conference of July 1945, he pointed out that, if left to their own devices, none of the disputed countries would elect a Soviet-friendly government. (Potsdam is a city near Berlin in Germany.) Britain and the United States realized that only a war would change Stalin's mind. Because they were in no position to fight another war, they had to agree to Stalin's terms. At Potsdam, a new British prime minister, Clement Attlee, replaced Churchill. Roosevelt had died in April 1945. Harry Truman, the vice president, replaced him.

Soviet Expansion and U.S. Response

As Western leaders watched the Soviet Union install Communist governments in Poland, Hungary, Romania, Bulgaria, and Albania, they became alarmed. They grew even more uneasy when the Soviet Union prevented the people of these countries from communicating with people in the West. This was the "iron curtain" that Churchill had warned about.

Although Americans disapproved of the Soviet Union's actions, they were reluctant to take a military stand against it. They wanted the soldiers who had fought so long overseas to come back home. Because the Soviet Union did not yet have an atomic bomb, many Americans felt that Soviet expansion was not a serious threat to their own freedom and safety.

Truman Doctrine. As time went on, however, the Soviet Union weakened this sense of security by becoming more and more aggressive. A civil war erupted in Greece at the end of World War II. Communist guerrillas received aid from Soviet satellite nations. The guerrillas wanted to overthrow the Greek government and replace it with a Communist government.

During the same period, the Soviet Union was pressuring Turkey and Iran to give up territory. Russia also wanted control of the Dardanelles, the passageway between the Black Sea and the Mediterranean Sea. Turkey and Iran asked the United States for help.

In March 1947, President Truman responded with military and economic aid to Greece, Iran, and Turkey. The aid program came to be called the *Truman Doctrine*. The doctrine stated that the United States would "support free peoples" who resist being taken over by outside forces. The Truman Doctrine kept Greece, Iran, and Turkey from becoming Communist.

Marshall Plan. After World War II, Communist political parties once more became active in Western Europe. Europe's slow economic recovery from the war made many people dissatisfied with capitalism and democracy. The United States wanted to prevent these people from turning to communism for relief and to help those who had suffered during the war. To achieve these aims, U.S. Secretary of State George C. Marshall introduced the *Marshall Plan* in June 1947. This program asked all the nations of Europe, including the Soviet Union, to work out a plan for their recovery. The United States pledged money to carry out the plan. The Communist countries chose not to participate in the Marshall Plan. Stalin accused the United States of using the aid to wage economic warfare on the Soviet Union. Between 1948 and 1952, the United States gave $12 billion to the 16 West European countries that joined the program. West Germany also received aid.

Western Europe recovered and went on to achieve the greatest prosperity it had ever known. It is believed that this American aid saved Western Europe from turning Communist.

Containment. The United States worried that the Soviets would try to spread communism to Africa, Asia, and Latin America. In 1949, President Truman established the Point Four Program to give technical assistance to developing nations.

With the Truman Doctrine, the Marshall Plan, and the Point Four Program, the United States put into effect its *containment policy* toward the Soviet Union. After 1947, the United States tried to block, or contain, Soviet moves to expand into areas it had not held in 1945.

Cold War. The new policy created tension between the two superpowers. The hostile attitudes deepened in the 1950s and became known as the *cold war* (1945–1990). Each side took steps just short of a shooting war to protect its own interests.

Berlin Blockade. In 1948, the Soviets again tested the will of the Western Allies to contain the spread of communism. In February of that year, Soviet troops helped the local Communists to turn out the elected government of Czechoslovakia. The Soviets then tried to take over the entire city of Berlin.

After the war, the Soviet Union controlled East Germany. The Allies controlled West Germany. Although Berlin was located in East Germany, the Soviets occupied and governed only one section of it. Britain, France, and the United States held the rest of the city, called West Berlin.

In an effort to force the British, French, and Americans out of Berlin, the Soviets shut down all highways and railroad lines to West Berlin from West Germany. The city was blockaded. It could not receive supplies by land. Rather than try to break the blockade by sending in troops and possibly starting a war, the United States and its allies decided to airlift supplies to Berlin.

Although the blockade caused Berliners much suffering, the Berlin Airlift kept them from starving. Planes landed at a rate of one a minute. They brought in more than 7,000 tons of food, fuel, and machinery every day. After 11 months, the Soviets ended the blockade and once again opened up the land routes across East Germany. The Berlin Airlift demonstrated Allied determination to oppose Soviet moves. It had been a dazzling technological achievement. Soviet experts had told their leaders that it could not be done.

Europe After World War II

Berlin children greet a U.S. plane flying in food over the Soviet blockade

Cold War Military Alliances

NATO. Fear of Soviet aggression caused 12 Western nations to band together in a mutual defense pact in 1949. The United States, Canada, Britain, France, Belgium, the Netherlands, Norway, Denmark, Italy, Luxembourg, Iceland, and Portugal formed the *North Atlantic Treaty Organization* (NATO). They stated that an attack on any one member was an attack on all. Later, Greece, Turkey, West Germany, and Spain joined NATO. U.S. troops under the direction of NATO were stationed in Europe, particularly in West Germany.

Warsaw Pact. In 1955, the Soviet Union and the Communist nations of Eastern Europe organized their own military alliance. The purpose of the *Warsaw Pact* was to protect Eastern Europe from aggression by the NATO countries. The members of the pact were the Soviet Union, Bulgaria, Czechoslovakia, East Germany, Hungary, Poland, and Romania. Albania belonged until 1968, when it became more closely allied with Communist China. Yugoslavia never joined. Josip Broz, called Tito, the Yugoslav leader, preferred to remain independent of the Soviet Union.

Although the Warsaw Pact was dissolved in 1991, after the collapse of the Soviet Union, NATO still exists. After East and West Germany reunited in 1990, the combined Germany joined NATO. Three Eastern European nations—the Czech Republic, Hungary, and Poland—were granted NATO membership in 1999.

The Cold War: Opposing European Alliances

NATO Members

Warsaw Pact Members

Nuclear Weapons and the Space Race

In order to deter the other from starting a war, the Soviet Union and the United States each rushed to develop the deadliest weapons. In 1949, the Soviet Union produced its first atomic bomb. In the early 1950s, both the United States and the Soviet Union developed the hydrogen bomb, which is much more powerful than the atomic bomb.

Because both countries now had almost equal nuclear power, each began to look for other ways to display its power. This led to the space race. Each side wanted to build satellites that could orbit the earth. The satellites would carry equipment to detect where the other side had positioned its bombs.

In 1957, the Soviets launched Sputnik 1, the first earth-orbiting satellite. Stung by this achievement, the United States sped up its own space program. The first U.S. satellite, Explorer 1, went up in 1958. In 1961, Soviet cosmonaut Yuri Gagarin was the first man to orbit the earth. The following year, John Glenn became the first American to orbit the earth. In 1969, the United States landed two men on the moon. (Chapter 31 describes how competition to explore space developed into a cooperative venture between the United States and Russia.)

INFO CHECK

1. Explain how superpower competition after World War II led to the cold war.

2. Define *containment policy*. List the steps taken by the United States to implement this policy.

3. Name the two great alliance systems of the cold war era. How did these alliance systems change in the early 1990s?

4. How did the space race begin? List the space race achievements of the United States and the Soviet Union.

COMPETITION FOR CONTROL OF DEVELOPING COUNTRIES

At the end of World War II, the United States insisted that its allies, as well as its enemies, must give up their colonies. The colonies themselves knew that the imperialist nations were now too weak to resist nationalist movements. In the first stages of independence, the former colonies remained politically and economically weak. They relied on stronger countries to give them aid and advice. Since the ruling countries no longer monopolized their trade, the new nations became open markets. The former European colonizers, however, expected the former colonies to repay their aid by giving them trade advantages and forming political alliances with them. Some of the inhabitants of the newly freed countries complained that the Western powers were now involving them in a new kind of colonialism.

Immediately after World War II, Stalin had been too preoccupied with his satellite nations and nearby Communist allies to pay much attention to places far from the borders of the Soviet Union. But when Stalin died in 1953 and Nikita Khrushchev took charge, the Soviets began to extend "friendship treaties" to the developing countries of Asia, Africa, and Latin America. They also began to offer military advice and other kinds of support to countries that had not yet won independence from foreign rulers.

North Africa and the Middle East

The Soviet Union and the Western powers competed for territory and influence in the oil-rich Middle East. Immediately after World War II, the Soviet Union tried to control parts of Iran and Turkey. The United States blocked that attempt by giving the threatened countries financial and military help.

Later, the United States lost the trust of the Arab nations by backing their enemy, Israel. The Soviet Union saw the growing distance

The Middle East

between the United States and the Arabs as an opportunity to strengthen its own position with Arab counties.

Egypt. In 1955, the Soviet Union and Gamal Abdel Nasser, the head of Egypt, entered an arms agreement. The Soviets also promised to help Egypt fight the Israelis. The United States tried to win Egypt away from the Soviet Union by offering to lend Nasser funds for building a huge dam at Aswan on the Nile River. (The dam would provide electric power and better irrigation for agriculture.) When Nasser continued to favor the Soviets, the United States took back its offer. In 1956, the Egyptian government *nationalized* (took over) the Suez Canal. Nasser wanted to keep the tolls paid by ships passing through the canal for the dam project. This important waterway was located in Egypt but owned by Britain and France. Outraged at its loss, Britain and France invaded Egypt and encouraged Israel to join them.

The Israelis seized the Gaza Strip, an Egyptian-owned area along the Mediterranean Sea. They then prepared to invade the Sinai Peninsula. At the same time, France and Britain were poised to capture the Suez Canal. The Soviet Union threatened to fight with Egypt against the invaders. Another world war seemed imminent.

At this point, the United Nations intervened. The United States joined with the Soviet Union in protesting the invasion. UN peacekeeping troops occupied the area around the canal and opened it to all ships except those of Israel. America's last-minute support of Egypt did not help the United States establish good relations with that country. The Soviet Union strengthened its ties with Egypt by providing it with money and technical aid to build the Aswan Dam.

Iraq. The Soviet Union also increased its control over Iraq. In July 1958, General Abdul Karim Kassem, a radical nationalist, led a revolt against the pro-Western government. After ordering the death of the prime minister and the royal family, Kassem set up a pro-Communist republic. He was assassinated in 1963. Three regimes followed, the last being that of Saddam Hussein, beginning in 1979. In 1972, Iraq entered into a formal alliance with the Soviet Union.

Africa

In many cases, turmoil followed independence in former colonies in Africa. The different groups that had fought for liberation of the colonies often quarreled over which would control the new nation. The United States and the Soviet Union each backed the factions it thought would follow its political agenda. For the most part African nations did not openly take sides in the cold war.

Republic of the Congo. In 1960, the Congo declared its independence from France. In the struggle for power that followed France's withdrawal, the Soviet Union supported a pro-Communist group. The Congo became a Communist state in 1964. Nonetheless, it kept its economic ties to France and other Western nations. In the long run, communism failed to benefit the Congo's economy. Strikes and other problems plagued the country. In 1990, the Congo's government installed a multiparty political system and abandoned Marxist ideology.

Angola. After Portugal freed Angola in 1975, the groups that had pressured for its independence could not put aside their differences and unite the country. Civil war broke out. The Soviet Union and Cuba backed the *Popular Movement for the Liberation of Angola* (MPLA). Cuba sent troops to help ensure a Communist victory. In reaction, the United States and South Africa allied with the *National Union for the Total Independence of Angola* (UNITA).

In 1976, the MPLA formed a Marxist government. UNITA refused to recognize the new government, and violence continued. Cuban troops remained in Angola. Finally, in 1991, Angola, Cuba, and South Africa signed a peace treaty. Cuban troops departed. All political parties were legalized. However, UNITA refused to accept the results of the elections held in 1992 and continued to oppose the MPLA government of Angola.

Latin America

Communism gained a strong foothold in several Latin American countries, where social injustice caused much unrest. The United States did not like the expansion of communism so close to its borders.

Cuba. When Cuba won independence from Spain in 1898, it became politically, militarily, and economically dependent on the United States. Although Cuba was one of the richest countries in Latin America, the vast difference between rich and poor disturbed many of its people. In 1959, Fidel Castro led Cubans in a successful revolution and established a Communist government. Having a close ally of the Soviet Union as a neighbor was very troubling to U.S. leaders. Their efforts to topple Castro later gave rise to one of the most frightening incidents of the cold war—the Cuban missile crisis of 1962. (See Chapter 31.)

Chile. Like Cuba, Chile had many social, political, and economic problems. U.S. corporations controlled its copper industry, inflation was high, and most of the country's wealth was in the hands of a few landowners. In 1970, Chileans elected Salvador Allende, a Marxist, to be president. Allende nationalized the U.S. copper companies and the banks and speeded up a program to distribute the land more equally.

The United States felt threatened at having another Communist government in the Western Hemisphere. The U.S. *Central Intelligence Agency* (CIA) began giving money and other help to anti-Allende forces. In 1973, Allende's government was overturned. A right-wing *junta* (governing group) under the leadership of General Augusto

Fidel Castro and fellow revolutionaries marching through Havana, Cuba

Pinochet took control of Chile and returned businesses and land to private owners. Pinochet also put Chile under military rule and imposed strict censorship in order to get rid of opposition to his government. His policies against opponents were sometimes so harsh that they attracted the criticism of international human rights groups.

In general, the Chilean economy did well under Pinochet. In 1988, he lifted the state of siege and granted amnesty to his political enemies. When he tried to force Chileans to elect him as president for an additional eight years, they rebelled and voted in his more moderate opponents in 1989. Chile has prospered under more democratic policies in the 1990s.

Guatemala. The United States also interfered in attempts by Guatemalan leaders to bring about social and economic reforms. In 1951, the president, who favored Communist ideas, started an agrarian reform program. When the Guatemalan government took land held by the United Fruit Company, an American firm, the United States supported rebel groups that opposed the government. In 1954, the military took over the government.

Leftist guerrilla groups, including Communists, struggled against the new repressive regime. The government responded by sending "death squads" to wipe out resistance in Indian villages. The squads

FIDEL CASTRO: CUBAN REVOLUTIONARY

Since 1959, Fidel Castro has been premier of Cuba. He is one of the best-known figures of the cold war. For many, he is the symbol of Socialist revolution.

Born in 1926 in Cuba, Castro received part of his education in the United States, graduating from New York's Columbia University in 1950 with a degree in law. After his return to Cuba, he represented the legal interests of the poor and attempted to bring political change to Cuba by constitutional means. He soon became disillusioned by his inability to accomplish much.

Cuban politics before 1959 were controlled by corrupt dictatorships. Poor administration, fiscal irresponsibility, bribery of public officials, and insensitivity to the problems of the poor, who were the majority of the population, made life in Cuba difficult for many.

By 1959, there was widespread dissatisfaction with the current dictator, Fulgencio Batista, even within the Cuban army. Many admired Fidel Castro because of his early opposition to the Batista dictatorship. Castro had become a revolutionary in the 1950s, leading a suicidal attack against a military fortress on July 26, 1953. Although the attack failed, the "26th of July" revolutionary movement had begun. With a few survivors, Castro went to Mexico and prepared for another action against Batista. This was attempted in December 1956. Again, the revolutionaries met defeat. Most of the group were killed or captured. The survivors retreated to the Sierra Maestra mountains in Cuba. From there, they fought a guerrilla war for two years. Victory came on January 1, 1959. With only 1,000 "Fidelistas," Castro succeeded in driving Batista from office. Most Cubans no longer supported the dictator.

Lacking administrative experience or firm political plans, the Fidelistas began a program to reshape Cuba politically and economically. It appealed to the lower economic classes by giving them equality and social justice through educational and social reforms. The new government was modeled on those of the Communist nations. Although a president was chosen in July 1959, Castro kept firm control of the government as premier and as head of the Cuban Communist Party. It was the only political party allowed.

Conflict with the United States became inevitable. The nationalization of hundreds of millions of dollars of American-owned property ended foreign control of the Cuban economy. An angry U.S. government responded by declaring a total trade embargo. Diplomatic relations with Cuba were broken in 1961. The United States then supported an unsuccessful invasion by Cuban exiles at the Bay of Pigs in April 1961 and voted for the expulsion of Cuba from the Organization of American States in 1962.

Castro turned to the Soviet Union for aid. It became Cuba's major trading partner and source of funds and military supplies. However, the Soviets were unable to supply desired consumer products. Cuba's economy started to decline. Individual Cubans began to feel the effects of the economic problems, especially after 1962, when the rationing of certain products began.

For many, sacrifice became a permanent way of life. A great many left or tried to leave for a better life in other Latin American countries or the United States. By 1990, the collapse of the Soviet Union and disappearance of the "Communist-bloc" in Europe dealt the Cuban economy a severe blow. Stiffer trading restrictions imposed by the United States in 1992 made economic conditions even worse.

Through all the difficulties, Castro remained in power. However, anti-government demonstrations in August 1994 caused him to loosen emigration restrictions. More than 30,000 people left Cuba in 1995.

Castro's revolution continues, although it has failed to solve many of Cuba's problems. Nevertheless, it gave Cubans a national pride and social consciousness that was lacking before 1959. As Castro ages, many wonder what course the revolution will take in the future.

1. Has the Cuban revolution been successful? Why or why not?

2. Why do you think every U.S. president since 1959 has opposed Fidel Castro? Do you agree with this policy? Give reasons for your answer.

murdered many innocent people, including foreign diplomats. More moderate leaders came into power in the mid-1980s and tried to stop the political murders. But opposition forces continued their violence. Amnesty International and the United Nations Commission for Human Rights objected. Repeated pressure to end the killings finally resulted in the arrest of people suspected of "death squads" activity. In 1993, Guatemalans elected a president whose past work to promote human rights was generally respected. Three years later, a treaty between the government and the rebels ended the civil war.

INFO CHECK

1. How did the conflicts between Israel and the neighboring Arab nations affect cold war competition in the Middle East?

2. Why do you think historians regard Angola's long civil war as an outgrowth of the cold war?

3. How did U.S.-Soviet competition affect events in Cuba and Chile?

THE COLD WAR HEATS UP

The Korean War

In 1945, U.S. troops took over southern Korea from the defeated Japanese. Soviet troops occupied the north. The dividing line between South Korea and North Korea was the 38th parallel (line of latitude). The south developed an anti-Communist, representative form of government that soon turned into a dictatorship. The North became

The Korean War

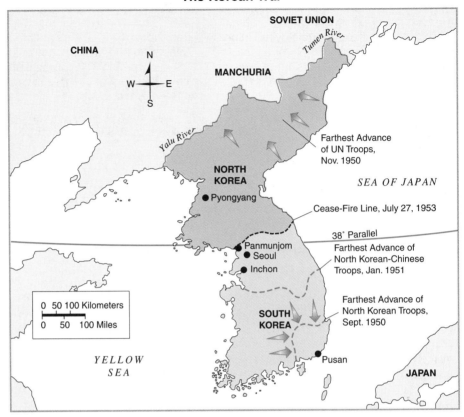

Communist. Each section hoped to unite the whole country under its rule. U.S. troops remained in South Korea until 1949.

Attack. On June 25, 1950, North Korean troops crossed the 38th parallel and invaded South Korea. U.S. President Harry S. Truman did not want Communists to take over more territory. He called on the United Nations to take action. (The vote in the Security Council was taken when the Soviet Union was not present. The vote favored the U.S. request.) The UN then asked members for troops to fight in Korea. The United States rushed in U.S. soldiers from bases in Japan. Fifteen other UN member nations also sent fighting units. U.S. General Douglas MacArthur was appointed commander of the UN forces.

Fighting. By early September, the North Koreans had nearly pushed the UN forces off the Korean peninsula. Within three weeks, a counterattack swept the North Koreans back across the 38th parallel. UN forces moved toward the Yalu River, the border between North Korea and Manchuria. At this point, in November 1950, Chinese soldiers poured into North Korea. The Chinese wanted a Communist victory. They also wanted to prevent UN troops from coming too close to their own border. Chinese and North Korean forces pushed the UN troops back toward the 38th parallel, where the war had started. For the rest of the war, the fighting was centered on this location.

In July 1951, truce talks began. Throughout 1952 and into 1953, the talks and the fighting went on. Finally, in July 1953, an armistice was signed. North and South Korea did not formally end the war until 1996.

After the War. Since the end of the Korean War, South Korea has developed considerable economic power and moved toward a democratic form of government. In contrast, North Korea has remained a rigid Communist dictatorship. The United States continues to keep armed forces in South Korea.

Vietnam

Another area of conflict between democratic and Communist nations was Vietnam. After World War II, France wanted to resume control of its colonies in Indochina. In Vietnam, a nationalist group led by Ho Chi Minh opposed the French. A Communist and a nationalist, Ho Chi Minh wanted to free his country from imperialist control. The Soviet Union aided the Vietnamese, and the United States backed the French. Fighting between the French and Vietnamese lasted for eight years. In 1954, the Vietnamese won an important battle and the war at Dien Bien Phu.

Representatives from Vietnam, Laos, Cambodia, France, China,

Vietnam nationalist and
Communist leader
Ho Chi Minh

Southeast Asia

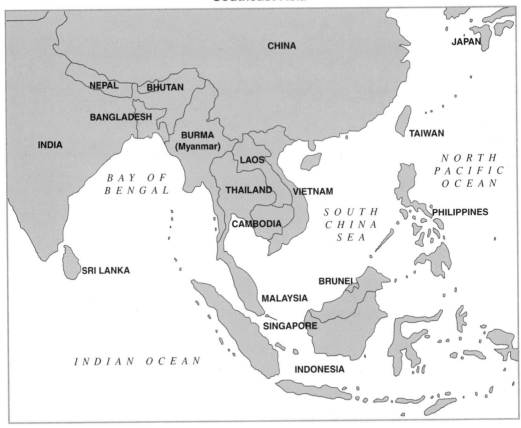

Britain, the United States, and the Soviet Union met in Geneva, Switzerland, to draw up a peace agreement. Completed in July 1954, the Geneva Agreements made Laos and Cambodia independent states and divided Vietnam at the 17th parallel. Communists controlled North Vietnam, and anti-Communists controlled South Vietnam. Elections were to be held in 1956 to choose a government for the whole of Vietnam. The United States and South Vietnam did not sign the agreements. They felt that the documents favored the Communists.

The elections were never held because the government of South Vietnam claimed that the vote would not be open and honest in the North. The president of South Vietnam was a dictator, whom many of the Vietnamese did not support. Chapter 30 describes how this increasingly tense situation developed into a long, destructive war.

Trouble in Eastern Europe

Nikita Khrushchev replaced Stalin as head of the Soviet Union in 1953. As he tried to win new allies for the Soviet Union in the devel-

oping countries, some of the satellite nations began to seek more independence. Stalin had been an iron dictator. Khrushchev's regime
seemed more relaxed.

Hungary. Hungarians began to feel that the time was ripe to
replace their Soviet-controlled regime with a government more to
their own liking. In October 1956, an uprising of students and workers took place. These idealistic revolutionaries persuaded their fellow
Hungarians to elect a liberal Communist reformer to lead the government. The new government promised to hold free elections and to
cancel Hungary's military alliance with the Soviet Union. Fearing
that other satellite nations would follow Hungary's example, Khrushchev sent troops and tanks to put down the new government.

Czechoslovakia. Twelve years later, when Leonid Brezhnev had
succeeded Khrushchev, the Czechs also tried to establish a more liberal government. In 1968, Soviet control of the satellite had loosened
somewhat. A reformist group in the Czechoslovak Communist Party
replaced the Soviet-backed leader with the more liberal Alexander
Dubcek. Although Dubcek was a Communist, he believed that socialism could work under a less dictatorial government. He lifted censorship and put economic planning in the hands of trade unions, managers, and consumers. Although Dubcek made no attempt to break
the military alliance with the Soviet Union, Brezhnev saw his reforms
as a threat. He was afraid that other satellite countries would demand self-government. In August 1968, Brezhnev reasserted Soviet
authority by sending a force of 500,000 soldiers to occupy Czechoslovakia. Keeping the fate of the Hungarians in mind, the Czechs surrendered. The new head of government canceled the reforms.

INFO CHECK

1. Compare the causes of the Korean War (1950–1953) with the beginning
   of conflict in Vietnam in the 1950s. What were the similarities and
   differences?

2. Describe the developments in Hungary and Czechoslovakia in the 1950s
   and 1960s. Why do you think the Western democracies took no action to
   aid the revolts?

ECONOMIC ISSUES IN THE COLD WAR
AND POST-COLD WAR ERA

Nearly all the democracies had capitalistic or free-market economic systems, while the Communist countries had command economies. These two economic systems played an important part in the
cold war. When offered the choice between communism and democracy, the leaders of developing countries took into consideration the
kind of economic system each used. Great numbers of people in de-

veloping countries were poor and either unemployed or confined to jobs that did not pay a living wage. Their leaders felt that industrialization would create jobs that paid well. They tried to determine whether a command economy or a free-market system would best help them to industrialize.

Free-Market Economy v. Command Economy

In capitalism, private individuals own the means of production. *Capitalism* is called a free-market economy because it is controlled by the market, not by a government or even by the people who own the means of production. The forces that rule the marketplace are supply and demand and competition. These forces decide what products will be made, who will make them, and what their prices will be.

In a command economy, the government has complete control over the country's means of production. Stalin's Five-Year Plans were carried out under a command economy. The government set production quotas for the manufacturers and determined what goods would be made and what price they would sell for. In agriculture, Stalin instituted the system of state-owned, collective farms. Like the manufacturers, the farmers had to follow Stalin's instructions.

The Soviet Union began to lose the cold war in the late 1980s. To a large extent, its command economy caused its defeat. As Western nations grew richer, Russia and its satellites grew poorer. One cause of this was the government's refusal to let Soviet industries produce enough consumer goods. Westerners could buy a variety of goods. For Eastern Europeans, even food and clothing were scarce. Industries in the Soviet Union concentrated on producing military weapons and the technology needed for the space race, such as satellites.

To be sure that the United States was strong enough to counter any Soviet threat, U. S. President Ronald Reagan (1981–1989) increased military spending. He also gave nuclear missiles to allies in Europe. The Soviets could not keep up the competition. Their economy was not strong enough. Furthermore, huge sums were being spent on the fighting in Afghanistan. Soviet forces had invaded that country in 1979 to aid a pro-Communist government. The troops stayed until 1989.

Economic Progress in India

When India became independent in 1947, the new government made industrialization one of its priorities. India now produces automobiles, airplanes, satellites, computers, and nuclear reactors. Its textile industry, for which it has always been famous, has been especially successful.

The Green Revolution yields a bountiful wheat harvest in India

The Green Revolution boosted India's agricultural output. Scientists created this revolution by developing better fertilizers, new kinds of seeds that grow well in tropical climates, and more efficient means of irrigating fields. By adopting these improvements, Indian farmers increased their crop yield. But the fertilizer, seeds, and pesticides to kill harmful insects are expensive. Not every farmer can afford them.

Although more food is produced, some has to be imported. It is often too expensive for many people to buy. Poor diets, widespread illiteracy, and a rapid population growth keep India poor.

Economic Progress in Latin America

The Latin American countries have been slow to industrialize. As colonies, they had to send raw materials to the home country and to buy its manufactured goods. After they won their independence, most continued this pattern, but with a wider selection of markets.

Many Latin American countries that did try to industrialize, failed to develop a variety of industries. This made their economies very vulnerable. For example, if a country based its wealth almost entirely on mining a certain metal, its economy would be ruined by a drop in the price of that metal in the world market.

Industrialization. Industrialization was slowed by other problems as well. After World War II, Brazil and Mexico worked hard to build factories. Although they managed to produce enough goods to export, they could not build up a domestic market. Not enough Latin Americans could afford to buy their products.

Exploitation. Without enough domestic consumers, the industries of many Latin American countries could not support themselves. Industrialists often turned to foreign investors for help. Unfortunately, the outsiders tended to take advantage of the situation. Many of them grew rich on Latin America's natural resources and gave little in return. Because most of these investors were from the United States, Latin Americans began to distrust their wealthy neighbor. This exploitation of Latin American industries by U.S. investors caused several Latin American countries to adopt Socialist-style governments.

Unrest. Some countries, of course, did have moderate success in building industries. Even in these countries, political unrest occurred. A new class arose from the urban industrial workers. Unlike upper- and middle-class people, the workers wanted social change. They tended to vote for left-wing governments that favored Socialist reforms. The middle and upper classes feared that these governments would take away their privileges and strengthened their support for very conservative leaders. Thus, in some cases, industrialization increased Latin American political instability.

Agriculture. The uneven distribution of wealth also affected Latin America's agriculture. Most of the best land was in the hands of a few wealthy landowners. They made larger profits by growing cash crops, such as bananas and coffee, than by growing a variety of food to feed their fellow Latin Americans. Therefore, much of the food had to be imported. This measure worked for the wealthy. The poor, however, could not buy expensive imported items.

Land Distribution. In order to give everyone a fair share of their countries' wealth, left-wing governments initiated land-distribution programs. They divided large plantations among the poor farmers. This procedure was bad for economies based almost entirely on the export of a single crop. The loss of the big plantations meant the loss of the cash crop. Land distribution also angered the landlords and the American companies that made their profits from fruit grown in Latin America. (In order to profit from a cash crop, a large amount of land has to be devoted to the crop to raise the quantity needed for a substantial return. Breaking up the property would make it more difficult to reach this goal.) The U.S. government helped the landlords overthrow the reform governments in Chile and Guatemala.

Economic Progress in Africa

Economic reforms were largely unsuccessful in the newly independent African nations. The new governments believed that they could best help their people by industrializing their countries as quickly as possible. Many felt that nationalizing their industries would speed up the process of modernization. Unfortunately, the colonizing countries had not allowed many of their African subjects access to schools and universities. The new companies lacked trained managers and skilled workers. Poor decision making, low-quality products, and changing world markets caused many businesses to fail.

Food Production. African leaders frequently concentrated on industrialization at the expense of agriculture. The old methods of agriculture could not produce enough food to feed Africa's expanding population. These methods also caused the land to erode or become infertile. In addition to these problems, Africa underwent a period of drought. More and more farmland dried out. The process in which fertile land becomes desert is known as *desertification*. This problem occurs particularly in West Africa. Famines occurred in many countries, including Ethiopia, Somalia, and the Sudan. The misery, disease, and political rivalries caused unrest. Bloody conflicts continue to trouble Africa.

Economic Recovery in Europe and Japan

With Marshall Plan aid, Western Europe prospered. Communism did not advance beyond East Germany. Japan also prospered under the American occupation forces.

Germany. At first, the victorious Allies adopted a punitive attitude toward Germany. A large portion of eastern Germany was given to Poland. Consequently, millions of Germans were relocated to Soviet-occupied Germany where housing and food were scarce. The Soviets took possession of German factories and other valuable property. Economic recovery in East Germany proceeded at a slow pace.

The West Germans owed much of their economic recovery to Marshall Plan aid and government policies that favored a free-market economy. The "economic miracle" in Germany turned the country into a leading industrial power in the 1950s.

Common Market. The cooperation required to follow the Marshall Plan strengthened ties among the countries of Western Europe. In 1957, six of these countries, agreeing to follow common policies to increase trade among them, created the *European Economic Community* (EEC). Also known as the *Common Market*, the EEC, later joined by six more members, has become a major economic force in the world. Its goals include a single currency and a unified banking system. In 1991, the EEC took steps toward merger with another group of European countries. The combined organization, called the European Economic Area, now involves 19 nations. In 1994, the organization became the *European Union* (EU). Economic interests have proved to be a powerful force in the integration of Europe.

Comecon. In 1949, the Soviet Union and its satellite countries in Eastern Europe formed the *Council for Mutual Economic Assistance* (COMECON). It encouraged trade among its member nations, all Communist. The organization was not as successful as the EEC. In 1991, COMECON disbanded as Eastern European governments sought economic ties with Western Europe after the collapse of the Communist system.

Japan. At the end of World War II, most of Japan's industries and cities lay in ruins. The U.S. occupation force acted quickly to put Japan back on its feet. A new constitution, calling for a democratically elected legislature (the Diet), was put in effect in 1947. A prime minister directed the government.

Japan and the Allies signed an official peace treaty in 1951. The Soviet Union signed a separate agreement with Japan in 1956. The 1951 treaty took away all of Japan's colonial possessions and allowed Japan to rearm for defensive purposes only. In 1972, however, Okinawa and some other possessions were returned to Japan. The United States and Japan signed a mutual defense pact in 1952. It allowed U.S. troops to stay in Japan for an indefinite time.

With aid from the United States, Japanese industry grew rapidly after the 1950s. The automobile and electronics industries were especially successful. The country became the second largest economy in the world, just behind the United States. By the 1990s, Japanese products dominated Asian and other markets around the world.

Emergence of Pacific Rim Economies

Japan's successful economy set an example for other Pacific Rim countries. South Korea, Taiwan, Hong Kong, and Singapore developed such powerful economies that they were called the "four tigers" of East Asia.

At first, these countries produced mainly textiles for export. They had to import most other manufactured goods. Their leaders realized that to improve their economies, they would have to develop strong domestic markets. Before they made goods for export, therefore, they freed themselves from relying heavily on foreign imports. Once they were able to satisfy the needs and wants of their own people, they went on to develop industries that made goods for foreign markets. They now export such items as radios, televisions, computers, and electronic devices around the world.

In the mid-1990s, this rapid economic growth slowed. Inefficient banking practices and other problems caused an economic crisis. The crisis spread beyond Asia to Europe, Latin America, and to the United States. In response, the Pacific Rim nations began programs to reform and improve their banking and other economic practices.

OPEC and the Oil Crisis of the 1970s

As the Arab nations become more independent, they found that their rich reserve of oil gave them a great deal of influence in the world. To consolidate their strength, Iran, Kuwait, Saudi Arabia, and Venezuela formed the *Organization of Petroleum Exporting Countries* (OPEC) in 1960. In the next ten years, eight other nations also became members. Once the oil-producing countries united, they were able to regulate both the rate of production and the price of oil. This ability gave the Arab members of OPEC a powerful weapon against Israel and the countries that supported it.

The Arab nations have refused to recognize Israel's right to exist. Starting in 1948, the two sides engaged in frequent wars. In one of these, the Six-Day War of 1967, Israel took Egypt's Sinai Peninsula, Syria's Golan Heights, Jordan's West Bank, and the Jordanian half of Jerusalem. The Israelis said they would return these territories only if the Arab nations signed a peace treaty that recognizes Israel's right to exist. The Arabs refused, and the conflict simmered on as a series of border raids and limited bombing attacks.

In October 1973, the hostilities erupted into another full-scale war. It is called the Yom Kippur War because the Arabs attacked the Israelis on Yom Kippur, the holiest day of the year for religious Jews, in order to catch them off guard. Aided by supplies from the United States, Israel managed to get the upper hand. The Arabs decided to weaken Israel, the United States, and other countries that helped Israel by limiting or cutting off their supplies of oil.

This strategy proved very effective. Almost all industries depend on oil as a source of fuel. The world economy was therefore severely

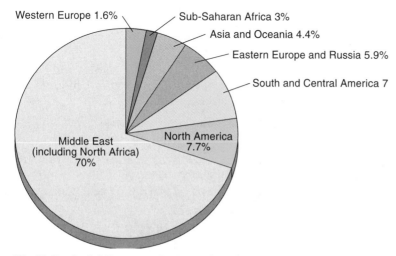

World Crude Oil Reserves, by Region   1996

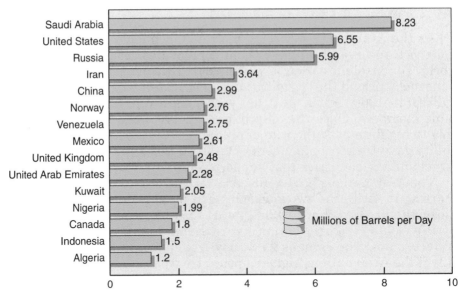

Major Crude Oil Producers   1995
(millions of barrels per day)

damaged by the oil embargo. The United States realized with a shock how much it relied on outside sources of oil. It began to take steps to cut oil use by conservation measures.

To prevent the Arabs from imposing more embargoes, U.S. leaders began to work harder to promote peace talks between the Arab nations and Israel. The United States also tried to be more even-handed in its relations with Arab nations. Most had felt that the United States had favored Israel.

INFO CHECK

1. Explain the difference between free-market economies and command economies. Which type of economic system did the Soviet Union have? What problems did this cause for the Soviet Union?

2. PROVE or DISPROVE: Too much reliance on cash crops and foreign investment has caused widespread poverty in Latin America.

3. Explain why economic recovery from World War II in Germany and Japan was faster and better than in other countries.

4. Define the terms *Pacific Rim* and *Four Tigers*. How did these countries develop strong economies after World War II?

5. What is the connection between the Western nations' dependence on oil and their desire for peace in the Middle East?

THE CHINESE COMMUNIST REVOLUTION

China is a vast and powerful country with a population of over a billion. Its size and central location in Asia make it a dominant force among the nations of the world.

Background. Many Chinese resented foreign interference in their country. Because they thought that a Communist government might offer effective resistance to the Western nations and Japan, they formed a Communist Party in 1921. This began a long struggle between the Communists and the ruling Nationalist Party for control of China. The leader of the Nationalist Party, General Jiang Jieshi, drove the Communists out of the cities controlled by his party. Thereafter, they settled in rural areas. Under the leadership of Mao Zedong, they spread Communist ideas among the peasants. As the Nationalists began taking over China's rural areas, Jiang again attacked the Communists—this time driving them into northern China.

When the Japanese invaded China in 1937, the Communists and Nationalists agreed to join forces against their common enemy. When World War II ended in 1945, the two groups resumed their civil war.

Jiang Jieshi lost the support of many people. They considered his government to be corrupt and dictatorial. The Nationalists favored the landlords and factory owners over the peasants and workers.

The Communists, led by Mao Zedong and Zhou Enlai, had the support of the peasants. When the Communists took over an area, they reinforced this support by executing landowners and distributing their property among the local farmers.

In 1949, the Communists won the conflict. The Nationalist forces escaped to Taiwan, an island off the coast of China, and set up a government there under the rule of Jiang Jieshi.

Communism Under Mao Zedong

The Communists created the People's Republic of China on the mainland. Mao ran the government as a dictator. Zhou served as the premier. Mao quickly moved to nationalize existing industries and create new business operations under government control. In 1958, the "Great Leap Forward" began. Mao forced the peasants to combine their lands in huge communes or agricultural communities. In these communes, the state owned everything. The peasants owned nothing. Mao was attempting to increase agricultural production. Instead, strong peasant resistance to the economic system reduced output. Those who protested were "reeducated" in prison camps or killed.

Red Guards. Although industrial production did increase somewhat, Mao was unable to modernize China as fast as some people wanted. To quiet his critics, Mao launched the "Great Cultural Revolution" in 1966. He closed schools and universities and sent out

Mao Zedong overlooks
Tiananmen Square, Beijing

groups of students, called Red Guards, to force people to live by his ideas and rules. Thousands were persecuted, imprisoned, or killed for not acting in a way acceptable to the Red Guards. One goal of the revolution was to create a classless society. Some peasants and sections of the army fought against the Red Guards. Law and order were breaking down. Mao called a halt to the revolutionary actions in 1968.

Mao v. Confucius. The Communists discouraged the study of the ideas of Confucius. They replaced the Confucian principle of loyalty to the family with the dictatorial principle of loyalty to the state. Mao's teachings became the main guide for Chinese thinking and living. All Chinese were expected to live and work for the success of the revolution.

Relations With the Soviet Union. When Mao Zedong first set up the Communist government in China, the Soviet Union gave him aid. For more than ten years, the two countries presented a united front against the Western democracies. But in the late 1950s, China began to disagree with Soviet Communist aims. China also resented Soviet efforts to cooperate with the United States. Disputes over ter-

Time Line

Year	Dates and Events
A.D. **1941**	**1945:** Potsdam Conference recognizes Soviet control of Eastern Europe
	1945: U.S. occupies South Korea; Soviet Union occupies North Korea
	1946–1954: Indochina War: Laos, Cambodia independent; Vietnam divided
	1947: Truman Doctrine: U.S. aids Greece, Turkey, Iran; vows to face down threats from communism
	1948–1952: Marshall Plan: U.S. economic aid to recovering European nations
	1948: Berlin Blockade: Soviets cut off Western supply lines to Berlin
	1948–1949: Berlin Airlift
1950	**1949:** Point Four Program: U.S. technical assistance to developing nations
	1949: Organization of NATO, defense pact of 12 (later 19) Western nations
1951	**1949:** Communists win control of China; Nationalists flee to Taiwan
	1949: Soviet Union develops atomic bomb
	1950–1953: Korean War: South Korea a democratic government; North Korea a Communist dictatorship
	1951–1954: Pro-Communist Guatemala opposed by U.S.-supported rebels
	1952: U.S. develops hydrogen bomb
	1955: Soviet Union develops hydrogen bomb
	1955: Warsaw Pact of Soviet Union and satellites in Eastern Europe
1960	**1955:** Soviet Union, Egypt sign arms agreement
1961	**1956:** Egypt takes Suez Canal; France, Britain, Israel attack Egypt; U.S. insists on their withdrawal
	1956: Uprising by anti-Soviet Hungarians put down by Soviet troops, tanks
	1957: Soviet Union launches first artificial satellite, *Sputnik 1*
	1957: Six (later 12) Western European nations organize EEC
	1959: Castro leads Cubans in revolt against dictator Batista; sets up Communist state allied to Soviets
1970	**1960:** Iran, Kuwait, Saudi Arabia, Venezuela organize OPEC
	1961: Soviet cosmonaut Gagarin, first man to orbit earth
1971	**1963:** Communist China, Soviet Union end diplomatic relations
	1966–1968: "Great Cultural Revolution" in China
	1967: Six-Day War: Israel occupies East Jerusalem, parts of Syria, Jordan, Egypt
	1968: Czech moderate Dubcek's reforms cause Soviet Union to occupy Czechoslovakia
	1969: U.S. lands two astronauts on moon
1980	**1970:** Allende heads new Communist government of Chile
	1972: Nixon visits mainland China
1981	**1973:** U.S. helps Pinochet's military regime take control of Chile
	1973: Yom Kippur War: Arabs attack Israel; lose war; OPEC imposes oil embargo on Israel and allies
	1976: Chinese leader Deng initiates economic advances; more trade with West
	1979: U.S. and Communist China establish diplomatic relations
	1979: Saddam Hussein becomes dictator of Iraq
	1981–1989: U.S. military spending under Reagan forces Soviets to compete
1990	**1989:** Chinese student protest in Tiananmen Square put down harshly
1991	**1990s:** China becomes world's fastest growing economy
	1994: EU (EEC members and 7 more nations) takes further steps toward economic integration of Europe
	1997: Britain returns Hong Kong to China
2000	

ritory grew into armed clashes on the long Soviet-Chinese border. Finally, in 1963, the Chinese broke off relations with the Soviets.

China and the West. When Canada, France, Great Britain, and others established diplomatic relations with Communist China, the United States refused to do so. It continued to support Nationalist China on Taiwan as the legitimate government of China. Then, in the early 1970s, U.S. President Richard Nixon took steps to recognize the People's Republic of China. In 1972, he became the first American president to visit mainland China. In 1977, the United States and China established full diplomatic relations with each other. Nationalist China was stripped of its UN seat in 1971 in favor of Communist China. It then became one of the five permanent members of the Security Council.

When the United States recognized Communist China, it broke off official relations with Nationalist China (Taiwan). But the United States and Taiwan remained friendly. Taiwan continued to receive some military aid from the United States and favorable trading terms.

Communism Under Deng Xiaoping

Two developments made the United States willing to recognize Communist China—the growing ill-will between China and the Soviet Union and the death of Mao Zedong. A more moderate leader, Deng Xiaoping, took office in 1976. He initiated a program called the "Four Modernizations." This program was designed to bring about advances in four areas—science and technology, agriculture, industry, and national defense. The changes it produced in these areas significantly improved the Chinese people's quality of life.

Agriculture. Deng's policies were most successful in agriculture. The government no longer forced peasants to work on large collective farms. Instead, it allowed them to farm in small family units and to decide which crops to grow. Under this more liberal system, food production increased by more than 50 percent in six years.

Industry. Deng then gave a limited freedom to industry. He permitted Western manufacturers to open factories in China. Goods were produced more cheaply than in the West. The resulting lower prices appealed to consumers. The sale of Chinese products around the world gave a substantial boost to China's economy. Chinese citizens also had more freedom in the marketplace. They were now encouraged to set up small businesses, such as snack shops and beauty parlors. Capitalistic ideas began to take hold in China.

Limited Freedom. By the mid-1990s, the new policies had made China into the world's fastest growing economy. But Deng did not allow freedom to exceed certain limits. The state still owned most large industries. The government discouraged cultural and political change by keeping control of the media. After some time, Deng feared that China was becoming too Westernized and began to check the trend toward a freer economy. The inflation that followed caused widespread unrest.

Tiananmen Square Massacre. The young people of China began to demand more personal freedom. In April 1989, university students demonstrated against government restrictions and corruption. People of all ages supported them. On May 17, over a million Beijing citizens gathered in Tiananmen Square. When the government sent soldiers and tanks to stop the demonstrations, unarmed people blocked their entrance into the city. For two weeks, the army leaders hesitated to drive the tanks past the human blockade. Finally, on June 4, 1989, the army pushed its way in. Many of the demonstrators were either killed outright or arrested and executed. More than 700 students died. Hundreds more were sent to prison for long terms.

Reforms. The democratic nations condemned this violation of human rights. To justify the actions to the Chinese, Deng and his associates claimed that the demonstrators had been plotting to destroy national unity. To convince his people that he had their welfare at heart, Deng resumed economic reforms. China's economic prosperity continued. At the same time, he tightened restrictions on political expression and continued to mistreat political prisoners.

The United States threatened to revoke China's special trading privileges if the human rights of the government opponents were not observed. To avoid losing their markets in the United States, the Chinese government promised reforms. Evidence that the reforms have taken place is scant. The United States continues to urge China to treat political protesters fairly. The Chinese continue to resent this interference, they say, in their internal affairs. Even after Deng's death in 1997, the issue caused friction between the two countries.

Hong Kong. China's repressive regime and its apparent indifference to human rights are of concern to the people of Hong Kong. Hong Kong is an island located at the mouth of the Canton River in China. It was a British crown colony from 1898 to 1997. In 1997, it reverted to Chinese rule. The Chinese have promised that they would not interfere with either Hong Kong's free-market economy or its democratic government for 50 years. Nonetheless, democratic countries are watching China's activities in Hong Kong for signs of repression. Some experts believe that China will not interfere with Hong Kong's successful economy.

The Role of Women in Communist China

A vivid symbol of women's status in traditional Chinese society was the practice of stunting the growth of little girls' feet. This was done by binding a girl's feet with the toes bent against the soles of the feet. The process was crippling and extremely painful. Parents did it because, at the time, women with tiny feet and a tottering gait were considered attractive among the upper classes. Foot binding prevented women from moving freely and put them almost entirely under their husband's control.

In traditional China, parents arranged their daughters' marriages. Once married, a girl became the property of her husband. Men were allowed to have more than one wife, but women could have only one husband. Being one of several wives lessened a woman's value. Because girls were given little or no education, running away from a cruel husband usually meant starvation or a life of servitude. Sometimes even a life of servitude was closed to them. Their deformed feet disqualified them from many menial jobs.

After 1911, under the Nationalists, the position of women improved. The government banned foot-binding. More and more women were allowed to marry men of their own choice. They were permitted to go to school, to own property, and to enter the business world. Nonetheless, life for poor women and for women who lived in rural districts remained restricted. Tradition still ruled that women should be subservient to men.

When the Communists took power in 1949, they gave women equal rights with men. They tried to eradicate the tradition of keeping women subservient to men through education and indoctrination. They opposed arranged marriages and outlawed polygamy, or the practice of having more than one spouse. The women of Communist China now go to the same schools as the men and are encouraged to get jobs. They can become Communist officials and enter the professions.

In China, the government still controls the lives of both men and women. As the massacre of the demonstrators in Tiananmen Square illustrates, the Chinese do not have freedom of speech. The government dictates the subjects that students can study. Some students complain that high school and university teachers discourage original ideas and critical thinking. Couples are allowed to have only one child. This rule is strictly enforced by local Communist officials.

Nevertheless, the development of a type of free-market economy made possible the growth of a middle class, especially in the cities. Opportunities to earn more money and enjoy a higher standard of living have increased in the 1990s.

After World War II, life for people all over the world changed drastically. Although many improvements occurred, new problems emerged. The West worried about communism becoming the basis of more governments. Everyone worried about the possibility of a nuclear war. But expanding prosperity made life easier for a great many more people throughout the world.

Chapter 30 provides a closer look at the changes that occurred in Africa, Asia, and the Middle East after World War II.

INFO CHECK

1. Identify: Jiang Jieshi, Mao Zedong, Zhou Enlai, Deng Xiaoping.

2. Explain why you AGREE or DISAGREE with these statements:

   - The long struggle between Communists and Nationalists had little effect on China's political and economic development after World War II.

   - By the 1990s, China developed a free-market economy while remaining a political dictatorship.

3. Describe the changing role of women in China.

CHAPTER REVIEW

Multiple Choice

1. Winston Churchill referred to the Soviet Union's shutting down of Western contacts with the nations of Eastern Europe as the descent upon these nations of

   1. an iron curtain
   2. a plague
   3. a boycott
   4. none of the above.

2. The Truman Doctrine meant that the United States would

   1. assist all war-torn nations of the world with food and clothing
   2. assist only our former World War II allies with humanitarian aid
   3. use military force to stop the spread of Nazism
   4. support nations fighting against Communist-supported guerrillas.

3. To aid the economic recovery of post-war Europe, the U.S. secretary of state developed the

   1. policy of containment
   2. "Dollar diplomacy"

3. Marshall Plan
4. Roosevelt Corollary.

4. Immediately after World War I, the United States refused to join the League of Nations and followed a policy of isolationism. After World War II, it joined the United Nations and followed a policy of

   1. neutrality
   2. containment
   3. aggression
   4. isolationism.

5. The importance of the Berlin Airlift was that it

   1. moved needed men and machines to the battle zone
   2. demonstrated Allied determination to prevent the Soviets from taking over West Berlin
   3. showed the value of airpower as a military weapon
   4. provided cheap plane tickets for tourists to West Berlin.

6. Prior to World War II, the major powers formed alliances that were

called the Triple Entente and the Triple Alliance. After World War II, they were called the

1. Communist League and the Alliance for Progress
2. Warsaw Pact and NATO
3. Arab League and the American League
4. ZYO and the PLO.

7. The Middle East was valued by both the Soviet Union and the Western democracies for two major reasons

1. the Panama Canal and uranium deposits
2. naval coaling stations and military airports
3. the Suez Canal and oil deposits
4. military alliances and rich diamond reserves.

8. In Latin America, military dictators often ruled the countries with support from the

1. military, wealthy landowners, and foreign investors
2. League of Nations and foreign capitalists
3. peasants and the Catholic Church
4. United Nations and Amnesty International.

9. The nations of Western Europe formed the Common Market. The Soviet Union and its Eastern European satellites formed the COMECON. These organizations were formed to create

1. military alliances
2. soccer leagues
3. consumer research companies
4. trade and economic cooperation.

10. In order to create heavy industries in Russia, Stalin had his Five-Year Plans. To increase agricultural production in China, Mao had his

1. "Great Cultural Revolution"
2. Red Guards
3. reeducation policy
4. "Great Leap Forward."

11. The map on page 660 suggests that:

1. NATO and Warsaw Pact nations had equal military power
2. the world was dominated by two opposing European alliances
3. the nations of Africa formed a third alliance
4. the Soviet Union had greater power and influence than the United States.

12. Use the time line on page 654 to select the most accurate statement.

1. Yeltsin became the Russian president before Gorbachev became the Soviet leader.
2. Both NATO and the Warsaw Pact were created in the same year.
3 The Soviet Union collapsed after many nations of Eastern Europe held free elections in which the Communist party was defeated.
4. The Cold War ended when Gorbachev became Soviet leader.

Thematic Essays

1. China has undergone many changes. Discuss the differences and similarities in the economic and governmental policies and practices of Mao Zedong and Deng Xiaoping. *Task:* Include the Great Leap Forward, reeducation, Red Guards, Four Modernizations, and Tiananmen Square.

2. Compare and contrast free-market and command economies. *Task:* Explain the role of government in each type of economic organization. Give examples of countries that have practiced one or the other of these economic systems. State the importance

of this issue in the cold war and post-cold war eras.

Document-Based Questions

Use your knowledge of Global History and Geography and the documents to assist you in answering the questions.

1. Study the photo on page 680.

   Explain, using several reasons, why such a large picture of Mao would appear in this busy, capital city square.

2. Mao Zedong wrote in 1952:

   ". . . the present rulers of Great Britain and the United States are still imperialists. Internationally we belong to the side of the anti-imperialist front, headed by the Soviet Union. . . . Who are the people? They are the working class, the peasantry and . . . the bourgeoisie. . . . Under the leadership of the working class and the Communist Party these classes unite to create their own state . . . so as to enforce the dictatorship over the henchmen of the imperialist—the landlord class and the bureaucratic capitalist class. . . ."

   Discuss what Mao is saying about the differences between China and the West and the reason for tension between China, the Soviet Union, Great Britain, and the United States.

3. Study the photo on page 659.

   How does this photo illustrate the post-World War II cold war between the Soviet Union and its Communist allies versus the United States and its allies?

Identify the operation in progress. Explain why it was a political and technological victory for the West.

4. President Truman speaking before the first session of the 80th Congress in 1947:

   ". . . The very existence of the Greek State is today threatened by the terrorist activities of several thousand armed men, led by Communists. . . . the United States must supply this assistance. . . . No other nation is willing and able to provide the necessary support for a democratic Greek Government. . . . Greece's neighbor, Turkey, also deserves our attention . . . one of the primary objectives of the foreign policy of the United States is the creation of conditions in which we and other nations will be able to work out a way of life free from *coercion* [pressure]. . . . At the present moment in world history, nearly every nation must choose between alternative ways of life. The choice is too often not a free one. . . . I believe we must assist free peoples to work out their [futures] in their own ways."

   What conflict is being discussed here, and what role does Truman plan for the United States?

Document-Based Essay

Task: Explain why the former World War II allies—the Soviet Union and the United States—became postwar adversaries. Include in your essay: political power and economic competition.

CHAPTER
30

Postwar Developments in Africa, Asia, and the Middle East

Enos looked at his watch. Eric was late. The club was already full. Soon Pieter-Dirk Uys would begin his show. Enos wished he had been old enough to have watched the famous comedian in the years when apartheid had been in effect in South Africa. It must have been so exciting when Uys made fun of prominent political figures while they were in power. He still did, of course. But now it was safer.

Most things were easier now. A young black man like Enos could afford to go to an expensive club. He could sit openly with a white friend. (Enos looked at his watch again. Where *was* Eric?) He could have a good government job and live in a mixed neighborhood.

Still, things could be a lot better. Few of Enos' black friends could afford to come to this club. And some of those who could, wouldn't. They felt uncomfortable around white people. Many whites hadn't given up their apartheid attitudes.

Enos sighed and glanced around at the other tables. As he did, he caught sight of Eric hurrying toward him, smiling and waving. Enos felt a wave of warmth and hope. He and Eric worked for a government agency designed to help black people get better jobs. Surely, they and others like them would make South Africa a true rainbow society.

T his young black man is experiencing the benefits and discomforts of post-apartheid South Africa. South Africa became independent from Britain in 1961. Nonetheless, the system of apartheid kept many of the evils of colonialism alive in that country for a long time. *Apartheid* means the separation of black people from white people through laws and political and social policy. Apartheid ended in 1991 and a multiracial government took power in 1994. But many injustices remain.

Almost all of the post-colonial countries are not as industrialized as the Western nations that once colonized them. Latin American countries threw off their colonial yokes earlier than did the countries of Asia and Africa. But they have many of the same troubles.

During the cold war, it became common to refer to three worlds. The Western capitalist countries and Japan were the *First World*, and the Communist countries were the *Second World*. Nations that were not industrialized became known as the *Third World*. The less developed countries are located in Africa, Asia, Latin America, and the Middle East. Because they are in various stages of becoming industrialized, they are often referred to as *developing nations*.

THE COLLAPSE OF WESTERN IMPERIALISM

Before World War II, many of the Third World nations located in Asia, Africa, and the Middle East were the colonies of Western countries. The maps on pages 690 and 694 show the former colonies in these regions, their ruling countries, and the dates on which they won their independence.

Following the end of World War II in 1945, nationalist groups in most colonized countries stepped up their demands for independence. They knew that the time had come when they could achieve this end. The ruling European countries had to rebuild their cities and convert their factories from wartime to peacetime production. They lacked the time and money to govern other countries. Then, too, they could no longer claim that racial superiority gave them the right to dominate other peoples. The theories of Nazi Germany's leaders about a "master race" had shown this claim to be inaccurate, arrogant, and cruel. Therefore, moved by both practical and ethical motives, the imperialist nations agreed to prepare their colonies for self-government.

Independence Gained

The United States freed the Philippines in 1946. India, which gained its independence in 1947, was the first European colony to do so. By 1954, most other colonized Asian countries had also gained their freedom.

Some of the Middle Eastern countries took somewhat longer. The last of these, Bahrain, Qatar, and the United Arab Emirates, ended British rule in 1971.

France fought to keep control of Algeria in North Africa, but fi-

Asia After World War II

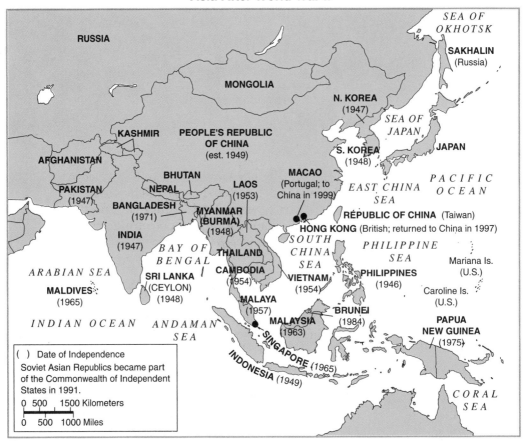

( ) Date of Independence
Soviet Asian Republics became part of the Commonwealth of Independent States in 1991.

0 500   1500 Kilometers

0   500 1000 Miles

nally set it free in 1962. Most of the colonies in Africa south of the Sahara won their independence from France and Britain without fighting. They continued to keep close economic ties with their former rulers.

Great Britain and its former colonies formed an association called the Commonwealth. The 53 members meet periodically to exchange views on economic, scientific, educational, and other issues. After Britain became part of the European Union, it loosened its economic ties with the Commonwealth members.

Belgium was reluctant to give up its territory in the Congo. But in 1959, unrest forced the Belgians to withdraw.

Bangladesh

After gaining its independence in 1947, Pakistan faced internal conflicts. The new state was divided into a western province and an eastern province. These provinces were at opposite ends of India. Besides their shared faith (Islam), the people who lived in the provinces had little in common. They did not even speak the same language.

East Pakistan had the larger population, but West Pakistan had more representation in the Pakistan government. East Pakistanis felt that the West Pakistanis were treating their part of the state as a colony. In the late 1960s, East Pakistani leaders demanded independence. The West Pakistan government then put East Pakistan under martial law. In 1971, the East Pakistanis rebelled. After a hard struggle, in which they were aided by India, they gained their freedom. East Pakistan became the nation of Bangladesh in 1973.

Postindependence Development of India

India's first prime minister (1948–1964), Jawaharlal Nehru, faced many problems. Independence stirred up conflicts that had been quiet during India's years as a colony. These conflicts centered around religious differences. Besides its wars with Pakistan, India also fought a border war with China in 1959 and 1962. Nonetheless, Nehru's government managed to integrate the vast subcontinent with its many different cultural groups into a single nation. Indians speak 16 major languages and more than 1,000 minor ones.

Democratic Socialism. The new government's priorities were economic improvement and industrialization. To bring about these changes, it adopted a mixed economy. The system, called democratic socialism, is a combination of free market and Socialist planning. Under this system, the government owns and operates such industries as railroads, automobile manufacturing, and banking, while private individuals or firms own consumer-goods industries and agriculture.

Kashmir. A dispute over control of the northern province of Kashmir broke out between India and Pakistan in 1947. A cease-fire was arranged by the UN in 1949. But the dispute remains unresolved. Fighting still breaks out occasionally.

Indira Gandhi. Indira Gandhi (who was Nehru's daughter and unrelated to Mohandas Gandhi) became prime minister in 1966. (She served until 1977 and again between 1980 and 1984.) She confronted many problems. In an effort to lower India's birth rate, she attempted to institute a birth control program. At the same time, she tried to fight the corruption in her government. As both these campaigns met resistance, Gandhi proclaimed a state of emergency in 1975. With her temporary dictatorial powers, Gandhi began to prosecute dishonest officials, tax evaders, and black marketeers. She also tried to force impoverished farmers to use state-endorsed methods of birth control.

When Gandhi called for free elections, Indians showed their disapproval of her methods of rule by voting her out of office. Her fall from power was only temporary, however. The leaders who succeeded her were unable to cooperate with each other. Gandhi was reelected prime minister in 1980.

Indira Gandhi among Indian supporters

During this term of office, Gandhi tried to deal with the new nationalist groups that had become active in India at the end of British rule. Besides Muslims and Hindus, India's population includes Buddhists, Jainists, Christians, Parsis, and Sikhs.

These different religious groups also have different cultures. The members of one, the Sikhs, are strongly nationalistic and want more independence for their state, the Punjab. In 1984, some of the more radical Sikhs turned to violence to back up their demands. Gandhi sent an army to the Punjab to control the situation. At her orders, the Indian soldiers stormed the Sikh's Golden Temple at Amritsar. The Sikhs took revenge by ordering her assassination. The deed was carried out by members of her bodyguard. Outraged, Hindus formed mobs and began a random slaughter of Sikhs.

Rajiv Gandhi. Indira Gandhi's son, Rajiv, succeeded her as prime minister. He managed for a while to calm the violence. Nonetheless, he could not remove the roots of the problem—extreme nationalism and intolerance of cultural and religious differences. Sikh separatists continued to agitate for self rule. Other problems reasserted themselves. Because of India's large population, economic growth slowed. Corruption in high government positions continued. Dissatisfaction with the economy and lack of respect for the government spurred more nationalist groups to demand independence for their states. Rajiv Gandhi resigned as prime minister in 1989. While campaigning again in 1991 to become prime minister, Rajiv Gandhi was assassinated by a nationalist group, the Tamils.

Rao. In 1991, Narasimha Rao became prime minister. His term of office was troubled by the efforts of an opposition party to stir up religious strife. Such strife caused economic instability. Evidence of corruption and incompetence in Rao's party, the Congress party, reflected badly on Rao. There were periodic demands for his resignation.

Rao rejected the Socialistic economic ideas of Nehru. He privatized many industries once controlled by the government and invited more foreign investment. The economy grew faster. But with the new industrialization, air pollution became a bigger problem. After Rao left office in 1996, no one political party controlled the government until the 1997 victory of the Hindu Nationalist Party.

INFO CHECK

1. Why do you think so many colonies of European nations and the United States gained their independence after, rather than before, World War II?

2. Identify two countries in which ethnic or religious conflicts led to violence after independence had been won. Select one of these countries and explain how the problem developed.

AFRICAN INDEPENDENCE MOVEMENTS AND PAN-AFRICANISM

African nationalism emerged as a serious force in the 1920s but was not successful in attaining its goals until after 1945. Western nations also had second thoughts about imperialism. The charter of the United Nations included the principle of self-government. Great Britain's Labor Party government strongly favored gradual independence for Britain's colonies. While not quite endorsing independence for its African possessions, France felt that the time had come to reform the economic and social systems there.

The new African leaders, however, wanted immediate independence. Unable to invest much energy in hanging on to their colonies, postwar France and Britain gave in to the African leaders. By 1964, almost all of western, eastern, and central Africa had peacefully won independence.

With independence, internal conflicts arose. The African leaders built their states within the boundaries set by the former European

Africa and the Middle East: Dates of Colonial Independence

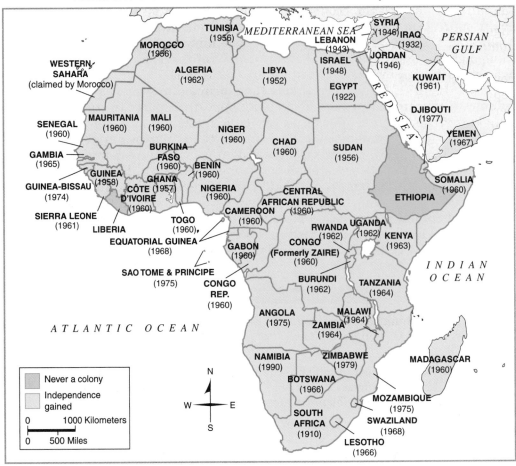

rulers. Because these boundaries broke up ethnic groups and tribes, tribal chiefs often objected. Sometimes, these objections led to civil wars.

From Colonialism to Independence

Ghana. Ghana led the other African colonies in winning independence. In 1948, Britain responded to the demands of Ghanaians for freedom by proposing a gradual transition to self-rule. A new African leader, Kwame Nkrumah rejected their proposal. His Convention People's Party incited Ghanaians to riot and strike against their British rulers. Although jailed by the British, Nkrumah won the national elections of 1951. In the free elections that followed the departure of Britain, he defeated his more moderate African rivals as well as the tribal chiefs.

Nigeria. Nigerian nationalists negotiated with Britain and, in 1954, accepted its offer of a gradual transition to self-rule. In 1960, Nigeria achieved independence. In spite of their period of preparation, Nigerians were to have a difficult time building their state.

East and Southern Africa. In other states, such as Kenya and Southern Rhodesia (now Zimbabwe), Africans did not win their independence easily. These states had a large population of white settlers, who enjoyed privileged positions. They were more determined than British government officials to keep their country under British control. Nonetheless, the white settlers in Kenya and Zambia (formerly Northern Rhodesia) were too few to postpone decolonization permanently. Southern Rhodesia, however, had a high percentage of white settlers. In 1965, they defied both the African nationalists and Britain by setting up an independent government. In 1980, after a long guerrilla war, black African nationalists defeated the whites and named the new country Zimbabwe.

Western Africa. In the late 1950s, President Charles de Gaulle of France realized that the decolonization of Africa was inevitable. He tried to insure that French possessions in Africa would continue to cooperate with France following independence. Before freeing French West Africa and French Equatorial Africa in 1960, de Gaulle divided them into 13 separate territories. Elections were held in each to decide whether it would continue ties with France after independence. If a territory voted against this continued relationship, France would no longer support it in any way.

Most educated French Africans had been treated well by France and had great affection for the country. They also needed French financial aid to help build their new states. Consequently, all but Guinea voted to continue ties with France. Guinea was able to govern itself without French financial or political support. Soon, the other territories that had voted to remain close to France sought greater self rule. They still enjoy friendly relations with their former ruler.

Central Africa. The Belgians had treated the Congolese harshly and kept them poor and subservient. They did not build up a group of educated African bureaucrats. The Congolese were forced to fight hard for their independence. In 1959, the Belgians left. The Congolese, however, were unable to govern themselves. Their new state was overwhelmed by tribal conflict, civil war, and foreign interference. (See Chapter 32.)

Tribalism v. Nationalism in Nigeria

Trouble between tribal chiefs and nationalist leaders plagued African independence movements from the start. In building their new states, nationalist leaders wanted to keep the boundaries set by the colonizing powers. The tribal chiefs wanted new ones based on ethnic and tribal loyalties. Because it was most convenient to use the existing boundaries, the nationalist leaders got their way. Nonetheless, tribal conflicts continued to play an important and destructive role in African politics.

Ethnic Rivalries. Ethnic rivalries turned Nigeria from a hopeful, prosperous country into one wasted by war and famine. The area the British named Nigeria was a collection of kingdoms peopled by many different ethnic groups. Two of the most powerful were the Yoruba and the Ibo. The Yoruba of the southwest were known as powerful warriors. The Ibo in the southeast had the reputation of being good businesspeople. Two other powerful groups were the Hausa and Fulani, who occupied northern Nigeria. These groups had different ideas about how political power in their newly independent state should be distributed. Nonetheless, they hammered out a compromise. Nigeria became a federation of states. The national government was situated in the southern capital of Lagos. It shared power with state governments in the north, west, and east. The most powerful tribe in each region headed its political party. Although powerful tribes had political leadership, the law protected the rights of Nigeria's minorities.

Tribal Wars. Unfortunately, ethnic rivalries were stronger than Nigeria's new laws. The Yoruba tried to dominate the minority ethnic groups in the Western Region. To avoid subjection to the Yoruba, the weaker groups sought to form their own region in the midwest. Soon the Western Region was torn by tribal wars.

Dictators. In the midst of this turmoil, a military group took control of the national government in Lagos and ordered the execution of all the leading politicians. In order to stop the fighting in the Western Region, the military did away with the regional governments and put the entire country under martial law.

At first, the new military dictators were popular. Many Nigerians resented the heads of the national government. These leaders were suspected of being corrupt and too easily influenced by the United States and European nations. The Hausa and Fulani of the north, however, distrusted the intentions of the military coup that was led primarily by Ibo officers. The two northern tribes had long been envious of the Ibos' success in business and the professions. When the military council officially declared itself a dictatorship, the Hausa and Fulani rose in protest and slaughtered thousands of Ibos. Some military officers of those tribes then took over the national government.

Biafra. Fearing a government controlled by hostile ethnic groups, the Ibos seceded from Nigeria and set up the Eastern Region as the independent state of Biafra. The revolt of the Ibos caused a war that lasted three years. The Nigerian forces outnumbered the Ibos, however, and finally succeeded in surrounding Biafra. Besieged and starving, the Ibos surrendered. Biafra once more became part of Nigeria.

For a while after this civil war, Nigeria remained at peace. Money earned by exporting oil brought the country prosperity. After 13 years, the military government returned political power to a civilian regime. Unfortunately, falling oil prices on the world market plunged the country into poverty. A coup in 1983 put the country under military rule again. Until 1998, Nigeria was governed by a succession of military dictators. Then efforts were made to establish a democratically elected government.

Tribalism in Kenya and Rwanda

In other parts of Africa, tribal leaders helped their countries attain freedom. After independence, they influenced the distribution of political power.

Kenya. The British minority in Kenya refused to give up their hold on the nation's government and wealth. During the 1940s, the leader of the Kikuyu tribe, Jomo Kenyatta, challenged the white colonists' right to own most of his country's best farmland. At the same time, a terrorist group called the Mau Mau were raiding European-owned farms and murdering the white owners and their black workers. The British accused Kenyatta, who was not associated with the Mau Mau, of ordering the group's terrorist activity and jailed him.

When the raids continued, the British realized that they had lost control of Kenya. They gradually shifted power to the Kenyans to

President Jomo Kenyatta at a
state occasion in Mombasa,
Kenya, 1976

prepare them for self-rule. In the 1963 national election, Kenyatta was chosen to be Kenya's first prime minister. He served until his death in 1978.

Daniel arap Moi succeeded Kenyatta as president. Moi is a member of the small Kalenjin tribe. Larger tribes, such as the Kikuyu, Luo, and Luyha resent the new group. They wanted to have more influence in the government. Even though the government has legalized other parties, opposition groups are suppressed. Moi's party remains dominant.

Rwanda. Strife between the Hutus and the Tutsis in Rwanda began when Rwanda was still a Belgian colony. Although a minority, the Tutsis controlled Rwanda. The Hutus made up the majority of the population. When the Tutsis pressed Belgium for independence, the Belgians tried to curb their power by aiding the Hutus in a rebellion. The Hutu revolt developed into a wholesale slaughter, or genocide, of the Tutsis. To escape being massacred, the Tutsis took refuge in neighboring countries, such as Zaire.

After Rwanda gained independence in 1962, Tutsi refugees formed a guerrilla army called the *Rwandan Patriotic Front* (RPF). The RPF eventually took over small areas of Rwanda and forced the Rwandan government to sign a cease-fire in 1993. With the arrival of peacekeeping troops sent by the United Nations, calm seemed to be restored.

Ethnic Warfare. Unfortunately, when the president was killed in a plane crash in 1994, Rwanda again became a scene of violence and chaos. Many people suspected extremist Hutus had killed the president in order to prevent him from reaching a permanent peaceful settlement with the Tutsis. At any rate, the act plunged the nation back into civil war. Hutu extremists once more began to kill Tutsis and moderate Hutus.

The Tutsis and moderate Hutus seeking safety in the refugee camps of Zaire and other neighboring countries died of cholera and other diseases. Those remaining in Rwanda were frequently hunted down and slaughtered.

Meanwhile, the Tutsi guerrilla army, the RPF, seized Rwanda's capital, Kigali, and set up a new government. Although the government was a coalition of Tutsis and Hutus, fighting between the two groups continued. The predominately Tutsi army gained strength. In 1996, the UN peacekeeping troops left. The Rwandan government sought out individuals suspected of genocide and had them tried by a UN-sponsored tribunal. During this period of uneasy peace, both Hutu and Tutsi refugees returned home.

South Africa

Apartheid. Unlike most African nations after independence, South Africa was ruled by a white minority. Until 1994, its government put severe economic and political restrictions on the black majority through a policy called *apartheid*. Apartheid is the Afrikaans word for "apartness." The policy maintained strict separation of the races. Laws required all blacks to carry passes, prevented them from voting, and made them subject to arrest at any time. South Africa's Asian population also suffered from discrimination. Great tensions developed between whites and blacks. In the 1980s, moderate groups in South Africa tried to find an acceptable and peaceful way to let blacks participate fully in the government. Protest demonstrations became common in black areas. Desmond Tutu, a black archbishop in the South African Anglican church, led many of these protests. Following the teachings of Mohandas Gandhi, Tutu urged his followers to use nonviolent tactics. He was awarded the 1984 Nobel Peace Prize for his work.

Sanctions. The white South African government responded harshly to black African resistance. Many Western nations became indignant at its disregard of the black Africans' human rights. To discourage this abuse of human rights, several countries imposed trade *sanctions* on South Africa. (Sanctions are laws prohibiting a nation's businesses from buying or selling goods to a country that violates international law.) As poverty in South Africa increased, violence between blacks and whites became more frequent. Foreign businesspeople lost confidence in South Africa's economy and withdrew their investments.

By 1990, a more moderate leadership began to respond to foreign pressure and the demands of black leaders by reducing the level of discrimination in South Africa. Then, in 1992, a majority of white South Africans voted to end apartheid and minority rule. Following the writing of a new constitution, multiracial elections were held for the first time in April 1994.

The ANC. The struggle by the black majority to achieve equality and political power was led by the *African National Congress* (ANC). The South African government of President F. W. de Klerk recognized the ANC in 1990 and cooperated with its leader, Nelson Mandela. De Klerk released Mandela from prison. Since 1962, Mandela had been serving a life sentence for sabotage. However, violent clashes between rival black groups and attacks on blacks by white extremists made reform difficult.

Mandela. As a result of the 1994 elections, Nelson Mandela became president. De Klerk became one of two vice presidents in this new multiracial government. The new government's primary concern was to improve the lives of black South Africans without losing the support of other groups. One of the government's first steps in stabilizing South Africa was to repair its damaged economy. Mandela promised to preserve its system of free enterprise. With the ending of economic sanctions, trade with other African nations resumed, and the economy soon improved.

NELSON MANDELA'S LONG STRUGGLE

In May 1994, a slender, white-haired, black African became president of the Republic of South Africa. It was an historic event for both the nation and its new leader, Nelson Mandela. For decades, South Africa had been ruled by a white minority kept in power by the rigid system of racial separation called apartheid. All this had been ended by a long revolutionary struggle. A new constitution made South Africa into a multiracial democracy. As the long serving leader of the African National Congress (ANC), Nelson Mandela had been in the forefront of that struggle.

Mandela was born in the Transkei region of South Africa in July 1918. He was trained from a young age to hold high office in the tribal government. However, influenced by cases that came before the chief's court, he decided to become a lawyer. Mandela was also influenced by the tribal elders' stories of the heroism of his ancestors during the wars of resistance to imperialist domination. He dreamed of making his own contribution to the struggle of black Africans for greater freedom and equality.

Mandela became a lawyer. Then, in 1942, he entered politics by joining the ANC.

Mandela helped transform the ANC into a mass movement and turn it into a radical organization. In 1949, it adopted a policy of opposing apartheid through strikes, boycotts, and civil disobedience.

In 1952, Mandela was arrested for his leadership role in the Campaign for the Defiance of Unjust Laws. This was a mass civil disobedience campaign. Although convicted, he was given a suspended prison sentence. However, he was prohibited from attending public meetings and was confined to the city of Johannesburg for six months. During this period of restricted movement, Mandela opened a law practice in Johannesburg.

During the 1950s, South African authorities attempted to repress Mandela's political activities and his legal work. He was banned, arrested, and imprisoned. By 1961, the ANC had been declared illegal. Its leadership went underground. Mandela had to live apart from his family and move from place to place to avoid detection by government informers and police spies. Inevitably, he concluded that the use of force by the government to repress those opposed to apartheid made violence unavoidable. Mandela became commander-in-chief of the newly established military force of the ANC. In 1962, he left South Africa illegally and traveled to other countries for several months. During this trip, Mandela arranged for military training for ANC guerrillas. The armed struggle had begun.

Shortly after his return to South Africa, Mandela was again arrested. In his trial, he based his defense on the premise that he had no duty to obey the laws of a white parliament in which he was not represented. Mandela was convicted and sentenced to five years imprisonment. While serving this sentence, he was also charged with sabotage, convicted, and sentenced to life imprisonment. Mandela remained in prison from 1962 to 1990. He spent much time at hard labor and in isolation. Instead of breaking him, the experience strengthened his resolve to gain justice for black South Africans.

A moderate white government started negotiations with Mandela as a leader of the ANC and a man of great moral authority. The goal was to give a greater voice in government to blacks. In 1991, Mandela, now out of prison, was elected president of the ANC and began to direct the transformation of South Africa. In 1993, Mandela and President F.W. de Klerk were jointly awarded the Nobel Peace Prize. Mandela accepted on behalf of all South Africans who suffered and sacrificed to bring peace to South Africa.

- The following statement was made by Nelson Mandela at the conclusion of his trial for sabotage. Explain why you AGREE or DISAGREE with the decision of the Nobel Committee to award him the peace prize.

"I have fought against white domination, and have fought against black domination. I have cherished the ideal of a democratic and free society in which all persons live together in harmony and with equal opportunities. It is an ideal which I hope to live for and achieve. But, if needs be, it is an ideal for which I am prepared to die."

Many other problems remained, however. Unemployment among black South Africans was high. Housing was inadequate. Crime was common. Experts predicted that it would take many years to repair the damage that apartheid and violence had done to South Africa.

Pan-Africanism

As more and more African countries achieved independence, a number of African leaders recognized the necessity of promoting unity among the new nations. In May 1963, 32 African countries established the *Organization of African Unity* (OAU). Through the OAU, they hoped to coordinate cultural, scientific, political, and economic policies, to end colonialism in Africa, and to promote a common

Nelson Mandela, just released from prison, speaking in Soweto, South Africa, 1990

defense of its members' independence. Today the organization has 53 members. It meets annually in Addis Ababa, Ethiopia.

In many ways, the OAU has been frustrated in its attempts to solve the severe problems affecting Africa. It avoids controversial issues, such as human rights violations, in order to avoid alienating any of its members. Because it cannot force its members to pay dues, it remains underfinanced. It has no armed forces, so it cannot enforce its decisions.

Nonetheless, the OAU has made major contributions to maintaining peace in Africa. Its diplomatic campaigns have been particularly effective. During the 1960s, the organization successfully mediated territorial disputes between Algeria and Morocco as well as in both Zaire and Nigeria. It helped the African National Congress to end apartheid and white minority rule in South Africa. Similar assistance was given to the Southwest African People's Organization in its struggle for Namibia's independence. The Zimbabwe National Union-Patriotic Front was also aided in its struggle to end white colonialism in Zimbabwe.

INFO CHECK

1. Describe the roles played in African independence movements of each of the following: Kwame Nkrumah, Jomo Kenyatta.

2. Explain why you AGREE or DISAGREE with the following: Tribalism has been more of a problem in Kenya than it has been in Nigeria and Rwanda.

3. Why do many students of African history regard Nelson Mandela and F.W. de Klerk as heroes?

NATIONALISM AND COMMUNISM IN SOUTHEAST ASIA

In the late 1800s, the Vietnamese, like the Cambodians and Laotians, became part of the French empire called Indochina. Although the Vietnamese emperor was permitted to maintain his court in the region called Annam, the French governed Vietnam directly. The French also took control of the mineral resources and rubber plantations of the area.

End of French Rule

After World War II, France wanted to resume control of its colonies in Indochina. Ho Chi Minh, a Communist nationalist leader, wanted to free his country from French control. The Soviet Union aided Ho Chi Minh, and the United States backed the French. Fighting between the French and Vietnamese lasted for eight years. In

1954, the Vietnamese won an important battle and the war at Dien Bien Phu. France agreed to leave Vietnam, Cambodia, and Laos. Vietnam was divided into two parts—North and South Vietnam.

The Beginning of the Vietnam War

In 1957, North Vietnam, under the leadership of Ho Chi Minh, encouraged South Vietnamese Communists to begin guerrilla warfare against the U.S.-backed government in South Vietnam. Known as the Vietcong, the guerrillas hoped to bring down the government of the south and unite the country under Communist rule.

The South asked the United States for help. At first, a few hundred nonfighting advisers were sent by U.S. President Dwight Eisenhower. By 1962, under President John Kennedy, the number of American advisers in Vietnam had increased to several thousand.

In the 1960s, the United States believed that it had to stop the Communist advance in Southeast Asia. It feared that Communist

Vietnam, Laos, and Cambodia   1954–1965

China might take over the area. It was also afraid that the Soviets might gain influence over Ho Chi Minh. If all of Vietnam went Communist, U.S. officials, said, the rest of the countries in Southeast Asia would also turn Communist. They would go down just like a row of falling dominoes. The "Domino Theory" greatly influenced U.S. policy decisions throughout the 1960s.

In 1964, U.S. Navy destroyers in the Tonkin Gulf off the coast of North Vietnam reported that they had been fired upon. The destroyers were acting in support of South Vietnamese attacks on the North Vietnam coast. This report later proved to be inaccurate. But President Lyndon Johnson believed it and asked Congress for extensive war powers. Congress granted them. The Gulf of Tonkin Resolution was almost a declaration of war against North Vietnam. Johnson ordered U.S. planes to bomb North Vietnam. The pace of the war stepped up. More and more U.S. troops were sent to Vietnam, eventually reaching a high of some 536,000. These U.S. soldiers went into combat against the Vietcong and North Vietnamese forces.

The End of the Vietnam War

As Americans took over most of the fighting for South Vietnam, a strong antiwar movement developed in the United States. Increasing doubt of eventual victory and the loss of large numbers of American soldiers caused many American citizens to demand peace. Many nations around the world criticized the United States for becoming involved in another nation's civil war.

After 1969, President Richard Nixon began the process of turning the fighting over to the South Vietnamese. He slowly withdrew almost all of the U.S. forces by 1972. Efforts to reach a peace settlement increased. Finally, in January 1973, an agreement was signed. A cease-fire was arranged. Prisoners of war were exchanged. All U.S. troops left Vietnam by April 1973.

The Vietnamese civil war continued until 1975. Without American help, the South Vietnamese effort became weaker. The soldiers loyal to North Vietnam defeated the South and turned Vietnam into one country ruled by Communists. Communists also took over control of the governments of Cambodia and Laos. But the kind of Commu-

CASUALTIES IN VIETNAM WAR

	Dead in Battle	Wounded in Battle
United States	58,000	300,000
South Vietnam	1,000,000*	N.A.
North Vietnam	500,000–1,000,000*	N.A.

*N/A.: not available;   *estimate*

nist unity feared by the Americans failed to develop in Southeast Asia.

After the War

The Communist Vietnamese government was flexible in its economic policies. In an effort to relieve the widespread poverty of their country, Vietnamese leaders loosened the government's hold on the economy and began to encourage free enterprise. *Doi moi*, a program to return farms from collective management to private ownership, increased food production. New businesses arose in such cities as Ho Chi Minh City (formerly Saigon).

At the end of the cold war, the former Soviet Union stopped giving financial aid to Vietnam. The Vietnamese then looked to the United States and other Western nations for economic help and investment. In 1992, several reforms designed to make the Vietnamese more democratic improved relations between Vietnam and the United States. In 1994, Vietnam returned the remains of soldiers killed during the Vietnam War. The United States then ended a 19-year-old trade embargo with that nation. Along with other Asian nations, Vietnam suffered economic problems in the late 1990s.

Cambodia

The Khmer Rouge, a Communist group led by Pol Pot, took control of Cambodia in 1975. They persecuted anti-Communists and others. City dwellers were forced to move to the countryside. Thousands of people lived in slave labor camps. About one million people were killed. This brutality ended in 1979 after Vietnamese forces invaded Cambodia. While in Cambodia, the Vietnamese put a moderate Communist government into office and kept it under Vietnamese supervision.

The Vietnamese forces were withdrawn from Cambodia in 1989. In 1991, the leaders of Cambodia's four rival political groups, including the Khmer Rouge, agreed to form a national council. Rivalry among the four groups led to civil war. The Khmer Rouge opposed UN peace efforts and attempted to increase its territory.

Despite Khmer Rouge opposition, UN-sponsored elections were held in May 1993. The new national assembly quickly adopted a constitution that provided for a coalition government under a monarchy. Prince Norodom Sihanouk, a veteran Cambodian leader, was chosen king. His son, Prince Ranariddh, became prime minister. The UN agreed to assist the new government. In 1997, Deputy Prime Minister Hun Sen drove Ranariddh out of the country and took control of Cambodia.

The UN discouraged the new coalition government's efforts to share power with the part of the Khmer Rouge led by Pol Pot. The

Khmer Rouge then set up camps along the border with Thailand. They continued to attack the Cambodian government.

Part of the Khmer Rouge reached an agreement with the government in 1997 to join in political affairs. Another Khmer Rouge group that opposed Pol Pot put him on trial for murdering rival officials. He was sentenced to house arrest for the duration of his life. He died in 1998.

The Cambodian government abandoned strict control of the economy. By the mid-1990s, a majority of its economic resources were in the hands of private businesspeople. Another goal was the improvement of education. During the Khmer Rouge regime of 1975–1979, schools were closed and teachers killed. To raise educational standards and develop new professional people and government leaders, Cambodia needed a period of political and economic stability.

INFO CHECK

1. Should the United States have become involved in Vietnam's civil war? Why or why not?

2. Explain why Cambodia has had so many problems since 1975.

CONFLICTS AND CHANGE IN THE MIDDLE EAST

The Middle East traditionally includes a part of North Africa and southwest Asia. Most North African countries have much in common with the countries of the Middle East. They have similar geographic features and share Arab traditions as well as the Islamic religion.

Following the creation of Israel in 1948, Egypt sided with the Arab nations of the Middle East in their effort to destroy Israel. The *Organization of Petroleum Exporting Countries* (OPEC) also played a role in weakening the support of Western allies for Israel.

Israel and Egypt negotiated a peace treaty in 1979. Egypt has since worked to help establish better Israeli-Palestinian relations. Nonetheless, the distrust between Israel and its neighbors remains severe. This distrust also heightened the ill will between the Western nations that support Israel and the Arab nations of the Middle East.

Civil War in Lebanon

The Israeli-Arab wars influenced internal events in several Middle Eastern countries. Lebanon's population is a mixture of Muslims and Christians. At the time of independence from France in 1943, the two religious groups agreed to share government power. The cooperation lasted until the 1970s. Fighting broke out between Christians and Muslims over support for the militant *Palestine Liberation Organization* (PLO). Then, Palestinian refugees began streaming into Lebanon. Muslims came to outnumber the Christians. Moreover, the

Time Line

Year	Dates and Events
A.D. **1941**	**1947:** Pakistan becomes independent from India
	1948–1964: Nehru controls Indian government as prime minister
	1951: After riots and strikes, Nkrumah wins control of Ghana through first free elections
	1954: Vietnamese defeat French at Dien Bien Phu; Vietnam divided into the North and South
	1957: Vietcong begin guerrilla war against South Vietnam; U.S. "advisers" sent to support government
1950	**1959–1960:** Congo becomes independent, initiating years of civil war
1951	**1960:** French West Africa, Equatorial Africa vote to retain ties to France; Guinea votes for independence
	1962: Algeria gains independence from France
	1963: Kenyatta elected first prime minister of independent Kenya
	1964: Gulf of Tonkin Resolutions give President Johnson power to wage war against North Vietnam
1960	**1965–1980:** White Southern Rhodesians finally defeated by African nationalists of renamed Zimbabwe
1961	**1967–1970:** Ibos in Nigeria set up independent Biafra; rejoin Nigeria
	1971–1973: East Pakistan becomes independent nation of Bangladesh
	1971–1981: Shah of Iran ousted by Muslim revolutionaries; U.S. supports shah in exile; Iran militants occupy U.S. embassy; take 53 Americans hostage for 444 days
	1972: PLO terrorists kill 28 people in Tel Aviv, 11 Israeli Olympic athletes in Munich
	1973: U.S.–North Vietnam peace: cease-fire, withdrawal of U.S. troops
1970	**1975:** North Vietnam defeats the South; Communist governments in place in Vietnam, Laos, Cambodia
1971	**1975–1976:** Civil war in Lebanon; intervention by Syria provokes more fighting
	1980–1988: Iran-Iraq War over boundary disputes, religious differences
	1980s: Archbishop Tutu leads peaceful effort to end apartheid in South Africa
	1982–1984: Israel invades Lebanon to destroy PLO; peacekeeping force fails to end violence; withdraws
	1983: After coup, Nigeria is controlled by military group
1980	**1984:** I. Gandhi orders storming of Sikh's Golden Temple; is assassinated
1981	**1990–1998:** Operation Desert Storm (28 nations) drives Iraq from Kuwait; Saddam Hussein bans UN weapons inspections; on-and-off military actions taken by UN and U.S.
	1991: Syrian-Lebanese force reestablishes peace; Syria and Israel maintain troops in Lebanon
	1991: End of apartheid in South Africa
	1991: R. Gandhi is assassinated by Tamil nationalists
1990	**1991–1996:** Rao's term as India's prime minister marked by political oppression, economic instability, corruption, privatization of industry
1991	**1992–1995:** Vietnam returns U.S. war dead; U.S. ends embargo, reestablishes diplomatic relations
	1993: PLO signs peace accord with Israel
	1993: UN-supervised election in Cambodia
	1994: Multiracial government rules South Africa for first time, with Mandela as president
2000	**1994–1996:** Tutsis and Hutus renew civil war, slaughter of Tutsis and moderate Hutus; uneasy peace

Palestinians were more militant than the original Lebanese Muslim population.

The PLO used Lebanon as a base for border raids on Israel. In response to these raids, Israel attacked Lebanon. In the mid-1970s, conflict broke out between Lebanese Christians, who opposed the attacks on Israel, and Lebanese Muslims, who favored the guerrilla activity. In 1976, Syria, backed by the Soviet Union, attempted to stop the war by sending in troops.

In June 1982, Israel invaded Lebanon in an attempt to destroy the PLO. The PLO leader, Yasir Arafat, escaped to Tunisia. Israel succeeded mainly in increasing the political disorder in Lebanon. When a right-wing Christian militia group massacred hundreds of civilians in two refugee camps, a peacekeeping force consisting of American, French, British, and Italian soldiers arrived in Lebanon. Suspecting that these troops had come to support the Lebanese Christians, Muslim terrorists planted bombs that killed 241 American and 58 French soldiers. The international force was removed in 1984.

Peace of sorts finally came in 1991. The Syrian-backed Lebanese Army disarmed various private armies that had been operating there. Although Syria and Israel continued to maintain troops there, life in Lebanon began to return to normal. The country turned to repairing the great destruction caused by the many years of conflict. Prime Minister Rafiq al-Hariri, elected in 1993, began to rebuild Lebanon's economy and to restore law and order. Clashes between Lebanese and Israeli forces continued until 1996. After a 17-day Israeli attack, Lebanon and Israel agreed to limit military conflict and spare civilians. Syria and the United States supported this pact.

The Iranian Revolution

Under Shah Mohammad Reza Pahlavi (ruled 1941–1979), Iran began to modernize. Women gained the right to vote. Using the wealth brought in by its vast oil wells, Iranians developed new industries.

Many Iranians were dissatisfied, however. Some complained that the shah was a dictator. They pointed out that only a small portion of the population benefited from the new prosperity. Devout Muslims resented their government's many departures from Islamic tradition. A group of Muslim revolutionaries under the leadership of Ruhollah Khomeini ousted the shah in 1979.

Khomeini, who was a high official of the Iranian Muslims, replaced the shah as the head of a strict religious government. Now called by his religious title *ayatollah*, Khomeini tried to wipe out all Western influences.

Because the United States had supported the shah and had served as a model for Iran's Westernization, the followers of Ayatollah Khomeini hated Americans. In 1979, Iranian militants protested against

Iranian woman standing before a poster of Ayatollah Khomeini, Teheran, 1993

the United States for supporting the shah. They attacked and occupied the American embassy, taking its occupants hostage. The 53 Americans remained prisoners for 444 days, until January 1981.

When Ayatollah Khomeini ignited a revolution in neighboring Iraq, the Iraqi leader, Saddam Hussein, responded by invading Iran in September 1980. (The dispute was over boundary questions and religious rivalries among various Muslim factions.) The Iranians managed to force the Iraqis back across the border but did not totally defeat them. Although deadlocked, with neither side able to defeat the other, the Iraqis and Iranians fought on for eight years. The death of Ayatollah Khomeini in 1989 raised hopes for more peaceful relations between Iran and Iraq and the United States.

The Persian Gulf War

Although the Iraq-Iran War ended without a distinct winner, the Iraqi army had been strengthened. President Saddam Hussein decided to expand Iraqi territory by invading Kuwait in August 1990. Iraq had long claimed that Kuwait was part of Iraq. The takeover gave Iraq rich oil fields and a valuable seaport on the Persian Gulf. Hussein then moved his military forces to the border of Saudi Arabia. It seemed possible that he would order an invasion of that oil-rich nation also.

U.S. President George Bush led worldwide opposition to the Iraqi aggression. He sent military forces to Saudi Arabia to protect it. The United Nations also took action. It condemned Iraq and demanded its withdrawal from Kuwait by January 15, 1991. The UN authorized the use of military force if Iraq did not meet the deadline.

Iraq did not withdraw, and Operation Desert Storm began on January 17, 1991. A UN coalition of 28 nations used overwhelming military power (mostly U.S.) to drive Iraq out of Kuwait. The forces had the advantage of the latest technology in terms of weapons guidance systems and weapons.

The coalition victory, however, did not end Saddam Hussein's control over Iraq. Nor did it bring peace to the region. UN forces had to protect the Kurds, a minority group within Iraq, from Hussein's troops. UN inspection teams had to search Iraq to ensure that Iraq was dismantling its nuclear, chemical, and biological weapons factories. The UN monitoring of Iraq's weapons potential continued throughout the 1990s. Hussein frequently refused to cooperate. Strict economic sanctions were placed on Iraq. It had to reveal all of its weapons sites before the sanctions would be lifted. The people suffered because of the short supplies of food, medicine, and other supplies. Saddam Hussein's continuing refusal to cooperate with UN inspectors increased suspicion that he was secretly building weapons of mass destruction. In December 1998, U.S. President Clinton responded to this threat by ordering four days of intensive bombing of Iraqi military targets. The raids caused moderate to severe damage to Hussein's military capability.

Extremism and Terrorism

Throughout the late 20th century, extremist Muslim groups hostile to the Western powers caused unrest in the Middle East. Their hostility was often expressed in acts of terrorism. One Middle East terrorist movement is known as the Islamic Jihad, which means Islamic Holy War. It has claimed responsibility for numerous bombings in Lebanon and Kuwait. Some believe this name is used by many groups and does not designate a single organization. Others feel that it is a group backed by the governments of Iran and Syria. Libya and Syria have also sponsored terrorist actions by other groups against Western countries that support Israel.

More easily identified are terrorist groups associated with such political organizations as the Palestine Liberation Organization. The PLO is a collection of Palestinian groups dedicated to driving Israel out of the Middle East. When Yasir Arafat became the chairman of the PLO in February 1969, he brought his Al Fatah guerrilla group into the organization. In 1972, PLO-backed terrorist groups killed 28 people at the airport in Tel Aviv, Israel. They also murdered 11 Israeli athletes during the summer Olympics of that year. After 1993, PLO-backed terrorist actions diminished when that organization signed a peace accord with Israel.

The Hamas is a militant branch of the Muslim Brotherhood, a nationalist group founded in Egypt in 1928. A rival of the PLO, the Hamas denounced that organization for signing the peace accord with Israel.

Terrorism is an active force in North Africa as well. In 1995, a group of Muslim terrorists from Algeria was blamed for a series of bombings in French cities. These acts punished the French for supporting the Algerian government's attempts to prevent a group of extremists from winning an election. Some people also believed that Muslim radicals were responsible for the wholesale slaughter of innocent Algerian villagers in 1997 and 1998.

During the 1990s, Muslim militants targeted Egyptian celebrities and leaders. They stabbed the 1988 Nobel Prize-winning writer, Naguib Mahfouz in 1994. In 1995, they made an unsuccessful attempt to murder President Hosni Mubarak. Attacks on tourists occurred frequently in 1997 and 1998.

The gaining of independence brought disorder to many former colonies. The nationalist fervor that gave impetus to the fight for independence sometimes got out of control. Different ethnic groups struggled with one another to rule the new states. In some cases, such as in the Middle East, nationalist groups felt that the Western powers were continuing to interfere in the region. The backing of Israel by the United States and other Western countries has often outraged the Arab countries and intensified their nationalistic feelings.

Chapter 31 covers the end of the cold war and how the breakup of the Soviet Union affected Eastern Europe. In that area, nationalism frequently changed from a unifying into a divisive force.

INFO CHECK

1. Identify the countries that have been involved in Lebanon's civil war. Which of these countries do you think did the most to bring peace to Lebanon? Give reasons for your answer.

2. Why did Iran not come to the aid of Iraq during the Persian Gulf War?

3. Explain what each of the following have in common: Islamic Jihad, Al Fatah, Hamas.

CHAPTER REVIEW

Multiple Choice

1. The nations of the world that were formerly victims of imperialism and did not align themselves with either the West or the Communist powers are today called

1. First World countries
2. Second World countries
3. underdeveloped nations
4. developing nations.

2. After World War II, European imperialism on the continents of Asia and Africa began to end because

   1. European nations realized the need to treat former colonial people as equals
   2. native peoples turned to imperialism
   3. exhausted by the war, Europeans nations could not spare the money or military forces to overcome nationalistic demands
   4. the United Nations ordered them to give up all their colonial empires.

3. Disputes between India and Pakistan are of concern to the rest of the world because both

   1. have the ability to use nuclear weapons
   2. have larger armed forces than the major powers
   3. are highly industrialized nations
   4. supply a major portion of the world's rice.

4. Periods of genocide occurred in

   1. South Africa and Kenya
   2. Rwanda and Cambodia
   3. Vietnam and Kenya
   4. India and Bandgladesh.

5. Apartheid was ended in South Africa because of

   1. economic sanctions and withdrawal of foreign investments
   2. the activities of Desmond Tutu and the ANC
   3. the courage of moderate white leaders to take actions unpopular with so many whites
   4. all of the above.

6. India's constitution outlawed discrimination based on caste and granted full citizenship and equality to women. The problems of caste and women's rights still exist because

   1. not all Indian parties signed the constitution
   2. conservative women's groups protested against the changes
   3. traditional beliefs and practices are very hard to end by legislation
   4. India's rapid growth made the laws unenforceable.

7. The development of the newly independent African nations was hampered by

   1. European imperialism
   2. tribalism
   3. Pan-Africanism
   4. communism.

8. A successful, nonviolent tactic used by the world community to force the South African government to change its apartheid policy was

   1. economic sanctions
   2. letters of protest
   3. guerrilla movements
   4. United Nations' inspections.

9. Lenin's NEP policy and Vietnam's economic policy of *Doi moi* were similar in that they

   1. were strictly command economies
   2. relied on barter for exchange of goods and services
   3. encouraged free enterprise, particularly in farming
   4. both developed five-year plans.

10. The clash of traditional religious beliefs with the needs of a secular state occurred in

   1. Israel and England
   2. Japan and China

3. Egypt and Lebanon

4. Turkey and Iran.

11. The map on page 694 indicates that:

   1. many African nations achieved independence during the 1960s

   2. Ethiopia never achieved full independence

   3. the nations of the Mideast all achieved independence by 1948

   4. by 1970, imperialism no longer existed in Africa.

12. Use the time line on page 707 to identify the correct chronological order of the following events:

   1. Mandela elected president of South Africa
      Pakistan independence from India
      Gulf of Tonkin Resolutions
      assassination of Rajiv Gandhi

   2. assassination of Rajiv Gandhi
      Gulf of Tonkin Resolutions
      Mandela elected president of South Africa
      Pakistan independence from India

   3. Pakistan independence from India
      Gulf of Tonkin Resolutions
      assassination of Rajiv Gandhi
      Mandela elected president of South Africa

   4. Gulf of Tonkin Resolutions
      assassination of Rajiv Gandhi
      Mandela elected president of South Africa
      Pakistan independence from India.

Thematic Essays

1. Gandhi's policy of nonviolence, together with the strain of World War II, succeeded in ending British rule in India. Since gaining independence, India's political and social history has been filled with violence. *Task:* Explain the reasons for that violence.

Consider the religious, political, and nationalistic causes for the violence.

2. African nationalism often relied on the ability of one man to unify the peoples of his nation. *Task:* Select any two African leaders and describe their policies as well as the forces they had to overcome to unify their nations. Consider economics, tribalism, imperialism, superpower rivalry, racism, and individual leadership qualities.

Document-Based Questions

Use your knowledge of Global History and Geography and the documents to answer the questions.

1. Gamal Abdel Nasser discusses the strengths of the Arab peoples:

   ". . . there are three main sources that should be taken into account. The first . . . is that we are a community of neighboring peoples . . . and a civilization which has given rise to three holy religions. . . . As for the second source of strength it is our land itself and its position on the map—that important strategic position which embraces the crossroads of the world, and thoroughfare of its traders. . . . There remains the third source: oil. . . ."

   Of the three sources of strength Nasser refers to, which has been the one that the Arab nations have used against their enemies? Describe how it was used and whom it was used against.

2. From the Proclamation of Independence of the State of Israel:

   "The land of Israel was the birthplace of the Jewish people. Here their spiritual, religious and national identity was formed . . . here they wrote and gave the Bible to the world . . . the Balfour Declaration reaffirmed . . . the historic connection of the Jewish people with Palestine and their right to reconstitute their National Home-

ANYONE SMELL ROPE BURNING?'

MIDDLE EAST CRISIS

grew, developed and excelled. The Palestinian people was never separated from or diminished in its ... bonds with Palestine ... the Palestinian Arab people never faltered and never abandoned its conviction in its rights of return and independence. ... It calls upon Arab compatriots [fellow Arabs] ... to intensify efforts whose goal is to end Israeli occupation ..."

Compare the continued needs stated in this declaration with those of the Israeli declaration. Do you think there will be conflict between the Israelis and Palestinians? Why?

4. Study the photo on page 709.
    The Iran-Iraq War lasted eight years. Planes, rockets, and poison gas were used and the only result was the deaths of hundreds of thousands. Explain the factors that caused two neighboring Islamic nations to engage in combat. Identify the leader of Iraq during the Iran-Iraq War. How were he and the Ayatollah Khomeini similar in their attitudes toward the United States?

5. Study the cartoon.

    Who or what does the figure on the rope represent? Identify a Middle East crisis during the 1990s.

land. The recent holocaust, which engulfed millions of Jews in Europe, proved anew the need to solve the problem of the homelessness and lack of independence of the Jewish people by means of reestablishing of the Jewish State ..."

What are some of the cultural, political, and social justifications given for the Israeli Proclamation of Independence?

3. From the Palestinian Declaration of Independence of November 15, 1988:

    "... Palestine, the land of three monotheistic faiths, is where the Palestinian Arab people was born, on which it

Document-Based Essay

Did the cold war superpower rivalry start the conflict in the Middle East or simply add fuel to a fire that already existed? *Task:* Explain the roles of conflicting nationalistic and religious beliefs, strategic location, and natural resources.

C H A P T E R

31

Late 20th-Century
Developments in Europe

Inge took Joachim's hand and let him pull her to the top of the wall. Only five years ago, her uncle had been arrested for doing what she was doing so lightheartedly today. There before her lay West Berlin with its cafés, clubs, and university buildings—all places where she could meet young people like herself—her fellow Germans. To think that all this time, these strangers had been neighbors. Inge couldn't wait to get to know them.

Joachim hugged her and together they danced on top of the wall, while the other students laughed and cheered. Then down they all scrambled again to help the ones below chop away its heavy stones.

These exhilarated young East Germans are celebrating an event that signaled the end of the cold war—the tearing down of the Berlin Wall in 1989. Almost simultaneously, other countries in Eastern Europe and the republics of the Soviet Union were also shaking off the grip of communism. What caused the iron curtain to lift at this time? How did the "sudden" breakup of the Soviet Union affect the world?

THE END OF THE COLD WAR

The Nuclear Threat

For decades after the United States dropped atomic bombs on Japan in 1945, the world lived in fear that nuclear weapons would be used in another war. The hostility and suspicion that caused the cold war increased the chances of such a disaster. The Soviet Union and the United States developed ever more powerful weapons in greater and greater quantities. Other nations also learned how to make nuclear devices. During the 1960s, a number of countries agreed to limit above-ground testing of nuclear devices. These tests resulted in fallout pollution that could be dangerous. The fallout affected the health of humans, animals, and plants. Diplomats also tried to prevent countries that did not yet possess nuclear weapons from acquiring them.

Soviet Actions

In the first years after World War II, the Soviet Union seemed to exercise absolute control in Eastern Europe. In 1953, Soviet tanks ended protests by East Berlin workers. Many East Germans fled to

"Let's Get A Lock For This Thing"

John F. Kennedy and Nikita Khrushchev uniting against the nuclear menace, inspired by the Cuban Missile Crisis

the West through West Berlin. To halt the loss of its labor force, the East German government built the Berlin Wall in 1961. East Berliners became prisoners in their own city.

The fear that the cold war would develop into a nuclear conflict was almost realized in the autumn of 1962 during the Cuban Missile Crisis. The crisis began when the Soviet Union placed nuclear missiles in Cuba, an island just 90 miles from Florida. The Cuban leader, Fidel Castro, was an ally of the Soviet Union. U.S. President John F. Kennedy asked the Soviets to remove the missiles. When they did not, he set up a naval blockade of Cuba. The world did not know how Soviet leader Khrushchev would react. Many feared that he would fire off a missile at a target in the United States, which would set off World War III. After a brief standoff, during which the world held its breath, Khrushchev agreed to remove the missiles. In return, Kennedy promised not to invade Cuba and to remove obsolete U.S. missiles in Turkey. War had been avoided.

Although Khrushchev's successor, Leonid Brezhnev, tightened party rule within the Soviet Union, he tried to improve relations with the West. This policy of increased cooperation with the United States and Western Europe was called *détente*. In 1972, President Richard Nixon became the first U.S. president to visit Moscow. During his stay, he and Brezhnev agreed to cooperate in science and technology, exploration of outer space, and trade relations.

Even before Nixon's visit, the two leaders had discussed ways to lessen the nuclear threat. These talks, the *Strategic Arms Limitation Talks* (SALT I), led to an agreement to reduce the numbers of certain nuclear weapons, both offensive and defensive.

In 1973 and 1979, Nixon and Brezhnev held talks that produced the SALT II treaty. In this treaty, the Soviet Union and the United States agreed to place limits on the number of long-range bombers and missiles. Unfortunately, the Soviet Union aroused U.S. suspicion that it did not really want peaceful coexistence. The Soviet Union ignored the human rights of the people in the countries it controlled and continued to try to take over countries in Asia and Africa. When Soviet troops invaded Afghanistan in late 1979 to settle a civil war, the United States regarded the aggression as evidence of the Soviet Union's bad faith. Believing that the Soviet Union had no intention of living up to the SALT II treaty, the United States refused to sign it. For the time being, détente was at an end.

Gorbachev and the Era of Reform (1985–1991)

In 1985, Mikhail Gorbachev became the Soviet leader. To improve social and economic conditions, Gorbachev developed two new programs. One, *perestroika* (restructuring), was a program to make the Soviet economy more efficient. Citizens gained the right to set up their own businesses. Heads of large factories were told to make their plants profitable. Another reform, *glasnost* (openness), granted increased freedom of speech and the press to Soviet citizens.

Because of these reforms, relations with the West improved. In 1987 and in 1991, the United States and the Soviet Union signed major nuclear arms reduction treaties. Gorbachev ordered Soviet forces out of Afghanistan in 1989. He also stopped supporting Marxist governments and movements around the world to end the economic drain on the country.

Some Communists opposed Gorbachev, believing that his reforms were ruining the Soviet Union and violating the teachings of Marx. In August 1991, these Communists led an unsuccessful coup against Gorbachev. To lessen the power of the Communists, Gorbachev resigned from the party. The Soviet Parliament suspended all party activities. The Communist party no longer controlled the government, the economy, or the military.

Gorbachev continued his reforms. In spite of his efforts, Russia, Ukraine, and the 13 other republics that had once formed the Soviet Union declared their independence. At the end of 1991, Gorbachev resigned as president. Most of the former Soviet republics then

The Commonwealth of Independent States

formed the *Commonwealth of Independent States* (CIS). The Soviet Union no longer existed. Russia was the dominant state in the CIS. This succession of events in 1991 ended the cold war.

After the fall of the Soviet Union, the leaders of the newly independent republics struggled to develop new political systems and to solve severe economic problems. Eager to promote democracy and free-market economies in the East, the United States and other Western nations supported their efforts with financial aid and advisers.

Boris Yeltsin was elected president of the Republic of Russia in 1990. He had been a leader in the Communist Party and had supported Gorbachev's reforms. In Russia, Communists and ultranationalists opposed Yeltsin's attempts to establish democracy and a free-market economy. In October 1993, these "hard-liners" unsuccessfully tried to remove Yeltsin from office. New national elections were held in December 1993. Yeltsin won and a new constitution was approved. Although in poor health, Yeltsin was elected as president again in 1998. He continued his efforts to move toward capitalism and maintain good relations with the West. Severe economic problems hampered his efforts.

The Fall of Communism in Eastern Europe (1989–1990)

Until 1989, the Soviet Union closely supervised the governments of its Eastern European allies. It crushed revolts against the Communist system by groups within the satellite countries. Soviet troops put down prodemocracy movements in Hungary in 1956 and in Czechoslovakia in 1968. Protests and strikes by Polish workers, students, and intellectuals in 1956, 1968, 1970, and 1976 were also quickly put down.

Solidarity. In 1980, Lech Walesa became head of Solidarity, a trade union organization in Poland. Walesa was an electrician in the shipyards in Gdansk. Solidarity demanded trade unions free of Communist control and a reexamination of Poland's alliance with the Soviet Union. At first, the government agreed to some changes. The workers continued to make demands. Then, Polish authorities, encouraged by the Soviets, outlawed Solidarity in 1981. They arrested Walesa and thousands of others and imposed military rule on the country. These harsh actions drew strong criticism from the United States and other Western countries. Walesa was released in 1982, and martial law was lifted in 1983.

Rising prices and shortages of consumer goods led to protests in Poland. The Communist Party yielded to the people's demands for free elections in 1989, which the Solidarity movement won. It formed the first non-Communist government in a former satellite country. In 1990, Lech Walesa was elected the president of his country.

Soviet Reaction. Mikhail Gorbachev changed the way the Soviet Union dealt with its satellites. He abandoned the Brezhnev

Doctrine. It had stated the right of the Soviets to interfere in any satellite state to protect communism. Thus, when the people of Eastern Europe protested against their Communist governments in 1989, the Soviet Union did little in response.

Reaction in Other Countries. In addition to Poland, other Eastern European countries recognized that Soviet-led communism was a failure. It could not provide goods, services, and freedom equal to what was enjoyed in the West. In Hungary, Czechoslovakia, Albania, and Bulgaria, demands for free elections led to the peaceful end of Communist rule between 1989 and 1991. In Romania, when the Communist rulers did not agree to free elections, they were overthrown. The president, Nicolae Ceausescu, a brutal ruler, was executed.

East Germany. In East Germany, too, the people demanded greater personal freedoms and economic opportunity. In 1989, they forced the East German government to open the Berlin Wall and allow unrestricted travel across its borders. In 1990, free elections in East Germany led to the fall of the Communist Party from power. In October 1990, East and West Germany were reunited. The unified Germany has again become the leading economic and political power in Europe.

Germans from East and West Berlin taking over the hated wall, 1989

INFO CHECK

1. What was the great fear of people all over the world during the cold war? What steps did the United States and the Soviet Union take to make the world safer?

2. List the succession of events that ended the cold war in 1991.

3. Who do you think did most to cause the fall of the Soviet Union—Mikhail Gorbachev or Boris Yeltsin? Give reasons for your choice.

4. How did abandonment of the Brezhnev Doctrine lead to change in Eastern Europe?

THE RISE OF THE NEW EUROPE

Commonwealth of Independent States

By 1992, the Commonwealth of Independent States (CIS) had developed into a grouping of independent states without a strong central authority. Russian President Yeltsin and the leaders of the other republics decided to establish the commonwealth's headquarters in Minsk, the capital of Belarus. They chose the Russian ruble as a standard currency. They also agreed to work for nuclear disarmament and to permit each republic to organize its own military forces.

Western nations quickly recognized the independence of the post-Soviet republics and opened diplomatic relations with them. To assist the new states in their efforts to establish democratic governments and free-market economies, the Western industrialized nations sent substantial economic and humanitarian aid. They were particularly eager to help Russia, which is by far the largest of the republics and the cornerstone of stability in the region.

Yeltsin's Policies. Yeltsin wished to turn Russian factories, farms, and other businesses over to private owners who would run them for a profit. Such an economic reform is called *privatization*. Privatization was carried out by selling and giving away shares of stock to private individuals. Each Russian received a certificate, or voucher, that he or she could trade for stock. To win support for its reforms, the government gave managers and workers free shares of stock in the companies where they worked. Under communism, in theory, the people own everything. Thus, when businesses were sold, the people received the proceeds.

Opposition. Not all Russians approved of Yeltsin's policies. Although many were excited at the new opportunities to make money, others felt threatened by the introduction of private enterprise. People who had enjoyed prosperity and power under communism felt that the new system would take away their privileges. Under the Communist system, workers had enjoyed job security whether they were productive or not. The free market requires businesses to be as efficient as possible. Workers feared that as the new owners stream-lined the businesses, they would lay off many workers. Russians also feared large cutbacks in social services.

Hardship. The reforms did, in fact, bring hardship to many. Production dropped lower than it had in the United States during the Great Depression of the 1930s. As food and consumer goods became scarce, their prices rose sharply. Millions lost their jobs. Crime increased. Racketeers extorted money from small businesses. Drug dealers found new customers, and armed gangs roamed the streets. Day after day, the press carried news of corrupt dealings in business and government.

Many Russians became convinced that democracy and private enterprise did not work. They doubted their president's ability to transform the defective economy.

The Struggle to Develop a Democratic Government

By late 1992, a bitter power struggle was under way. On one side stood Boris Yeltsin. On the other stood his political enemies in the Russian parliament, elected before the breakup of the Soviet Union. Old-style bureaucrats, former Communist bosses, and ultranationalists in parliament were determined to slow privatization and undermine Yeltsin's power. Yeltsin asked for constitutional changes that would give him greater control of the economy. Instead, parliament reduced his presidential powers.

Crisis. In March 1993, Yeltsin announced that he was taking emergency powers and would govern Russia by issuing decrees. This move brought on a constitutional crisis. Communists and other parliamentary opponents of Yeltsin called for his impeachment and removal from office. Russia's top judicial body, the Constitutional Court, agreed that Yeltsin's moves had gone against the constitution. But the court did not try to remove him from office, and Yeltsin's opponents had too few votes in parliament to impeach him.

Finally, legislators accepted the idea of a referendum. Across Russia, 65 percent of the eligible voters turned out. They gave clear support to Yeltsin. Immediately, Yeltsin proposed a new constitution that would strengthen the presidency and limit the parliament's powers. Before the new constitution could be accepted, however, the power struggle took a new and explosive turn. Yeltsin touched off the crisis by suspending his vice president, with whom he had quarreled. Then Yeltsin announced that he was dissolving the parliament and calling for new legislative elections. Parliament reacted angrily, claiming that Yeltsin's actions were illegal. They voted to replace him with the vice president. Yeltsin refused to yield.

Revolt. With parliament holding round-the-clock sessions in its headquarters, known as the "white house," Yeltsin surrounded it with police and military forces. He threatened to arrest parliamentary leaders. After several days of standoff, civilians who supported the parliament charged the police with clubs and guns. This set off a bloody battle in the heart of Moscow on October 3, 1993. After 26 hours, heavily armed soldiers blasted their way into the parliament. They arrested the parliament chairman, the vice president, and dozens of their supporters.

Problems. Despite Yeltsin's victory, economic problems and crime continued to worsen. In December 1993, Russian voters approved the proposed constitution. However, a large number of seats in the State Duma (the new lower house of parliament) went to ultranationalists and others opposed to Yeltsin's reforms. Clashes between the president and parliament continued.

Prices spiraled upward at a dizzying pace. Economic officials tried to ease people's hardship. They slowed down privatization, printed more paper money, and sought ways to increase production. Some reformers feared that Russia might turn back to its old methods of rigid central control.

War With Chechnya

A rebellion in Chechnya, a small region of southern Russia, flared into all-out war in 1994. It is one of dozens of separate territories that

Chechen women protest the killing of their leader by a Russian missile

make up the Russian federation. The Chechen people are mainly Muslim and non-Russian. They have been under Russian rule since the 1860s.

When Chechnya declared full independence, Russian leaders responded with overwhelming force. The Russian army destroyed the Chechen capital, Grozny, and much of the territory's industry. The war killed some 1,400 Russian soldiers and 20,000 civilians. In a 1995 peace settlement Russia gave Chechnya its own government within the Russian federation.

In 1999, hostilities erupted once more. By early 2000, Russia was in the process of trying to crush Chechen self-determination altogether.

Western Reaction to Yeltsin

Although Western leaders expressed alarm at the bloody battles in Chechnya, they generally sided with Yeltsin in his domestic struggles. They praised Yeltsin for helping to end the cold war. In January 1993, he signed a new arms-reduction treaty with U.S. President George Bush. *START II*, as the treaty was called, provided for eliminating land-based missiles having more than one warhead. Two thirds of the nuclear warheads on each side were to be destroyed by the year 2003.

Rise of Ultranationalists

Seeing Yeltsin as a democrat Western leaders preferred him to the former Communists and the nationalists. One ultranationalist, Vladimir Zhirinovsky, feared by some as a budding Hitler, had won strong support in the 1993 parliamentary elections. Zhirinovsky called for a revival of Russia's empire and said he would end the "humiliation" of Russia by Western powers. He also expressed anti-Semitic ideas and prejudice against nonethnic Russians.

Seeking to cut into Zhirinovsky's support, Yeltsin began to take a tougher line on international issues. Nonetheless, he generally cooperated with Western nations on most matters.

New Elections

Yeltsin lost ground in the 1995 parliamentary elections, but Zhirinovsky's party slipped even more. A revived Communist party won nearly one-third of the seats.

Nonetheless, Yeltsin won the 1996 presidential election. He changed cabinet ministers several times, but massive aid from the West failed to prop up the economy. By 1999, many businesses were not paying taxes. To prevent total economic collapse, the *International Monetary Fund (IMF)* committed even more money to Russia. But confidence in Yeltsin declined.

On December 31, 1999, Yeltsin surprised the world by resigning the presidency in favor of Vladimir Putin. Putin, who had spearheaded the renewed crackdown on Chechnya, received a slender majority of votes in the March 2000 election.

INFO CHECK

1. Describe the problems of Russia in the 1990s. If you were a Russian citizen at this time, would you oppose or support Boris Yeltsin? Give reasons for your answer.

2. Why do you think the leaders of the United States and other Western nations have supported President Yeltsin?

3. Why do the people of Chechnya want independence from Russia? Why do you think the Russian government has refused to give Chechnya its independence?

BEYOND RUSSIA: NATIONALISM AND ECONOMIC REFORM

Issues of nationalism and economic disarray also flared up in other republics of the Commonwealth of Independent States. Many had economic troubles similar to those that Russia experienced. Ethnic and religious differences became more important. In addition, the former Soviet republics worried about the possible revival of Russian imperialism. Some republics, such as Ukraine, Kazakhstan, Azerbaijan, Armenia, and Belarus had special challenges to overcome.

Ukraine

From czarist times down to the collapse of the Soviet Union, Ukrainians resented Russian rule. During World War II, Ukrainian nationalists fought both the Germans and the Soviets. Ukraine's 52 million people finally broke away in 1991. In a national referendum, more than 90 percent of Ukrainian voters favored independence.

The break stirred up many disagreements between Russia and Ukraine. The two states quarreled over how to divide the fleet of ships that the Soviet navy had kept in the Black Sea. After long negotiations, they agreed that Russia would get the bulk of the fleet. In return, part of Ukraine's debt for purchases of Russian natural gas would be canceled.

The region of Crimea led to another dispute. Crimea was traditionally part of Russia, and today, two thirds of its 2.7 million people are Russians. In 1954, Soviet leader Nikita Khrushchev turned Crimea over to Ukraine as a gesture of friendship. After 1991, Russian nationalists in Crimea demanded that Ukraine give the region back to Russia—or at least allow self-rule. Nationalists in Russia's State Duma supported such demands. Nonetheless, Russia's government adopted a hands-off policy.

Despite mutual distrust, Russia and Ukraine remained dependent on each other. Most of Ukraine's oil and gas came from Russia. In turn, Russia got much of its food from Ukraine and needed the large Ukrainian market for its exports.

Some Ukrainians wanted to keep the nuclear missiles that the Soviet Union had stationed on Ukrainian territory. They believed the weapons would offer protection against any Russian attack. In the end, however, Ukraine agreed to allow its nuclear weapons to be destroyed, as called for by the START II agreement. So did its neighbors, Belarus and Kazakhstan. This meant that, of all the former Soviet republics, only Russia would have nuclear weapons.

Ukraine launched its own free-market reforms. Like Russia, Ukraine experienced sharp price rises and other economic shocks. Western nations supported Ukraine's reforms by offering large loans. They also offered to help Ukraine shut down the nuclear power plant at Chernobyl and build a safer plant in its place. Chernobyl was the site of the world's worst nuclear accident in 1986. This accident had spewed radiation over the local area and across Europe.

Kazakhstan

Oil-rich Kazakhstan is one of the luckier states to have emerged from Soviet Central Asia. It not only has oil but it also contains a modern space-launching facility at Baikonar. Russia took out a 20-year lease on the facility, providing extra income for Kazakhstan.

Some 17 million people live in Kazakhstan. The country produces vast amounts of cotton and grain. In addition to oil, its mineral resources include gas, iron, gold, silver, copper, and chromium.The potential for economic growth has attracted Western investors. Kazakhstan is ruled by an authoritarian president. He introduced a policy of gradual privatization. But some major economic enterprises were to remain state property.

Kazakhstan came under Russia's control in the 18th century. It has two main ethnic groups—Kazakhs (42 percent) and Russians (37 percent). Ethnic Kazakhs speak a Turkic language and follow the Sunni Muslim religion. Ethnic Russians have dominated the industrial cities for more than 100 years. Kazakhstan's economy has remained closely tied to Russia's. Along with Belarus, Kazakhstan joined Russia in a customs union, or free trade zone.

Azerbaijan and Armenia

The collapse of the Soviet Union rekindled old quarrels between two former Soviet republics, Azerbaijan and Armenia. Violence erupted within Azerbaijan in 1988.

Azerbaijan and Armenia are small countries. They are important because of their natural resources and their position at the southeastern tip of Europe. Turkey, Iran, and Russia have long competed for power and influence in the Caucasus region.

The people of Azerbaijan, known as Azeris, speak a language related to Turkish. They were under Turkish rule for the greater portion of their history. Therefore, their culture and their social institutions are largely Turkish. Azeris were also once under Persian (Iranian) rule. Like today's Iranians, most Azeris belong to the Shiite sect of Islam, rather than the Sunni sect that is popular in Turkey.

The Armenians are mainly Christians. In the 19th century, they looked to Christian Russia for protection against the Turks and Persians. The traditional territory of Armenia was split in two, with half ruled by Turkey and half by Russia.

Both Armenia and Azerbaijan came under Soviet rule after the Russian Revolution of 1917. Each became a Soviet republic. Large numbers of Armenians lived within the borders of Azerbaijan.

It was in the Armenian section that trouble erupted in 1988. The Armenians resented Azeri rule and wanted to become part of Armenia. Armenia's government shared that goal. Mass demonstrations by Armenians demanding political change touched off riots between ethnic Armenians and Azeris in Azerbaijan. Outright warfare erupted.

The war redrew the lines of influence in the southern Caucasus. Armenia turned more and more toward Russia. Azerbaijan forged links to Turkey. Using its great oil and gas wealth as leverage, Azerbaijan cut off fuel shipments to Armenia and began an economic blockade. That damaged the Armenian economy. Militarily, however, the Armenians had the upper hand.

By 1994, the war had taken at least 20,000 lives and caused more than a million people to flee their homes. Late in the year, Russian mediators helped to arrange a cease-fire, and peace negotiations began. Both sides kept their guns ready for more fighting. No resolution to the dispute had been reached by 1999.

Belarus

The Belarussians are a Slavic people whose culture is similar to the Russians and Ukrainians. Their strongest link with those nationalities is the Eastern Orthodox religion.

Belarus's poor soil was damaged by the radioactive contamination that resulted from the Chernobyl nuclear accident in 1986. Belarus was once thought to have few valuable minerals. Recently, however, rich deposits of coal and oil have been discovered there. Belarus is now a parliamentary republic with close economic ties to Russia.

Eastern Europe

Since the fall of communism, the former Soviet satellite nations have struggled to develop democracy and free-market economies.

Czech President Vaclav Havel (right) meeting Elie Wiesel, Holocaust survivor and spokesman against oppression

They have also attempted to negotiate closer relations with the economically stronger nations of Western Europe.

Czech Republic and Slovakia. Created in 1918 by the uniting of Czech and Slovak lands, Czechoslovakia was occupied and dissolved by the Nazis during World War II. When Soviet armies drove out the Nazis, an elected Czechoslovak government took office in 1946. Communists seized power in 1948 and installed a harsh regime. All dissent was repressed.

In 1968, an invasion of Soviet troops supported by Polish, East German, Hungarian, and Bulgarian forces crushed a movement for democracy. Repressive policies remained in force. Czechoslovak demands for more human rights led to another crackdown in 1977.

In 1989, tens of thousands of people took to the streets of Prague, Czechoslovakia's capital, to demand free elections. Millions went on strike. The Communist Party leadership resigned. Vaclav Havel, a Czech playwright and human rights advocate, was elected president of a non-Communist government.

The Slovaks had been independent during World War II. Their demands for a separate state, in 1992, were opposed unsuccessfully by President Havel. He failed to win reelection as a result. But after Slovakia became a a separate nation in 1993, the Czech parliament elected Havel to the presidency of the new Czech Republic.

Traditionally, the Czechs have been oriented toward the West. The Slovaks have looked to Hungary and Russia for trade and support.

Poland. Although Poland welcomed democracy with enthusiasm, it faced immense economic problems. Poland tried what was called "shock therapy," or an economic stimulus. That meant introducing free-market capitalism all at once, rather than step-by-step as in some other countries of Eastern Europe.

"Shock therapy" brought a rush of Western consumer goods and a sharp rise in foreign trade. Polish businesses, however, found it hard to withstand the international competition. At first, industrial production fell, wages dropped, and unemployment soared. Many Poles were alarmed and angry to find their standard of living threatened. Opinion polls showed a sharp drop in the popularity of President Lech Walesa, who spearheaded the changes.

In 1993, the largest block of seats in the Polish parliament went to former Communists. They were able to assemble a majority and elect a new prime minister. Under Poland's system of parliamentary democracy, President Walesa had to share power with the new government, although he sharply criticized it. In the presidential election of 1995, Polish voters replaced Walesa with a former Communist.

Despite the initial pain, Poland's "shock therapy" has begun to pay off. In the early 1990s, Poland led the former Communist nations of Eastern Europe in economic growth. By the mid-1990s, private enterprise accounted for more than half of Poland's output. But inflation and unemployment remained high.

Poland was the first nation to free itself from communism. Its methods of pursuing a free-market economy helped to guide other nations of Eastern Europe.

Hungary. Hungary followed Poland and Czechoslovakia in separating from the Soviet Union. Hungary has not found the transition to independence easy. At first, it established close ties to Poland and Czechoslovakia. When Czechoslovakia split up, Hungary became concerned about the status of the Hungarian minority in Slovakia.

The change to a free-market economy brought many hardships. Later, the economy recovered. Privatization of industries continued, and foreign investment increased.

NATO and Eastern Europe

After the cold war, many of the countries that had once been part of the Soviet empire wanted to avoid falling under Russian domination again. Therefore, they sought membership in NATO. But if they joined NATO, American and West European troops would be required to defend any former Warsaw Pact member threatened by Russia. At first, the NATO allies were not prepared to make this commitment or offend Russia. The United States and other NATO members urged the East Europeans to be patient. They should work toward the goal of full NATO membership by first joining a "Partnership for Peace."

Gradually, Russian leaders began to accept the idea of membership of East European countries in NATO. In 1997, Yeltsin signed an agreement that prepared the way for East European countries to become full members of NATO. The Czech Republic, Hungary, and Poland joined in 1999. The agreement also gave Russia a voice in issues involving NATO. Russia also promised not to put nuclear weapons in East European countries.

NATO—MOVEMENT TOWARD THE 21ST CENTURY

The *North Atlantic Treaty Organization* (NATO) was formed in 1949 as a cold war military alliance of the United States and its allies. Originally, the mission of NATO was to defend Western Europe from aggression by the Soviet Union and its Communist allies. The fall of the Soviet Union and the end of the cold war brought changes in mission, organization, and membership to NATO in the 1990s.

When the United States Senate voted its approval of the expansion of NATO in May 1998, President Bill Clinton emphasized the historic importance of the decision:

> By admitting Poland, Hungary, and the Czech Republic, we come even closer than ever to realizing the dream of a generation—a Europe that is united, democratic, and secure for the first time since the rise of nation states on the European continent.

Adding the three countries to NATO required the approval of the 16 existing NATO members. Many regard the enlargement of NATO as a redrawing of the boundaries of Europe. It would push the direct influence of the military alliance 400 miles eastward toward Russia. Also, the expansion of NATO committed American, Canadian, and European military forces to the defense of Prague, Warsaw, and Budapest for the first time in the history of the alliance. Among the benefits to be gained by the existing NATO allies were the strengthening of security by nurturing new democracies in Europe, a stronger barrier against any possible Russian aggression, and the enlargement of NATO military forces by 200,000 troops.

For those cautious about NATO enlargement, the matter of extending membership to the nine nations seeking to become a part of the alliance raised other issues. The cost of assisting the new NATO members to acquire sophisticated weapons and military equipment needed to meet strict NATO military standards would be great. But weapons manufacturers in the United States and Europe looked forward to significant profits.

Supporters of NATO expansion have had to consider carefully the reaction of Russia to the movement of the alliance closer to its borders. In the late 1990s, NATO and Russia struggled to develop a genuine partnership. Russian and NATO troops conducted joint peacekeeping patrols in Bosnia. A select group of young Russian colonels attended the NATO Defense University. A NATO-Russia council was established to discuss peacekeeping, terrorism, nuclear weapons, and other security matters.

Achieving political and military stability in southern Europe has been a NATO priority since the war in Bosnia began. The more recent crisis in the Serbian province of Kosovo, where ethnic Albanians wish to gain independence from Serbia, intensified peacekeeping problems in the region. NATO also began to focus on the Mediterranean as an area in which future security challenges are likely to occur. A dialogue developed between NATO authorities and Egypt, Israel, Jordan, Mauritania, Morocco, and Tunisia. Political, social, and economic pressures in these non-NATO countries have the potential to create problems for the alliance. Violent radical groups, population growth, and immigration to NATO countries may affect the stability of Europe. In addition, the possible disruption of the flow to Europe of oil and natural gas from the Mediterranean region is also of concern.

Since 1996, the alliance has been directed by Dr. Javier Solana, the Secretary General of NATO. A physicist, Solana has had many years of government service in his native Spain. General Wesley Clark, an American, has been Supreme Allied Commander Europe since July 1997. General Klaus Naumann, a German, has been Chairman of the North Atlantic Military Committee since February 1996.

Respond to the following arguments:

1. NATO is a cold war military alliance for which there is no need today.

2. NATO should be expanded to include every country in Europe.

INFO CHECK

1. Why does Kazakhstan have a better economic future than most of the other republics of the CIS?

2. Identify the two major goals of the Eastern European nations after the cold war. What was the role of Poland during this period?

CHANGE IN WESTERN EUROPE

Germany and Austria

Germany's economic and political strength gave it a leading role in European affairs. Recently, however, Germany has had problems arising from the nation's reunification in 1990.

Effects of Reunification. East Germany was far less developed economically than the western portion of Germany. Its markets in the former Soviet Union were gone, and East Europeans were no longer interested in buying East Germany's heavy machinery. To overcome eastern Germany's widespread poverty and unemployment, the West German government, led by Chancellor Helmut Kohl, offered far-reaching economic assistance, ranging from business subsidies to welfare payments for families.

Germany had to raise taxes to help finance the aid to eastern Germans. Both western and eastern Germans found much to criticize. Some western Germans thought eastern Germans were "freeloaders." Many eastern Germans resented the attitude of the richer westerners. These tensions were made worse by a recession in 1992 and 1993. The economy improved, but unemployment remained high in the eastern section. Elections in 1998 turned out Kohl and put in Gerhard Schröder, a Social Democrat.

Nationalistic Feelings. During the 1970s and 1980s, West Germany's expanding industries had hired large numbers of "guest workers" from Turkey and other countries. At the same time, crises in the Middle East and elsewhere sent large numbers of refugees flooding into Germany to escape war and hunger. With unemployment, resentment of foreigners grew. One result was a surge in activity by *neo-Nazis*—people who seek to bring back the "Germany-for-Germans" policies of Hitler's time.

Chancellor Kohl's government introduced measures to curb extremist violence. Also, Germany's parliament voted to limit the number of foreign job seekers permitted to enter Germany.

In Austria, feelings against immigration were also strong. In October, 1999, Austrians gave enough votes to the anti-immigration Freedon Party to include it in a coalition government. Most world leaders distrusted its leader, Jorg Haider, who had expressed approval of Hitler's labor policies. When the European Union suspended diplomatic relations with Austria, Haider resigned as party leader.

France

Although France was one of the victors in World War II, postwar political and economic instability made recovery difficult. Problems were made worse by costly colonial wars in Southeast Asia and Algeria from 1946 to 1958.

De Gaulle. General Charles de Gaulle became prime minister and then president in 1958. Under a new constitution, de Gaulle had greatly expanded powers as president. He encouraged economic and technological advances and supported European unity. France, he hoped, would play a leadership role in postwar Europe. De Gaulle resigned from office in 1969 after losing a national referendum on changes to the constitution that would have strengthened presidential powers.

Under de Gaulle, France experienced economic growth and urbanization. Cities were rebuilt. Consumer goods became more widely available. More students went to universities. Such changes had been under way before 1958, but Gaullist economic reforms helped them along. Also, de Gaulle turned France away from colonialism in Asia and Africa, negotiating independence for Algeria in 1962. Instead of colonialism, increased trade with the rest of Europe became France's priority.

Socialists. De Gaulle was succeeded as president by Georges Pompidou (1969–1974) and Valéry Giscard d'Estaing (1974–1981). Both were conservatives and supporters of Gaullist policies. But in 1981, economic problems resulting from a global oil crisis brought a Socialist victory. François Mitterrand became president with backing

Time Line

Year	Dates and Events
A.D. **1951**	**1953:** Soviet tanks suppress protesters in East Berlin
	1956: Soviets suppress prodemocracy movement in Hungary
	1956–1976: Soviets suppress repeated protests and strikes by Poles
	1958–1969: French president De Gaulle supports economic, technological advances, European unity
	1961: East Germany builds Berlin Wall to stop citizen flight to West Berlin
	1962: France grants independence to Algeria
	1962: Cuban Missile Crisis ends when Soviets remove missiles
	1968: Soviets suppress prodemocracy movement in Czechoslovakia
1960	**1972:** SALT I: U.S.-Soviet agreement to reduce nuclear weapons
1961	**1972:** Nixon visits Moscow; he and Brezhnev plan cooperation in technology, space exploration, trade
	1973: Britain joins European Economic Community
	1974–1981: Giscard d'Estaing, conservative and supporter of de Gaulle's policies, is president of France
	1979: SALT II: U.S.-Soviet agreement to limit long-range bombers, missiles
	1979: Soviets invade Afghanistan; U.S. refuses to sign SALT II
	1979–1990: As Conservative prime minister of Britain, Thatcher privatizes industry; reduces government spending; starts Falklands War
1970	**1981–1983:** Walesa, leader of Poland's Solidarity trade union, imprisoned
1971	**1985:** Gorbachev becomes Soviet leader; perestroika (economic reforms), glasnost (openness)
	1986: In Chernobyl, Ukraine, nuclear accident spreads radiation across Europe
	1988–1994: War between Muslim Azerbaijan and Christian Armenia
	1989: Gorbachev withdraws Soviet troops from Afghanistan
	1989–1990: Poles elect first non-Communist government in a former satellite, with Walesa as president
	1989–1991: Hungary, Czechoslovakia, Albania, Bulgaria, East Germany hold free elections; turn out Communists; Berlin Wall opened
1980	**1990:** Reunification of East and West Germany
1981	**1990–1998:** Yeltsin elected president of Russian Republic; survives attempted coup; holds new national election; new constitution approved; initiates policy of industrial privatization
	1991: 15 Soviet republics demand independence, form Commonwealth of Independent Nations (CIS); Gorbachev resigns; end of cold war
	1993: Czechoslovakia is divided into Czech Republic and Slovakia
	1993: START II: U.S.-CIS treaty to eliminate two-thirds of land-based missiles
	1994–1995: Chechnya fights for independence from Russia; peace settlement grants partial self-rule
1990	**1995:** France conducts underground test of nuclear weapons in South Pacific
1991	**1995:** Former Communist replaces Walesa as Polish president; government's successful free-market economy is model for East Europeans
	1997: Blair, head of Labour party, becomes prime minister of Britain; improves education, reforms health care system; forms closer ties with Europe
	1998: Schröder elected German chancellor
	1999: Czech Republic, Hungary, Poland become members of NATO
	1999: Yeltsin resigns as president of Russia, is succeeded by Putin
2000	**1999:** Chechnya's rebellion against Russia is crushed

from French Communists. A socialist prime minister served with him. Mitterrand held the presidency until 1995.

For a time, the Socialists increased government control of the economy. They added more tax-supported public services and utilities. They gave workers and unions more power in the workplace and increased social welfare benefits. However, in the face of high inflation and rising unemployment, the Socialists switched gears in 1984. They cut taxes sharply and reduced government spending.

Conservatives. When economic conditions remained poor, voters turned to the more conservative political parties. The conservatives had called for privatization of industry and deregulation of the economy. Growing resentment of foreign workers, especially those coming from the former French colonies in North Africa, also strengthened the conservatives. The Socialist-led government focused on strengthening France's ability to compete economically in world markets and on building European unity. However, the Socialists were unable to solve France's economic problems.

Socialists and conservatives alternated in power throughout the 1990s. Strikes plagued France in the 1990s. France was criticized for conducting underground tests of nuclear weapons in the Pacific in 1995.

Jacques Chirac, the Conservative mayor of Paris, became president in 1995. His efforts to strengthen the economy by raising taxes and reducing government spending on education aroused strong protests. As a result, Lionel Jospin, a Socialist leader, was elected prime minister in 1997. France began another period of divided government leadership.

Great Britain

After World War II, the Labour Party set government policy in Great Britain. To help people suffering from the economic deprivation caused by the war, it increased Britain's already extensive social services. The most important of these was the National Health Service, a system of socialized medicine. (The government paid the costs of medical services for the citizens.) The government also nationalized such vital economic enterprises as the Bank of England and the coal and steel industries.

Problems. During the 1960s and 1970s, Britain's economy declined. Its colonial markets were gone, and it had fallen behind other countries in manufacturing productivity. Britain hoped to find new markets by becoming part of the European Economic Community in 1973.

Britain also experienced conflicts within its population. Many members of the white majority resented the large influx of non-white immigrants. In the 1960s, the British government tried to reduce racial tensions by restricting immigration from commonwealth countries. Trouble in Ireland was another source of ethnic hostility. The struggle between Protestants and Catholics to control Northern Ireland led to acts of political terrorism in British cities.

Thatcher. In the 1980s, a Conservative government led by Prime Minister Margaret Thatcher reversed the Socialist policies of the Labour Party. Nationalized industries were returned to private ownership, and government spending was reduced. The influence and power of labor unions was also reduced. Thatcher pursued an aggressive foreign policy. Britain went to war with Argentina over control of the Falkland Islands. Gorbachev received Thatcher's support in his efforts to improve the Soviet economy and open up Soviet society. But Thatcher, along with U.S. President Ronald Reagan, opposed the spread of communism and pursued efforts to limit nuclear arms. Not since Queen Elizabeth I had England had such a strong and influential female leader.

Thatcher remained in power until 1990. She lost public support by persuading Parliament to pass an unpopular tax called the poll tax. When her opposition to integration with Europe was challenged by other party leaders, she resigned.

Rise of the Labour Party. In 1997, the Labour Party, headed by Tony Blair, won an overwhelming victory over the Conservative Party. It was a very different Labour Party than the one that had governed Britain in the years after World War II. Nationalization of industry was no longer part of its program. In fact, two of its most important campaign promises were to support business and to limit government spending. Its platform had been designed to appeal to ordinary people who were trying to do better financially. Some of the new prime minister's goals were to raise standards in British education, to reform the National Health Service, to help Scotland and Wales form new legislatures, and to establish closer ties with Europe. He also planned to put into effect measures to prevent crime, such as prohibiting handguns and increasing penalties against juvenile crim-

Margaret Thatcher after winning a third election as British prime minister

inals. Bringing about a permanent peace in Northern Ireland also claimed Blair's attention.

The last decades of the 20th century brought great changes all over the world. Many countries shook off foreign oppression, only to find themselves overwhelmed with internal conflict and economic difficulties. Others established themselves after a relatively short period of confusion and adjustment. The more stable Western nations also had economic difficulties that altered the political orientation of their populations. People in the United States and Western Europe became increasingly aware of how dependent they were on the well-being of small remote countries. Chapter 32 describes how events in developing nations in the late 20th century affected the rest of the world.

INFO CHECK

1. Explain why you AGREE or DISAGREE with the following: The reunification of Germany in 1990 gave rise to economic and social problems.

2. How did French government leadership become divided in the 1990s? Why did French voters do this?

3. Identify some of the differences between the Labour Party and the Conservative Party in Britain. State two goals of Prime Minister Tony Blair.

CHAPTER REVIEW

Multiple Choice

1. Leonid Brezhnev's policy of cooperation with the United States and Western Europe was called the

   1. Good Neighbor policy
   2. policy of appeasement
   3. policy of containment
   4. policy of détente.

2. The purpose of the SALT I and II treaties was

   1. to spread the use of natural seasonings
   2. agreement by the superpowers to protect the seas and the environment
   3. agreement by the superpowers to limit the use and number of nuclear weapons

   4. agreement by the superpowers to support the UN.

3. Two exceptions to the Communist Party's reliance on command economic principles took place at the beginning and the end of the Soviet Union. They were

   1. Lenin's NEP and Gorbachev's Perestroika policies
   2. Stalin's collectivization and Five-Year Plan
   3. Gorbachev's Glasnost and Trotsky's Red Guards
   4. Czar Alexander's Serf Emancipation and Czar Peter's Westernization.

4. In the 20th century, the major power in Eastern Europe changed its name

several times. It was first called Russia, next

1. the USSR and in 1990 the Republic of Russia
2. the USSR and today the Soviet Union
3. Soviet Russia and today the USSR
4. the Peoples' Republic and today the Commonwealth of Nations.

5. Yeltsin's attempt in Russia to move from a command economy to individual ownership of businesses, factories, and farms is known as

1. collectivization
2. Great Leap Forward
3. privatization
4. Five-Year Plan.

6. One of the biggest differences between a command economy and a market economy is that

1. jobs are not guaranteed and efficiency and profits are necessary
2. heavy industry is more important than consumer goods
3. success in the marketplace is controlled by the government
4. production decisions are based on government decisions not profit margins.

7. The Soviet leader who did most to end the cold war was

1. Joseph Stalin
2. Nikita Khrushchev
3. Leonid Brezhnev
4. Mikhail Gorbachev.

8. Economic growth of the reunited Germany has

1. speeded up, due to the joining of the two economically powerful sections
2. ceased, as each section fights for military control of the other

3. moved ahead, as East and West joined economic forces to control the world computer market
4. had problems because of East Germany's high poverty and unemployment levels.

9. When the Soviet Union fell apart, the non-Communist nations of the world were very concerned about

1. immigration of Communists into their nations
2. invasion of the former Soviet Union
3. the many nuclear weapons of the former Soviet Union
4. payment of debts owed to them by the former Soviet Union.

10. Political and economic changes in Eastern Europe, the collapse of the Soviet Union, and economic problems in the West have resulted in

1. a worldwide depression
2. rise of military dictatorships
3. more military alliances being formed among nations
4. nations realizing that events anywhere in the world can affect their economies.

11. Use the information contained in the map on page 718 and your knowledge of Global History and Geography to select the most accurate statement.

1. Georgia, Belarus, Ukraine, and Russia are now independent nations.
2. The Soviet Union continues to exist.
3. Russia has colonized Estonia and Latvia.
4. Mongolia, China, Sweden, and Denmark have joined in a military alliance with the former Soviet Union.

12. The photographs on pages 720 and 723 show that

    1. Communists continue to hold and control former Soviet satellites

    2. people in areas formerly controlled by Communists now may feel a greater freedom to assemble and speak their minds

    3. women continue to be oppressed in most nations of the former Communist bloc

    4. oppression, even by as strong an organization as the Communist party, cannot last long.

Thematic Essays

1. The last two Soviet leaders, Brezhnev and Gorbachev, tried to do three things: maintain Communist power, improve the economy, and achieve better relations with the West. *Task:* For each of the leaders, select one of the goals and describe the efforts made to reach that goal. Consider in your answer the Brezhnev Doctrine; Salt I and II; Afghanistan invasion; perestroika; glasnost; and the Commonwealth of Independent States.

2. The collapse of the Soviet Union allowed the reunification of the German nation. *Task:* Imagine that you are a reporter who, one year after the reunification, interviewed factory workers from the former East and West Germany. What positive and negative things would each tell you about the reunified Germany? Consider political, social, and economic issues and concerns in your answer.

Document-Based Questions

1. Gorbachev explained the need for reform:

    "The Soviet Union, the world's biggest producer of steel, raw materials, fuel and energy, has shortfalls in them due to wasteful or inefficient use. . . . Our rockets can find Halley's comet and fly to Venus with amazing accuracy, but side by side with these scientific and technological triumphs is an obvious lack of efficiency in using scientific achievements for economic needs, and many Soviet household appliances are of poor quality . . . the improvement in living standards was slowing down and there were difficulties in the supply of foodstuffs, housing, consumer goods and services. . . ."

    Explain why the Soviet economy was a mixture of success and failure.

2. Milovan Djilas, a Yugoslavian and a former Communist, wrote a book titled *The New Class* in 1957. He stated:

    "The Communist East European countries did not become satellites of the USSR because they benefited from it, but because they were too weak to prevent it. As soon as they become stronger, or as soon as favorable conditions are created, a yearning for independence and for protection of 'their own people' from Soviet hegemony [control] will rise among them. . . ."

    Have the words of this man proved to be correct? Explain.

3. From a 1990 New Year's Day address to the Czechoslovakian people by President Vaclav Havel:

    ". . . entire branches of industry are producing things for which there is no demand while we are short of the things we need. The state, which calls itself a state of workers, is humiliating and exploiting them instead. Our outmoded economy wastes energy, which we have in short supply. . . . We have spoiled our land, rivers and forests, inherited from our ancestors, and we have, today, the worst environment in the whole of Europe. . . ."

    Is President Havel praising or condemning Czechoslovakia's command economy in 1990? Explain your answer.

"WE INTERRUPT THIS BULLETIN FROM BULGARIA – WHICH INTERRUPTED THE BULLETIN FROM EAST BERLIN–WHICH INTERRUPTED THE BULLETINS FROM MOSCOW AND POLAND AND HUNGARY, TO BRING YOU THIS FROM CZECHOSLOVAKIA–"

NEWS ON THE HOUR OR LESS

©1989 HERBLOCK

4. Study the photo on page 723.
   What caused the fighting between the Russian and Chechen forces?

5. Study the cartoon.
   What events is the cartoonist trying to portray?

Document-Based Essay

Was the collapse of the Soviet Union caused by the efforts of the United States and its allies, or internal causes, or some combination of both? *Task:* Use the documents and your knowledge of Global History to present a factually supported answer. Explain why you AGREE or DISAGREE with the claim of some Americans that the United States won the cold war.

C H A P T E R
32

The Developing World in the Late 20th Century

Fifteen-year-old Juan looked down from his bedroom window. His heart sank as he watched his mother join the other women on their march to the Plaza de Mayo. They were demonstrating against the Argentine government's practice of kidnapping people suspected of opposing its policies. His father and older brother had disappeared just five months ago. Juan told himself over and over again that they were dead but couldn't help hoping for their return. It was too horrible to imagine the kind of deaths they must have suffered.

Juan was the only man left in his family now. He felt ashamed to think that his mother was exposing herself to danger while he stayed at home. The women of Argentina were brave. His mother would dare anything for herself. But Juan knew that it would break her heart if anything happened to him.

J uan's mother was one of many courageous women whose demonstrations called the world's attention to the inhumanity of Argentina's military regime. During the late 20th century, more and more ordinary people throughout the world began to take a stand against human rights abuses. The belief that governments must respect their citizens' rights motivated the people of developing countries to struggle against oppressive rulers.

POLITICAL UNREST IN LATIN AMERICA

Social and political problems have troubled most Latin American countries throughout their history. These problems—poverty, inequality, and political repression—are widespread in Latin America. In large part, they originated in the region's colonial past.

Economics

All too often the wealth of Latin American countries has depended on one or two cash crops or on a single mineral. The plantations and mines that produce these products are usually in the hands of a few wealthy, politically powerful landowners. This narrow concentration of power and ownership plus a sharp class division between Indians and people of European extraction have resulted in an unequal distribution of wealth, health services, and education. The rich landlords have often treated the people who work for them in much the same way that medieval landlords treated their serfs.

Most Latin American countries pushed industrialization after World War II. Unfortunately, industrialization has brought few benefits to the Latin American poor. Many factory workers are paid very low wages. They are forced to live in slums, called *favelas*, on the edge of cities. Their tiny houses, made of cardboard or tin, have no heat or running water. Because of crowding, lack of plumbing, and poor nutrition, the slum dwellers are susceptible to diseases, which they cannot afford to have treated.

U.S. Involvement

Resentment bred by such inequalities made revolutions common in Latin America in the 19th and 20th centuries. The United States has frequently intervened in Latin America's internal affairs to prevent foreign countries from taking advantage of its political disorder and gaining a foothold there. Fear of communism during the cold war prompted the United States to support a number of anti-Communist dictatorships. At the same time, U.S. leaders spoke out in favor of democracy and respect for human rights. Most recently, the United States has joined Latin American governments in their struggle against the growing power of drug *traficantes* (dealers).

Preventing the shipment of narcotics from Latin American laboratories and processing plants to criminal distributors in North America has been a major goal of the United States. U.S. military and law enforcement personnel have worked closely with their Latin American counterparts in the war against the *traficantes*. Although many Latin American governments have cooperated with their powerful northern neighbor, they have done so reluctantly. Their resentment of Yankee interference grew especially strong in the 1990s.

Military Influence

Throughout Latin America, the military has continued to wield immense political power. Venezuela experienced two military coup attempts in 1992. Rumors of takeovers swept other nations from time to time. The civilian government of Chile, elected in 1989, was unable to remove General Augusto Pinochet, the former dictator, from his post as commander-in-chief of the army until 1998. In Uruguay, Bolivia, and Paraguay, high-ranking military officers have repeatedly warned civilian governments not to investigate past human rights abuses. In all cases, the growth of democracy occurred only when the determination of the people for more political power was stronger than the determination of military leaders to retain their special status.

Argentina

Perón. Juan Perón, an army colonel, was elected president of Argentina in 1946. The Roman Catholic Church, industrial workers, and city residents were his main supporters. Once in office, Perón was able to assume dictatorial power by increasing his popularity. He did this by giving workers a stronger political voice and by increasing social benefits for the poor. Of great help in appealing to the poorer classes was his wife, Evita. Her projects won for her a deep devotion that continued until she died in 1952. Perón won over other parts of the population by appealing to nationalist feelings. His policies of rapid industrialization, reduction of foreign economic influence, and raising wages also appealed to large numbers. Those who opposed his policies, he silenced by repression.

Unfortunately, Perón had to change his popular economic policies. Like many Latin American countries, Argentina did not have a diversified economy. When world prices for Argentine wheat and beef dropped in the early 1950s, Perón had to freeze wages and cut spending on welfare programs. The resulting public dissatisfaction paved the way for a military takeover in 1955.

After Perón. In the following 18 years, Argentina had a series of weak leaders, none of whom was able to complete a full term of office. Perón, meanwhile, retained his influence over the Argentineans. They elected him president again in 1973. Perón no longer had a solid backing, however. His regime was weakened by conflicts among his followers and by his own failing health. (He died in 1974.) A troubled economy with an inflation rate of over 300 percent added to the unrest.

In 1976, the first of a series of generals took over the government of Argentina and ruled harshly. They sent out "death squads" to kill people they suspected of opposing them. The government did not take responsibility for these executions. Political dissidents, many of them young college students, simply disappeared. Their families were left in a state of permanent suspense, fearing the worst but hoping against hope for their relatives' return.

Mothers, calling themselves the Mothers of the Plaza de Mayo, began to demonstrate against the disappearance of their children. (Juan in the opening story witnessed one of these demonstrations.) They gathered in the Plaza de Mayo, the square in Buenos Aires on which the presidential palace is situated. There, with pictures of their missing sons and daughters, they bore witness to the cruelty of Argentina's rulers. By attracting the support of international human rights groups and the attention of foreign presses, the mothers' demonstrations did much to weaken the military regime.

Falkland Islands War. The period of tyranny finally ended in the spring of 1982. At that time, Great Britain and Argentina disputed the ownership of the Falkland (Malvinas) Islands off the coast of Argentina. The quarrel developed into a brief war that Britain won. Disgraced by this defeat, the ruling general gave up his office in mid-1982. The Argentine people took advantage of the lapse in military power and brought about a return to civilian rule in 1983.

Menem. In May 1989, Carlos Saúl Menem was elected president. Menem's top priority was improving Argentina's shaky economy. His financial plan, designed to reduce inflation and deregulate industry, was not immediately successful. But by 1995, Menem's reforms had brought about moderate improvement. These reforms included the privatization of government-owned industries, reduction of the national debt, and attracting foreign investments. Argentina's economic growth rate increased signficantly. On the strength of the improvement, he was reelected.

Cuba

Soviet aid to Cuba continued until the dissolution of the Soviet Union in 1991. When aid was cut off, the Cuban economy went into a sharp decline. A drop in trade with Eastern Europe made Cuba's problems worse. Serious shortages of fuel developed, limiting both industrial and agricultural production.

In 1993 and 1994, President Fidel Castro and the Communist Party leadership introduced limited free-market reforms similar to those in China. People were allowed to form small private businesses, legally possess foreign currency, and establish their own agricultural cooperatives. However, the reforms caused little immediate improvement in Cuba's economy.

Boat People. In August 1994, some 35,000 Cubans crowded into flimsy boats and headed for the United States. The Cuban government did nothing to stop them. After secret talks with Cuban representatives, President Bill Clinton announced in May 1995 that he was ending a 35-year-old policy of granting Cuban refugees free entry

Eleven Cuban boat people afloat off their island's coast in 1994

to the United States. The United States also toughened its long-standing embargo on Cuban trade in early 1996 after the Cuban air force downed two planes owned by U.S. citizens. In 1999, the United States eased the embargo somewhat. Because of continuing political and economic challenges, Cuba's future remains uncertain.

Haiti

In the 1990s, the Caribbean island nation of Haiti began to break free from years of oppression. A path to greater freedom opened in 1986, when unrest provoked by crop failure and famine put an end to 28 years of dictatorship under the Duvalier family. Four years of military rule followed.

Aristide. In 1990, a left-wing Catholic priest named Jean-Bertrand Aristide became the first democratically elected president of Haiti since 1950. Aristide ruled only briefly. His proposed democratic reforms alarmed both the military and Haiti's small, educated elite. They saw the changes as a threat to their power and wealth. In September 1991, the military arrested Aristide and expelled him from Haiti. A military group assumed power.

Embargo. Some U.S. officials distrusted Aristide for his leftist ideas. But the United States and the Organization of American States demanded that he be restored to power as Haiti's rightful leader. They placed an embargo on Haiti in October 1991 in the hope of unseating the military rulers. The embargo caused serious damage to Haiti's economy, the poorest in the Americas. The damage worsened after the United Nations put an embargo on oil and arms sales to Haiti in June 1993.

Even before the embargoes, the majority of Haitians had lived in poverty. They crowded into urban slums or scratched out meager livings on small farms. An upper class of less than 5 percent of the population controlled Haiti's limited wealth. The embargoes made life even harder for most Haitians. Unemployment and starvation spread. Despite the suffering brought by the embargo, many Haitians supported it, in the hope that it would bring back Aristide.

Refugees. Fearing rebellion, the army terrorized the slums and countryside. Thousands of Haitians attempted to flee to the United States by boat. Presidents Bush and Clinton refused to admit most of the boat people, saying that the Haitians were seeking economic gain rather than fleeing political oppression. The U.S. Coast Guard returned many boatloads to Haiti. It took others to "safe havens" in Latin America. Some critics claimed the U.S. policy was racially biased.

Negotiations. The United Nations tried to work out an agreement between the military and Aristide for a peaceful return of the president to power. A tentative agreement in 1993 did not hold up. In May 1994, UN sanctions were tightened.

The United States positioned Marines on ships near Haiti and announced they were practicing for an invasion. That news inspired mixed reactions among Haitians. Even Aristide's supporters were worried about U.S. military action. They recalled that U.S. soldiers had occupied Haiti from 1915 to 1934. To some Haitians, U.S. intervention smacked of old-fashioned imperialism. Others saw it as the only way to restore Aristide to power.

In July 1994, the UN Security Council authorized the use of force against Haiti. On the eve of an announced U.S. invasion, a team of U.S. negotiators persuaded the military to let U.S. troops land peacefully. General Raoul Cedras, the military dictator of Haiti, agreed to leave the country.

Return of Aristide. On October 15, 1994, President Aristide returned to Haiti. Cheering crowds greeted him. The president urged his supporters not to seek revenge against Haitian soldiers for their past acts. "No to violence, no to vengeance, yes to reconciliation," Aristide declared.

Rebuilding. Haiti began the long, slow process of rebuilding its economy and strengthening its democratic institutions. UN peacekeeping troops arrived, replacing most of the U.S. soldiers. Elections were held to choose a new parliament in June 1995. Voters went to the polls again six months later to elect Aristide's successor. (By law, Aristide could not succeed himself.) René Preval, a close associate of Aristide's, won. In 1997, Aristide formed a new political party and reentered Haitian politics. The road ahead seemed long and hard. When UN troops left the country in late 1997, Haiti was still suffering from extreme poverty and political instability. But the prospects for democracy in Haiti were brighter than they had been in a long time.

Nicaragua

In 1979, the Sandinista National Liberation Front overthrew the U.S.-supported military dictatorship that had ruled Nicaragua for 50 years. The United States and some Latin American countries opposed the Sandinistas because they were Marxists. The Sandinistas received aid from Cuba and sent weapons to revolutionary groups in neighboring countries. In the 1980s, the United States aided anti-Sandinista rebels, known as the Contras. Using weapons provided by the United States, the Contras fought to overthrow the Nicaraguan government. In 1989, President George Bush and the U.S. Congress agreed to limit Contra aid to medical supplies, food, and clothing. Sandinista rule ended peacefully in 1990 when Violetta Barrios de Chamorro, an opponent of the Sandinistas, became president of Nicaragua.

Nonetheless, Nicaragua remained a sharply divided society. Continuing poverty and unemployment caused strikes and political kidnappings. In an attempt to strengthen the nation's fragile democracy, President Chamorro and the often hostile National Assembly agreed on constitutional changes in 1995. The changes strengthened the legislature at the expense of the presidency and barred Chamorro from running for reelection. A new president, Arnaldo Alíman Lacayo, took office in 1997 and set about improving the economy.

Guatemala

Another Central American country that has experienced interference from the United States for decades is Guatemala. In the 1950s, Guatemala had an elected president. When he nationalized the property of powerful U.S. companies and bought arms from a Communist country, U.S. agencies secretly backed an invasion. The invading force quickly overthrew the government.

From 1954 to 1986, a succession of Guatemalan military officers held power, with the support of the United States. Power often changed hands in military coups. Leftists organized a guerrilla army in the mountains and hills of rural Guatemala, demanding social reforms to aid the desperately poor peasants. The army responded with brutal repression. Many rural people fled across the Mexican border and spent years in refugee camps.

Democratic government returned in 1986 under a new constitution. But the war in the countryside went on, and civilian presidents had little control over the military. In 1993, an elected president tried to suspend constitutional rights. The military forced him to step down. A weak caretaker president took over but was replaced when Alvaro Enrique Arzú Irigoyen was elected in 1995. In December of the following year, the government signed a peace treaty with guerrilla rebels. After 36 years of civil war and 140,000 deaths, Guatemala looked forward to peace and stability.

Meanwhile, U.S.–Guatemalan relations suffered a setback with revelations about secret, illegal operations. A U.S. Congressman revealed that the U.S. Central Intelligence Agency had made payoffs to Guatemalan military officials. One of these officials was alleged to have been involved in the slayings of an American and of a guerrilla leader married to an American.

Mexico

In 1993, Mexico drew closer to its northern neighbors (Canada and the United States) by entering into the North American Free Trade Agreement (NAFTA). But tension continued between officials of the U.S. Drug Enforcement Agency (DEA) and Mexican security forces. The U.S. officials, who were trying to stop the flow of drugs across the Mexican border, were frustrated to see Mexican *traficantes* living in open luxury in their own country.

Carlos Salinas de Gortari, Mexico's president from 1988 to 1994, cooperated with U.S. officials in their war on drugs. Salinas declared that drug trafficking should be regarded as a threat to national security. He created military and police organizations to carry out antinarcotics operations.

Under Salinas, Mexican agents worked closely with U.S. officials. Mexican agents destroyed crops of marijuana and opium poppies. They intercepted drugs being smuggled from South America through Mexico to the United States. However, drug lords sometimes were able to bribe Mexico's antidrug officials. U.S. agents suggested that corruption reached into high levels of the Mexican government. In 1998, ex-President Salinas' brother, a high-ranking police official, was accused of cooperating with *traficantes*.

Some Mexicans objected to U.S. involvement in their country's internal affairs. Others worried that the military would become too powerful as a result of the antidrug campaign.

Ernesto Zedillo, who succeeded Salinas in 1994, continued the policy of close cooperation with the United States. He had little choice. Mexico's economy took a sharp nose-dive soon after President Zedillo took office. President Clinton offered him a multibillion-dollar rescue package if he cooperated more closely in the drug war.

Zedillo also had to deal with a challenge from leftist rebels who launched a guerrilla war in the southern state of Chiapas in 1994. The rebels called themselves Zapatistas (after the early 20th-century Mexican revolutionary Emiliano Zapata). The government persuaded the Zapatistas to suspend military operations and enter into peace talks. Nonetheless, the two sides remained far apart.

INFO CHECK

1. Identify the Latin American country led by each of the following: Juan Perón, Carlos Saúl Menem, Fidel Castro, Jean-Bertrand Aristide, Ernesto Zedillo.

2. Which of the above leaders do you regard as most admirable? Which do you regard as least admirable? Give reasons for your choices.

3. Name two Latin American countries that experienced revolutionary movements in the 1990s. Which revolution was most successful in achieving its goals? Why do you think so?

POST-COLD WAR "HOT SPOTS"

The rivalry of the two superpowers in the cold war had blinded the world to the problems of smaller nations. Some, such as North Korea, felt isolated from the rest of the world. In other nations, governments stirred up ethnic and racial problems instead of solving them. The needs of the officials became more important than the needs of the citizens. The resulting troubles caused instability in many regions. The UN and the United States feared that the instability in certain areas might affect world peace.

North Korea

Despite aid from China, the economic development of the Democratic People's Republic of Korea was limited. The country became largely self-sufficient in food production. Some 36 percent of the labor force is engaged in agriculture, and rice is the major crop. Because North Korea remains committed to continuing the Communist struggle against Western capitalism, its economic resources have been largely directed toward military production. In the 1990s, a severe fuel shortage reduced industrial and agricultural output, hampered fishing, and caused a serious shortage of food. The shortages became especially severe in the late 1990s. The cause was drought and other weather-related problems.

North Korean farmers, beset by famine and poverty, working the soil

For North Korea's first 46 years, supreme power was in the hands of Communist Party leader, Kim Il Sung. Kim died in July 1994 at the age of 82. His son, Kim Jong Il, who had been commander of North Korea's military forces, took his place. Thus, North Korea became the world's first Communist dynasty.

The country kept to itself. It did not encourage visitors. Except for China and Russia, few other countries knew much about life in North Korea.

Nuclear Program. During the 1990s, North Korea's nuclear program alarmed both Western and Asian governments. A crisis erupted in 1993, when North Korea rejected international demands for inspection of its nuclear power facilities and announced its intention to withdraw from the 1968 Nuclear Nonproliferation Treaty. That agreement has been the mainstay of efforts to prevent the spread of nuclear weapons. North Korea was the first nation to threaten to withdraw from the treaty.

After U.S. warnings of harsh actions if North Korea went ahead with its plans, North Korea and the United States reached an agreement in October 1994. North Korea promised to freeze its nuclear weapons development program and then shut it down. In return, the United States promised to arrange more than $4 billion in energy

NORTH KOREA'S DANGEROUS MILITARY

In August 1998, North Korea fired a ballistic missile across Japan. The missile firing indicated that North Korea had greatly increased the range of its missiles. An older missile could reach only part of Japan. The new missile has the capability to reach all of Japan with either nuclear or chemical warheads. Obviously, the Japanese felt threatened by the test. The event also caused serious global concern about the role of North Korea in the international trade in weapons of mass destruction.

North Korea's missile-development program has attracted much attention because that nation is suspected of possessing a few nuclear weapons. North Korea is also believed to have large quantities of chemical weapons, which are easy to deliver by missile. Some experts believed that the 1998 firing of the missile over Japan was an advertisement to the Middle East and other developing countries shopping for cheap, effective weapons. Ballistic missiles remained the only North Korean product that could be sold for foreign currency.

In addition to its missile-development program, North Korea's military power worries its Asian neighbors and other nations. With a one-million-member army, the economically underdeveloped Communist nation has one of the largest military forces in the world. Added to its huge army is an air force of approximately 50,000 members, a navy of close to 40,000, and local militia forces with nearly 5 million members. Although the militia members serve part time, the total number of people engaged in military service represents a large portion of North Korea's population of approximately 22 million in the late 1990s.

Military service in North Korea is compulsory for men who are 20 to 25 years of age. Those who are drafted into the army must serve five to eight years. The air force requires three to four years of service, and members of the navy are required to serve for five to ten years. Women join the armed forces as volunteers.

The bulk of North Korea's huge army has been concentrated in the Demilitarized Zone. This zone has marked the border with South Korea since the end of the Korean War (1950–1953). Military experts agree that any hostile move by the Communist forces would be very difficult and costly to contain. For this reason, the South Korean military is kept at readiness by regular joint training exercises with U.S. forces.

Periodic actions by the North Korean military create tensions in the region. In 1998, for example, a small submarine, used by the North Koreans for spy missions, ran aground in South Korea. Its crew committed suicide rather than be taken into custody and questioned by South Korean authorities. The missile firing across Japan in the same year was regarded by many Japanese analysts as a political statement. The North Korean government had demonstrated that its military capabilities were continuing to advance.

- Write a newspaper article to accompany the following headline: *Asians Fear North Korean Military Power.*

assistance for North Korea, mainly from Japan and South Korea. Included in the assistance would be two nuclear reactors for producing electricity. The United States said that these would be so-called light-water reactors. Their by-products would be hard to use in a nuclear weapons program. Prior to the agreement, North Korea had been building a type of nuclear reactor with by-products that would be relatively easy to use in weapons. Work on the new reactors began in 1997.

Negotiations on how to carry out the nuclear agreement began late in 1994, but quickly ran into problems. New disputes between North and South Korea have delayed a final agreement.

South Korea

For years after the Korean War, South Korea was a dictatorship. It became a police state under the control of a military group. In 1987, weeks of protest by middle-class workers, businesspeople, and students against authoritarian rule resulted in the election of a president by direct popular vote. Since 1990, South Korea has evolved toward a relatively stable state in which two parties compete for votes.

Economic Boom and Downturn. In contrast to North Korea, South Korea experienced extensive economic growth. Textiles and automobiles were the major industries. Some 79 percent of the labor force is engaged in manufacturing and service industries. Since World War II, the economy has been controlled by *chaebol*, large family-run business organizations with great political influence.

In October 1997, the financial crisis that had earlier hit Southeast Asian countries started to affect South Korea's economy. Corporations began to fail and South Korea's currency, the *won*, fell sharply in value. South Korea was forced to request an emergency economic rescue package from the International Monetary Fund (IMF). Expressing their dissatisfaction with the economic crisis, South Koreans elected Kim Dae Jung as president in 1997. Kim is a former dissident and political prisoner. He began the task of restoring international confidence in the South Korean economy.

Reunification on Hold. In 1972, South and North Korea agreed on a common goal of reunifying their two nations by peaceful means. They made little progress toward that goal until 1985, when they reached an agreement to discuss economic issues. The two countries opened trade relations, and South Korea began investing in North Korea. In 1991, North and South Korea signed a non-aggression treaty that formally ended the Korean War. Three years later, the two Koreas set a date for the first summit meeting between their two leaders. However, North Korean dictator Kim Il Sung died and the meeting was put off indefinitely. The Korean peninsula remained a hot spot throughout the 1990s.

Congo (Formerly Zaire)

Sewage flowed in open ditches through the streets of Congo's capital, Kinshasa. In the countryside, highways were so full of potholes that trucks moved only at a crawl. Hospitals lacked medicines. The government barely functioned.

In the first half of the 1990s, Congo was a case study in disintegration. Billionaire President Mobutu Sese Seko was widely denounced as a money-hungry dictator. Observers blamed his repressive policies for military mutinies, destructive riots, and economic ruin. At a time when other African nations were struggling to turn dictatorships into democracies, Congo seemed lost in a time warp.

Background. Congo has known many hardships since the late 1800s. Under Belgian control from 1885 to 1960, the country was known as the Belgian Congo. The Belgian authorities treated the people cruelly and did little to prepare them for self-government. As a result, when Belgium granted independence in 1960, the new nation (called Congo-Kinshasa) plunged into political chaos.

Almost at once the mineral-rich province of Katanga (now called Shaba) attempted to secede. The Congo-Kinshasa government asked the United Nations to help it keep the country united. When the UN sent troops to help end the provincial rebellion, fighting broke out between UN forces and the Katanga army. Not until 1963 did Katanga come under the control of the Congolese central government. (It tried unsuccessfully to break away again in the 1970s.)

Civil War. During the civil war, a young nationalist named Patrice Lumumba was prime minister of the Congo. In order to unite the Congo, he took steps to win back the Katanga province. First he asked the UN for help. Dissatisfied with the way in which the UN proposed to help him, he persuaded the Soviet Union to strengthen his army. Western anti-Communist powers felt threatened by this association with the Soviet Union. They criticized Lumumba and backed one of his rivals. In 1961, political rivals imprisoned Lumumba and assassinated him.

Although a new government was formed in 1964, continuing civil strife made this country one of Africa's bloodiest battlegrounds. Taking advantage of the disorder, an ambitious young army general named Joseph Mobutu seized power in 1965. He later Africanized his name to Mobutu Sese Seko. Mobutu changed the country's name to Zaire in 1971. He ruled until 1997.

Natural Resources. Congo has been one of the world's major producers of diamonds, copper, and cobalt. With its plentiful rainfall and good soil, the country is suitable for growing a variety of crops. Its forests are full of valuable timber, and its rivers are good for generating hydroelectric power. Unfortunately, much of Congo's modern industry was destroyed by government-sponsored arson and looting in 1991 and 1993. Exports dropped drastically. Prices rose 5,000 percent in just one year. As a result, the people became increasingly poor. Corrupt and inefficient government also contributed to the decline in the nation's standard of living.

Rule of Mobutu. Mobutu's personal wealth was legendary. His opponents say that control of the state-owned diamond, copper, and cobalt mines enabled Mobutu to divert billions of dollars for his own use. During the 1970s and 1980s, the rest of the world did not seem to mind. The United States, France, and other Western nations found Mobutu a useful tool in the cold war politics of Africa. But as the cold war drew to an end, Western nations began pressing for economic reforms and democratization.

In 1990, Mobutu responded to this pressure by allowing new political parties to be created in opposition to his own party. Dozens of new parties sprang up. One opposition leader tried to take control of the government away from Mobutu.

But Mobutu held the main power centers. In particular, he controlled the army and other security forces. They were composed mainly of people from Mobutu's native province. The president used the security forces to stir up trouble among Congo's major ethnic groups, in a policy of "divide and rule." Support for Mobutu seemed weak. But no one else gathered enough power to unseat him.

Kabila Takes Over. Bloodshed between the Hutus and Tutsis in Rwanda spilled over into Congo in 1994. The Congo army became

Rwandan refugees sheltering in a camp in Congo

involved in the conflict. This encouraged a group of Congo rebels led by a Marxist general named Laurent Kabila to rise up against Mobutu's government. Mobutu's army could not hold off the rebel army, which was receiving aid from Rwanda, Uganda, and Angola.

General Kabila and his army took over Congo in May 1997. Mobutu fled to Morocco and died later that year. The new rulers changed its name to the Democratic Republic of the Congo. Shortly after becoming president, Kabila banned political parties and public demonstrations. In 1998, rebels helped by Rwanda and Uganda challenged Kabila's leadership. By 1999, aided by Angola, Namibia, and Zimbabwe, he had put down the revolt. Kabila's relations with world powers remained uneasy.

China

During the 1990s, China's economy moved toward a type of free-market system. But its government continued to rule repressively. Censorship and propaganda discouraged new ideas. The threat of prison and labor camps kept opposition quiet.

Continued Repression. The 1989 massacre in Tiananmen Square had provoked international outrage. Nevertheless, Deng Xiaoping, China's senior leader, tightened control over cultural and media activities. The Communist Party officials wanted to discourage further demands for democracy. Deng also allowed the torture of political suspects until they confessed and informed on their associates. Deng's policies reflected his belief that the people would continue to accept Communist rule as long as their standard of living kept rising and the country's economic growth persisted.

MFN Status. In May 1993, President Bill Clinton signed an executive order stating the improvements that he wanted China to make in the area of human rights before he would renew its trade benefits. Since the 1970s, China has enjoyed "most favored nation" (MFN) status. This has allowed China to send its products to the United States at the lowest available tariff. MFN status must be renewed annually.

Clinton's order called for China to stop using prison labor to make goods exported to the United States. It also required China to allow certain dissidents (opposition leaders) to leave the country.

The presidential order touched off a debate within the administration and in Congress. Some leaders wanted the president to stand by his executive order. Others argued that withdrawal of China's trade benefits would cost thousands of American jobs and billions of dollars in contracts. They claimed that trade had become an important instrument for opening up Chinese society and for promoting the rule of law and freedom of movement in that country. Trade was also viewed as a means of encouraging the Chinese government to allow

Time Line

Year	Dates and Events

A.D.
1941

1946: Perón elected president of Argentina, assumes dictatorial power
1955: Military takeover of Argentina after Perón
1960–1965: Congo civil war between Katanga and central government
1961: Imprisonment and murder of Congo president Lumumba
1965–1997: Mobutu seizes power in Congo (Zaire); overthrown by Kabila
1976–1983: Harsh military dictatorships subject Argentines to "death squad" terrorism; Britain wins Falklands War; military dictator steps down; civilian rule returns

1950

1979: Sandinistas overthrow U.S.-supported military dictatorship in Nicaragua

1951

1980s: U.S. aids Nicaraguan Contras with weapons, supplies in fight against Marxist Sandinistas
1986–1990: Haitians end dictatorship of Duvalier; military junta takes over
1988–1994: Mexico and U.S. wage war on Mexican drug trafficking
1989: Massacre in Tiananmen Square provokes international outrage
1990s: North Korean economy hurt by fuel shortage, drought
1990s: Chinese government remains repressive; economy gradually transformed into free-market system

1960

1990: Sandinista opponent Chamorro becomes president of Nicaragua after peaceful election

1961

1990–1991: Aristide elected president of Haiti; is expelled by military junta
1991: Collapse of Soviet Union ends aid to Cuba
1991–1994: North and South Korea sign treaty ending Korean War; reunification talks put off indefinitely
1993: U.S.-supported dictator in Guatemala replaced by democratic government
1993: Clinton holds up U.S. renewal of China's MFN trade status pending human rights reforms

1970

1993: North Korea agrees to freeze nuclear weapons program

1971

1993: Mexico joins U.S. and Canada as member of NAFTA
1993–1994: Castro's government begins free-market reforms in Cuba; no economic improvement
1994: Under pressure from U.S. officials, Clinton renews China's MFN status unconditionally
1994: North Korea's Communist leader Kim Il Sung dies, is succeeded by son Kim Jong Il

1980

1994: Collapsing Mexican economy rescued by huge U.S. loan

1981

1994: 35,000 Cuban boat people refused free entry into U.S.
1994: UN authorizes use of power against Haiti; U.S. troops land peacefully; Aristide reclaims presidency
1994–1995: Haitian boat people returned by U.S. to Haiti or "safe havens" in Latin America
1995: Menem reelected Argentina's president on strength of economic reforms, improved economy

1990

1995–1996: Temporary cease-fire in Guatemala, followed by UN-supervised peace accords

1991

1996: Cuba shoots down two private U.S. planes; U.S. tightens trade embargo on Cuba
1997: China reclaims Hong Kong; promises to retain free-market economy
1997: New Chinese president Jiang visits U.S. to improve economic relations; warns U.S. not to interfere in internal Chinese affairs
1997: Southeast Asian financial crisis hits South Korea; nation is forced to request rescue by IMF

2000

1998: Pinochet steps down as Chilean army's commander-in-chief

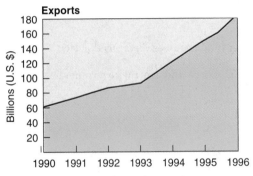

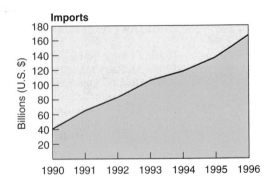

China's Foreign Trade in the 1990s

its citizens to acquire a wide variety of products, including satellite dishes and foreign newspapers.

In May 1994, President Clinton decided unconditionally to renew China's MFN status. U.S.-Chinese relations remained uneasy, especially after the fall of 1996, when the Chinese sentenced a young dissident to long-term imprisonment for his democratic views.

Jiang's Visit to the United States. By 1997, relations between China and the United States had improved somewhat. Deng died in February. A new president, Jiang Zemin, continued Deng's economic policies and curbs on human rights. But he wanted to have good relations with the United States for economic reasons. Jiang visited the United States in October. It was the first official visit by a Chinese leader since 1985.

Jiang and Clinton pledged to discuss differences on human rights. He claimed that China had already begun to control the export of nuclear and nuclear-related materials and would strengthen these controls in upcoming years. He also objected to U.S. interference in the internal affairs of China.

While Jiang was in the United States, U.S. officials told him that President Clinton would be unable to return the visit in 1998 if leading political dissidents were still in prison. In November 1997, the Chinese released Wei Jingsheng, one of China's most influential dissidents. Clinton did visit China in June 1998. In televised speeches, he urged more liberal human rights policies. He also renewed China's MFN status before the visit. Many in the United States had urged him not to do so.

Military. China's military policies also disturbed U.S. leaders. Determined to be the dominant military power in East Asia, China used some of its new wealth to build up its naval and air forces. U.S. strategists saw the Chinese buildup as a challenge to U.S. and Japanese interests in the region. The United States was one of many nations that protested Chinese underground nuclear tests in the mid-1990s.

Population Curbs. China's population-control policies also drew U.S. protests. With about 1.2 billion people, China has the largest population of any country in the world. The government strongly encourages only one child per couple, hoping to bring about a population decline in the 21st century. The United States denounced China's use of harsh methods to enforce birth control, including compulsory sterilization, forced abortions, and fines for unauthorized pregnancies.

Under a so-called responsibility system, local officials were held accountable for meeting family planning targets in their districts. As a result, the birthrate dropped drastically. Government planners achieved goals they had not expected to reach until the year 2010.

Developments in Hong Kong and Taiwan

On July 1, 1997, Hong Kong transferred from British to Chinese rule. China promised to let Hong Kong retain its free-market economy for 50 years but imposed other changes. Hong Kong's Legislative Council was replaced by a Provincial Legislature. This body has placed limits on opposition to the Chinese government and reduced the number of political candidates in elections.

Hong Kong's previously healthy economy was affected by the financial crisis that hit Asia in July 1997. The Chinese government announced that Hong Kong was responsible for managing its own economy. It did, however, reassure its new province that China's bank, the People's Bank, would help if necessary.

Raising of the Chinese flag in Hong Kong, 1997

In the new century, the people of Taiwan distanced themselves from both Communist China and the Nationalist Chinese. In March, 2000, they elected Chen Shiu-bian as president in defiance of China's threats of war should they do so. Chen's Democratic Progressive Party had long advocated independence from China. After his victory, Chen soft-pedaled his stance on independence, and China's threats subsided.

In Unit VII, the narrative described how many countries moved from dictatorships to more democratic governments. At the end of the 20th century, many of these countries were still struggling to establish stable governments and economies. Unit VIII focuses on how conditions in one region can influence all other parts of the world. Chapter 33 describes global economic trends. Chapter 34 covers efforts to make the world a more secure place. Chapter 35 discusses advances in technology, environmental protection, and women's rights.

INFO CHECK

1. Explain why you AGREE or DISAGREE with the following: The United States should not have interfered with North Korea's nuclear development program.

2. Why have U.S. leaders been concerned about China's human rights and military policies in the 1980s and 1990s? Do you think Chinese President Jiang Zemin was right to object to U.S. interference in China's internal affairs in 1997? Why or why not?

3. If you were a citizen of Hong Kong, would you approve or disapprove of the transfer from British to Chinese rule in July 1997? Give reasons for your answer.

CHAPTER REVIEW

Multiple Choice

1. Latin America's economic problems were often caused by

   1. too much dependence on only one or two cash crops
   2. bad weather conditions that destroyed the crops
   3. a worldwide depression
   4. high import tariffs on its products.

2. Many Latin Americans of Indian descent do not benefit from their nations' wealth because

   1. their nations are all very poor and lack natural resources
   2. the Indians do not care to live in Western-style houses
   3. wealth and political power are limited to the military and the descendants of the Spanish
   4. Indians live so far from the capital that their governments do not know where they are.

3. Latin Americans still resent or are fearful of the U.S. government and its actions because

1. Americans polluted the waters of the Amazon River

2. past U.S. governments intervened in the running of many Latin American countries

3. U.S. businesspeople are still being given unfair trading advantages in Latin America

4. American missionaries are transported in U.S. military airplanes.

4. The Plaza de Mayo in Argentina and Tiananmen Square in China are famous because they are places where

1. tourists get information

2. famous churches are found

3. fast-food restaurants can be found

4. human rights demonstrations were held.

5. Military rule in Argentina ended in 1982, after the defeat of the military in the brief, but costly, war with Great Britain. The war was fought over control of

1. the Panama Canal

2. the Falkland (Malvinas) Islands

3. Easter Island

4. Jamaica.

6. The United States has supported military dictatorships in Latin America because they

1. were anti-Communist governments

2. sent troops to fight in the Persian Gulf War

3. built advanced military equipment for the United States

4. loaned the United States money to pay off foreign debts.

7. North Korea is a "hot spot" because of

1. the unrest of the people

2. its wish to reunite with South Korea

3. its development of nuclear weapons

4. its self-imposed isolation.

8. Mobutu Sese Seko, the ruler of Congo (then Zaire), was noted for

1. his ability to accumulate a personal fortune

2. stirring up ethnic unrest

3. no reason presented in the chapter

4. turning over power to Laurent Kabila.

9. Restoring Aristide as president of Haiti was important in order to show

1. Cuba's power in the Caribbean

2. that democratically elected officials should be allowed to hold office

3. the weakness of the OAS

4. that Haiti was a major Caribbean country.

10. The Chinese allowed the people of Hong Kong to keep their

1. own government for 50 years

2. free-market economy for 50 years

3. British governor for 50 years

4. tax-free status for 50 years.

11. Which of the following is the best generalization to be made about events on the time line on page 755?

1. Efforts at democratic reform have collapsed in Latin America but show signs of progress in Asia.

2. The global economy has steadily improved since 1946.

3. The period represented has seen a range of events that include conflict, cooperation, democracy, and repression.

4. The United States has played a diminished role in global affairs.

12. The photograph of North Korean farmers on page 749 shows us that

1. the Communist regime has industrialized agriculture in North Korea
2. North Korean farmers face famine because of their refusal to work under communism
3. weather-related problems and a fuel shortage have caused hardships for North Korean farmers
4. North Korean farmers refuse to cooperate with one another.

Thematic Essays

1. The cold war affected almost all parts of the world. *Task:* Describe how the rivalry between the United States and the Soviet Union affected Central American countries. Consider social, political, economic, and military policies in your answer.

2. The Korean peninsula continues to be a focus of world concern. *Task:* State the economic and strategic reasons in your answer.

Document-Based Questions

Use your knowledge of Global History and Geography and the documents to answer the questions.

1. Former Prime Minister Nehru of India explaining his nation's foreign policy in 1955:

   ". . . As we all know, Asia is no longer passive today; it was passive enough in the past. It is no longer a submissive Asia; it has tolerated submissiveness too long. The Asia of today is dynamic. . . ."

   What do you think is meant by the repeated reference to Asia no longer "being submissive"?

2. From a 1963 report by A.M. Rosenthal, a reporter from *The New York Times*, regarding the changing role of the Japanese emperor and Japan.

   "Japan set about recasting the image of the emperor to fit her new needs. A nation that had died economically now ranks as the fourth industrial power in the world. . . . Japan, the defeated enemy is eagerly called one of the three pillars of the free world. . . . There is a part of Japan that reaches out to the emperor in memory of what he used to be. . . ."

   Why are the Japanese proud of the post-World War II development of their country?

3. Study the photo on page 757.
   Why is the flag ceremony representing the end of British control of Hong Kong a sign of changing relations between China and the West?

4. Study the photo on page 744.
   How many "boat people" fled Cuba in 1994? Why did they do so?

Document-Based Essay

Great changes occurred in the "developing" world in the late 20th century. *Task:* List three (3) developing nations. For each, identify a political or economic change that occurred in the 1990s.

UNIT REVIEW

Thematic Essays

1. After winning their struggle against European imperialism, many former colonies continued to have widespread fighting in their homelands. *Task:* Select two nations, each from a different region treated in this era. Discuss the reasons peace and governmental stability have not occurred in each country. Consider in your answer reli-

gious, tribal, racial, or political factors.

2. Economics played a major role in 20th-century politics. Economic factors greatly affected the struggle between the Soviet Union and the Western powers over developing countries. They contributed to the successful revolt of satellite countries against the Soviet Union. *Task:* Identify and explain those economic factors in a well-thought-out essay. Consider why developing countries were attracted to a command economy and why Eastern European countries wished to change to a free-market economic system.

Document-Based Questions

Use readings from the chapters and your knowledge of Global History and Geography to answer the questions.

1. Study the cartoon on page 716. Why were the countries of the world so afraid of nuclear weapons?

2. Study a map of North America and the Caribbean. Why would the United States be afraid of Soviet missiles in Cuba?

3. Winston Churchill, in a speech given at Westminster College in Fulton, Missouri, on March 1946, said

"... From Stettin in the Baltic to Trieste in the Adriatic, an iron curtain has descended across the Continent. Behind that line lie all the capitals of the ancient states of Central and Eastern Europe ... all those famous cities and their populations lie in what I must call the Soviet sphere. ..."

What was happening in Eastern and Central Europe behind the "iron curtain"?

4. Ayatollah Ruhollah Khomeini gave a speech titled *Message to the Pilgrims* on September 13, 1980, in Teheran, Iran. In it, he said:

"... Muslims who are now sitting next to the House of God, engaged in prayer! Pray for those who are resisting America and other superpowers, and understand that we are not fighting against Iraq. The people of Iraq support our Islamic revolution; our quarrel is with America, and it is America whose hand can be seen emerging from the sleeve of the Iraqi government.

According to the Ayatollah, who are the Iranians fighting? Why are the Iraqis and Iranians fighting if the Iraqi people support the Islamic revolution?

Document-Based Essay

Identify two nonmilitary 20th-century occurrences that you believe were turning points in Global History. *Task:* Discuss these changes. Consider for inclusion religion, nationalism, colonialism, economics, technology, and the competition between different political systems.

UNIT VIII

Global Connections and Interactions

C H A P T E R

33

Global Economic Trends

Sighing, Lizaveta left the electronics store in Moscow empty-handed. She had wanted to buy so many things. But she'd settle for a radio and headphones. Everyone in America had one. Kids there, she thought, strolled around the streets as if in their own livingrooms. They not only listened to music, but they also talked to friends on their cellular phones, watched their favorite shows on tiny TV sets, and consulted pocket organizers to see if they had any dates. And she couldn't even afford a simple radio.

Lizaveta remembered her father's sad smile when she had asked him to buy her one. "Too expensive," he had said. "Under communism, I didn't have much money, but things were cheap. Of course, then they weren't selling American-made headsets. I could have bought you a nice toy tractor, though. Now we have many things in stores, but no money to buy them."

Lizaveta laughed and shrugged. Even if consumer goods were expensive, at least they were available now. And things would change. She was young and very smart. Last term, she'd placed at the top of her class in computer programming. In a few years, she'd be designing software. She might even own her own business one day, selling computer games to Americans. Then she could buy whatever she liked. She wondered whether her father longed for a special electronic gadget. She'd find out and one day surprise him with it.

This girl is experiencing some of the frustration the new economic system is causing Russians and others who once lived under Communist regimes. Under communism, a command economy, manufacturers did not make many consumer goods, such as televisions, radios, and computers. They turned out weapons and farm machinery instead. The consumer goods that were available, however, were priced so that most people could afford them.

Now that former Soviet Union and Eastern European countries are trading with the West, their stores carry a wide range of consumer goods. Unfortunately, not everyone can afford them. Wages are lower and jobs less secure than they used to be. Eastern European products do not sell as well as Western products. Often, factories have to close down, leaving their employees without work. Many people long for the security they had known under communism. Some, however, are beginning to realize that in a free market economy (like the capitalist countries), they can open their own businesses. Like Lizaveta, they are looking forward to the time when they can benefit from the new economic order that is emerging in the world.

GROWTH OF A NEW ECONOMIC ORDER IN THE 1990s

The trend toward this new economic order started when the countries in Asia, Latin America, and Africa decided to industrialize.

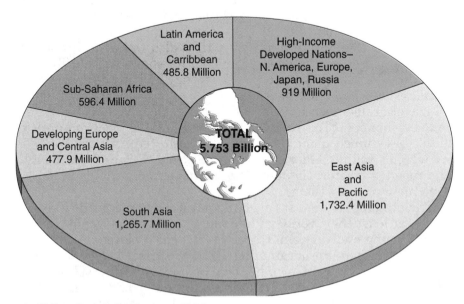

World Population, by Region   1996
(millions of people)

These countries became known as the Third World or the developing nations.

The leaders of some developing countries adopted command economies. They felt that government-controlled decision making would speed up the process of industrialization. Then, too, Communist countries gave financial and military aid to encourage them to do so. The developing countries also sold their goods profitably to Communist nations.

The new economic order took on shape when the Soviet Union and Eastern Europe abandoned communism for free-market economies in the late 1980s and early 1990s. The changeover did not always go smoothly. They could no longer give financial and trade support to developing countries. These countries soon decided to improve their economies by adopting the free-market capitalistic system.

Integration of Developing Nations Into the Global Economy

The industrialized nations encouraged Communist countries to adopt free-market economies. Unfortunately, when the change took place, the industrialized nations were having economic problems of their own. Although they continued to be the most prosperous nations in the world, the growth rates of their economies declined in the early 1990s. Britain, the United States, and Canada showed little growth. In France, unemployment soared. Japan's economy was weaker than it had been in the previous 40 years. As a group, the industrial countries had growth rates that stayed in the range of 2 to 3 percent per year.

New Competitors in the World Market

Many leaders of industrialized countries began to realize that their countries' high unemployment had a more serious cause than an economic slump. They began to see the developing nations as rivals in the world market. With more than 3 billion inhabitants hungry for a better life, new free-market countries stepped up their competition with the industrialized nations. Developing nations in Asia, for example, began to rival Japan. The *Chinese Economic Area* (CEA), which includes China, Hong Kong, and Taiwan, dramatically increased its exports. It moved from eleventh place in world trade ranking in 1973 to fifth place in 1990. It rose even higher in the mid-1990s.

Eastern Europe was slow to win a place in the world market. As time went on, however, some Eastern European countries began to export more goods to Western Europe. Poland, Hungary, the Czech Republic, and Slovakia were the quickest to move toward free-market economies and to build trade with the West. Those nations agreed to create a free trade area by 1999.

In 1992, they signed trade agreements with the *European Union*

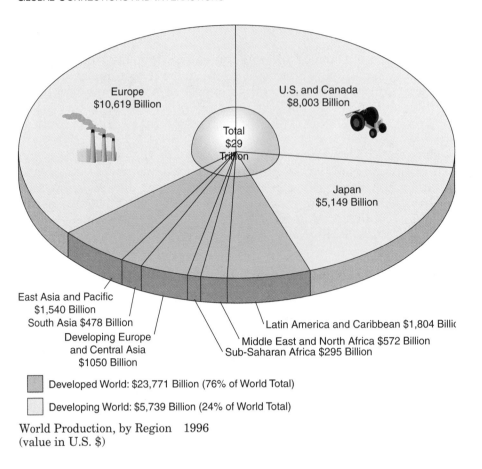

Developed World: $23,771 Billion (76% of World Total)

Developing World: $5,739 Billion (24% of World Total)

World Production, by Region   1996
(value in U.S. $)

(EU). The EU is a group of Western European nations that cooperate economically with one another. About 40 percent of Eastern European exports to the EU nations, such as food, textiles, steel, and chemicals, competed with similar Western European goods. Alarmed at this competition, some unhappy competitors in the EU called for trade barriers. Tariffs on products imported from non-EU countries would raise the prices of these goods, making them unattractive to consumers.

Competition for Investment

Developing countries began to edge out the industrialized ones in other areas besides trade. Investment, for example, began to shift away from the West. Regions such as Southeast Asia offered lower labor costs, greater productivity, and more rapidly growing markets than those in the West. As they privatized their industries, many countries in Eastern Europe and Latin America sold government-owned businesses to foreign as well as to domestic investors. (Economists regard privatization as an important step in the transition from command to free-market economies. It usually results in more efficient and profitable industries.)

As the developing nations attracted more investors, they sent new waves of goods and people to the nations of the West. To stay competitive, many Western business firms *restructured*, or *downsized*. This means that they lowered their expenses by eliminating jobs and asking senior (older) employees to retire before age 65.

Some firms reduced costs by moving their factories to developing countries, where they saved vast sums of money on wages. Taiwanese workers earned one fifth the wages of workers in industrialized countries. Brazilian and Mexican workers earned one tenth.

Investment in technology also moved abroad. American and Japanese investors, for example, made India a center for the manufacture of computer microchips. When South Korea, Taiwan, Hong Kong, and Singapore—the Four Tigers of Asia—created high-tech industries, multinational corporations built factories there. Investors poured billions of dollars into the stock markets of India, Korea, Mexico, and other Third World nations.

INFO CHECK

1. Define the following: Third World, command economies, free-market economies, Chinese Economic Area (CEA), European Union (EU).

2. Why do you think many of the developing nations began to build free-market economies in the 1980s and 1990s?

3. Describe the competition between developing and industrialized nations that grew in the 1990s. How did this cause problems for businesspeople and their employees in the industrialized nations?

4. Identify the Four Tigers of Asia. How did they attract investment by multinational corporations?

ECONOMIC DECISION MAKING IN DEVELOPING COUNTRIES

In order to keep their governments stable, political leaders have to make economic policies that promote the general welfare. They must constantly change these policies to adjust to new conditions both within their countries and abroad.

India

When India gained independence from Britain in the late 1940s, one of its first priorities was rapid industrialization. To accomplish this aim, the government decided to adopt an economic system that combined features of a free-market economy with features of Socialist planning. Under *democratic socialism*, as this system is called, the government owns large industries, such as railroads, automobile manufacturing, and banking. Private individuals and companies own the consumer goods and agricultural industries.

While this system helped India to modernize, it did not increase its prosperity. In the early 1990s, the government tried to make the economy more productive by privatizing government-controlled industries. It sold them to private business persons to run them for their own profit. It also encouraged more foreigners to invest in India. By the mid-1990s, India had begun to export computers and other high-tech goods. Foreign investment increased. For example, United States' investments in India grew to over $1.14 billion in the late 1990s.

Argentina and Brazil

In the early 1990s, the leaders of Argentina and Brazil hoped to turn their countries into economic success stories. At that time, many countries in Latin America wished to achieve low inflation, balanced budgets, smaller bureaucracies, deregulation of industry, and lower tariff barriers. Argentina and Brazil decided to outdo all of them.

Argentina launched its free-market economic reform in 1991. The reform brought Argentina's inflation rate down from 1,344 percent in 1990 to less than 5 percent in 1994. Argentina's debt dropped to 25 percent of its *gross domestic product*. (GDP is the total value of goods and services produced in a country in one year.) The lowering of import barriers brought in foreign investment and foreign goods. The government sold almost all of its state-owned businesses. Tax collections rose sharply.

In the first half of the 1990s, Argentina had one of the highest rates of economic growth in Latin America, topping 6 percent for four years in a row. Its growth rate was among the best in the world. One international economic agency pointed to Argentina as a model from which other developing countries might learn.

In the early 1990s, Brazil, Latin America's largest democracy, had taken only a few steps toward economic restructuring. Its pace picked up in 1994, however, when Fernando Enrique Cardoso was elected president. Cardoso persuaded Brazil's congress to add a number of free-market amendments to the constitution. He made Brazil's economy more attractive to investment by foreigners, introduced a new currency, and curbed inflation. Cardoso found it unnecessary to privatize the state-owned telephone and electricity companies. Instead, he ended their monopolies by allowing private firms to compete with them for business.

Although Argentina and Brazil won praise from international investors and agencies, their reforms brought pain to many of their citizens. Unemployment remained high in both countries. Cuts in Argentina's social services hurt the poor. In December 1994, Mexico had a financial crisis. This made investors nervous about risking their money anywhere in Latin America. During 1995, Argentina plunged into a deep recession. The government raised taxes and borrowed money to try to make ends meet. Nonetheless, Argentina's voters re-elected President Carlos Menem, who vowed to carry on with the restructuring.

Egypt

Political problems have interfered with the efforts of Egypt's leaders to improve their country's economy. In 1961, the Egyptian government had hoped that a Socialist economic system would speed up industrial development. The government nationalized (took over control of) the banking, insurance, mining, power production, and transportation industries. After the 1967 war with Israel, however, this policy no longer worked. In 1970, Egyptian leaders replaced government control with private enterprise. Egypt looked to the West for increased trade.

In 1972, after dismissing its Soviet advisers, Egypt lost Soviet aid. In 1979, it also lost Arab aid by signing a peace treaty with Israel. The United States and other Western nations stepped in to give financial help. After that, the Egyptian economy expanded.

This improvement was not universal. During the 1990s, President Hosni Mubarak's government faced internal political problems that severely hurt the economy. A fundamentalist organization called the Islamic Group launched a campaign of violence throughout Egypt. In an attempt to damage Egypt's important tourism industry, terrorists attacked and killed tourists. They also tried unsuccessfully to assassinate Mubarak. This unrest discouraged foreigners from investing in and visiting Egypt.

Nigeria

Falling oil prices on the world market damaged Nigeria's economy in the early 1980s. Other factors that caused the economy to slide disastrously were its large foreign debt and high inflation rate. The military government, led by Major General Mohammed Bhari, tried to correct the damage by introducing a variety of austerity measures. It also tried to diversify Nigeria's industries by encouraging agriculture. Unfortunately, only the military elite benefited from the improvements that resulted by these changes. The majority of Nigerians remained impoverished. Military dictators continued to control Nigeria's government and economy in the 1990s.

Asian Economic Crisis in 1997

Increasingly, economic decision making has become an international affair. This is because economies all over the world have become dependent on one another. An economic crisis in Asia that began in 1997 demonstrates this dependency.

The crisis began in the spring of 1997 when, for the first time in ten years, Thailand owed more money than it had in its treasury. The *baht*, the basic unit of Thai currency, lost its value in the world market. The Bank of Thailand was forced to spend $10 billion to protect the baht. In July, the bank discontinued this support. As a result, the baht fell, and the Bangkok stock market plunged.

The crisis spread through Southeast Asia, hitting Malaysia, Indonesia, and the Philippines. By October, it had affected Hong Kong's stock market, which in turn caused markets all over the world to drop. Japan also experienced an economic downturn. Although the Western stock markets recovered, financial experts predicted that the continuing crisis in Asia would slow economic growth for some years to come. With less money for foreign goods, Asian nations were less able to import Western products. Also, a lowering of prices on Asian goods resulted in higher sales of these goods in the West.

INFO CHECK

1. If you were a citizen of Argentina or Brazil in the 1990s, would you approve or disapprove of the economic reforms practiced by the leaders of those countries? Give reasons for your answer.

2. How did the 1997 Asian economic crisis begin? How and why were the economies of the Western nations affected?

GLOBAL AND REGIONAL ECONOMIC ORGANIZATIONS

The Group of Seven

The *Group of Seven* (G-7) is an organization of the world's leading industrial nations. Its members are Britain, Canada, France, Germany, Italy, Japan, and the United States. These nations' top leaders have been holding annual meetings since 1975 in an attempt to keep the global economy healthy. The following quotation from a professor of government at Harvard gives some idea of how important this group is: "If the [seven] don't talk, it's a more dangerous world."

A Hazard in the Global Market. One of G-7's main concerns is the speed with which money moves around the world. On a weekday evening when people in San Francisco are getting ready for bed, businesses in Tokyo are well into their next workday. Before turning in, a San Francisco investor can sit down at a computer, check the prices on the Tokyo stock market, and instruct a broker to buy shares in a Japanese company. Before the investor wakes up, the transaction will be completed. In the same manner, an investor in Japan or Hong Kong can place overnight orders on the U.S. stock and currency markets. It is through these markets that the *currency* (money) of one country, such as the U.S. dollar, can be traded for the money of another country, such as the Japanese yen. Like your neighborhood convenience store, some of the world's financial markets stay open 24 hours a day.

The speed with which financial transactions take place can lead to danger. When a crisis, such as the one in Southeast Asia, occurs, it can have an almost immediate effect on other stock markets. Every 24 hours, $1 trillion changes hands on the world's currency markets. A trillion dollars is a lot of money to be moving back and forth. Sometimes, it moves too fast and turns a small crisis into a big one or a big crisis into a disaster.

Goals of the G-7. At its Halifax, Canada, summit in June 1995, G-7's leaders tried to work out ways of checking economic crises. They issued a statement that said, in part:

> The world economy has changed beyond all recognition over the last fifty years. The process of *globalization* [trade between almost all the countries of the world], driven by technological change, has led to increased economic interdependence. . . . The prevention of crisis . . . requires an improved early warning system, so that we can act more quickly to prevent or handle economic shocks.

The leaders also proposed creating a new emergency source of funds to help countries in financial crisis.

The G-7 has other important goals. It aims to lower tariffs in order to stimulate world trade, to prevent recessions (or at least keep their effects from spreading), and to reduce chronic unemployment. It also has political goals: It hopes to promote human rights, limit nuclear proliferation, and find solutions to political crises, such as regional wars.

The G-7 worked to help Russia in its efforts to become a democracy and to develop a free-market economy. During the early 1990s, G-7 members contributed billions of dollars to aid the Russian economy.

The G-7 has also intervened when it felt that its member countries were acting unwisely. It put pressure on Japan and the United States to change some of their policies. The issue with Japan was trade. Japan was exporting more goods to Europe and North America than it was importing from them. G-7 urged it to buy more from those regions in order to restore a balance. The issue with the United States was its federal budget deficit: It was spending more money every year than it was taking in tax revenues. G-7 pressed the United States to balance its budget.

The discussions held at the G-7's annual conferences reflect the economic interdependence of nations in the 1990s. To achieve prosperity, countries must coordinate their policies through a variety of international and regional organizations.

The World Bank

The World Bank stimulates economic growth in developing nations by means of loans and advice. Created after World War II, the World Bank became the largest single lender to developing countries. Between 1947 and 1990, the funds lent to nations in Asia, Latin America, the Middle East, and Africa totaled $186 billion. The World Bank usually granted those loans to higher income developing countries, since these were more likely to pay the money back.

Organization of the World Bank. One hundred and eighty-member nations own and finance the World Bank. Its board of governors consists of one governor from each member country. Since the board meets only once a year, a 22-member board of executive directors actually runs the bank. These directors work full time at the bank's headquarters in Washington, D.C. The nations that own the most shares in the bank have the most voting power. Since G-7 nations own 45 percent of the shares, they control the bank's policies.

The United States has a strong influence on the World Bank. The U.S. president selects the bank's president, who has always been an American. The bank has undertaken no major programs without U.S. approval.

A New Trend. In recent years, the World Bank has tried to help nations find private sources of capital. In 1990, the bank and other official development aid groups put more money into developing countries than did private investors. By the mid-1990s, private investment in developing nations was more than three times larger than aid from official organizations.

The International Monetary Fund

The work of the *International Monetary Fund* (IMF) is closely connected to that of the World Bank. Established in 1944, the IMF oversees the rules governing money. It also ensures orderly currency arrangements among the industrial nations. When no other source is available, it lends money to both rich and poor nations.

Organization of the IMF. Like the World Bank, the IMF is controlled by the wealthy nations, especially the United States, France, Britain, Germany, and Saudi Arabia. These and other nations provide the financial resources of the IMF. Each member government is represented on the board of governors. The board delegates many of its powers to 22 executive directors in Washington. The managing director is usually a European.

Through the years, the role of the IMF has changed. Today, its primary mission is to assist developing nations with troubled economies. Its aid comes with conditions, though. IMF requires that nations first develop free-market economies. Also, it insists on cutting budget deficits, which often means sharp cuts in social programs.

The IMF's policies are highly controversial. Critics say the IMF's insistence on strict free-market policies exposes developing nations' economies to greedy international corporations, corruption, social unrest, and political instability. Supporters of the IMF admit that free-market remedies can cause confusion and hardship at first. Nonetheless, they argue that developing nations will build healthier economies by encouraging competition.

Activities of the IMF. In the 1990s, the IMF supervised economic reform programs in more than 50 countries. The countries included Russia, other former Soviet republics, the nations of Eastern Europe. The IMF helped those countries make the change from Communist-style central planning to free-market economic systems. It also helped Southeast Asian nations that suddenly ran into difficulties.

During the Asian economic crisis of 1997 and 1998, the IMF developed an aid package of $50 billion for South Korea. The country's banks were failing and its debts mounting, while its foreign currency reserves dwindled. Conditions for IMF assistance included the sale to private investors of inefficient government-owned businesses and improvement of their banking systems. Russia's economy was also in danger. By mid-1998, the value of its currency was declining, as was Russia's ability to pay its debts. The IMF instructed Russia either to raise its taxes or reduce its *budget deficit* (the gap between government income and government spending).

At this time, the IMF was running short of cash. It looked to the governments of the United States and other wealthy nations to increase the size of their contributions.

The World Trade Organization

Its Origins. The *World Trade Organization* (WTO) developed in the 1990s from another group called the *General Agreement on Tariffs and Trade* (GATT). GATT was created at a time when national tariffs were limiting world trade. (A tariff is a tax a country places on imported goods.) GATT aimed to expand world trade by reducing such barriers. The World Trade Organization serves a similar purpose. The WTO, however, goes beyond GATT. It tries to open up trade in services (for example, banking and insurance) as well as trade in goods. The WTO has a membership of 117 countries. It is a specialized agency of the United Nations.

Goals of the WTO. The WTO requires each member to treat all other members equally, a rule known as the most-favored-nation-clause. Under this clause, if Country A grants a trade benefit to Country B, it has to extend the same benefit to all other member countries. In other words, each nation has the same benefits as the most-favored nation. The rule aims to make global trade freer for all.

RUSSIA IN CRISIS

By September 1998, the Russian economy was plunging toward collapse. The ruble had been devalued, sending prices of consumer goods soaring and reducing the purchasing power of the ordinary Russian. Unable to pay debts to investors or depositors, banks were closing their doors. The prices of Russian stocks and bonds dropped, as investors withdrew their money. As many business firms refused to pay either debts or taxes, the financial resources of the government diminished. The chairman of the central bank resigned, after writing a harsh letter criticizing the government for failing both to collect taxes and maintain financial discipline.

As imports declined, consumer goods became harder to obtain. In Moscow, many stores were picked clean by shoppers who rushed to buy whatever was available. Lines at gas stations grew as motorists tried to fill their tanks in advance of price increases of as much as 40 percent. Skyrocketing prices and shortages of goods also occurred in other cities. In Omsk, the price of some Russian food staples doubled. In Novgorod, the cost of medicine greatly increased. Hospitals throughout Russia experienced shortages of drugs and medicines. Some regional governors tried to institute price controls.

The causes of Russia's problems were similar to those that had caused the economic crisis in many Asian nations in 1998. Poor banking practices undermined the efforts to develop a modern market economy. Bank managers were allowed to operate their companies like high-flying speculative ventures. They made bad loans of huge sums of money to businesses that could not repay them. In some cases, the bankers themselves had interests in these businesses. In the end, the banks were left with worthless securities. And because the bankers often had political influence, loans were made from the nations' central bank to prop up failing banks. Other factors also contributed to the crisis, especially the declining world price of oil, a product vital to the Russian economy, and the government's admission that its tax collections were not reaching the goal it had set.

As panic spread, Russians desperately sought solutions. Much hope was placed on a $22.6-billion rescue plan developed by the International Monetary Fund. IMF aid was supposed to protect both private investors and the Russian people from hardship and to restore faith in the government's ability to deal with the crisis. But these benefits were slow to develop. Foreign investors continued to withhold their money, causing the ruble to lose more value.

Russia's out-of-power Communist Party made political use of the economic chaos to launch new attacks on President Boris Yeltsin. As threats of impeachment were made by Yeltsin's enemies in the Duma, or parliament, the Communists presented themselves as champions of the poor and downtrodden. Declaring their willingness to form a new government of "national unity," the Communists promised low-interest loans to businesses in difficulty and taxes on imports to protect Russian industries from foreign competition. They also pledged to pay salaries, protect savings, and crack down on financial speculation. Renationalization of major industries (restoring government ownership) was another proposal that seemed to many to reflect the Communists' desire to return to the programs and policies of the former Soviet Union.

While the future of Russia remained uncertain, world leaders sought ways to help the nation continue developing a democratic government and a functioning market economy.

- Respond to those who argue that a return to Communist leadership would be the best course of action for Russia in the 21st century.

Additional WTO goals are to encourage development in developing countries, to keep tariffs low to give greater access to markets, and to promote fair competition.

The European Union

The interdependence of the world's nations has led to the rise of regional economic bodies as well. One of the oldest and most successful of these bodies is the *European Union* (EU). There are now 15 members in the EU. Six other countries are waiting to join.

Origin of the EU. The European Union traces its roots back to 1957, when six nations organized the *European Community* (EC), or *Common Market*. The Common Market's goal was to encourage economic cooperation among the major non-Communist industrial countries of the region. They wanted to form a single market by eliminating trade barriers.

Over the years, the EC moved beyond the status of a common market. In 1992, the members signed a treaty in the Dutch city of Maastricht that changed the EC into the European Union as of 1994. The *Maastricht Treaty* removed almost all barriers to the movement of people, goods, and services across national borders in Western Europe. The treaty also committed members to establish a single European currency, the euro, by 2002, and to coordinate foreign and defense policies. One of its key goals was to enable the region to compete more successfully with the United States and Japan. Eleven nations began using the euro in banking and trade transactions in January 1999.

Pros and Cons of the EU. The creation of a single market not only strengthened Western Europe economically, but it also set the stage for political unification in the 21st century. Many people viewed the 1992 treaty as an important step toward a federal Europe. It increased the powers of European Union institutions, such as its executive offices in Brussels, Belgium. Many Europeans feared such a development, however. They worried that stronger European Union institutions would threaten the independence of individual nations.

Britain and several other countries opposed giving the European Union too much power.

EU Membership. Many nations have applied to join the EU. One of the most persistent has been Turkey. Turkey first applied in 1987. For years, the EU discouraged Turkey, saying that it was not yet ready economically. The EU also felt that Turkey's government was not democratic enough. In 1995, however, EU leaders agreed to allow free trade between Turkey and the EU. This step improved Turkey's chances of becoming a full member.

The EU gave the Czech Republic, Slovakia, Poland, Hungary, Romania, and Bulgaria some access to its market. But negotiations on a trade agreement between the EU and Russia were deadlocked. Several EU members felt threatened by competition from the lower-priced steel, textiles, and farm products produced in Eastern Europe. Most believed, however, that the EU should expand in order to compete successfully with the United States and Japan.

Organization of the EU. The European Parliament is the legislative body of the European Union. It meets in Strasbourg, France. The members are elected every five years. There are 567 members of the European parliament. The number elected from each country depends on its population. In the legislative chamber, however, members are seated by party, not by nationality.

The parliament has authority over the budget of the EU. It can pass laws that apply to all EU nations. A council of ministers, which represents the governments of the member nations, must approve all laws and budgetary decisions. There is also a 20-member European Commission, which acts as the executive branch of the EU. It is responsible for carrying out the laws and decisions of the council and the parliament. Under the Maastricht Treaty, the parliament gained the power to approve or reject candidates nominated by the council as members of the European Commission. The parliament must also approve the appointment of the commission's president.

Another EU organization, the *European Monetary Institute* (EMI), began operations in 1994. The EMI became the European Central Bank in 1999. As the regulator of banks in the EU and the euro currency, it will be one of the most powerful of EU bodies. The Central Bank has its headquarters in Frankfurt, Germany. It regulates the EU's economy just as the U.S. Federal Reserve Bank regulates the American economy.

The Organization of Petroleum Exporting Countries (OPEC)

The *Organization of Petroleum Exporting Countries* (OPEC) was founded in 1960. By 1997, it included Algeria, Gabon, Indonesia, Iran, Iraq, Kuwait, Libya, Nigeria, Qatar, Saudi Arabia, United Arab Emirates, and Venezuela. At first, OPEC was primarily concerned with gaining more profits for its members. Foreigners controlled the oil resources of many Middle Eastern countries. By uniting in OPEC,

LEADER OF THE FREE WORLD

The United States was humbled by OPEC's control of oil production and pricing in the 1970s

©1979 HERBLOCK

these countries gained control of oil production and were able to set oil prices.

Rapid price increases in oil during and after 1974 led to higher profits for the OPEC nations. This enabled them to develop new sources of oil. The larger supplies of oil that resulted, however, drove down prices in the early 1980s. Since then, OPEC has used production quotas to limit the supply of oil on the market and to stabilize prices. Saudi Arabia, the largest and most influential oil producer, has encouraged this policy.

In the 1990s, changes in the oil market began to affect the status of OPEC. The discovery of new oil sources in countries that are not members of OPEC weakened its power. Then, too, other countries reduced their dependence on OPEC oil by using such energy sources as gas, coal, and nuclear energy. In 1998, OPEC reduced oil production in an effort to reverse a long drop in oil prices.

North American Free Trade Agreement (NAFTA)

As Europe moves toward economic unity and the establishment of a single market, similar efforts have started in the Americas. In 1991, the governments of Canada, the United States, and Mexico

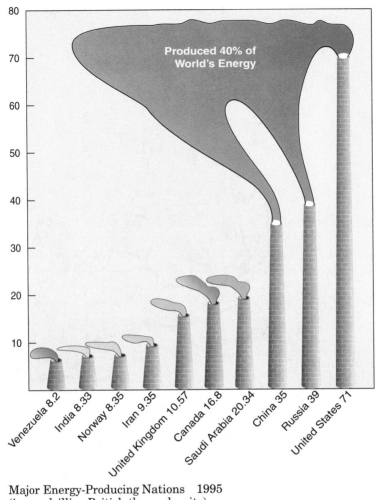

Produced 40% of World's Energy

Major Energy-Producing Nations   1995
(in quadrillion British thermal units)

Venezuela 8.2
India 8.33
Norway 8.35
Iran 9.35
United Kingdom 10.57
Canada 16.8
Saudi Arabia 20.34
China 35
Russia 39
United States 71

negotiated the *North American Free Trade Agreement* (NAFTA). This agreement aims to eliminate tariffs and other trade barriers among the three nations within 15 years. The first tariff reductions went into effect in 1994. NAFTA will eventually create a single market of more than 380 million people.

A lively discussion took place before the U.S. Congress voted its approval of NAFTA in November 1993. Supporters said North America had to establish a free-trade area if it was to compete with the European Union and other regional economic blocs. They argued that free trade under NAFTA would make the economies of the United States, Mexico, and Canada more efficient. In each nation, access to larger markets would help the most competitive industries grow. Supporters also argued that NAFTA would expand U.S. exports, create high-technology jobs in the United States, promote democratic

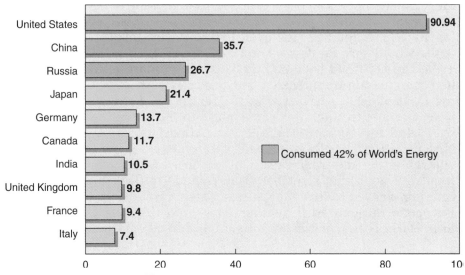

United States 90.94
China 35.7
Russia 26.7
Japan 21.4
Germany 13.7
Canada 11.7
India 10.5
United Kingdom 9.8
France 9.4
Italy 7.4

Consumed 42% of World's Energy

0   20   40   60   80   10

Major Energy-Consuming Nations   1995
(in quadrillion British thermal units)

reforms in Mexico, and reduce illegal immigration from Mexico to the United States. The administrations of presidents George Bush and Bill Clinton both strongly supported NAFTA.

Legislators in Canada and Mexico held similar discussions. Critics argued that NAFTA would give U.S. multinational companies political power in their countries. NAFTA supporters claimed that, without NAFTA, the three North American countries could not stand up to the fierce competition from Europe, Japan, and the developing nations.

Mexico faced an economic crisis in December 1994, which made it harder to measure the effects of NAFTA. Over a six-week period, the

Autoworker on an assembly
line in Mexico City, 1995

Mexican currency, the peso, dropped from a value of 29 U.S. cents to 17 U.S. cents for one peso. That meant that Mexican wages, already low by U.S. standards, fell even lower. It also meant that Mexican pesos would buy far fewer imported goods than before. Earlier in 1994, the U.S. had been selling $1.3 billion more to Mexico than it had been buying from Mexico. The peso crisis reversed the flow. During most of 1995, U.S. exports to Mexico ran more than $1 billion lower per month than Mexican exports to the United States.

Plans for Expanding NAFTA. Almost immediately after the NAFTA accord had been signed, U.S. officials began talking about enlarging the free-trade area. One proposed a Western Hemisphere free-trade zone that stretched from Canada to Chile and Argentina. Another wanted to link the United States, Canada, and Mexico with European nations. Still another suggested that the United States form closer economic ties with Asian and Pacific nations.

Commonwealth of Nations

The Commonwealth consists of Great Britain and most of the countries that were once its colonies. Because Britain strongly influenced the way of life in its former colonies, most Commonwealth members have many traditions in common. Most of their governments are modeled on Britain's parliamentary government. Although only a few member countries pledge allegiance to the Britain monarch, they all acknowledge the monarch as the Commonwealth's symbolic head.

Commonwealth members have cooperative trade relations with one another. In this respect, the Commonwealth was an important forerunner of the European Union. Britain once lowered tariffs for the goods Commonwealth members brought to the British market. When Britain became a member of the European Union in 1973, however, it had to stop this preferential treatment. Commonwealth nations continue to enjoy trade advantages with Britain, though. Great Britain's membership in the EU makes it a better market for the goods of the other Commonwealth countries. Then, too, Britain's ties to the EU make it easier for Commonwealth countries to enter trade agreements with the EU nations.

INFO CHECK

1. Summarize the functions of each of the following: Group of Seven (G-7), World Bank. How does the United States exercise influence in these organizations? Is this good or bad for the global economy?

2. Briefly explain the role of each in regulating the global economy: International Monetary Fund (IMF), World Trade Organization (WTO), European Union (EU), Organization of Petroleum Exporting Countries (OPEC), North American Free Trade Agreement (NAFTA), Commonwealth of Nations.

3. Why would developing nations with troubled economies be more dependent on the IMF than upon any other economic organizations listed above?

4. Why might it be argued that NAFTA was established to accomplish in the Americas what the EU is accomplishing in Europe?

MODERNIZATION VERSUS TRADITION: FINDING A BALANCE

A community's economy does much to shape its culture. Remember the cultural transformation that occurred in hunting-and-gathering societies when their members turned to farming. New technology, such as complex irrigation systems, changed small farming villages into cities. Long-distance trade spread fresh ideas and more efficient tools from one region to another. Much later, the Industrial Revolution increased the power of the middle classes.

Changes in the world's economy continue to affect the ways that people live and think. This is especially true in non-Western countries. With very little preparation, the people of Africa, much of Asia, and Latin America have had to adapt to new ways of working, new technology, and new social relationships.

Changes in China

Some Western business experts predict that, as Chinese leaders put free-market concepts into effect, their political system will become more democratic. These experts claim that in order to increase the productivity of their workers. Chinese businesspeople will have to give them the freedom to plan. Once they are used to making important decisions on the job, Chinese workers may demand the right to make political decisions as well.

Some commentators claim that liberalizing tendencies are already at work in China. As the Chinese government has eased its control over people's economic decisions, people have formed business and professional groups. They have begun to elect village councils and to publish newspapers and magazines not controlled by the state. By 1998, economic expansion had resulted in more personal freedoms. The Chinese people were able to travel, change jobs, and marry, for example, without government permission. China's Communist leaders had found that strict control of their society was not practical in a market economy.

Capitalism Versus Tradition in Corporate Japan

For many years, the Japanese managed to blend Western business techniques with their traditional culture. The leaders of Japanese corporations and their workers felt a loyalty to one another that was comparable to that between samurai warriors and their lords.

Employees were willing to work long hours for rather moderate pay. In return, they enjoyed job security and the sense that they were connected to a powerful and protective institution.

Toward the end of the 1990s, experts saw signs that this "samurai work ethic" was beginning to weaken. New generations of workers were unwilling to work the long hours that their fathers and mothers had taken for granted. Many began to express a desire for more leisure time, larger homes, and a greater share of the wealth they created. More and more, the Japanese were unwilling to remain "poor people in a rich country," as some began to call themselves.

Indian Tradition Yields to Technology

Nationalist feelings often create a longing for old ways of life that are no longer productive. When Gandhi and other Indian leaders planned a free India, they envisioned an economic system that included the cottage industries that were once common in India. In cottage industries, craft items are produced by small groups of people in their homes. Indian leaders felt that creating traditional crafts would keep people mindful of traditional values. This dream was never realized, however. In the late 20th century, India's most important industries were the manufacture of such high-tech products as computers. Some Indians and many world leaders felt that India was going too far along the technological path when its government tested nuclear weapons for the first time in 1998. This increased tension with Pakistan, India's traditional enemy.

The Effect of the Economy on Politics in Egypt and Algeria

Problems in the economy strongly influence political and social behavior. In Egypt and Algeria, such problems have left many young people without employment. Young Algerians who cannot find work are nicknamed *haitists*, which means "people who prop up walls." It is easy to imagine how such a name might make these young people feel. In search of a purpose to their lives, they often join fundamentalist Islamic movements. Such groups soothe their hurt pride and reconnect them to their traditional culture. In belief that they are working to change society for the better, some carry out acts of terrorism for their groups.

Some young Egyptians join radical Islamic groups for the same reason. Western advisers have counseled President Hosni Mubarak to supplement police action with political and economic reforms. Such action would create more employment opportunities.

Change in the Traditional Roles of Women

In Saudi Arabia. Sometimes, economic difficulties can bring positive changes for at least some members of society. The decrease in oil revenues during the 1990s put Saudi Arabian women in a position to gain more power.

Once Middle Eastern oil was no longer the world's most important source of energy, the Saudi economy fell. Its government had to call for austerity measures. Prices rose and incomes fell. In many families, two salaries were necessary to make ends meet. Men began to encourage their wives to work. Observing this trend, Saudi liberals began to hope that women would be able to obtain more freedom in their working lives. As they became more necessary to the economy, women might be able to negotiate better pay, an end to sexually segregated workplaces, and careers in fields now open only to men.

Women in most Muslim countries do not enjoy the freedom and rights that men have. For example, men can divorce their wives simply by saying, "I divorce you" three times. Women, on the other hand, must take legal proceedings to get a divorce. Even when they do so, the law seldom grants it to them. When in public, they must cover themselves from head to foot and veil their faces. They cannot travel without written permission from their husbands or male relatives. They are even discouraged from venturing out on the streets without a male escort.

In some Muslim countries, however, women are allowed to work. Saudi Arabia is one such country. Saudi women, however, must work only in jobs that will bring them into contact with other women. They frequently become doctors and teachers, because in these professions they can limit their patients and students to people of their own sex. They also open shops that cater only to women. In spite of these restrictions, Saudi women have done well. In 1996, it was estimated that women owned at least 40 percent of Saudi Arabia's private wealth.

In Afghanistan. Poverty and political unrest worsened the position of women in Afghanistan. Like Saudi Arabia, Afghanistan is a Muslim country. Throughout its history, it has endured countless invasions.

In 1978, a Marxist group, called the *People's Democratic Party of Afghanistan* (POPA), took over the Afghan government. It was so extreme and repressive that the Afghan people were constantly on the verge of revolt. The Soviet Union sent in troops to support the Marxists in 1979.

Strong nationalist feelings, aroused by the Soviet invasion, strengthened Afghan resistance. Aided by Pakistan and the United States, the Afghan guerrilla fighters, who called themselves the *mujahadin* (Islamic warriors), managed to take over large parts of the country. The fighting continued for 11 years, devastating the country's already weak economy. Soviet troops finally withdrew in February 1989.

Peace did not return to Afghanistan, however. During their war against the Soviets, the mujahadin had broken up into several rival parties. These continued to struggle with one another for control of

Schoolgirls in Afghanistan receiving a traditional Muslim education

Afghanistan. In 1995 and 1996, a fundamentalist Islamic group called the Taliban captured two important cities, Heart and Kabul. Although not officially recognized as the ruling party, the Taliban set government policies for Afghanistan, which it renamed the Islamic Emirate of Afghanistan.

The Marxist government had been oppressive. It did, however, allow women to go to school and enter the work force. Interpreting Islamic law in its strictest sense, the Taliban took these advances away from women. They not only denied women the right to work, they did not even permit them to leave their homes without a male escort. Some women had lost all their male relatives during the long war. The law made no exceptions for these women, reducing them to misery and, sometimes, starvation.

INFO CHECK

1. Compare economic and cultural change in China and Japan in the late 20th century. How has the process of change been similar in these countries? How has it been different?

2. Explain why you AGREE or DISAGREE:

   - Economic change must always cause cultural and political change.
   - The economic changes of the 1990s resulted in more rights and political and economic power for women in developing nations.

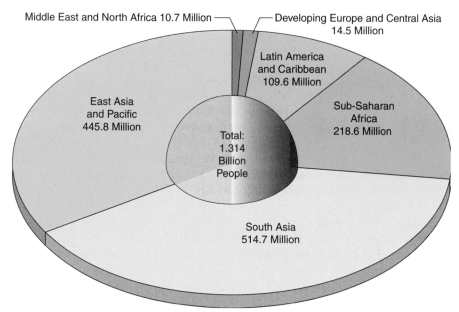

Extreme Poverty, by Region   1993
(people living on less than $1 U.S. a day)

CONTINUING SOCIAL PROBLEMS AND CRISIS

World Hunger

Countries in Asia, Africa, and Latin America have made great strides in industrialization and modernization. Nonetheless, large segments of their populations remain malnourished and illiterate. In many of these countries, only the members of a small group own the wealth brought by their improved economies. To get a true picture of a country's economic condition, experts now measure its wealth in terms of how well all of its people are living.

Some important factors that affect a country's standard of living are population size and political stability. A large and growing population can strain a country's food supply and send food prices skyrocketing. Ways exist, however, to increase the food supply and slow down the population growth. In countries such as India, the Green Revolution substantially boosted crop production. Government programs have put some limit on high birthrates.

The problem of political instability, however, is harder to solve. When several leaders struggle over the control of a region, they are not concerned about the suffering of its inhabitants. In fact, they usually feel that it is in their interest to increase this suffering. The case of Somalia illustrates the difficulty of helping people when leaders are concerned only with gaining power.

The Famine in Somalia

In the early 1990s, world attention focused on the extreme suffering of the Somali people. Located on the Indian Ocean, in the mainly desert area known as the Horn of Africa, British Somaliland was given its independence in 1960. Shortly after, it joined with the Italian-held portion of Somaliland to form the larger nation of Somalia.

In the 1970s and 1980s, the United States and the Soviet Union competed for influence in the Horn of Africa region. During that period, Somalia laid claim to Ogaden, a section of neighboring Ethiopia largely inhabited by Somalis. The Soviet Union tried to gain influence in Ethiopia by sending Cuban troops to help Ethiopia protect Ogaden. Also looking for allies in the region, the United States sent weapons to the Somalis. During the long war that followed (1977–1988), Somali forces were defeated by the Soviet-equipped Cubans.

Internal Conflict in Somalia. Taking advantage of their country's weakened state, Somali leaders began to battle one another and their official government for control of Somalia. By late 1992, Somalia had almost ceased to exist as a nation. All government had been destroyed. Drought and famine increased the misery caused by war. Several hundred thousand people died from disease and starvation.

Humanitarian organizations, such as the International Committee of the Red Cross, worked with the United Nations to bring supplies of food, fuel, and medicine to Somalia. Unfortunately, rival warlords prevented this by attacking the relief workers and looting their convoys and warehouses.

UN Intervention. In December 1992, the United Nations approved a plan to send United States and other military forces to Somalia to protect relief workers as they distributed food. They also intended these forces to stop the warlords from fighting one another. By early 1993, large numbers of troops from the United States, France, Britain, and Italy had arrived in Somalia.

Efforts were made to disarm the warlords and persuade them to shift from military to political competition. The strongest Somali warlord, General Muhammad Farah Aydid, opposed these measures. To remove this obstacle, U.S. and UN forces carried out attacks against Aydid's supporters and attempted to capture him. The UN intervention suffered a setback in October 1993, when 18 U.S. soldiers died in a fight with Aydid's forces. The United States withdrew all its forces by March 1994.

Several nations were troubled that UN troops had fought against one Somali faction, rather than acting as a neutral peacekeeper. Consequently, in March 1995, the UN pulled out its troops. The Somali factions fought on, with no end to the war in sight.

The Problems of Urbanization

One of the most striking developments in the newly industrialized nations is the rapid growth of their cities. In the ten years following

World War II, many developing nations' cities expanded to twice and even three times their former size. In the 1990s, they grew even faster.

North American and European cities have also grown larger since 1945. But the growth of these cities was less of a problem than the growth of developing nations' cities. Western cities had been established for a long time. They already had advanced infrastructures, such as sewage systems and power sources, and institutions to help the poor. Until the middle of the 20th century, most developing nations had been primarily rural. They were poorly prepared for urbanization.

Many factors account for the sudden growth of developing nations' cities. Two of the most important are the population explosion and industrialization. In rural areas, a larger population meant that more people had to share limited amounts of farmland. Much of this land was already in the hands of a few wealthy landlords. They began to use new machines that reduced the number of people needed to work the large farms. People with no land of their own competed with one another for farm jobs. The landlords often took advantage of this large and desperate labor force and offered very low wages. As factories sprang up in the cities, rural people flocked to them, hoping to find work that paid a living wage.

Conditions in the Developing World's Cities

Developing nations do not have as many cities as countries in the West. Often, a single "supercity" possesses most of the country's industries, hospitals, and schools. Consequently, it draws vast numbers of people. Affordable housing in such cities is so scarce that large squatter settlements have mushroomed on their outskirts. The cities' limited plumbing and lighting systems cannot serve them. Their schools and hospitals do not have the equipment, the staff, or the money to accommodate their many poor inhabitants.

Nonetheless, the people who live in these squalid settlements consider themselves more fortunate than those who remain in the countryside. Although factory jobs are scarce, they pay better than equally scarce farm jobs. Squatters cling to the hope that they will eventually get such work. Meanwhile, the jobless participate in what is known as the "bazaar economy." They set up street corner markets and sell articles that they have found or made. Others hire themselves out to mend tools or do other odd jobs. Still others turn to crime. Many people consider the squatter settlements breeding places for crime and violence.

Most squatters, however, are simply disadvantaged people doing the best they can for themselves. Not only have many of them helped themselves by engaging in the "bazaar economy," they have also improved their makeshift dwellings. Some families have replaced their houses' mud or tarpaper walls with concrete blocks. Others have joined together to pressure the city to provide their communities with water pumps and schools. These enterprising people have much in common with those slum dwellers of 19th-century Western cities who worked their way out of poverty during the Industrial Revolution.

The International Drug Trade

The extreme poverty of much of the developing world has helped to foster an international trade in illegal narcotic drugs. The drug lords can easily recruit impoverished farmers and unemployed city people to grow or process drugs and smuggle them to other countries. Those who have lost hope of improving their lives often become customers. These penniless addicts turn to theft and other crimes to get money for drugs.

The Problems of Controlling Illegal Drugs. For many reasons, government attempts to control drug trafficking have not met with great success. Political corruption often makes it difficult for official agencies to fight this crime. Then, too, it is difficult to target the people who are at the head of the organizations. Drug lords have influence in the business world and can easily use world financial markets to "launder," or camouflage, the source of the money they make. Advanced technology makes money laundering easy. Electronic fund transfer systems on computers make it possible to send huge amounts of money around the world almost instantaneously. Messages can be encrypted, or changed into unbreakable codes, on fax machines and cellular telephones. As a result, drug lords can make long-distance deals without being detected. The use of violence by the members of drug cartels also makes it difficult to control them. When the officials of drug-fighting organizations, cannot be bribed, the cartels threaten to kill them and their families.

United States and the War on Drugs. The United States has tried to work with Latin American governments to control drugs. But economic problems make it difficult for Latin American leaders to crack down on drug production as hard as the United States would like. To avoid direct confrontation with the cartel members, leaders have tried to control drug trafficking in other ways. For example, Peruvian President Alberto Fujimori has requested additional U.S. aid. He wants to subsidize peasant farmers as they switch from growing coca leaf to the cultivation of such legal crops as rice and corn.

Bolivian leaders have had limited success in using these alternative measures. The peasants of that nation live in grinding poverty. They have the shortest life span in the Americas. Less than half the population of Bolivia has access to safe drinking water. The sale of coca leaves to drug traffickers has kept whole communities of farmers alive.

The *United Nations Drug Control Program* (UNDCP) has tried to help some Bolivian farmers switch from growing coca to growing legal crops. It gave them the tools and training needed to cultivate tea, bananas, and livestock. It funded the building of roads to take the crops to market. It also tried to reduce the farmers' poverty by providing hospitals and basic medical services.

Coca growing has declined in many parts of Bolivia. Much of the decline, however, is due to a U.S.-trained antidrug police force. It has made the farmers fear the police more than the drug lords. U.S. officials working in Bolivia say a combination of tactics must be used if the war against drugs is to be won. Alternative development must be combined with tough policing and the destruction of drug-processing factories.

In recent years, U.S. officials have concentrated on reducing the flow of illegal drugs into North American cities. U.S. agencies, such as the Drug Enforcement Agency (DEA), have sent officers to Latin American countries to work with local security services. The U.S. officers have participated in raids on coca farms, factories, and illegal airstrips and in the arrest of drug traffickers. Such joint efforts have won some support but have also aroused resentment.

Latin American Objections to U.S. Intervention. Many Latin Americans blame the United States for causing Latin America's drug problems. They resent U.S. meddling in their affairs. Critics want U.S. officials to focus on reducing the demand for cocaine in their own country. Then they would not have to attack the sources of supply in Latin America.

Political leaders in drug-producing countries point to the economic and political sides of the drug problem. Many people involved in the drug trade are taxpayers and voters. Many of these people have no other source of income. The leaders of drug-producing countries have to consider those realities. They also have to use military resources to combat politically motivated terrorism. Therefore, they often prefer to negotiate with the drug lords rather than continue destructive wars against them.

Many Latin American governments are reluctant to cooperate with the United States in the drug war for other reasons. In the 1990s, their resentment of the U.S. military presence in their countries and suspicion of its motives strengthened. Then, too, they point out that, even after a decade, U.S. drug policies have not stopped the flow of narcotics into North America.

Privatization in the former Communist countries and industrialization in developing countries have resulted in a new economic order. The economies of the world are both more competitive with one another and more dependent on one another. The complexity of their relationships has contributed much to the instability of the world. In response to this, world leaders have established organizations that try to foster international cooperation and prevent financial crisis.

Chapter 34 will discuss potential causes of violence in the world and peace-keeping organizations that attempt to control violence.

INFO CHECK

1. Why is Somalia regarded as an example of the difficulties of dealing with hunger in the Third World?

2. Define the term urbanization. Why has this been more of a problem in developing nations than in industrialized nations?

3. What suggestions would you make to leaders in the United States and Latin America for dealing with the international drug trade?

CHAPTER REVIEW

Multiple Choice

1. Nations that used the Soviet-style command economy tended to place the majority of their natural, monetary, and labor resources into the areas of

   1. consumer and civilian industries and products
   2. heavy industries and military products
   3. educational and housing developments
   4. civilian-oriented, technological, and communication industries.

2. In the 1990s, developing nations and Pacific Rim countries received investment monies because

   1. the developed nations needed places to safeguard their excess funds
   2. the developed nations wanted to assist the poorer nations in improving their standards of living
   3. Western and Communist nations were competing for allies in the Third World and Pacific Rim countries
   4. they had lower labor costs, greater productivity, and growing markets for sales.

3. An economic system that combines elements of private- and government-ownership of business is known as

   1. command economy
   2. capitalism
   3. democratic socialism
   4. privatization.

4. The economies of Nigeria and Egypt suffered because both nations

   1. depended too heavily on a single economic resource
   2. became involved in costly foreign projects
   3. depended on foreign assistance to balance their budgets
   4. suffered severe droughts that destroyed their agricultural exports.

5. Economic problems in one area of the world affect other parts of the world because

   1. all nations borrow money from one another
   2. having less money means fewer sales or less money to spend
   3. some nations only sell finished goods
   4. some nations have nothing of value to sell.

6. The EU, OPEC, G-7, and the IMF are all examples of

   1. military alliances
   2. political parties
   3. global or regional communication companies
   4. regional or global economic organizations.

7. If you represented a developing nation and needed economic advice or a loan, you could turn to the

   1. Warsaw Pact
   2. Truman Plan
   3. World Bank
   4. Federal Credit Union.

8. The WTO, the EU, and NAFTA all seek to

   1. encourage trade and reduce tariff barriers
   2. promote development of the former republics of the Soviet Union
   3. promote development of the nations of Latin America
   4. develop military technology in the area of space travel.

9. Examples of problems that still exist in developing nations are

   1. overspending on consumer and luxury goods
   2. famine and fighting between local warlords or militias
   3. natural disasters destroying the economy
   4. how to safely destroy their stockpiles of atomic weapons.

10. The slum dwellers of the 20th-century developing world and the slum dwellers of the 19th-century Western world both

    1. joined the military as a way out of their poverty
    2. fought against the machines that caused them to lose their jobs and self-respect

    3. left their villages to see the big cities and visit the museums
    4. lived in unhealthy conditions while they sought jobs in the cities, hoping to end their poverty.

11. A comparison of the graphs on pages 780 and 781 shows that

    1. the industrial nations need a synthetic petroleum product
    2. Japan is both a major producer and consumer of energy
    3. China, Russia, and the United States produce and consume the most energy
    4. India produces more energy than it consumes.

12. The cartoon on page 779 shows that, during the 1970s,

    1. the United States dominated the Arab nations
    2. the United States was dependent on imported oil
    3. OPEC was only able to manipulate the United States by controlling its oil exports
    4. the nations of the West turned to the production of synthetic oil.

Thematic Essays

1. The economic system in the newly independent states of the former Soviet Union brought good news and bad news. The good news was that consumer goods were being produced and people could open their own businesses. The bad news was that wages and job security were not guaranteed in a free-market economy. *Task:* Describe some reasons for the problems in those countries and what they and the nations of the world are doing to resolve their economic difficulties.

2. Economic competition among nations, regions, and Communist and Western nations has slowly given way in the face of global interdependence. *Task:* Describe any two examples of eco-

nomic activities that would support that statement. Consider for inclusion in your essay regional or world-wide economic unions, world banking, or economic regulatory agencies.

Document-Based Questions

Use the documents and your reading of the chapter to assist you in answering the questions.

1. From a discussion including Drs. Athayde, Facio, and former U.S. Senator Morse dealing with change in Latin America:

    Dr. Athayde: ". . . we feel that it is necessary to establish an effective system of economic cooperation among all the nations . . ."

    Dr. Facio: ". . . a greater effort toward an economic development that will permit an increase in the wealth in order that it may be more widely distributed. Economic progress and social justice must go hand in hand . . ."

    Senator Morse: ". . . I think land reform is probably the first step that needs to be taken. . . . In many parts of Latin America there is not a fair tax system . . . a narrowing of the economic gap, the gap between the great masses of poverty-stricken people and the small number of very, very rich people. . . . The rich people have also got to show confidence in Latin America. They've got to get their money out of New York and Swiss banks and back into Latin America, and invest their money in the future of Latin America . . ."

    ("Today's Revolution," from *Americas* magazine)

    What actions do the three speakers claim are necessary for economic change in Latin America?

2. From a book about Soviet communism by Louis Fisher.

    ". . . The twentieth century's biggest problem is the control of personal, group and national power. My acceptance of Soviet Russia was, I suspect, a by-product of my protest against the power over human beings which accumulated-wealth and property have given to their owners. . . . Then Soviet Russia emerged, promising to break forever the power of landlords, trusts, big business exploiters and private capital generally. . . . I now realize that Bolshevism is not the way out because it is itself the world's biggest [massing together of] power over man. . . . The Kremlin [dominates] its citizens not only by the police and prison power but also by the greater power [natural to] the ownership and operation of every economic enterprise in the nation . . ."

    Why did Fisher first accept but later reject the Communist economic system?

3. Study the pie chart on page 787.

    Identify the world region in which poverty affects the most people. Would you describe the nations of this region as "developing" or "industrialized"? Which global economic organization might help them to reduce poverty? What actions might this organization take?

4. Look at the cartoon on page 779.

    How does the cartoon show the power of a group to cripple the economies of the world's most developed nations? In your answer describe the factors that make it possible.

Document-Based Essay

In the late 20th century, many developing nations altered their economic systems. *Task:* For each of two developing nations, describe a change in the economic system and the problems or benefits that resulted.

C H A P T E R

34

The Search for Global Security

Shondra loved jogging through Tribeca on Sunday mornings. No other neighborhood in New York was so peaceful at this time. There was hardly any traffic. Today was a bright spring day. A few joggers, bikers, and roller bladers were also out enjoying the mild weather.

Exhilarated by the sense of space and the soft spring air, Shondra broke into a sprint and nearly ran into a police barrier. Beyond it, people were screaming, running around, and writhing on the ground. Were they making a movie? Or was it a real disaster? Shondra remembered that, several years ago, terrorists had bombed the World Trade Center.

She joined a cluster of roller bladers near the barrier. It was a drill, they told her, to make sure that the city was prepared to handle a poison gas attack by terrorists. Shondra shuddered. If this had been real, she would have been killed or badly injured.

Like many Americans, Shondra is becoming aware that her world is a more dangerous place than it used to be. Once it seemed that only faraway countries were troubled by violent events. Now they were happening in the United States. Both foreign and domestic terrorists, for example, were attacking ordinary Americans. In this chapter, you will learn about the problems and conflicts that have given rise to terrorist groups. You will also learn what individual countries, the United Nations, and smaller international organizations are doing to keep peace and to fight terrorism.

THE STRUGGLE TO KEEP THE PEACE

At the end of World War II, the world placed its hopes for global peace on the United Nations. That hope was somewhat frustrated during the long decades of the cold war. The hostility between democratic states and Communist states frequently paralyzed the United Nations. It could not prevent wars between Communists and anti-Communists from breaking out in several Third World countries. Some of these were Korea, Vietnam, Afghanistan, Cuba, El Salvador, and Nicaragua.

The cold war came to an end in the early 1990s. The friendlier relationships among world leaders did not bring security, however. Power struggles continued throughout the developing nations. In parts of Eastern Europe, long-smoldering conflicts erupted into violence.

The Peacekeeping Role of the United Nations

In the 1990s, the United Nations sent peacekeeping missions to the hotspots of the world. In Africa, UN troops kept peace while Namibia changed from a South African colony to an independent state. In Mozambique (Africa), El Salvador (Central America), and Cambodia (Southeast Asia), troops helped put an end to devastating civil wars. In Haiti (Caribbean), they helped maintain peace while a democratic government replaced a military dictatorship.

In other cases, however, the UN's peacekeeping forces failed. In 1994, they were unable to prevent the people of Rwanda (Africa) from slaughtering one another. In 1995, they withdrew from Somalia (Africa) while that country's civil war still raged. They struggled for years to bring order to Bosnia (Europe). As one UN officer in Bosnia observed, "It's much easier to come in and keep peace when there's some peace around."

Why Peacekeeping Missions Fail. One reason for these failures was that people expected the UN forces to be more than peacekeepers. Ideally, the forces would have moved in only after the warring factions had agreed to stop fighting. Then their job would have been straightforward. They would have made sure that all sides in the dispute observed the peace settlements or truces. They would have run free elections and brought supplies to civilian populations. But in places such as Rwanda, Somalia, and Bosnia, the peacekeepers found themselves in the midst of ongoing wars. At times, they themselves took part in the fighting.

The UN's peacekeeping role expanded greatly in the early 1990s. In 1988, the United Nations had only five active peacekeeping oper-

UN peacekeeping forces in Somalia, beset by rival factions

ations. By 1993, it had 28. By the mid-1990s, the number had dropped into the mid-teens.

In earlier years, most UN peacekeeping forces mediated between the armies of rival nations—for example, between Israel and its Arab neighbors. In the 1990s, the United Nations also sent peacekeepers into domestic conflicts in Somalia and Bosnia. Out of nine peacekeeping operations, seven involved civil wars.

Composition of the Peacekeeping Forces. UN troops increased from 9,500 in 1988 to 70,000 in the mid-1990s. Individual countries supplied soldiers to the United Nations. They came from dozens of countries—from Venezuela and Canada, from Ukraine and Bangladesh, from Egypt and Nepal. The soldiers were usually lightly armed and were instructed to return fire only if attacked. The soldiers did not always follow instructions, however. Military experts felt that they needed more discipline.

Lack of Cooperation Among Member Nations. Peacekeeping operations do not come cheap. In 1994 alone, the United Nations spent about $3.6 billion for peacekeeping (far more than its general budget of $1 billion). UN member nations were supposed to cover peacekeeping expenses, as well as those of the general budget. Many nations felt that they had to pay too large a percentage. The U.S. Congress, for example, wanted to cut the U.S. share from 33 percent to 25 percent of the total. It refused to pay its dues until this change had been made. Other nations also refused to pay. The United States, however, was the United Nations' biggest debtor. It owed more than $1 billion.

Decisions in the UN

Several UN members objected to the way the United Nations made its decisions. UN membership grew from 53 countries in 1945 to 185 in the 1990s. Nonetheless, the 15-member Security Council made most peacekeeping decisions. As permanent members, the United States, Russia, Britain, France, and China had veto power. They were the nations that won World War II and had the most power during the cold war period. In the post-cold war era, Japan and Germany requested admission to the Security Council. India, Egypt, Brazil, and other large developing nations also wanted to take part in the decision-making process.

Social and Economic Programs

The rise of Nazism in Germany after World War I taught the world a valuable lesson. It demonstrated that dangerous political movements often arise when poor economic and social conditions exist. The founders of the United Nations wanted to prevent the people of any country from feeling deprived and angry. Therefore, they set up the *Economic and Social Council* (ECOSOC). The General Assembly supervises this council and elects its 54 members. These members meet at least twice a year.

ECOSOC agencies study and recommend ways of improving economic and social cooperation. They are also concerned with human rights, the status of women, and the control of illegal drugs. A well-known voluntary program under ECOSOC supervision is the *United Nations Children's Fund* (UNICEF).

A People-Centered World Order

In 1990, ECOSOC launched the United Nations Development Program. This program explores ways to achieve a "people-centered world order." In such an order, a nation's economic development brings prosperity to its private citizens as well as to its leaders. Only the powerful groups of a nation benefit when its economy expands without creating new jobs. The experts in the United Nations Development Program suggested a variety of solutions for this problem. Many of these solutions are based on the principle that money should not be saved at the expense of the general welfare. For example, governments should not throw people out of work by shutting down unnecessary industries. Instead, they should find ways to convert the outdated industries to new uses. Governments should also invest more in education and give aid to small enterprises.

The Human Development Scale

The United Nations Development Program rates nations according to their ability to improve their citizens' quality of life. Each nation's rating is based upon such criteria as life expectancy, educational standards, and individual income. Among the industrialized nations, for example, Japan received a high rating. Compared to other countries, more of its citizens enjoyed a high personal income. The United States was in sixth place. The report noted a broad gap between the living standards of white Americans and Americans of other races.

Several developing countries scored higher on the human development scale than did more industrialized ones. Uruguay, for example, ranked above Poland. The lowest human development scores went to the poorest African nations. In Somalia, Mali, and Sierra Leone, only small groups of people enjoyed the national wealth.

The United Nations Development Program does not equate a high per capita (per person) income or gross national product with a high quality of life. The average Brazilian, for example, earns more than the average Costa Rican. Nonetheless, the United Nations Development Program gives Costa Rica a higher human development rating than Brazil. The average Costa Rican lives longer, is better educated, and enjoys better sanitation than does the average Brazilian.

The experts also point out differences in quality of life between men and women. They have observed that no country treats its female citizens as well as it does its males. In most nations, women have fewer job opportunities and lower earnings than men. In the developing countries, women also have inferior health care, nutrition, and education.

ECOSOC encourages all nations to ensure that their economic growth improves the quality of life for their people. By so doing, they will help make the world more secure.

The North Atlantic Treaty Organization

The *North Atlantic Treaty Organization* (NATO) was created in 1949. Its original purpose was to defend Western Europe and North America from attack by the Soviet Union.

New Strategies and Organization. In November 1991, the leaders of the NATO countries met in Rome to reorganize NATO's military forces. Although the cold war was over, new problems had arisen, for which new approaches were needed.

The alliance's 16 member nations focused on three troubled areas—Eastern Europe, the Balkans, and the Middle East. The former satellite nations of Eastern Europe wanted to join NATO for protection from Russia. NATO promised to defend them should the need arise. National and ethnic rivalries were simmering in the former

Yugoslavia. NATO feared that these conflicts would spread throughout the Balkans. The Middle East posed several problems. Iraqi dictator Saddam Hussein threatened the security of the region. Iran was identified as a supporter of terrorist organizations. Tension continued between Israel and its neighbors. Controlling hostilities in that region was especially important, because it contained much of the world's oil supplies.

To deal with the new dangers, NATO leaders took a number of steps. Formerly, they had massed most of their forces in Germany to meet threats from Eastern Europe and the Soviet Union. Since many new conflicts were now arising in southern areas, they had to adopt a more flexible strategy. Therefore, they divided their forces into smaller units, backed by highly mobile reserves.

Both the U.S. government and NATO allies agreed that it was important to keep American soldiers in Europe. Conflicts in the Middle East affect the United States as much as they do Europe. In case of war there, American soldiers would have to intervene. They could do so more quickly if they were based in Germany. In 1998, President Clinton said he would keep 100,000 U.S. troops in Europe.

Expansion of NATO. While the Eastern European nations were eager to join NATO, NATO members felt that they were not ready. Eastern Europe's democratic governments were new and inexperienced. Their economies and military systems were also weak. If they joined NATO, all NATO members would have to defend them should they be attacked. The leaders of the NATO nations were not sure that they wanted their young soldiers to "die for Bratislava" (the capital of the Slovak Republic). Moreover, Russia adamantly opposed any extension of NATO into Eastern Europe. It saw such an extension as a potential threat to its own security.

On the other hand, NATO leaders believed that some sort of link to NATO was necessary to stabilize Eastern Europe. In 1994, they invited interested countries to join the Partnership for Peace. Countries that participated in this partnership could enjoy increased political and military cooperation without the burdens of full membership. Although it first rejected the idea, Russia signed on in 1995. It was one of 27 countries to join the Partnership for Peace. NATO leaders promised the major Eastern European nations that eventually they could become full NATO members. In July 1997, NATO nations began discussions on making Poland, Hungary, and the Czech Republic full-fledged members in 1999. The U.S. Senate voted approval of this step in a historic 1998 vote. It was recognized that enlarging NATO would move the alliance 400 miles eastward toward Russia.

NATO's Nuclear Strategy. Another subject discussed at the 1991 conference in Rome was NATO's nuclear strategy. NATO members decided to continue its existing policy. This meant that, in the event of a conventional war, they could threaten to make first use of nuclear weapons. However, NATO leaders also agreed to reduce the nuclear weapons based in Europe by 90 percent.

1. List the difficulties encountered by the United Nations in its peacekeeping operations in the 1990s.

2. How would you respond to those who argue that UN military forces should not be involved in dangerous peacekeeping missions?

3. Explain the Human Development Scale of the United Nations Development Program. Why has Japan received a higher rating than the United States?

4. How has the North Atlantic Treaty Organization (NATO) changed in mission and composition since the end of the cold war?

EFFORTS TO LIMIT NUCLEAR PROLIFERATION

In August 1945, the United States ended World War II by dropping atomic bombs on two Japanese cities. Horrified by the destruction and suffering caused by this new weapon, the Japanese government surrendered. This was the beginning of the nuclear age.

Nuclear weapons have not been used in warfare since 1945. The Soviet Union did not use them in Afghanistan. The United States did not use them in Vietnam or Iraq. Nonetheless, the possibility that they might be used caused general concern.

Cold War Strategies

Throughout the late 1940s and 1950s, the United States had overwhelming nuclear superiority. By 1960, however, the Soviet Union had enough nuclear weapons to retaliate fully against any attack. By the late 1960s, the Soviet Union's nuclear arsenal was roughly equal to that of the United States. Out of this balance of power arose the belief that *mutual assured destruction* (MAD) would prevent a nuclear holocaust. Neither power would bomb the other if it thought it would be destroyed in the process. The safety of the world depended on both powers having equal stockpiles of deadly weapons.

The United States and the Soviet Union worked together to keep this balance. From 1963 until the Soviet Union collapsed in 1991, they negotiated arms control agreements. Limitations on antiballistic missile systems, for example, were established in 1972 and 1974.

Nuclear Arms Control

Popular movements protesting nuclear weapons arose all over the world. They reached a peak between 1982 and 1984. Eighty-one percent of U.S. citizens polled in April 1982 voted in favor of banning nuclear weapons. Peace groups in the United States reached out to peace groups in Western Europe, Eastern Europe, and the Soviet

Union. These movements declined, however, after the 1984 reelection of President Ronald Reagan.

Antinuclear Agencies and Treaties

Private citizens were not alone in opposing nuclear weapons. International and national organizations formed to protect the world against nuclear destruction.

An independent United Nations agency, the *International Atomic Energy Agency* (IAEA), was founded in 1957. It has 122 member countries. They work to encourage peaceful uses of atomic energy. The agency attempts to discourage the building of nuclear weapons and to prevent the conversion of nuclear plants from civilian to military use.

In 1968, more than 175 nations signed the *Nuclear Nonproliferation Treaty* (NNT). Its purpose was to halt the proliferation, or spread, of nuclear weapons. The signers of the treaty also agreed to allow inspections of their nuclear power facilities. Officials of the International Atomic Energy Agency conduct those inspections.

The *London Suppliers Agreement* was made in 1976. It tries to stop the spread of nuclear materials and nuclear technology to nations that have no nuclear weapons. *EURATOM* is an authority that controls nuclear proliferation in Western Europe. It is legally responsible for preventing nations or groups from changing nuclear material into nuclear weapons. The EURATOM Commission can bring an offending nation before the European Court of Justice. Unfortunately, despite these agreements and safeguards, nuclear proliferation continues.

The Spread of Nuclear Arsenals

At the end of the cold war, only five nations admitted to possessing nuclear weapons. These were the United States, Russia, China, France, and Britain. Parts of the Soviet nuclear stockpile remained in Ukraine and in Kazakhstan.

Several other nations are suspected of having nuclear arms. India exploded what it described as a "peaceful nuclear device" in 1974. It conducted a nuclear test in 1998. It may have a small nuclear arsenal for possible use against Pakistan. Pakistan has developed its own nuclear weapons and also conducted a nuclear test in 1998. Israel reportedly has built several hundred nuclear weapons for use as a last resort against its Arab enemies. South Africa's white minority government built atomic weapons in the 1980s. It gave them up voluntarily, however, when it ended apartheid in 1991. Libya, North Korea, Iraq, Iran, and Argentina may also have started programs to develop nuclear weapons.

Nuclear weapons may eventually be used to settle one of the bitter

NATIONS WITH NUCLEAR WEAPONS IN 1997

Country	Estimated Number of Warheads
Russia	12,000
United States	10,000
France	480
China	450
United Kingdom	200
India	not available
Pakistan	not available

political rivalries that exist in today's world. Some leaders have no scruples about using lethal weapons against civilians. Iraq, for example, has used poisonous chemicals against Iran and some of its minorities. And nuclear technology is becoming more accessible. This increases the threat of nuclear blackmail or terrorism.

INFO CHECK

1. Explain how each protects the world from nuclear war: International Atomic Energy Agency (IAEA), Nuclear Nonproliferation Treaty (NNT), London Suppliers Agreement, EURATOM.

2. Why do you think prevention of the spread of nuclear arsenals has been so difficult? What do you think might be a solution?

NUCLEAR-CONTROL CRISES

Ukraine: No More Missiles

When the Soviet Union broke apart, 1,800 of the country's nuclear warheads were in Ukraine. Newly independent Ukraine suddenly became a nuclear power. Russian and U.S. leaders quickly set to work to persuade the Ukrainians to give up its new weapons.

Suspicious of Russia. Many Ukrainians were unwilling to do this. For one thing, they were deeply suspicious of Russia. How could Ukraine protect itself if Russia tried to build up a new Russian empire? Moreover, Ukrainian nationalists wanted their country to be a powerful state in its own right. What better way to these goals than to keep the weapons it had inherited from the Soviet Union?

Support From Major Powers. Ukrainian leaders became more and more convinced that their country needed the nuclear weapons. To shake this belief, Western powers promised to support Ukrainian independence. They sweetened their promise by offering economic aid. Then the United States, Russia, and Britain jointly promised that they would respect Ukraine's borders. They also pledged that they would not use economic sanctions against Ukraine. In exchange, they asked Ukraine to give up its nuclear weapons. They also requested it to sign the START I arms-reduction treaty and the Nuclear Nonproliferation Treaty.

Signing the Treaty. The Ukrainian president, a former rocket engineer, accepted the bargain. In November 1994, the parliament ratified the Nuclear Nonproliferation Treaty.

Before the end of 1994, Ukraine had started dismantling its nuclear missiles. The warheads went to Russia to be destroyed. The missiles stayed in Ukraine to be cut apart. The resulting cylinders were then used as farm silos and fuel tanks. In Ukraine, at least, the turning of "swords" into "ploughshares" had begun.

Crisis in Korea

In March 1993, North Korea announced its intention to withdraw from the Nuclear Nonproliferation Treaty. Before this, no nation had backed out of the treaty. Would North Korea become the first to do so?

Background. North Korea had signed the treaty in 1985. It then began allowing *International Atomic Energy Agency* (IAEA) inspectors to check on its civilian nuclear power program. But when the IAEA proposed an inspection of two special sites, North Korea stopped cooperating. The IAEA expected to find spent, or used, nuclear fuel at these sites. They wanted to determine whether North Korea had diverted any nuclear materials to military use. North Korea refused to allow the inspection. When the IAEA insisted on it, North Korea said it would withdraw from the pact.

Reaction in the United States and Japan. That threat set alarm bells ringing in Washington and other world capitals. The North Koreans had a plant for recycling used nuclear fuel. Normally, such a plant would turn out fuel for civilian nuclear power plants. But it might also turn the used fuel into weapons-grade plutonium. The specialists feared that North Korea might have already produced enough plutonium to make one or two nuclear weapons. Such a possibility would threaten stability in Asia and the rest of the world. Two months later, North Korea tested its first medium-range missile. Specialists said the missile was capable of carrying a small nuclear device. Japanese officials expressed fears that such a missile might reach some of their most heavily populated cities.

The Crisis Is Defused. Legally, North Korea had a right to withdraw from the treaty after a three-month waiting period. World reaction to its withdrawal was so strong, however, that North Korean leader Kim Il Sung had second thoughts. The crisis dragged on for a year and a half. The United States threatened economic sanctions unless North Korea allowed the inspections. North Korea warned that it would view sanctions as an act of war. A military confrontation seemed possible. U.S. and North Korean diplomats held round after round of meetings to avoid such a disaster.

In October 1994, shortly after Kim Il Sung's death, the two sides arrived at a resolution. The plan was so complex that it would take ten years to complete. North Korea agreed not to pursue a nuclear weapons program. It would also shut down its existing nuclear power stations and close its reprocessing plant. In return, the Western nations promised North Korea two new nuclear power reactors and other economic aid. South Korea and Japan agreed to pay for most of the aid. The new reactors would produce much less plutonium than the older type. And the plutonium would be used only for electric power. The new power plants would be built in South Korea because the South Koreans were bearing most of the cost. Reluctantly, the North Koreans agreed.

Monitoring Iraq

Iraq's case was unusual. A UN-sponsored military force had defeated Iraq in the Persian Gulf War in 1991. As part of the peace terms, the Iraqi government agreed to let a group called the United Nations Special Commission inspect their factories. The United Nations wanted to make sure Iraq was destroying its programs to build nuclear, biological, and chemical weapons.

The commission made a number of startling discoveries. Iraq was preparing to use advanced computer-controlled machinery to build nuclear weapons. A British firm had provided precision equipment and technology to the Iraqis. German companies had also contributed some sophisticated machinery.

Ease of Obtaining Equipment. This incident demonstrated how hard it is to prevent nuclear proliferation. Iraq had signed the Nuclear Nonproliferation Treaty. So had Britain, the United States, and Germany. Nevertheless, Iraq started a nuclear weapons program. It had little trouble buying the highly specialized equipment it needed from other countries that had also signed the treaty. Iraqi officials later stated that Iraq was within four months of producing its first nuclear bomb when the Persian Gulf War began.

New Threats from Iraq. UN inspectors believed that the Iraqis were manufacturing and storing weapons in structures referred to as "presidential properties." In the fall of 1997, the Iraqi government refused to allow the inspectors to search these sites. It claimed that the sites must remain closed to preserve national security.

First, Iraqis barred the Americans' participation in inspection tours. Then they expelled the Americans from Iraq. As Iraq grew more uncooperative and defiant, the U.S. government made preparations to attack. During the Persian Gulf War, most of Iraq's Arab neighbors

TWO DICTATORS OF THE 1990s

Kim Jong Il, leader of the Communist state of North Korea, took control of his country's government upon the death of his father, Kim Il Sung, in 1994. The elder Kim had held supreme power for 46 years. When his son took his place, North Korea became the world's first Communist dynasty.

Born in February 1948, Kim was his father's firstborn son. When he was six years old, his father became dictator of the newly created Communist nation. Kim attended elite schools in Pyongyang, the North Korean capital, while his father built up his political power. In 1964, Kim began working for the Korean Workers' Party, as the country's Communist party is known. He became a member of the Politburo, the nation's governing body in 1975, and was officially named his father's successor in 1980. The young man was made supreme commander of the armed forces in 1991. Long before his father's death in 1994, Kim was in charge of the day-to-day operations of the nation's government.

North Korea is a country with many problems. At the time Kim became dictator, the economy was in decline, the government's funds were depleted, and the nation's nuclear-development program was under attack by world leaders. The new leader had made a practice of avoiding contact with foreign diplomats and officials and had done little travel outside North Korea. Nor had he taken part in the high-level negotiations concerning his father's threat to withdraw from the Nuclear Non-Proliferation Treaty. As a result, little was known about Kim. Some described him as a bloodthirsty terrorist responsible for a 1983 bombing that killed seventeen South Korean officials in Myanmar, and as a power-hungry tyrant. Others regarded him as a friendly man who liked to attend parties, and who made jokes about his small stature.

Kim dropped out of sight for awhile after his father's state funeral. This caused rumors that he was seriously ill as a result of a car accident and that he was unable to gain the support of military leaders needed to consolidate his power. Speculation ended in October 1997, when Kim officially assumed the title of General Secretary of the Korean Workers' Party.

North Korea has long been known as one of the world's most isolated and secretive nations. This continued under Kim, who inherited the "personality cult" that had idolized his father. He is called by North Koreans, for example, "Dear Leader," "Guiding Focus," and "Bright Star of the Country."

Saddam Hussein, dictator of Iraq, has maintained a repressive police state since 1979. He is best known as the leader who ordered his forces to invade Kuwait in 1990, and was then compelled to withdraw from the tiny nation by a U.S.-led coalition of allied troops in the Persian Gulf War.

Born in 1937 to a peasant family in northern Iraq, Hussein entered politics at age 20 by joining the Ba'th Arab Socialist Party. Following an unsuccessful attempt to assassinate Iraq's military dictator in 1959, Hussein spent several years in exile in Egypt. In 1963, army officers and members of the Ba'th Party took control of Iraq. Hussein returned from exile. He gained power and influence in the government, holding important party and government posts. Upon the resignation of Iraq's president in 1979, Saddam Hussein was selected to succeed him.

One of Hussein's first actions as president was to order the execution of 500 opponents in the Ba'th Party. In 1980, Hussein launched an attack on neighboring Iran in an effort to increase Iraq's power in the Persian Gulf region. Before a cease-fire ended the war in 1988, an estimated 150,000 Iraqi soldiers died. Iraq's economy was severely damaged by the war, and Iranian air attacks killed many Iraqi civilians. After the war, Hussein began rebuilding Iraq and strengthened his brutal dictatorship. Despite the damage caused by the Iran-Iraq war, Hussein was able to maintain a huge, well-trained military force. Included in the armed forces were Republican Guard units fiercely loyal to Hussein.

Because many Iraqis suffered from poverty, disease, and starvation, Hussein took steps to protect himself from a popular revolution. He repressed rebellions by Shi'ite Muslims and Kurds and rotated senior army officers to prevent a military takeover. Despite another humiliating defeat and more damage to Iraq in the Persian Gulf War in 1991, Hussein retained his political power. He was the sole candidate in the presidential election of October 1995 and was reelected by 99.9 percent of the voters.

Under Hussein's dictatorship, the president and the Ba'th Party control all branches of the Iraqi government. The secret police assist the government by restricting the political activities of anyone who is not a member of the Ba'th Party. Government policies are determined by the Revolutionary Command Council, which is made up of ten top officials of the Ba'th Party. Hussein is chairman of the council.

1. Explain how Kim Jong II and Saddam Hussein have influenced global history in the late 20th century.

2. Would you like to live in either North Korea or Iraq? Why or why not?

had supported the Western nations. This time they were unwilling to fight or cooperate in any other way. While France and Great Britain supported the United States, Russia stated that it would not allow an assault on Iraq for fear of setting off a world war.

In February 1998, U.S. troops were poised to bomb strategic targets in Iraq. Meanwhile, diplomatic efforts to defuse the situation continued. Kofi Annan, the UN secretary general, finally succeeded in overcoming Iraq's resistance. He persuaded its president, Saddam Hussein, to allow UN inspectors access to eight restricted presidential sites.

U.S. President Bill Clinton accordingly called off the attack. He was not entirely reassured by the agreement, however. He asked other nations to join him in a serious warning: If Iraq did not continue to allow inspectors unlimited access to all suspected weapon storage sites, it would be attacked.

Efforts to End Nuclear Testing

The Nuclear Nonproliferation Treaty came up for renewal in 1995. The nations that had signed the treaty met to discuss its future.

Should the treaty be extended indefinitely? That was what the United States and other nuclear powers wanted. Or should its extension be limited to 25 years? That was what many smaller nations proposed. They would only agree to an indefinite extension if the nuclear powers promised to give up their own nuclear arms. All nations eventually agreed to extend the treaty indefinitely. In order to win the extension, the nuclear powers had repeated their old promise to give up their weapons. They also made a new pledge to conclude a comprehensive ban on nuclear testing by the end of 1996.

Efforts to halt nuclear testing have been under way since the 1950s. At the time, most people were concerned about the harmful radiation that aboveground nuclear tests release into the atmosphere. In 1963, the United States, Britain, and the Soviet Union signed the Limited Nuclear Test-Ban Treaty. The treaty banned the testing of nuclear weapons in the atmosphere, underwater, or in space. It allowed tests to be conducted underground, however. In recent years, China and France have observed the same restriction. India and Pakistan conducted underground nuclear weapons tests in 1998.

The Comprehensive Test-Ban Treaty

In October 1992, a moratorium, or temporary halt, in nuclear weapons testing went into effect. It was the result of an agreement among the United States, Russia, France, and Britain. Meanwhile, representatives of 38 nations met in Geneva, Switzerland, to discuss a comprehensive test-ban treaty. A comprehensive treaty would ban all types of tests, including those underground.

A key issue at the Geneva talks was whether or not to continue to allow very small underground nuclear tests. The United States and Russia said that they were necessary to check the reliability of their weapons. Nonnuclear states strongly opposed any such loopholes. In August 1995, President Clinton promised not to conduct small tests.

Saddam Hussein protesting his innocence while stockpiling chemical weapons

That put pressure also on Russia to agree to a comprehensive test ban.

Support for a comprehensive test-ban treaty seemed to be strong. Many nations condemned China and France. They felt that these countries should not stage underground tests while the test-ban treaty was being discussed. China began new tests in 1993, France in 1995. Both nations said they intended to conduct a limited number of tests that would be finished before the end of 1996. Both said they would then sign a comprehensive test-ban treaty.

By April 2000, over 150 nations had signed the treaty but only 52, including Russia, had ratified it. The United States had signed the agreement in October 1999, but the U.S. Senate voted against ratification.

INFO CHECK

1. How did the United States and other nations respond to nuclear weapons crises in Ukraine and North Korea? How successful were these efforts?

2. Why did U.S. President Bill Clinton order an air and missile attack on Iraq in 1998? Why do you think British Prime Minister Tony Blair ordered British warplanes to support the American attack? Explain why you AGREE or DISAGREE with the actions of these leaders.

3. How does the Comprehensive Test Ban Treaty differ from the Nuclear Nonproliferation Treaty?

THE INTERNATIONAL TRADE IN WEAPONS

When Rwandan rebels and government forces clashed in the early 1990s, each side had a large stash of weapons. They had mortars from France, assault rifles from Romania and Russia, and machine guns and grenades from South Africa. Each year, buyers from many nations spend tens of billions of dollars for weapons sold on the world arms market.

Many nations have arms-exporting industries. China leads in the production of light arms, such as rifles and hand grenades; it also sells missiles. Sweden sells everything from fighter planes to submarines. But the United States outsells almost everyone.

While the world's leaders often denounce the arms trade, they also encourage it. U.S. administrations have actively assisted U.S. corporations in winning arms contracts from allied nations. After the cold war ended, the U.S. government cut back its purchases from U.S. arms manufacturers. The manufacturers had to lay off workers, cut back research, and merge with one another. The arms industry was on the verge of collapse. To prevent further economic hardship, the government stepped up the promotion of sales to other countries.

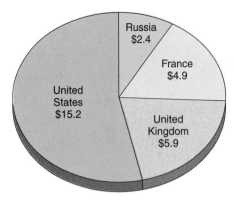

Major Arms-Selling Nations   1997
(value of sales in U.S. $)

Attempts to Limit Arms Sales

The major nations try to put limits on the sale of certain weapons, especially such destructive ones as missiles. They also try to control sales of technology that might have military applications. The *Missile Technology Control Regime* (MTCR) helps to coordinate these controls. The United States, Canada, France, Germany, Italy, Japan, and the United Kingdom started this organization in 1987. Several other nations have signed on since. The MTCR limits exports of all but the shortest-range ballistic and cruise missiles. A separate agreement restricts sales of arms and military technology to such "troublesome" states as Iraq, Iran, North Korea, and Libya.

In 1993, the Clinton Administration attempted to stop Russia from selling missile technology to India and dangerous chemicals to Libya. It also barred Americans from doing business with Russian firms that violate the international limits on missile exports. The ad-

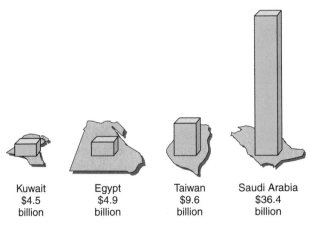

Major Arms-Buying Nations   1994–1997
(value of purchases in U.S. $)

ministration also refused to cooperate with Russia in science projects. For example, it made construction of a U.S. and Russian space station dependent on Russia's agreement to abide by the controls.

Although China did not sign the MTCR, it did agree to observe the controls. Nevertheless, Beijing sold missile technology to Pakistan in the 1990s. China also purchased advanced military technology from Israel. In order to stop such activities, the United States has occasionally cut off exports of high-tech American goods to China.

Overall, the sale of weapons to developing nations has declined since the end of the cold war. From a peak of $61 billion in 1988, arms sales dropped to around $25 billion a year in the mid-1990s.

The Arms Buildup in Asia

Weapons suppliers in the United States, Russia, France, and Germany compete for business in Asian countries. Starting in 1988, China steadily increased its military spending. It purchased sophisticated fighter aircraft from Russia and expressed interest in buying Russian aircraft carriers. China's arms buildup threatens its neighbors. Japan, China's chief rival for markets, investments, and resources, fears that it might be its target. Taiwan leaders are concerned that, when China grows strong enough, it might invade their country.

The Asian nation that posed the most serious threat to peace in the early 1990s was North Korea. As discussed in an earlier section, it had been developing its nuclear capability. It had also increased its arsenal of conventional weapons and built up its armed forces. Sixty-five percent of its one million troops had been stationed close to the *demilitarized zone* on its South Korean border. Military analysts predicted that any hostile actions by North Korea would force Japan to increase its military forces. This, in turn, would cause further buildup in China.

Concern about the growing military power of Asian nations caused the United States to seek new defense arrangements. In 1993, with the help of the Association of Southeast Asian Nations, the United States arranged a multinational discussion. It focused on achieving mutual security in the region by slowing down the purchase of weapons.

INFO CHECK

1. Explain why you AGREE or DISAGREE with the following: "The United States is opposed to the international trade in weapons, but also participates in it!"

2. China and North Korea have both increased their military forces in 1990s. Which country do you think presents the greatest threat to world peace? Give reasons for your answer.

HUMAN RIGHTS: ISSUES AND PROBLEMS

In June 1993, the United Nations hosted a two-week-long World Conference on Human Rights in Vienna, Austria. It was attended by 5,000 delegates from 160 countries. Representatives of 1,000 nongovernmental organizations also attended. The participants debated the rights of women, minority groups, native peoples, migrant workers, the handicapped, and other groups. They also discussed political and economic rights.

The Debate Over Human Rights

The Western nations favored strengthening the United Nations' authority to defend human rights. Several Asian nations, however, wished to keep Westerners from interfering in their internal affairs. Western delegates argued that human rights should be guaranteed to the people of all nations. They rejected the idea that governments can withhold such rights from citizens for any reason.

The leaders of many developing nations strongly objected to this idea. They classified some human rights as "Western." For example, they did not consider living under a democratic government to be a human right. Western beliefs in human rights derive from the period of the Enlightenment (Chapter 19). John Locke argued that people have three basic "natural rights"—to life, liberty, and property.

At the end of the conference, the delegates adopted an agenda for international action on human rights and liberties. The United States proposed that a new United Nations High Commissioner for Human Rights be appointed. This was endorsed by Nigeria, Uganda, and Gambia. *Amnesty International*, a nongovernmental human rights organization, led several groups in criticizing the conference. They claimed that it had added nothing new to earlier United Nations human rights declarations. Others felt that the conference had identified the important global issues related to human rights.

Human Rights: An International Concern

After World War II, people were horrified to learn of the atrocities that the Nazi regime had committed in Europe. They began to feel that other nations should intervene when a government abuses its citizens and others.

The founders of the United Nations made the issue of human rights a priority. The UN Charter, adopted in 1945, stated that the organization should promote "universal respect for . . . fundamental freedoms for all without distinction as to race, sex, language, or religion." In 1948, the United Nations issued the Universal Declaration of Human Rights. The UN General Assembly adopted this statement of commitment unanimously.

In subsequent years, the nations of the world made a number of international agreements that focused on human rights. These included: the European Convention on Human Rights (1950); the International Covenant on Civil and Political Rights (1966); the American Convention on Human Rights (1969); the Helsinki Accords (1975); and the African Charter on People's and Human Rights (1981).

Measures Taken to Protect Human Rights

Private citizens began to form nongovernmental organizations, or NGO's, to support those agreements. NGO's did much to educate people about human rights abuses. They spoke out against nations that abused their citizens. Nevertheless, most governments did not try to stop other governments from abusing human rights until the 1980s.

During the 1980s, several governments joined in making foreign policies that promoted human rights in other countries. The Scandinavian countries and the Netherlands issued reports on denying economic aid to countries that violated human rights. The European Community based its economic transactions with countries on their human rights practices. Canada and Australia announced that the promotion of human rights would affect their participation in international projects. The Council of Europe refused to accept Turkey as a member unless it improved its human rights practices.

During the 1980s, U.S. policy on human rights focused on the establishment of free elections. The United States took steps to oppose anti-Communist dictators it had once supported. For example, it helped turn General Augusto Pinochet out of Chile in 1989.

The spotlight on human rights issues made it difficult for dictators to crush their citizens' protests against abuse of power. To keep Western economic aid, a number of countries installed democratic governments. Argentina did so in 1983; Uruguay followed suit in 1985.

The international community's growing concern for human rights also encouraged people to revolt against oppression. In 1986, popular revolts removed dictators in Haiti and the Philippines. Fear of international censure forced the military regime in South Korea to permit democratic elections.

In 1989, the Chinese government violently put down a demonstration for democracy by college students. News photographs and reports of the Tiananmen Square massacre touched off worldwide condemnation. This condemnation did not soften Chinese policy. Nonetheless, the world's sympathy for the Chinese dissidents encouraged other Asian people to reject their Communist regimes. Mongolians made a peaceful transition from communism to multiparty democracy. The people of Nepal also moved toward democracy.

The human rights revolution continued into the 1990s. Public awareness of human rights issues increased. Nongovernmental organizations became more active in protesting violations. Under this combined pressure, governments made human rights a key factor in international policy.

Human Rights and Refugees

The 1990s saw a dramatic increase in the number of people fleeing their homelands to avoid war or persecution. Millions of refugees fled from the former Yugoslavia, several republics of the former Soviet Union, Iraq, Rwanda, Somalia, Ethiopia, Mozambique, and Liberia. The civil war in Bosnia and Croatia alone produced 3.5 million refugees by 1995.

Immigrants and Aliens in Europe

More than 750,000 refugees crowded into Western European countries in the peak year of 1992. The region's population of legal immigrants soared to nearly 20 million. The number of illegal immigrants was estimated at 2 million. In later years, the flow of aliens eased somewhat. *Aliens* are people who do not have citizenship in the country where they reside. Thus, all immigrants are aliens until they become citizens.

Most of the new arrivals required economic support from their host nations. Unfortunately, they came to Western Europe when it was experiencing an economic downturn. Funding for UN refugee-assistance programs was tight. Levels of unemployment were high, and housing was scarce. The local people resented having to compete with new arrivals for jobs and homes. The newcomers were poor, lacking in marketable skills, and different in culture and race. Many West Europeans felt threatened by them. Some even attacked them. Others demanded that the government restrict immigration.

Approximately half the immigrants to Europe in the 1990s were Muslims. The majority of these were North Africans. Others were Bosnians, Turks, Pakistanis, and Somalis. In France, where most people are Roman Catholics, Islam replaced Protestantism as the second largest religion.

In Belgium, Austria, and Italy, anti-immigrant political parties gained new public support. In Spain, nationalist groups called for the expulsion of Arabs and Africans. Demonstrations against foreigners increased in Britain and Sweden. In all these countries, gangs made violent attacks on immigrants and people of foreign extraction.

German Reaction to Immigrants. In Germany, foreigners made up 7 percent of the population. This percentage was higher than in any other Western European country. Economic and social problems had followed the unification of East and West Germany in 1991. Some Germans accused the immigrants of adding to these problems.

Neo-Nazis and other ultranationalists attacked foreigners. Most Germans opposed the attacks and criticized their government for not doing more to prevent them. In response, the government cracked down on the neo-Nazis. In 1999, the German government proposed legislation to permit resident aliens to become citizens. However, it also moved to restrict new immigration to Germany.

Italian Reaction to Immigrants. Italy experienced an economic expansion in the 1980s. As a result, approximately one million immigrants entered the country. A large number of them came from Morocco and other African nations. The immigrants took jobs that native Italians did not want. Even after ten years, many of the foreigners still lived in poverty. When hard times struck in the 1990s, Italians turned against them. Still, 25,000 Albanians were allowed to enter Italy in 1991.

During the 1990s, most European nations took steps to restrict illegal immigrants. Governments introduced rigorous checks to identify and expel foreign residents who took jobs illegally. They were strict in monitoring short-stay visitors and people who came to be reunited with their families.

French Reaction to Immigrants. In France, a population of 57 million people included 4 million foreigners. Immigration became a

French students demonstrating against the National Front's
anti-immigration stance

hot issue in French political campaigns. In 1993, the parliament toughened laws on immigration. One measure repealed a policy of granting French citizenship to anyone born on French soil. Prior to this, even a child born to foreign parents on a visit to France was legally a French citizen. Another law made it easier for the government to expel illegal aliens. Still another made it harder for foreigners to acquire residency papers.

Human rights advocates called the changes discriminatory. However, French people who were worried about high unemployment supported them. In France's 1995 presidential election, Jean-Marie Le Pen, leader of the far-right National Front Party, won more than 15 percent of the vote. Le Pen proposed many policies against immigrants.

Immigrants and Aliens in America. The United States has long been considered a nation of immigrants and a haven for refugees. This view is not entirely accurate, however. It is true that people from all corners of the globe populated and built America. Nonetheless, the United States had in the past put *quotas*, or limits, on the numbers of people that can be accepted from each country. During the early 20th century, these quotas favored immigrants from Western Europe. In 1965, this discriminatory system was changed to give applicants from all nations a chance to become U.S. citizens. In the 1990s, quotas were again put on immigrants.

Among the latest arrivals, Asians, Africans, and Latin Americans outnumbered Europeans. The number of people hoping to settle in the United States continues to increase. In the mid-1990s, nearly 2.5 million people were on lists awaiting admission. Many did not wait. Illegal immigrants entered the United States at double the rate of legal entrants. According to estimates, almost 40 percent of America's population growth over the next decade will come from immigration.

Negative reaction to immigrants focused on possible increases in taxes to pay for social services and education. Some protested that immigrants took jobs away from citizens. Often, though, immigrants filled jobs that no one else wanted to take. The newcomers' energy revitalized rundown areas in many cities.

The Haitian Boat People

In 1993, a decision of the U.S. Supreme Court intensified concern over refugees. It ruled that Haitians attempting to enter the United States illegally would be returned to Haiti. International law prohibits the return of refugees to a place where they could suffer persecution. During the Vietnamese War, the United States had recognized this law. It criticized Hong Kong for returning Vietnamese boat people without checking to see if they were fleeing from persecution.

Nevertheless, in May 1992, the U.S. Coast Guard began stopping

Haitian boats. It returned the refugees to Haiti without allowing them to request political asylum. In 1994, President Clinton modified this policy by ordering the Coast Guard to check the political status of the refugees. The flow of Haitians to the United States tapered off in 1994 when Haiti regained its civilian government.

President Clinton's modification of the policy toward the Haitian refugees did not appease the members of human rights organizations. They feared that it would be used against other groups. The UN High Commissioner for Refugees also disliked the policy. It showed that the United States placed protection of its borders above international law.

African Migrations: Hutu and Tutsi

The most recent conflict between the Hutus and the Tutsis in Rwanda started in 1994. The trigger was the assassination of the Hutu president, allegedly by Tutsis. Rwandan government soldiers and Hutu militia took revenge by slaughtering Tutsis and moderate Hutus.

As the killing spread, swarms of refugees fled to neighboring countries. In one 24-hour period, 250,000 people poured into Tanzania. More than a million fled to Zaire (now the Democratic Republic of the Congo), where tens of thousands died of cholera. In Rwanda, UN peacekeepers found huge piles of corpses.

During 1997, the conflict between Hutus and Tutsis continued in Rwanda and neighboring countries. Hutu and Tutsi refugees still looked for sanctuary from mass killings and famine.

INFO CHECK

1. Define the term human rights.

2. Identify three international agreements to protect human rights.

3. Explain why each of the following has become a matter of concern to the UN and other human rights organizations: political dissidents, refugees and aliens, ethnic minorities.

TERRORISTS AND ULTRANATIONALISTS

The Threat to Global Security

Terrorism is the systematic use of violence to achieve political goals. In modern times, individuals or small militant groups have engaged in terrorist acts against governments and dominant majorities. Although they are meant to affect powerful groups, acts of terrorism frequently kill and injure innocent bystanders. Governments and international organizations regard terrorism as a major threat to domestic and international security. They have been forced to apply more and more of their resources to combat this menace.

Ultranationalists feel that a particular national or ethnic group should dominate their country. Their aggressive behavior toward people of other cultures marks them as racists. Since they use violence in the same way that terrorists do, right-wing extremists threaten both domestic and world peace.

Major Events of the 1990s

Terrorism in the United States. In the 1990s, the United States began to experience acts of terrorism. A powerful car bomb exploded in New York City's World Trade Center in 1993. It caused six deaths and extensive damage to the building. Two years later, a truck bomb demolished the Alfred P. Murrah Federal Building in Oklahoma City, killing 168 people, including 15 children. The first incident was attributed to international terrorists, the second, to homegrown extremists.

Terrorism in the Middle East. The Middle East has long been a hotbed of terrorism. Arab-Israeli differences have caused much of the violence. In the 1990s, however, other terrorist movements became active. Algerian Islamists launched attacks that killed tens of thousands of people in 1992. They were angry because their government had not recognized an Islamic party's electoral victory. A sect of militant Egyptian Islamists attempted to bring down the government of President Hosni Mubarak. They hoped that their attacks on tourists would destroy Egypt's tourist trade and weaken its economy. The militants considered Mubarak to be hostile to Islam and too friendly to the United States and Israel.

The nature of Middle Eastern terrorism changed in the late 1990s. Some organizations, such as the Popular Front for the Liberation of Palestine, concluded that terrorism would not work. Other groups grew extremely weak. They no longer had the support of Libya, Syria, and other Arab nations. They now sought to improve their global image. More important, Arab leaders now had to protect their own governments from Islamic terrorist attacks.

Many terrorist groups wanted to replace secular Arab governments with Muslim fundamentalist regimes. In pursuit of this objective, militant Islamists struck at targets in the Arab world, Europe, and the United States. The fundamentalist regimes of Iran and Sudan were believed to be the key sponsors of the new terrorism.

Terrorism in Other Areas

In 1995, French cities were disrupted when bombs exploded in subway cars and garbage cans. Authorities blamed the Islamic opponents of the Algerian government. The Islamists were angry that the French had cooperated with Algerian leaders.

In South America, a bomb set off by drug gangs or leftist guerrillas killed 30 people at a festival in Bogotá, Colombia, in 1993.

In 1996, terrorists in Lima, Peru, took about 500 people hostage. They had been guests at a diplomatic reception. All but 72 were released. Peruvian commandos stormed the residence where the hostages were being held and freed them. The terrorists were killed in the raid.

In 1995, Japanese terrorists released a nerve gas called sarin in five Tokyo subway cars during rush hour. Twelve people died as a result. Officials placed responsibility for the attack on the members of a religious cult.

In many areas of the world, terrorist campaigns drag on for years. During the 1960s, a terrorist organization known by the initials ETA began terrorist operations in Spain. They were still active in the 1990s. Its members demanded that the Basque provinces of northern Spain be allowed to rule themselves. In 1999, the Spanish government warned the ETA that violence would not be tolerated.

Also in the 1990s, Kurdish rebels mounted a wave of assaults on Turkish diplomatic missions and businesses throughout Europe. They had been struggling for more than a decade to gain independence from Turkey.

From 1983 into the 1990s, Tamil rebels used terrorist tactics in a war for independence from Sri Lanka (South Asia). For more than two decades, Muslim rebels in the Moro Front waged a guerrilla war for independence from the Philippines.

In some parts of the world, terrorist campaigns have tapered off and even stopped. This happened in Canada, where Quebec separatists resorted to terrorism in the 1960s and 1970s. They later turned to more peaceful methods.

A lessening of attacks happened in Northern Ireland. The Irish Republican Army (IRA) had begun a campaign of terror in the 1970's. In 1994, the Roman Catholic IRA and its Protestant opponents called for a halt to the violence so that political negotiations could begin. But outbreaks of violence continued to take place even as the peace agreement was being carried out in 1998.

Ultranationalist Violence

Ultranationalist, or right-wing, violence is another threat to world peace. Usually, this kind of violence is directed against ethnic or religious groups. It may also be aimed at governments seen as hostile to ultranationalist goals.

Right-wing extremists known as Neo-Nazis were active in Germany and other countries. They wanted to reestablish the Third Reich, Hitler's Nazi government. Neo-Nazis often direct their attacks at minority group members and foreigners. Skinheads, another extremist group, often follow the ideas of the Neo-Nazis.

The Balkans

Ultranationalism and racism played a part in the disintegration of Yugoslavia in the 1990s. Hatred between Muslims and Christians in the Balkan region dates back to the 1400s. At that time, the area was a battleground between the Muslim sultans of the Ottoman Empire and the Christian rulers of Europe. Because of atrocities committed by both sides, hatred between the two groups has smoldered for centuries. When Yugoslavia broke apart in 1991, this hatred flared into violence. In 1995, the Bosnian Serbs overran the UN-protected city of Srebrenica. Afterward, 4,000 to 6,000 Bosnian Muslims were reported missing. Satellite photos showed large mounds of freshly turned soil in the area. After examining these pictures, U.S. leaders suspected that Bosnian Serbs had shot and buried many of the missing Muslims. Bosnian Serbs accused the Croatians and Muslims also of committing mass murder.

The United States

Ultranationalism is also to be found beyond Europe. Neo-Nazi groups in the United States have committed a number of racially motivated murders and vandalized synagogues. The Aryan Brotherhood and the Nation have attacked minority members who are prominent in the government and the arts.

Efforts to Control Terrorism and Ultranationalism

The United Nations urged all countries to cooperate in combating the threat of terrorism and ultranationalism. In January 1997, the General Assembly adopted a resolution on measures against international terrorism.

The UN resolution required nations to cooperate with one another in the struggle against terrorism. It suggested that they exchange information about terrorist groups and conduct joint investigations of their activities. It encouraged them to research methods of detecting harmful substances or devices hidden in public places. It advised them to develop ways to prevent the use of electronic and other high-tech communication systems in terrorist acts. It recommended that they investigate organizations suspected of providing cover or funds for terrorism. The resolution also repeated an earlier appeal to governments not to support terrorist groups or provide them with refuge.

Chapter 35 will describe the technological advances that have brought the world closer together and how experts in a variety of countries are cooperating to solve shared problems.

INFO CHECK

1. Explain why you approve or disapprove of the methods used by *terrorists* and *ultranationalists* to achieve political change.

2. PROVE or DISPROVE:
   a. Terrorism came to the United States in the 1990s.
   b. Terrorism and ultranationalism are global problems.
   c. Terrorists and ultranationalists are often *racists*.

3. Describe the methods used in the 1990s to combat terrorism and ultranationalism.

CHAPTER REVIEW

Multiple Choice

1. United Nations peacekeeping efforts succeeded in Haiti, El Salvador, and Cambodia but failed in Bosnia, Rwanda, and Somalia because UN forces

   1. took sides in the conflict
   2. were placed in the midst of ongoing wars
   3. left because they ran out of money
   4. were militarily unprepared.

2. Recently, the UN has had difficulty maintaining a peacekeeping force because

   1. Soviet and U.S. conflict prevented forming such a force
   2. the smaller, less powerful nations did not want to participate in peacekeeping efforts
   3. many nations did not want to pay the high costs needed to support the peacekeeping force
   4. the United States did not want to send its forces in support of a UN peacekeeping effort.

3. The United Nations Development Program rates a nation's ability to improve its citizens' quality of life. It uses such standards as

   1. life expectancy, education, and quality of life

   2. per capita income, male-to-female births, and size of families
   3. type of government and whether the economy is agricultural or industrial
   4. government stability, number of people receiving welfare, and food stamps.

4. The reorganization of NATO in the 1990s provided for the

   1. defense of Western Europe
   2. ability to respond to Middle Eastern crises
   3. stabilization of Eastern Europe
   4. all of the above.

5. The nuclear balance of power between the Soviet Union and the United States resulted in

   1. environmental destruction
   2. both sides cooperating in arms negotiations and limitation agreements
   3. both sides assisting their allies in building atomic weapons
   4. the nonaligned nations becoming allies of either the Soviet Union or the United States.

6. The nations of the world were concerned about the military and nu-

clear weapons of the former Soviet Union because

1. many nuclear weapons needed to be safeguarded or destroyed
2. their generals and soldiers were hiring out as mercenary armies
3. threats of nuclear war were made against the West by those who did not want the breakup of the Soviet Union
4. the Soviet military might destroy the oil supplies needed for world industries and commerce.

7. Along with conventional and nuclear weapons, another major issue for the world community has been

1. a ban on smoking
2. a ban on violence in movies
3. human rights abuses
4. women demanding voting rights.

8. Recently, in Europe, immigrants and aliens were not always accepted because

1. they were smarter than the local people and got the best jobs
2. they brought with them strange new languages and beliefs
3. local people feared they would cause political turmoil
4. many came needing assistance, and economic hard times placed them in competition with citizens for jobs and housing.

9. Africa has seen a continuing flood of refugees and violence because

1. imperialist nations were forcing out the native peoples
2. UN forces were fighting against apartheid
3. Nigerian government forces were seeking to end the Biafran separatist movement
4. fighting continued between the Hutu and Tutsi peoples.

10. One of the most persistent obstacles to world peace has been those who use terror tactics. These terrorists are

1. all located in the Middle East and are religious fanatics
2. all located in Eastern Europe and are religious fanatics
3. to be found worldwide and have religious as well as nationalistic goals
4. radicals who have grudges against a few people, governments, or companies.

11. The photograph on page 797 shows that the UN

1. failed to keep peace in Somalia
2. sometimes uses a military force in peacekeeping operations
3. no longer uses the General Assembly
4. has in itself become a major military power.

12. A conclusion suggested by the charts on page 810 is that

1. major arms-buying nations purchase weapons from each other
2. the United States is the leading exporter of arms while Saudi Arabia is the leading buyer
3. Asians have purchased most of the arms on the world market
4. Europeans sell weapons exclusively to nations of the Middle East.

Thematic Essays

1. During the cold war, the world was afraid that conflict between the two superpowers would lead to nuclear destruction. *Task:* Explain why that did not occur and describe the efforts of two superpowers and the UN to prevent nuclear destruction. Consider for inclusion in your answer balance of power, MAD, IAEA, and NNT.

2. The United Nations has met with limited success in trying to achieve world peace. *Task:* Using specific examples, identify and explain the reasons for peacekeeping success or failure.

Document-Based Questions

1. In 1963 a nuclear test ban treaty was drafted and signed by the United States, Great Britain, and the Soviet Union. It stated:

"... as their principal aim the speediest possible achievement of an agreement on general and complete disarmament under strict international control ... which would put an end to the armament race.... Each of the parties to this treaty undertakes to prohibit, to prevent, and not to carry out any nuclear weapon test or explosion. ..."

What was the goal of the three nations that signed this treaty, and why do you think other nations have failed to follow their lead?

2. Refer to the discussion of nations possessing nuclear weapons, on pages 802–803.

While the U.S. and the former Soviet Union's nations are limiting or destroying their nuclear weapons, developing nations of the world are testing or developing nuclear weapons.

Select any developing nation from the discussion. Briefly discuss two reasons for nuclear weapons development.

3. Selections from the United Nations Charter:

"... to unite our strength to maintain international peace and security, ... to employ international machinery for the promotion of the economic and social advancement of all people ... to take effective and collective measures for the prevention and removal of threats to the peace and for suppression of acts of aggression or other breaches of the peace."

Describe the main purpose of the United Nations and how it appears to be different from the League of Nations.

4. Look at the cartoon of Saddam Hussein on page 808.

Identify the symbols on the containers and over Hussein's head. Explain why the cartoonist used them in the picture.

5. From an article by Michael T. Klare on global security:

"... it is apparent that the problem of preventing and controlling local, ethnic, and regional conflict has become the premier world security concern of the post-cold war era. Because such conflicts are likely to [grow] in the years ahead, and because no single group is willing or able to guarantee global peace and stability, United States and world leaders will be forced to [enlarge] existing peacekeeping instruments and to develop new techniques. ..."

Describe the writer's view of the future and the suggestions he makes for future peace.

Document-Based Essay

Task: Identify any two major causes of world conflict. Describe what actions individual nations and peacekeeping organizations have taken to resolve the two problems you identified.

C H A P T E R
35

Global Trends and Issues of the Late 20th Century

After finishing his algebra, Adam sat down at his computer. Now he could work on his social studies project. Quickly he logged onto the Internet and accessed the chat room he had set up with his overseas pen pals. He was hosting an international conference on the environment.

Tonight, he and Pablo were going to discuss ways that Brazil could preserve the Amazon rain forests. Mitsuo from Japan and Inge from Germany had said they'd join in. Adam was glad. He and Pablo would need referees. When Adam had proposed the topic, Pablo had seemed annoyed. What Brazil did with its forests was its own business, he had said. And anyway, look at the United States. It produced most of the carbon dioxide gas that caused global warming. Adam decided that Pablo had a point. Maybe before they discussed the rain forests, they could brainstorm antipollution measures that the United States might take.

Adam hoped the other kids would like his report. He planned to use a lot of graphics and maybe some music to accompany the video clips. Putting it together would be the fun part.

J ust ten years ago, no high school student had the educational resources that Adam takes for granted. Computer software helps him to create multimedia reports. The Internet makes it possible for him to get current information about all sorts of subjects. It also enables him to discuss important issues with people of other cultures. This, in turn, teaches him diplomacy and cooperation.

Chapter 35 discusses advances in communication that are making the world a more closely knit community. The chapter also discusses international organizations and projects designed to promote global cooperation.

SCIENCE AND TECHNOLOGY

Since the 1940s, an important technological advance has given us new tools for work and leisure activities. The compact electronic computing machine makes it possible to process and store information rapidly. In 1970, scientists introduced the microchip, a small silicon chip that can store thousands of transistors. A *transistor* is a device that conducts electrical signals. The *microchip* makes it possible for computers to operate more quickly and store huge amounts of information. Because these microchips are so tiny, computers can be built in convenient sizes. By the 1990s, computers had become essential tools in every field of human activity.

Information Superhighway

Computers have transformed the economies of the industrialized nations. One way that they have done this is by rapidly sending large

The Electronic Numerical Integrator and Computer (ENIAC), introduced in 1946

Thumbnail-sized microchip, designed to handle all of ENIAC's functions

amounts of information across long distances. They allow investors to get up-to-the-minute news about foreign currencies and stock markets. They make it possible for manufacturers to send pictures and descriptions of their latest models to faraway customers. They help market researchers discover what kinds of products different consumers tend to buy. People speak of the flow of information through computers as the *information superhighway*.

Information has become an important source of wealth. By 1990, the production and sale of information accounted for 50 percent of the gross domestic product of the United States. Approximately half of all workers in the United States today have jobs in the information business.

The Internet. Corporations have been competing frantically to offer commercial services over the worldwide Internet. The *Internet* is a form of information superhighway that is already available to the public. It links computers in far-flung locations into one giant network. Individuals in their homes or cars can reach the Internet by using telephone signals. All they need is a phone, a computer, and a modem. (A *modem* converts digital computer signals into sounds that telephone equipment can process.) Businesses and universities can connect to the Internet over direct lines that give speedier service than those used by private individuals. People use the Internet to exchange messages (electronic mail, or *E-mail*), to share the information that they have stored on their computers, and to search for new information.

Lately, the fastest-growing segment of the Internet has been the World Wide Web. In addition to the printed word, it delivers sound, still pictures, and moving video images. Many businesspeople hope to turn the World Wide Web into a global shopping mall. They have introduced many different kinds of electronic cash and online credit cards. The big problem has been security. Many people have found ways to counterfeit the cash and steal the credit card numbers.

data on the geology of Mars, *Pathfinder* fell silent on September 27, 1997. It could not withstand the cold of the Martian winter. The lander and the little rover, which had been designed to last about one month, had lasted almost three.

Jupiter. The planet Jupiter, largest in the Solar System, has been another space target. *Galileo*, an American spacecraft launched in cooperation with Germany, carried cameras that recorded a spectacular collision between Jupiter and a flurry of comet fragments in 1994. *Galileo* later went into orbit around Jupiter to study the dense clouds in Jupiter's atmosphere and the planet's many moons.

Space Platform. Another key project of the 1990s was the beginning of joint construction of an international space platform that will be larger than a football field. It will include seven laboratories to be used by Americans, Europeans, Russians, Japanese, and Canadians. Facilities will allow a crew to stay aboard permanently. Space shuttles will come and go from the Earth's surface. In 1995, a U.S. space shuttle carrying seven astronauts docked with Russia's three-person *Mir* space station. It was the first joint docking of U.S. and Russian spacecraft since a one-time event in 1975.

Scientists and political leaders considered the U.S. and Russian space project a valuable experience. One of the project's most important experiments, a study of the effects of low gravity on the human body, was successfully completed. In general, the venture has been an exercise in cooperation between Russian and American astronauts and scientists. The space platform should be completed in 2002.

Health and Medical Technology

Research, funding, and technological developments in the late 1990s have focused on AIDS, cancer, heart disease, and other global threats to human life. Advances were made in these and other areas critical to the quality of life.

AIDS. At international AIDS conferences in the 1990s, the difficulty of achieving early detection of the HIV virus, which causes AIDS, was a major topic of discussion. The ability of the virus to remain hidden in the blood cells for long periods of time has increased the difficulty of treatment. Researchers have concentrated efforts on developing antibodies to combat AIDS. Of the 18 such drugs produced, AZT, developed by the Glaxo Wellcome Company, a British firm, has received the most attention. AZT, however, appears to do little for patients who have the HIV virus but have not developed symptoms. For people with AIDS, AZT has provided definite benefits. Researchers have recently begun to study natural immunity to the HIV virus, hoping to duplicate the biochemical process in those without the immunity.

Alzheimer's. To combat the debilitating memory loss of Alzheimer's disease, scientists at Cytotherapeutics Inc. in Rhode Island have developed a miniature biotech factory that is inserted directly into the brain. The capsule, no bigger than a grain of rice, contains thousands of cells that produce a brain hormone called *nerve growth factor* (NGF). The lack of NGF is believed to cause Alzheimer's. The capsule is made from a special plastic membrane that has been engineered to shield its cells from attack by the body's immune system yet permits NGF to escape. Testing with rats and primates is in progress.

ALA. A team of British doctors discovered a useful acid called ALA. This natural compound sensitized cancer cells to light for a few hours. Used with ALA, a low-powered laser can destroy cancers near the surface of the skin without leaving a patient sensitive to sunlight for weeks. Researchers are trying to determine correct drug dosages and laser intensities.

Lasers. Surgeons have found laser technology a valuable tool. Because laser beams can be focused with great precision, they can be used to detect the exact location of a problem and to remove or repair it with less damage to the surrounding tissue. For this reason, lasers are an invaluable tool in eye surgery. When used with an endoscope, an instrument that allows the doctor to look inside tubular organs, a laser beam can be aimed from within the body. To take advantage of this possibility, researchers are working to develop lasers that can unblock clogged arteries.

Lung Cancer. Lung cancer kills about a million people a year. The cancer must be detected while still small, before it spreads. Canadian researchers have experimented with photosensitive drugs that make tumors glow under ultraviolet (UV) light. The drugs do not destroy cancer cells, but they make it possible to detect cancer cells earlier than do other methods. The Canadians discovered that all cells have a pale red glow in the presence of UV light. Healthy cells also emit green light. To help detect the difference between healthy and cancerous cells, a group of doctors started a company to build LIFE (lung-imaging fluorescent endoscope) machines.

Genes. Scientists and corporate executives predicted that the 21st century will usher in a new era of genes as drugs. They made this prediction after an American researcher developed a genetic treatment for cystic fibrosis, a disease that attacks the lungs. The treatment involves the use of an engineered gene that stimulates the lungs to make a protein to fight the disease. Efforts were also begun to develop genetic treatments for other diseases, such as cancer and diabetes.

It has been estimated that *mutations* (errors in the coding of genes) are responsible for 3,000 to 4,000 hereditary diseases. Recognizing that human DNA holds the genetic instructions to make and operate the human organism, biologists began the Human Genome Project in 1990. The goal of this ambitious 15-year effort is the decoding of all of the genetic information found in DNA. This genetic script, or *genome*, is the basis for much of what scientists can hope to

Scientist Ian Wilmut and his creation, the cloned sheep Dolly

explain about the physical aspects of human life, including the causes and treatment of disease.

Cloning. Cloning is a result of *genetic engineering*—the manipulation of DNA (the basic genetic material) in order to change traits or produce organisms. In 1997, a sheep made news all over the world. Her name was Dolly, and she was the first clone of an adult animal. Cloning is the process by which an organism is reproduced from only one parent, without fertilization. This means that the genetic structure of the clone is exactly the same as that of its parent. The Scottish scientists who created Dolly, and the scientific community as a whole, hope that cloning will lead to important medical advances—for example, the creation of animals whose organs could be successfully transplanted into humans.

INFO CHECK

1. Describe the computer revolution of the late 20th century. How has it changed the ways in which we live and work?

2. Define the following: information superhighway, Internet.

3. Explain the relationship among the microchip, the modem, and the flow of information and ideas.

4. List some of the uses of satellite technology.

5. Identify a significant late 20th-century development in each of the following areas: telecommunications, space explorations, health and medical technology.

THE ENVIRONMENT

Causes and Consequences of Environmental Destruction

The increase in industrialization and the advances in technology that have accompanied it have not been unmixed blessings. The chemicals used in fertilizers, factories, and such products as lead batteries and paper pollute soil and water. The burning of carbon fuels to produce heat for homes and energy for industries has not only poisoned the air but caused the world's temperatures to rise. Scientists predict that this change in the climate will melt the polar ice caps, which will then flood coastal areas of the world's continents.

Nuclear Safety. Finding safe ways to store radioactive byproducts from nuclear plants is difficult. Leaks from these wastes can contaminate crops and water supplies. Then, too, the plants that generate nuclear energy are not accident-proof. In March 1979, the operators of the U.S. Three Mile Island reactor misread a signal and turned off a cooling device. The core of the reactor melted, spilling radioactive material. Luckily, only a few harmful gases escaped beyond the containment building.

A more serious accident occurred in Ukraine in April 1986, when one of the reactors of the Chernobyl nuclear power plant exploded. Although authorities carried out a massive cleanup campaign, large areas in the vicinity remained heavily contaminated a decade later. During that time, the people living in those areas experienced a higher than normal incidence of thyroid cancer, leukemia, and other radiation-related illnesses.

Acid Rain and Deforestation. Acid rain, which is a combination of moisture and airborne chemicals from factories and cars, has damaged the forests of industrialized nations. Even more harm has been done by harvesting large numbers of trees or clearing forests so that the land can be used in other ways. *Deforestation* is occurring all

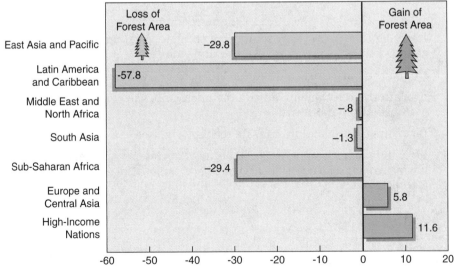

Annual Loss or Gain of Forest Areas, by Region,   1990–1995
(thousands of square kilometers)

over the world. The most dramatic example is the destruction of the Amazon rain forest. Its 5 million square kilometers comprise the largest continuous expanse of tropical rain forest remaining in the world. Although such forests cover only 7 percent of the planet's land surface, they contain approximately 50 percent of the plants and animals found on the globe. Of these, thousands of species face extinction each year as a result of forest destruction. (Trees are being felled at the rate of 4,500 acres every hour.)

Desertification. *Desertification* is the process by which farmland or grassland becomes desert. It is caused by drought, allowing animals to overgraze in an area, and cutting down too many trees and bushes. The roots of trees and bushes hold down the topsoil so that it cannot be blown away. This problem is common in Africa, where the Sahara is expanding at an alarming rate into the Sahel, a grassland on its southern border.

Although poisoning by chemical and other pollutants takes a heavy toll on wild plants and animals, environmental changes, such as land development, deforestation, and desertification, are the main threats to wildlife.

International Efforts to Preserve the Environment

Rio Conference. The *United Nations Conference on Environment and Development* (UNCED), the Earth Summit, held in Rio de Janeiro, Brazil, in 1992, was attended by delegates and diplomats from 178 countries. Thousands of representatives of nongovernmental organizations also participated. The conferees drew up a list of global policies for the protection of the environment. These included: (1) a proposal for environmental development; (2) the Rio Declaration, a list of environmental and economic-development concerns; and (3) statements about the prevention of global climatic changes and the protection of threatened forests.

Kyoto Convention. On December 1, 1997, delegates from more than 150 nations arrived in Kyoto, Japan, to attend the Conference of the Parties to the United Nations Framework Convention on Climate Change. They met to devise the first international treaty on ways to reduce the emission of carbon dioxide gas into the atmosphere. Carbon dioxide is a gas that is released when such fuels as coal, gasoline, and wood are burned. In the atmosphere, it serves as a sort of one-way windowpane, like the glass in a greenhouse. The sun's radiation passes down through the windowpane to warm the earth. Some of the heat from the earth's surface is radiated to the atmospheric windowpane, however, and is trapped on the earth, creating a *greenhouse effect*.

At the Kyoto convention, the delegates discussed the results of a two-year negotiation process that followed the Earth Summit held in Brazil. The final treaty, known as the Kyoto Protocol, laid out a specific strategy for combating global warming. This strategy required 38 industrialized nations to reduce their combined greenhouse-gas emissions to more than 5 percent below 1990 levels. Developing nations, which release fewer carbon dioxide gases into the atmosphere, could set their own limits on such emissions. Those industrialized nations that were unable to meet the limits set for them could apply for emission-reduction credits from industrialized nations that achieved reductions greater than that called for by the treaty. Since forests absorb large quantities of carbon dioxide, industrialized nations could receive emission credits by planting new forests and protecting existing ones.

U.S. lawmakers who attended the conference stated that the U.S. Senate would never ratify the Kyoto Protocol. Opponents of the treaty argued that to cut the use of carbon fuels to the extent it required would cause energy prices to soar and would damage the U.S. economy.

Air Pollution Controls

Throughout the 1990s, the United States has taken many measures to reduce its use of carbon fuels. The 1990 Clean Air Act stiffened antipollution laws that applied to cars, trucks, and buses. Since motor vehicles account for more than half of all air pollutants, air quality improves as older cars go out of use. Models on sale in the mid-1990s emitted only one percent as much pollution as those made 20 years earlier. California and 12 other states were planning to introduce still tougher standards in the late 1990s.

Restricting Auto Emissions. The American automobile industry has been under pressure to develop a high-performance *zero-emission* car—one that offers the convenience of any other car but gives off no pollutants. General Motors announced plans to sell an electric car in areas of the western United States. In Europe, an Environmental Concept Car (ECC) model has been developed by Volvo, a Swedish automobile manufacturer. The ECC is driven by a high-efficiency electric motor. The motor can operate on power supplied by on-board batteries, making the ECC a zero-emission vehicle for use in congested cities. When more range and performance are required, the driver can dial in a hybrid mode. This starts up a gas turbine engine that drives an ultra-efficient, high-speed generator. Even when the car is operating in the hybrid mode, emission levels are low.

The ECC and other electric models may be the environmental cars of the future. One carmaker has displayed an electric race car. It combines a turbine and flywheel, providing 500 horsepower for quick acceleration. Will everyone be driving electric cars in the future? Perhaps that won't be necessary. Automakers are finding new ways to cut the emissions from gasoline-powered engines. And they are also experimenting with other kinds of fuels.

Ideal Fuel. During the past 200 years, the demand for energy in industrialized countries has soared. Large future increases in global energy demand are expected from developing countries. The ideal fuel should be domestically supplied, renewable, and nonpolluting. Ultimately, a combination of solar energy and nuclear fusion to supply electricity and hydrogen gas may meet this need. Until such systems are developed, however, environmentalists are paying increased attention to natural gas, or methane.

Natural gas is abundant in North America, Europe, Asia, and elsewhere. It is the least polluting of the hydrocarbons. Currently, the United States relies primarily on coal for generating electricity and on petroleum for transportation. Because of declining U.S. petroleum production, the country has had to import more than half of its crude oil since 1994. The cost of that oil adds to U.S. trade deficits. It is argued, therefore, that increased use of natural gas would have both environmental and economic benefits.

In recent years, natural gas has gained ground in the transportation field. In some places, it powers buses, mail delivery trucks, and other vehicles. Since 1992, a few natural gas-powered sanitation trucks have operated in New York City. In addition, gas furnaces heated over half of American homes in the 1990s, and natural gas was used as a fuel to produce electrical energy more cleanly and efficiently than oil or coal.

Recycling

Technology has made it possible to increase the use of recycled paper. Several major American business firms have joined with the *Environmental Defense Fund* (EDF) in a long-range project to further improve the production of paper made from recycled trash. Their goal is to reduce the use of landfills (places where garbage is permitted to be dumped). A similar effort by the EDF and a fast-food chain led to the replacement of plastic foam hamburger boxes with a less bulky paper wrapper. Paper products make up one third of all municipal trash.

The appearance and strength of recycled paper have been problems that scientists are attempting to overcome. Recycled paper is often not as bright as virgin paper because not all the ink is removed in reprocessing. It is sometimes weaker, causing rolls of paper to break in printing presses. Paper containing 10 percent wood fiber recovered from trash is now available, however, thus enabling publishers to use more recycled paper.

INFO CHECK

1. Why are environmentalists today more concerned about the future of our planet than they were in earlier decades? Do you agree with their concern? Why or why not?

2. Why were global warming and the greenhouse effect major concerns at the Kyoto Convention of 1997? What did the delegates decide to do about this problem?

3. How are improvements in automobile design related to the effort to reduce air pollution?

POPULATION PRESSURES AND POVERTY

A common cause of poverty in the developing countries of Africa, Asia, and Latin America is rapid population growth. On an average, women in the Third World have five to seven children. The population of Asia, Africa, and Latin America, taken together, grew from 1.750 billion to 3 billion between 1950 and 1975. In the year 2000, experts predict that it will increase to 5.2 billion.

Will these countries be able to feed so many people? The 18th-century economist Thomas Malthus believed that since the increase in a country's food supplies does not keep pace with the increase in its population, famines must occur periodically. Few modern economists agree that starvation inevitably follows rapid population growth, however. Modern technology has, to some extent, increased the production of food. But this increase has mainly benefited the richer nations.

Family Planning

In the developing countries, large numbers of poor people are going hungry and living in makeshift shelters. Their governments have been trying for many years now to establish family-planning programs. People who live according to some traditional cultures, however, resist birth control. Catholicism in Latin America, Islam in Muslim countries, and Hinduism in India encourage their followers to have many children. Many people in Africa believe that supernatural spirits inhabit natural features and forces. Followers of such animistic religions place a high value on fertility.

Most governments have to battle old customs and values in implementing family planning programs. Chinese leaders have attempted to limit couples to one child. While many urbanized married couples have accepted this limit, it is highly unpopular with people who live according to tradition. Such people want sons. If the first child is a girl, they feel that they should be allowed to try again for a boy. Many Indian people take great pride in having many children. Whether Hindu or Islamic, they feel that it is the will of god that they have large families. When India's prime minister Indira Gandhi tried to force sterilization on poor people, she lost her political following.

Experts claim, however, that more people now see the advantages of having smaller families and are beginning to cooperate with their governments' policies on birth control. Even in Africa, where these

WORLD POPULATION GROWTH, 1980 TO 2050

| Year | Population (mil.) | AVERAGE ANNUAL* | |
		Growth Rate (percent)	Population Change (mil.)
1980	4,458	1.71	76.7
1985	4,855	1.69	82.5
1990	5,282	1.58	83.9
1995	5,691	1.41	80.5
1996	5,771	1.38	80.2
2000	6,090	1.28	78.6
2010	6,858	1.09	75.5
2020	7,593	0.92	70.2
2030	8,265	0.77	63.7
2040	8,865	0.61	54.6
2050	9,356	(NA)	(NA)

Source: U.S. Bureau of the Census. NA Not available. *Represents change from year shown to immediate succeeding year.

policies have met with the least success, women are beginning to have fewer children. In 1994, the typical African woman had about six children, as opposed to an average of eight children only a few years earlier.

Experts do not expect the world's population to stabilize until the middle of the 21st century. By then, they believe, there will be between 9 billion and 10 billion people on Earth. Although, these multitudes will strain the world's resources, experts are hopeful that advances in technology and conservation techniques can help solve the problem of limited resources. They point to the high standards of living in such small, densely populated countries as Belgium and the Netherlands. They suggest that the economies and social programs of these countries be studied and used as a model.

Policies and Programs

International conferences are valuable for guiding countries in their efforts to make sure that growing populations do not bring down standards of living. In 1994, representatives from 179 nations attended the *International Conference on Population and Development* (ICPD) in Cairo, Egypt. They met together to devise a program of action on population and development for the next 20 years.

Some of the topics discussed were the relationship between population and poverty, the status of women, the role of the family in society, reproductive health and rights, population distribution, education, research on health, social, and economic issues, and

THE GRAYING OF EUROPE

In the 1970s, a set of studies sponsored by the *Club of Rome*, a global think tank, predicted that rising population levels would devastate the world by the mid-1990s. Nothing of the sort has come to pass. The authors of that grim forecast could not have foreseen that by 1998 women in industrialized countries like Italy would be having an average of fewer than 1.2 children, the lowest figure ever recorded among humans. Nor could they have known that the end of communism in Europe would create both political freedom and economic uncertainties that would freeze birthrates from Germany to Russia. Instead of being overwhelmed by population pressures, the world has experienced a fundamental social revolution in the late 20th century.

Driven largely by prosperity and freedom, women throughout the industrialized world are having fewer children than ever before. They stay in school longer, put more emphasis on professional and financial advancement, and marry later. As a result, birthrates in many industrialized countries went into a sustained decline by the 1990s.

Once regarded as an important goal to be achieved, low birthrates have become a cause for alarm in the developed nations. With people living longer at the same time that fertility drops, most developed countries may soon find themselves with lopsided societies that will be difficult to sustain. They will consist of a large number of elderly people and not enough young people working and paying taxes to support them. Such a demographic shift will affect every government program that requires public funds, including health care, education, pension plans, and military spending.

By 1998, there was not a single country in Europe in which people were having enough children to replace themselves when they die. Italy became the first nation in history, in the late 1990s, to have more people over the age of 60 than under the age of 20. Germany, Greece, France, and Spain have been moving in the same direction. Government officials and researchers in these countries have worried about the shrinkage of their populations.

These trends have reached beyond Europe. In 1997, Japan's *fertility rate* (the number of children born on average) fell to 1.39, the lowest level it had ever reached. In the United States, a large pool of new immigrants keeps the fertility rate higher than in any other industrialized country. Nevertheless, the American birthrate in 1998 was slightly below an average of 2.1 children per woman. This is the number needed to keep the population from shrinking.

Even in the developing nations, where overpopulation has long been a cause of poverty and disease, population growth has slowed. In Bangladesh, for example, the fertility rate fell from 6.2 children per woman to 3.4 in the 1990s. Despite this decline, however, control of population growth in Asia, Africa, and Latin America still remains a goal related to the improvement of health and living standards. In most of Africa, six births per woman remained the average in 1998.

Although the global birthrate has been falling, the world's population continues to grow rapidly. In the late 1990s, the populations of Europe and Africa reached roughly equal levels. If the trends discussed above continue, Africans will outnumber Europeans by three to one in the year 2050. In that year, 50 percent of the population of Italy will be over the age of 50. Half the people of Iraq will be younger than 25.

Traditionally, the nations of Europe have been less receptive than the United States to immigrants from the developing nations. As European countries become "grayer," however, increased immigration may prove to be the only means of keeping their societies economically functional by maintaining a balance of different age groups. Young people from Asia, Africa, and Latin America will be needed to offset the shrinkage of European populations.

- Select an industrialized nation of Europe. Write a letter to a real or imaginary friend explaining why and how the population of that country is likely to change in future decades.

international cooperation on plans of action. One of the key issues discussed under reproductive health and rights was family planning. It was recommended that governments educate people, especially women, to make their own reproductive choices, including the decision to prevent unwanted pregnancies. To help people carry out their decisions, governments were urged to provide affordable, high-quality health facilities and educational and counseling services. They were also urged to coordinate family-planning programs.

The *Population Information Network* (POPIN), is a group of international, regional, and national population institutions. Founded in May 1979, POPIN is funded mainly by the United Nations and the world body's *Department of Economic and Social Affairs* (DESA).

POPIN distributes information on population issues, such as migration and population control, and helps different regions and nations coordinate activities intended to deal with these issues. It provides a community where representatives of developed and developing nations can meet and share information.

INFO CHECK

1. Explain the relationship between rapid population growth and poverty, especially in the Third World's developing nations.

2. List the measures to maintain standards of living recommended to the governments of the world at the International Conference on Population and Development in 1994. Which of these measures do you think will be most effective?

THE STRUGGLE FOR WOMEN'S RIGHTS

Increasingly, people from different nations are realizing the value of discussing social and economic problems with one another. In the late 20th century, women's rights became an important international issue.

Women's Conference in Beijing

In 1995, the Fourth World Conference on Women was held in Beijing, China. The delegates found much to celebrate. Female literacy was on the rise. Governments were paying greater attention than in the past to women's rights. But the delegates also found much to protest—from systematic rape during the wars in Bosnia and Rwanda to deeply entrenched social, economic, and legal discrimination against women. During the conference, the delegates drew up a "platform for action." They urged the governments they represented to use the document as a guideline for guaranteeing the "full enjoyment by women of their human rights."

One of the lessons of the Beijing conference, and of earlier UN conferences, was that women of different cultures could unite to pursue common goals. Representatives of women's groups from all over the world flocked to China. The nongovernmental organizations held their own, separate conference in a Beijing suburb. They wanted to make themselves heard by government delegates at the official conference.

Of course, the women's groups didn't always agree. Often, they

Representatives attending the international conference on women, Beijing, 1995

Aung San Suu Kyi, under
guard in Myanmar for
opposing its military
dictatorship

emphasized different issues. In some developing countries, key issues include the selling of women as slaves and the ritual mutilation of girls. In the United States, women's groups typically focus on such issues as reproductive rights and sex discrimination. Issues of sex discrimination include unequal employment and promotion opportunities, salary differences, and sexual harassment. Many issues were common to all the women's groups, however. In every country, women experience sex discrimination and are victims of domestic violence (physical abuse within family situations).

Women World Leaders

In the 1990s, women's rights groups were encouraged by the fact that women in several nations had achieved leadership positions. At the start of 1995, women headed ten of the world's 191 nations. The proportion of women in legislatures and other political bodies, however, was lower than it had been in the 1980s. This is largely because of the collapse of European communism. Communist nations had set quotas of up to 30 percent for women in office.

Ireland. President Mary Robinson of the Republic of Ireland, in office since 1990, was one of Europe's most popular heads of state. On one occasion, a poll of Irish voters gave President Robinson a 93 percent approval rating, compared to the 28 percent rating of the Irish prime minister of the time. In late 1997, Robinson accepted the post of UN High Commissioner for Human Rights. Mary McAleese, a law professor, became president of Ireland in October 1997.

Canada. In 1993, Kim Campbell became the first woman to serve as Canada's prime minister. Campbell served only briefly, however.

The Conservatives were defeated in national elections later in 1993. Several other women have reached high office in Canada, holding such positions as premier of Prince Edward Island, mayor of Ontario, leader of the New Democratic Party, and deputy leader of the Liberal Party.

Iceland and Norway. President Vigdis Finnbogadottir was Iceland's head of state from 1980 to 1996. Gro Harlem Brundtland has served as prime minister of Norway and then as head of the UN *World Health Organization* (WHO).

Turkey. Muslim societies are traditionally *patriarchal* (ruled by men). Yet, in 1993, Tansu Ciller, a former economics professor and economics minister, became the first woman to hold the office of prime minister of Turkey. Her election reflected the desire of many Turks that Europe and America regard them as modern and secular. They also supported her plans to lower Turkey's high inflation rate and to privatize state-owned businesses, which had been losing money. The defeat of her party by an Islamic party in 1995 general elections forced Ciller to resign.

Pakistan and Bangladesh. In South Asia, three of the seven national leaders who gathered for regional summits in the mid-1990s were women. They were Prime Minister Benazir Bhutto of Pakistan, Prime Minister Khaleda Zia of Bangladesh, and President Chandrika Kumaratunga of Sri Lanka. All were members of political dynasties started by fathers or husbands.

Both Bangladesh and Pakistan are mainly Muslim countries. Bhutto became prime minister of Pakistan in 1989, lost an election, then returned to power in 1993. She opened Pakistan's first all-women police station and started a women's bank. Zia became prime minister of Bangladesh in 1991. She aggressively promoted the education and economic self-sufficiency of women. The leader of the country's political opposition, Sheik Hasina Wazed, was also a woman. So were at least 10 percent of the members of parliament.

Sri Lanka. In Sri Lanka, a majority of the people are Buddhists. Kumaratunga won a 1994 election that was called "the battle of the widows." Her rival was the widow of an opposition leader killed two weeks before the election by a suicide bomber. Kumaratunga's father served as Sri Lanka's prime minister in the 1950s. He had been assassinated in 1959, when she was 14. Her husband had also been a political figure who had also been assassinated. Immediately after her election as president, Kumaratunga appointed her 78-year-old mother, Sirimavo Bandaranaike, as prime minister. (In 1960, Bandaranaike had been the first woman in the world to become prime minister. She led her political party to an election victory a year after her husband's assassination.)

Unit VIII has covered many of the 20th-century problems that will continue to trouble us in the 21st century. The great disparity in the quality of life between the populations of developing countries and those of industrialized countries is an important cause of the world's unrest. This inequality helped to bring about the radical nationalist and fundamentalist movements that opposed various forms of colonialism. After the end of colonialism, inequality intensified conflicts between those movements and the Western nations.

As these final three chapters have pointed out, the regions of the world are now more intricately connected than they have ever been. This means that both good and bad events can have global repercussions. Economic crises, drug trafficking, environmental damage, and terrorist activities that take place in one area often affect people far away. Recognizing this fact, world leaders increasingly hold conferences on how to confront these dangers. International organizations, such as the United Nations, provide forums in which experts from different countries can discuss solutions to shared problems. This spirit of cooperation has benefited the scientific community, whose members now have access to a pool of ideas and techniques.

INFO CHECK

1. Explain the phrase "full enjoyment by women of their human rights." Which human rights do you think are most important for women to achieve?

2. State the differences in goals between women's groups in the United States and those in the developing nations.

3. Select two (2) women leaders whom you find most impressive. Give reasons for your choices.

CHAPTER REVIEW

Multiple Choice

1. The modern computer operates quickly and can store vast amounts of information in small spaces because of
   1. the information superhighway
   2. transistors
   3. corporate downsizing
   4. silicon chips called microchips.

2. Examples of how science and technology have benefited individual lives include

   1. laser-guided surgery
   2. personal computers
   3. electronic mail
   4. all of the above.

3. Mir, NASA, and space shuttles are all related to
   1. cold war spy technology
   2. joint scientific study and space-exploration efforts
   3. United States efforts to build antimissile defenses
   4. joint Canadian, French, and Japanese space exploration efforts.

4. Technology can be harmful to the environment and humans if not carefully supervised. Examples of these dangers are

1. acid rain and AIDS
2. Chernobyl and Three Mile Island
3. desertification and deforestation
4. Alzheimer's disease and laser technology.

5. The "greenhouse effect" refers to the environmental situation caused by the

1. growing of onions indoors during the winter months
2. growing of flowers throughout the year
3. warming of the earth's atmosphere caused by carbon dioxide gas
4. loss of water in the Earth's atmosphere when the moon rises in the midnight sky.

6. Japan and the United States have many differences with regard to trade and economic concerns. However, an area where they both agree is

1. the need to find usable, environmentally safe nonfossil fuels
2. the number of automobiles produced and traded in each other's country
3. the number of items imported into each other's country
4. the need to develop and test nuclear weapons.

7. Thomas Malthus, after observing the recent famines caused by overpopulation, would have probably

1. suggested the use of family-planning clinics
2. agreed with the population-control programs established by the Chinese government
3. said he knew that a country's food

supply does not keep pace with increases in population
4. all of the above.

8. The election of women to high political offices is particularly significant in Southeast Asian nations because their societies are

1. traditionally patriarchal
2. traditionally matriarchal
3. formerly Communist-dominated
4. recently freed of colonial rule.

9. The late 20th-century inequality between the developed and developing nations caused the rise of

1. the cold war and nuclear arms races
2. radical nationalistic and religious fundamentalist movements
3. imperialism and colonial empires
4. international peacekeeping organizations.

10. The fact that economic crises, drug trafficking, and environmental concerns can affect all regions of the world highlights the

1. power of the Internet
2. power of worldwide communication
3. global economic and social interactions of today's world
4. need for moral leadership and a return to family values.

11. The bar graph on page 832 illustrates

1. that most of the world's nations are facing the problem of deforestation
2. that high-income nations and the nations of Europe and Central Asia are adding more woodland than they are losing
3. that nations of the third world suffer the most loss of forest areas
4. all of the above.

12. The photograph on page 840 illustrates that

1. women's issues now receive an international focus
2. women from the United States and Western Europe no longer participate in international women's conferences
3. third world nations have little interest in the women's movement
4. women from traditional societies are more likely to be affected by the women's movement than those in industrialized nations.

Thematic Essays

1. The regions of the world have become more directly affected by each other. *Task:* Identify and describe one positive and one negative consequence of that fact and explain what the world community is doing to either continue the positive or eliminate the negative situation. Consider regional associations, world bodies, and scientific inventions, technology and communication developments in your answer.

2. It was only in the 20th century that many of today's developing nations overthrew their colonial rulers. Free of colonial rulers, they sometimes resent interference from environmentalists and foreign economists. *Task:* Select one real-life situation and describe a problem environmentalists and/or economists pointed out in the developing nation. What is being done by the developing nation and the world community to resolve that problem? Consider for inclusion in your answer the various regional or United Nations agencies, and environmental and economic issues.

Document-Based Questions

1. Look at the illustrations of an early computer and a modern microchip on pages 825 and 826. Compare and contrast the two pictures. What scientific and technological implications for humankind can you draw from those two pictures?

2. Professor Abelardo Villegas, referring to the work of the Alliance for Progress in Latin America:

"No radical transformation of Latin American society can be expected is so short a time as 20 years. Many South American countries have not changed substantially since colonial days and it is futile to hope that they will do so by 1984."

Why do you think Professor Villegas was pessimistic about the progress of the Latin American people toward freedom and a higher standard of living? Consider geography, societal classes, and types of governments.

3. From the historian Hans Kohn:

". . . interest in the classics is growing; hundreds of thousands of copies of books about ancient Greece and Rome are sold in paperback editions. . . . Records and FM radio make available the finest music of all periods to a much wider public then ever before. While the West studies Oriental [Asian] and African music and sculpture, the East learns to master Western techniques in all arts. . . . Is it too much to hope that the new spirit developing out of the world revolution of our time will produce more lasting results that will benefit mankind?"

How has late 20th-century technology increased cultural diffusion?

Document-Based Essay

Science and technology have the potential to improve human life or create horrible weapons of mass destruction. *Task:* What actions has the world community taken that show it is attempting to prevent the misuse of science and technology? Relate this to the struggle to stop global environmental destruction.

Thematic Essays

1. The recent economic problems of Pacific Rim nations, e.g., Japan and Korea, and the former nations of the Soviet Union have affected the stock markets and economies of the entire global community. *Task:* Identify and briefly discuss two reasons why this has occurred and explain two actions that world bodies or regional associations have taken to deal with these crises. Factors to consider include technology, communications, global investments, the World Bank, and the International Monetary Fund.

2. Developing nations often experience many societal and cultural conflicts as they seek to modernize their economies and ways of life. The influence of religion, women's rights and roles, family size, and traditional customs are some of the issues they must confront. *Task:* Select any two developing nations and identify a problem of modernization and the programs or policies developed to deal with that issue. Include in your essay whether the nations have succeeded in overcoming the conflicts or, if not, why they are having continued difficulty with them.

Document-Based Questions

1. Public Announcement, U.S. Department of State, Office of the Spokesman, Bangladesh, September 11, 1998.

   Bangladesh is experiencing the most devastating flooding in its history. Approximately seventy percent of the country is under water, and many areas are inaccessible. Many people have drowned, and hundreds of thousands are suffering from flood-re-

lated diseases. U.S. citizens should consider deferring nonessential travel to Bangladesh because of the severity and the extent of the flooding, the deteriorating health conditions, and the breakdown of essential services.

Public Announcement, U.S. Department of State, Office of the Spokesman, China. August 18, 1998.

Serious flooding of the Yangtze River continues in the Wuhan region of China. U.S. citizens contemplating travel on the Yangtze River should consider this information until flooding subsides.

In what region of the world are these events occurring? Who is issuing the warning? What is the cause of the problem?

2. *Worldwide Caution.* September 24, 1998.

   In light of the August 7 bombings of the U.S. embassies in Nairobi, Kenya, and Dar es Salaam, Tanzania, the August 20 U.S. air strikes in Afghanistan and Sudan, and the apprehension of persons believed to have been involved in the U.S. embassy bombings, the potential for retaliatory acts against Americans and American interests overseas continues to exist. In addition, terrorists . . . continue their threats against the United States and have not distinguished between military and civilian targets.

   Identify the reasons for the "worldwide caution" and explain why it involves citizens of other nations.

3. October 1998

   (a) Top Story: *Conflict/Yugoslavia: U.S. warns of looming NATO attack* Western diplomats said Thursday an attack on Yugoslavia by North Atlan-

tic Treaty Organization forces appeared imminent, unless Yugoslav security forces withdraw from Kosovo.

(b) *Human Rights/Bolivia: 3,000 peasants demand title deeds*
Three thousand peasant farmers from various regions of Bolivia began a march "For Water, Land, and Life" Thursday in the capital La Paz, demanding title deeds to their land and protesting a draft law which they say will force them to pay fees for the use of water.

Identify the world problems and proposed solutions that each of these articles describes.

4. Look at the cartoon.

Who are the "kids" in front of the store and why are their toys so dangerous?

Document-Based Essay

The global community is confronted by both man-made and natural dangers. *Task:* Identify any two of those dangers, explaining why so many nations are affected and what the global community is trying to do to control or end those threats.

INDEX

848

English in North America, 388–389
Enlightened despots, 415–416, 418
Enlightenment in Europe, 411–418
Entente Cordiale, 575
Entertainment, public, 563–567
Environment; causes and consequences of destruction of, 832–833; civilization and, 55–56; global, 17; international efforts to preserve, 833–834
Environmental Defense Fund (EDF), 835
Ephors, 95
Epicureans, 101
Epigraphical evidence, 4
Equestrians, 124
Essenes, 142
Estates, 428
Ethiopia, 627
Ethnic cleansing, 448
Ethnocentrism, 535
Etruscans, 104
Euclid, 102
EURATOM, 802
Euripides, 94
Europe, 199–200; Eastern, see Eastern Europe; economic recovery in, 675–676; Enlightenment in, 411–418; German aggression in, 626–627; graying of, 838–839; immigrants and aliens in, 814–816; late 20th century developments in, 715–736; Medieval, see Medieval Europe; after Napoleon, 448–451; new, rise of, 721–725; revival after Middle Ages, 271–272; after Treaty of Versailles, 584; urban centers in Middle Ages in, 251–254; Western, change in, 731–736; in World War I, 572–572; after World War II, 659
European Community (EC), 777
European Economic Community (EEC), 675
European imperialism, colonial response to, 614–619
European Monetary Institute (EMI), 778
European nation-states, rise of, 298–318
European Union (EU), 25, 676, 767–768, 777–778
Europeans: in Africa, 364–367; in North America, 388–391; slavery and, 368–369; in South America, 382–388
Evolution, 508
Excommunication, 210
Existentialism, 646
Exploration, Renaissance and, 376–377

Expressionism, 647
Extraterritorial rights, 536

Factories, 499–501
Factory towns, 504
Falkland Islands War, 743
Family planning, 836–837
Famine in Somalia, 788
Farming communities, 54–55
Fascism, 30; in Italy, 606–607
Fatimids, 186
Ferdinand and Isabella, 382–383
Fertile Crescent, 56
Fertility rate, 838
Feudal peasants, 201
Feudalism, 215–219, 299–300
First World, 689
Five-Year Plans, 600
Flagellants, 264
Florence, 279–280
Forest areas, annual loss or gain of, 833
France, 207; Bourbons of, 302, 304–305; change in, 732, 734; colonies of, 530, 531–532; empire building by, 381; exploration and discovery in Africa by, 378–379; reforms made in, 519–520
Franco, Francisco, 627–629
Franco-Prussian War, 472
Frankfurt National Assembly, 453
Frankish Empire, 204–207
Franz Ferdinand, 575–576
Frederick the Great, 415–416
Free-market economy, command economy versus, 672
French and Indian War, 381, 425
French in Africa, 366–367
French in North America, 389–390
French reaction to immigrants, 815–816
French realism, 513
French Revolution, 428–431
Freud, Sigmund, 556–557

Galileo Galilei, 282, 406–407, 409–410
Gandhi, Indira, 691–692
Gandhi, Mohandas K., 481–482
Gandhi, Rajiv, 692–693
Garibaldi, Giuseppe, 474, 476–477
General Agreement on Tariffs and Trade (GATT), 775
General Assembly, UN, 642
Generalizations, 10
Genetic engineering, 831
Genetics, 508
Genghiz Khan, 241, 242
Genocide, 632
Genome, 831
Geocentric solar system, 404
Geography, 12

George III, 425–426
German aggression in Europe, 626–627
German reaction to immigrants, 814–815
Germanic peoples, 134
Germany, 207; change in, 731–732; colonies of, 530, 534; divided, 642; economic recovery in, 675; Habsburgs of, 306–308; after unification, 477; unification of, 471–473; unified, 720
Ghana, 694
Ghana Empire, 357–359
Ghettos, 371
Glasnost, 718
Global balance of power, search for, 656–661
Global communications, 827–828
Global depression, 607–610
Global developments in late 20th century, 740–758
Global economic interdependence, 24–25
Global economic organizations, 772–775
Global economy, 523, 767
Global environment, 17
Global hunger, 787
Global markets, 772–773, 767–768
Global migrations, 520
Global nationalism, 468–492
Global population, 766, 837
Global production, by region, 768
Global security, 795–821, 817–818
Global trade: Greek and Roman, 119–121; Middle Ages, 250–266
Global trends and issues of late 20th century, 824–843
Globalization, 773
Glorious Revolution, 318, 423
Gold Coast, 366
Gold trade, 259
Gorbachev, Mikhail, 717–718
Gothic style, 209
Government, 27; in Athens, 89–91; centralized, 299–300; earliest, 60–63; purposes of, 28–29
Graphic evidence, 4
Gravity, 283, 410
Graying of Europe, 838–839
Great Britain, 424, 498; change in, 734–736; colonies of, 530, 532; empire building by, 381; reforms made in, 518–519. See also British entries; England
Great Depression, 607–610
Great Plains, peoples of the, 346–347
Great Schism, 266
Great Wall of China, 85, 86

recovery in, 676; geography of, 230–231; as global power, 545–546; Western imperialism and, 542–543, 545–546

Japanese culture, 231–233

Japanese imperialism, 545

Japanese militarism and expansion, 613–614, 634

Jelia music, 360

Jenner, Edward, 509

Jesus, 142–144

Jewish homeland, 485–486, 586

Jews: intolerance toward, 371; persecution of, 612, 613; in Reformation, 294–295

Jiang Jieshi, 613, 614, 679

Jiang Zemin, 756

Jinnah, Muhammad Ali, 482

Joan of Arc, 303

John, King of England, 212, 312

Joint-stock company, 190, 274

Joseph II, 416

Joyce, James, 589

Judaism, 140–141

Judgment, 10

Julius Caesar, 107, 126–127

Jung, Carl Gustav, 557

Junta, 664

Justinian, 169–170

Ka'ba in Mecca, 144, 145

Kabila, Laurent, 754

Kabuki, 238

Kandinsky, Wassily, 647

Karma, 136

Kashmir, 691

Kayaks, 351

Kazakhstan, 726

Keats, John, 513

Kemal, Mustafa, 485, 586–587, 604–605

Kenya, 695, 697–698

Kenyatta, Jomo, 697–698

Kepler, Johannes, 406

Khmer Rouge, 705–706

Khomeini, Ayatollah, 708–709

Khrushchev, Nikita, 670–671

Kievan Russia, 176

Kilwa, 362

Kim Jong Il, 806

Kivas, 344

Knighthood, 217, 219

Koch, Robert, 509

Korea, 751

Korean War, 667–669

Kosovo, 488–489

Kristallnacht, 632, 633

Kumaratunga, Chandrika, 842–843

Kumbi-Saleh, 359

Kush, 75–76

Kyoto convention, 833–834

Labor union movement, 517–518

Laborers, 503

Labour Party, 518, 734–735

Laissez faire, 415, 502

Lamaism, 245

Landforms, 13

Lao-tzu, 140

Las Casas, Bartolomé de, 386

Laser technology, 830

Latin alphabet, 41, 119

Latin America: Catholic Church in, 459–460; class system in, 460; economic progress in, 673–674; economic structure of, 460, 462; economics in, 741; political unrest in, 741–748; Spain and, 438; United States and, 443, 741, 791–792; after World War II, 664–667

Latin American revolutions, 436–443

Latins, 102–104

Law, earliest, 60–63

Law enforcement, 31

Lay investiture, 211

League of Nations, 584–585, 602

Lebanon, 618, 706, 708

Lebensraum, 625

Leeuwenhoek, Anton van, 410–411

Legalism, 85

Legitimacy, principle of, 450

Lend-Lease Act, 634

Lenin, Vladimir I, 598–599

Leonardo da Vinci, 279

Lewis, Sinclair, 646–647

Liberals, 448, 451–459

Liberia, 535

Life expectancy, 558

Limited Nuclear Test-Ban Treaty, 808

Lister, Joseph, 509

Literacy, 40

Literary evidence, 4

Literature, 512–513; in early 20th century, 589–590; Renaissance, 280–281; during World War II, 645–647

Little Ice Age, 260–261

Locke, John, 412–413, 812

London Suppliers Agreement, 802

Louis Philippe, 451–452

Louis XIII, 304

Louis XIV, 304–305

Louis XVI, 430

Lunar calendar, 70

Lung cancer, 830

Lupercalia, 129

Luther, Martin, 285–287

Maastricht Treaty, 777

Macedonia, 98

Machiavelli, Niccolo, 281–282

Machu Picchu, 340, 387

Madagascar, 367

Madero, Francisco, 462–463

Magadha, 158

Magellan, Ferdinand, 377

Magistrates, 105

Magna Carta, 312

Magyars, 214–215

Mahabharata, 160

Mali Empire, 359–361

Malraux, André, 590

Malthusian economics, 522

Mammoths, 14

Mandarins, 165

Mandate of Heaven, 83

Mandela, Nelson, 699–701

Mandingo society, 360

Manifest Destiny, 478

Mann, Thomas, 645

Manorial system, 219–221

Mansa Musa, 8, 9, 359, 361

Mao Zedong, 613, 679–680, 682

Maps, 12–13

Marcus Aurelius, 128

Maria Theresa, 307–308, 416

Marius, 125

Market economy, 20–21, 23–24

Married women, 503–504

Mars, 828–829

Marshall Plan, 657–658

Martel, Charles, 205

Martial arts, 166

Martyrdom, 210

Marx, Karl, 516, 598

Mass-production system, 501

Maurya Empire, 82, 112–113

Mayas, 13, 333–336, 385

Mazzini, Giuseppe, 473–474

Mecca, 144, 145

Mechanistic world view, 410

Medical advances, 508–509, 554–558, 829–831

Medicis, 278–279

Medieval Europe, 198–223; culture of, 208–209; after fall of Rome, 200–204; invaders and conquerors in, 212–215; spatial organization and geography, 199–204

Medieval feudal society, 216

Meiji reign, 543

Meitner, Lise, 560, 561

Menem, Carlos Saúl, 743

Mental health, 556–558

Mercantilism, 275–276, 501

Mesoamerica, cultures of, 329–338

Mesopotamia, 28; Assyrians and, 74–75; city-states of, 56–58, 60–61, 63, 66, 67, 69, 70; trade between Egypt and, 74

Messiah, 141

Mestizos, 438

Metternich, Klemens von, 449–450

Mexican Revolution, 462–464

Mexico, 747–748; conquest of, 383–385

Michelangelo, 279–280

Microchip, 825

Microlith, 53
Middle Ages, 199; end of, 270–276; global trade in, 250–266
Middle class, role of, 274
Middle East, 662–663, 706; conflicts and change in, 706, 708–711; nationalism in, 484–485; terrorism in, 818
Middle Passage, 392, 393
Middle Stone Age, 52–53
Midwives, 162
Migrations, global, 520
Militarism, 574–575
Mill workers, 500
Ming Dynasty, 254–256
Minoans, 86–87
Miranda, Francisco de, 439
Missile Technology Control Regime (MTCR), 810–811
Mobutu Sese Seko, 752–754
Modem, 826
Modernization versus tradition, 783–786
Moi, Daniel arap, 698
Monarchy, 299–300
Monasteries, 150, 203–204
Money, 20
Mongol Empire, 241–246
Mongols, 235
Monotheism, 140
Monroe Doctrine, 443
Montesquieu, Baron de, 413
Moravians, 175
Morton, William T. G., 509
Moses, 140
Most favored nation (MFN) status, 754, 756
Motherwell, Robert, 648
Movable type, 240
Movies, 563–565
Muhammad, 182
Mujahadin, 785
Mummies, 66, 71
Music, 512
Muslim Empire, rise of, 182–183
Muslim invasions, 215
Muslim League, 481, 615
Muslim society, 186–195
Muslim trade and commerce, 189–190
Muslim women, 187
Muslims, 35–36, 144–145
Mussolini, Benito, 606–607
Mutual assured destruction (MAD), 801
Mycenaeans, 86–87
Mystery cults, 142

Napoleon Bonaparte, 433–436
Napoleonic Wars, 434–435
Narcotic drugs, illegal, 790–792
Nasser, Gamal Abdel, 663
National Aeronautics and Space; Administration (NASA), 828
National Assembly, 430–431

National Union for the Total Independence of Angola (UNITA), 664
Nationalism, 418, 450, 529, 573; African, 693; Arab, 586, 617–618; in Asia, 480–486; global, 468–492; historians' view of, 469–470; in India, 480–484; influence through the ages, 470; liberals fight for, 451–459; in Middle East, 484–485; power of, 469–470; Russian, 456–457; in Southeast Asia, 702–706; western, 470–478
Nationalization, 663
Native American tribes, 341–352
Natural law, 108
Natural rights, theory of, 29
Navajos, 345–346
Nazi state, 624–625
Nazism, 30, 610–612
Neanderthals, 49–51
Nehru, Jawaharlal, 482, 691, 692
Neo-Nazis, 732, 819
Neolithic period, 9
Neolithic Revolution, 52, 53
Neolithic tools, 4
Nepotism, 286
Nero, 128
Netherlands: empire building by, 381; exploration and discovery in Africa by, 378. *See also* Dutch
Neuroses, 557
New Amsterdam, 390
New Deal, 609
New Economic Policy (NEP), 599, 600
New Spain, 386
New Stone Age, 9, 53
Newton, Isaac, 283, 410
Nicaragua, 746
Nigeria, 695–697, 771
Nightingale, Florence, 458
Nile River, Egypt and, 58, 61–62, 63–64, 66, 67–68, 69, 70
Ninjas, 237
Nirvana, 138
Nomadic groups, 48–49
Normandy, 214
North Africa, 662–663
North America: Europeans in, 388–391; geography of, 326, 327, 328; slavery in, 395
North American cultures, 341–352
North American Free Trade Agreement (NAFTA), 25, 747, 779–782
North Atlantic Treaty Organization (NATO), 660, 729–731, 799–800
North German Confederation, 471–472
North Korea, 748–751, 804–805

Northern Ireland, 489–491
Northern Rhodesia, 695
Northwest Coast peoples, 348–349
Northwest Passage, 377–378
Norway, 842
Nubia, 75–76
Nuclear arms control, 801–802
Nuclear arsenals, spread of, 802–803
Nuclear-control crises, 803–809
Nuclear fission, 560
Nuclear Nonproliferation Treaty (NNT), 802, 807–808
Nuclear safety, 832
Nuclear testing, efforts to end, 807–808
Nuclear weapons, 661, 716

Octavian, 127–128
Oil crisis, 677–678
Oligarchy, 88
Olmecs, 330–332
Olympic games, 97
Omar Khayyam, 194
Open Door Policy, 538
Open-field system, 496
Opium War, 536
Oppenheimer, J. Robert, 561
Oral histories, 8
Organization of African Unity (OAU), 701–702
Organization of Petroleum Exporting Countries (OPEC), 677–678, 706, 778–779
Orozco, José, 592
Orthodox Christian Church, 171, 173
Ottoman Empire, 171, 484–485, 585–587
Owen, Robert, 515–516

Pacific Rim economies, emergence of, 676
Painting, 510–512
Pakistan, 483, 484, 617, 690–691, 842
Palestine, 485–486
Palestine Liberation Organization (PLO), 491–492, 706, 708, 710
Palladio, Andrea, 280
Pan-Africanism, 701–702
Pan-Germanism, 574
Pan-Slavism, 458, 574
Panama Canal, 539
Pandemic, 581
Papal power, 209–212
Papal States, 205, 210, 475–477
Paris Commune, 520
Parliament, 312–313, 315–317
Parthenon, 93
Passive resistance, 482
Pasteur, Louis, 509
Pastoral societies, 54, 76–78
Patriarchal society, 63, 842
Patriarchs, 203
Patricians, 105

Saudi Arabia, 485; change in traditional roles of women in, 785
Scandinavia, 212
Scarcity, 20
Schleswig-Holstein, 471
Science and technology, 3, 559–567, 587, 589; development of, 41; earliest, 70–72; in late 20th century, 825–831; World War II and, 640–641
Scientific advances, 507–508
Scientific method, 282, 404; Renaissance and, 404–411
Scotland, 424
Scott, Walter, 513
Seanachies, 8
Second Republic, 452–453
Second World, 689
Secretariat, UN, 642
Secretary General, UN, 642
Sectionalism, 478–480
Secularism, 279
Security Council, UN, 642
Semitic nomads, 76–77
Senate, Roman, 105
Sepoy Mutiny, 480–481, 531
Serbia, 488
Serfs, 219–220, 272
Seven Years' War, 381, 425
Sexual harassment, 193
Shaka, 532, 533
Shakespeare, William, 281
Shamans, 351
Shang Dynasty, 62–63, 65, 67, 68, 69–70, 71–72, 76
Shaw, George Bernard, 514
Shelley, Percy Bysshe, 513
Shi Huangdi, 85–86
Shi'ites, 184
Shinto, 232
Shogunate, 233–235
Shotoku, 232
Sibelius, Jean, 512
Sikhs, 692
Silk Road, 110, 121–122
Sinclair, Upton, 646
Sino-Japanese War, 546
Skalds, 7–8, 213
Slash-and-burn farming, 13
Slavery: in Africa, 367–368; in Americas, 391–395; Europeans and, 368–369; evils of, 369, 371; in Muslim society, 185–186, 188; rise of, 367–372; triangular trade in, 392–393; in United States, 479; in West Indies, 393, 395
Slovakia, 728
Smallpox, 385
Smith, Adam, 501
Social changes, 502–504
Social contract, 412
Social Darwinism, 522–523
Social sciences, 3
Social structure, earliest, 63–65
Socialism, 448

Socialist movement, 515–516
Socrates, 94–95
Solar system, 282
Solidarity, 719
Solomon, 140
Solon, 90
Somalia, 788, 796, 797
Songhai Empire, 361–362
Sophocles, 94
South Africa, 5, 532, 698–701
South America: Europeans in, 382–388; geography of, 326, 327, 328; Incas of, 338–340; after wars of independence, 459–464
South Korea, 751
Southeast Asia, nationalism and communism in, 702–706
Southern Rhodesia, 695
Soviet Union, 22–23, 599, 601; control of Eastern Europe, 656–657; expansion of, United States response to, 657–661. See also Commonwealth of Independent States; Russia
Space exploration, 828–829
Space platform, 829
Space race, 661
Spain: colonies of, 534–535; empire building by, 380–381; exploration and discovery in Africa by, 377; Habsburgs of, 306–308; Islamic, 194–195; Latin America and, 438
Spanish Armada, 289, 301
Spanish Civil War, 627–629
Spanish Inquisition, 295
Sparta, 95–96
Specialization, 60
Spender, Stephen, 646
Sphere of influence, 535
Spice trade, Portuguese, 256–260
Sputnik, 828
Sri Lanka, 842–843
Stalin, Joseph, 599–602, 641–642
Stamp Act, 425–426
Standard of living, 567
Steam engine, 499
Steamships, 504
Stein, Gertrude, 589
Still, Clyfford, 647
Stoics, 101
Stone Age, 9, 13–14, 52
Strategic Arms Limitation Talks (SALT), 717
Strikes, 517
Sub-Saharan Africa, 357
Suez Canal, 532
Suffrage movement: in United States, 519; women's, 605–606
Suharto, 31
Sui Dynasty, 163
Sulfa drugs, 554
Sumerian civilization, 56–58, 60–61, 63, 66, 67, 69, 70

Sun-centered universe, 405
Sun Yixian, 538–539, 614
Sundiata, 359
Sung Dynasty, 239–241
Sunni Ali, 361
Sunnites, 184–185
Superpowers, 656
Supply and demand, 20, 501–502
Surgery, advances in, 555–556
Surrealism, 591–592
Swahili culture, 362–363
Syria, 618

T'ai Tsu, 254
Taiping Rebellion, 536
Taiwan, 679, 758
Tale of Genji, 233
Tamerlane, 243
Tang Dynasty, 163–167
Taoism, 140
Tariffs, 25, 275, 479
Tchaikovsky, Peter Ilich, 512
Technology, see Science and technology
Telegraph, 506
Telephone, 506
Telescope, 283
Television, 506, 567
Teller, Edward, 561
Tennyson, Alfred, Lord, 513
Tenochtitlán, 384, 385
Teotihuacán, 332–333
Terrorism, 710–711
Terrorists, 817–821
Thatcher, Margaret, 735
Theodosius, 202
Third Reich, 612, 624–625
Third World, 689
Thirty Years' War, 291
Three Kingdoms, 132
Tiananmen Square massacre, 683
Timbuktu, city of, 39–40, 359
Time frames, 8–9
Tithes, 210
Tokugawa Shogunate, 236, 238–239, 542
Tolstoy, Leo, 514
Toltecs, 336
Tories, 317
Totalitarianism, 610–614; democracy versus, 30–31
Toussaint L'Ouverture, 437–438
Trade: earliest, 72; global, see Global trade
Traditional economy, 20–22
Transportation, improvements in, 504–506
Treaty of Versailles, 582–584, 602, 624
Trench warfare, 578
Triple Alliance, 541–542, 575
Triple Entente, 575
Troy, 87
Truman Doctrine, 657
Trusteeship Council, UN, 643
Tudors of England, 300–302

Turkey, 221, 604–605, 842; civil conflicts in, 585–586; founding of, 485
Turkish Empire, 484–485
Tutsis, 698, 817
Twain, Mark, 514
Tyranny, 88, 90

Ukraine, 725–726, 803–804
Ulema, 186
Ulster Defense Association (UDA), 489
Ultranationalists, 724, 818, 819–821
Umayyad Dynasty, 184–185
Unions, 517
United Nations, 642–643, 812; decisions in, 798; peacekeeping role of, 796–799
United Nations Children's Fund (UNICEF), 798
United Nations Conference on Environment and Development (UNCED), 833
United Nations Development Program, 798–799
United Nations Drug Control Program (UNDCP), 791
United States, 23, 108, 110, 478; China and, 682; Constitution, 28; economy in, 608; House of Representatives, 29; immigrants and aliens in, 816; imperialism and, 539–540; Latin America and, 443, 741, 791–792; response to expansion of Soviet Union, 657–661; sectionalism in, 478–480; slavery in, 479; suffrage in, 519; terrorism in, 818; war on drugs in, 790–791; women's suffrage movement in, 605–606; after World War I, 592; World War I and, 579–580; World War II and, 632, 634, 636–640
Urbanization, problems of, 789
Utopianism, 515–516

Vassals, 216–217
Venice, 252

Verdi, Giuseppe, 512
Versailles, palace of, 305
Vesalius, Andreas, 283, 408, 409
Veto, 105
Vietnam, 669–670
Vietnam War, 703–705
Vikings, 201, 212–214, 351
Vindolanda, England, 6
Virgin Islands, 540
Voltaire, 413–414
Voyager 2, 828

Wagner, Richard, 512
Warsaw Pact, 660
Weapons, global trade in, 809–811
Weimar Republic, 610
West Africa, 371
West Indies, slavery in, 393, 395
West Pakistan, 691
Western civilization, 37
Western Europe, change in, 731–736
Western nationalism, 470–478
Whigs, 317
White-collar workers, 503
Wiesel, Eli, 728
Wilberforce, William, 454
Wilhelm, Kaiser, 471, 473
William of Orange, 318
William the Conqueror, 214, 300
Wilson, Woodrow, 582–584
Witch hunts, 292–293
Women: change in traditional roles of, 785–786; in Communist China, 683–684; in guilds, 273; in Gupta Empire, 162; Iroquois, 342–343; married, 503–504; Muslim, 187; Protestantism and, 292; in Sung Dynasty, 241; world leaders, 841–843; after World War I, 592
Women's conference in Beijing, 840–841
Women's rights, struggle for, 840–843
Women's suffrage movement, 605–606
Wordsworth, William, 513

Works Progress Administration (WPA), 609
World Bank, 774
World Trade Organization (WTO), 775, 777
World War I, 546, 571–592; casualties in, 580; causes of, 573–577; China after, 614; end of, 580, 582–585; era following, 596–619; immediate causes of, 575–577; Indian response to, 615, 617; popular culture after, 592; Russia after, 597–598; United States and, 579–580
World War II, 486, 623–648; Asia after, 690; beginnings of, 626–629; casualties in, 640; course of, 629–641; Europe after, 659; planning after, 641–643; technology and, 640–641; United States and, 632, 634, 636–640
World Wide Web, 826
Writing systems, earliest, 67–68
Written history, 8
Written languages, civilization and, 40–41
Wu Zhao, Empress, 167

Yalta, 642, 656
Yamato emperors, 232
Yeltsin, Boris, 719, 721–725
Yom Kippur War, 677
Yuan Dynasty, 243, 245–246
Yugoslavia, 488

Zaire, 752
Zambia, 695
Zapata, Emiliano, 463
Zedillo, Ernesto, 747–748
Zemstvos, 456
Zen, 230, 235–236
Zeno, 101
Zero, concept of, 160
Zero-emission car, 834
Zheng He, 256
Zhou Dynasty, 83–85
Zhou Enlai, 679
Ziggurats, 69
Zimbabwe, 364, 695
Zionism, 485–486

PHOTO CREDITS

3 Scala/Art Resource **4** Erich Lessing/Art Resource **5** Kenneth Garrett/National Geographic Image Sales **6** ©Vindolanda Trust **7** AKG **13** American Museum of Natural History **17** Borromeo/Art Resource **21** Novosti/Liaison **22** Steve Raymer/National Geographic Image Sales **23** M. Setboun/Sygma **28** Scala/Art Resource **29** Joseph Bailey/National Geographic Image Sales **30** P. Parrot/Sygma **36** Liz Gilbert/Sygma **37** Borromeo/Art Resource **38** Borromeo/Art Resource **39** Library of Congress **40** Corbis-Bettmann **51** World Photo Service Ltd/Superstock **52** Bridgeman Art Library **60** Louvre/Giraudon/Art Resource **61** Rijksmuseum/ Erich Lessing/Art Resource **62** British Museum/Bridgeman Art Library **64** Giraudon/Art Resource **86** Yat Min Chan/Image Bank **93** W. Hille/Leo de Wys **100** Alinari/Art Resource **110** Peter Baker/Leo de Wys **126** Alinari/Art Resource **127** Louvre/Bridgeman Art Library **137** Adam Woolfitt/Woodfin Camp **139** Stapleton Collection/Bridgeman Art Library **143** Louvre/ Bridgeman Art Library **145** Photo Researchers **161** Ravi Shekhar/Dinodia Picture Library **165** Werner Forman/Art Resource **167** China Stock **169** Alinari/Art Resource **170** Oronoz, Madrid **181** Alexander Low/Woodfin Camp **188** Bibliothèque Nationale, Paris **189** Bibliothèque Nationale, Paris **192** Freer Gallery of Art **201** Victoria and Albert Museum/Bridgeman Art Library **204** Corbis **206** Scala/Art Resource **217** Superstock **220** New York Public Library **232** Bibliothèque Royale Albert I, Brussels **233** Chester Beatty Library and Gallery of Oriental Art, Dublin/Bridgeman Art Library **234** Laurie Platt Winfrey Inc. **236** Laurie Platt Winfrey Inc. **239** Laurie Platt Winfrey Inc. **243** National Palace Museum, Taipei/Laurie Platt Winfrey Inc. **252** Bodleian Library, Oxford **257** *top:* Bibliothèque Nationale, Paris/Superstock; *bottom:* Science Museum, London/Bridgeman Art Library **262** Bibliothèque Royale Albert I, Brussels **272** Bibliothèque Royale Albert I, Brussels **280** Alinari/Art Resource **283** Science Museum, Florence/Scala/Art Resource **284** The Granger Collection **286** Corbis **287** Foto Marburg/Art Resource **293** North Wind Picture Archive **294** North Wind Picture Archives **302** Private Collection/Bridgeman Art Library **305** Giraudon/Art Resource **308** Schloss Schonbrunn, Vienna/ Bridgeman Art Library **309** Hermitage/Bridgeman Art Library **310** Schloss Ambras, Innsbruck/ Erich Lessing/Art Resource **315** Bridgeman Art Library **316** Corbis **331** Fritz Henle/Photo Researchers **332** Werner Forman/Art Resource **335** American Museum of Natural History **340** Leo de Wys **342** British Museum/Bridgeman Art Library **344** Fritz Henle/Photo Researchers **348** A. Ramey/Woodfin Camp **361** Bibliothèque Nationale, Paris **363** Marc and Evelyne Bernheim/Woodfin Camp **368** The Granger Collection **369** The Granger Collection **384** Courtesy Department of Library Services, American Museum of Natural History **385** Courtesy Department of Library Services, American Museum of Natural History **404** Art Resource **405** *top:* Corbis; *bottom:* The Granger Collection **407** Corbis **409** Corbis **415** The Granger Collection **426** John Carter Brown Library **429** Corbis **433** Giraudon/Art Resource **437** Corbis **439** Schalkwijk/Art Resource **443** Corbis-Bettmann **452** Corbis **453** The Granger Collection **456** Brown Brothers **463** Museum of Modern Art, New York. Abby Aldrich Rockefeller Fund **474** Corbis **475** Corbis-Bettmann **482** UPI/Corbis-Bettmann **491** White House **500** Mary Evans Picture Library **508** Corbis **510** Art Resource **511** Metropolitan Museum of Art, Bequest of Mrs. H. O. Havemeyer, 1929 **515** Mary Evans Picture Library **530** Corbis-Bettmann **538** Stock Montage **540** Theodore Roosevelt Collection, Harvard University Library **555** Museum of Modern Art **556** The Granger Collection **559** UPI/Corbis-Bettmann **561** UPI/Corbis-Bettmann **562** The Granger Collection **563** UPI/Corbis-Bettmann **575** UPI/Corbis-Bettmann **576** ©John McCutchson/*Chicago Tribune*, 1914 **578** Brown Brothers **582** Mary Evans Picture Library **590** © 1999 Artists Rights Society (ARS), New York/ADAGP, Paris/Estate of Marcel Duchamp Philadelphia Museum of Art/Bridgeman Art Library **591** Museum of Modern Art **598** Novosti/ Corbis-Bettmann **604** Mary Evans Picture Library **606** Corbis-Bettmann **611** UPI/Corbis-Bettmann **612** Bildarchiv Preussicher Kulturbesitz **613** Corbis-Bettmann **631** Holland, *Nashville Banner*, 1940 **638** Bachmann/Photo Researchers **641** Library of Congress **652** The Granger Collection **653** Robert Nickelsburg/Gamma Liaison **659** Corbis-Bettmann **665** Sygma **669** Roger Viollet/Gamma Liaison **673** Robert Nickelsburg/Gamma Liaison **680** J. Langevin/ Sygma **692** e. t. Archive **697** Pascale Villiers Le Moy/Sygma **701** P. Durand/Sygma **709** A. Johannes/Sygma **714** © Shanks, *Buffalo News* **716** © 1962 *Herblock: A Cartoonist's Life*, Times Books, 1998 **720** D. Aubert/Sygma **721** D. Aubert/Sygma **723** J. Abraityte/Sygma **728** Les Stone/Sygma **735** D. Hudson/Sygma **738** © 1989 by Herblock in the *Washington Post* **744** Philippe Caron/Sygma **749** UN photo/Gamma Liaison **753** Jean-Michel Turpin/Gamma Liaison **757** Aventurier-Buu-Hires/Gamma Liaison **763** Jerome Delay/AP/Wide World **779** © 1979 Herblock **797** Liz Gilbert/Sygma **808** AUTH © 1998 *Philadelphia Inquirer*. Reprinted with the permission of Universal Press Syndicate **815** Jerome Delay/AP/Wide World **825** Corbis **826** Gamma Liaison **831** Murdo Mac Leon/Sygma **840** Anat Givon/AP/Wide World **841** Sonon/Gamma Liaison